THE WEST POINT ATLAS
OF AMERICAN WARS

Volume I   1689-1900

Compiled by

**THE DEPARTMENT OF MILITARY ART
AND ENGINEERING
THE UNITED STATES MILITARY ACADEMY**

WEST POINT, NEW YORK

Chief Editor

**BRIGADIER GENERAL
VINCENT J. ESPOSITO**

FORMER PROFESSOR AND HEAD OF THE DEPARTMENT
OF MILITARY ART AND ENGINEERING
THE UNITED STATES MILITARY ACADEMY

With a prefatory letter by DWIGHT D. EISENHOWER
Foreword by GENERAL JOHN R. GALVIN

HENRY HOLT AND COMPANY • NEW YORK

Henry Holt and Company, Inc.
Publishers since 1866
115 West 18th Street
New York, New York 10011

Henry Holt ® is a registered trademark
of Henry Holt and Company, Inc.

Published in Canada by Fitzhenry & Whiteside, Ltd.,
195 Allstate Parkway, Markham, Ontario L3R 4T8.
Originally published in 1959 by Frederick A. Praeger, Inc., Publishers.

Library of Congress Cataloging-in-Publication Data

United States Military Academy. Dept. of Military Art and Engineering.
The West Point atlas of American wars / compiled by the Department
of Military Art and Engineering, the United States Military Academy;
chief editor Vincent J. Esposito; with prefatory letter by Dwight D. Eisenhower;
foreword by John R. Galvin. — 1st ed. 1995. [rev. and updated from 1959 ed.]
      p. cm.
Originally published: New York: Praeger, 1959.
Contents: v. 1. 1689–1900.
1. United States—History, Military—Maps.   I. Esposito. Vincent
J. (Vincent Joseph), 1900–1965.   II. Title.
  G1201.S1U5   1995 <G&M>   95-6753
  912.73—dc20   CIP
                                    MAP

ISBN 0-0850-3391-2

Henry Holt books are available for special promotions and premiums.
For details contact: Director, Special Markets.

First Revised and Updated Edition—1995

Printed in Hong Kong
All first editions are printed on acid-free paper. ∞

10 9 8 7 6 5 4 3 2 1

ACKNOWLEDGMENTS

The editors of this new edition owe a debt of gratitude to the original editors, authors and cartographers of this venerated volume, who are identified in the Introduction and whose work has made our task an unusually pleasant one. We also wish to express our appreciation to Captain John Dougherty for supervising the project, and to Majors Steven Hawley and Frank Siltman and Captains Douglass Whitehead and Michael Wooley for their contributions to the sections on the Civil War, the Colonial Wars, the War of 1812 and the Mexican-American War, and the Spanish-American War respectively. Colonel (Retired) John R. Elting, an important contributor to the original volume, and Professor Charles Roland of the University of Kentucky, a former Visiting Professor at the Military Academy, also provided helpful advice. To Jim Charlton, whose belief in the importance of the project helped make it go on, goes our special thanks.

COLONEL ROBERT A. DOUGHTY
COLONEL CHARLES F. BROWER IV

West Point, New York

Like a true friend and mentor, *The West Point Atlas of American Wars* has been my boon companion ever since I pored over these maps in earlier pamphlet versions of the book during my schooling at the Military Academy. More than four unbelievable decades later I still find myself turning the pages of my worn and dog-eared copy to refresh myself on the framework of a battle or campaign, or to place in perspective a book I'm reading.

I'm always impressed with the arrangement of the atlas—clear map on the right, concise text on the left carrying you quickly into a specific moment in time, laying out for you the essential elements of a battle, commenting just enough to give you the gist of what happened, providing you with the wherewithal to allow you to apply yourself to the aspects that are pertinent to your interest. The maps are strongest in their unique ability to portray the dynamics of warfare in the maneuver of opposing forces. With subdued terrain and highlighted unit symbols, the *Atlas* emphasizes action—move and countermove—with an amazing economy of simple graphics. The accompanying critical summaries, themselves masterpieces of brevity and concentration, move chronologically as you turn the pages. The time charts in the front of the volume assist you in placing an event with reference to other actions. As for the many ramifications of war—social impacts, technological development, psychology of leadership, battle planning, logistics, and much else, including most of what falls in the category of "the fog of war"—the *Atlas* leaves these things to your more specialized study, confining itself to maps and skeletal essays, superb in their eloquently frugal delineation of what occurred and why.

It is the Civil War, with its endless variety of situations and lessons, that has become the storehouse of American battle lore and has continued to enthrall the public in this country and in others. The *Atlas* recognizes this phenomenon, this extraordinary interest, by devoting the major part of this volume to that war.

Military leaders know that they should live a life immersed in the history of human conflict, garnering an ever greater store of knowledge of what war is like, not because any situation or even any event will precisely repeat itself, but because a deep comprehension will provide a context, a setting against which any new happening can be judged. The search for understanding of the profession of arms begins and ends with the history of human conflict, and this book is unmatched as a guide in what for many of us has been and will be a lifelong quest for mastery of leadership in battle.

Battle leaders past, present, and future do not, however, have exclusive domain over the world of military history: a surprising number of people show great and abiding interest in the field of combat studies, probably because in war the stakes are so high that concomitant activities become heightened, even transcendent. Because of this the *West Point Atlas*, originally created to assist cadets in understanding the face of war, appeals to readers in all walks of life who want to know more about what happens and why, when human beings engage in mortal combat. As a concise and dependable battlefield guide, nothing has ever served as well as this collection of maps and associated analytical narratives.

JOHN R. GALVIN
GENERAL, UNITED STATES ARMY (RETIRED)

Mershon Center
The Ohio State University

April 22, 1959

TO THE CORPS OF CADETS, UNITED STATES MILITARY
ACADEMY

I am glad to learn of the forthcoming publication of The West
Point Atlas of American Wars, for use in cadet instruction -- and
indeed for use by all military personnel in the study of military
history.

Through a careful and objective study of the significant campaigns
of the world, a professional officer acquires a knowledge of military experience which he himself could not otherwise accumulate.
The facts of a given battle may no longer serve any practical purpose except as a framework on which to base an analysis; but when
the serious student of the military art delves into the reasons for
the failure of a specific attack -- or soberly analyzes the professional qualities of one of the responsible commanders of the past --
he is, by this very activity, preparing for a day in which he, under
different circumstances, may be facing decisions of vital consequence to his country.

The "principles of war" which this atlas will assist you in studying
are broad. They apply to air and naval warfare as well as to land
combat.   They are not, in the final analysis, limited to any one
type of warfare, or even limited exclusively to war itself.   But
principles as such can rarely be studied in a vacuum; military
operations are drastically affected by many considerations, one of
the most important of which is the geography of the region.   Thus,
it is important that these campaigns be studied in conjunction with
the very best available in clear and accurate maps.

I am confident that The West Point Atlas of American Wars will
prove a tremendous aid in instructing -- and inspiring -- the minds
of those whose profession it will be to defend the frontiers of the
Free World against all enemies.

Dwight D. Eisenhower

The Origin and Purpose of the Work

This atlas is especially designed for the cadets of the United States Military Academy as an aid in their initial studies in the History of the Military Art. It is equally appropriate for the civilian student of military history, while the advanced and experienced reader will find the text accompanying the maps to be valuable summations and the abundance of maps to be a boon. In a sense, this combined text and atlas is revolutionary in the field of military writing. Here the theme is carried along by the maps and the narrative is supplemental; in the normal work the reverse is generally the case.

The first step in the study of any military operation is to ascertain precisely what occurred and what factors influenced the course of the action and its outcome. These factors include: the quality of the leadership; the plans, the preparations, the training, and the morale; weather and terrain conditions; armament and equipment differentials; tactics and battle techniques; and contemporary political, economic, and sociological considerations. With this background clearly in mind, one can then proceed to the more exciting task of analysis, criticism, and, perhaps, speculation. The many splendid works on military history generally combine such background material with discussion and analysis as events progress, and this arrangement is excellent for the experienced reader who is able to relate the many factors and proceed without loss of continuity. Unfortunately, however, such is not the case with the new student. He must pause frequently for reflection and comprehension; many questions arise. Soon he begins to be confused as to the exact sequence of events described and is forced to go back to establish their continuity. In so doing, he encounters formidable obstacles. Military works are almost universally lacking in adequate maps. Many have the maps interspersed with the text so that, since many pages relate to one map, a constant turning of pages becomes necessary if the reader is to achieve any correlation. More frequently, the novice will find it necessary to work back through the narrative in order to pick up the lost strands. The new student eventually masters these problems, but initially they are time-consuming and at least somewhat frustrating.

The time available to the cadets of the United States Military Academy for study is severely budgeted. That allotted in the Academy curriculum to the Course in the History of the Military Art is limited, and the subject matter of the course covers an extensive field which expands constantly. It is therefore necessary to make sure that the cadets derive maximum benefit from the limited time at their disposal, and to this end, the course material has been progressively modified to facilitate study. In 1938, this department began the development of a series of atlases to accompany the several historical works used as texts. The first of these to deal with American wars was compiled in order to supplement *American Campaigns,* by Matthew Forney Steele (which, though published more than fifty years ago, remains one of the best works on American military operations prior to 1900). The maps of this first atlas covered the Colonial and Revolutionary Wars, the War of 1812, the Mexican War, the American Civil War, and the Spanish-American War. Revised throughout the years, these maps now form the content of Volume I of this publication. Another atlas was compiled to accompany a department text on World War I. During World War II, pamphlets were hastily prepared on operations as they progressed; and these were provided with fold-in maps at the back. Eventually, the pamphlets and maps were revised, corrected, and incorporated into a formal text and atlas comparable to the others of the series. With the advent of the Korean War, a department pamphlet was compiled, including appropriate maps. The maps of the atlases on World War I and World War II and of the Korean pamphlet comprise the content of Volume II of this work.

The title of these volumes—*The West Point Atlas of American Wars*—may mislead some into believing that only engagements in which Americans participated are considered. This is not the case. Though emphasis may be given to American actions, wars are treated as a whole. For example, most of the maps in the World War I section cover events prior to the entry of the United States into that war, and, in the World War II section, many of the maps concern engagements in which United States forces did not participate, while others portray operations undertaken jointly with our allies.

With few exceptions, the maps depict operations of the land forces. There is no intention to slight the splendid achievements of the air and naval forces; these are given appropriate recognition in the narrative. Air and naval operations are intricate and highly specialized; and since they do not lend themselves to the type of map portrayal employed in this general work, they must perforce be the subjects of separate detailed studies. Our Army, Navy, and Air Force (and their individual components) can be proud of their traditions and accomplishments in defense of the United States and its ideals; each can prove itself to have been *a* decisive force in operations in which it has participated. But which was *the* decisive force is sometimes the subject of controversy that will long endure.

In the present work, every effort has been made to eliminate or reduce time-consuming processes and inconveniences to study. The narrative pertaining to each map is specially "tailored" to fit on the blank page opposite the map. Thus, side by side, text and map are most conveniently arranged for joint study; only on rare occasions will it be necessary to turn back to another map. The narrative is carefully designed to avoid involving the reader in a fruitless search for material not included on the map. Similarly, where places on the map are difficult to locate, the narrative includes direction guides.

The text is made brief not only for convenience in map-text reference but also for another highly important educational purpose. The novice engaged in the study of a standard work stands in awe of the author and is likely to accept his views and analyses without question. Eventually, with greater experience and broader background, he is able to evaluate the author's case properly; but, initially, his efforts do not go far beyond an exercise in memory. It is our purpose at the Military Academy to develop in the cadets an intellectual curiosity—the facility to question, to analyze, and to arrive at their own conclusions. The text is designed with this end in view. Its brevity permits the application of much of the cadets' limited study time to reflection rather than to reading. It is recognized that they will encounter difficulty at first in ascertaining which elements are worthy of consideration. Accordingly, they are provided with a list of pertinent subjects, illustrated by the particular campaign under study, for discussion. At the classroom sessions, which are conducted in round-table fashion with the instructor acting as moderator, the cadets express their views and contest those with which they are in disagreement. At times, compromises are reached (though more often they are not).

The study of a military campaign is not an end in itself; rather, it is a vehicle which introduces the student to the contemplation of many facets of the military art. For example, the German invasion of Flanders in 1940 presents for consideration a great number of subjects. The list of study topics for this campaign, if reduced to simple subject statements, would read: Military Geography and Topography, Military Organization and Doctrine, The Influence of Political Factors on Military Planning, The Role of Permanent Fortifications in Modern Warfare, The Influence of Technological Advances, The Influence of Naval Power in War Strategy, The Relationship of Time and Space Factors, The Conduct of Airborne Operations, The Attack of Fortified Strong Points, Mobility as a Factor in Operations, Air Support of Ground Operations, Tactics and Techniques of River Crossings, The Command Structure in Combined Operations with Allies, Analysis of Principal Military Leaders, Advances in Submarine Warfare, and The Influence of Present-Day and Future Weapons Systems. It is, of course, impossible to cover fully all of these subjects in a single classroom session, but these, and many others, arise again and again as different campaigns are studied. In the end, a fairly comprehensive field of knowledge has been assimilated.

A Guide to Study

The reader will find his study much easier if he will first become acquainted with the symbols employed to depict information on the maps. Most of the basic symbols are similar for all wars, but there are others peculiar to particular periods. There is a page of symbols in the front of Volume I which is applicable to the maps of the entire volume; Volume II contains a page of symbols pertaining to World War I and another for use with the World War II and Korean War maps.

The narrative accompanying a map will be easier to follow if a few moments are first spent examining the map to ascertain what is represented and, most important, the timing. The title block of each map contains a summation of this information. The troop dispositions at the specific time indicated are shown on the map in solid lines. On some maps, actions and movements, as shown by appropriate route lines and symbols, will lead to the positions shown in solid lines; on others, the solid lines indicate an initial location, and route lines emanating therefrom signify subsequent movements.

On the first map of most campaigns, numerals appear in parentheses under the names of commanders. These signify the numerical strength of the commanders' units. Their strengths are not shown on each map, but they are shown where significant changes from the initial strength have taken place.

The conduct of every campaign is strongly influenced by the topography of the area involved. Frequently, this topography dictates the course of action, and it often introduces significant hazards. An initial study of the ground over which the campaign or battle was fought—rivers, mountains, roads, railroads, vegetation—will prove most helpful in understanding the reasons for many of the actions.

Some of the first sixteen maps of Volume I, which contain much more than the average amount of material, will require special concentrated study.

Charts of chronology are provided for events of each of the major wars: the Civil War, World War I, and World War II. These charts are valuable in correlating events in other areas with those in the particular area under study. We have found from experience that the best way to study wars which are extensive in scope is to study by campaign areas rather than by chronology of events. Consequently, the maps in this atlas are grouped according to campaign areas. However, if the reader desires to study events by time sequence, he can do so by following the charts of chronology and referring to the appropriate maps.

After a period of study, the novice will develop confidence in his ability to master standard works in military history. He may wish to expand his investigation of a particular aspect of this work or to delve into related fields. To assist him, there is provided at the end of each volume a comprehensive list of books, conveniently arranged, which are recommended for further reading.

Acknowledgments

This department is deeply indebted to the many officers who, throughout the years, participated in preparing the material incorporated in this work. Some have passed on, others have retired from active service, and the remainder are expecting grade changes; for these reasons, the grades of those hereafter mentioned are not indicated. All are, or were, officers of the United States Army—except for those whose names are given in italics to indicate that they are members of the United States Air Force.

Research and preparation of the initial drafts of the maps were accomplished by the following: the Civil War section—Allen F. Clark, Jr., Ellsworth I. Davis, John C. B. Elliott, Clayton S. Gates, Lawrence J. Lincoln, Theodore M. Osborne, Alfred D. Starbird, David H. Tulley; all other maps of Volume I —John R. Elting; the World War I section—*Richard C. Boys,* Charley P. Eastburn, Philip L. Elliott, Walter J. Fellenz, Ralph R. Ganns, Earl F. Holton, Cecil E. Spann, Jr., *Daniel F. Tatum,* George P. Winton, Jr.; the World War II section—Raymond W. Allen, Jr., Allen F. Clark, Jr., Edmund K. Daley, Thomas Q. Donaldson, 4th, Charley P. Eastburn, John R. Elting, Clayton S. Gates, Ronan C. Grady, Jr., Charles L. Hassmann, Robert A. Hill, Max S. Johnson, Lawrence J. Lincoln, John J. Outcalt, William H. Roedy, Alfred D. Starbird, Harrison G. Travis; the Korean War—Philip L. Elliott, Cecil E. Spann, Jr.

The text is the product of the collaborative efforts of John R. Elting, Thomas E. Griess, and the undersigned, with the burden of research, initial manuscript drafting, and review of final manuscript falling to the first two mentioned. Many sources have been used in the preparation of the text, particularly official histories. For the World War II and Korean War text, the splendid publications prepared to date by the Office of the Chief of Military History, Department of the Army, have been drawn on heavily as primary sources.

Special acknowledgment is made of the contributions of: T. Dodson Stamps, former head of the department, who initiated the department atlas project; Robert A. Hill, formerly assistant professor, who supervised the preparation of the maps in most of the initial department pamphlets of World War II operations from which the corresponding maps in this work were developed; John R. Elting and Thomas E. Griess, who, in addition to bearing the major burden of text preparation, assisted in the many tasks incident to publication; Edward J. Krasnoborski, department cartographer, who so competently translated the final drafts of the maps into production copy; and James Glover, department secretary, who performed the tedious task of typing the manuscript.

Though many hands have labored in the production of the material which eventually has found its way into this work, the undersigned planned, supervised, and nurtured the original component atlases from their inception, and he either approved or prepared the final drafts of text and maps alike. He must therefore assume full responsibility for any deficiencies which may exist in these volumes.

VINCENT J. ESPOSITO

West Point, New York
June, 1959

TABLE OF CONTENTS

1862	EAST	WEST	
JAN.		HENRY AND DONELSON CAMPAIGN	
FEB.	PENINSULAR CAMPAIGN	Fort Henry / Fort Donelson — SHILOH CAMPAIGN	
MAR.	Troops Embark	Battle of Pea Ridge	
APR.	Siege of Yorktown — VALLEY CAMPAIGN	Shiloh — STONES RIVER CAMPAIGN	Capture of New Orleans
MAY	Seven Pines — McDowell — Winchester		
JUNE	Port Republic / Jackson Leaves the Valley — Seven Days' Battles	Corinth Captured — Buell Starts	Combined Fleet and Land Operations Against Vicksburg
JULY	2D BULL RUN CAMPAIGN	Buell Halted	
AUG.	Withdrawal — Cedar Mountain — 2d Bull Run — ANTIETAM CAMPAIGN	Kirby Smith Starts North — Bragg Starts North	
SEPT.	Antietam	Buell at Louisville	GRANT'S FIRST ADVANCE ON VICKSBURG — Corinth
OCT.	FREDERICKSBURG CAMPAIGN	Perryville	
NOV.	McClellan Relieved	Buell Relieved	Grant Reaches Oxford
DEC.	Fredericksburg	Rosecrans at Nashville — Stones River	Holly Springs — Chickashaw Bluffs

1863	EAST	WEST	
JAN.	Hooker Replaces Burnside	VICKSBURG CAMPAIGN	
FEB.		Period of Unsuccessful Attempts	
MAR.			OPERATIONS AGAINST PORT HUDSON
APR.	CHANCELLORSVILLE CAMPAIGN		Operations West of New Orleans
MAY	Chancellorsville — GETTYSBURG CAMPAIGN	Grant Crosses the Mississippi — Jackson / Champion's Hill / Siege Begins	Siege of Port Hudson Begins
JUNE	Lee Crosses the Potomac — Meade Replaces Hooker	TULLAHOMA CAMPAIGN	
JULY	Gettysburg / Lee Recrosses the Potomac	Surrender	Surrender
AUG.	CHICKAMAUGA CAMPAIGN — Bragg Evacuates Chattanooga	OPERATIONS IN EAST TENNESSEE	
SEPT.	OPERATIONS ALONG ORANGE & ALEXANDRIA RY. — Chickamauga — Union Retreat to Chattanooga	Burnside Captures Knoxville	
OCT.	Lee Crosses the Rapidan — Confederates Retire	CHATTANOOGA CAMPAIGN — Thomas Replaces Rosecrans — Supply Line Cleared	
NOV.	Lee Recrosses the Rapidan — Mine Run	Lookout Mountain and Missionary Ridge	Longstreet Sent to Knoxville — Confederate Assault
DEC.			Siege Raised

1864	EAST			WEST
JAN.				
FEB.				
MAR.	**ARMY OF THE JAMES**	**ARMY OF THE POTOMAC**	**OPERATIONS IN THE SHENANDOAH VALLEY**	
APR.				Red River Expedition
MAY	Butler Advances / Butler "Bottled Up" at Bermuda Hundred	Grant Advances / Wilderness / Spottsylvania / North Anna / Cold Harbor	Sigel Advances / Newmarket	Sherman Advances
JUNE	Attack on Petersburg	Crossing of the James	Lynchburg	Kenesaw Mountain
JULY		The Mine	Monocacy / Washington / Kernstown	Chattahoochee Crossing / Hood Replaces Johnston / Battles North and East of Atlanta
AUG.			Sheridan in Command	Sherman Swings to the West / Combat South of Atlanta
SEPT.			Winchester / Fisher's Hill	Hood Evacuates Atlanta / Hood Moves West to Alabama / Sherman Follows Hood North
OCT.		Siege of Petersburg	Cedar Creek	Operations Against Union L of C / Sherman Returns to Atlanta / Hood to Tuscumbia
NOV.				March to the Sea / Hood Invades Tennessee / Spring Hill
DEC.				Savannah / Franklin / Nashville / Hood Back in Alabama
1865 JAN.				Sherman Moves North
FEB.				Columbia
MAR.		Lee's Assault / Five Forks	Sheridan Joins Grant	Fayetteville / Goldsboro
APR.		Lee Surrenders		Armistice / Johnston Surrenders

BASIC SYMBOLS:

Company or troop	I	Infantry	⊠
Battalion or squadron	II	Cavalry	⊘
Regiment	III	Cavalry covering force	• • • • • •
Brigade	X	Artillery	▣
Division	XX	Artillery in position	⊔⊔⊔
Corps	XXX	(Symbol does not indicate type or quantity)	
Army	XXXX	Trains	⎕

Examples of Combinations of Basic Symbols:

Small infantry detachment ⊠

2d Regiment, Virginia state troops ⊠ 2 Va.

1st Division, regular troops ⊠ 1

Cheatham's infantry division of Polk's corps ⊠ Cheatham (POLK)

Williams infantry division of Slocum's XII Corps ⊠ Williams (XII)

Shafter's V Corps ⊡ SHAFTER

Stuart's cavalry corps ⊘ STUART

Jackson's infantry division, less unit commanded by Winder ⊠ Jackson (−Winder)

Garrard's cavalry division, with unit commanded by Croxton attached ⊘ Garrard (+Croxton)

Army commanded by Meade ⎕ MEADE

OTHER SYMBOLS:

	Actual location	Prior location
Troops on the march	➤	⇢
Troops in position	▬	⊏ ⊐
Troops in bivouac or reserve	⬭	⬭
	Occupied	Unoccupied
Field works	∿∿∿	∧∧∧
Strong prepared positions	⊓⊔⊓	⊓⊔⊓

Troops displacing and direction of movement

Troops in position under attack

Route of march - - ➤ - - ➤ - - ➤

Boundary between units ——— XXX ———
(Appropriate basic symbol)

Fort ⊠

Swamp

THE WEST POINT ATLAS
OF AMERICAN WARS

Volume I   1689-1900

The American colonies were born, and grew, in an atmosphere of war. Many of them barely survived the early Indian wars. Then, from 1689 to 1815, came six world-wide wars between England and France. America was involved in all of them. This map shows the principal operations carried out within the American colonies prior to 1758.

In 1689, the colonies were encircled by a line of French forts extending along the rivers and lakes from the Gulf of St. Lawrence to New Orleans. Indian tribes were aligned with both sides; those friendly with the English are indicated in blue on the map; those allied to the French, in red. After 1700, the Spaniards in Florida and Texas joined the French.

In North America, the War of the Grand Alliance (1689-97)—called King William's War by the colonists—and the War of the Spanish Succession (1701-13)—or Queen Anne's War—were largely a series of minor, but bloody, French and Indian raids (*not shown*) against the frontier settlements. The War of the Austrian Succession (1740-48)—King George's War—was marked by a successful expedition of Massachusetts volunteers under Col. William Pepperell, supported by a small British squadron, against the important French fortress of Louisbourg (*see inset sketch*). Its garrison, mutinous and short of ammunition, hastily evacuated their key Grand Battery, whose guns the colonists quickly turned against the main fortress. (In the southern colonies, which are not shown here, Governor James Oglethorpe of Georgia successfully defended his colony against the Spanish.) At the end of the war, Louisbourg was returned to the French. Port Royal (*large map, upper right*), and later Halifax (founded 1749), became the British northern bases.

The French and Indian War (1754-63) began when the French seized a Virginia trading post, which they renamed Fort Duquesne (now Pittsburgh, Pennsylvania). A small force of Virginia militia, under Lt. Col. George Washington, advanced into the disputed area (*lower center*). Though successful in an opening skirmish, Washington eventually was forced back into Fort Necessity where, after a three-day siege, he was compelled to surrender.

In 1755, Maj. Gen. Edward Braddock landed in Virginia with two understrength British regiments, which he partially filled with colonial recruits. His plan of campaign included four widely separated operations: he himself was to move against Fort Duquesne along Washington's original route; a colonial column was to advance up the Mohawk River against the French posts on Lake Ontario (*see map 2*); another was to attack Crown Point (*this map, right center*); and a third was to capture Forts St. John and Beausejour in Canada (*upper right*). It should be noted that in those days few roads existed in North America. Therefore, military operations were generally along lakes and rivers. For example: the traditional invasion route from Canada to New York was by way of the Richelieu River, Lake Champlain, Lake George, and the Hudson River.

Braddock's column advanced to within eight miles of Fort Duquesne before the French commander there could persuade his reluctant Indian allies to join him in an attack. Unfamiliar with forest fighting and shaken by heavy losses, most of Braddock's troops panicked during the Battle of Monongahela which followed (*inset sketch*). The survivors were eventually withdrawn to Philadelphia. Braddock was mortally wounded. Washington, serving as one of his aides, distinguished himself by his cool courage. The hostile Indians, now convinced that their French ally would win the war, began raiding savagely along the frontier.

The two center expeditions in New York likewise failed to take their objectives (*see* the text of *map 2* for a detailed account of their experiences and of the 1758 expedition against Louisbourg), but the expedition against St. John and Beausejour took these forts with ease and reinforced the British base at Port Royal. The local population of the surrounding area—the Arcadians—were forcibly deported to prevent their support of the French garrison at Louisbourg.

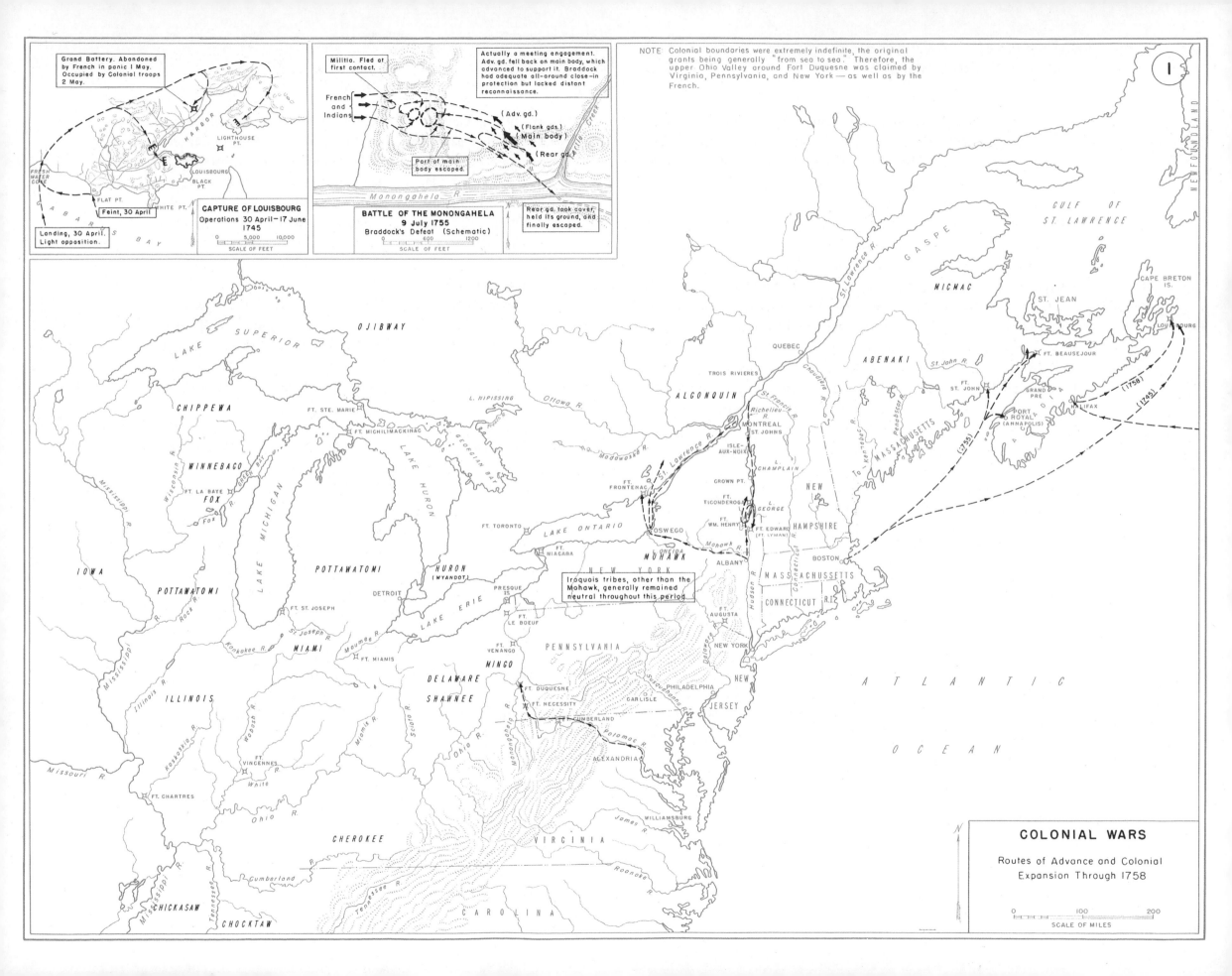

CAPTURE OF LOUISBOURG
Operations 30 April – 17 June 1745

Grand Battery. Abandoned by French in panic 1 May. Occupied by Colonial troops 2 May.

Militia. Fled at first contact.

Feint, 30 April

Landing, 30 April. Light opposition.

SCALE OF FEET
0   5,000   10,000

BATTLE OF THE MONONGAHELA
9 July 1755
Braddock's Defeat (Schematic)

Actually a meeting engagement. Adv. gd. fell back on main body, which advanced to support it. Braddock had adequate all-around close-in protection but lacked distant reconnaissance.

French and Indians

(Adv. gd.)
(Flank gds.)
Main body
(Rear gd.)

Part of main body escaped.

Rear gd. took cover, held its ground, and finally escaped.

Monongahela R.

SCALE OF FEET
0   600   1200

NOTE: Colonial boundaries were extremely indefinite, the original grants being generally "from sea to sea." Therefore, the upper Ohio Valley around Fort Duquesne was claimed by Virginia, Pennsylvania, and New York — as well as by the French.

Iroquois tribes, other than the Mohawk, generally remained neutral throughout this period.

COLONIAL WARS

Routes of Advance and Colonial Expansion Through 1758

SCALE OF MILES
0   100   200

Governor William Shirley of Massachusetts led the 1755 expedition up the Mohawk River, his initial objective being Fort Niagara. On reaching Oswego (*center*), he halted, fearing that the French troops at Fort Frontenac might cut his line of communications behind him. Fort Frontenac being too strong to attack, he reinforced the Oswego garrison and returned to Albany.

The command of the column marching on Crown Point (*right center*) in 1755 was assigned to William Johnson because of his influence with the Mohawk Indians. After building Fort Lyman (later renamed Fort Edward) to command the portage between Lake George and the upper Hudson River, Johnson continued his advance to the head of Lake George. There he was attacked by General Ludwig August Dieskau, the French commander at Crown Point, who had moved south to surprise him. Although Dieskau successfully ambushed one of Johnson's detachments, he could not persuade his Indians and the Canadian militia to join in an attack on the hastily fortified colonial camp. Undaunted, he attacked the camp with a few French regulars. His troops were repulsed and retreated to Ticonderoga; Dieskau was wounded and captured. Johnson failed to follow up his success; instead, he built Fort William Henry on the site of his camp and disbanded most of his troops.

In 1756 this frontier bickering grew into an overt major conflict—The Seven Years' War (in America, the French and Indian War)—in which England and Prussia stood against all Europe. The Marquis de Montcalm arrived in Canada to command the French forces; a new British commander, Lord Loudoun, concentrated his forces at Albany. In August, Montcalm made a swift raid across Lake Ontario and overwhelmed the Oswego garrison. Otherwise, fighting took the form of increasingly ferocious raids by French irregulars and Indians and of counterraids by Loudoun's rangers.

In 1757, the forceful William Pitt became the British prime minister. He increased the British forces in North America and began cutting Canada off from France by a tightening naval blockade. That same year Loudoun stripped the frontier of its best troops to organize a force for an attack on Louisbourg, but he abandoned his plan on learning that the fortress had been reinforced. Meanwhile, Montcalm suddenly struck south along Lake Champlain and Lake George and forced the surrender of Fort William Henry. He permitted the garrison to march out with the honors of war but lost control of his Indian allies, who massacred part of it.

The British plan for 1758 provided for three operations: Maj. Gen. Jeffrey Amherst, with Brig. Gen. James Wolfe as one of his subordinate commanders, was to take Louisbourg (*inset sketch*) and then move against Quebec; Maj. Gen. James Abercrombie was to advance northward from the vicinity of Albany (*lower right*) while part of his command, under Col. John Bradstreet, moved up the Mohawk against Fort Frontenac; and Brig. Gen. John Forbes was to capture Fort Duquesne (*not shown*). Amherst captured Louisbourg; but Abercrombie blundered into a frontal attack on Montcalm's fortified position at Ticonderoga and sacrificed his best troops in repeated assaults before ordering a retreat. Amherst therefore abandoned his proposed movement on Quebec. Forbes eventually arrived at Fort Duquesne and found it deserted. Bradstreet's raid on Fort Frontenac was successful and undoubtedly hastened the French evacuation of Fort Duquesne. The Indians then began to desert the French.

Amherst then took command of all the British forces in North America. He planned to lead an advance from Albany northward in 1759, while Wolfe sailed up the St. Lawrence River to attack Quebec and a small expedition moved west to reoccupy Oswego and capture Fort Niagara. Amherst's march was slow but inexorable. The French were forced to abandon first Ticonderoga and then Crown Point. At the latter place, Amherst halted for the winter and built a flotilla of gunboats with which he gained control of Lake Champlain. The expedition against Oswego and Fort Niagara was completely successful.

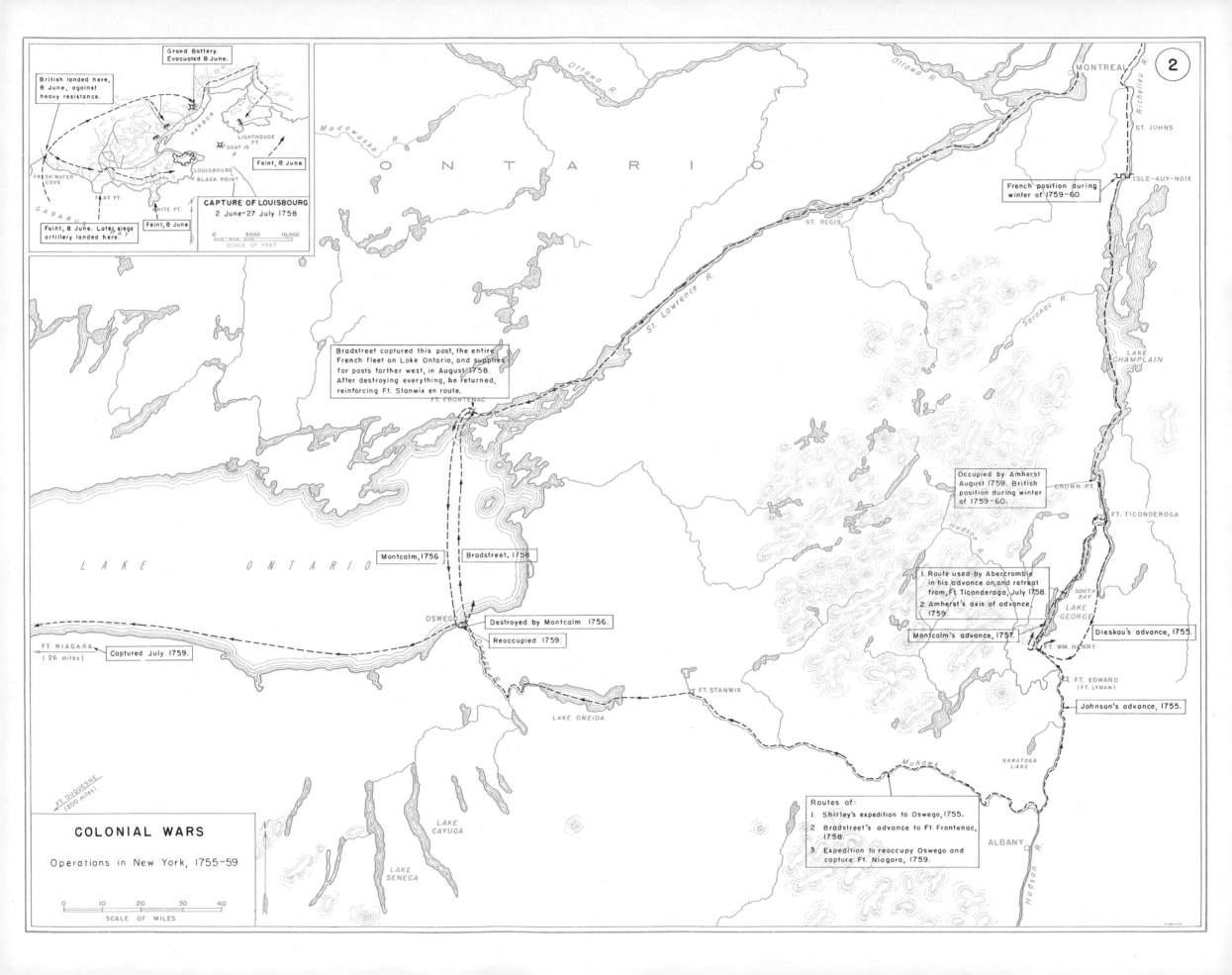

2

CAPTURE OF LOUISBOURG
2 June–27 July 1758

Grand Battery. Evacuated 8 June.

British landed here, 8 June, against heavy resistance.

Feint, 8 June

Feint, 8 June. Later siege artillery landed here.

Feint, 8 June

FRESH WATER COVE

GABARUS BAY

FLAT PT.

WHITE PT.

HARBOR

LIGHTHOUSE PT.

GOAT IS.

LOUISBOURG

BLACK POINT

0   5000   10,000
SCALE OF FEET

O N T A R I O

Madawaska R.

Ottawa R.

Ottawa R.

Richelieu R.

MONTREAL

ST. JOHNS

ISLE-AUX-NOIX

French position during winter of 1759-60

ST. REGIS

St. Lawrence R.

Saranac R.

LAKE CHAMPLAIN

Bradstreet captured this post, the entire French fleet on Lake Ontario, and supplies for posts farther west, in August 1758. After destroying everything, he returned, reinforcing Ft. Stanwix en route.

FT. FRONTENAC

Occupied by Amherst August 1759. British position during winter of 1759-60.

CROWN PT.

FT. TICONDEROGA

Hudson R.

Montcalm, 1756

Bradstreet, 1758

L A K E   O N T A R I O

OSWEGO

Destroyed by Montcalm 1756.

Reoccupied 1759.

1. Route used by Abercrombie in his advance on, and retreat from, Ft. Ticonderoga, July 1758.
2. Amherst's axis of advance, 1759.

Montcalm's advance, 1757.

SOUTH BAY

LAKE GEORGE

Dieskau's advance, 1755.

FT. NIAGARA
(26 miles)

Captured July 1759.

Oswego R.

FT. WM. HENRY

FT. EDWARD
(FT. LYMAN)

Johnson's advance, 1755.

FT. STANWIX

LAKE ONEIDA

Mohawk R.

SARATOGA LAKE

FT. DUQUESNE
(200 miles)

LAKE CAYUGA

LAKE SENECA

COLONIAL WARS

Operations in New York, 1755-59

Routes of:
1. Shirley's expedition to Oswego, 1755.
2. Bradstreet's advance to Ft. Frontenac, 1758.
3. Expedition to reoccupy Oswego and capture Ft. Niagara, 1759.

ALBANY

Hudson R.

0   10   20   30   40
SCALE OF MILES

Meanwhile, on 26 June, 1759, Wolfe landed on the Island of Orleans, just downstream from Quebec (*inset*). The French commander, Montcalm, had the stronger army numerically, but most of his troops were unsteady Canadian militia. Furthermore, he was hampered by interference from the Marquis de Vaudreuil, the arrogant and incompetent French Governor General. Montcalm carefully fortified his position and hoped to defend it until the approach of winter would force the British to leave the St. Lawrence River. His attempts to burn the British fleet by means of fire ships failed. Wolfe could neither find a weak spot in the French lines nor tempt Montcalm into an erroneous move. Finally, he tried to storm the French position on the north bank of the river, but was repulsed with heavy losses. Then, on 3 September, Wolfe evacuated his Montmorenci position and moved more ships and men upstream above Quebec. A trail up the cliffs was located at Anse-au-Foulon, some two miles upstream from Quebec, and Wolfe decided to make a surprise attack there. Events favored his venture: his deceptive operations along the French defenses led Montcalm to expect an attack at Beauport; the French sentinels along the river mistook the boats carrying Wolfe's assault force for some French vessels they had been told to expect; and, finally, the Canadian guard on the trail at Anse-au-Foulon allowed itself to be surprised. Wolfe advanced and drew up his forces on the Plains of Abraham. Montcalm, affected by his own eagerness and by Vaudreuil's meddling, attacked before all available French troops had joined him—particularly a large detachment from farther up the river at Cap-Rouge. The short battle which followed was in the formal eighteenth-century European style. Massed English volleys of one-ounce balls fired at forty yards shattered the French advance. Montcalm was mortally wounded; Wolfe received three wounds in rapid succession and died on the battlefield. His victorious troops had to halt their pursuit of Montcalm's troops to check the approaching Cap-Rouge force.

The command of French troops around Quebec then fell to Vaudreuil. Although Quebec was a fortified town and the troops at his disposal still outnumbered the English, Vaudreuil became panic-stricken and fled upstream to Jacques Cartier (*large map*). A week later, Quebec surrendered. Through the winter there was constant skirmishing around the city, the British suffering severely from cold and sickness. In April, General de Lévis, Montcalm's successor as military commander, marched on Quebec from Montreal. Brig. Gen. James Murray, Wolfe's successor, came out to meet him and was defeated by superior numbers. However, he managed to hold Quebec until the breakup of the river ice in May allowed passage of the British fleet with reinforcements and supplies. Lévis fell back for a last stand around Montreal.

Amherst then began his final offensive. It included: an advance by Murray up the St. Lawrence River from Quebec; another by Brig. Gen. William Haviland from Crown Point (*lower left*) northward along the Richelieu River; and an advance by his own column by way of Oswego and down the St. Lawrence. All three forces converged on Montreal on 6 September, 1760. Two days later Vaudreuil capitulated, and Canada became a British colony.

Thus fighting subsided in North America until 1763, when Pontiac led a general revolt of western Indian tribes. All the western forts were devastated except Detroit and Fort Pitt (formerly Fort Duquesne), which managed to hold out. Settlers were massacred and several detachments of troops destroyed. Col. Henry Bouquet, a Swiss soldier of fortune who became an expert Indian fighter, finally crushed the rebellion in 1764.

Though Washington and other colonial officers had gained valuable training, the war was actually won by English troops and English commanders. Few colonial officers had distinguished themselves, and the bickering colonies had never managed to cooperate in exploiting the great superiority in manpower they had enjoyed over the Canadians.

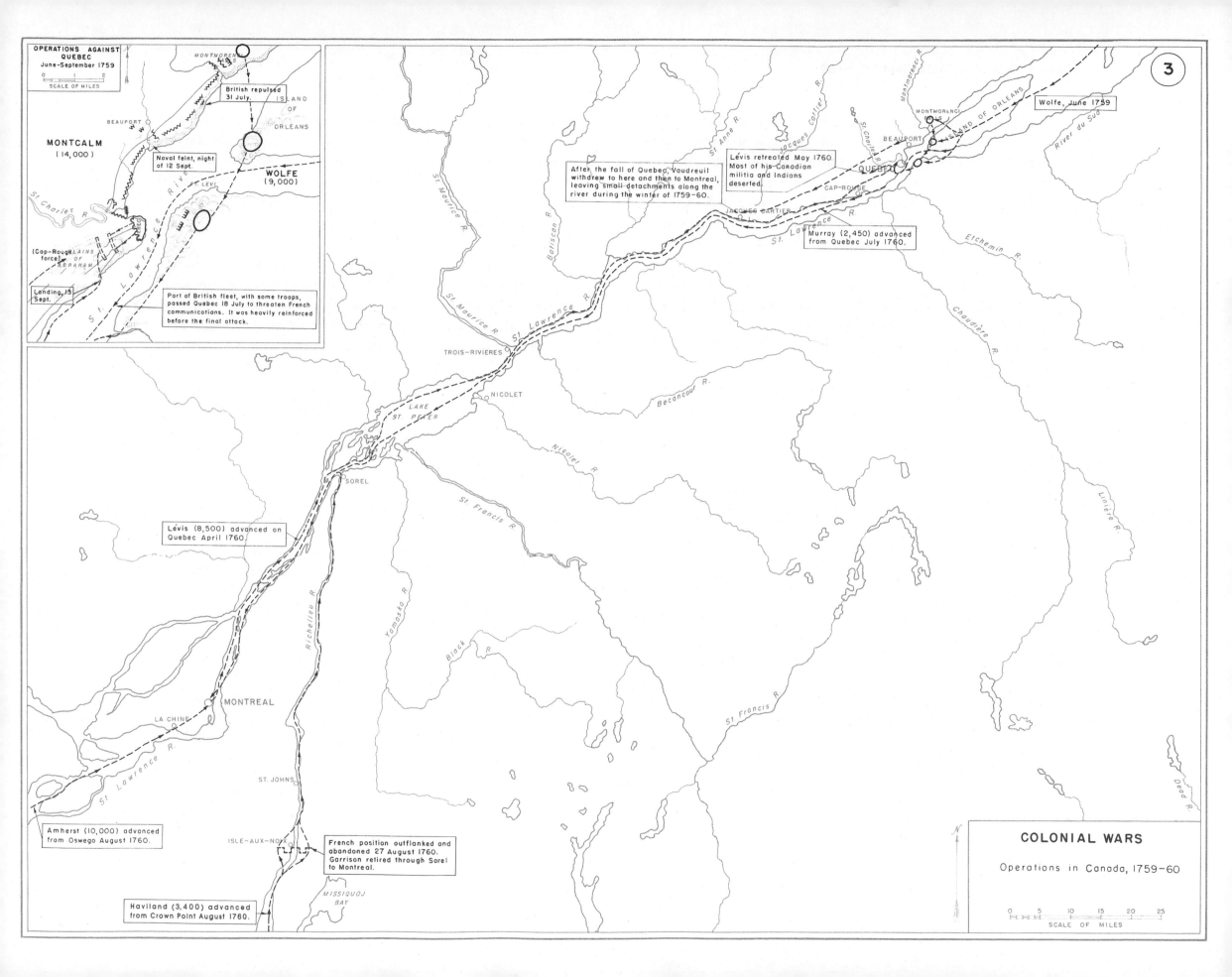

3

OPERATIONS AGAINST QUEBEC
June–September 1759

SCALE OF MILES

MONTCALM
(14,000)

WOLFE
(9,000)

MONTMORENCI FALLS

British repulsed 31 July.

BEAUPORT

ISLAND OF ORLEANS

Naval feint, night of 12 Sept.

St Charles R.

(Cap-Rouge force)

PLAINS OF ABRAHAM

Landing, 13 Sept.

Part of British fleet, with some troops, passed Quebec 18 July to threaten French communications. It was heavily reinforced before the final attack.

Wolfe, June 1759

MONTMORENCI FALLS

BEAUPORT

QUEBEC

CAP-ROUGE

JACQUES CARTIER

Lévis retreated May 1760. Most of his Canadian militia and Indians deserted.

After the fall of Quebec, Vaudreuil withdrew to here and then to Montreal, leaving small detachments along the river during the winter of 1759–60.

Murray (2,450) advanced from Quebec July 1760.

St Anne R.

Jacques Cartier R.

St Charles R.

St. Lawrence R.

Montmorenci R.

River du Sud

Etchemin R.

Chaudiere R.

Batiscan R.

St Maurice R.

St. Lawrence R.

TROIS-RIVIERES

NICOLET

LAKE ST. PETER

Becancour R.

Nicolet R.

SOREL

Lévis (8,500) advanced on Quebec April 1760.

St Francis R.

Linière R.

Richelieu R.

Yamaska R.

Black R.

St Francis R.

MONTREAL

LA CHINE

St Lawrence R.

ST. JOHNS

Amherst (10,000) advanced from Oswego August 1760.

ISLE-AUX-NOIX

French position outflanked and abandoned 27 August 1760. Garrison retired through Sorel to Montreal.

MISSIQUOI BAY

Dead R.

Haviland (3,400) advanced from Crown Point August 1760.

N

COLONIAL WARS

Operations in Canada, 1759–60

SCALE OF MILES

In the early morning of 19 April, 1775, a British detachment, en route from Boston to destroy colonial military supplies at Concord, found the Lexington militia drawn up across its line of march. An attempt to disarm the militia brought on a brief skirmish. The militia scattered; the British proceeded to Concord where they destroyed such supplies as the colonists had not hastily removed. Meanwhile, the countryside was warned by William Dawes, Paul Revere, and other American riders. Militia units emerged from neighboring communities, stalked the British back to Boston, and placed them under siege. On 10 May, Ethan Allen and Benedict Arnold surprised and captured the small British garrison at Fort Ticonderoga, seized Crown Point, and successfully raided St. Johns.

The British over-all plans for the suppression of this colonial uprising appear to have had four basic purposes (*sketch* a): to separate the New England colonies, the principal fomenters of rebellion, from the other colonies by seizing the line of the Hudson River northward through Lake Champlain; to isolate the food-producing central colonies by occupying the line of the Chesapeake Bay and the lower Susquehanna River; to control the southern colonies by holding Charleston, Georgetown, and the line of the Santee River; to maintain a naval blockade of the coast to prevent the importation of weapons and supplies. A plan for a drive westward from the Boston area to the Hudson River to split the New England colonies apparently was considered but was abandoned in favor of operations to capture Newport, Rhode Island, which would provide a convenient naval base.

If conducted with determination and with adequate force, these plans could have been executed successfully. But the British government and the principal military commanders, hopeful of conciliatory measures, failed to act with resolution; nor were adequate forces provided. War with the colonists was unpopular in England; hence recruiting was unsuccessful. Even the hiring of 30,000 German mercenaries failed to provide the essential manpower requirements. As a result, the British were never able to control an invaded area, due to the necessity for shifting the limited forces available to operations in other areas. Also, the long, irregular coastline of the colonies was difficult to blockade effectively.

While fortifying their positions around Boston (*sketch* b), the colonists occupied Breed's Hill, bringing on the action known as the Battle of Bunker Hill (*sketch* c). Batteries there would threaten British shipping in Boston Harbor, so the British immediately attacked the hastily constructed American entrenchments. These attacks were very costly, but they caused the colonists to withdraw into their original lines.

On 2 July, 1775, Washington assumed command of the militia around Boston. The remainder of the year he spent in enlisting and training a new army as the militiamen were discharged progressively in accordance with their terms of service. At the same time, an improvised and ambitious two-pronged invasion of Canada was conducted by Brig. Gen. Richard Montgomery and Col. Benedict Arnold (*sketch* a). Despite great hardships, the two columns eventually reached Quebec. However, the British had just reinforced the town, and the American assaults were repulsed. Montgomery was killed and Arnold was wounded. The next spring, though reinforced, the invasion collapsed.

In the meantime, Col. Henry Knox transported to Boston by sled heavy artillery captured at Ticonderoga. Early in March, 1776, Washington occupied Dorchester Heights (*sketch* b); later he extended his siege work to Nook's Hill. Thus Boston Harbor was rendered untenable for the British, who evacuated the city and sailed to Halifax.

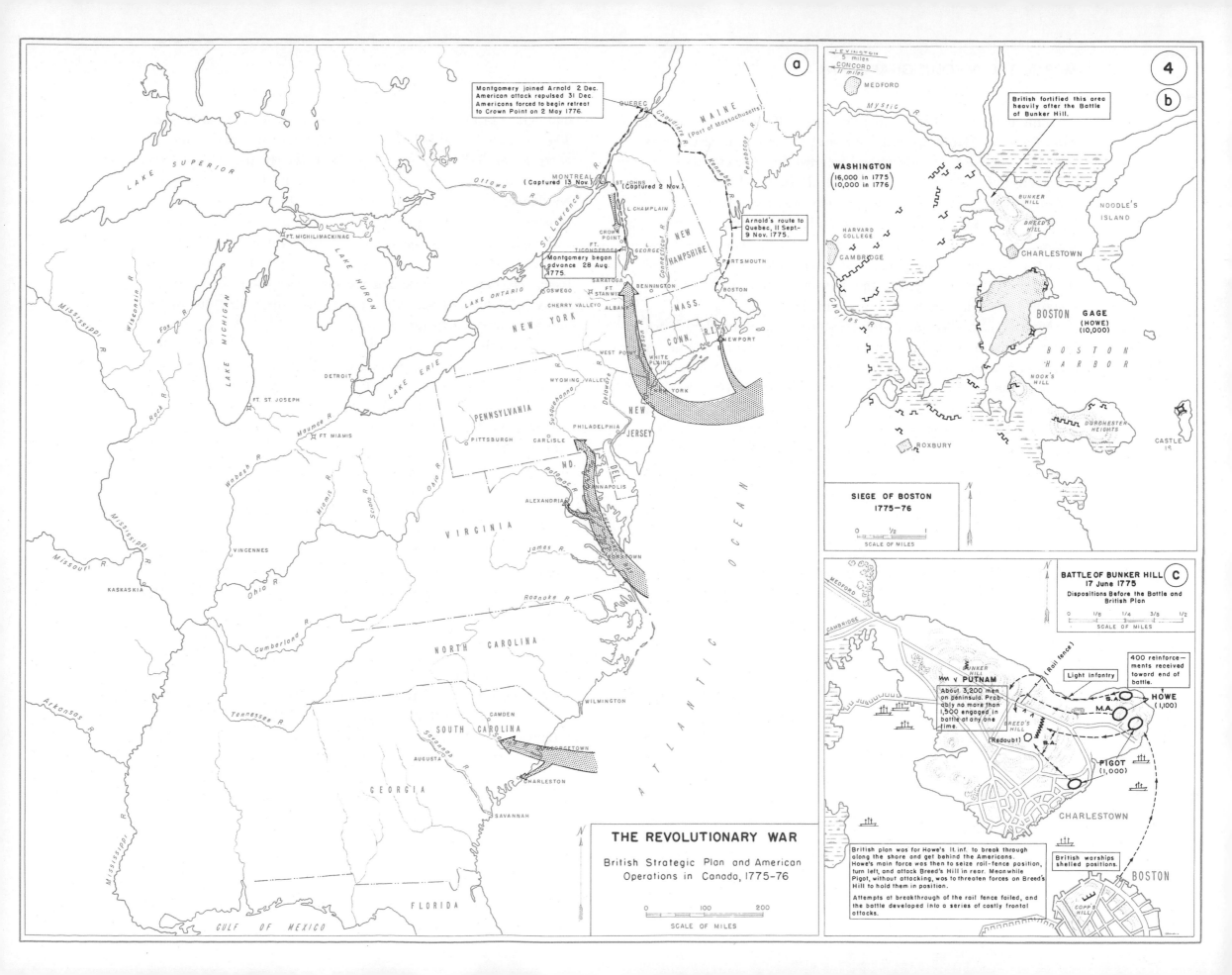

a

Montgomery joined Arnold 2 Dec.
American attack repulsed 31 Dec.
Americans forced to begin retreat
to Crown Point on 2 May 1776.

Arnold's route to
Quebec, II Sept-
9 Nov. 1775.

Montgomery began
advance 28 Aug.
1775.

QUEBEC (Port of Massachusetts)

MAINE

MONTREAL (Captured 13 Nov.) ST. JOHNS (Captured 2 Nov.)

CROWN POINT

FT. TICONDEROGA L. GEORGE

NEW HAMPSHIRE

PORTSMOUTH

SARATOGA FT. STANWIX BENNINGTON

ALBANY BOSTON

MASS.

OSWEGO CHERRY VALLEY

CONN. R.I.

NEW YORK NEWPORT

LAKE SUPERIOR

LAKE MICHIGAN LAKE HURON

FT. MICHILIMACKINAC

LAKE ONTARIO

LAKE ERIE

DETROIT

FT. ST. JOSEPH

WEST POINT WHITE PLAINS

NEW YORK

PENNSYLVANIA

NEW JERSEY

PITTSBURGH CARLISLE PHILADELPHIA

WYOMING VALLEY

FT. MIAMIS

VINCENNES

MD. DEL.

ANNAPOLIS

ALEXANDRIA

VIRGINIA

KASKASKIA

James R. YORKTOWN

Roanoke R.

NORTH CAROLINA

WILMINGTON

CAMDEN

SOUTH CAROLINA GEORGETOWN

AUGUSTA CHARLESTON

GEORGIA

SAVANNAH

FLORIDA

ATLANTIC OCEAN

GULF OF MEXICO

THE REVOLUTIONARY WAR

British Strategic Plan and American
Operations in Canada, 1775-76

0   100   200
SCALE OF MILES

4

b

LEXINGTON 5 miles
CONCORD 11 miles

MEDFORD

MYSTIC R.

British fortified this area
heavily after the Battle
of Bunker Hill.

WASHINGTON
(16,000 in 1775)
(10,000 in 1776)

BUNKER HILL

NOODLE'S ISLAND

HARVARD COLLEGE

BREED'S HILL

CAMBRIDGE

CHARLESTOWN

Charles R.

BOSTON

GAGE
(HOWE)
(10,000)

BOSTON HARBOR

NOOK'S HILL

ROXBURY

DORCHESTER HEIGHTS

CASTLE IS.

SIEGE OF BOSTON
1775-76

0   1/2   1
SCALE OF MILES

BATTLE OF BUNKER HILL **c**
17 June 1775
Dispositions Before the Battle and
British Plan

0   1/8   1/4   3/8   1/2
SCALE OF MILES

MEDFORD

CAMBRIDGE

BUNKER HILL PUTNAM

About 3,200 men
on peninsula. Prob-
ably no more than
1,500 engaged in
battle at any one
time.

(Rail fence)

Light infantry

400 reinforce-
ments received
toward end of
battle.

S.A. HOWE
M.A. (1,100)

BREED'S HILL

(Redoubt) S.A.

PIGOT
(1,000)

CHARLESTOWN

British warships
shelled positions.

BOSTON

COPP'S HILL

British plan was for Howe's lt. inf. to break through
along the shore and get behind the Americans.
Howe's main force was then to seize rail-fence position,
turn left, and attack Breed's Hill in rear. Meanwhile
Pigot, without attacking, was to threaten forces on Breed's
Hill to hold them in position.

Attempts at breakthrough of the rail fence failed, and
the battle developed into a series of costly frontal
attacks.

The initial British offensive in 1776 was in the Carolinas, where Maj. Gen. Sir Henry Clinton's attempt to seize Charleston was severely repulsed. Washington meanwhile concentrated his army around New York (*sketch* a). Defense of the city presented a difficult problem, for not only was its area dominated by Brooklyn Heights, but the surrounding navigable waterways allowed the British navy to join in an attack. The Americans built fortifications, sank hulks, and installed batteries to control the rivers. They garrisoned the harbor islands and stationed one-third of their troops on Long Island.

Maj. Gen. Sir William Howe wished to capture New York intact for use as winter quarters for his troops, so he avoided a direct attack on the city and began operations by landing on Long Island (*sketch* b). Here, by clever maneuvering, he outflanked the American position south of Brooklyn Heights. Complete victory was in sight but, perhaps fearful of another Bunker Hill, Howe halted the attack and planned to resort to siege operations with the help of the British fleet. However, a northwest wind prevented the warships from operating in the East River and a heavy morning fog permitted Washington to complete the withdrawal of his troops to New York.

Howe now lost two weeks in fruitless peace negotiations with a Congressional committee. Then he renewed his amphibious advance by landing on Manhattan Island at Kip's Bay (*sketch* a), scattering the American troops there. This maneuver forced Washington to abandon New York. He established a new position at Harlem Heights and repulsed the expected British attack. Howe then executed another turning movement by landing at Throg's Neck, but his maneuver was frustrated by the destruction of an essential bridge. He then landed at Pell's Point; Washington countered by taking up a defensive position at White Plains. An indecisive engagement ensued, after which the Americans retired to a stronger position at North Castle.

Howe suddenly turned about and attacked Fort Washington, which threatened his line of communications. Washington had delayed too long in ordering evacuation of the isolated post. The overwhelming British attack captured the place and its garrison of 3,000. A few days later the British crossed the Hudson and made a surprise attack on Fort Lee. Maj. Gen. Nathanael Greene and his garrison barely made their escape. Washington sought to protect New Jersey and cover the American capital at Philadelphia, but the small force under his command was harried across New Jersey as far as the Delaware River. He prepared to defend the several crossings of the river, but was highly relieved when the British suspended operations and went into winter quarters.

Meanwhile, a British expedition (*not shown*) from New York captured Newport, Rhode Island, and its excellent harbor. Also, during this period Sir Guy Carleton, Governor of Canada, advanced south as part of the plan to isolate the New England colonies. No effective American force could be brought against him, but Benedict Arnold, with an improvised fleet, fought an effective delaying action against Carleton's squadron on Lake Champlain. Carleton later captured Crown Point, but concluded that the season was too late for operations against Ticonderoga and returned to Canada.

The arrival of reinforcements bolstered Washington's strength and permitted him to undertake a three-pronged Christmas offensive across the Delaware (*sketch* c). Only his own column completed the crossing, but it surprised and overwhelmed Col. Johann Rall's Hessian brigade at Trenton. Maj. Gen. Lord Charles Cornwallis advanced to surround Washington's troops in Trenton, but the Americans slipped away at night by a back road, shattered Cornwallis' rear guard at Princeton, and then took up a strong position at Morristown. Only the fatigue of his troops prevented Washington from seizing the main British depot at New Brunswick.

Harassed by American raids, the British evacuated all of New Jersey except New Brunswick, Perth Amboy, and Paulus Hook.

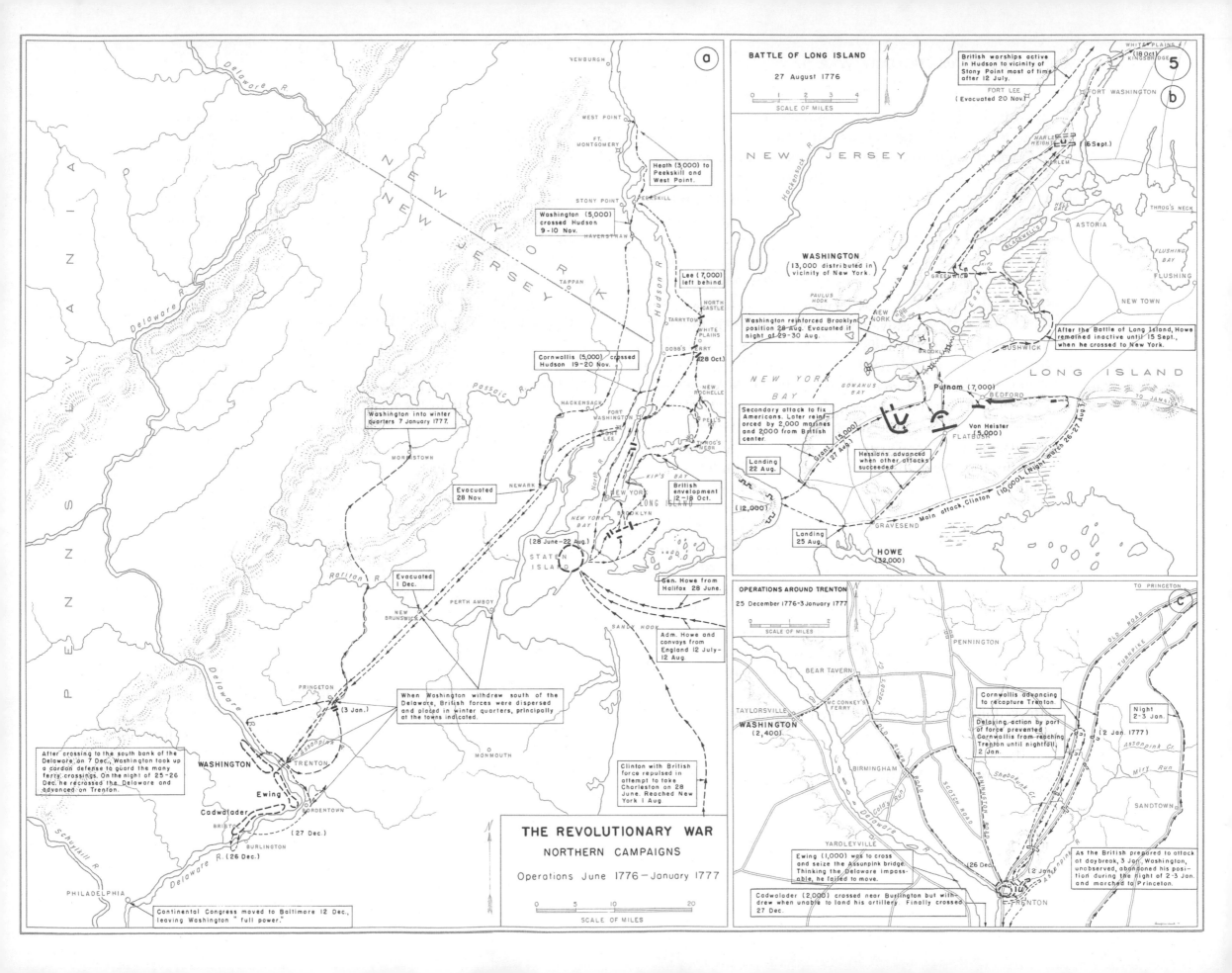

THE REVOLUTIONARY WAR

NORTHERN CAMPAIGNS

Operations June 1776 – January 1777

Map a (left panel):

- Heath (3,000) to Peekskill and West Point.
- Washington (5,000) crossed Hudson 9-10 Nov.
- Lee (7,000) left behind.
- Cornwallis (5,000) crossed Hudson 19-20 Nov.
- Washington into winter quarters 7 January 1777.
- Evacuated 28 Nov.
- British envelopment 12-18 Oct.
- Evacuated 1 Dec.
- Gen. Howe from Halifax 28 June.
- Adm. Howe and convoys from England 12 July-12 Aug.
- When Washington withdrew south of the Delaware, British forces were dispersed and placed in winter quarters, principally at the towns indicated.
- After crossing to the south bank of the Delaware on 7 Dec., Washington took up a cordon defense to guard the many ferry crossings. On the night of 25-26 Dec. he recrossed the Delaware and advanced on Trenton.
- Clinton with British force repulsed in attempt to take Charleston on 28 June. Reached New York 1 Aug.
- Continental Congress moved to Baltimore 12 Dec., leaving Washington "full power."
- WASHINGTON
- Ewing
- Cadwalader
- (27 Dec.)
- (26 Dec.)
- (3 Jan.)
- (28 June-22 Aug.)

Map b (upper right): BATTLE OF LONG ISLAND, 27 August 1776

- British warships active in Hudson to vicinity of Stony Point most of time after 12 July.
- Fort Lee (Evacuated 20 Nov.)
- (6 Sept.)
- After the Battle of Long Island, Howe remained inactive until 15 Sept., when he crossed to New York.
- WASHINGTON (13,000 distributed in vicinity of New York)
- Washington reinforced Brooklyn position 28 Aug. Evacuated it night of 29-30 Aug.
- Putnam (7,000)
- Von Heister (5,000)
- Secondary attack to fix Americans. Later reinforced by 2,000 marines and 2000 from British center.
- Grant (5,000) (27 Aug.)
- Hessians advanced when other attacks succeeded.
- Landing 22 Aug.
- Landing 25 Aug.
- (12,000)
- Main attack, Clinton (10,000) (Night march 26-27 Aug.)
- HOWE (32,000)

Map c (lower right): OPERATIONS AROUND TRENTON, 25 December 1776-3 January 1777

- TO PRINCETON
- Cornwallis advancing to recapture Trenton.
- Night 2-3 Jan.
- Delaying action by part of force prevented Cornwallis from reaching Trenton until nightfall, 2 Jan.
- (2 Jan. 1777)
- WASHINGTON (2,400)
- Ewing (1,000) was to cross and seize the Assunpink bridge. Thinking the Delaware impassable, he failed to move.
- Cadwalader (2,000) crossed near Burlington but withdrew when unable to land his artillery. Finally crossed 27 Dec.
- As the British prepared to attack at daybreak, 3 Jan., Washington, unobserved, abandoned his position during the night of 2-3 Jan. and marched to Princeton.
- (26 Dec.)
- (2 Jan. night)

The British plan for 1777 provided for three separate offensives converging on Albany (*sketch* a): Maj. Gen. John Burgoyne was to advance south from Canada by way of Lake Champlain; Lt. Col. Barry St. Leger, at Fort Oswego, was to move east down the Mohawk River Valley; and Howe was to proceed north from New York. Burgoyne and St. Leger advanced according to plan. Howe, however, launched an expedition to capture Philadelphia and lure Washington into battle rather than support Burgoyne. Howe left only a small garrison in New York under Clinton.

Burgoyne's advance was hampered by a shortage of transportation and an excessive number of cannon. His Indian allies, angered by efforts to make them observe the rules of war, deserted him after his first reverses. Moving down Lake Champlain, Burgoyne discovered that Mount Defiance, a steep hill that commanded Fort Ticonderoga, was unoccupied. He installed a battery on the hill, whereupon Maj. Gen. Arthur St. Clair, commander at Ticonderoga, recognized his danger and evacuated the fort. Next, Burgoyne elected to continue his advance south by way of Skenesboro and Fort Anne instead of following the easier Lake George route. Maj. Gen. Philip Schuyler, commander of the American northern army, immediately destroyed all bridges along this road, felled trees across it, dammed streams to create swamps, burned crops, and drove off all cattle. As a result, Burgoyne could advance but twenty miles in twenty days and could find no food on the way. A detachment of German mercenaries was ordered to Bennington (*lower right*) to seize American stores and horses there; a second column followed it in support. New Hampshire and Vermont militia, enraged by the killing of an American girl by a party of Burgoyne's Indians, attacked in force, destroyed the first detachment, and routed the second.

By now, none but ominous signs presaged the fate of Burgoyne's venture. American reinforcements of regular troops were arriving from the east and south. New York and New England militia units had turned out in large numbers: some were across Burgoyne's supply line to Canada; others had captured all the small British posts around Ticonderoga. He could entertain little hope of assistance, for Howe had not been heard from, and St. Leger had returned to Oswego after an abortive attempt to capture Fort Stanwix (*lower left*). Nevertheless, Burgoyne persisted in his undertaking. He crossed the Hudson and marched south of Saratoga, where his advance was blocked by American forces under Maj. Gen. Horatio Gates, entrenched at Bemis Heights (*sketch* b). An attack (Battle of Freeman's Farm) to capture the high ground that dominated the left flank of the American position ended in a very limited and costly success. Depleted in strength and short of supplies, Burgoyne made one final effort (Battle of Bemis Heights) to dislodge his opponents (*sketch* c). However, his maneuver was disrupted by American counteraction and he withdrew to Saratoga where, surrounded by constantly increasing American troops, he was forced to capitulate (*sketch* a).

Clinton, at New York, was aware of Burgoyne's plight after the Battle of Freeman's Farm and moved up the Hudson to divert the attention of the Americans (*see map* 7a). He captured the forts below West Point, broke through the West Point river defenses, and, on the day before Burgoyne surrendered, his forces had reached Kingston, which they burned. After Burgoyne's surrender, Clinton returned to New York.

The American success at Saratoga was the deciding factor in persuading France to enter the war against England. Spain and Holland soon followed. Thus the American Revolution engendered a world war that raged from the East Indies, through India, across the Atlantic into the Caribbean, and through North America to the Mississippi.

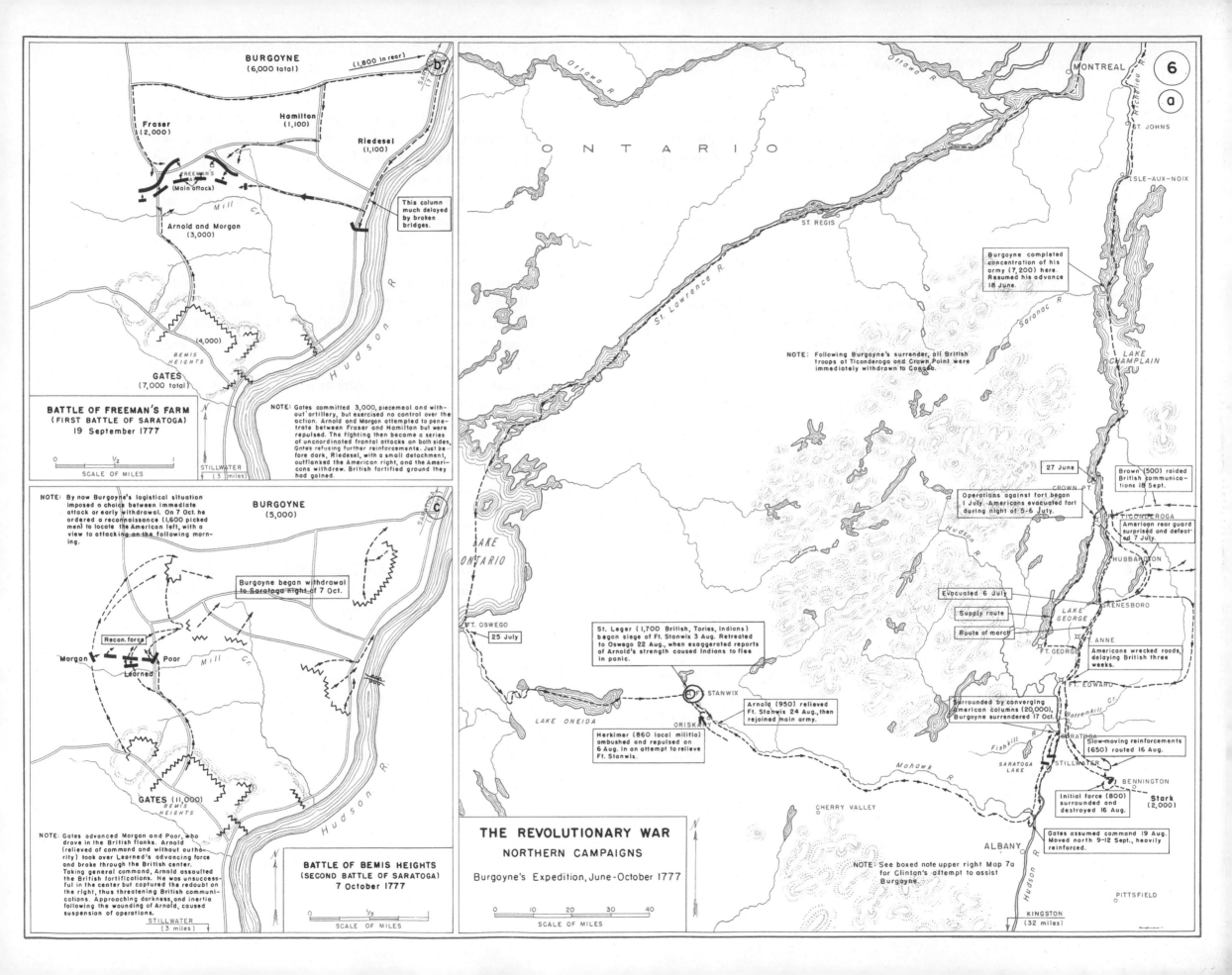

Howe opened the 1777 campaign by attempting to lure Washington into a decisive battle. To this end he concentrated some 18,000 men around New Brunswick (*sketch* a), as if in preparation for a drive on Philadelphia. Washington, with about 8,000 troops, countered by taking up a strong position that threatened the flank and rear of any British advance. After two weeks of fruitless maneuvering through a hostile countryside, Howe retired to New York, abandoning practically all of New Jersey.

Howe then embarked most of his forces but remained afloat in the vicinity of New York, leaving Washington uncertain as to whether his destination was Philadelphia, Boston, or Albany. Fearing that it would be Albany, Washington moved his forces to the Hudson Valley, only to shift them toward the Delaware when Howe finally sailed south. He was on the point of marching north again when he received word of Howe's landing near Elkton, at the head of Chesapeake Bay (*lower left*).

Washington occupied a good position at Brandywine (*sketch* b) across Howe's route to Philadelphia, but in the ensuing battle he was driven off the field by better generalship. A period of maneuvering followed, in which Howe retained the upper hand and eventually occupied Philadelphia. The Delaware River would provide a better line of communications, so he detached about half of his army to aid the British fleet in reducing the American river fortifications; the remainder he stationed around Germantown (*sketch* c). Here Washington surprised him and was repulsed only after heavy fighting, in which the British were roughly handled. Thereafter, the British spent the winter comfortably in Philadelphia while the American forces froze and starved at Valley Forge, only twenty-four miles away (*sketch* a).

During this winter the American Army several times approached the verge of breaking up but somehow held together. News of the French alliance helped morale; Greene reorganized the quartermaster department; Joseph Wadsworth got the commissary department functioning efficiently; and Baron von Steuben introduced discipline, organization, and training. The army that marched from Valley Forge in the spring of 1778 was a good one by any standard.

Meanwhile, Howe resigned his commission and was replaced by Clinton. The latter then received a confused set of orders from the British Colonial Secretary. These included the evacuation of Philadelphia, the return of the British forces to New York by water, and the diversion of a considerable part of them to the West Indies. Knowing that a powerful French fleet, under Admiral d'Estaing, was in the Atlantic, and fearing that a slow sea voyage might either expose him to its attack or enable Washington to reach New York ahead of him, Clinton chose to return overland (*sketch* a). Washington's pursuit was slow, but he came upon Clinton at Monmouth Court House. Here (*sketch* d), Maj. Gen. Charles Lee's erratic behavior upset Washington's plans, and as a result his attack proved indecisive. Clinton regained New York, and Washington took up his former position at White Plains. Thus, at the end of two years of campaigning, both armies were about where they had begun.

Further actions in 1778 were limited in scope. In May, Clinton made a sudden attack up the Hudson and captured Stony Point (*sketch* a). In July, he made a series of destructive amphibious raids against Connecticut and Virginia seaports (*not shown*). Washington, however, refused to be drawn into a general engagement. Instead, he launched Brig. Gen. Anthony Wayne and Major Henry Lee in very successful raids against Stony Point and Paulus Hook. An independent expedition, sent out by Massachusetts against a British post at Castine, Maine, failed miserably; but Maj. Gen. John Sullivan and Col. Daniel Brodhead defeated the Iroquois, and Lt. Col. George Rogers Clark completed seizure of the Ohio River towns by defeating Lt. Col. Henry Hamilton at Vincennes.

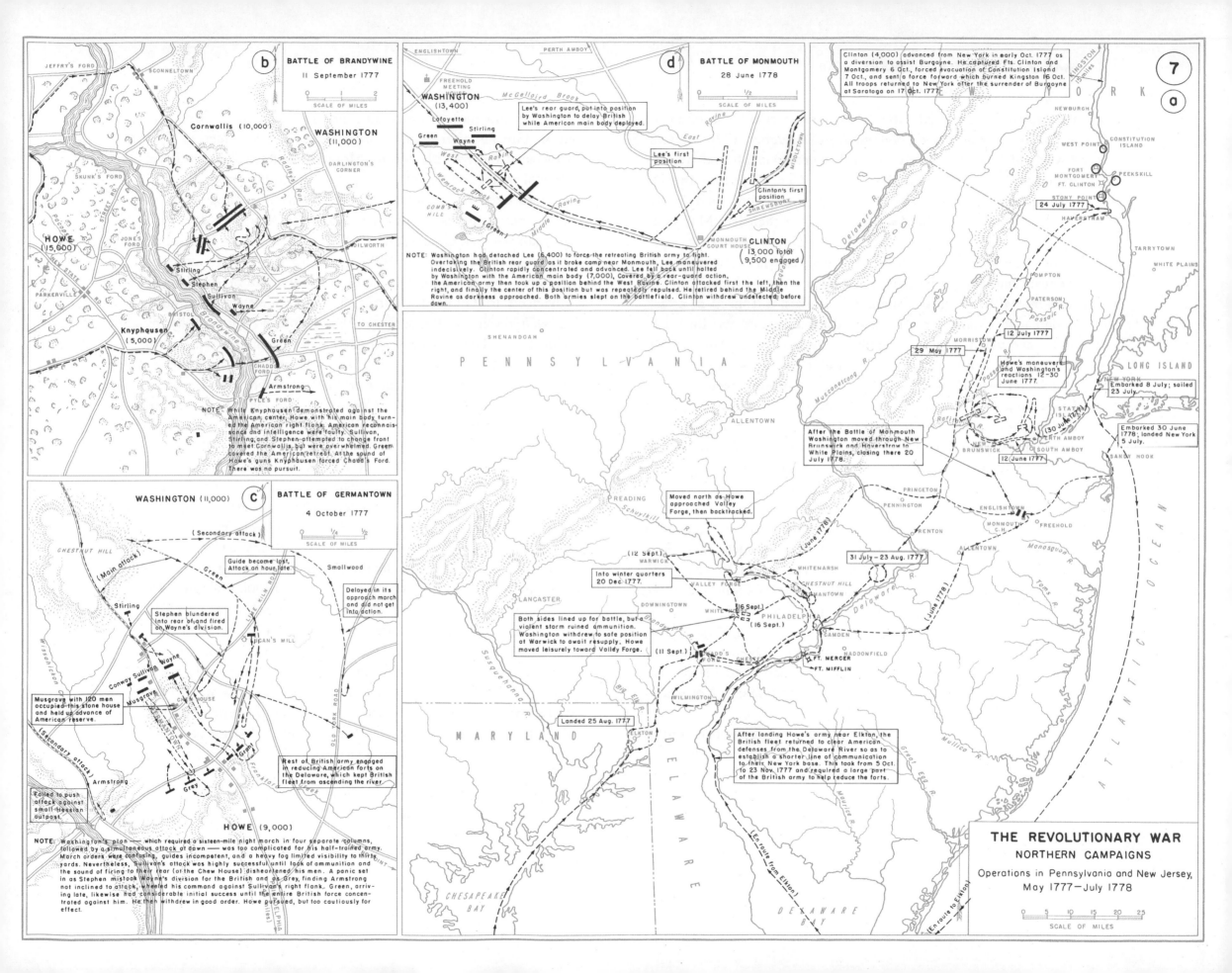

THE REVOLUTIONARY WAR
NORTHERN CAMPAIGNS
Operations in Pennsylvania and New Jersey,
May 1777 – July 1778

Frustrated in the north, the British transferred their offensive to the southern colonies (*sketch* a). In December, 1778, Lt. Col. Archibald Campbell's force landed near Savannah and wrested the city from the militia defenders. Maj. Gen. Augustine Prevost arrived from Florida (then a British possession) and joined Campbell in overrunning Georgia. Congress then sent Maj. Gen. Benjamin Lincoln to expel the British. Lincoln sent Brig. Gen. John Ashe from Charleston into Georgia, where he recovered Augusta but was badly defeated at Briar Creek. Lincoln himself then moved to Augusta, whereupon Prevost advanced to attack undefended Charleston. He reached the city, but was forced to withdraw when Lincoln rapidly returned from Augusta. In October, Lincoln, aided by Admiral d'Estaing's French fleet, attacked Prevost's forces in Savannah, but was repulsed with heavy losses. In January, 1780, Clinton and Cornwallis arrived at Savannah and moved to capture Charleston. Here, under great public pressure to defend the city, Lincoln occupied its fortifications and resisted stubbornly for a month before being forced to capitulate. Clinton returned to New York, leaving Cornwallis in command.

Congress then gave the command in the south to Gates who advanced slowly to attack Cornwallis at Camden (*sketch* a, *center*). The latter concentrated his forces and moved north to meet Gates. The two armies collided north of Camden (*sketch* b), where the American forces were badly defeated. Cornwallis continued north to Charlotte (*sketch* a), sending Maj. Patrick Ferguson on a raid to the west. Ferguson's advance stirred up the frontier militia, who surrounded and destroyed his detachment at Kings Mountain. On learning of this defeat, Cornwallis retired to Winnsborough.

Greene then received the task of restoring American control in the south. After assembling the small army available at Charlotte, he sent Brig. Gen. Daniel Morgan west with about half these men and moved east to Cheraw with the remainder. Cornwallis thereupon sent Lt. Col. Banastre Tarleton against Morgan and moved northwest with his main body, hoping to draw Greene after him. Morgan and Tarleton met at The Cowpens (*sketch* c), where Morgan conducted a battle of tactical perfection, almost wiping out Tarleton's force.

Infuriated by Tarleton's defeat, Cornwallis made a determined but unsuccessful attempt to intercept Morgan (*sketch* a). Morgan rejoined Greene, and together they withdrew into southern Virginia. The British followed up to the Dan River, then withdrew to Hillsboro as a base. Heavily reinforced, Greene advanced to Guilford Court House and took up a position (*sketch* d) much the same as that employed successfully by Morgan at The Cowpens. Though badly outnumbered, Cornwallis attacked; the courage and skill of his troops broke Greene's first two lines. Rather than risk his last unbroken regiments, Greene chose to withdraw. Cornwallis, however, had suffered heavy losses and withdrew to Wilmington (*sketch* a); later he marched north into Virginia.

Greene followed as far as Ramsay's Mill, then turned south and reentered South Carolina, where Thomas Sumter, Francis Marion, and other partisan leaders were waiting to cooperate with him. At Hobkirk's Hill, near Camden, Greene met and was defeated by Lt. Col. Francis Rawdon (*sketch* e). However, Marion had cut Rawdon's line of communications at Fort Watson, and Rawdon was forced to retire to Monk's Corner. He then moved to rescue the garrison at Ninety-Six, after which he returned to Orangeburg. Greene took station in the High Hills of Santee, twenty miles to the north. In August, Greene advanced suddenly on Orangeburg, forcing Lt. Col. Alexander Stuart (who had replaced Rawdon) back to Eutaw Springs. Here, with the battle almost won (*sketch* f), the famished Americans fell to looting the British camp, allowing Stuart to reorganize and counterattack successfully. Nevertheless, Stuart's army had been shattered and he withdrew to Charleston. This was the last pitched battle in the south, though guerrilla war dragged on for another year.

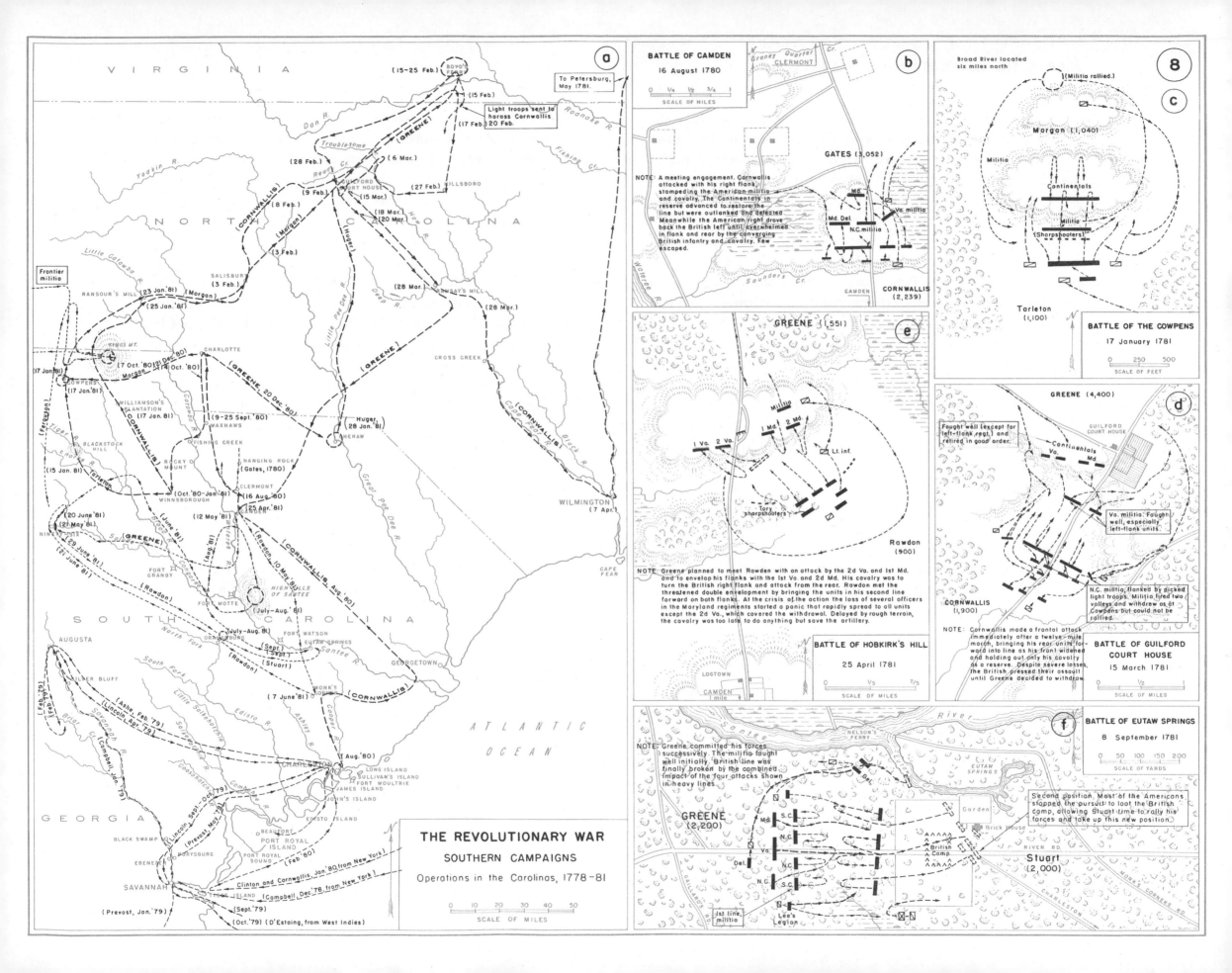

(a)

VIRGINIA

(15-25 Feb.)
BOYD'S FERRY

To Petersburg, May 1781.

(15 Feb.)
Light troops sent to harass Cornwallis 20 Feb.

Dan R.

(17 Feb.)

Troublesome Cr.

(GREENE)

(28 Feb.)
Reedy Cr.
(6 Mar.)

(9 Feb.)
GUILFORD COURT HOUSE
(15 Mar.)

(27 Feb.)
HILLSBORO

CORNWALLIS

(8 Feb.)

(Morgan)

(18 Mar.)
(20 Mar.)

NORTH CAROLINA

Yadkin R.

(Huger)

(3 Feb.)

Haw R.

(28 Mar.)
RAMSAY'S MILL

(GREENE)

SALISBURY
(3 Feb.)

Little Pee Dee R.

Deep R.

(28 Mar.)

(28 Mar.)

Little Catawba R.

Frontier militia

RANSOUR'S MILL (23 Jan.'81) (Morgan)
(25 Jan.'81)

CHARLOTTE

CROSS CREEK

Pee Dee R.

Cape Fear R.

(GREENE)

CORNWALLIS

KINGS MT.
(7 Oct.'80) (1 Dec.'80)
Morgan (14 Oct.'80)

(GREENE 20 Dec.'80)

CORNWALLIS

WILMINGTON
(7 Apr.)

(17 Jan.'81)
COWPENS

(17 Jan.'81)

WILLIAMSON'S PLANTATION
(17 Jan.'81)

(9-25 Sept.'80)
WAXHAWS

Huger,
28 Jan.'81

CHERAW

(Ferguson)

Tiger R.

BLACKSTOCK'S HILL

Enoree R.

FISHING CREEK

ROCKY MOUNT

HANGING ROCK
(Gates, 1780)

Great Pee Dee R.

(15 Jan.'81)
Tarleton

(Oct.'80-Jan.'81)

CLERMONT
(16 Aug.'80)

WINNSBOROUGH

CAMDEN
(25 Apr.'81)

(20 June'81)
(21 May'81)

(12 May'81)

(June'81)

(GREENE)

FORT GRANBY

(Aug.'81)

Wateree R.

(Rawdon)

CORNWALLIS

(29 June'81)

(21 June'81)

(Rawdon)

NINETY SIX

SOUTH CAROLINA

FORT MOTTE

Broad R.

HIGH HILLS OF SANTEE

(July-Aug.'81)

Congaree R.

EUTAW SPRINGS
(Sept.)
(Sept.)
(Rawdon) (Stuart)

GEORGETOWN

North Fork

AUGUSTA

ORANGEBURG

(July-Aug.'81)
FORT WATSON

Santee R.

CAPE FEAR

SILVER BLUFF

South Fork

Edisto R.

Little Saltcatcher R.

Ashley R.

Cooper R.

MONK'S CORNERS

(7 June'81)

CORNWALLIS

(Feb.'79)
(Ashe, Feb.'79)

(Lincoln, Apr.'79)

(Campbell, Jan.'79)

GEORGIA

Savannah R.

Brier Cr.

BLACK SWAMP

EBENEZER

PURYSBURG

BEAUFORT
PORT ROYAL ISLAND

PORT ROYAL SOUND

(Lincoln, Sept.-Oct.'79)
(Prevost, May '79)

(Feb.'80)

CHARLESTON
(Aug.'80)

LONG ISLAND
SULLIVAN'S ISLAND
FORT MOULTRIE
JAMES ISLAND
JOHN'S ISLAND

Edisto Island

ATLANTIC OCEAN

SAVANNAH

TYBEE ISLAND

(Sept.'79)

(Oct.'79) (D'Estaing, from West Indies)

Clinton and Cornwallis, Jan.'80 from New York
Campbell Dec.'78 from New York

(Prevost, Jan.'79)

N

THE REVOLUTIONARY WAR
SOUTHERN CAMPAIGNS
Operations in the Carolinas, 1778-81

0 10 20 30 40 50
SCALE OF MILES

(b)

BATTLE OF CAMDEN
16 August 1780

Graney Quarter Cr.

CLERMONT

0 1/4 1/2 3/4 1
SCALE OF MILES

GATES (3,052)

Md.

Va. militia

Md. Del.
N.C. militia

Wateree R.

Saunders Cr.

CAMDEN

CORNWALLIS (2,239)

NOTE: A meeting engagement. Cornwallis attacked with his right flank, stampeding the American militia and cavalry. The Continentals in reserve advanced to restore the line but were outflanked and defeated. Meanwhile the American right drove back the British left until, overwhelmed in flank and rear by the converging British infantry and cavalry. Few escaped.

---

(8)

(c)

Broad River located six miles north

(Militia rallied.)

Morgan (1,040)

Militia

Militia

Continentals

Militia

(Sharpshooters)

Tarleton (1,100)

BATTLE OF THE COWPENS
17 January 1781

N

0 250 500
SCALE OF FEET

(e)

GREENE (1,551)

Militia

1 Md. 2 Md.

1 Va. 2 Va.

Lt. inf.

Tory sharpshooters

Rawdon (900)

NOTE: Greene planned to meet Rowden with an attack by the 2d Va. and 1st Md. and to envelop his flanks with the 1st Va. and 2d Md. His cavalry was to turn the British right flank and attack from the rear. Rowdon met the threatened double envelopment by bringing the units in his second line forward on both flanks. At the crisis of the action the loss of several officers in the Maryland regiments started a panic that rapidly spread to all units except the 2d Va., which covered the withdrawal. Delayed by rough terrain, the cavalry was too late to do anything but save the artillery.

LOGTOWN

CAMDEN 1 mile

N

BATTLE OF HOBKIRK'S HILL
25 April 1781

0 1/5 2/5
SCALE OF MILES

(d)

GREENE (4,400)

GUILFORD COURT HOUSE

Fought well (except for left-flank regt.) and retired in good order.

Continentals
Va.   Md.

Va. militia: Fought well, especially left-flank units.

N.C. militia, flanked by picked light troops. Militia fired two volleys and withdrew as at Cowpens but could not be rallied.

CORNWALLIS (1,900)

NOTE: Cornwallis made a frontal attack immediately after a twelve-mile march, bringing his rear units forward into line as his front widened and holding out only his cavalry as a reserve. Despite severe losses, the British pressed their assault until Greene decided to withdraw.

BATTLE OF GUILFORD COURT HOUSE
15 March 1781

0 1/2
SCALE OF MILES

(f)

Santee River

NELSON'S FERRY

EUTAW SPRINGS

NOTE: Greene committed his forces successively. The militia fought well initially. British line was finally broken by the combined impact of the four attacks shown in heavy lines.

GREENE (2,200)

Md.   S.C.

N.C.

Va.   N.C.

Del.

N.C.   S.C.

Garden

Brick House

British Camp

Second position. Most of the Americans stopped the pursuit to loot the British camp, allowing Stuart time to rally his forces and take up this new position.

Stuart (2,000)

1st line militia

Lee's Legion

Gaillard's

RIVER RD.

MONK'S CORNERS RD.

CHARLESTON RD.

BATTLE OF EUTAW SPRINGS
8 September 1781

0 50 100 150 200
SCALE OF YARDS

While Cornwallis was engaged with Greene in the Carolinas, the British were also operating in Virginia, with Portsmouth (*lower right*) as a base. From there, Arnold (turned traitor) raided and ravaged the countryside. Steuben gathered all available Virginia militia and forced Arnold back to Portsmouth. Clinton sent large reinforcements from New York to Portsmouth; Washington countered by sending the Marquis de Lafayette with some crack Continental infantry to Virginia.

Upon his arrival at Petersburg, Virginia (*lower center*), on 20 May, Cornwallis assumed command of all British forces in the state. He made repeated efforts to crush Lafayette and Steuben while Tarleton raided across Virginia, almost capturing Virginia's Governor Thomas Jefferson at Charlottesville. Lafayette, reinforced by Wayne from the north, maneuvered successfully, eluding Cornwallis' attacks and harassing his withdrawals. At Williamsburg (*bottom right*), Cornwallis received orders from Clinton to send part of his forces to New York. He thereupon started for Yorktown, sending Tarleton on another long raid and brushing aside an attack by Lafayette en route.

Meanwhile, in the north, Washington had been joined by the Comte de Rochambeau and his French troops at White Plains and was preparing an attack on New York. Clinton was mounting an amphibious attack against the small French fleet stationed at Newport. A large French fleet, under Admiral de Grasse, carrying a strong contingent of French troops, was expected off the American coast momentarily. Washington hoped to obtain its cooperation in his planned attack on New York.

But de Grasse dictated the strategy of the coming campaign when he wrote that he was sailing from the West Indies to the Chesapeake and urged Washington to be prepared to employ him immediately, for he would have to return to the West Indies by the middle of October. Washington thereupon rapidly and skillfully converted his plan for an attack on New York into a feint to cover his march to Virginia (*inset sketch*). Maj. Gen. William Heath was left to hold the Hudson River forts. While the Americans and French marched south, de Grasse arrived in the Chesapeake, landed his troops, and beat off the English fleet.

Clinton, at New York, was caught by surprise. His expedition to Newport found that the French squadron, loaded with siege artillery, had sailed to join de Grasse. Frantically, he tried to assemble a force strong enough to relieve Cornwallis, but he could not gather sufficient shipping in time. As a diversion, Arnold raided and burned New London and Groton.

Reinforced by de Grasse's troops, Lafayette took up a position around Yorktown on 8 September (*inset sketch*), the same day that the British at Eutaw Springs were forced to withdraw to Charleston. Upon the arrival of Washington, regular siege operations were begun against Cornwallis' isolated troops. After several weeks, with the Americans and French drawing closer and closer and with no prospect of outside assistance, Cornwallis capitulated.

This surrender virtually ended the war in America, though fierce Indian fighting continued on the Ohio frontier and in western New York. Receiving reinforcements, Greene sent Wayne to Georgia to clear out the remaining British and their Indian allies. Wayne succeeded, except at Savannah. In 1782, Carleton, who had assumed the British command in North America, evacuated first Savannah and then Charleston. Washington held his army in the West Point area until the British evacuated New York at the end of the war.

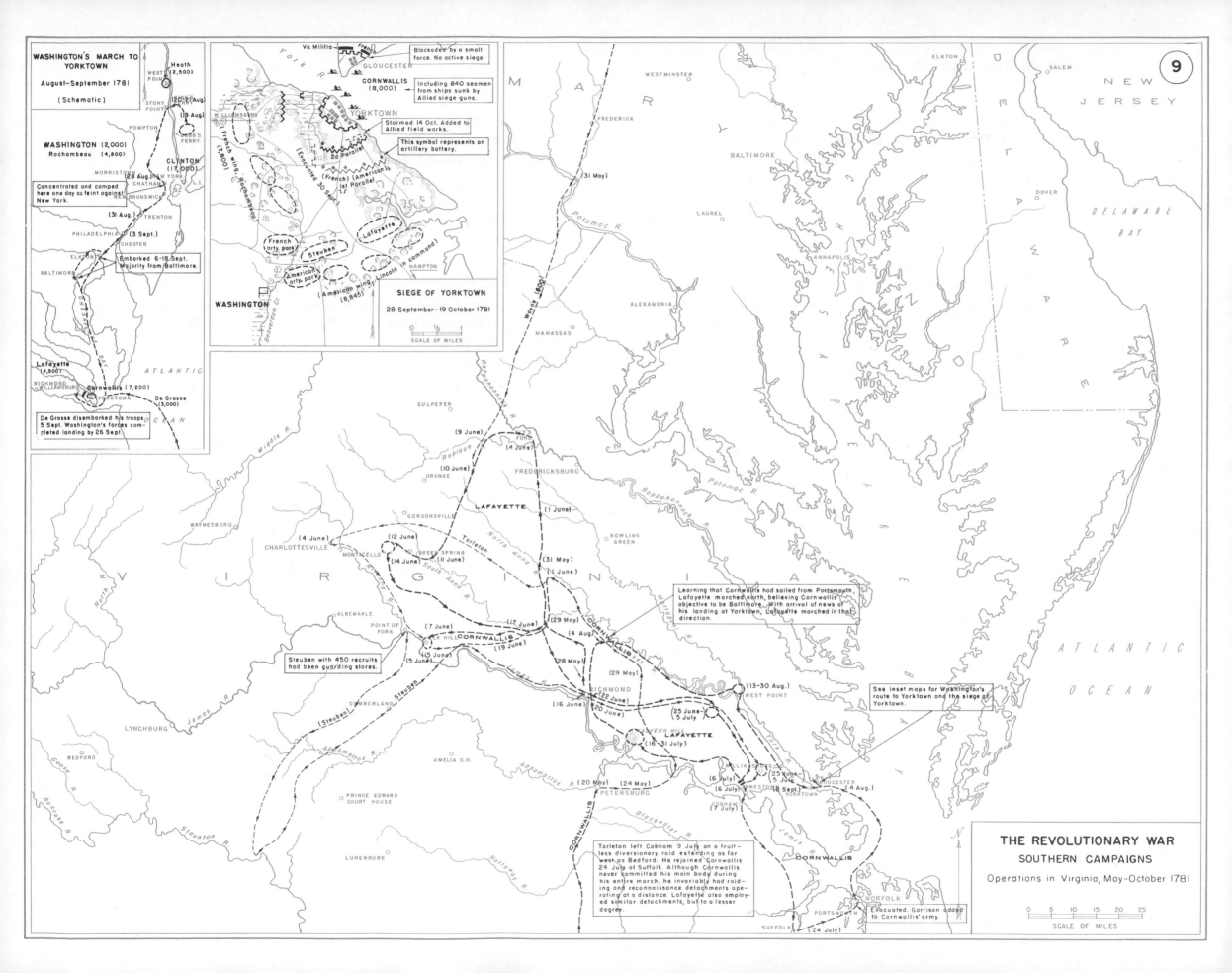

WASHINGTON'S MARCH TO YORKTOWN

August–September 1781

(Schematic)

WASHINGTON (2,000)
Rochambeau (4,800)

CLINTON (17,000)

Heath (2,500)
WEST POINT

(20 Aug.)

(19 Aug.)

WEBB'S FERRY

STONY POINT

POMPTON

MORRISTOWN

CHATHAM

(28 Aug.) NEW YORK

L. I.

Concentrated and camped here one day as feint against New York.

NEW BRUNSWICK

(31 Aug.) TRENTON

PHILADELPHIA (3 Sept.)

CHESTER

Embarked 6–18 Sept. Majority from Baltimore.

ELKTON

BALTIMORE

Lafayette (4,500)

RICHMOND
WILLIAMSBURG

Cornwallis (7,200)
YORKTOWN

De Grasse (3,000)

De Grasse disembarked his troops 5 Sept. Washington's forces completed landing by 26 Sept.

ATLANTIC OCEAN

SIEGE OF YORKTOWN

28 September–19 October 1781

Va. Militia

French

GLOUCESTER

Blockaded by a small force. No active siege.

CORNWALLIS (8,000)

Including 840 seamen from ships sunk by Allied siege guns.

YORKTOWN

WILLIAMSBURG

Stormed 14 Oct. Added to Allied field works.

This symbol represents an artillery battery.

2d Parallel

(French) (American) 1st Parallel

(Evacuated 30 Sept.)

(French wing, Rochambeau)

(French arty. park)

Steuben

Lafayette

American arty. park

(American wing, Lincoln in command) (8,845)

WASHINGTON

HAMPTON

YORK R.

SCALE OF MILES

MARYLAND

NEW JERSEY

ELKTON
SALEM
WESTMINSTER
FREDERICK
DOVER
DELAWARE BAY
LAUREL
BALTIMORE
ANNAPOLIS
ALEXANDRIA
MANASSAS
(31 May)
Potomac R.
Wayne (800)
Rappahannock R.

CULPEPER

(9 June)
(4 June)
(10 June)
ORANGE
FREDERICKSBURG

LAFAYETTE (1 June)

BOWLING GREEN

GORDONSVILLE

(4 June)
(12 June)
(14 June)
GREEN SPRING (11 June)
CHARLOTTESVILLE
MONTICELLO
Tarleton
North Anna R.
South Anna R.
(31 May)
(1 June)

ALBEMARLE

POINT OF FORK
(7 June)
(17 June)
(29 May)
CORNWALLIS
(5 June)
(19 June)
(15 June)
(5 June)
Steuben
(4 Aug.)

Learning that Cornwallis had sailed from Portsmouth, Lafayette marched north, believing Cornwallis' objective to be Baltimore. With arrival of news of his landing at Yorktown, Lafayette marched in that direction.

Steuben with 450 recruits had been guarding stores.

CUMBERLAND

(Steuben)

(28 May)
(29 May)
RICHMOND
(22 June)
(16 June)
(20 June)

(13–30 Aug.)
WEST POINT

See inset maps for Washington's route to Yorktown and the siege of Yorktown.

LYNCHBURG
BEDFORD
AMELIA C.H.

MALVERN HILL
LAFAYETTE
(16–31 July)

(25 June–5 July)

(6 July)
WILLIAMSBURG
(25 June–5 July)
GLOUCESTER
(4 Aug.)

Goose R.
Roanoke R.
Staunton R.
PRINCE EDWARD COURT HOUSE
LUNENBURG

Appomattox R.
(20 May) (24 May)
PETERSBURG
Blackwater R.

(6 July)
JAMESTOWN (8 Sept.)
(6 July)
COBHAM (7 July)
YORKTOWN

James R.

Tarleton left Cobham 9 July on a fruitless diversionary raid extending as far west as Bedford. He rejoined Cornwallis 24 July at Suffolk. Although Cornwallis never committed his main body during his entire march, he invariably had raiding and reconnaissance detachments operating at a distance. Lafayette also employed similar detachments, but to a lesser degree.

CORNWALLIS

NORFOLK
PORTSMOUTH
SUFFOLK
(24 July)

Evacuated. Garrison added to Cornwallis' army.

ATLANTIC OCEAN

THE REVOLUTIONARY WAR

SOUTHERN CAMPAIGNS

Operations in Virginia, May–October 1781

0 5 10 15 20 25

SCALE OF MILES

VIRGINIA

The United States entered the War of 1812 determined to conquer Canada. Four separate, uncoordinated offensives were envisaged. The main army was to advance up the old Lake Champlain invasion route (*upper right*) to capture Montreal; three other columns, composed chiefly of militia, were to invade Canada from Detroit, Niagara, and Sackett's Harbor. There were few competent commanders or trained soldiers or supplies available. However, England was desperately engaged with Napoleon and could not spare reinforcements for Canada. The local British forces could only await the American attacks, meanwhile stirring up the Indian tribes along the frontiers.

The advance from Detroit was assigned to William Hull, the aging governor of Michigan Territory. After constructing 200 miles of road from Dayton (*lower left*), Hull reached Detroit, crossed the river, and approached Fort Malden. But he did not attack. When Indians began to raid his line of supply, he returned to Detroit. Meanwhile Brig. Gen. Isaac Brock sailed to the relief of Fort Malden. He arrived after Hull had returned to Detroit, followed him there, and bluffed him into a disgraceful surrender. The capture of Fort Mackinac by local forces and the massacre of the garrison of Fort Dearborn completed the American defeat in the west. Brock returned to the Niagara frontier.

Nothing came of the three other contemplated advances. At Niagara, Maj. Gen. Stephen van Rensselaer's advance guard made a surprise night crossing and captured the heights at Queenstown. But the militia refused to follow across the river, leaving the advance guard to be overwhelmed and captured. Brig. Gen. Alexander Smyth, who replaced Rensselaer, made no attempt to renew the offensive. Maj. Gen. Henry Dearborn advanced from Plattsburg, marched twenty miles to the Canadian border, then marched back. The proposed advance from Sackett's Harbor never materialized.

Maj. Gen. William Henry Harrison organized a number of columns of militia and made several unsuccessful efforts to retake Detroit. One of his columns, under Brig. Gen. James Winchester, captured Frenchtown, but was practically destroyed in a surprise counterattack by Col. Thomas Proctor's troops. Proctor made two unsuccessful attacks on Fort Meigs and was also repulsed with heavy loss at Fort Stephenson. Land activity was suspended by the Americans until Commodore Oliver Hazard Perry completed construction of his fleet and defeated the British navy on Lake Erie. Perry then ferried Harrison's troops across the lake. Proctor withdrew to the north, but was overtaken and routed at Moravian Town. This action ended serious fighting in the west.

In the east, instead of moving to Montreal according to plan, Dearborn crossed Lake Ontario, raided York, and then turned to attack Fort George. Though initially successful, this offensive collapsed. The British countered with an unsuccessful raid on Sackett's Harbor. Dearborn was replaced by Maj. Gen. James Wilkinson. The latter proceeded down the St. Lawrence toward Quebec, expecting to be joined en route by Maj. Gen. Wade Hampton's troops advancing north from Plattsburg. At Christler's Farm, Wilkinson suffered a humiliating defeat at the hands of a small British force. He then withdrew and went into winter quarters; Hampton did likewise. In December, the British forced the evacuation of Fort George. For no apparent reason, the retreating Americans burned Queenstown and nearby Newark. The British retaliated by ravaging a thirty-mile stretch of the American border, burning Buffalo, Black Rock, and several smaller towns. They also captured Fort Niagara, which they held to the end of the war.

In early 1813, British Admiral George Cockburn carried out a series of punitive raids along the Chesapeake. Repulsed at Norfolk, he retaliated by brutally sacking the Virginia town of Hampton.

In March, 1814, Wilkinson fought his last battle—a shameful one. His attack at La Colle Mill with 4,000 men was repulsed by a British outpost of 200 men. The British constructed a superior fleet and gained control of Lake Ontario. They successfully raided Oswego, but failed to attack the main American depot some twelve miles inland.

Prevost's operations in August-September, 1814, are described in the text for map 11.

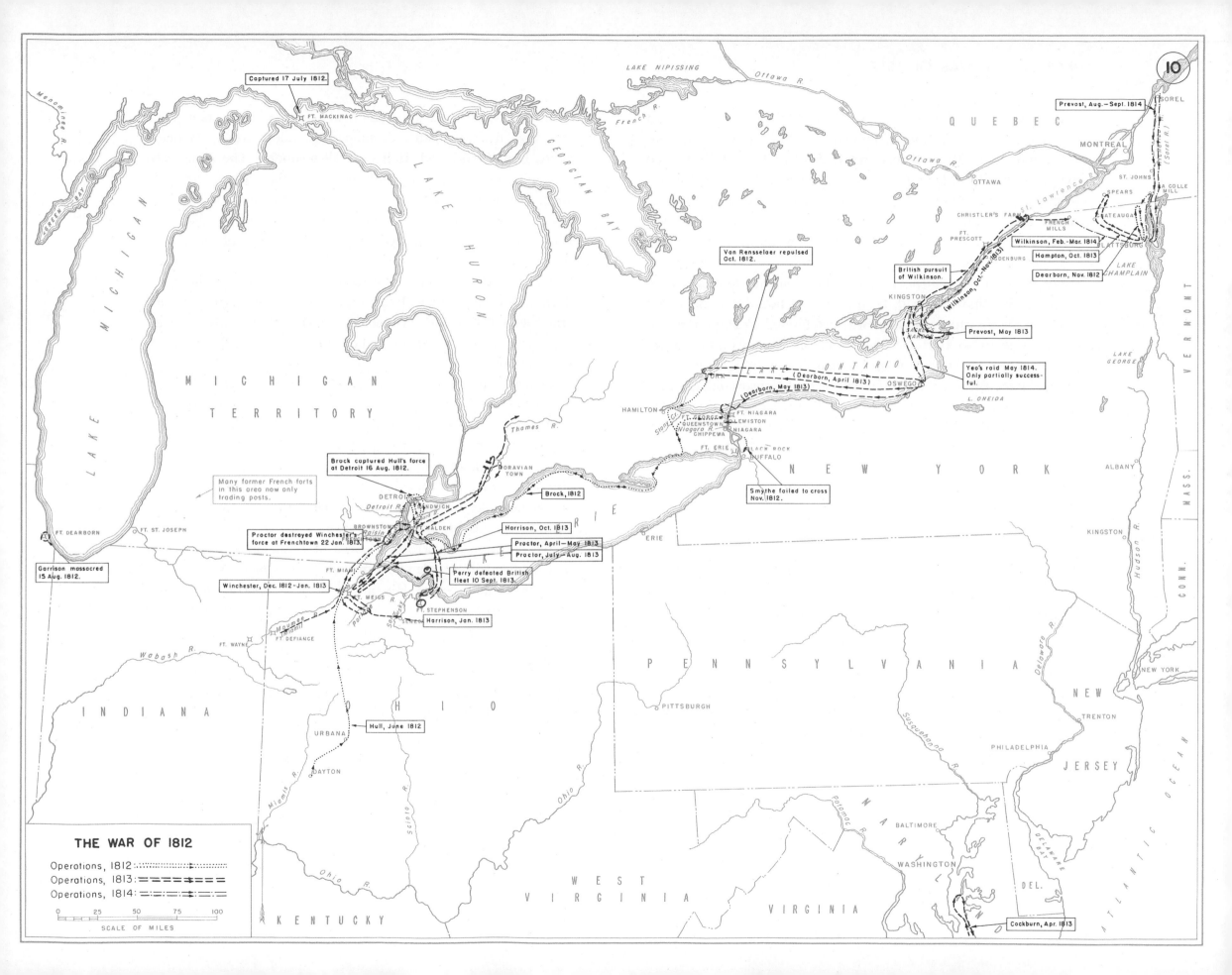

THE WAR OF 1812

Operations, 1812 ....
Operations, 1813 ━━━━━━━━━━
Operations, 1814 ━━━━━━━━━

0   25   50   75   100
SCALE OF MILES

Captured 17 July 1812.

Prevost, Aug.—Sept. 1814

Van Rensseloer repulsed Oct. 1812.

Wilkinson, Feb.—Mar. 1814
Hampton, Oct. 1813
Dearborn, Nov. 1812

British pursuit of Wilkinson.

Prevost, May 1813

Yeo's raid May 1814. Only partially successful.

Brock captured Hull's force at Detroit 16 Aug. 1812.

Many former French forts in this area now only trading posts.

Brock, 1812

Smythe failed to cross Nov. 1812.

Proctor destroyed Winchester's force at Frenchtown 22 Jan. 1813.

Harrison, Oct. 1813

Proctor, April—May 1813
Proctor, July—Aug. 1813

Perry defeated British fleet 10 Sept. 1813.

Garrison massacred 15 Aug. 1812.

Winchester, Dec. 1812—Jan. 1813

Harrison, Jan. 1813

Hull, June 1812

Cockburn, Apr. 1813

Following their pointless raid on York, General Dearborn and Commodore Isaac Chauncey launched in May, 1813, a successful amphibious attack to capture Fort George (*sketch* a). To avoid being cut off, Brig. Gen. John Vincent withdrew his British forces west to Hamilton. After much vacillation American forces, under Brig. Gen. Henry Winder and Brig. Gen. John Chandler, began a pursuit. About ten miles east of the city they made camp for the night, neglecting to establish outposts. Vincent and a small force made a surprise night attack on the exposed camp. In the melee that followed, both sides lost heavily; Winder and Chandler were captured. The British retreated to Hamilton and the Americans to Fort George. Dearborn then withdrew from Fort George, leaving a small garrison of militia. Fearing an attack by the British, the militia later burned Newark and Queenstown, crossed the river, and returned to their homes. In retaliation, the British surprised Fort Niagara and ravaged the American side of the river.

Operations were resumed on the Niagara front in July, 1814, when Maj. Gen. Jacob Brown's small but well-trained army captured Fort Erie (*bottom*). The Americans advanced north to Chippewa, where Brig. Gen. Winfield Scott's brigade defeated the British, under Maj. Gen. Phineas Riall, in a brief but fierce battle (*sketch* b). Brown then pushed the British back toward Fort George (*sketch* a). However, finding them reinforced (and Commodore Chauncey being slow to support his operations), he retired to Chippewa.

Lt. Gen. Sir Gordon Drummond now prepared to advance on the east bank from Fort Niagara. Brown, worried about this threat to his communications, sent Scott toward the British position at Queenstown to force the British to concentrate their troops on the west bank of the river. Scott's brigade collided with Drummond's advance guard at Lundy's Lane (*sketch* c). A savage five-hour battle developed in which Brown, Winfield Scott, Drummond, and Riall were all wounded. The Americans withdrew to Fort Erie (*sketch* a), which they hastily strengthened. Drummond followed cautiously and began a formal siege. On 3 August, a British raid on the American supply depots at Black Rock was routed by American riflemen. An assault on Fort Erie on 14 August was repulsed with heavy losses. On 17 September, Brown made a successful sortie; Drummond withdrew a few days later. In October, Maj. Gen. George Izard and over 6,000 troops arrived to aid Brown. He advanced on Chippewa with an excellent chance of overwhelming Drummond, but suspended operations upon learning that Commodore Chauncey had retired into Sacket's Harbor. Fort Erie was therefore abandoned on 5 November, and the Americans went into winter quarters near Buffalo.

Meanwhile, the fall of Napoleon in April, 1814, enabled the British government to shift large forces of veteran troops to North America. Several offensives were envisaged, including one along the Lake Champlain route. The Americans, preoccupied with operations on the Niagara front, had left this route practically open. In August, Sir George Prevost, Governor General of Canada, with a splendid army of 11,000 men and a strong fleet, began an advance. His only immediate opposition on land was a force of about 1,500 American troops, under Brig. Gen. Alexander Macomb, in a strong line of defenses at Plattsburg. However, when Commodore Thomas Macdonough's small fleet defeated the larger British fleet in a hard-fought battle in Plattsburg Bay, Prevost returned precipitously to Canada. Thus ended major operations in the north.

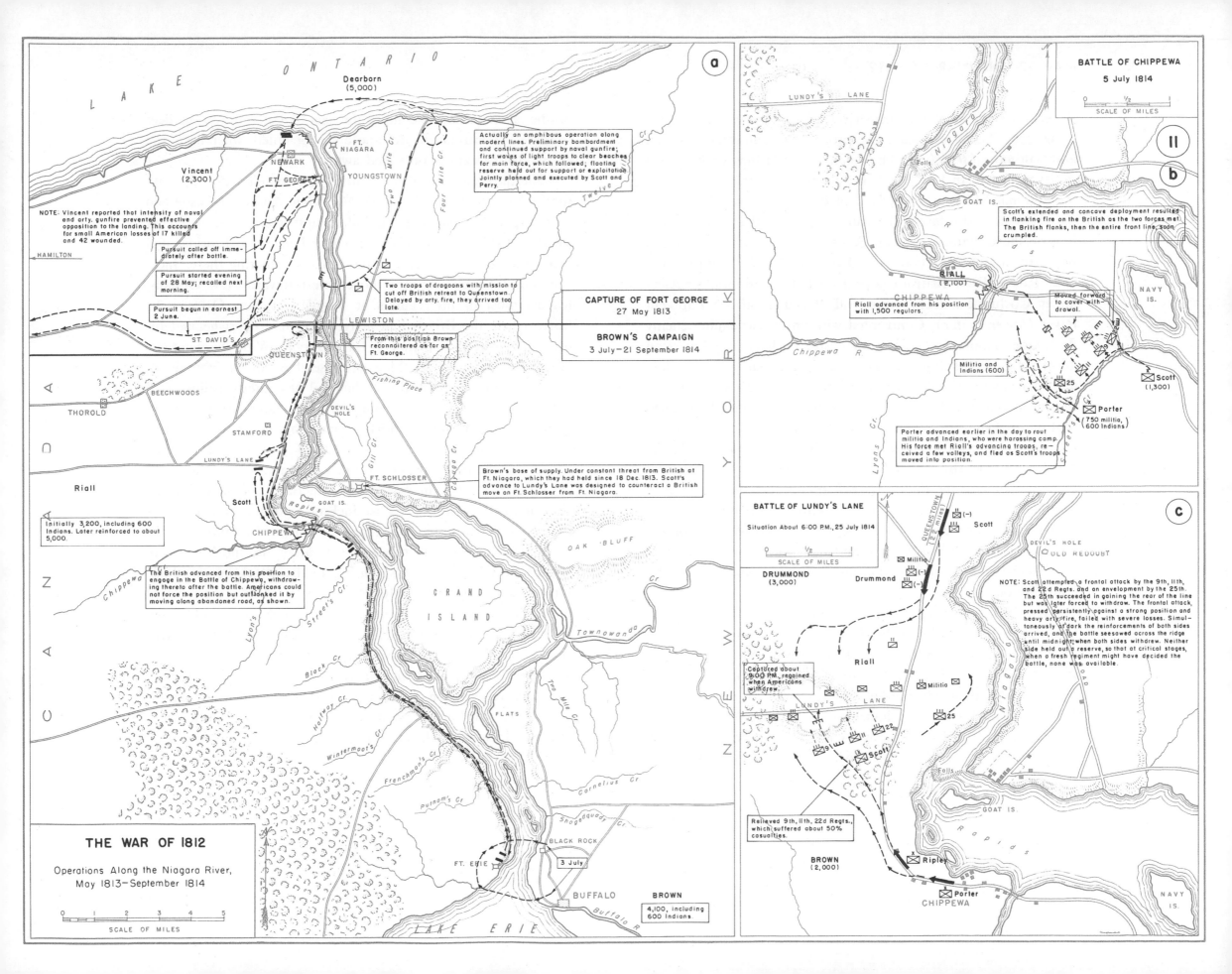

a

LAKE ONTARIO

Dearborn
(5,000)

Vincent
(2,300)

NEWARK

FT. NIAGARA

YOUNGSTOWN

FT. GEORGE

NOTE: Vincent reported that intensity of naval and arty. gunfire prevented effective opposition to the landing. This accounts for small American losses of 17 killed and 42 wounded.

HAMILTON

Pursuit called off immediately after battle.

Pursuit started evening of 28 May; recalled next morning.

Pursuit begun in earnest 2 June.

Actually an amphibous operation along modern lines. Preliminary bombardment and continued support by naval gunfire; first waves of light troops to clear beaches for main force, which followed; floating reserve held out for support or exploitation. Jointly planned and executed by Scott and Perry.

Two troops of dragoons with mission to cut off British retreat to Queenstown. Delayed by arty. fire, they arrived too late.

CAPTURE OF FORT GEORGE
27 May 1813

LEWISTON

From this position Brown reconnoitered as far as Ft. George.

BROWN'S CAMPAIGN
3 July–21 September 1814

ST. DAVID'S

QUEENSTOWN

BEECHWOODS

THOROLD

STAMFORD

DEVIL'S HOLE

Fishing Place

LUNDY'S LANE

Riall

Scott

Brown's base of supply. Under constant threat from British at Ft. Niagara, which they had held since 18 Dec. 1813. Scott's advance to Lundy's Lane was designed to counteract a British move on Ft. Schlosser from Ft. Niagara.

FT. SCHLOSSER

Initially 3,200, including 600 Indians. Later reinforced to about 5,000.

CHIPPEWA

GOAT IS.

Rapids

OAK BLUFF

The British advanced from this position to engage in the Battle of Chippewa, withdrawing thereto after the battle. Americans could not force the position but outflanked it by moving along abandoned road, as shown.

GRAND ISLAND

Townowanda Cr

Street's Cr

Black Cr

Halfway Cr

Wintermoot's

Frenchman's Cr

FLATS

Putnam's Cr

Snapedquady Cr

Cornelius Cr

Two Mile Cr

BLACK ROCK

FT. ERIE

3 July

BUFFALO

Buffalo R

THE WAR OF 1812

Operations Along the Niagara River,
May 1813–September 1814

0 1 2 3 4 5
SCALE OF MILES

BROWN
4,100, including 600 Indians.

LAKE ERIE

b

BATTLE OF CHIPPEWA
5 July 1814

0 ½
SCALE OF MILES

LUNDY'S LANE

Falls

Niagara R

GOAT IS.

NAVY IS.

RIALL
(2,100)

Scott's extended and concave deployment resulted in flanking fire on the British as the two forces met. The British flanks, then the entire front line, soon crumpled.

CHIPPEWA

Riall advanced from his position with 1,500 regulars.

Moved forward to cover withdrawal.

Militia and Indians (600)

25

Scott
(1,300)

Porter
(750 militia, 600 Indians)

Porter advanced earlier in the day to rout militia and Indians, who were harassing camp. His force met Riall's advancing troops, received a few volleys, and fled as Scott's troops moved into position.

II

c

BATTLE OF LUNDY'S LANE

Situation About 6:00 P.M., 25 July 1814

0 ½
SCALE OF MILES

QUEENSTOWN (2½ miles)

Scott

Militia

DRUMMOND
(3,000)

Drummond

DEVIL'S HOLE

OLD REDOUBT

NOTE: Scott attempted a frontal attack by the 9th, 11th, and 22d Regts. and an envelopment by the 25th. The 25th succeeded in gaining the rear of the line but was later forced to withdraw. The frontal attack, pressed persistently against a strong position and heavy arty. fire, failed with severe losses. Simultaneously at dark the reinforcements of both sides arrived, and the battle seesawed across the ridge until midnight, when both sides withdrew. Neither side held out a reserve, so that at critical stages, when a fresh regiment might have decided the battle, none was available.

Riall

Captured about 9:00 P.M., regained when Americans withdrew.

Militia

LUNDY'S LANE

9th

22d

Scott

25

Relieved 9th, 11th, 22d Regts., which suffered about 50% casualties.

Scott

Falls

GOAT IS.

Rapids

BROWN
(2,000)

Ripley

Porter

CHIPPEWA

NAVY IS.

A second element of the British plan for 1814 was a series of raids along the eastern seaboard, principally against Washington and Baltimore (*sketch* a). The defenses of Washington had been sadly neglected. In July, 1814, President James Madison created the Potomac Military District and placed General Winder in command. Winder displayed the same ineptitude that had marked him on the Canadian frontier. Some militia were called up, but no fortifications were constructed or planned. In August, Maj. Gen. Robert Ross' British troops, escorted by Admiral Sir Alexander Cochrane's fleet, arrived off Benedict on the Patuxent River (*lower center*). Confronted with an overwhelming enemy fleet, Commodore Joshua Barney destroyed his small American flotilla of gunboats in the upper Patuxent and marched his sailors and marines to join Winder. The latter, in a high state of confusion, marched and countermarched his troops until he learned that the British were on the road to Bladensburg; then he rushed to interpose himself between the British and Washington. In the Battle of Bladensburg that followed (*sketch* a, *inset*), Barney's men and some of the militia fought stubbornly; the former even counterattacked successfully. But, lacking leadership, the unseasoned militia broke and fled. The British burned most of the public buildings in Washington and then withdrew. Meanwhile, a British naval expedition laid all the Potomac River towns under contribution.

The British then moved against Baltimore (*sketch* a). Maj. Gen. Samuel Smith of the Maryland militia and other local leaders had worked diligently to fortify the town. When the British landed at North Point, Smith sent Brig. Gen. John Stricker forward to delay their advance. In an engagement at Godly Wood, Ross was killed and heavy losses were inflicted upon his troops before Stricker finally withdrew. A reconnaissance of the Baltimore defenses convinced the British that the fortifications could not be taken without the aid of the fleet. An attempt by the fleet to force the entrance to Baltimore harbor failed, whereupon the entire British expedition sailed away.

The third element of the British plan contemplated the capture of New Orleans (*sketch* b). Maj. Gen. Andrew Jackson had been engaged in suppressing Indian uprisings in the south. A small British force established itself at Pensacola, Florida, and proceeded to arm and supply the Indians gathering there. Jackson seized Pensacola, then moved west toward New Orleans, leaving most of his regulars at Mobile. At New Orleans, he learned that the British had arrived and had overwhelmed his little squadron of gunboats on Lake Borgne. With characteristic energy he declared martial law and assembled all available forces —mostly militia, stiffened by a handful of regulars, sailors, and the Baratarian pirates and smugglers. He made a furious night attack on the advancing British columns, but was repulsed. Jackson then prepared for defense behind the Rodriguez Canal, which was dry at the time (*sketch* c). On 1 January, 1815, Maj. Gen. Sir Edward Pakenham brought on the Battle of New Orleans with an artillery attack against Jackson's position, but his guns were soon silenced. On 8 January, he launched infantry attacks on both sides of the river and a naval attack up the Mississippi against Fort St. Phillip (*sketch* b). In the attack against Jackson's canal position, the 44th Regiment failed to bring forward the scaling ladders and fascines needed to enable the main attack to cross the canal. Nevertheless, Pakenham pressed the attack. It was made with great bravery; it was repulsed with great loss. The naval attack failed; the British succeeded on the left bank, but later retired. On 18 January, 1815, the British withdrew completely and began operations against Mobile, only to learn that the Treaty of Ghent, ending the war, had been signed on 24 December, 1814.

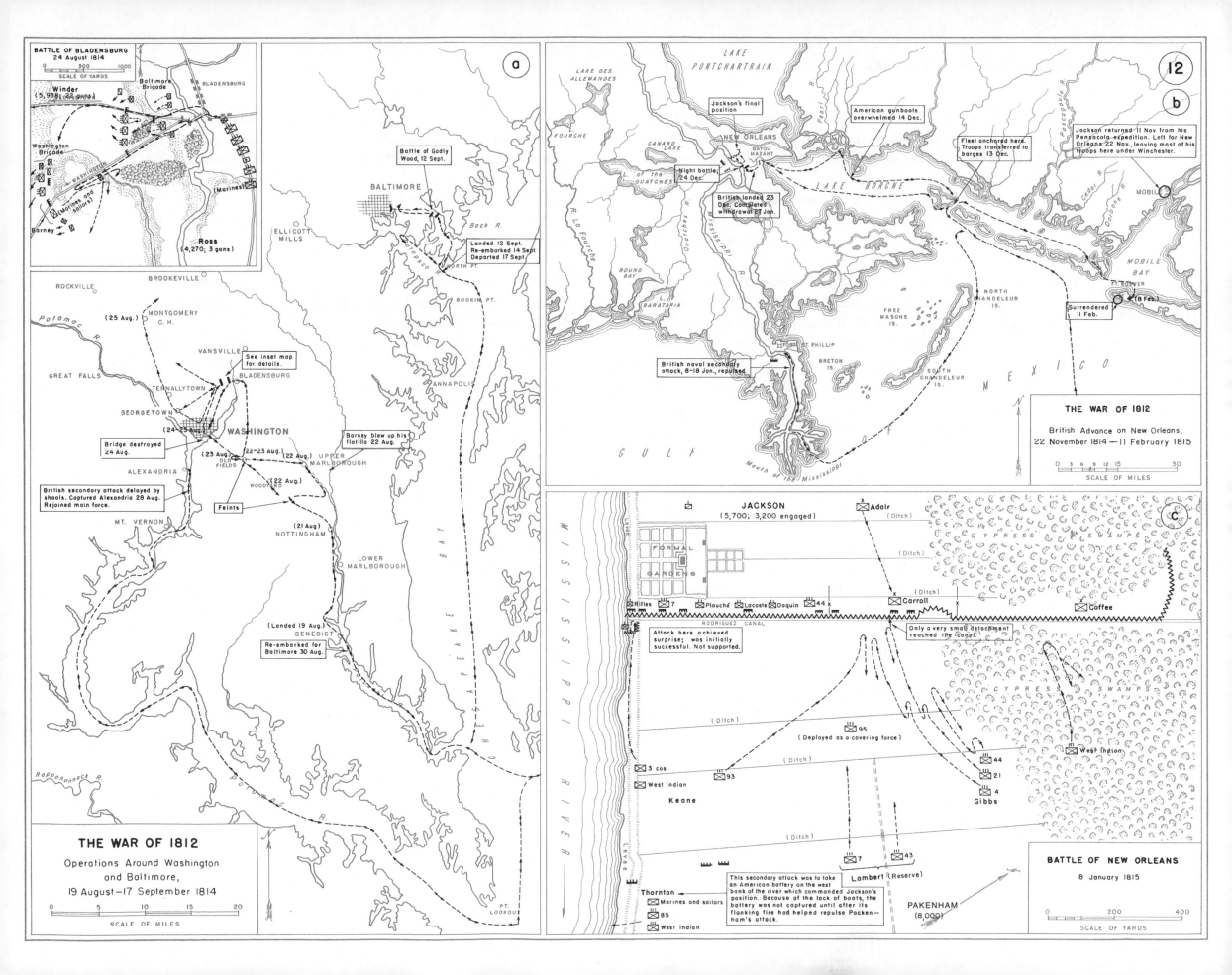

BATTLE OF BLADENSBURG
24 August 1814

SCALE OF YARDS
0   500   1000

Winder
(5,930)

Baltimore Brigade

BLADENSBURG

Washington Brigade

(Marines)

Marines and sailors

Barney

Ross
(4,270; 3 guns)

---

a

Battle of Godly Wood, 12 Sept.

BALTIMORE

Back R.

Landed 12 Sept.
Re-embarked 14 Sept.
Departed 17 Sept.

ELLICOTT MILLS

BROOKEVILLE

ROCKVILLE

NORTH PT.

BODKIN PT.

Patapsco R.

MONTGOMERY C.H.

(25 Aug.)

VANSVILLE

See inset map for details.

GREAT FALLS

TENNALLYTOWN

GEORGETOWN

BLADENSBURG

ANNAPOLIS

WASHINGTON
(24-25 Aug.)

Bridge destroyed 24 Aug.

(24-25 Aug.)

(23 Aug.)

OLD FIELDS

(22-23 Aug.)

(22 Aug.)

UPPER MARLBOROUGH

Barney blew up his flotilla 22 Aug.

ALEXANDRIA

British secondary attack delayed by shoals. Captured Alexandria 28 Aug. Rejoined main force.

Feints

WOODYARD

(22 Aug.)

CHESAPEAKE BAY

MT. VERNON

(21 Aug.)

NOTTINGHAM

LOWER MARLBOROUGH

Potomac R.

Rappahannock R.

(Landed 19 Aug.)
BENEDICT

Re-embarked for Baltimore 30 Aug.

PT. LOOKOUT

THE WAR OF 1812
Operations Around Washington and Baltimore,
19 August–17 September 1814

SCALE OF MILES
0   5   10   15   20

12

b

LAKE PONTCHARTRAIN

LAKE DES ALLEMANDES

L. FOURCHE

CANARD LAKE

NEW ORLEANS

Jackson's final position

BAYOU MAZANT

American gunboats overwhelmed 14 Dec.

Fleet anchored here. Troops transferred to barges 13 Dec.

Jackson returned 11 Nov. from his Pensacola expedition. Left for New Orleans 22 Nov., leaving most of his troops here under Winchester.

Pearl R.

Pascagoula R.

Cedar R.

MOBILE

L. of the Ouatches

Night battle 24 Dec.

British landed 23 Dec. Completed withdrawal 27 Jan.

LAKE BORGNE

Ouatches R.

R. La Fourche

ROUND BAY

L. de BARATARIA

FREE MASONS IS.

NORTH CHANDELEUR IS.

MOBILE BAY

FT. BOWYER

(8 Feb.)

Surrendered 11 Feb.

FORT ST. PHILLIP

BRETON IS.

SOUTH CHANDELEUR IS.

G U L F   O F   M E X I C O

British naval secondary attack, 8–18 Jan., repulsed.

Mouth of the Mississippi

THE WAR OF 1812
British Advance on New Orleans,
22 November 1814 – 11 February 1815

SCALE OF MILES
0   3   6   9   12   15   30

---

c

JACKSON
(5,700; 3,200 engaged)

Adair
(Ditch)

CYPRESS SWAMPS

FORMAL GARDENS

(Ditch)

(Ditch)

Carroll

Coffee

Rifles   7   Plauché   Lacoste   Daquin   44

RODRIGUEZ CANAL

Only a very small detachment reached the canal.

Attack here achieved surprise; was initially successful. Not supported.

MISSISSIPPI RIVER

(Ditch)

95
(Deployed as a covering force)

West Indian

3 cos.

(Ditch)

44

West Indian

93

21

Keane

4

Gibbs

(Ditch)

7

43

Lambert (Reserve)

Thornton

Marines and sailors

85

West Indian

PAKENHAM
(8,000)

This secondary attack was to take an American battery on the west bank of the river which commanded Jackson's position. Because of the lack of boats, the battery was not captured until after its flanking fire had helped repulse Pakenham's attack.

BATTLE OF NEW ORLEANS
8 January 1815

SCALE OF YARDS
0   200   400

Though for some time disputes over the territory north of the Rio Grande, claimed by Mexico, had indicated the probability of war, the United States government had no plans for such a war. In the hope that a show of force would bring on a satisfactory negotiated peace, President James K. Polk in March, 1846, ordered Maj. Gen. Zachary Taylor into the disputed area. Taylor was instructed to defend Texas against invasion; but his orders implied authority to invade Mexico if necessary. In the Pacific, Commodore John D. Sloat's instructions required him to seize the California ports if war broke out. Clashes in the vicinity of Fort Brown soon made it evident that open hostilities could not be avoided. Polk, striving for a small and quick war, decided to blockade the coasts of Mexico and to occupy her northern provinces. These were believed ready to revolt against their central government.

Accordingly, a number of offensives were set in motion. Brig. Gen. John E. Wool was ordered to proceed to the important trading center of Chihuahua (*center*)—which he never reached. At Parras, he was diverted to Taylor's command. Col. Stephen W. Kearny was dispatched from Fort Leavenworth to occupy Santa Fe (*top center*) and other New Mexico towns, then to proceed to California if he felt capable of so doing. He was successful in New Mexico and moved on to California, detaching Col. Alexander W. Doniphan to pacify the warlike Indian tribes in the southern part of New Mexico and then to march south to Chihuahua (which Kearny assumed Wool would have occupied by that time). After defeating two Mexican forces en route, Doniphan arrived at Chihuahua. Taylor later ordered him to Saltillo; eventually his command boarded transports on the Rio Grande to return home. Doniphan's entire movement from Fort Leavenworth onward covered 3,500 miles—one of the most remarkable marches in military history. Meanwhile, on the way to California, Kearny learned that the Navy, aided by local American settlers, had seized the California ports. Sending most of his troops back to New Mexico—where they became involved in suppressing revolts that had broken out after his departure—he pushed on to California. There he encountered considerable opposition, but soon restored order.

The principal operation was entrusted to Taylor, who captured Monterey. One of his columns, under Brig. Gen. John A. Quitman, occupied Victoria. Meanwhile the Navy had occupied Tampico (*lower right*) which was later garrisoned by the troops of Brig. Gen. James Shields. In February, 1847, Taylor defeated the Mexicans at Buena Vista.

Despite all these reverses, the Mexican government did not offer to surrender. Further, the ineptness of American rule had induced revolts and guerrilla warfare in the occupied areas. It appeared necessary to march directly on the capital, Mexico City, to attain a decision. But problems of terrain and supply precluded such an operation by Taylor's forces from the Monterey area. President Polk finally had to accede to the plan that Maj. Gen. Winfield Scott and others had been urging upon him for some time—an advance on Mexico City directly from Vera Cruz. Scott himself was to undertake its execution.

Scott was joined at Tampico by part of Taylor's force under Maj. Gen. Robert Patterson and Brig. Gen. David E. Twiggs. He then proceeded to Vera Cruz, landed successfully, and, in the face of many difficulties, carried his offensive on to victory. His capture of Mexico City forced the Mexican government to capitulate and ended the fighting, except for scattered guerrilla actions.

Throughout the war the American Navy played a prominent role. In addition to its actions in blockading and seizing ports, it provided strategic mobility to the ground forces and assisted in the solution of their extremely serious supply problems.

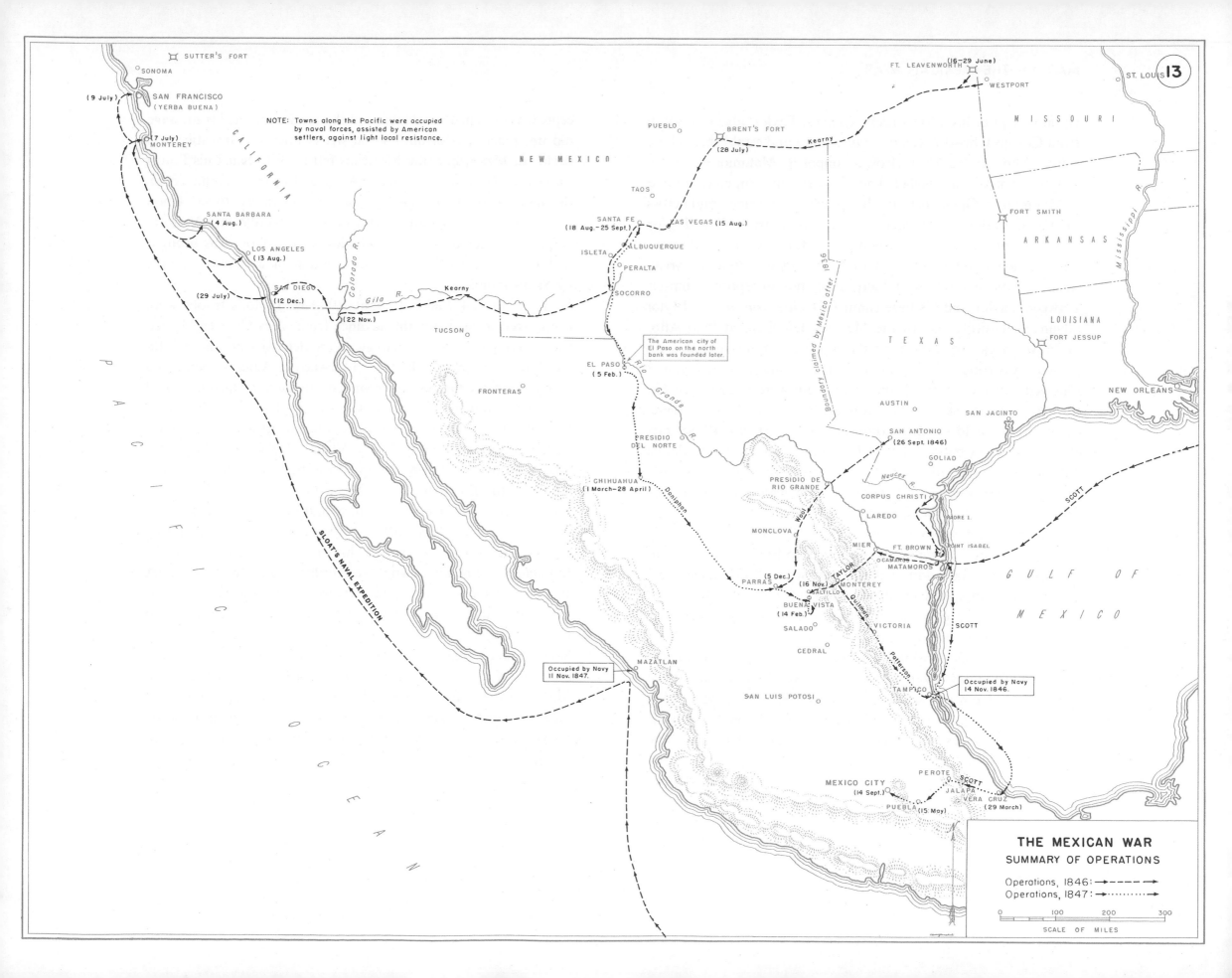

NOTE: Towns along the Pacific were occupied by naval forces, assisted by American settlers, against light local resistance.

The American city of El Paso on the north bank was founded later.

THE MEXICAN WAR

SUMMARY OF OPERATIONS

Operations, 1846: ------→

Operations, 1847: ·······→

SCALE OF MILES

0   100   200   300

Upon receipt of his initial orders, General Taylor advanced south from Corpus Christi (*sketch* a, *top center*) and established a base camp—later called Fort Brown—opposite Matamoros, and a supply depot at Point Isabel. The Mexicans, in turn, concentrated at Matamoros. Open hostilities began when a Mexican raid across the Rio Grande overwhelmed an American patrol. While Taylor was at Point Isabel with the bulk of his force, General Mariano Arista made an attempt to capture Fort Brown. Repulsed, Arista then took up a position at Palo Alto, thus interposing himself between Taylor and his base camp (*sketch* a, *top inset*). Taylor advanced leisurely against the Mexican left flank at Palo Alto. A Mexican cavalry attack on the American right rear was repulsed. A strong infantry attack on the American left and a renewed cavalry attack on the other flank were both driven off, principally by the skill of American artillery. The Mexicans thereupon left the field in some confusion. The next day Taylor met the Mexicans in battle a few miles south at Resaca de la Palma (*sketch* a, *bottom inset*). Attacks against the Mexican center and left in heavy chaparral caused the Mexican army to collapse and flee across the Rio Grande.

Arista withdrew to Linares (*sketch* a, *center*); Taylor followed for about sixty miles, then returned to Fort Brown to await reinforcements and additional transportation. When these were received, he established an advance base at Camargo and marched to Monterey. The city was well fortified, but the Mexican line of supply from Saltillo was poorly protected. Brig. Gen. William J. Worth took his division on a turning movement around the west end of the city (*sketch* b) to cut the Saltillo road and attack the defenses from the west and south. Meanwhile, Taylor threw Twiggs' and Maj. Gen. William O. Butler's divisions against the north and east faces of the city. General Pedro de Ampudia (who had replaced Arista) proposed surrender on terms highly favorable to himself, including an eight-week armistice. Taylor accepted. President Polk denounced the armistice, but his message did not reach Taylor until seven weeks after the armistice was declared. Meanwhile, the Mexicans fell back to San Luis Potosi (*sketch* a, *bottom left*), where Antonio Lopez de Santa Anna, the new Mexican president, began to reorganize them. Upon receiving Polk's decision, Taylor occupied Saltillo and Victoria and sent Shields to garrison Tampico. Later, Wool was brought in from Parras to Saltillo in anticipation of a rumored attack by Santa Anna.

Early in 1847, all but about 5,000 of Taylor's troops were transferred to Scott for the advance from Vera Cruz to Mexico City. Taylor was instructed to go on the defensive around Saltillo and Monterey; instead, he moved forward to Agua Nueva. Santa Anna intercepted a message from Scott to Taylor which disclosed the American plans and the weakness of Taylor's force. He therefore advanced north from San Luis Potosi against Taylor; Taylor withdrew to a position at Buena Vista (*sketch* c). Santa Anna arrived with 14,000 men and on 23 February launched his main attack in the Battle of Buena Vista. General Blanco's division was shattered by American artillery and General Pacheco's was routed; but the others pushed forward bravely, concentrating against the American left. At this crisis, an officer of the 2d Indiana, for some unknown reason, ordered his men to retreat. A stampede ensued, in which the Arkansas and Kentucky mounted regiments joined. Fortunately, Taylor then arrived from Saltillo with his dragoons and Mississippi Rifles. Repulsed everywhere, Santa Anna committed his reserve, General Ortega's division, only to have it checked by Capt. Braxton Bragg's guns. General Miñon's cavalry attacked Saltillo, but was repulsed. Santa Anna then retreated to San Luis Potosi (*sketch* a); Taylor returned to Monterey. Except for guerrilla actions, this ended the war in the north.

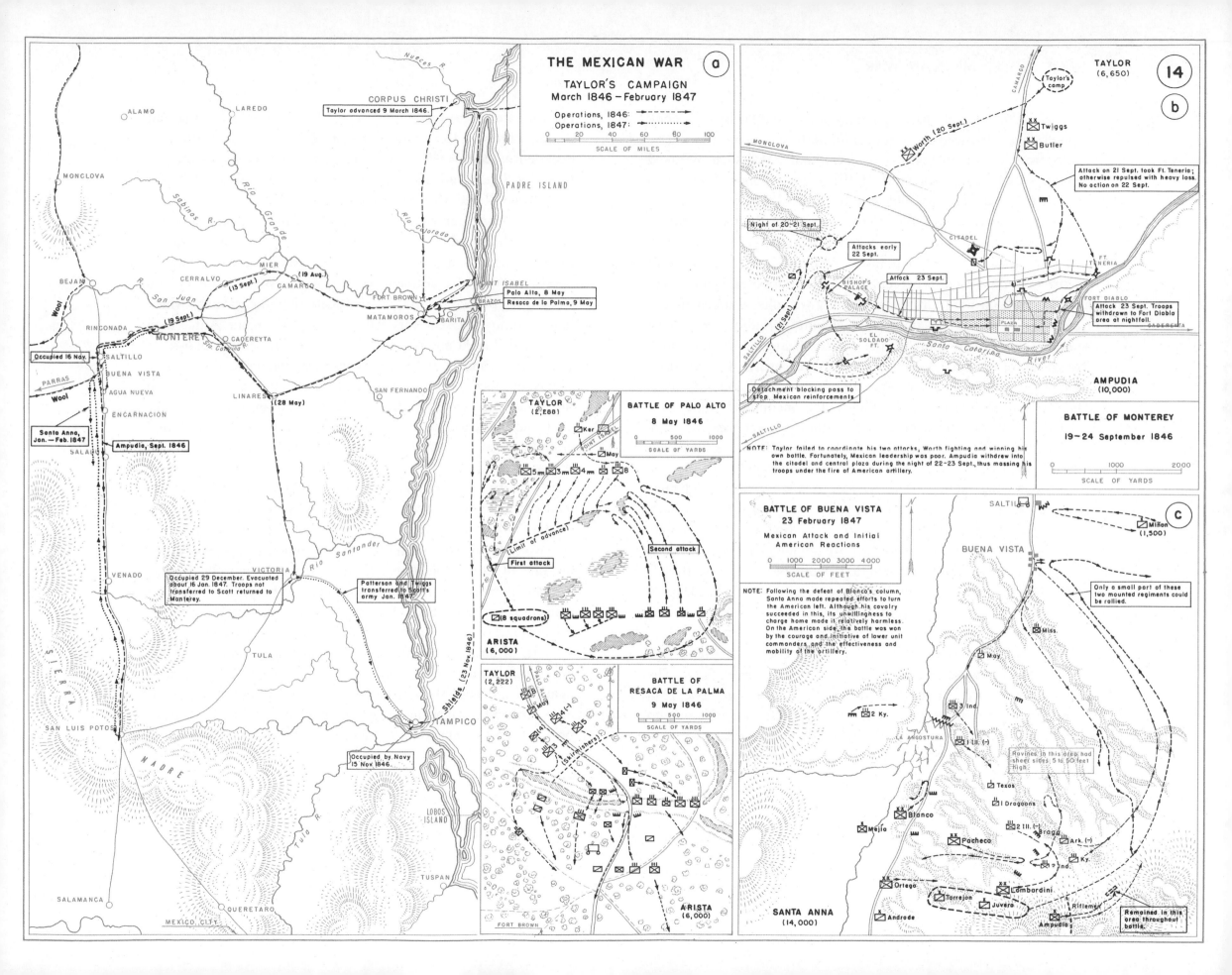

THE MEXICAN WAR

TAYLOR'S CAMPAIGN
March 1846 — February 1847

Operations, 1846
Operations, 1847

SCALE OF MILES
0   20   40   60   80   100

Taylor advanced 9 March 1846.

Palo Alto, 8 May
Resaca de la Palma, 9 May

(19 Aug.)
(13 Sept.)
(19 Sept.)

Occupied 16 Nov.

Santa Anna, Jan. — Feb. 1847

Ampudia, Sept. 1846

Patterson and Twiggs transferred to Scott's army Jan. 1847

Occupied 29 December. Evacuated about 16 Jan. 1847. Troops not transferred to Scott returned to Monterey.

Occupied by Navy 15 Nov. 1846.

Shields (23 Nov. 1846)

a / **14**

TAYLOR (6,650)
Taylor's camp

Twiggs
Butler
Worth (20 Sept.)

Attack on 21 Sept. took Ft. Teneria; otherwise repulsed with heavy loss. No action on 22 Sept.

Night of 20-21 Sept.

Attacks early 22 Sept.

Attack 23 Sept.

Attack 23 Sept. Troops withdrawn to Fort Diablo area at nightfall.

Detachment blocking pass to stop Mexican reinforcements

AMPUDIA (10,000)

NOTE: Taylor failed to coordinate his two attacks, Worth fighting and winning his own battle. Fortunately, Mexican leadership was poor. Ampudia withdrew into the citadel and central plaza during the night of 22-23 Sept., thus massing his troops under the fire of American artillery.

BATTLE OF MONTEREY
19-24 September 1846

SCALE OF YARDS
0   1000   2000

b

TAYLOR (2,288)
Ker
May
5m   3m   4   8

BATTLE OF PALO ALTO
8 May 1846

SCALE OF YARDS
0   500   1000

(Limit of advance)
First attack
Second attack

(8 squadrons)

ARISTA (6,000)

TAYLOR (2,222)
May
4(-)
5
(Skirmishers)

BATTLE OF RESACA DE LA PALMA
9 May 1846

SCALE OF YARDS
0   500   1000

ARISTA (6,000)
FORT BROWN

BATTLE OF BUENA VISTA
23 February 1847

Mexican Attack and Initial American Reactions

SCALE OF FEET
0   1000   2000   3000   4000

NOTE: Following the defeat of Blanco's column, Santa Anna made repeated efforts to turn the American left. Although his cavalry succeeded in this, its unwillingness to charge home made it relatively harmless. On the American side, the battle was won by the courage and initiative of lower unit commanders and the effectiveness and mobility of the artillery.

SALTILLO
Miñon (1,500)

BUENA VISTA

Only a small part of these two mounted regiments could be rallied.

Miss.

May

2 Ky.

3 Ind.

LA ANGOSTURA

1 Ill. (-)

Ravines in this area had sheer sides; 5 to 50 feet high.

Texas

I Dragoons

2 Ill. (-)

Braga
Ark. (-)

Blanco

Mejia

Pacheco

Ky.

2 Ind.

Ortega

Torrejon

Lombardini

Juvera

Riflemen

Andrade

Ampudia

Remained in this area throughout battle.

SANTA ANNA (14,000)

c

Place names on main map: CORPUS CHRISTI, Nueces R., PADRE ISLAND, ALAMO, LAREDO, MONCLOVA, Rio Grande, Sabinos R., San Juan, MIER, CERRALVO, CAMARGO, POINT ISABEL, FORT BROWN, BRAZOS, BARITA, MATAMOROS, BEJAN, RINCONADA, MONTEREY, CADEREYTA, Sta. Catarina R., SALTILLO, BUENA VISTA, AGUA NUEVA, ENCARNACIÓN, LINARES, SAN FERNANDO, PARRAS, Wool, SALADO, VENADO, VICTORIA, Rio Santander, TULA, SIERRA MADRE, SAN LUIS POTOSI, TAMPICO, LOBOS ISLAND, SALAMANCA, TUSPAN, QUERETARO, MEXICO CITY, Tula R.

President Polk sought to assign Senator Thomas H. Benton, completely inexperienced in military affairs, to command the operations from Vera Cruz to Mexico City. Finally, Maj. Gen. Winfield Scott, Commanding General of the United States Army, was given the task. He assembled a force of 13,000, including a large part of Taylor's force. Though much of the equipment he had requisitioned—siege guns, wagons, lighters—never appeared, he proceeded in close cooperation with the Navy against Vera Cruz (*sketch* a). On 9 March, 1847, an unopposed landing was made south of Vera Cruz, and the city was placed under investment (*sketch* b). An immediate assault probably could have taken the city, but only at the risk of heavy casualties which might have crippled Scott's already small army. The garrison could eventually have been starved out by a land and sea blockade, but speed was essential to avoid the oncoming yellow fever season. Scott therefore opened a sustained bombardment, supplementing his few guns with guns borrowed from the fleet. On 29 March, the Vera Cruz garrison surrendered.

Meanwhile, Santa Anna moved to oppose Scott's advance inland and began to construct defenses at Cerro Gordo (*sketch* a). The rapid fall of Vera Cruz did not allow time for their completion before the Americans arrived. Reconnaissance by American engineers showed that the position could be turned on its left by moving along a rough trail (*sketch* c). Scott's battle plan was for Twiggs to move along the trail and cut the Mexican line of retreat; Shields and Worth (*lower right*) were to follow. As soon as they were engaged, Brig. Gen. Gideon J. Pillow was to make a secondary attack against the Mexican right flank. The cavalry was held on the highway ready for pursuit. The plan was excellent, but its execution was poor. Instead of going to the Mexican rear as ordered, Twiggs cut in to attack at La Atalaya and El Telegrafo. Only Shields reached the road in rear,

but too late to cut off the retreat of the Mexican left wing and center. Pillow, a former law partner of Polk with little military experience, completely mismanaged his attack. However, the threat of Shields' advance and the drive of Twiggs' attack broke the morale of the Mexican army, and it fled.

Santa Anna gathered what forces he could at Puebla (*sketch* a). Scott followed, but, at Jalapa, he had to release for return to the United States almost all of his volunteer troops whose one-year terms of enlistment were expiring. With his remaining troops, he pushed on to Puebla, scattering the cavalry which Santa Anna had sent forward against him. Santa Anna then evacuated Puebla and retired to Mexico City. Scott remained at Puebla for three months, awaiting reinforcements; these came slowly in small columns, frequently under guerrilla attack. In the meantime, he established excellent relations with the local civil and clerical authorities, and managed to obtain food and clothing for his army from local sources. During this period Santa Anna reestablished control over the Mexican central government, troops were brought into Mexico City, and capable Mexican engineers worked on fortifying the approaches to the city.

On 7 August, 1847, Scott left Puebla and advanced on the Mexican capital (*left center*). Lacking sufficient troops to guard his line of communications, he abandoned it entirely, leaving a small garrison in Puebla to protect his hospitals there. No resistance was encountered up to Ayotla, but, just beyond, the fortified hill of El Peñon blocked the direct road to Mexico City. A series of daring reconnaissances revealed a passable trail leading south around Lake Chalco. While Twiggs demonstrated against El Peñon, the remainder of the army took the trail. It arrived at San Augustin—eight miles south of Mexico City—on 17 August. Santa Anna shifted his forces to meet this advance.

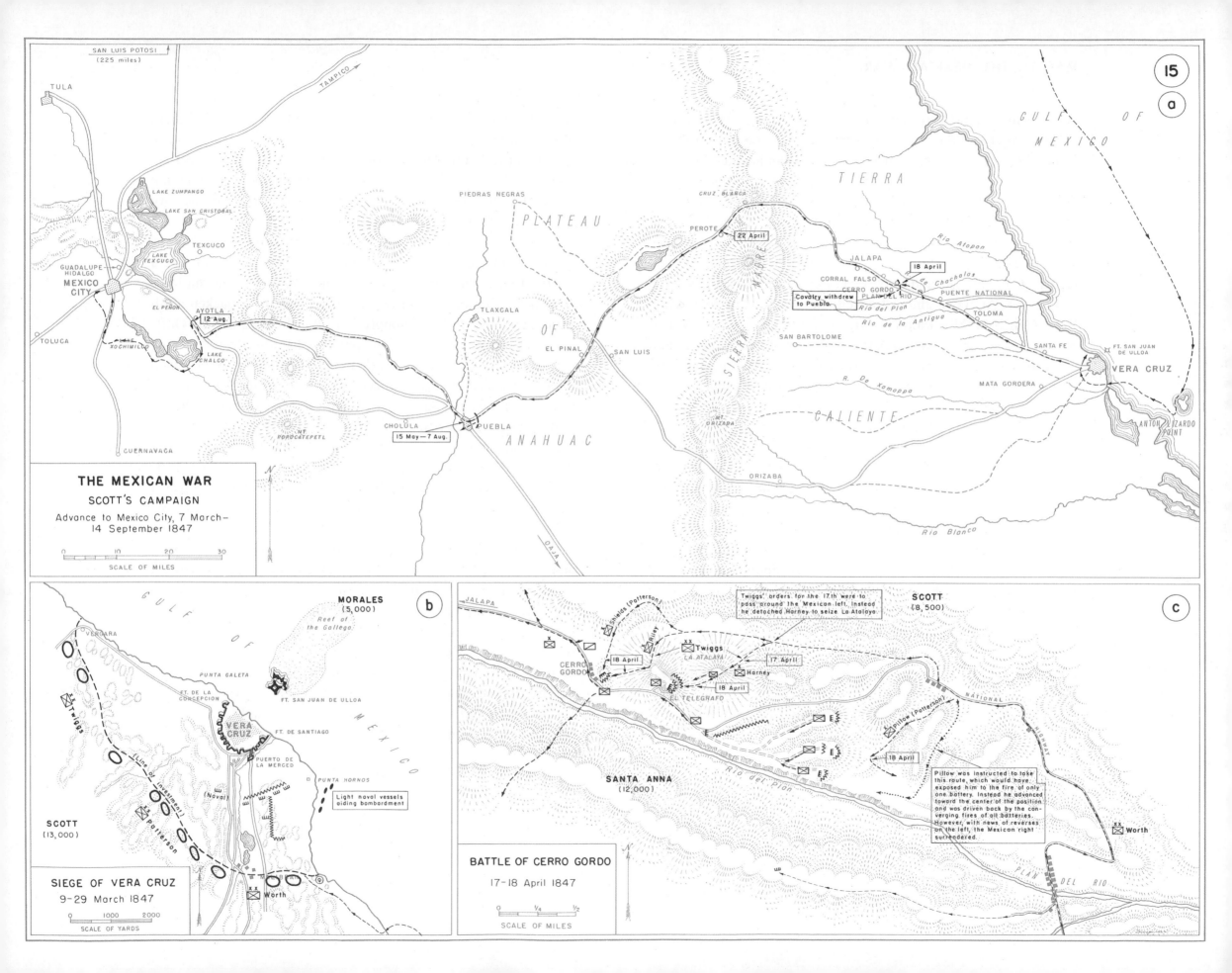

15 (a)

THE MEXICAN WAR

SCOTT'S CAMPAIGN

Advance to Mexico City, 7 March–
14 September 1847

SCALE OF MILES
0   10   20   30

San Luis Potosi
(225 miles)

TAMPICO

TULA

GULF OF MEXICO

TIERRA

PLATEAU

LAKE ZUMPANGO
LAKE SAN CRISTOBAL
TEXCUCO
LAKE TEXCUCO
GUADALUPE HIDALGO
MEXICO CITY
EL PEÑON
AYOTLA — 12 Aug.
LAKE XOCHIMILCO
LAKE CHALCO
TOLUCA

MADRE

PIEDRAS NEGRAS
CRUZ BLANCA
PEROTE — 22 April
JALAPA
CORRAL FALSO — 18 April
CERRO GORDO
PLAN DEL RIO
Cavalry withdrew to Puebla
Rio del Plan
Rio de Chachalas
PUENTE NATIONAL
TOLOMA
Rio Atopan
Rio de la Antigua

TLAXCALA
EL PINAL
SAN LUIS
SAN BARTOLOME
SANTA FE
FT. SAN JUAN DE ULLOA
R. De Xamappa
MATA GORDERA
VERA CRUZ

SIERRA

CHOLULA
PUEBLA — 15 May — 7 Aug.
ANAHUAC

OF

CALIENTE

MT. POPOCATEPETL
GUERNAVACA
OAJA
ORIZABA
MT. ORIZABA
ANTON LIZARDO POINT

Rio Blanco

(b)

SIEGE OF VERA CRUZ

9–29 March 1847

SCALE OF YARDS
0   1000   2000

MORALES
(5,000)

Reef of the Gallega

GULF OF MEXICO

VERGARA
PUNTA GALETA
FT. DE LA CONCEPCION
FT. SAN JUAN DE ULLOA
VERA CRUZ
FT. DE SANTIAGO
PUERTO DE LA MERCED
PUNTA HORNOS

SCOTT
(13,000)

Twiggs
(Line of Investment)
(Naval)
Patterson

Light naval vessels aiding bombardment

Worth

(c)

BATTLE OF CERRO GORDO

17–18 April 1847

SCALE OF MILES
0   ¼   ½

SCOTT
(8,500)

JALAPA

Shields (Patterson)
Riley
Twiggs' orders for the 17th were to pass around the Mexican left. Instead he detached Harney to seize La Atalaya.

CERRO GORDO
18 April
Twiggs
LA ATALAYA
17 April
Harney
18 April
EL TELEGRAFO

Pillow (Patterson)
18 April

NATIONAL HIGHWAY

SANTA ANNA
(12,000)

Rio del Plan

Pillow was instructed to take this route, which would have exposed him to the fire of only one battery. Instead he advanced toward the center of the position and was driven back by the converging fires of all batteries. However, with news of reverses on the left, the Mexican right surrendered.

Worth

PLAN DEL RIO

Santa Anna intended to defend the approaches to Mexico City at San Angel and San Antonio (*sketch* a), but the insubordinate General Gabriel Valencia moved forward to an isolated hill position at Contreras. Pillow made an unauthorized attack on the position with his and Twiggs' divisions. The attack failed, primarily because of heavier Mexican artillery and rough terrain. A gulley was found that led to the rear of Valencia's position, along which the brigades of Lt. Col. Bennet Riley, Brig. Gen. George Cadwalader, and Brig. Gen. Persifor F. Smith advanced (*sketch* b). At dawn they attacked the position in rear while Brig. Gen. Franklin Pierce's brigade attacked in front. Valencia's force collapsed. Santa Anna, with 7,000 men from the Hill of Toro, came forward only in time to meet the fugitives. He then ordered all Mexican troops to concentrate along the inner defenses of the capital.

As the garrison of San Antonio retired in obedience to this order (*sketch* c), one of Worth's brigades struck them in flank and scattered them. The hot pursuit of the American columns converged on the fortified bridgehead at Churubusco, which Santa Anna had ordered held at all costs. One of the defending artillery battalions was composed largely of American deserters, who could expect no mercy. Repeated American attacks were beaten back with heavy loss. After initial repulses, Pierce and Shields got across the river. Some of Worth's troops likewise crossed and attacked the bridgehead from the rear. Mexican resistance thereupon collapsed, except at the San Pablo Convent, where the desperate garrison held out for some time. Shields and Pierce hit the retreating forces in flank, and Sumner's dragoons pursued them right up to the city.

Santa Anna then obtained an armistice for peace negotiations, in order to gain time to reorganize his forces. The negotiations naturally failed. Scott directed his next attack at El Molino del Rey (*sketch* d), under the mistaken belief that it was a cannon foundry. After a costly two-hour struggle, Worth carried the objective and forced the withdrawal of the defenders to Chapultepec.

The crucial problem of how to attack Mexico City still remained. At a council of war, the majority favored an attack along the causeways leading to the southern part of the city (*sketch* e); Scott elected to attack through Chapultepec. To draw Mexican troops away from the Chapultepec area, Twiggs made a feint against the San Antonio Garita. (A garita was a fortified stone building used as a police and customs station.) Quitman's division, supported by Smith's brigade, attacked north from Tacubaya. Pillow, supported by Worth and aided by Quitman's advance, attacked and captured Chapultepec in the face of gallant resistance. Quitman thereupon proceeded up the Belen Road and seized the Garita Belen. Worth passed through Pillow's troops and took the San Cosme Garita in a heavy action. When both columns renewed their advance the next morning, they found that Santa Anna and his troops had left the city during the night. Before leaving, he had freed and armed all the convicts in the city jails, who, with the local criminal element, opened fire on the Americans as they entered the city. Stern measures were necessary to suppress them.

Santa Anna now resigned his office as President of Mexico and moved with a small force to attack the American garrison at Puebla (*see map* 15a), already besieged by guerrilla units. Failing here, he attempted to intercept Brig. Gen. Joseph Lane's column moving up from Vera Cruz. Lane defeated him and relieved Puebla. For a period there was heavy guerrilla warfare along the highway, especially east of Jalapa, but Lane and other commanders eventually put an end to such activity.

American military occupation of a considerable area around Mexico City continued until after the ratification of the Treaty of Guadalupe Hidalgo. On 12 June, the last American soldier left the capital.

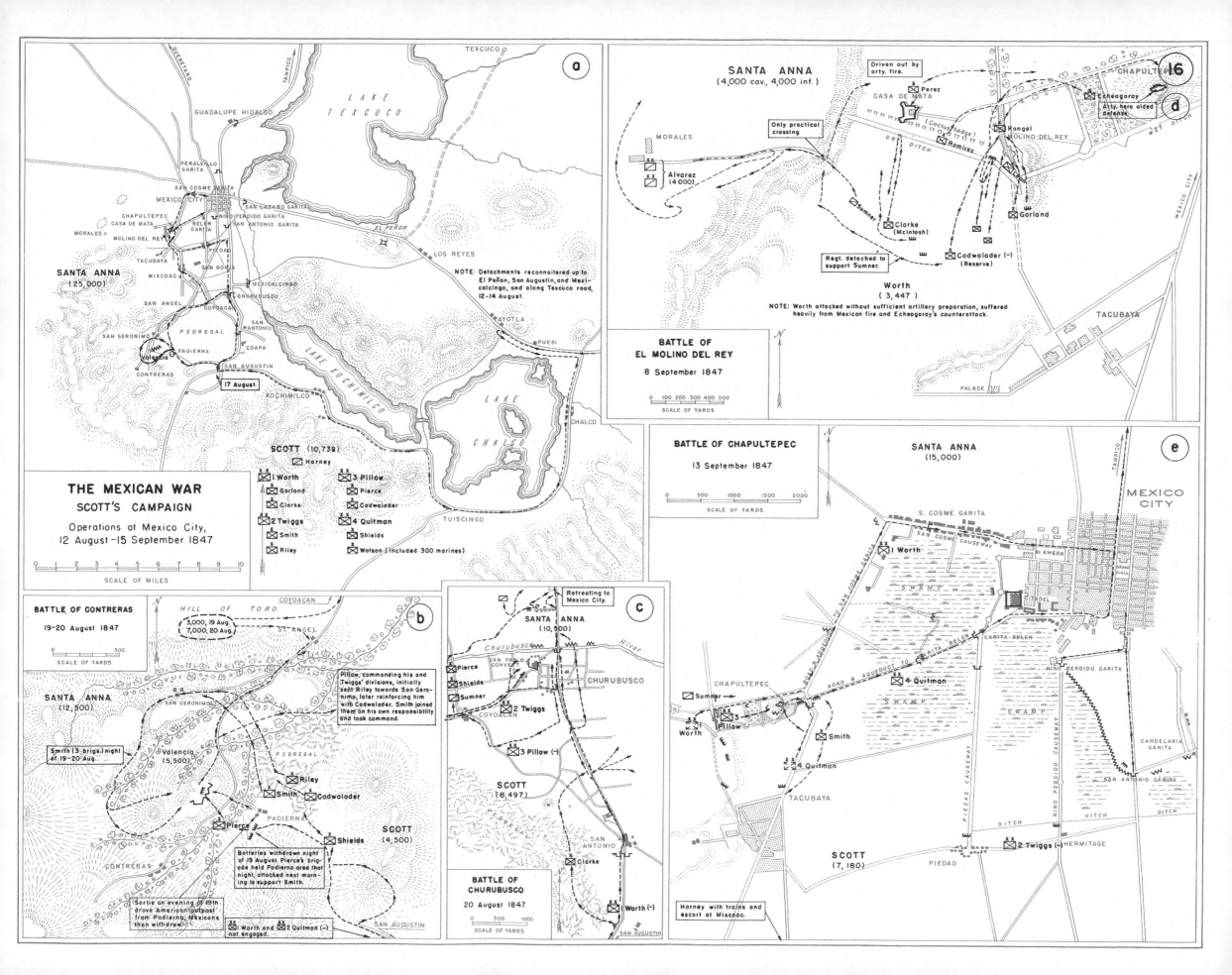

a

LAKE TEXCUCO

GUADALUPE HIDALGO

QUERETARO

TAMPICO

TEXCUCO

PERALVILLO GARITA

SAN COSME GARITA

CHAPULTEPEC

MEXICO CITY

SAN LAZARO GARITA

CASA DE MATA

NINO PERDIDO GARITA

SAN ANTONIO GARITA

BELEN GARITA

MORALES

MOLINO DEL REY

PIEDAD

TACUBAYA

SAN BORJA

MIXCOAC

MEXICALCINGO

EL PEÑON

LOS REYES

SANTA ANNA
(25,000)

SAN ANGEL

COYOACAN

CHURUBUSCO

SAN GERONIMO

PEDREGAL

PADIERNA

SAN ANTONIO

COAPA

AYOTLA

PUEBI

Valencia

CONTRERAS

SAN AUGUSTIN

17 August.

XOCHIMILCO

LAKE XOCHIMILCO

LAKE CHALCO

CHALCO

TUISCINGO

NOTE: Detachments reconnoitered up to El Peñon, San Augustin, and Mexi-calcingo, and along Texcuco road, 12-14 August.

THE MEXICAN WAR
SCOTT'S CAMPAIGN

Operations at Mexico City,
12 August -15 September 1847

0 1 2 3 4 5 6 7 8 9 10
SCALE OF MILES

SCOTT (10,738)

Harney

1 Worth
Garland
Clarke
2 Twiggs
Smith
Riley

3 Pillow
Pierce
Cadwalader
4 Quitman
Shields
Watson (included 300 marines)

16

SANTA ANNA
(4,000 cav., 4,000 inf.)

Driven out by arty. fire.

CHAPULTEPEC

CASA DE MATA

Perez

Echeagaray Arty. here aided defense.

(Cactus hedge)

d

MORALES

DRY DITCH

Rangel
MOLINO DEL REY

Ramirez

WET DITCH

Alvarez (4,000)

Only practical crossing

Sumner

Clarke (McIntosh)

Garland

Regt. detached to support Sumner.

Cadwalader (-) (Reserve)

MEXICO CITY

Worth (3,447)

NOTE: Worth attacked without sufficient artillery preparation, suffered heavily from Mexican fire and Echeagaray's counterattack.

TACUBAYA

BATTLE OF EL MOLINO DEL REY

8 September 1847

0 100 200 300 400 500
SCALE OF YARDS

N

PALACE

BATTLE OF CHAPULTEPEC

13 September 1847

0 500 1000 1500 2000
SCALE OF YARDS

N

SANTA ANNA
(15,000)

e

MEXICO CITY

S. COSME GARITA

SAN COSME CAUSEWAY

ALAMEDA

1 Worth

CITADEL

SWAMP

TAMPICO

ROAD 8 AQUEDUCT TO GARITA BELEN

GARITA BELEN

ROAD 8 AQUEDUCT TO SAN COSME GARITA

CHAPULTEPEC

Sumner

4 Quitman

SWAMP

NINO PERDIDO GARITA

3 Pillow

Worth

Smith

4 Quitman

SWAMP

CANDELARIA GARITA

SAN ANTONIO GARITA

TACUBAYA

PIEDAD CAUSEWAY

NINO PERDIDO CAUSEWAY

DITCH

DITCH

DITCH

SCOTT
(7,180)

PIEDAD

2 Twiggs (-) HERMITAGE

Harney with trains and escort at Mixcoac.

---

b

BATTLE OF CONTRERAS

19-20 August 1847

0 500
SCALE OF YARDS

N

HILL OF TORO

COYOACAN

ST. ANGEL

3,000, 19 Aug.
7,000, 20 Aug.

SANTA ANNA
(12,500)

SAN GERONIMO

Pillow, commanding his and Twiggs' divisions, initially sent Riley towards San Geronimo, later reinforcing him with Cadwalader. Smith joined them on his own responsibility and took command.

PEDREGAL

Valencia (5,500)

Smith (3 brigs.) night of 19-20 Aug.

Riley

Smith

Cadwalader

PADIERNA

Pierce

Shields

CONTRERAS

SCOTT
(4,500)

Batteries withdrawn night of 19 August. Pierce's brigade held Padierna area that night, attacked next morning to support Smith.

Sortie on evening of 19th drove American outpost from Padierna; Mexicans then withdrew.

Worth and 2 Quitman (-) not engaged.

SAN AUGUSTIN

---

c

Retreating to Mexico City.

SANTA ANNA
(10,500)

Churubusco River

San Pablo Convent

Pierce

Shields

Sumner

COYOACAN

2 Twiggs

CHURUBUSCO

3 Pillow (-)

SCOTT
(8,497)

SAN ANTONIO

Clarke

Worth (-)

BATTLE OF CHURUBUSCO

20 August 1847

0 500 1000
SCALE OF YARDS

SAN AUGUSTIN

On 12 April, 1861, Fort Sumter was fired upon, initiating the bloody conflict between the states which was to last four years. The major Civil War campaigns, except those of Banks and Farragut, are shown on this map and will be covered in detail on the maps which follow.

With the advent of war, both sides hastily began preparations, neither fully appreciating the tremendous problems involved. Some Confederates believed one sizable victory would discourage the Federal government; many Northerners expected the 75,000 militia, called for a period of three months, to win in that time a major victory which would restore the Union. Nor was either side ready for war. The Union, at least, might have been expected to be prepared; instead, it had a small regular army of only 16,000, scattered mostly in small units along the western frontier.

There were two major theaters of war: Virginia and the Mississippi-Tennessee River area. In 1861, neither side had an over-all strategy. Davis, the Confederate president, never developed one, being forced on the defensive early in the war and not fully understanding the significance of the western theater. Lincoln early appreciated the North's advantages in manpower, resources, and naval strength. He also saw the importance of a naval blockade and of taking the offensive. Later he appreciated the importance of the Mississippi Valley. But it was not until the emergence of Grant as commander in chief that a fully coordinated strategy was put into effect. General Scott, Lincoln's commander in chief when war came, foresaw the importance of coastal blockade and control of the Mississippi River, but his implementing strategy was a waiting rather than an offensive one. Both sides, particularly the Union, overrated the importance of the two capitals; hence the bloody campaigns in Virginia, which by themselves could not be decisive. Meanwhile, in the west, the foundation for Union victory was slowly being built by the battles along the great waterways. The campaign arrows trace the evolution of the Union strategy: first, a naval blockade of the Confederacy; second, the east-west cleavage of the Confederacy by subjugating the Mississippi River area; third, the drive across Georgia to split the previously severed eastern portion; and, lastly, the closing of the pincers on Lee and Johnston by Grant and Sherman.

An understanding of the geography of the area and of the railroad systems helps to explain the successes and failures during the war. Possessing naval superiority, the Union found it desirable to use the Ohio, Cumberland, Tennessee, Mississippi, and Potomac (via Chesapeake Bay) Rivers as axes of advance as well as supply routes. The many streams in Virginia were of great defensive value to Lee in his campaigns. The great Appalachian chain of mountains restricted the Union approach to the Confederate heartland around Atlanta. When it was turned at Chattanooga in 1863, the gateway to the South was laid bare. The Shenandoah Valley, hemmed in by mountains, was the scene of Jackson's brilliant exploits and was of inestimable value in Lee's defensive strategy. The railroads, though still in their infancy, made it possible for the armies to attain strategic mobility and to accomplish logistic miracles.

July, 1863, was the decisive month of the war. Lee's army was severely punished at Gettysburg and his second invasion of the North was driven back. Meanwhile, Grant broke the last Confederate link to the West by capturing Vicksburg—an event of at least equal importance. There were other important campaigns—Antietam, where Lee's first invasion was stopped and which led to Lincoln's issuance of the Emancipation Proclamation; and Chattanooga, which opened the gateway to Atlanta—but none was so decisive in its effects upon the Confederacy as were those of Gettysburg and Vicksburg.

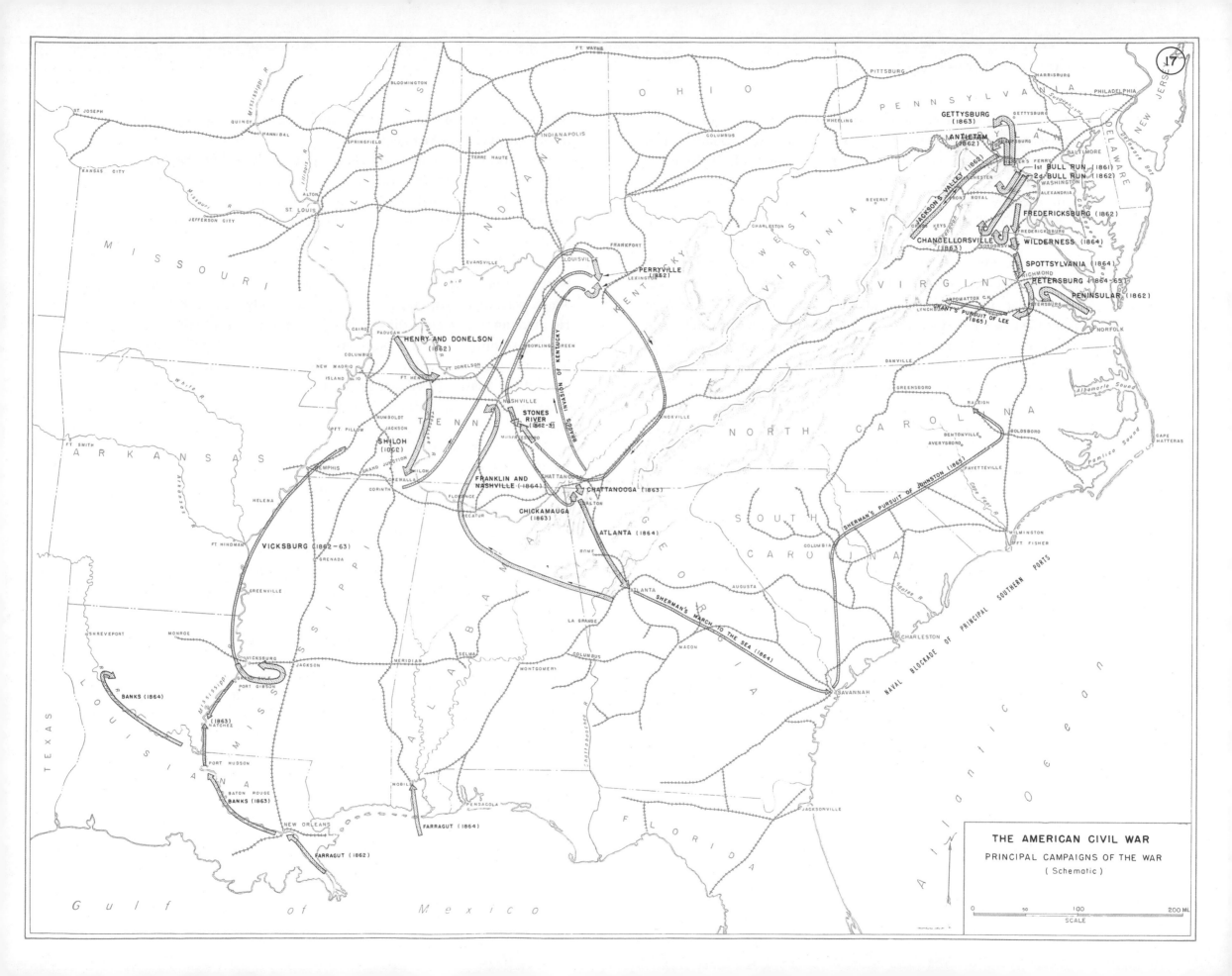

17

THE AMERICAN CIVIL WAR

PRINCIPAL CAMPAIGNS OF THE WAR

(Schematic)

GETTYSBURG (1863)
ANTIETAM (1862)
1st BULL RUN (1861)
2d BULL RUN (1862)
FREDERICKSBURG (1862)
CHANCELLORSVILLE (1863)
WILDERNESS (1864)
SPOTTSYLVANIA (1864)
PETERSBURG (1864-65)
PENINSULAR (1862)
GRANT'S PURSUIT OF LEE (1865)
JACKSON'S VALLEY (1862)
PERRYVILLE (1862)
HENRY AND DONELSON (1862)
BRAGG'S INVASION OF KENTUCKY
STONES RIVER (1862-3)
SHILOH (1862)
FRANKLIN AND NASHVILLE (1864)
CHATTANOOGA (1863)
CHICKAMAUGA (1863)
ATLANTA (1864)
SHERMAN'S PURSUIT OF JOHNSTON (1865)
VICKSBURG (1862-63)
SHERMAN'S MARCH TO THE SEA (1864)
NAVAL BLOCKADE OF PRINCIPAL SOUTHERN PORTS
BANKS (1864)
(1863) NATCHEZ
PORT HUDSON
BANKS (1863)
BATON ROUGE
FARRAGUT (1864)
FARRAGUT (1862)

0   50   100   200 MI.
SCALE

The first Bull Run campaign was the first major campaign of the war. The first engagement of the war had actually taken place on 10 June, 1861, at Big Bethel (near Fort Monroe, Virginia), where Col. John B. Magruder won a victory for the Confederacy. On 11–12 July, a small Confederate force had suffered humiliating defeat at Rich Mountain, near Beverly in western Virginia. As a result of this latter success, Maj. Gen. George B. McClellan, the Union commander, had attained an unwarranted prominence which inspired the belief that here was the leader the Union needed. Northwestern Virginia (West Virginia) had remained loyal to the Union cause, the Richmond authorities being unable to quell the Unionist sympathies in that part of the state by force of arms. The other border states were skillfully and successfully wooed by Lincoln, who undoubtedly was influenced by the fact that Missouri, Kentucky, and Maryland together had 517,000 men of military age—for whom the Confederacy certainly could find ample use.

The troop positions shown on the map are those occupied two days before Brig. Gen. Irwin McDowell began his march to Centreville (*upper center*) to do battle with Brig. Gen. Pierre G. T. Beauregard. The leaders were believed to be the best available. The colorful Beauregard, victor at Fort Sumter, was the man of the hour in the South; Brig. Gen. Joseph E. Johnston, one of the prewar army's outstanding officers, was now a ranking Confederate general; Magruder, Brig. Gen. Benjamin Huger, and Brig. Gen. Theophilus H. Holmes had also belonged to the "old army" as artillerist, ordnance specialist, and cavalryman, respectively. Arrayed against them were McDowell, lately a major, who by virtue of training in France had seemed to be best qualified to command a large body of troops; Patterson, a veteran of the Mexican War and the War of 1812; and Butler, no soldier, who owed his appointment to politics. The only officer on either side who ever had commanded as many as 5,000 troops was General Winfield Scott.

The locations of the capitals made it certain that the first campaign would be in Maryland or Virginia. Mistakenly influenced by the belief that seizure of the capital was more important than destruction of the enemy's army, Union leaders, goaded by public opinion, insisted that McDowell advance. Scott objected, wanting to wait until the army was larger and better trained, but to no avail. McDowell prepared a plan, which was approved, and he was directed to advance on 8 July. He had an army consisting largely of militia with only two months training, several subordinates who were good politicians but poor generals, and no staff to assist in supervision of the plan. But, reasoned Washington, the Confederacy faced the same problems—an unfounded assumption, for the major differential between the two armies was the care taken by the South in the selection of its officers.

Beauregard's force was located at Manassas, an ideal position from which to guard against the expected southward advance of McDowell via either Fredericksburg or Culpeper. It was also on a railroad which could be used to unite quickly Johnston's force with his own. Johnston originally had occupied Harper's Ferry, but had withdrawn on 15 June to Winchester, where he could better protect the entrance to the Shenandoah Valley. Patterson had been given the mission of capturing Harper's Ferry, but after its evacuation he was directed to follow Johnston. On 2 July, Patterson crossed the Potomac at Williamsport and, by 15 July, was in the vicinity of Charlestown. So, on the eve of the first major campaign, two forces were watching each other in the Valley; McDowell was preparing to advance to Centreville; and Beauregard, at Manassas, was busily preparing grandiose plans for the defeat of the Union.

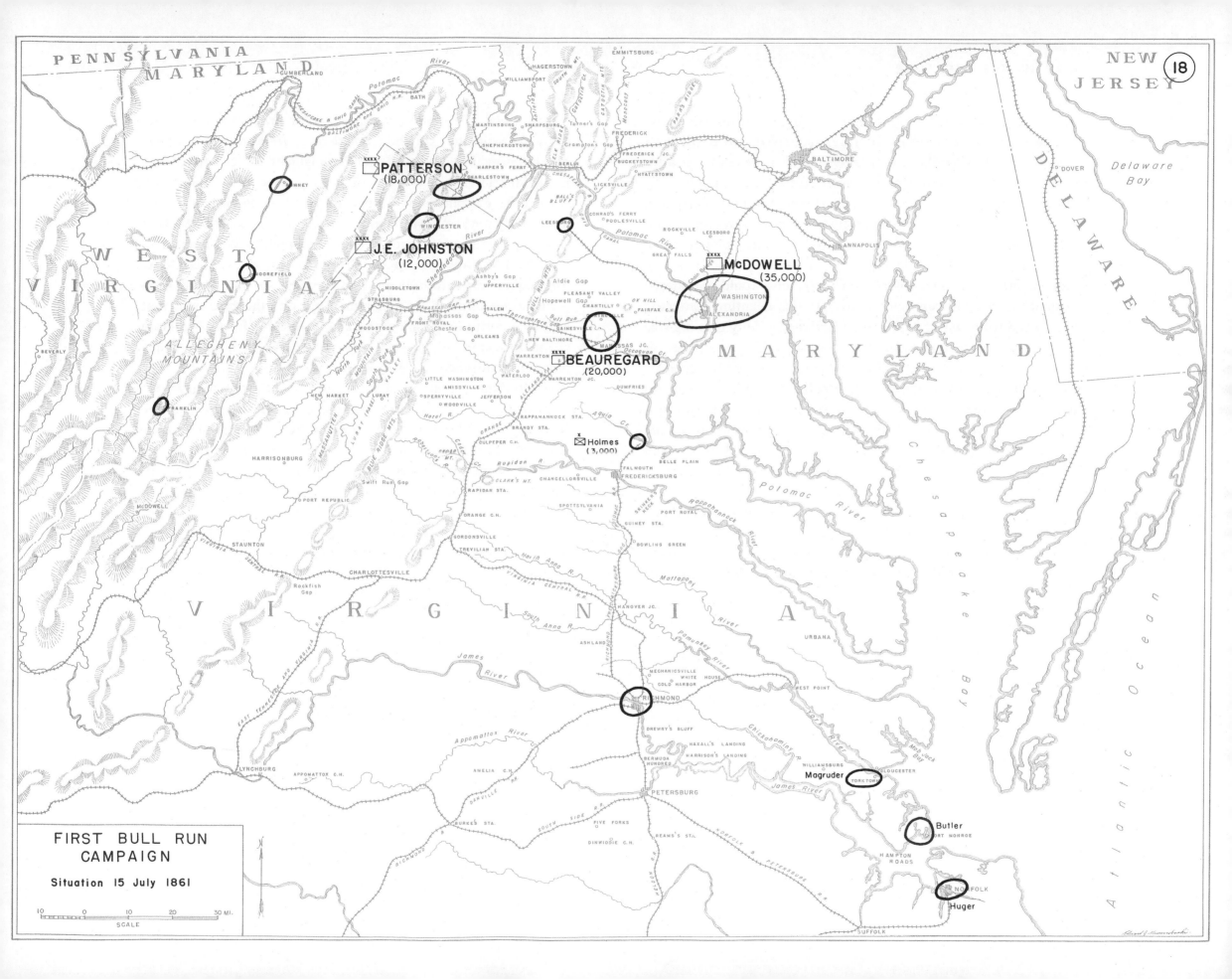

PENNSYLVANIA

MARYLAND

NEW JERSEY

WEST VIRGINIA

DELAWARE

Delaware Bay

XXXX
PATTERSON
(18,000)

XXXX
J.E. JOHNSTON
(12,000)

XXXX
McDOWELL
(35,000)

WASHINGTON

XXXX
BEAUREGARD
(20,000)

M A R Y L A N D

X
Holmes
(3,000)

FREDERICKSBURG

Potomac River

Chesapeake Bay

V I R G I N I A

RICHMOND

Magruder YORKTOWN

Butler FORT MONROE

HAMPTON ROADS

NORFOLK
Huger

Atlantic Ocean

FIRST BULL RUN
CAMPAIGN

Situation 15 July 1861

10   0   10   20   30 MI.
SCALE

McDowell's army left its encampment in the vicinity of Alexandria on the afternoon of 16 July. It arrived two and a half days later at Centreville, tired, hungry, and in need of rest after a march of twenty miles noted chiefly for lack of march discipline, overcaution, and confusion. (Only a month earlier, a small Union force had marched forty-six miles over mountain roads and inflicted defeat on the Confederates at Romney, West Virginia, all in slightly less than twenty-four hours. In a few more months hardened soldiers on both sides would consider it normal to march fifteen miles a day.) In the meantime Patterson exchanged wires with Scott, not understanding fully that his sole mission was to watch and detain Johnston. Having arrived at Bunker Hill on 15 July, he began to worry about his enemy's strength and his own supply line. Finally, taking counsel of his fears, but also believing that Scott sanctioned it, he withdrew to Charlestown on 17 July, where he sat in a perplexed state brought about partially by Scott's ambiguous telegrams and furthered by Confederate Col. James E. B. Stuart's fine cavalry work.

Nothing could have pleased Johnston more than this last movement, for shortly after midnight on 18 July, he received orders from President Davis to join Beauregard at Manassas. This message is the first of several we encounter throughout the war in which the discretionary phrase "if practicable" was employed. Fortunately for the Confederacy, Johnston was capable of exercising initiative and sound judgment in its application. Using Stuart's cavalry as a screen, he moved by foot to Piedmont, whence he entrained for Manassas. His leading brigade, commanded by Jackson, was headed for combat and immortality.

An efficient intelligence system had apprised Beauregard on 16 July of McDowell's departure from Alexandria. He had therefore requested reinforcements, and Holmes—as well as Johnston—had been directed to join him. This was the first time that lack of security in Washington made it possible for Confederate agents to obtain and transmit information of Union plans. Many more such instances were to follow.

Two things stand out in the actions of the Confederates just described: first, the wisdom of positioning the troops near the railroad, for without it Johnston could not have joined Beauregard in time to be of much assistance; and, second, Stuart so completely masked Johnston's movement with his regiment of cavalry that Patterson remained ignorant of it until 20 July— much too late for him to influence the action at Bull Run. In this, his first encounter, Stuart displayed the skill which was to make him famous in later campaigns.

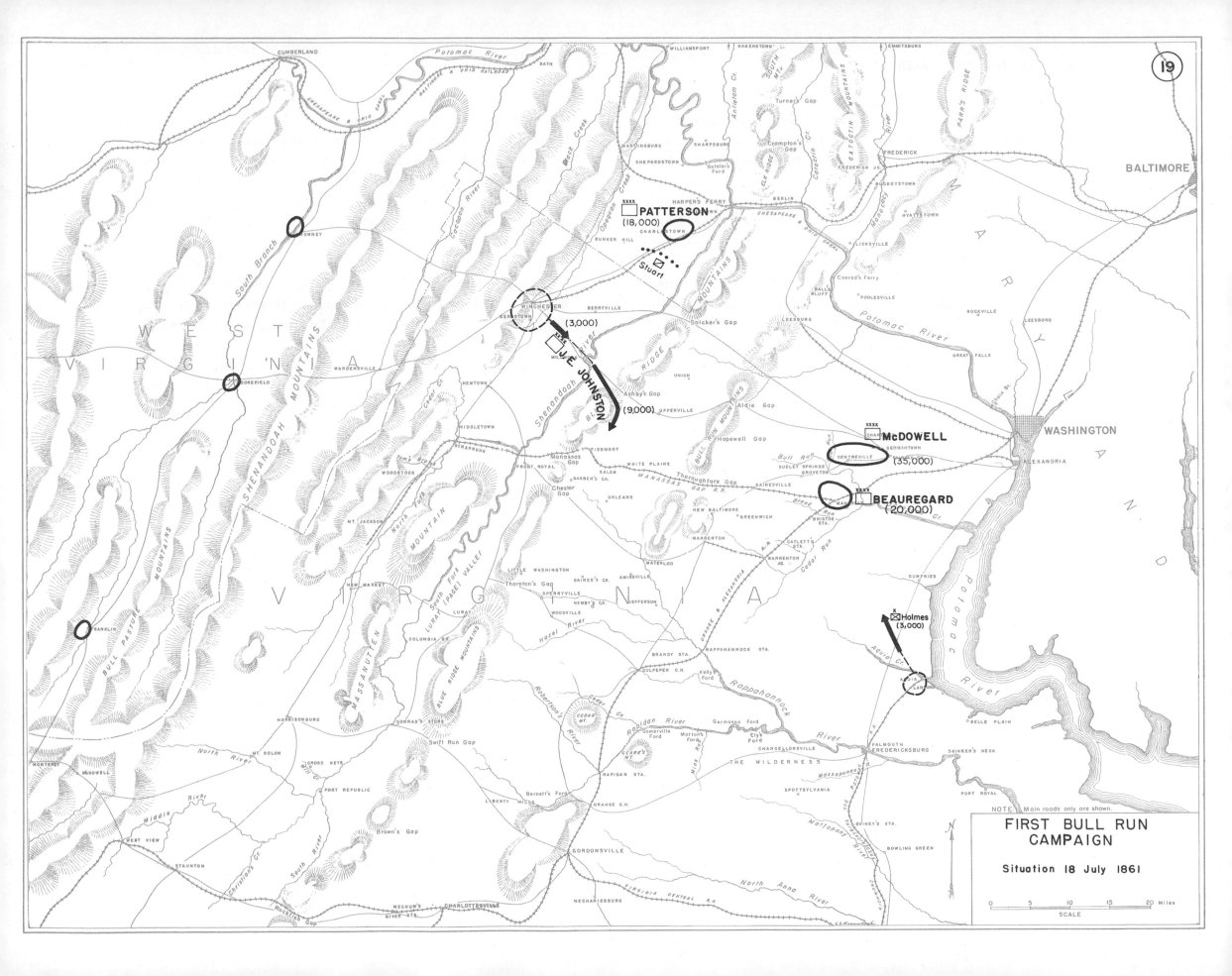

FIRST BULL RUN
CAMPAIGN

Situation 18 July 1861

NOTE: Main roads only are shown.

PATTERSON (18,000)

Stuart

J.E. JOHNSTON (3,000)

(9,000)

McDOWELL (35,000)

BEAUREGARD (20,000)

Holmes (3,000)

WEST VIRGINIA

VIRGINIA

MARYLAND

BALTIMORE

WASHINGTON

0   5   10   15   20 Miles
SCALE

A glance at Beauregard's dispositions along Bull Run shows his troops spread over a distance of ten miles in a cordon defense. He had no centrally located reserve until Johnston's troops arrived. Col. Jubal A. Early's brigade was a local reserve for the right flank, which Beauregard considered the part of his line most likely to be attacked by the enemy. He had also weighted this flank because he intended to launch an attack himself from Blackburn's and McLean's Fords.

McDowell originally had planned to turn his enemy's right flank, but Brig. Gen. Daniel Tyler's abortive attack at Mitchell's and Blackburn's Fords, plus the difficulty of the terrain as ascertained by personal reconnaissance, convinced him that the scheme was not feasible. Tyler's attack had been expressly forbidden by McDowell, who had specifically instructed Tyler to maintain only the impression that the Union army was moving on Manassas. Nevertheless, after sporadic artillery exchanges, Tyler had ordered Col. Israel B. Richardson to take his brigade down the ridge slope to the stream edge. This move was successful, but the Confederates, from good firing positions, had driven the Union troops back in disorder. The rebuff of Tyler's force lowered Union morale—particularly in Richardson's brigade—and served to encourage the Confederate troops on the eve of their first experience in a major engagement.

Bull Run could be forded at several points, but because of its steep banks and the heavily wooded approaches, cut up by many small tributaries, it was a formidable obstacle, particularly to the east of Stone Bridge. The dominant heights were the Centreville ridge, Henry House Hill (*upper left*), Bald Hill, and the hill to the southeast of Manassas Junction (*lower right*). Beauregard's extreme right was protected by Occoquan Creek, which ran east to the Potomac River.

Just prior to his departure from Washington, McDowell organized his army into five divisions. Thus, his span of control was less complicated than that of Beauregard, who was attempting to command seven separate brigades. But such a comparison is mainly academic, for Beauregard's brigade commanders were specially selected and well qualified, and the Union divisional organization had not yet had time to prove itself.

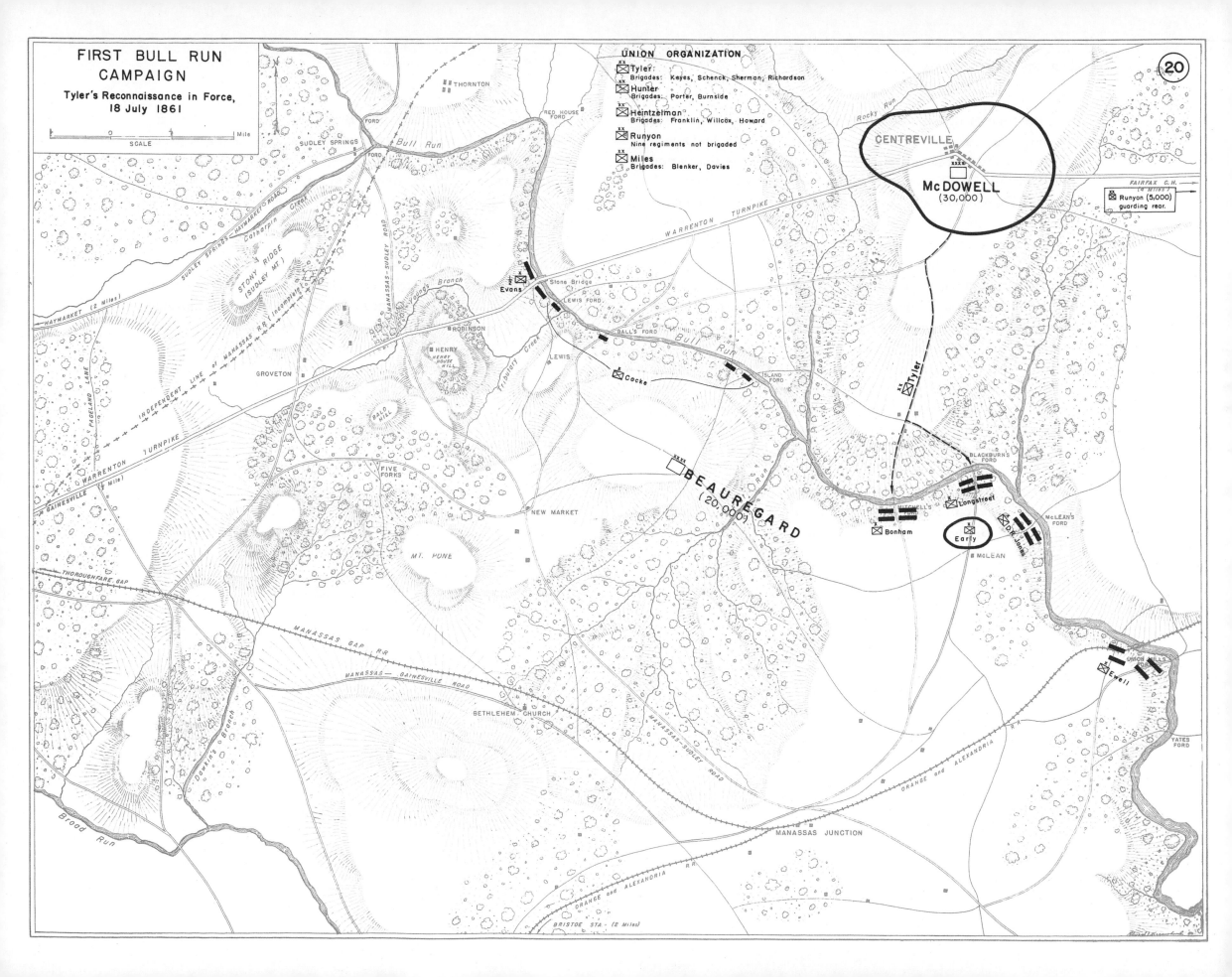

FIRST BULL RUN
CAMPAIGN

Tyler's Reconnaissance in Force,
18 July 1861

SCALE

UNION ORGANIZATION

Tyler:
  Brigades: Keyes, Schenck, Sherman, Richardson
Hunter
  Brigades: Porter, Burnside
Heintzelman
  Brigades: Franklin, Willcox, Howard
Runyon
  Nine regiments not brigaded
Miles
  Brigades: Blenker, Davies

CENTREVILLE

McDOWELL
(30,000)

FAIRFAX C.H.

Runyon (5,000)
guarding rear.

Evans

Stone Bridge

Cocke

BEAUREGARD
(20,000)

Tyler

BLACKBURN'S FORD

Longstreet

MITCHELL'S FORD

McLEAN'S FORD

Bonham

Early

D.R. Jones

McLEAN

Ewell

UNION MILLS

MANASSAS JUNCTION

BRISTOE STA. (2 Miles)

Since the time of the situation shown on the previous map, three days have passed—days which were critical to both McDowell and Beauregard, but in entirely different ways. During this period approximately 12,000 reinforcements had reached Beauregard, while McDowell—making timid reconnaissances and cooking extra rations—had frittered away his opportunity to attack while he still outnumbered the Confederates. It is true that McDowell needed at least one day to finish concentrating his army, but a vigorous reconnaissance all along the front would have given him the information he needed by 20 July. Furthermore, such activity would have confused the Confederates as to his intentions. But McDowell was a green commander of an even greener army.

McDowell's new plan, arrived at after Tyler's fiasco at Mitchell's Ford (*see map 20*), showed considerable skill. However, it was a rather complicated one for inexperienced commanders and, since McDowell was planning to attack a defensive position held by a force which he believed to be equal to his own, its success was completely dependent upon Patterson's ability to prevent Johnston from reinforcing Beauregard. Col. David Hunter and Col. Samuel B. Heintzelman were to turn the Confederate left by crossing at Sudley Springs and then move to sever the railroad to the Valley. This was to be the main effort. Tyler (less Richardson) was to make the secondary effort—an attack on Stone Bridge at daybreak. Richardson was to demonstrate at Blackburn's Ford in order to hold Brig. Gen. Milledge L. Bonham and Brig. Gen. James Longstreet in position. Col. Dixon S. Miles was the reserve.

It was in the execution that McDowell's plan went awry. Lack of experience and an inadequate staff upset things before he could even get started. As the Union army moved out early on 21 July, Tyler blocked the movement of the main column for several hours at Centreville; this delay, coupled with the slow movement over inadequately reconnoitered roads, made the main attack much later than planned. Tyler's attack at Stone Bridge jumped off at daybreak, but with so little energy that Col. Nathan G. Evans soon divined it to be just what it was—a secondary effort that offered no real threat.

In the interim, Beauregard had been joined by the bulk of Johnston's troops, and was busily planning an offensive movement toward Centreville by way of Blackburn's and McLean's Fords. Johnston, the senior of the two, approved the plan and delegated battlefield direction to the hero of Fort Sumter. But Beauregard's dreams of a great victory were rudely interrupted when one of the first rounds of the war hit the kitchen in McLean's house where his breakfast was being prepared—a rude announcement of the fact that McDowell had seized the initiative from him. (This same McLean also owned the house in Appomattox where Grant and Lee were to meet four years later.)

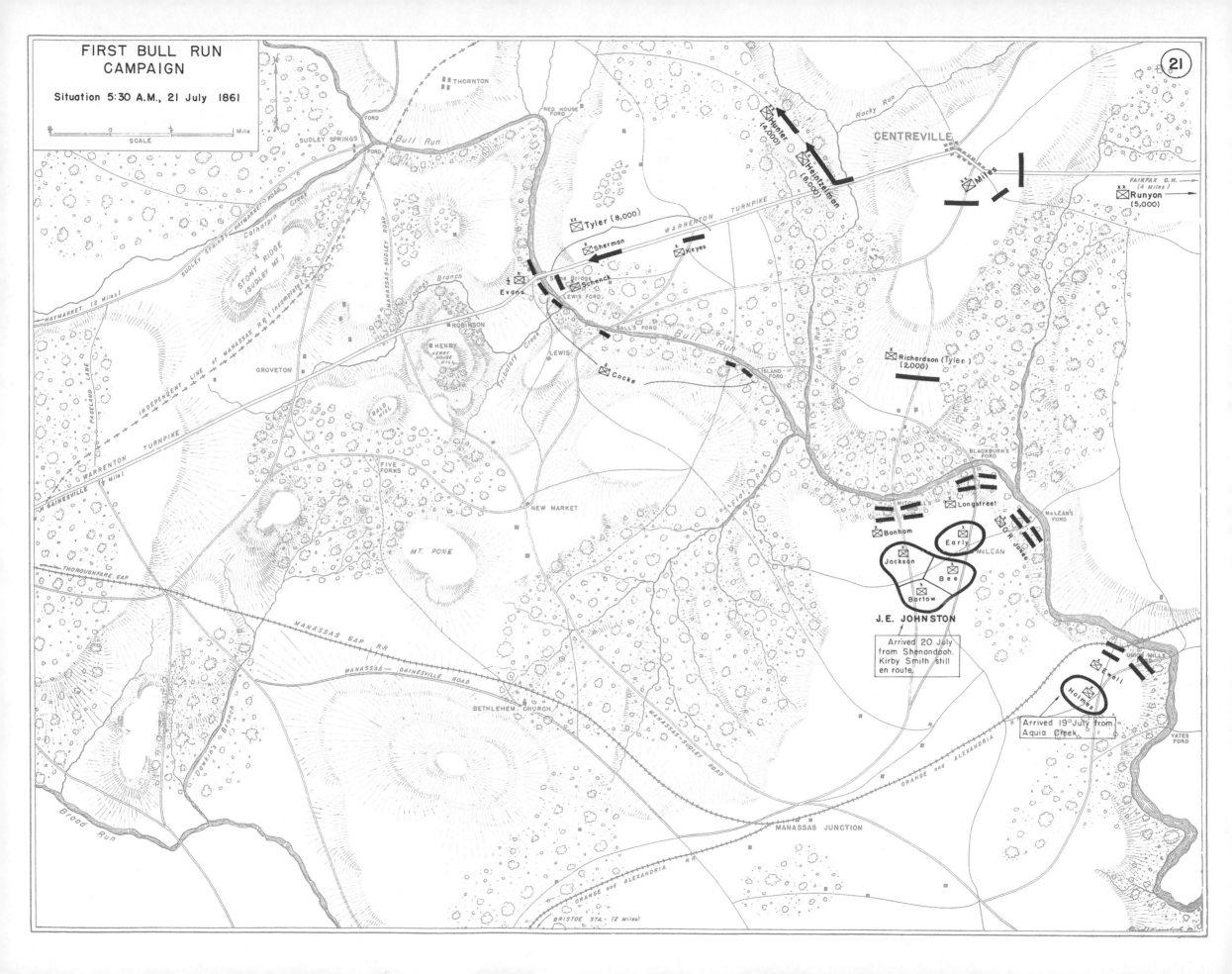

Learning that Federal forces were approaching the Stone Bridge and Mitchell's Ford, Beauregard, at 5:30 A.M., began issuing orders for an attack toward Centreville by his right-flank brigades. Between his own frequent counterorders and his amateur staff, the situation rapidly got out of hand. Brig. Gen. Richard S. Ewell (*lower right*), who was to lead this attack, was merely ordered to prepare to advance. Holmes, who was to support him, received no orders. Brig. Gen. David R. Jones received orders to attack to his front in order to extend Ewell's attack; he obeyed and found himself isolated. Meanwhile, Beauregard had begun shifting the troops of Brig. Gen. Barnard E. Bee, Col. Francis S. Bartow, and Brig. Gen. Thomas J. Jackson (whose forces included Capt. John D. Imboden's battery) toward the Confederate center. Then, at 10:30 A.M., while he was still attempting to get his attack underway, he became aware of violent fighting on his extreme left.

McDowell's main effort had reached and crossed Bull Run at Sudley Springs about 9:30 A.M., Hunter's division leading. As Hunter emerged from the woods a mile south of the creek, he found his route barred by Evans. The latter, warned of McDowell's turning movement by the Confederate observation post south of Manassas Junction and scorning the timorous advance of Brig. Gen. Robert C. Schenck's brigade of Tyler's division against Stone Bridge, had shown exemplary initiative in shifting most of his forces from Stone Bridge to a position commanding the Manassas–Sudley Springs road. Informed of this situation, Beau-

regard canceled his plans for an attack, ordered some of his right-flank units to demonstrate against the Federal left, and dispatched the rest of his forces toward Henry House Hill. Both he and Johnston followed.

Back in the vicinity of Young's Branch, Evans had been fighting valiantly and had even managed to force Hunter's division back somewhat. Eventually the Union leaders displayed some knowledge of tactics and began to outflank the Confederate line, now manned by Bartow, Bee, and the remnants of Evans' unit. To aid in carrying this position, McDowell had ordered Tyler to force his way across Bull Run. Col. William T. Sherman's brigade of Tyler's division can be seen doing just that at a hitherto undiscovered ford slightly upstream from Stone Bridge. Sherman immediately brought his brigade into action, threatening the Confederate flank. Shortly after 11:30 A.M., the Confederate forces were compelled to withdraw to Henry House Hill, as much from frontal pressure as from Sherman's attack. The movement was a hazardous one and toward the end degenerated into a rout, even though Imboden heroically attempted to cover the withdrawal from his position on the hill. (Note that, as this first action was being contested, Brig. Gen. E. Kirby Smith's brigade was arriving at Manassas Junction. This was another one of Johnston's units from the Valley, and one which was to play a decisive part in the day's fighting. Note also Jackson approaching Henry House Hill.)

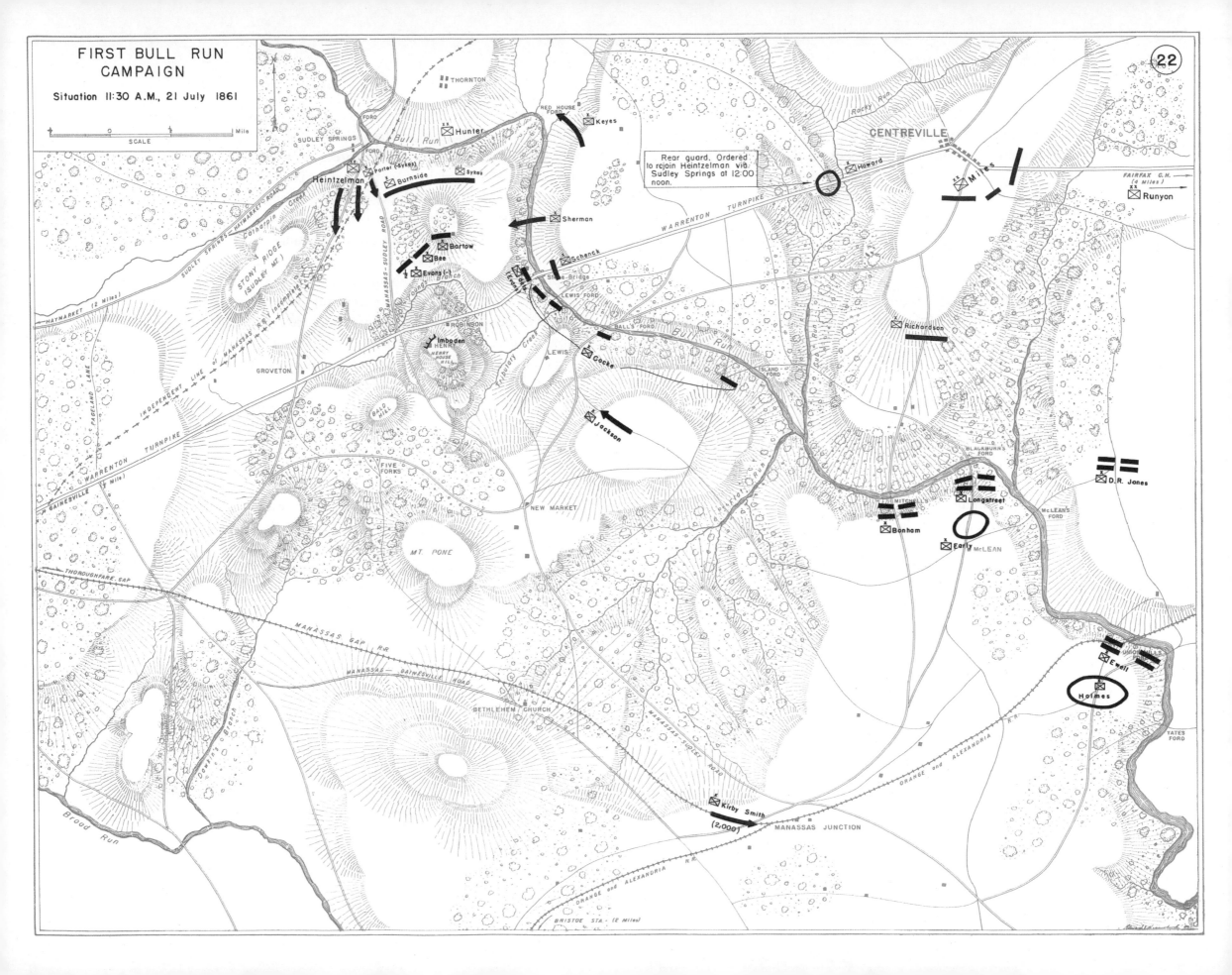

Beauregard and Johnston arrived at Henry House Hill just as the survivors of the earlier fight to the north were rallying there. They attempted to hearten the troops on the hill, with some success; but it was primarily the reassuring sight of Jackson's brigade, "standing like a stone wall," that gave renewed courage to the fleeing forces. Beauregard stayed at the scene of battle and, by personal example, continued to rally his troops. Meanwhile, Johnston, having arranged the command details with Beauregard, moved to the rear to coordinate and direct the movements of the Confederate units coming from Manassas Junction and the extreme right flank. McDowell, on the other hand, became ever more engrossed in personally leading brigades and regiments. His bravery and battlefield leadership were commendable, but they were displayed at the expense of his failure to exercise the duties of an army commander. Likewise, Hunter, Heintzelman, Burnside, and Franklin became involved in leading regiments, and their own commands suffered from lack of direction.

McDowell was determined to continue the assault and make his victory complete. Thus, at about 2:00 P.M., when the infantry he had in the immediate area of Henry House Hill still outnumbered the Confederates there by approximately two to one, he launched his attack up the slopes of the hill. The battle raged back and forth without either side gaining a substantial advantage.

Then the batteries of Capt. James Ricketts and Capt. Charles Griffin were emplaced on the hill and began to swing the tide of battle in favor of the Union forces. But these batteries were not destined to remain in action long. The 33d Virginia Regiment, still uniformed in blue, got close enough to the two batteries—which had held their fire because of the color of the uniforms—to suddenly shoot down the gunners and to drive off the battalion of marines and the regiment of zouaves which were supporting the guns. At about this same time, a small force of cavalry under Stuart made a successful charge against the flank of the zouaves. A renewed Union assault retook the position, but now Beauregard's reinforcements were beginning to arrive, while the exhausted Union troops had been reinforced only by Howard's brigade. McDowell had received little assistance from Tyler or Burnside and had not ordered Miles' reserve division forward.

As the critical point in the battle neared, Beauregard owed much to Jackson, who had skillfully selected and vigorously defended the original position on Henry House Hill.

(The mistake of Ricketts and Griffin in regard to the identity of the 33d Virginia was only one of several such during this battle. In addition to Confederate units in blue, there were a number of Federal regiments in gray, while several regiments on both sides wore similar gaudy zouave uniforms.)

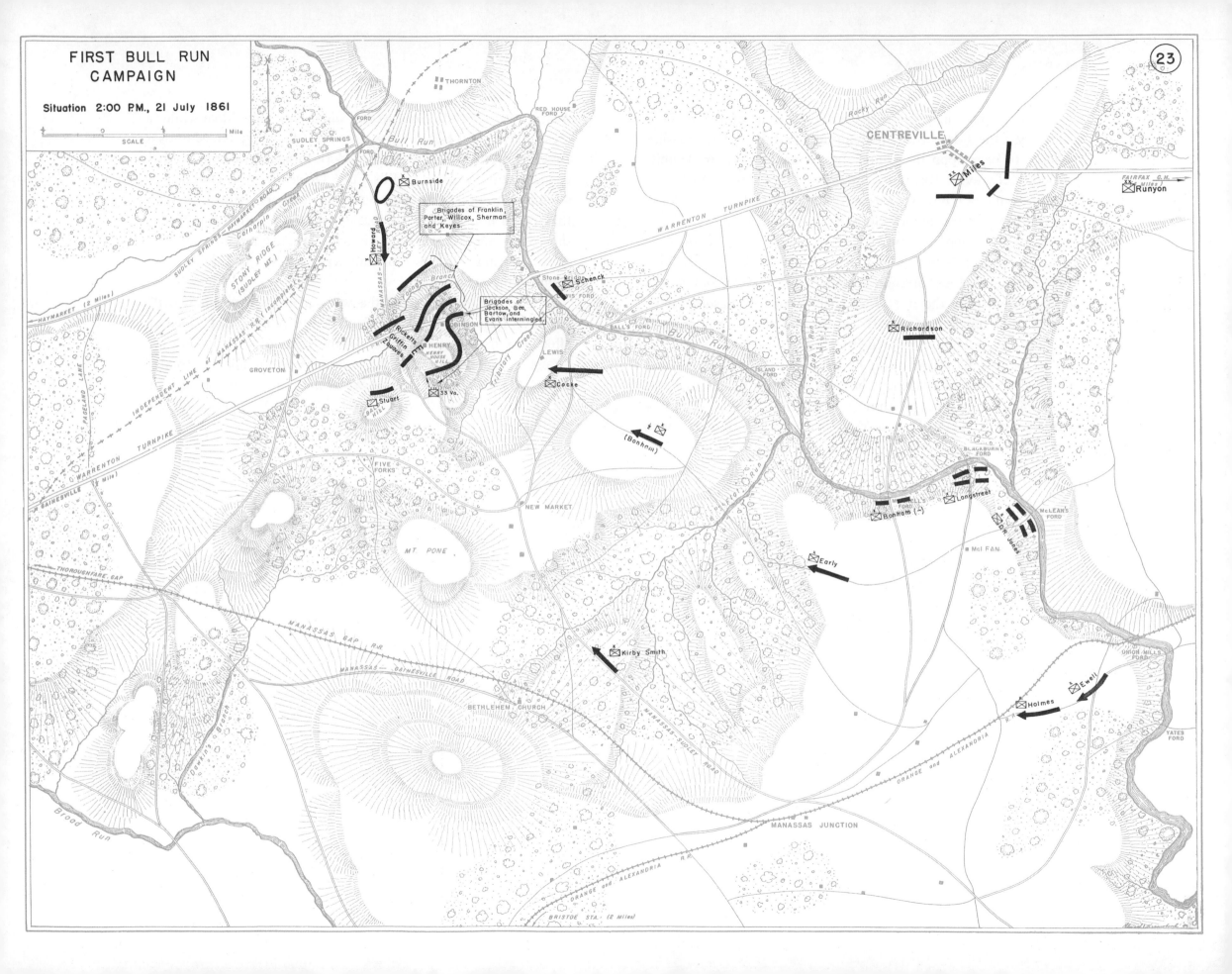

FIRST BULL RUN CAMPAIGN

Situation 2:00 P.M., 21 July 1861

SCALE
Mile

23

Brigades of Franklin, Porter, Willcox, Sherman and Keyes.

Brigades of Jackson, Bee, Bartow, and Evans intermingled.

THORNTON

RED HOUSE FORD

CENTREVILLE

FAIRFAX C.H.

Runyon

Miles

Burnside

Howard

SUDLEY SPRINGS

Bull Run

FORD

SUDLEY SPRINGS-HAYMARKET ROAD

Catharpin

Creek

STONY RIDGE (SUDLEY MT.)

WARRENTON TURNPIKE

Stone Bridge

Schenck

LEWIS FORD

BALL'S FORD

Richardson

Dogan's Branch

ROBINSON

HENRY HOUSE HILL

Ricketts Griffin Zouaves

HENRY

HAYMARKET (2 Miles)

MANASSAS R.R. (Incomplete)

INDEPENDENT LINE OF MANASSAS R.R. (Incomplete)

GROVETON

LEWIS

Tributary Creek

ISLAND FORD

Cocke

Bull Run

33 Va.

Stuart

WARRENTON TURNPIKE

GAINESVILLE (1 Mile)

FIVE FORKS

(Bonham)

BLACKBURN'S FORD

PAGELAND LANE

NEW MARKET

Flat Run

Longstreet

McLEAN'S FORD

Bonham (-)

MT. PONE

Early

D.R. Jones

McI FAN.

THOROUGHFARE GAP

MANASSAS GAP R.R.

Kirby Smith

UNION MILLS FORD

MANASSAS-GAINESVILLE ROAD

BETHLEHEM CHURCH

MANASSAS-SUDLEY ROAD

Holmes

Ewell

YATES FORD

Broad Run

Dawkins Branch

ORANGE and ALEXANDRIA R.R.

MANASSAS JUNCTION

BRISTOE STA. (2 Miles)

When Early and Kirby Smith arrived at the scene of action about 4:00 P.M., the tide turned in Beauregard's favor. The pressure brought to bear upon the Union right flank by these fresh units caused McDowell's forces to withdraw. Once begun, the withdrawal could not be stopped short of Centreville. The Union forces withdrew via Sudley Springs and Stone Bridge in fairly good order, though there were signs of panic and rout in some units and little supervision from senior officers. Under McDowell's direction, Miles' division formed a rear guard, but it was impossible to rally the rest of the army short of Washington.

On the Confederate side, there was an almost equal amount of confusion. Johnston ordered Bonham's and Longstreet's fresh troops on the Confederate right to cross at Blackburn's and Mitchell's Fords and take up the pursuit. Once across, the two commanders lost precious time in squabbling. Then a burst of artillery fire from the Federal rear guard caused Bonham, who was in over-all command, to call off the pursuit. Meanwhile, a false alarm that Federal troops were advancing on Manassas Junction from Union Mills caused Beauregard to order a new concentration at Union Mills Ford (*lower right*). The cavalry attempted to pursue at once, but their numbers were so few that they could not be a serious threat. Jackson felt that the pursuit should be renewed that night, but the exhaustion and confusion existing throughout the command kept Johnston and Beauregard from taking such action.

Thus, the first battle of the war—a battle between two ill-prepared forces—ended in a Confederate victory. But, since an effective pursuit was not initiated, the fruits of victory were not attained. Union losses in killed, wounded, and captured totaled 2,896; Confederate, 1,982. Among the many commanders on the field, three had shown definite promise: Jackson, Sherman, and Evans.

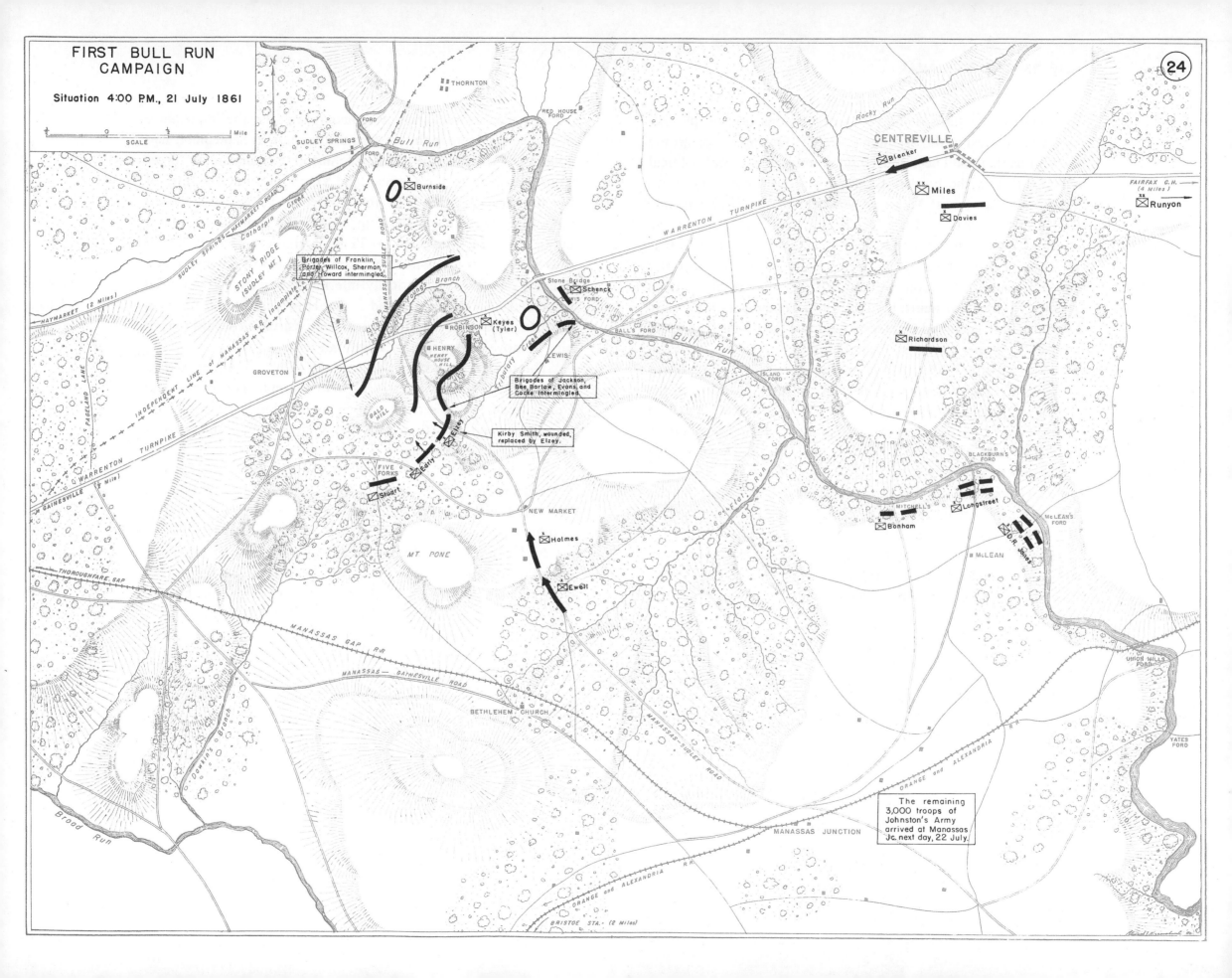

FIRST BULL RUN CAMPAIGN

Situation 4:00 P.M., 21 July 1861

SCALE

1 Mile

(24)

THORNTON

RED HOUSE FORD

Rocky Run

CENTREVILLE

Blenker

FAIRFAX C.H. (4 Miles)

Miles

Runyon

Davies

FORD

SUDLEY SPRINGS

Bull Run

SUDLEY SPRINGS FORD

WARRENTON TURNPIKE

Burnside

Brigades of Franklin, Porter Willcox, Sherman and Howard intermingled.

Young's Branch

Stone Bridge

LEWIS FORD

Schenck

BALL'S FORD

Bull Run

Richardson

ROBINSON

Keyes (Tyler)

HENRY

HENRY HOUSE HILL

LEWIS

ISLAND FORD

Gub Run

GROVETON

Brigades of Jackson, Bee Bartow, Evans, and Cocke intermingled.

Tributary Creek

BALD HILL

Elzey

Kirby Smith, wounded, replaced by Elzey.

BLACKBURN'S FORD

FIVE FORKS

Early

Stuart

NEW MARKET

Flat Run

MITCHELL'S

Longstreet

McLEAN'S FORD

Bonham

MT PONE

Holmes

McLEAN

D.R. Jones

Ewell

THOROUGHFARE GAP

MANASSAS GAP RR

MANASSAS — GAINESVILLE ROAD

BETHLEHEM CHURCH

MANASSAS—SUDLEY ROAD

UNION MILLS FORD

Dawkins Branch

Broad Run

ORANGE and ALEXANDRIA

YATES FORD

ORANGE and ALEXANDRIA RR

MANASSAS JUNCTION

The remaining 3,000 troops of Johnston's Army arrived at Manassas Jc. next day, 22 July.

BRISTOE STA. (2 Miles)

HAYMARKET (2 Miles)

STONY RIDGE (SUDLEY MT.)

Catharpin Creek

HAYMARKET ROAD

INDEPENDENT LINE OF MANASSAS RR (Incomplete)

WARRENTON TURNPIKE

GAINESVILLE (1 Mile)

PAGELAND LANE

This map shows the strengths and dispositions of the opposing forces in the west at the beginning of 1862. During the preceding six months there had been much minor activity and local political maneuvering in the border states as they faced the momentous question of secession. Missouri was held in the Union mainly through the efforts of Capt. Nathaniel Lyon, a regular army officer, and the influence of his victory at Boonville in June, 1861. In Kentucky, disagreement between a pro-Confederate governor and a legislature bent on preserving Union ties resulted in an attempt to maintain neutrality. But on 3 September, Maj. Gen. Leonidas Polk occupied Columbus, and two days later Brig. Gen. Ulysses S. Grant, displaying laudable initiative, seized Paducah. Thereafter, neither adversary respected the proclaimed status of the state. Kentucky's neutrality did have an indirect effect on the Henry and Donelson campaign in that the Confederates had had to build the two forts below the Kentucky-Tennessee border, whereas better and more defensible sites for the forts existed farther north in Kentucky.

The Union military command in the sprawling western theater was exercised through a series of departments. On 9 November, 1861, these were organized as—from west to east—the Department of Kansas, under Maj. Gen. David Hunter; the Department of Missouri, under Maj. Gen. Henry W. Halleck; and the Department of the Ohio, under Brig. Gen. Don Carlos Buell. Buell had replaced Brig. Gen. William T. Sherman, who had lost the confidence of the Administration. Now operations along the Mississippi and the lower reaches of the Tennessee and Cumberland would be solely under the command of Halleck. But if the Union geographical division had been improved, its command structure had not. Buell and Halleck were coequals, and each received his orders directly from McClellan in Washington.

The Confederacy, however, had recognized the importance of unified direction in the western theater and, in September, had appointed General Albert Sidney Johnston to command all forces from Arkansas to the Cumberland Gap. Johnston was one of the top-ranking generals in the Confederacy, and was looked upon by Davis as its outstanding soldier. His immediate subordinates, Polk and Maj. Gen. William J. Hardee, were then considered first-rate assistants. Johnston's problem of defense was a difficult one. With numerically inferior forces, he was required to defend an extremely broad front. However, he did have an excellent system of lateral communications, which would permit him to move troops rapidly where needed.

The terrain features in the area played an important part in the formulation of strategy. The Mississippi, Tennessee, and Cumberland Rivers served as avenues of approach for military operations and, together with the Ohio, supplemented other means of logistical support. The Appalachian chain of mountains, culminating in the Cumberlands, separated the eastern and western theaters. No east-west railroads traversed the mountains between Louisville and Chattanooga, a distance of more than two hundred miles.

In January, 1862, four different Union plans for offensive operations in the western theater were proposed—by Buell, Halleck, Lincoln, and McClellan—but none could be agreed upon. Buell, under pressure to invade eastern Tennessee, made half-hearted gestures, one of which resulted in a victory at Mill Springs by Brig. Gen. George H. Thomas. Halleck had Grant demonstrate up the Tennessee to divert attention from Buell's cherished plan to advance on Nashville, but Buell did not move. Finally on 1 February, Halleck, without arranging for Buell's cooperation, authorized Grant to proceed up the Tennessee against Fort Henry.

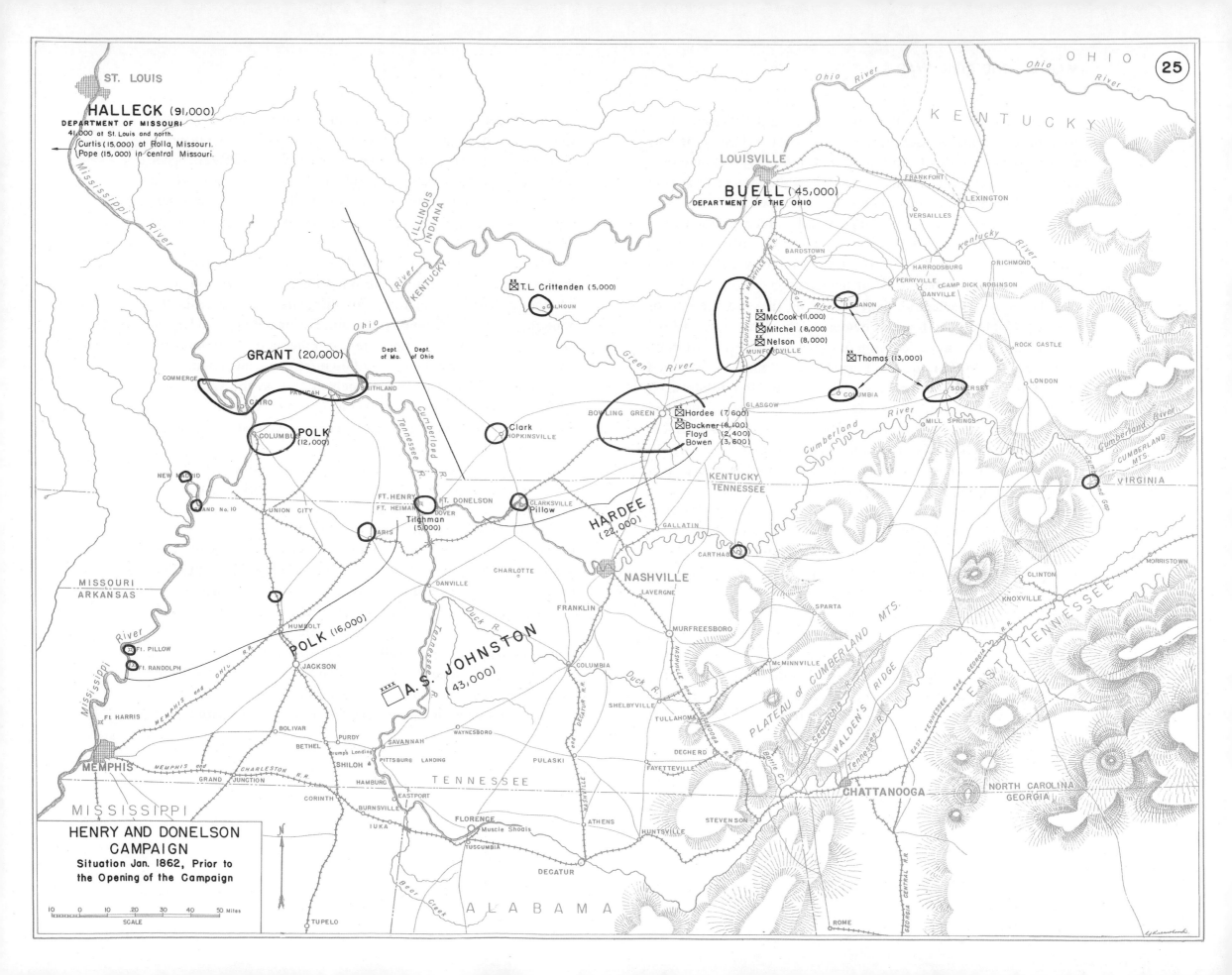

25

ST. LOUIS

HALLECK (91,000)
DEPARTMENT OF MISSOURI
41,000 at St. Louis and north.
Curtis (15,000) at Rolla, Missouri.
Pope (15,000) in central Missouri.

OHIO

KENTUCKY

LOUISVILLE

BUELL (45,000)
DEPARTMENT OF THE OHIO

FRANKFORT

LEXINGTON

VERSAILLES

BARDSTOWN

HARRODSBURG   RICHMOND

PERRYVILLE   CAMP DICK ROBINSON

⊠⊠ T.L. Crittenden (5,000)

DANVILLE

CALHOUN

LEBANON

⊠⊠ McCook (11,000)
⊠ Mitchel (8,000)
⊠⊠ Nelson (8,000)

ROCK CASTLE

GRANT (20,000)

MUNFORDVILLE

⊠ Thomas (13,000)

LONDON

Dept.   Dept.
of Mo.   of Ohio

COMMERCE

CAIRO   PADUCAH   SMITHLAND

Green   River

GLASGOW

Clark
HOPKINSVILLE

BOWLING GREEN   ⊠ Hardee (7,600)
⊠ Buckner (8,100)
Floyd (2,400)
Bowen (3,600)

SOMERSET

COLUMBIA

MILL SPRINGS

POLK
(12,000)   COLUMBUS

KENTUCKY
TENNESSEE

Cumberland   River

CUMBERLAND
MTS.

NEW MADRID

ISLAND No. 10

UNION CITY

FT. HENRY
FT. HEIMAN   FT. DONELSON
DOVER   CLARKSVILLE
Pillow
Tilghman
(5,000)

HARDEE
(22,000)

GALLATIN

CARTHAGE

VIRGINIA

Cumberland Gap

MISSOURI
ARKANSAS

PARIS

CHARLOTTE
DANVILLE

NASHVILLE

LAVERGNE

SPARTA

CLINTON

KNOXVILLE

MORRISTOWN

HUMBOLT

POLK (16,000)

FRANKLIN

MURFREESBORO

McMINNVILLE

EAST   TENNESSEE

⊠ FT. PILLOW
⊠ FT. RANDOLPH

JACKSON

A.S. JOHNSTON
(43,000)

COLUMBIA

SHELBYVILLE

TULLAHOMA

DECHERD

Plateau of Cumberland MTS.

FT. HARRIS

BOLIVAR

PURDY

BETHEL

SAVANNAH

PULASKI

FAYETTEVILLE

NORTH CAROLINA
GEORGIA

MEMPHIS

Crumps Landing   SHILOH   PITTSBURG LANDING

WAYNESBORO

CHATTANOOGA

STEVENSON

GRAND JUNCTION
HAMBURG   HAMBURG

TENNESSEE

CORINTH

BURNSVILLE

EASTPORT

FLORENCE
Muscle Shoals

ATHENS

HUNTSVILLE

MISSISSIPPI

IUKA

TUSCUMBIA

DECATUR

ROME

**HENRY AND DONELSON
CAMPAIGN**
Situation Jan. 1862, Prior to
the Opening of the Campaign

N

A L A B A M A

TUPELO

10 0 10 20 30 40 50 Miles
SCALE

Grant began the move up the Tennessee on 2-3 February, shuttling his divisions for lack of transports. By 6 February, he was in position four miles from Fort Henry and ready to launch his attack. When he had originally conceived the idea of attacking the fort, he had expected Commodore Andrew H. Foote's fleet alone to be able to reduce it, for an earlier reconnaissance by Brig. Gen. Charles F. Smith had revealed its vulnerability to gunboat fire. The movement of Grant's infantry columns was designed to cut off the retreat of the garrison.

The error in selecting Fort Henry as the site for one of the key Confederate forts is evidenced by Brig. Gen. Lloyd Tilghman's action upon learning of Grant's arrival downstream. Doubting his ability to defend Fort Henry, Tilghman abandoned Fort Heiman on 4 February and, early on the 6th, withdrew all of the Fort Henry garrison except seventy men. He dispatched the combined force of almost 2,500 men to Fort Donelson, without their having fired a shot in defense of Fort Henry. In justice to the Confederate commander, it should be noted that, although the fort was on a bend in the river and had seventeen guns, it was so low that the defenses were easy targets for gunboats. (Fort Heiman had been built across the river primarily to deny the high ground there which dominated Fort Henry.) Forts Henry and Donelson were about eleven miles apart. Two dirt roads connected them through rugged country of hills, marshes, streams, and thick woods, lately made more difficult by heavy rains.

Grant's infantry and gunboats moved out at 11:00 A.M. on 6 February. Two hours later, the gunboats had forced Fort Henry to surrender (Tilghman had remained behind with the seventy men); but, slowed by the rain-soaked terrain, Brig. Gen. John A. McClernand had not been in time to block the Confederate garrison's retreat, while Smith belatedly discovered that Fort Heiman had been abandoned. Grant now seized the opportunity to increase Johnston's difficulties and to drive his strategic penetration deeper by dispatching gunboats upstream to destroy the Memphis & Ohio Railway bridge over the Tennessee, thus severing Johnston's major means of communication between the wings of his army.

Grant's seizure of Fort Henry (and with it the initiative in the west) posed a real problem for Johnston. He had to decide whether to withdraw his forces all along the line or to resist the penetration by counterattacking Grant. Fortunately for the Union, he attempted to do both, with the result that neither attempt was very successful. Thus he sent 12,000 reinforcements under Brig. Gen. John B. Floyd to Fort Donelson and, at the same time, withdrew his right wing from Bowling Green to Nashville. In none of his actions was there a suggestion of any intent to move offensively against Grant's exposed force.

In the meantime, Grant was impatient to advance toward Fort Donelson, but the weather was so bad that his troops could not be supplied. Also, he had to wait for naval support to move into position on the Cumberland. Finally, on 12 February, he began the movement. By then a third division, Brig. Gen. Lew Wallace's, had joined him. On the evening of the 12th, his troops were in position on a commanding ridge around the entrenchments occupied by Floyd's troops. On that date Foote, at Grant's urging, attempted to repeat the aggressive tactics he had employed so successfully at Fort Henry. But here it was a different story. Since the Fort Donelson batteries were better located and more skillfully employed, they succeeded in inflicting heavy damage on Foote's fleet and forced it to withdraw.

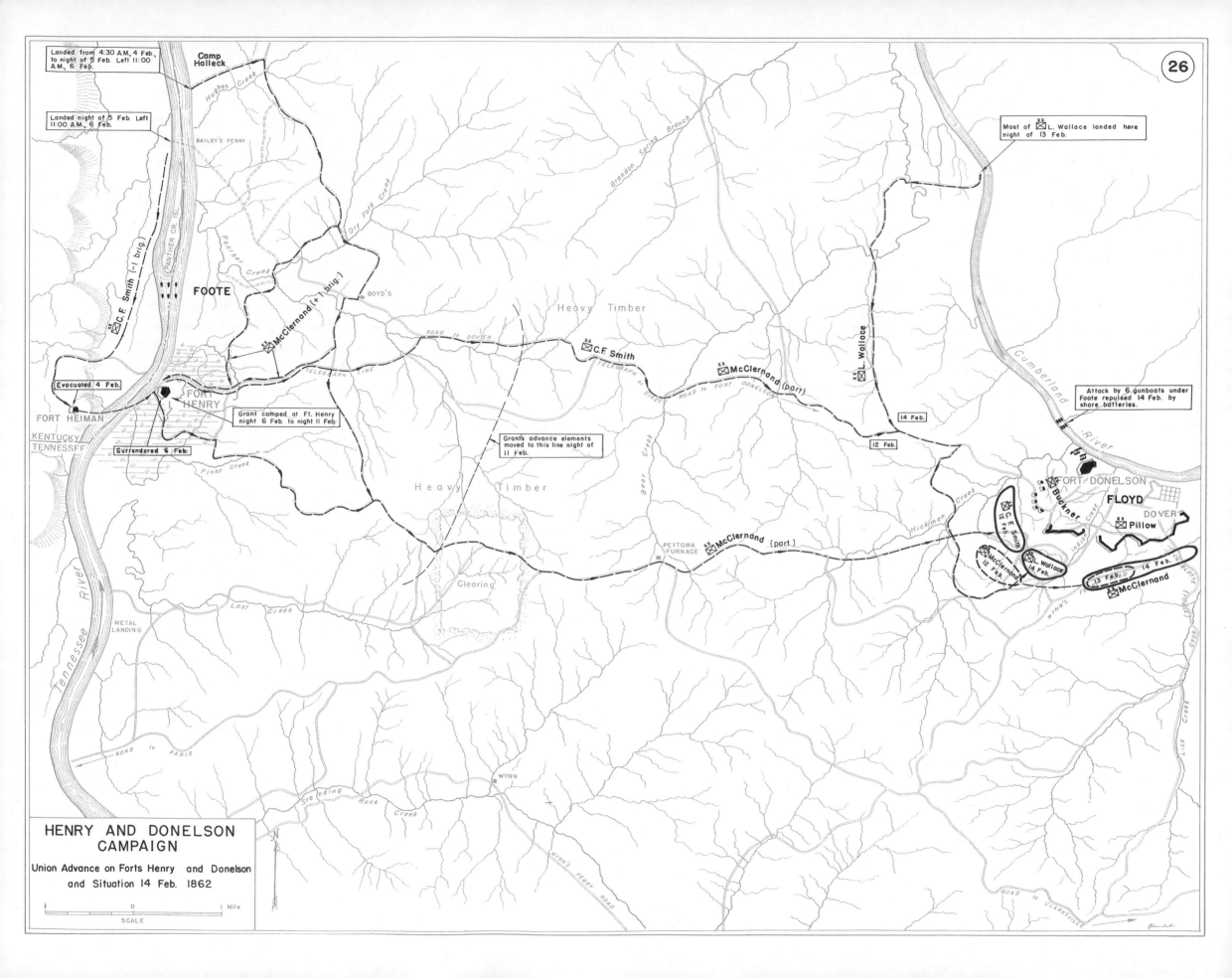

26

Landed from 4:30 A.M, 4 Feb, to night of 5 Feb. Left 11:00 A.M. 6 Feb.

Camp Halleck

Landed night of 5 Feb. Left 11:00 A.M. 6 Feb.

BAILEY'S FERRY

Most of L. Wallace landed here night of 13 Feb.

Hughes Creek

Brandon Spring Branch

FOOTE

Panther Creek

BOYD'S

Heavy Timber

ROAD to DOVER

C.F. Smith

L. Wallace

McClernand (+1 brig.)

C.F. Smith (-1 brig.)

TELEGRAPH LINE

TELEGRAPH or DIRECT ROAD to FORT DONELSON

McClernand (part)

L. Wallace

Attack by 6 gunboats under Foote repulsed 14 Feb. by shore batteries.

14 Feb.

12 Feb.

Cumberland River

Evacuated 4 Feb.

FORT HENRY

Grant camped at Ft. Henry night 6 Feb. to night 11 Feb.

FORT HEIMAN

KENTUCKY
TENNESSEE

Surrendered 6 Feb.

Piney Creek

Grant's advance elements moved to this line night of 11 Feb.

Heavy Timber

Bear Creek

Hickman Creek

FORT DONELSON

Buckner

FLOYD

DOVER

Pillow

C.F. Smith 12 Feb.

L. Wallace 14 Feb.

McClernand 12 Feb.

13 Feb.

14 Feb.

McClernand

PEYTOMA FURNACE

McClernand (part)

Clearing

Tennessee River

METAL LANDING

Lost Creek

WYNN'S FERRY ROAD

Lick Creek

ROAD to PARIS

WYNN

Standing Rock Creek

ROAD to CLARKSVILLE

HENRY AND DONELSON CAMPAIGN

Union Advance on Forts Henry and Donelson and Situation 14 Feb. 1862

0   1 Mile

SCALE

Fort Donelson was far stronger than its companion fort on the Tennessee. Its longest side measured about 500 yards, but, more important, it was on a commanding height. There were two main batteries on the river side, one just above the river level and the other 100 feet higher. It was the lower battery which inflicted most of the damage on Foote's fleet, primarily because he moved in to close range, thus failing to take advantage of the superior range and accuracy of his weapons.

The broken and irregular red line on the map represents the entrenchments erected by Pillow after the fall of Fort Henry. The line followed a commanding ridge and was backed up by artillery; but it should be noted that it was obviously sited to protect the main fort, not to serve as a base of maneuver or to protect an escape route. In this line of entrenchments, Floyd placed the bulk of his troops, probably contrary to what Johnston had in mind when he dispatched the reinforcements. Brig. Gen. Simon B. Buckner commanded the right of the line and Brig. Gen. Gideon J. Pillow the left.

The significant aspect of Grant's move from Fort Henry was the rapidity of march, due mainly to the fact that the indolent Pillow had made very little effort to oppose the advance. He was quite content to sit behind his breastworks, possibly reminiscing about his Mexican War experiences with a similar type of shelter. Had there been any kind of vigorous opposition, the vulnerability of Grant's columns as they traversed the broken country might have been noted, with the ultimate result that Pillow (or Floyd, who arrived on 13 February) might have launched a successful attack before the 14th, when Grant began to receive reinforcements.

Very little ground action occurred on 14 February. On the 13th, both Smith and McClernand had tested the Confederate defenses, and the latter had begun edging toward the river. On the following day, having been reinforced with Col. John McArthur's brigade, McClernand continued to extend his right in order to seal in Floyd's command completely. That night he reported that his right flank was within 400 yards of an impassable stream. Grant apparently paid little heed to this open flank, for, by this time, disappointed over the naval failure, he was resigned to a siege operation and was concerned about the welfare of his men. They were hungry, many were without adequate clothing, and all were enduring wintry blasts which had sent the thermometer to 12° F. that morning.

But in the Confederate camp it was equally cold the night of 14 February. Morale was low, and there was no leader of Grant's stature to take hold. Instead, Floyd resorted to a council of war which decided to abandon Fort Donelson and attempt a retirement to Nashville. An overestimation of Grant's strength and an underestimation of the damage inflicted on Foote's fleet thus set the stage for the attack which was to take place early the next morning.

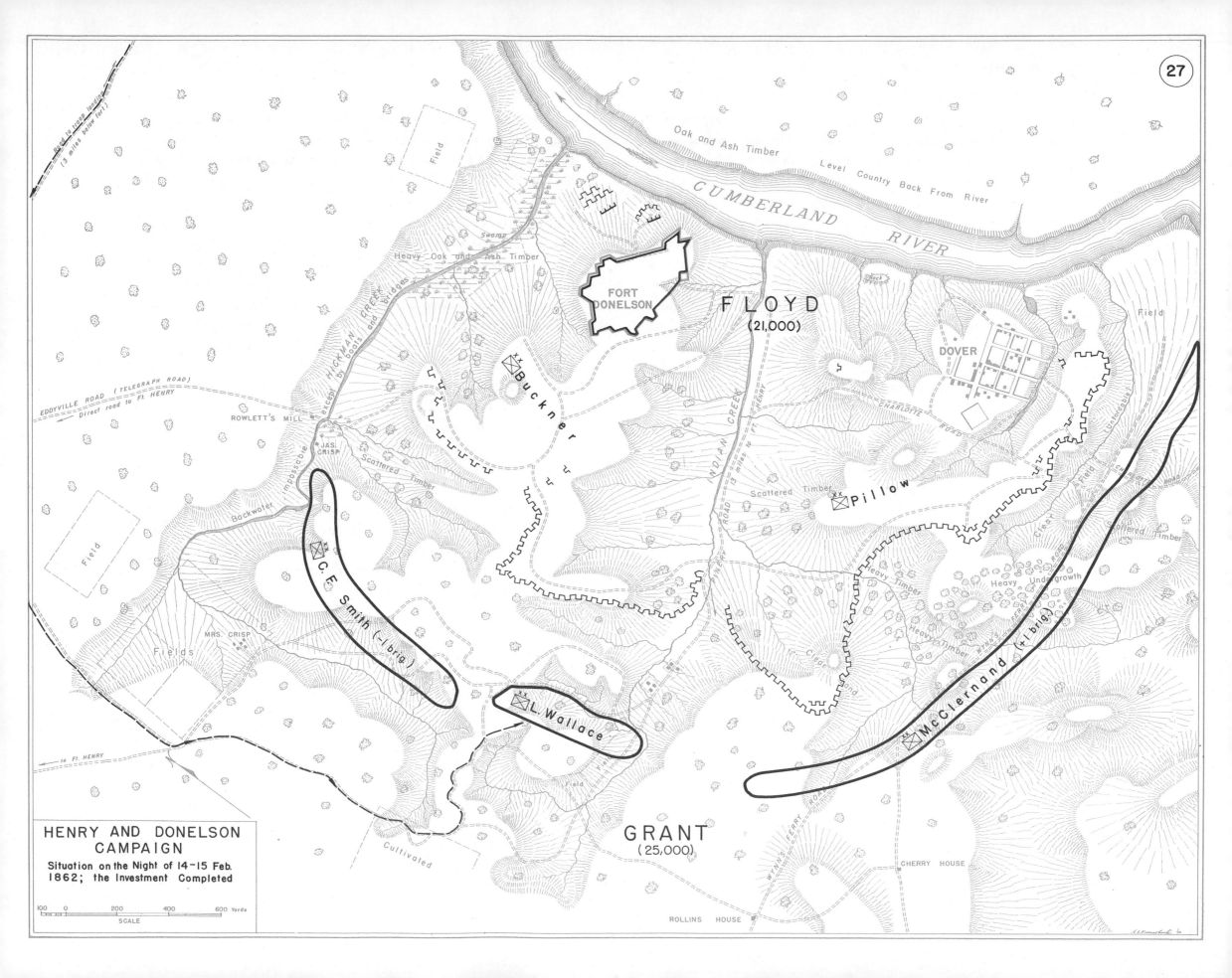

27

CUMBERLAND RIVER

Oak and Ash Timber

Level Country Back From River

Field

Swamp

Heavy Oak and Ash Timber

FORT DONELSON

FLOYD (21,000)

DOVER

Rock Point

Field

Buckner

EDDYVILLE ROAD (TELEGRAPH ROAD)

Direct road to Ft. HENRY

ROWLETT'S MILL

JAS. CRISP

Backwater (impassable except by boats and bridges)

Scattered Timber

CHARLOTTE ROAD

Scattered Timber

Pillow

Field

Unfordable

C. F. Smith (–1 brig.)

Scattered Timber

MRS. CRISP

Fields

Heavy Timber

Heavy Undergrowth

Heavy Timber

L. Wallace

McClernand (+1 brig.)

to Ft. HENRY

Field

Field

GRANT (25,000)

Cultivated

WYNN'S FERRY ROAD

CHERRY HOUSE

HENRY AND DONELSON CAMPAIGN

Situation on the Night of 14–15 Feb. 1862; the Investment Completed

100 0   200   400   600 Yards

SCALE

ROLLINS HOUSE

About daybreak on 15 February, the Confederate attack was initiated by Pillow's division. The plan, which had been worked out the previous night, envisioned a breakout on the Union right. Pillow was to make the main attack with the object of driving McClernand south of the Charlotte Road (*upper right*), thus opening an escape route. Buckner was to move out of his entrenchments and support the attack. When Pillow had opened the way, Buckner was to interpose his force across Wynn's Ferry Road and serve as rear guard to the withdrawing Confederates. To maintain a show of strength, a token force of one regiment was to remain in Buckner's entrenchments on the western end of the line.

The attack was successful; after several hours of hard fighting, Pillow broke McClernand's line and forced it to the south beyond the Charlotte Road. The offensive was aided considerably by the flank attack of Col. Nathan B. Forrest's cavalry and by the fact that McClernand's right, as pointed out earlier, was exposed. Thus, by noon, Floyd had opened an escape route and Buckner, with a relatively fresh force, was in position to cover the withdrawal. But the Confederate commander weakened at the critical moment and could not summon the courage to do something positive. After considerable vacillation and several conferences with Pillow and Buckner—and possibly influenced by Smith's threatening skirmisher and artillery action—he ordered the troops back to their entrenchments.

And what was Grant doing during this critical period? Early that morning Foote, unable to visit Grant because of a wound received in the fight the previous day, asked him to come aboard his flagship for a conference. Disappointed over the earlier naval failure and being desirous of shaping the strategy for the continuing fight, Grant rode downstream to see Foote. Before departing, he instructed his division commanders not to bring on an engagement but to maintain their positions. Grant obviously did not expect a Confederate attack. (However, had he appointed a second in command to serve during his absence, the initial Union defense against the Confederate breakout would have been better coordinated.) Having come to an understanding with Foote, Grant returned to his command to learn that his right was under fierce attack. He at once dispatched a request to Foote to make a show of force, adding significantly that part of his army was demoralized but that he believed the Confederates to be in an even greater state of demoralization which one concerted Union push could exploit to achieve final victory. Then he ordered Smith to attack to his front. Finally, about 3:00 P.M., he rode to his right and directed McClernand and Wallace (who had joined McClernand on his own initiative) to retake the lost position. Thus, the Union commander, acting coolly and without the least show of excitement, instantly regained the initiative so timorously relinquished by Floyd.

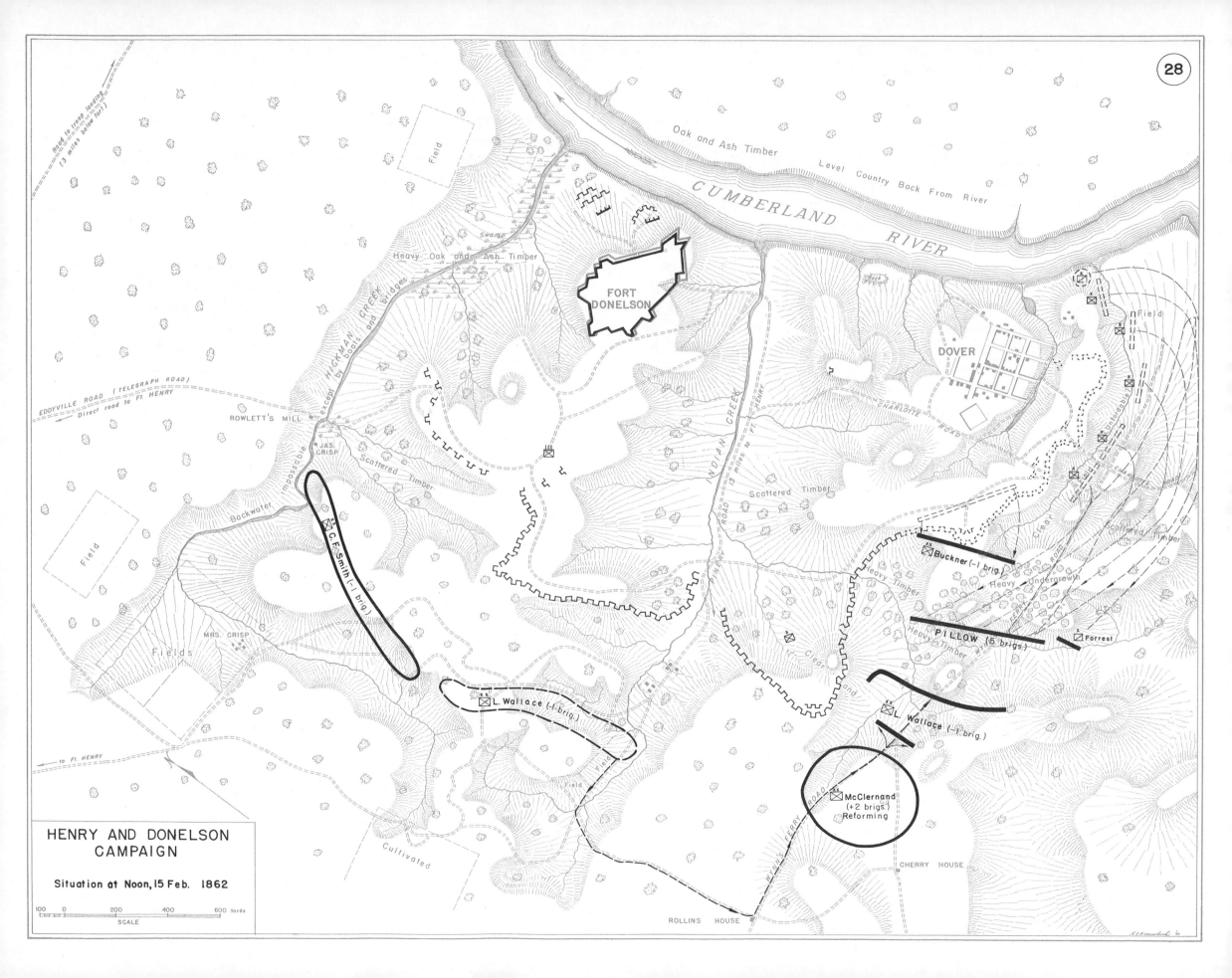

28

CUMBERLAND RIVER

Oak and Ash Timber

Level Country Back From River

Road to troop landing
(3 miles below fort)

Field

Heavy Oak and Ash Timber

Swamp

FORT DONELSON

DOVER

EDDYVILLE ROAD (TELEGRAPH ROAD)
Direct road to Ft. HENRY

ROWLETT'S MILL

CHARLOTTE ROAD

JAS. CRISP

Scattered Timber

Buckner (-1 brig.)

C. F. Smith (-1 brig.)

Scattered Timber

Backwater

PILLOW (5 brigs.)

Heavy Undergrowth

Forrest

MRS. CRISP

Fields

L. Wallace (-1 brig.)

Clear and

L. Wallace (-1 brig.)

to Ft. HENRY

Field

Field

McClernand
(+2 brigs.)
Reforming

**HENRY AND DONELSON
CAMPAIGN**

Situation at Noon, 15 Feb. 1862

Cultivated

ROLLINS HOUSE

CHERRY HOUSE

100 0   200   400   600 Yards
SCALE

Smith's attack succeeded in seizing the outer line of Confederate entrenchments from the regiment that had been left behind to maintain a show of force, while the remainder of Floyd's troops broke out. He was actually approaching Fort Donelson proper when Buckner, returning to his position on the right, as Floyd had ordered, drove him back to—but not beyond—the original Confederate line. Under comparable orders, Pillow had returned his forces as well, after about an hour of heavy fighting. By nightfall the investment was once again complete, though McClernand had not blocked the Charlotte Road. To the irresolute Floyd, it seemed an opportune time to call another council of war.

This conference resulted in a decision to surrender, with Buckner in command. Neither Floyd nor Pillow would consider surrendering personally because they feared Union reprisals; nor did they heed Johnston's orders directing evacuation of the command to Nashville, should it be impossible to hold the fort. Instead, they both made good their escape via river craft on the night of 15 February, leaving behind all but a fraction of their beleaguered troops. Forrest, the great cavalry leader, just beginning to learn his trade, also escaped, leading his entire command along a flooded trail paralleling the river, fifteen minutes before the escape route was cut by McClernand.

Early on 16 February, Grant received Buckner's note asking for terms. His now famous reply stating "no terms except unconditional and immediate surrender" shocked his old friend Buckner, but produced the desired results. In reality, Grant was not bluffing: Smith, being in good position after having taken the outer line of fortifications, was under orders to launch an attack, supported by the other divisions, the next day. Thus Grant no longer accepted the necessity for a siege; he meant to storm the fort. So Buckner surrendered his command of 11,500 men, along with forty cannon, considerable equipment, and foodstuffs which Grant needed badly, and went off to temporary captivity in the North. Johnston, his center now rent asunder, pondered how to recoup his losses and restore his injured reputation.

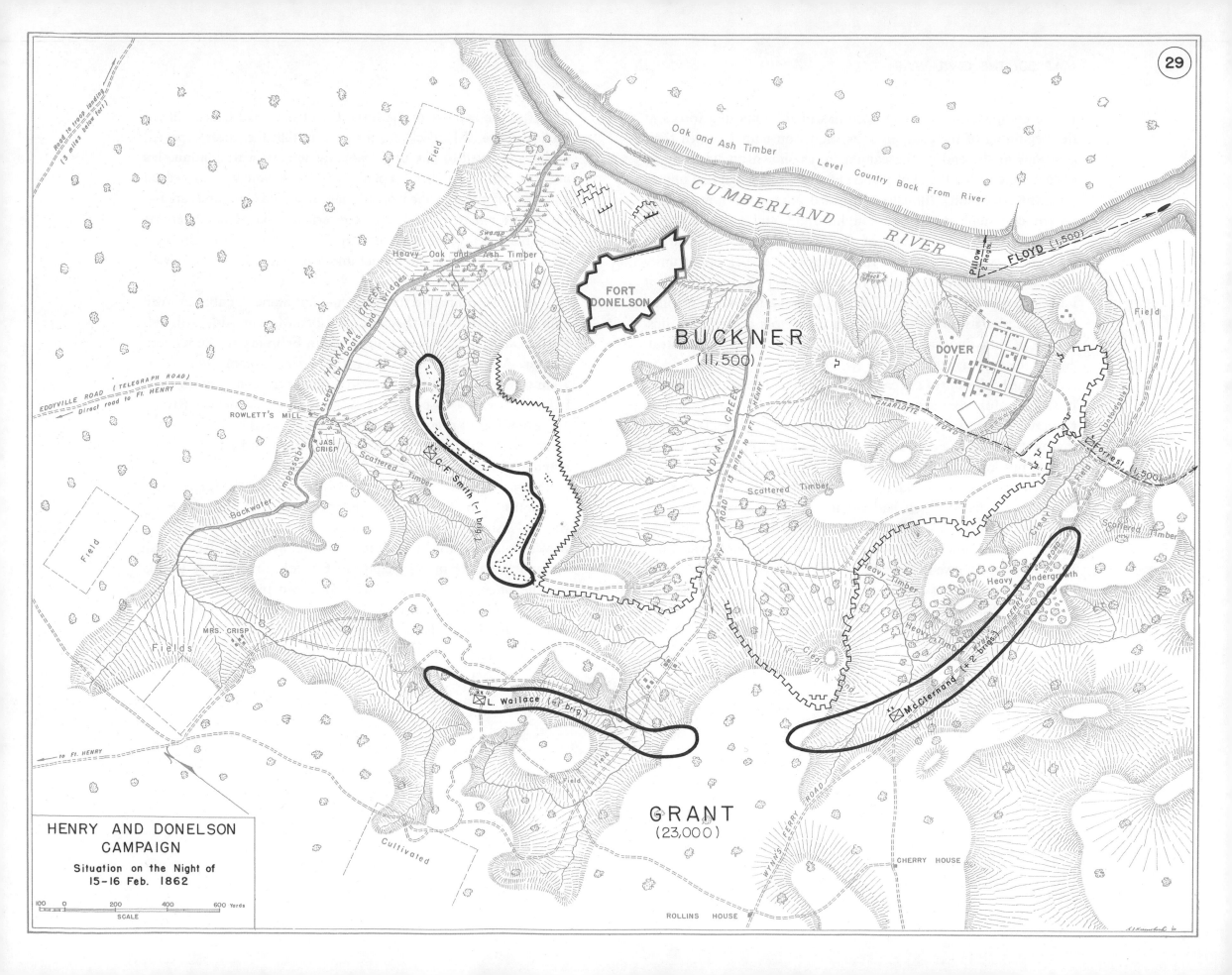

29

CUMBERLAND RIVER

Oak and Ash Timber

Level Country Back From River

Road to troop landing
(3 miles below fort)

Field

FORT
DONELSON

Pillow
(2 Regts.)

FLOYD (1,500)

BUCKNER
(11,500)

DOVER

Heavy Oak and Ash Timber

Swamp

EDDYVILLE ROAD (TELEGRAPH ROAD)

Direct road to Ft. HENRY

ROWLETT'S MILL

JAS CRISP

Scattered Timber

C.F. Smith (~1 brig.)

Backwater

CHARLOTTE ROAD

Forrest (1,500)

Unfordable

Scattered Timber

Scattered Timber

Heavy Undergrowth

MRS. CRISP

Fields

Heavy Timber

L. Wallace (~1 brig.)

McClernand (~2 brigs.)

to Ft. HENRY

Cultivated

Field

Field

GRANT
(23,000)

CHERRY HOUSE

HENRY AND DONELSON
CAMPAIGN

Situation on the Night of
15-16 Feb. 1862

100 0   200   400   600 Yards
SCALE

ROLLINS HOUSE

If one compares the relative positions of the opposing forces at the beginning of the campaign, as shown on map 25, with their positions at the end of the campaign, as shown on this map, it becomes clear that the Henry and Donelson campaign had important strategic results. Johnston's forward defense was now broken; lateral communications between his right and left wings had been severed by the cutting of the Memphis & Ohio Railroad by Grant, now a major general. Johnston's earlier opportunity to destroy Grant's then smaller force no longer existed, for Grant had been heavily reinforced. Further, Union gunboats controlled the Tennessee as far south as Florence (*bottom center*), an illustration of the important part the Navy played in the Union strategy in the western theater.

At the beginning of the campaign, Buell had been concentrated in the Munfordville area. Here he had been subjected to advice from two quarters. McClellan, now in over-all command in Washington, had advocated an advance into eastern Tennessee, though he was not insistent. Halleck, on the other hand, had pressed for Buell to advance to the Clarksville-Nashville area to cover Grant's exposed east flank. Buell had begun an advance south and, on 16 February (the day Buckner surrendered Fort Donelson), he had occupied Bowling Green, which Johnston had evacuated. He had then followed the retreating Confederates slowly, never exerting enough pressure to force a fight. Meanwhile, he had sent one division around by water, ostensibly to help Grant but also to move on Nashville. This unit was in possession of Nashville when the remainder of Buell's army arrived on 24 February.

After the capture of the forts, Grant occupied Clarksville at the insistence of Halleck, for it was here that the latter expected Grant and Buell to link up. Grant was impatient to continue his advance, but he was held in place by Halleck, who was concerned about an offensive by the Confederates from the Columbus area— which never materialized. This concern was based upon reports from his intelligence service that Beauregard, with reinforcements, had arrived in the theater and was to join Polk in a powerful drive northward.

General Beauregard had arrived—but alone. Unable to work with J. E. Johnston in the east, and somewhat at odds with Jefferson Davis, he had been transferred in February to the western theater. After a conference with the western commander, A. S. Johnston, he went to Jackson and assumed command of all Confederate troops between the Mississippi and Tennessee Rivers. Johnston, for all practical purposes, relinquished control of operations west of the Tennessee to Beauregard and acted as commander of the small force at Murfreesboro.

So, as one can see, on 27 February, Halleck's forces were concentrated in two locations under Pope and Grant, and Buell was at Nashville. The Confederates were much more widely dispersed, but Johnston, at Beauregard's urging, had evolved a plan for concentrating in the vicinity of Corinth, preparatory to taking the offensive. On the Union side, two plans to retain the initiative were being discussed. The one decided upon was to lead to the bloody fields of Shiloh.

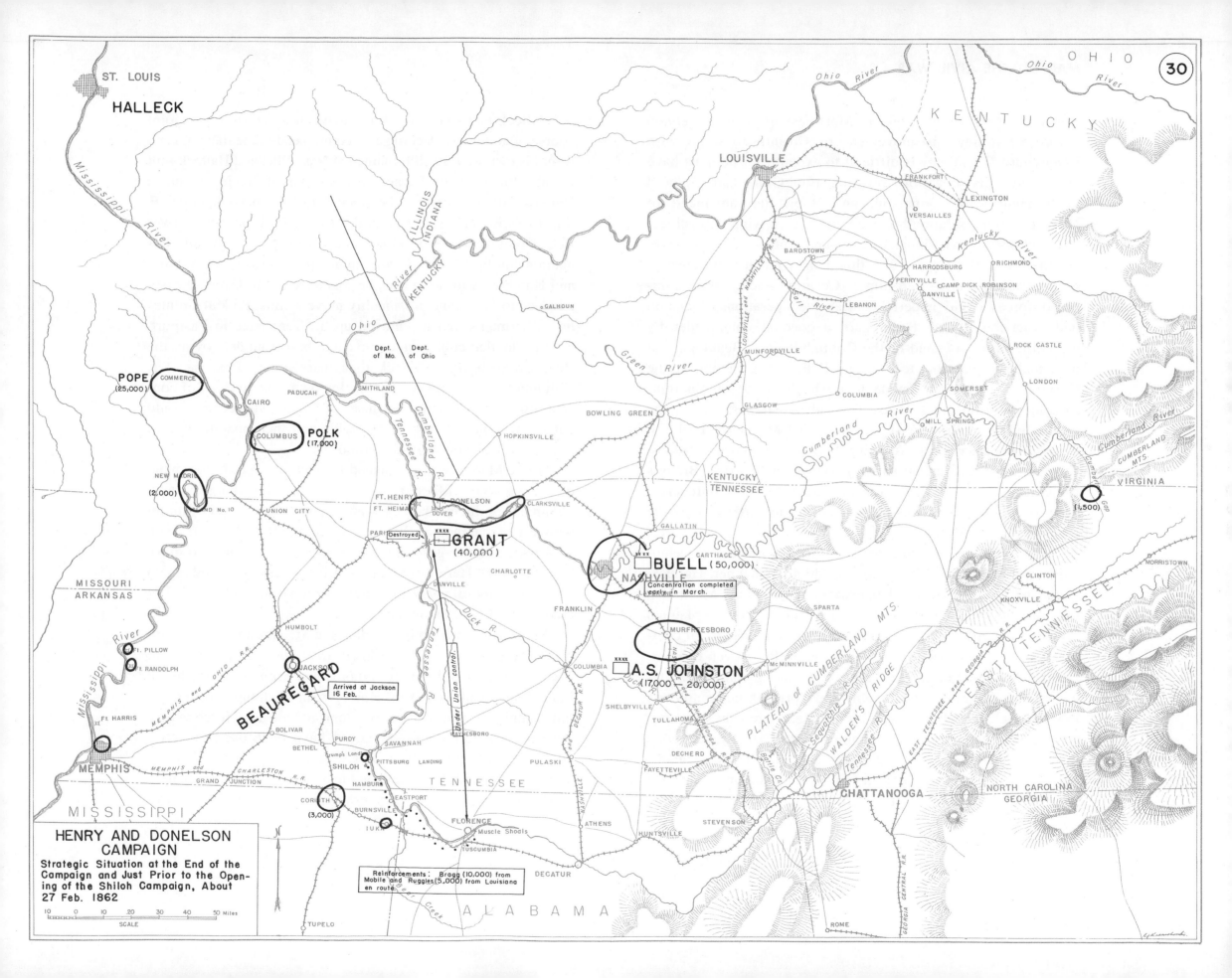

30

HALLECK

ST. LOUIS

KENTUCKY

OHIO

LOUISVILLE

POPE
(25,000)
COMMERCE

POLK
(17,000)
COLUMBUS

NEW MADRID
(2,000)

Dept.
of Mo.
Dept.
of Ohio

FT. HENRY
FT. HEIMAN
FT. DONELSON
DOVER
CLARKSVILLE

Destroyed

GRANT
(40,000)

BUELL (50,000)

Concentration completed
early in March.

MURFREESBORO

MISSOURI
ARKANSAS

A.S. JOHNSTON
(17,000 — 20,000)

BEAUREGARD

Arrived at Jackson
16 Feb.

MEMPHIS

Under Union control.

SHILOH
PITTSBURG LANDING
SAVANNAH

TENNESSEE

CHATTANOOGA

NORTH CAROLINA
GEORGIA

CORINTH
(3,000)

EAST TENNESSEE

MISSISSIPPI

FLORENCE
Muscle Shoals

DECATUR

ALABAMA

HENRY AND DONELSON CAMPAIGN

Strategic Situation at the End of the
Campaign and Just Prior to the Opening of the Shiloh Campaign, About
27 Feb. 1862

10   0   10   20   30   40   50 Miles

SCALE

Reinforcements: Bragg (10,000) from
Mobile and Ruggles (5,000) from Louisiana
en route.

TUPELO

Johnston spent eight days at Murfreesboro (*lower center*) before beginning his movement to Corinth to unite with Beauregard. This delay is difficult to explain, for he must have appreciated his precarious position after Grant had captured Forts Henry and Donelson, and Buell had advanced to Nashville, thus isolating his two wings. Each wing was subject to attack by overwhelming forces—and neither could possibly aid the other. Beauregard saw this danger much more clearly; he urged Johnston to join him at Corinth, whence their combined forces could undertake offensive operations. Johnston had practically made Beauregard a coequal commander by assigning him command of the Columbus area. Beauregard at once made preparations to withdraw Polk from Columbus to the Corinth area. Also, he made feverish efforts to obtain reinforcements from other areas. Through his imperiousness, he succeeded in cajoling local governors and Maj. Gen. Earl Van Dorn in Arkansas into providing him with additional troops, and also in effecting the shift of Maj. Gen. Braxton Bragg's force from Mobile. Thus was concentrated the Confederate army of 40,000 that Johnston was to lead in battle against the Union forces at Shiloh.

On the Union side, the preparations for the coming campaign were conducted in an equally dilatory manner. Halleck, elated by Grant's success but exasperated because McClellan maintained Buell on a status equal to his own, plagued Washington with requests for more troops and for unity of command in the west—with, of course, himself as over-all commander. While he talked vaguely about making war on "strategic points" (in this case Memphis and Corinth), he completely ignored the excellent opportunity to defeat Johnston's separated forces individually. Buell, thinking more logically, wanted to unite with Grant east of the Tennessee and to move against Johnston, fully realizing that the Confederate commander must soon recognize the necessity for concentrating his forces.

Halleck and Buell could not arrive at a decision on a joint course of action. So, lacking a directing head in the theater, each went his own way. Buell remained at Nashville, and Halleck sent Grant's force up the Tennessee River. Grant, having incurred Halleck's displeasure, had been temporarily superseded by C.F. Smith. Smith's mission was to destroy the railroad bridge over Bear Creek (between Florence and Corinth) and the rail connections on Polk's line of communications at Corinth, Jackson, and Humbolt; following this, he was to return to Danville, then advance to Paris, and presumably move against Polk at Columbus. Sherman's division moved up the Tennessee to Eastport, but the flooded countryside prevented him from destroying the Bear Creek bridge. Halleck then learned that Polk had left Columbus and had moved south. He now began to think of concentrating with Buell just northeast of Shiloh, whence they could cut the railroad leading to Memphis and then operate against Memphis itself, or other key points.

On 11 March, Lincoln placed Halleck in over-all command of the Knoxville-Missouri River area, thus resolving the area command problem. Halleck then ordered Buell to join Smith, who was encamped at Pittsburg Landing. It took Buell (who was made a major general on 26 March) thirteen days to move to Columbia. Here he found a bridge destroyed and again delayed an inordinately long time—a delay that almost led to the defeat of Grant's force.

Note that in attempting to hold the Mississippi, Beauregard had left a garrison at Island No. 10 (*left center*). The futility of occupying such isolated strongholds had been demonstrated at Forts Henry and Donelson. However, in so doing, Beauregard unwittingly led Halleck to leave Pope and his large force to deal with the island, when they could have been used to better advantage elsewhere. The loss, however, of its garrison of approximately 7,000 officers and men and much heavy artillery and supplies was still a considerable blow to the Confederacy.

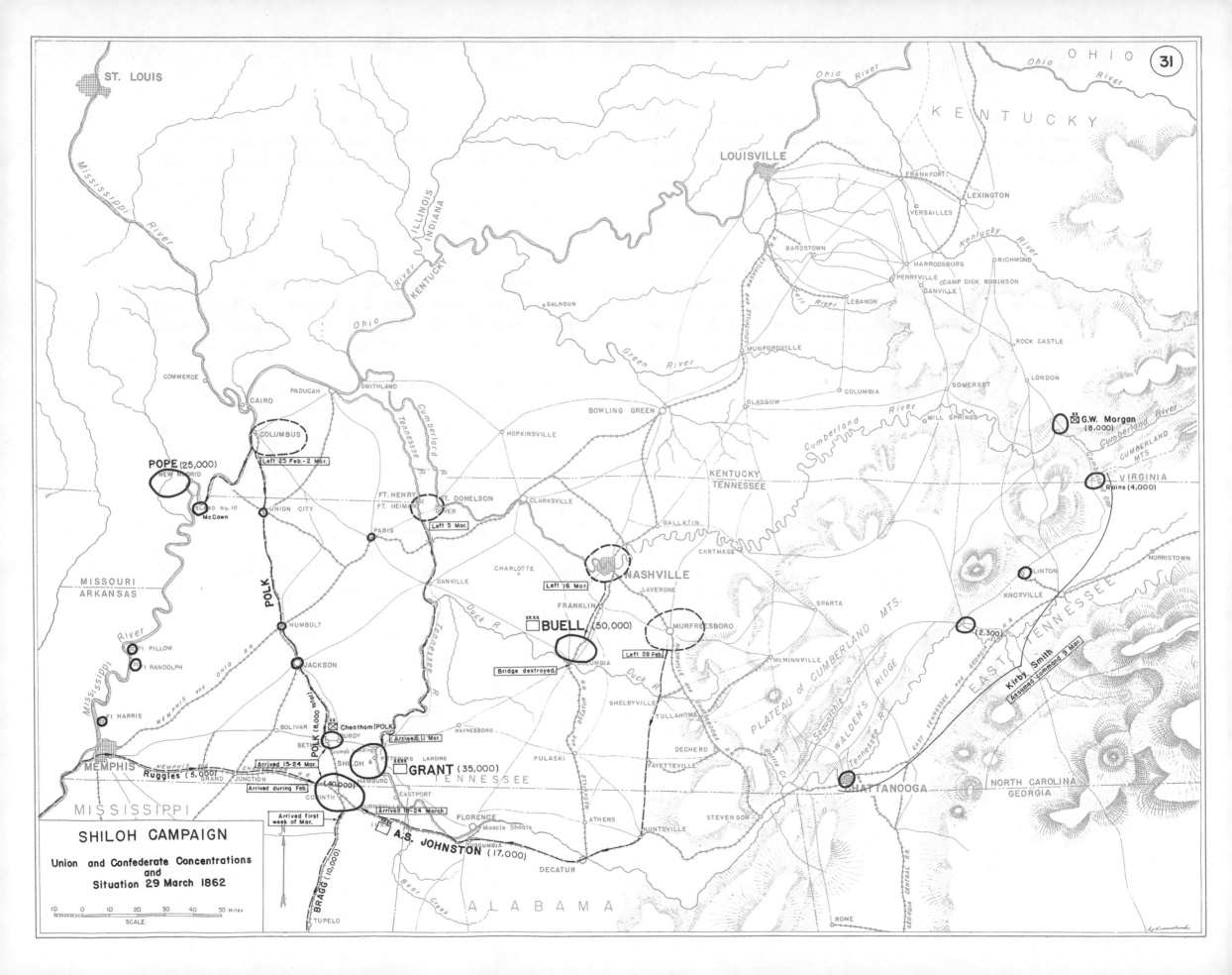

31

SHILOH CAMPAIGN

Union and Confederate Concentrations
and
Situation 29 March 1862

10 0 10 20 30 40 50 Miles
SCALE

By the evening of 5 April, the day before the Battle of Shiloh, Grant, now restored to command, had disposed his troops as shown. His force comprised six divisions; one, that of Maj. Gen Lew Wallace, had been left five miles downstream at Crump's Landing to prevent the emplacement of Confederate batteries, which could harass river traffic from that point. Wallace also had an offensive mission—to cut the railroad at Bethel, about ten miles west. Grant established his headquarters at Savannah, nine miles downstream from his troops. This unusual separation of headquarters and troops was to deprive the Union forces of his leadership during the important first two hours of the battle. Grant later explained that he had to be at Savannah to meet Buell, whose orders directed him to that place.

At Pittsburg Landing, Grant's army was merely camped wherever its units could find suitable clearings. No plans had been made for the defense of this position. Grant seems to have thought vaguely about fortifying it, but nothing had been done. (Actually, field fortifications were not highly esteemed by veterans of the Mexican War, who—having stormed many of them—felt that they merely reduced the fighting spirit of the troops behind them.) But the most inexplicable oversight was the almost complete lack of security. Only a sketchy line of infantry outposts covered the camp, and there was no effort at distant patrolling or reconnaissance. Even after a lively skirmish on 4 April, in which Confederate cavalry gobbled up a Union outpost and pursuing Union cavalry developed a Confederate force of all arms, Sherman could write Grant that he did not expect "any-thing like an attack" on his position. Neither Sherman nor Grant made any effort to find out more about these aggressive Confederates. Meanwhile, Johnston's army was concentrated a mere two miles in front of Sherman and Prentiss, and was preparing to attack the next morning.

The circumstances attending Grant's poor defensive and security measures against a surprise Confederate assault have been the subject of much debate. A general and perhaps most likely conclusion is that Grant, overconfident since his success at Fort Donelson and unsure of his mission as set forth in nebulous terms by Halleck, was careless in his intelligence effort and, furthermore, believed himself able to deal with any Confederate attack.

The area in which Grant's troops were encamped was triangular and was circumscribed by water courses. These were, in counterclockwise direction: the Tennessee River, Snake Creek, Owl Creek, Oak Creek, Locust Grove Creek, and Lick Creek. Except for a few cleared spaces, the ground was covered with forest and undergrowth, much of it impassable for horsemen. The highest terrain was a ridge running generally east to west, 200 feet above the Tennessee River on the north side of Oak and Locust Grove Creeks. This ridge sloped gradually in a northerly direction to the rearmost Union camps, which were about 100 feet lower. Tillman Creek divided the ridge into two plateaus. Note the swampy area along Owl Creek. The major roads in the area are shown in solid lines and are labeled.

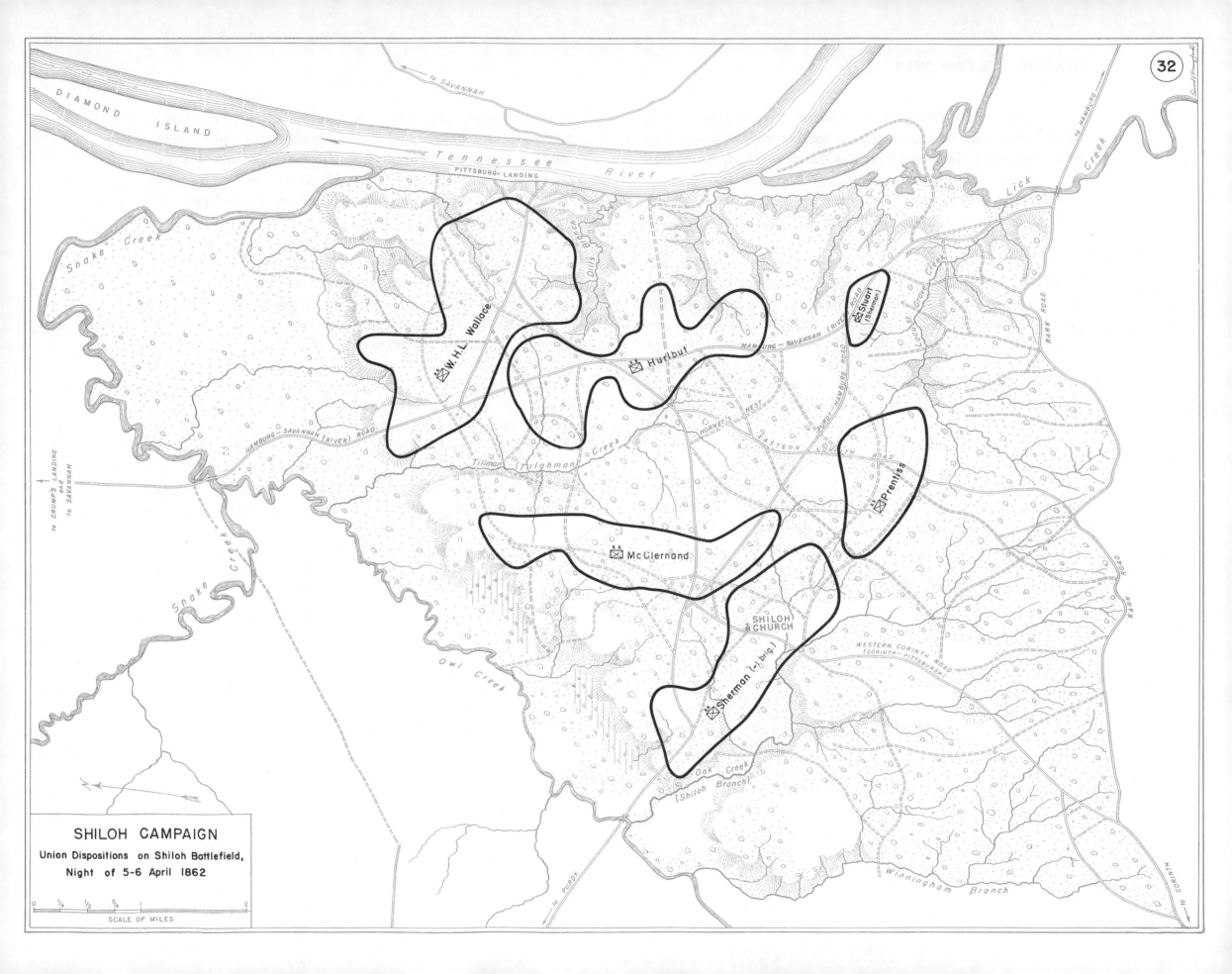

32

SHILOH CAMPAIGN

Union Dispositions on Shiloh Battlefield,
Night of 5-6 April 1862

0   ¼   ½   ¾   1   2
SCALE OF MILES

When Johnston finally arrived at Corinth, Beauregard insisted that offensive action was essential if the Confederate cause were to be preserved. To him, Grant was the ideal target, for he was well forward, unsupported, and occupied a poor tactical position. Johnston acquiesced, and Beauregard drew up the march order. The two roads used, moving north from Corinth, were the only suitable ones through the dense forest, though they were merely narrow dirt tracks. At Mickey, the routes converged and, as might be expected, a bottleneck developed as Bragg tried to fit his corps in between Hardee and Polk. Thus, owing to the delays encountered, the attack originally planned for 4 April was postponed to the 5th, and ultimately to the 6th; for it was not until 4:00 P.M. on 5 April that the troops, tired and hungry, were deployed for battle as shown. By then, Beauregard had begun to waver, fearing that, after all the confusion and delay, Grant must surely have been alerted for an attack. But Johnston insisted that the attack proceed as planned, even though he, too, had been angry over the delays.

Hence, the Confederate army bivouacked unobserved that night in order of battle two miles from the Union position, its front screened by infantry pickets. The army was formed in column of corps, with the two leading corps in line of divisions—that is, Hardee and Bragg had both placed their divisions in one long line (*see also map 34*). Hardee's line included one of Bragg's brigades. This peculiar and unwieldy attack formation will be seen to have caused considerable difficulty in Confederate command control during the battle.

Sherman did not suspect an attack from the south, and Grant was even less suspecting. He had been apprised by Lew Wallace that the Confederates were in strength at Purdy and had concluded that if any action took place it would be in Wallace's area. Actually, the enemy at Purdy had been Maj. Gen. B. Franklin Cheatham's division of Polk's corps, en route to join his corps at Mickey. On the night of 5 April, Grant reported to his superior, Halleck: "I have scarcely the faintest idea of an attack (general one) being made upon us, but will be prepared should such a thing take place."

Note that Brig. Gen. William Nelson's division, the vanguard of Buell's army, had arrived at Savannah on 3-4 April and was awaiting the remainder of Buell's army before moving upstream to bivouac in the vicinity of Hamburg (*center, right*).

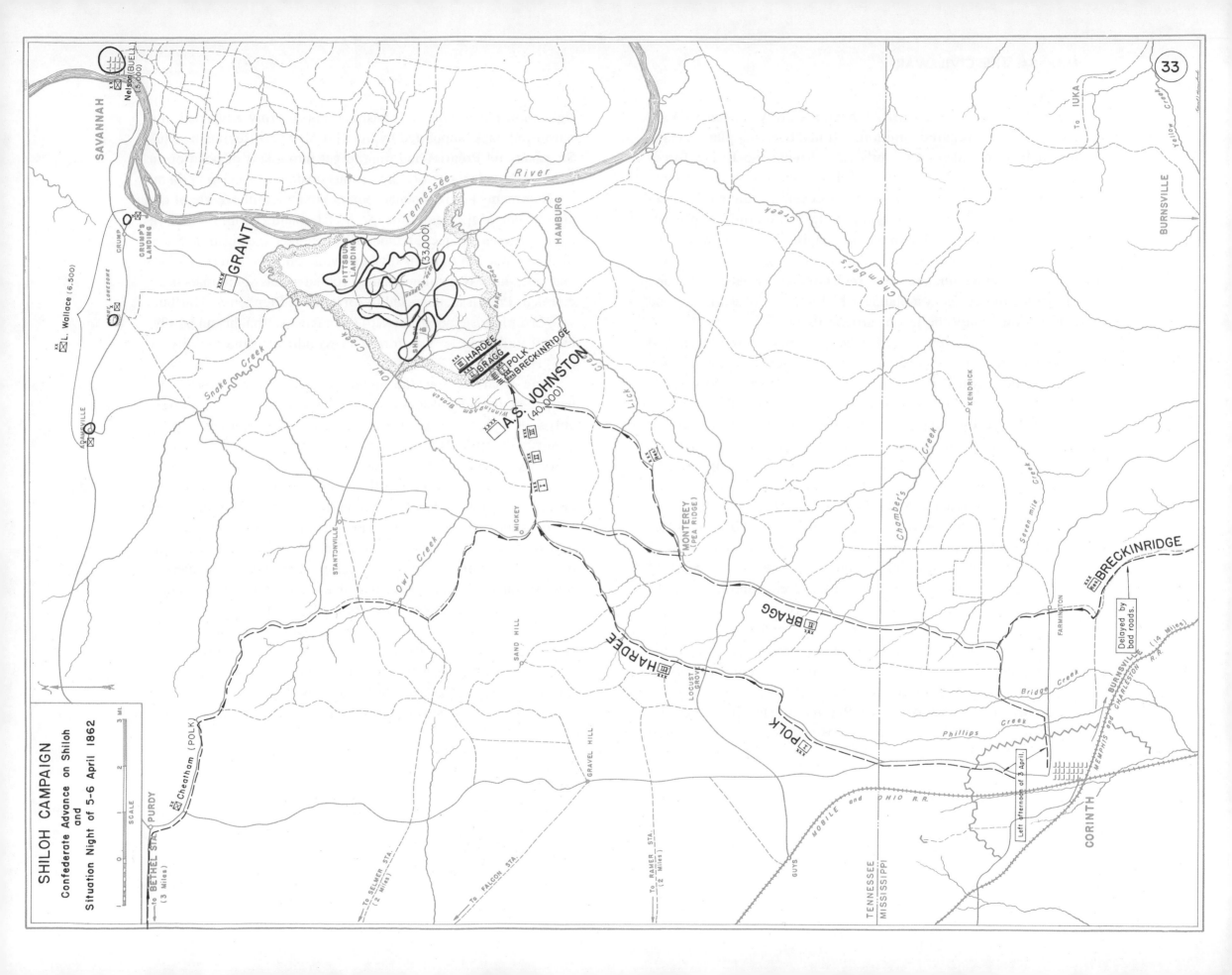

SHILOH CAMPAIGN

Confederate Advance on Shiloh
and
Situation Night of 5-6 April 1862

SCALE

3 MIL.
2
0
1

33

SAVANNAH

Nelson (BUELL) (5,000)

Tennessee River

BURNSVILLE

To IUKA

GRANT

CRUMP'S LANDING

L. Wallace (6,500)

PITTSBURG LANDING (33,000)

HAMBURG

HARDEE
BRAGG
POLK
BRECKINRIDGE

A.S. JOHNSTON (40,000)

MONTEREY (PEA RIDGE)

BRECKINRIDGE

Delayed by bad roads.

BRAGG

HARDEE

LOCUST GROVE

POLK

Left afternoon of 3 April.

CORINTH

SAND HILL

GRAVEL HILL

MOBILE and OHIO R.R.

MEMPHIS and CHARLESTON R.R.

TENNESSEE
MISSISSIPPI

STANTONVILLE

MICKEY

Owl Creek

Snake Creek

Cheatham (POLK)

To BETHEL STA. PURDY (3 Miles)

To SELMER STA. (2 Miles)

To RAMER STA. (2 Miles)

To FALCON STA.

GUYS

About 6:00 A.M. on 6 April, Johnston's army moved forward against the ill-prepared Union foe. It had been his plan to make the main effort against Grant's left, driving the Union forces against Snake and Owl Creeks and thus cutting them off from Pittsburg Landing (*top center*) and preventing their reinforcement by water. But the faulty attack formation did not provide the necessary extra strength on the eastern flank upon which the success of the plan depended. Consequently, as the first and second Confederate lines became intermingled in battle all along the front, the corps commanders had no reserve available and could control only the troops around them.

At 7:30 A.M., Beauregard, who as deputy commander had been left in rear to coordinate the movements of the reserve, ordered Polk and Brig. Gen. John C. Breckinridge forward to the left and right respectively. This merely had the effect of extending the line. By 9:00 A.M., though the reserve was not yet irrevocably committed, little chance remained to carry out the original plan. The attack had degenerated into a simple frontal assault, seeking to envelop both Union flanks and to penetrate the center simultaneously. Early in the battle Johnston had, in effect, left over-all control in Beauregard's hands by riding forward to lead the assault personally. For so doing he has been severely criticized, and rightly so; but, in a lesser sense, he should be credited with appreciating the fact that green, untrained troops need inspiring leadership—Johnston's forte.

If we go back to dawn, just before the Confederate offensive was launched, we find that Sherman and Prentiss had had some warning of the attack. The latter, uneasy over the negative findings of his patrols the previous day, had, at 3:00 A.M., sent forward part of the 25th Missouri Regiment. This force became engaged with the Confederate outposts at 5:15 A.M. A spirited fight took place, but, as Johnston's entire army advanced, the patrol fell back, supported by the 21st Missouri Regiment. Thus Sherman and Prentiss had time to get into a sort of position in front of their tents before the furious onslaught was upon them.

Sherman's left regiments soon broke under the weight of the attack, but Maj. Gen. John A. McClernand, coming forward upon Sherman's request, temporarily stabilized the position. Sherman continued to fight his division with coolness, determination, and skill; he was not immediately routed as has sometimes been claimed. Prentiss, supported by Brig. Gen. Stephen A. Hurlbut, who had likewise moved forward upon request, fought stubbornly, but by 9:00 A.M. he was forced to withdraw to the vicinity of the "Hornet's Nest."

And what of Grant during these critical early hours? We have seen that his division commanders were cooperating admirably—in part, this was probably due to instructions issued by Grant on 3 April. But he did not reach the field of battle until 8:30 A.M., having left his breakfast table at Savannah about 6:30 A.M., upon hearing gunfire. Now he labored with all his energy to restore balance to a situation which his earlier carelessness and overconfidence had permitted to develop. Before leaving Savannah, he had directed Nelson to move up to a point opposite Pittsburg Landing. At Crump's Landing he had alerted Lew Wallace, and, when he disembarked at Pittsburg Landing, he established a straggler line. He then went forward to see his commanders. Maj. Gen. William H. L. Wallace (promoted from Brig. Gen. on 21 March) was directed to send two regiments to secure the Snake Creek bridge—a precaution designed to expedite the arrival of Lew Wallace. Thus, as the Confederates vigorously pressed the attack, Grant struggled to position his forces to stop it.

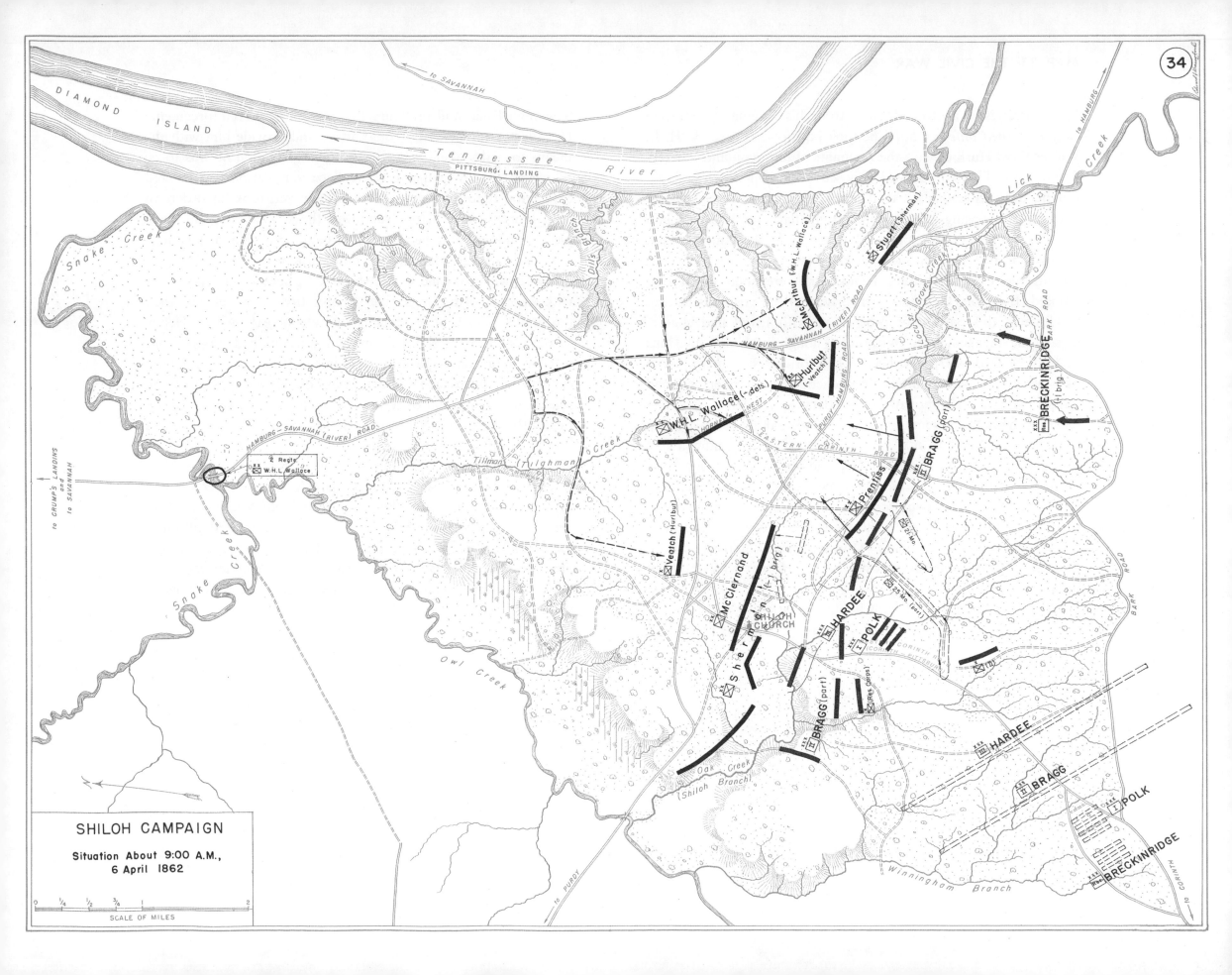

SHILOH CAMPAIGN

Situation About 9:00 A.M.,
6 April 1862

SCALE OF MILES

When Prentiss was forced back from his original line (*right center, dashed blue symbol*), he took position between W. H. L. Wallace and Hurlbut with the remnants of his command—barely 1,000 men. This withdrawal exposed McClernand's left flank, but he held tenaciously. At 10:30 A.M., Sherman was pushed back, thus exposing McClernand's right flank, and forcing him also to withdraw. At about the same time, Hurlbut's salient line was pushed inward. Sherman and McClernand took position behind the Purdy-Hamburg Road, but were soon again outflanked. By noon, they had been driven to the positions shown.

Indeed, this pattern of progressive withdrawal had characterized the engagement to this point. Though the Union divisions had cooperated, there had been a lack of cohesion in the force as a whole. Individual units, threatened with encirclement, had withdrawn when their own commanders so decided. Grant had been on the field for some time and had visited all of his division commanders, but had not yet succeeded in establishing a line which he could wholly control. But he had not been inactive: he had sent his only reserve (two regiments) to reinforce McClernand; orders had again been sent to Lew Wallace and Nelson to speed their movements to the field of battle; Buell had been urged to hurry reinforcements to the area; and Prentiss had been directed to "maintain that position [the Hornet's Nest] at all hazards."

In substance, all of Grant's actions seem to indicate that he was seeking to stabilize a line that would protect the Hamburg-Savannah Road and Pittsburg Landing until the reinforcements he expected momentarily could arrive and provide him with the means to strike offensively. But in this expectation he was to be disappointed, for neither Lew Wallace nor Nelson had reacted expeditiously to his orders. Prentiss, however, took his orders to hold literally; and before sundown, the sunken road he occupied at Shiloh was to become famous among Civil War positions —as were sunken roads in two other distant arenas.

Meanwhile, on the Confederate side, success had not been without its shortcomings. The troops, tired and hungry when the attack began, were reaching a state of exhaustion. Heavy casualties had been suffered, and many troops had dropped out to feast upon the ample rations found in the abandoned Union camps. The corps commanders, now directing sections of the line with almost total disregard for their original organization, rallied the troops and led them forward, striving to break Grant's line and achieve victory.

A survey of the over-all situation as it existed at this time will reveal three significant facts: though the Confederates had driven the Union forces back, they had nowhere achieved a decisive or overwhelming success; having committed all their forces to battle, the Confederates had no reserve to use in exploitation of that success, if it came, or to counter a Union offensive effort; and large Union reinforcements were present within a few miles of the battlefield.

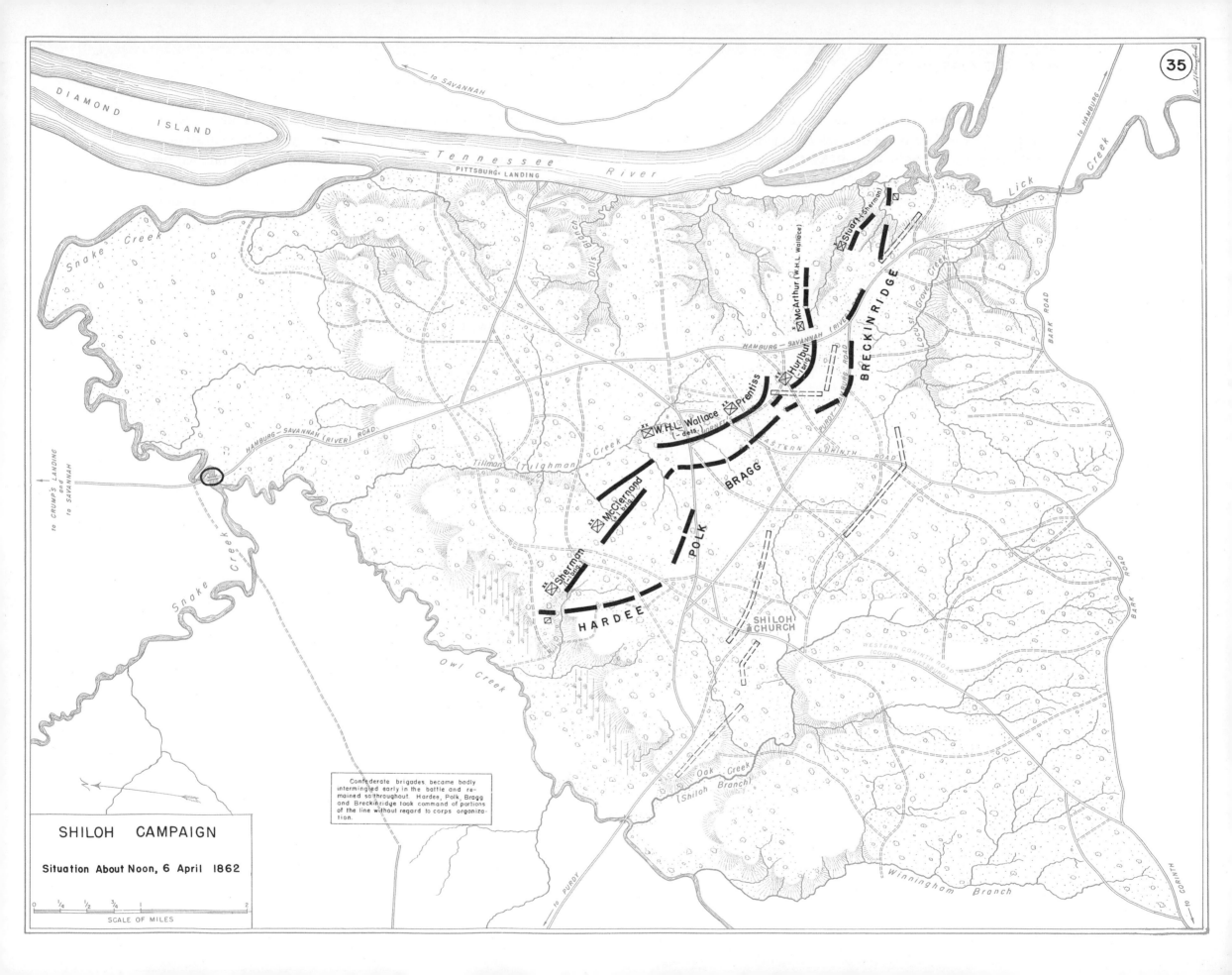

35

SHILOH CAMPAIGN

Situation About Noon, 6 April 1862

SCALE OF MILES

Confederate brigades became badly intermingled early in the battle and remained so throughout. Hardee, Polk, Bragg and Breckinridge took command of portions of the line without regard to corps organization.

Shortly after noon, Sherman's exhausted force, finding its flanks again imperiled, was forced to pull back still farther; at 1:00 P.M., it withdrew to the position shown. McClernand was similarly forced back by the hard-fighting Confederates. The two commanders held their new positions until shortly after 4:00 P.M., when they again withdrew to previously selected positions along the Hamburg-Savannah Road (*see map 37*). However, they dealt out heavy punishment in the interim to the forces of Hardee, which were now showing the effects of the severe and protracted fighting.

On Grant's left (*this map*), forces under Bragg and Breckinridge finally accomplished what the original Confederate plan had sought—the crumbling of that flank. About 3:00 P.M., Col. David Stuart and Brig. Gen. John McArthur found their left flank enveloped and withdrew all the way to Pittsburg Landing. Here was an excellent opportunity to move behind Grant's position and drive his troops against Owl Creek. But the Confederates, lacking a reserve, had no fresh troops available to exploit this momentary success.

Hurlbut, too, had been forced back by Bragg's assault, but he went into position to cover Prentiss' left flank. In the area of the Hornet's Nest, Wallace and Prentiss had been successfully holding their ground for the past five hours under incessant attack. Their position was an excellent one. It had withstood as many as twelve separate assaults, including at least one led personally by Johnston. Shortly thereafter, Johnston was mortally wounded, dying at about 2:30 P.M. Confederate morale undoubtedly suffered from this blow, but the general control of the Confederate attack did not, since Beauregard had been responsible for that since the beginning of the attack.

Prentiss' determined resistance had worked to Union advantage; the Confederates, instead of containing and by-passing the position, allowed it to attract all nearby units. Around the sunken road and the peach orchard behind it, sixty-two Confederate guns were massed to support the determined infantry assaults. And still Prentiss and Wallace held on. Meanwhile, Grant moved forward the two regiments covering the Snake Creek bridge and, for the third time, dispatched instructions to Lew Wallace to move without delay to the battlefield. Grant had met Buell at 1:00 P.M. at Pittsburg Landing and had reiterated his instructions of the morning for Nelson to move forward. But for some reason never satisfactorily explained, Nelson did not leave Savannah until 1:30 P.M. and consequently was just now nearing a point opposite Pittsburg Landing.

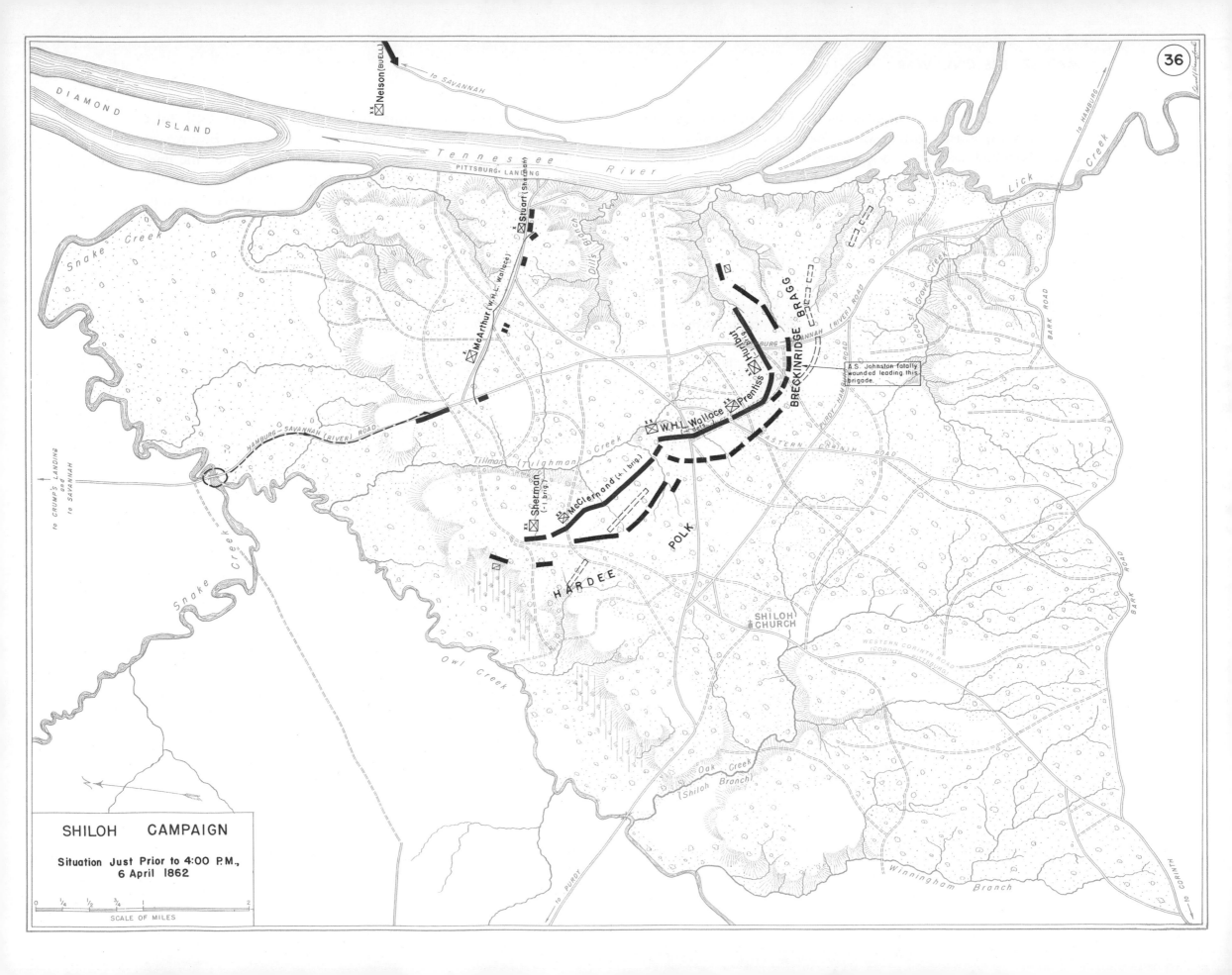

SHILOH CAMPAIGN

Situation Just Prior to 4:00 P.M.,
6 April 1862

Shortly after 4:00 P.M., Sherman and McClernand had, as was previously explained, withdrawn to the positions shown—positions which had been selected specifically to cover the Hamburg-Savannah Road, by which Lew Wallace's arrival had been expected since 1:00 P.M. Here, exhausted and decimated, the regiments of these two divisions prepared to make their final stand. This Union withdrawal allowed Hardee and Polk to swing their forces to the right to assist in the reduction of the Hornet's Nest.

Hurlbut had elected to withdraw from that area when his left flank, exposed by Stuart's retreat, had been enveloped. Shortly thereafter, W. H. L. Wallace and Prentiss were surrounded by the bulk of the Confederate army. Wallace, seeking to extricate his troops, faced his regiments to the rear; of these, two managed to cut their way through, though Wallace himself fell, mortally wounded. Prentiss drew back his flanks and, with the remnants of the two divisions, strove to execute Grant's order to hold—"as cool as if expecting victory" according to Grant, who last saw him about 4:30 P.M. Nevertheless, further resistance was futile. At 5:30 P.M., Prentiss, after having gained valuable time for Grant, surrendered his force of 2,200 men.

Earlier in the afternoon, Col. Joseph D. Webster, Grant's chief of staff, observing the Union left in a state of near-collapse, had begun—with Grant's approval—to assemble artillery on the commanding ridge overlooking Dill's Branch. By the time Prentiss surrendered, fifty guns were in position, supported by fragments of broken regiments under Hurlbut's command—about 4,000 men. After Prentiss' surrender, Bragg was eager to assault this new position, seize Pittsburg Landing, and thus give meaning to the battle which had raged so violently since dawn. But, again, the lack of a reserve was to frustrate the Confederate offensive. Bragg could muster only about 2,000 men, the understrength brigades of Brig. Gen. James R. Chalmers and Brig. Gen. John K. Jackson—and the latter was out of ammunition! Beauregard had dispatched orders to suspend the attack all along the line. Bragg had not yet received them, when, at about 6:00 P.M., he launched his brigades in the assault. Jackson's Alabamans, with no weapons but their bayonets, advanced heroically through heavy artillery fire. They reached the ravine beneath the crest on which the Union line was established, but could go no farther. Chalmers' efforts to storm the crest met with failure.

When two Union gunboats sought to support Webster's batteries, the high angle of fire necessitated by the bluffs along the river caused their fire to be relatively ineffective. (However, the gunboats interdicted Confederate rear areas with some success during the night.) As the fury of the battle abated, Col. Jacob Ammen's brigade of Nelson's division arrived and took position in line on Hurlbut's left, but it exerted little influence in the repulse of Bragg's attack. Lew Wallace finally arrived on Sherman's right, after the firing had ceased. His delay had been due principally to his having misunderstood Grant's orders—a mistake that caused him to make a slow and overcautious advance by the wrong road.

Thus, as a stormy, rainy night closed in, both sides bivouacked in the positions shown, thankful for a few hours of relatively uninterrupted rest. Beauregard, believing he had won a notable victory, informed Richmond of the events of the day in embellished terms and then went to bed in Sherman's captured tent. He had good reason to be proud of the achievements of his troops during the day, but an assessment of the over-all situation that existed that night would show little reason for complacency. True, Grant's army had been badly mauled and driven back, but it had remained intact, and before the next morning it would be reinforced with three fresh divisions.

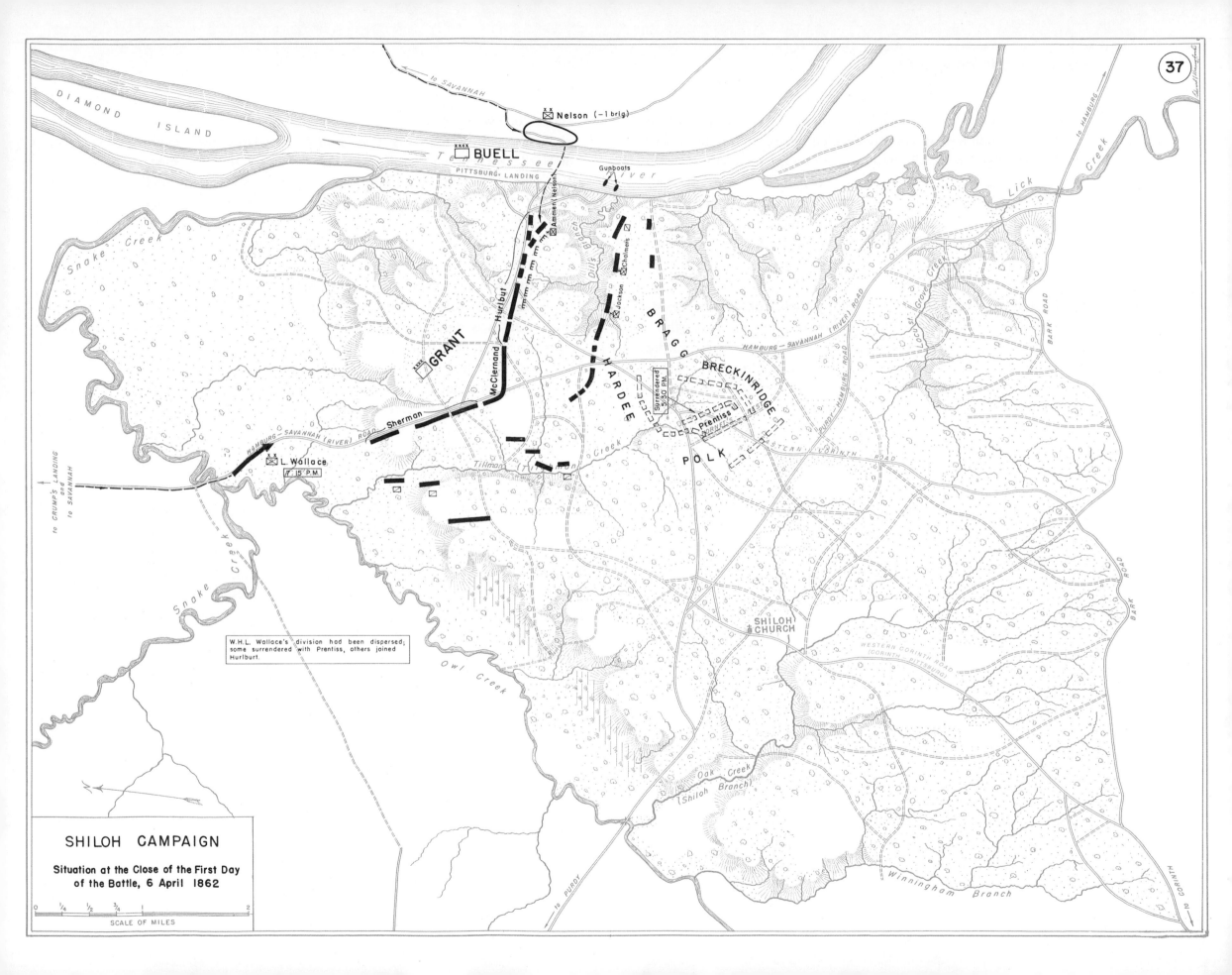

DIAMOND ISLAND

to SAVANNAH

Nelson (-1 brig)

BUELL

PITTSBURG LANDING

Gunboats

Snake Creek

Ammen Nelson

Duis Branch

Chalmers

Jackson

BRAGG

HARDEE

HURLBUT

GRANT

McClernand

BRECKINRIDGE

HAMBURG — SAVANNAH (RIVER) ROAD

PURDY — HAMBURG ROAD

Surrendered 5:30 P.M.

Prentiss

HORNETS

Sherman

HAMBURG — SAVANNAH (RIVER) ROAD

POLK

EASTERN CORINTH ROAD

L. Wallace
7:15 P.M.

to CRUMP'S LANDING
and
to SAVANNAH

Tillman

Tillman Creek

Snake Creek

LOCUST GROVE CREEK

BARK ROAD

Lick Creek

to HAMBURG

W.H.L. Wallace's division had been dispersed;
some surrendered with Prentiss, others joined
Hurlburt.

Owl Creek

SHILOH CHURCH

WESTERN CORINTH ROAD
(CORINTH — PITTSBURG)

Oak Creek
(Shiloh Branch)

BARK ROAD

to PURDY

to CORINTH

Winningham Branch

SHILOH CAMPAIGN

Situation at the Close of the First Day
of the Battle, 6 April 1862

0   1/4   1/2   3/4   1   2
SCALE OF MILES

The Union forces initiated their offensive at daylight on 7 April. Grant and Buell had apparently decided independently to attack, and hence coordination between their two armies could only be effected at the division level. Nelson began the action at about 5:00 A.M. with an advance along the Hamburg-Savannah Road. Before he encountered any serious resistance, he was halted by Buell in order to allow Brig. Gen. Thomas L. Crittenden and Brig. Gen. Alexander M. McCook (the major part of whose division had arrived at dawn) to move into line. The advance was resumed about 9:00 A.M., but by then Confederate resistance had stiffened and Buell's army found itself in a real fight.

On the other flank, Sherman, who had been alerted during the night, began his advance shortly after Nelson moved forward. He soon encountered sharp artillery fire which caused him to halt and await the resumption of Buell's attack. Grant's other division commanders received their attack orders by 8:00 A.M. and moved forward on either side of Sherman. By 10:00 A.M., Union forces were attacking all along the line. The weight of the attack, sparked by the 25,000 fresh troops, was too much for Beauregard's gallant but tired and outnumbered defenders. They were gradually forced back in fighting that was at times as intense as that of the previous day. Shortly after noon, Brig. Gen. Thomas J. Woods' division of Buell's army arrived and joined the fight.

By noon, Beauregard had apparently decided that he must retreat, though not until 2:30 P.M. did he issue the necessary orders. By 4:00 P.M., the Confederates had retreated behind Breckinridge's covering force of 2,000 men and were en route to Corinth. On this day the Confederate army, now reduced to about 20,000, had fought valiantly and stubbornly. As an example of the battle's toll, Brig. Gen. Patrick R. Cleburne's brigade of Hardee's corps entered the battle on 6 April with 2,750 men. It resumed the fight on 7 April with 900 men, and by the end of that day only fifty-eight remained. Similar appalling losses were suffered by some of Grant's units.

Once the Union army reached the line of its original camps, its aggressiveness seemed to dissipate. The troops and their commanders were content to allow the Confederates to escape relatively unmolested. No pursuit was initiated until 8 April, and that effort was handled roughly by Forrest's cavalry, thus discouraging any further attempts. So ended the Battle of Shiloh. Like Bull Run, it had been a clash between two raw armies which were being introduced to their trade. Both sides did extremely well under the circumstances. The total Union loss in killed, wounded, and missing was close to 13,700; the Confederate loss was 10,700.

The day of 7 April also saw another Confederate defeat. The forces left isolated at Island No. 10 (*see map 31*) on the Mississippi by Beauregard succumbed to a siege by Pope's troops —an outcome that Beauregard should have anticipated as inevitable. With the Mississippi now open almost to Memphis, the Union future in the western theater appeared bright. Halleck had a large, battle-seasoned force within twenty miles of Corinth; Beauregard had little strength to oppose a determined Union drive to the south. We shall soon see how Halleck failed to take advantage of this splendid opportunity for a decisive victory.

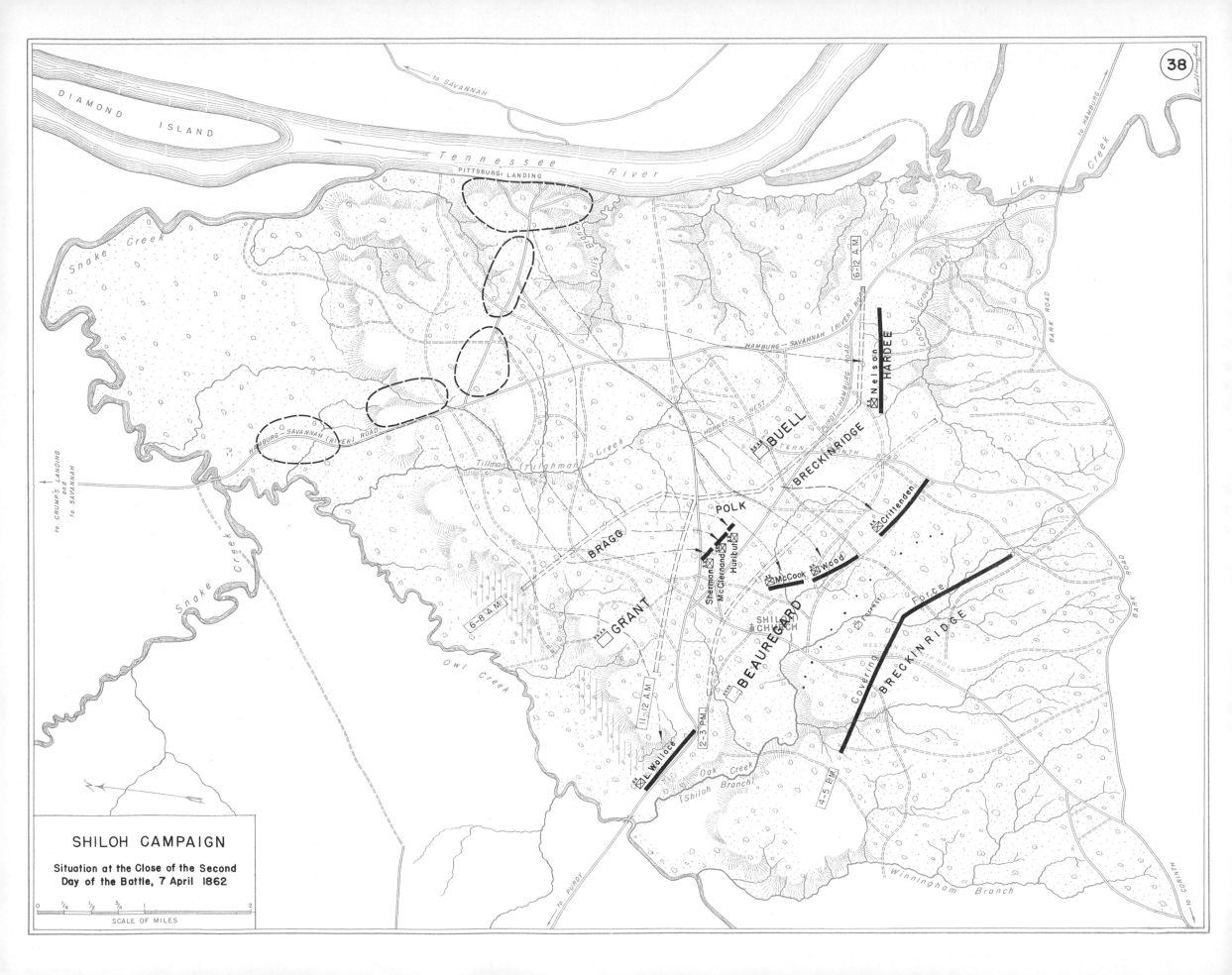

38

DIAMOND ISLAND

Tennessee River

PITTSBURG LANDING

to SAVANNAH

Snake Creek

to GRUMP'S LANDING and to SAVANNAH

Snake Creek

Owl Creek

HAMBURG – SAVANNAH (RIVER) ROAD

6-8 A.M.

GRANT

11-12 A.M.

2-3 P.M.

L. Wallace

Oak Creek

Shiloh Branch

Tillman (Tilghman) Creek

BRAGG

POLK

Sherman
McClernand
Hurlbut

BEAUREGARD

SHILOH CHURCH

McCook
Wood

Force

4-5 P.M.

BEAUREGARD

BRECKINRIDGE

HORNET'S NEST

BUELL

BRECKINRIDGE

Crittenden

Nelson

HARDEE

6-12 A.M.

Lick Creek

to HAMBURG

BARK ROAD

Locust Grove Creek

BARK ROAD

Covering Force

BRECKINRIDGE

WESTERN CORINTH ROAD (CORINTH-PITTSBURG)

Winningham Branch

to CORINTH

to PURDY

SHILOH CAMPAIGN

Situation at the Close of the Second
Day of the Battle, 7 April 1862

0   1/4   1/2   3/4   1   2

SCALE OF MILES

The day after the battle of Bull Run, Maj. Gen. George B. McClellan was summoned to Washington and given command of all forces in the vicinity—forces which were destined to become the Army of the Potomac. McClellan arrived fresh from his victories in West Virginia and enjoyed the complete confidence of the administration and populace. His first tasks were to strengthen the defenses of the capital and to build an army with which to take the offensive. The Union, far from being discouraged over the defeat at Bull Run, was now determined to make a supreme effort to stamp out the rebellion.

McClellan set about the organizing and training of the army with characteristic energy. However, his failure to do anything positive about General Joseph E. Johnston's army at Centreville, thirty miles away, began to create dissatisfaction in government circles. Criticism was accentuated by the abortive and badly managed operation at Ball's Bluff (on the Potomac near Leesburg) in which a small Union force was routed. Nor did the boldness of the Confederates in closing the Potomac to navigation with well-sited artillery improve his position. In November, 1861, Bvt. Lt. Gen. Winfield Scott retired, tired and chagrined at McClellan's undermining efforts. McClellan was then appointed to command all Union land forces. He developed no workable over-all strategy for the prosecution of the war, though he did make an attempt. In his own theater he planned to advance upon Johnston at Centreville as soon as he felt the army was sufficiently prepared. McClellan was a perfectionist, and this preparation was to consume an inordinate amount of time.

The plan to march directly upon Centreville was abandoned, primarily because McClellan, greatly overestimating Johnston's strength, shifted his objective from Johnston's army to the Confederate capital. He proposed to move by water to Urbana, on the Rappahannock, and thence overland to Richmond before Johnston could forestall the movement. For three months this plan was warmly debated. Lincoln favored the direct land ap-

proach and feared for the safety of Washington if the Union army moved away; McClellan argued that road conditions were intolerable, that the capital's defenses were adequate, and that Johnston would of necessity follow him. Finally, in early March, Lincoln approved McClellan's proposal. But on 9 March, Johnston, fearing a Union advance by way of Maryland, withdrew to Culpeper, and McClellan's plan became impracticable. He then proposed to move to Fort Monroe and thence up the Peninsula on Richmond; again Lincoln reluctantly assented.

Before embarking for Fort Monroe, McClellan moved his army to Centreville on a "shakedown" march. There it was discovered how weak Johnston's force and position had really been, and criticism of McClellan mounted. On 11 March, while McClellan was at Centreville, Lincoln relieved him of supreme command, primarily in order to allow him to devote his full attention to the extensive campaign to come. Lincoln assumed over-all direction of the Union armies for the next four months. The two political appointees, Maj. Gen. Nathaniel P. Banks and Maj. Gen. John C. Fremont, the latter recently relieved from western command, were thus McClellan's coequals, and their efforts could be coordinated only at the Washington level. This cumbersome arrangement was to be partly responsible for the subsequent Union failures. On 17 March, McClellan's army began to embark for Fort Monroe. (Note that Maj. Gen. John E. Wool's force at Fort Monroe was not subject to McClellan's command.)

Turning to the Confederate dispositions, it will be noted that Jackson has returned to Winchester, in the Shenandoah Valley, in order to protect that important supply source from Banks. Brig. Gen. Edward Johnson was stationed where he could oppose an advance by Fremont toward Staunton or Tennessee. Maj. Gen. John B. Magruder, Maj. Gen. Theophilus H. Holmes, and General Joseph E. Johnston blocked likely invasion routes to Richmond, while Maj. Gen. Benjamin Huger garrisoned the major base at Norfolk.

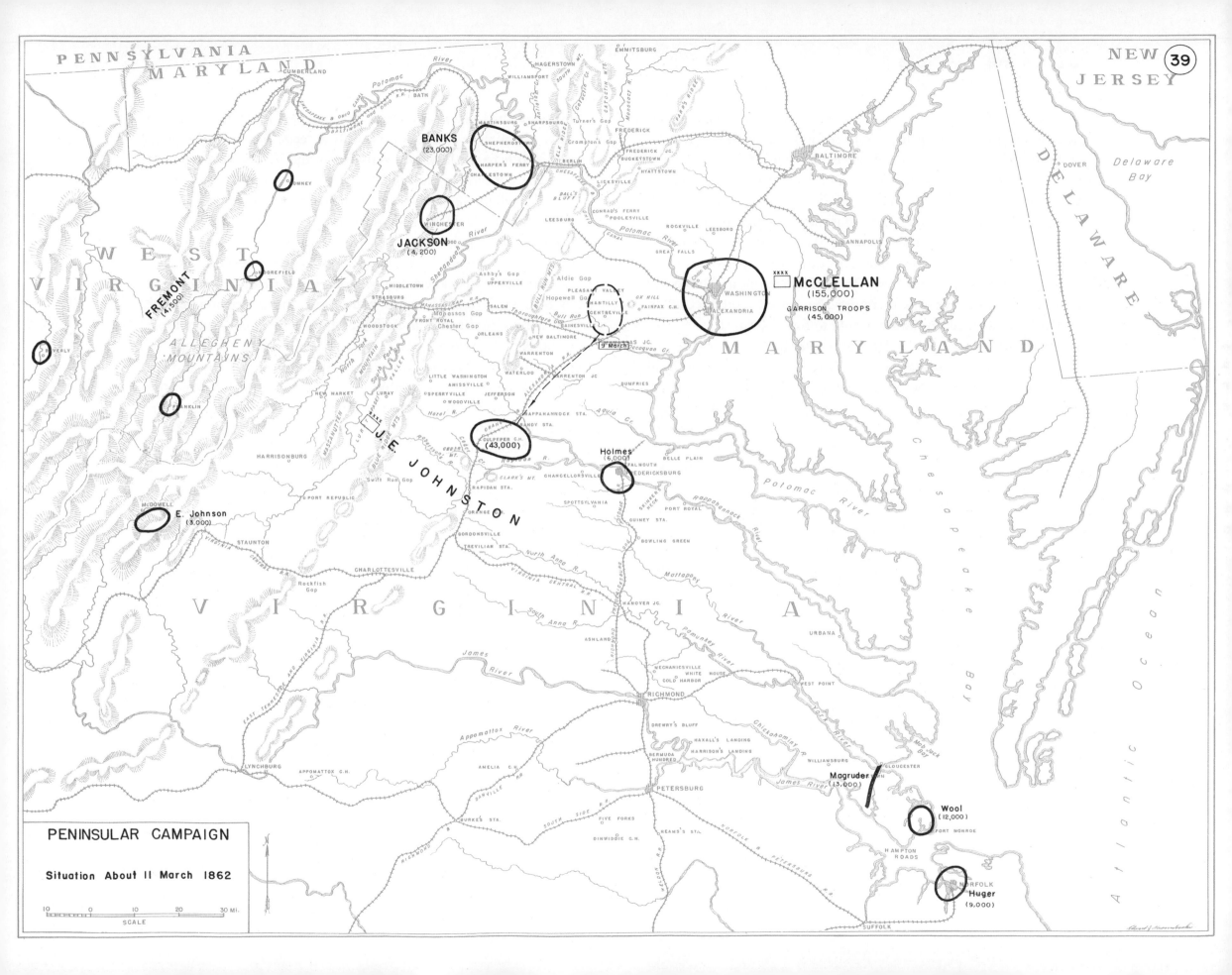

PENINSULAR CAMPAIGN

Situation About 11 March 1862

McClellan himself arrived at Fort Monroe on 2 April and found approximately 50,000 of his troops ready for combat. After consultation with the senior naval officer, he learned that the Navy could not offer more than token support of operations up either the York or the James Rivers. This fact he should, and could, have ascertained before embarkation at Washington. The difficulty stemmed from the presence of the powerful Confederate ironclad *Merrimack* in the James River and the Confederate batteries at the mouth of the York River. The idea of amphibiously enveloping Yorktown was therefore abandoned, and McClellan ordered an advance up the Peninsula to begin 4 April.

His plan envisioned the III Corps pinning the enemy to the Yorktown defenses while the IV Corps enveloped the position and blocked the Confederate retreat at Halfway House. But the plan went awry in execution because of a lack of adequate intelligence. McClellan's maps did not depict properly the course of the Warwick River, nor did he realize that it was a formidable obstacle. He was thus greatly surprised when informed that his corps were stopped by a line of fortifications which, instead of being concentrated in the Yorktown area, ran entirely across the Peninsula. He received this report on 5 April, the same day on which he was informed that Lincoln had canceled the movement of Maj. Gen. Irwin McDowell's corps to Fort Monroe. The President had taken this action because McClellan had failed to leave the number of troops previously agreed upon at Washington, and also because Jackson's activities in the Valley were a matter of some concern in the capital.

McClellan was now faced with his first major combat decision—how to deal with Magruder. He knew that Johnston would surely move reinforcements to the Peninsula. (In fact, the first division was already en route and was to arrive at Yorktown on 10 April.) He also knew that Magruder was greatly outnumbered by his own forces. Magruder had hastily improvised the defense line across the Peninsula. Although this line was extremely weak in places—Magruder did not have troops enough to occupy all of it—he succeeded in bluffing McClellan by constantly shifting the units he did have available and otherwise simulating the presence of a strong force. As a result, McClellan surrendered the initiative to the Confederates and prepared to lay siege to Yorktown. Meanwhile Johnston, after consultation with President Davis, was making haste to mass all possible strength on the Peninsula to oppose the Army of the Potomac. Jackson had already begun his brilliant diversion in the Valley. Magruder's boldness and deceptive measures had succeeded in frustrating McClellan's first move.

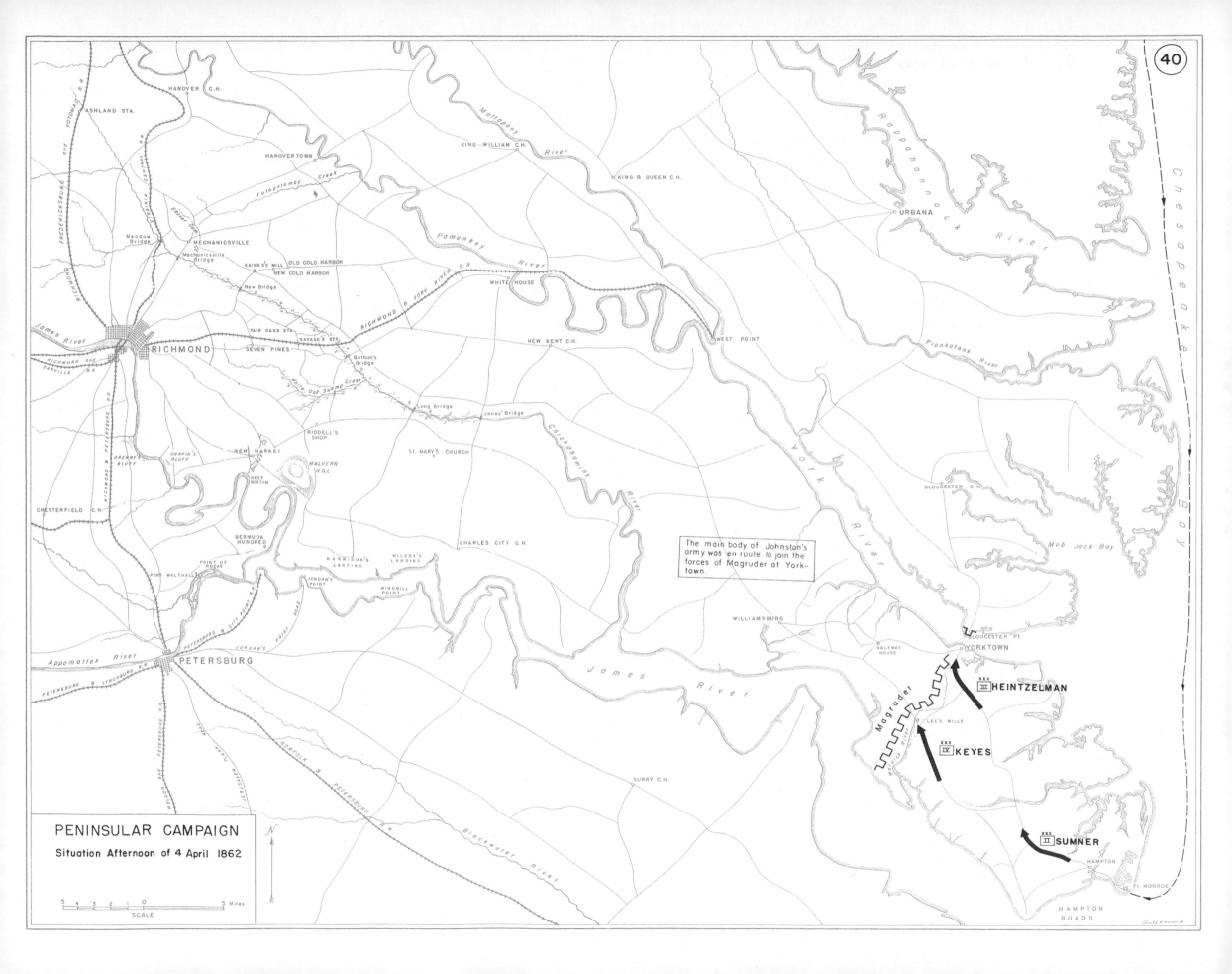

40

The main body of Johnston's
army was en route to join the
forces of Magruder at Yorktown.

GLOUCESTER PT.

YORKTOWN

HALFWAY
HOUSE

Magruder

LEE'S MILLS

XXX
III HEINTZELMAN

XXX
IV KEYES

XXX
II SUMNER

HAMPTON

Ft MONROE

HAMPTON
ROADS

PENINSULAR CAMPAIGN

Situation Afternoon of 4 April 1862

N

5 4 3 2 1 0   5 Miles
SCALE

Settling down in front of the Yorktown line, McClellan spent a month conducting regular siege operations. Having decided on this methodical approach, he completely renounced any attempt to assault Johnston's position. Thus, when on 16 April Brig. Gen. William F. Smith made a reconnaissance in force at Lee's Mills and captured a portion of the Confederate line, McClellan recalled him instead of making an effort to exploit the success. McClellan spent his entire time in preparing to open a major bombardment against Yorktown on 5 May, in demanding reinforcements and more artillery, and in arranging belatedly for transports for an amphibious flanking movement up the York River, once Yorktown fell.

But Johnston had no intention of testing the power of McClellan's heavy siege guns. On the night of 3 May, he began a withdrawal toward Richmond, his rear covered by Stuart's cavalry. The Union forces, under Sumner, took up the pursuit. Stuart was driven in by the Union cavalry, but Union infantry found the Confederate rear guard, under Longstreet, occupying a line of light field works previously constructed by Magruder two miles east of Williamsburg. Maj. Gen. Joseph Hooker attacked immediately. He was repulsed and counterattacked by Longstreet, but held out until Brig. Gen. Philip Kearny, slowed by muddy roads, came up to his relief. D. H. Hill's division came to Longstreet's assistance, and the fighting raged indecisively. In the early afternoon Brig. Gen. Winfield S. Hancock made a wide envelopment of the Confederate left with his brigade and seized two unoccupied redoubts on the flank and rear of Longstreet's position, defeating Hill's effort to drive him out. Longstreet, his escape route thereby endangered, withdrew unmolested under cover of darkness. He had conducted a good defense, gaining the time necessary to extricate the cumbersome Confederate supply trains.

Their movement, as well as that of the troops, had been hampered considerably during the last few days by the heavy rains and the poor—and now extremely muddy—roads.

The Union attack, on the other hand, had been mismanaged. McClellan, instead of riding with his advance guard, had remained at Yorktown to supervise the embarkation of the divisions which were to make the amphibious envelopment up the York River to West Point (*center*). From this place they would strike the flank of Johnston's retreating column. He did not reach the battlefield until late in the day, but reported, "I arrived in time." Sumner, meanwhile, had failed to commit at least half of the Union forces available. Only the three fighting division commanders—Hooker, Kearny, and Hancock—made a creditable showing.

McClellan's conception of the amphibious envelopment was sound, but his delay in requesting the necessary transports resulted in his securing only enough to move little more than one division at a time. Also, Johnston, an enterprising general, had foreseen this movement. When the first Union division (that of Brig. Gen. William B. Franklin, recently transferred to McClellan from McDowell's command) arrived at West Point, it was attacked and defeated by Maj. Gen. Gustavus W. Smith.

McClellan had at last broken through the Yorktown bottleneck and could now maneuver against Richmond. The Confederate withdrawal had left the York River open from its mouth to the head of navigation. Nevertheless, McClellan pursued slowly —in part, because of the heavy rains and muddy country roads. The full impact of his excessive delays was yet to be felt, and for the time being he had regained the initiative; but in this— his second move—McClellan had again been outgeneraled.

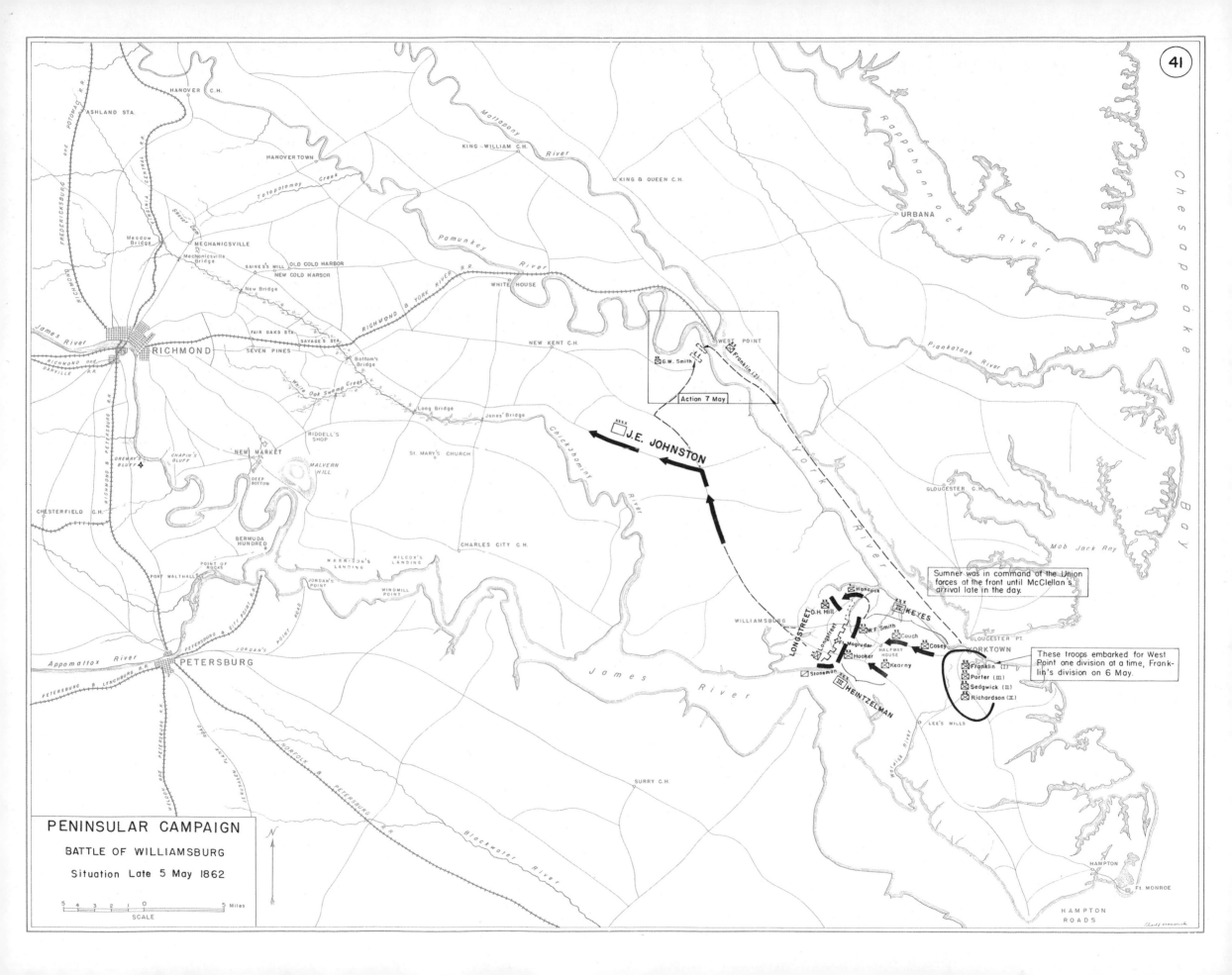

41

Action 7 May

G.W. Smith

Franklin (I)

WEST POINT

XXXX
J.E. JOHNSTON

Sumner was in command of the Union forces at the front until McClellan's arrival late in the day.

These troops embarked for West Point one division at a time, Franklin's division on 6 May.

Hancock

D.H. HILL

KEYES

Longstreet

W.F. Smith

Couch

Casey

LONGSTREET

Ft. Magruder

HALFWAY HOUSE

GLOUCESTER PT.

YORKTOWN

Hooker

Kearny

Stoneman

HEINTZELMAN

Franklin (I)

Porter (III)

Sedgwick (II)

Richardson (II)

WILLIAMSBURG

LEE'S MILLS

PENINSULAR CAMPAIGN

BATTLE OF WILLIAMSBURG

Situation Late 5 May 1862

5 4 3 2 1 0   5 Miles

SCALE

N

HAMPTON ROADS

FT. MONROE

HAMPTON

After the rebuff at Williamsburg, the Union forces advanced slowly up the Peninsula, taking fifteen days to reach a position astride the Chickahominy River. McClellan moved part of his army by water to White House (where he established his headquarters and base), but the greater part moved overland.

Meanwhile, Johnston prepared his defenses at Richmond, and the Confederate high command sought to reinforce him. After the battle at Williamsburg, Norfolk became isolated, so Huger was ordered to evacuate his forces from the city and join Johnston at Richmond. The evacuation of Norfolk had an important impact on the naval situation. It opened the James River to Union control as far upstream as Drewry's Bluff, only seven miles south of Richmond; and the *Merrimack,* now without a port and of too deep draft to move far up the James, had to be destroyed. In an attempt to exploit this advantage, the Union navy tried to reduce the Confederate forts at Drewry's Bluff on 15 May, but was unsuccessful. Thus the Confederates retained possession of the river approach to Richmond. This control would not be seriously contested for the ensuing three years.

It is important to relate events in the Valley to McClellan's operations against Richmond, for on several occasions they reacted to McClellan's distinct disadvantage. We have already seen that Jackson's activity in the Valley was partly instrumental in influencing Lincoln to retain McDowell's corps near Washington instead of sending it to join McClellan as had been planned.

But even at Washington or Fredericksburg, McDowell posed a threat to Johnston at Richmond, for, if McDowell should move south to join McClellan before Richmond, Johnston would be confronted with overwhelming numbers. This danger was perfectly clear to Robert E. Lee, now a full general and Davis' military advisor, who conceived Jackson's diversionary operations in the Valley specifically to thwart a juncture of the two Union forces. Actually, it was Lincoln's plan to send McDowell, reinforced by Brig. Gen. James Shields' division of Banks' command, south on 26 May to join McClellan.

On 23 May, Jackson attacked and practically wiped out Banks' flank guard at Front Royal. Banks retreated through Winchester with Jackson in pursuit. This turn of events had its effects in Washington. McDowell's orders to move south on 26 May to join McClellan were cancelled; instead, he was directed to dispatch the bulk of his force to Front Royal to aid Banks and Fremont in suppressing Jackson. For the moment, Johnston could make his plans with the assurance that his opponent would not be reinforced.

McClellan, though outnumbering Johnston five to three, rested before Richmond, again prepared to surrender the initiative to his opponent. Apparently he had accepted the estimates of his intelligence service portraying Johnston's strength as double his own. Meanwhile, existing climatic conditions were having a serious and detrimental influence on the health of his troops.

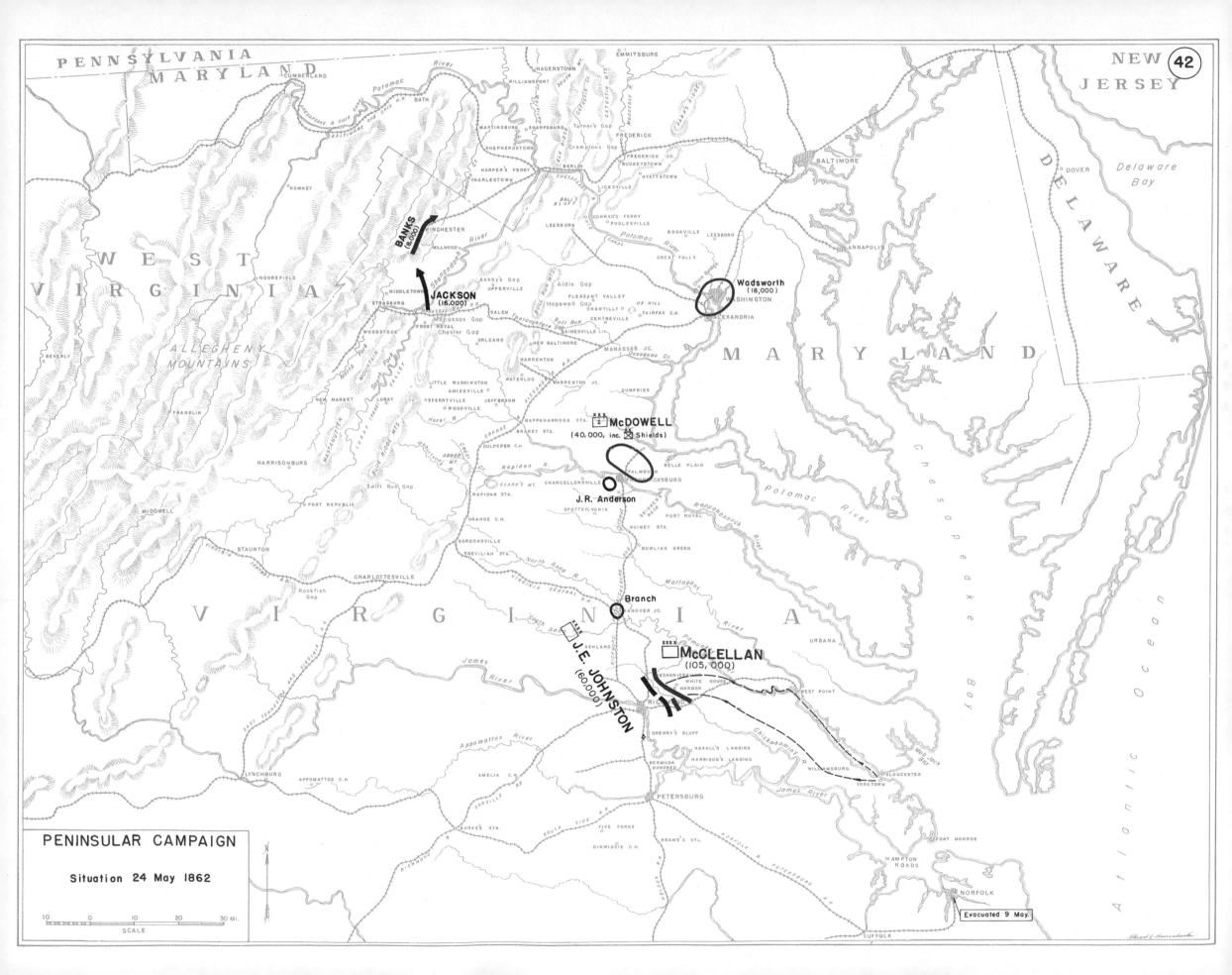

PENINSULAR CAMPAIGN

Situation 24 May 1862

PENNSYLVANIA
MARYLAND
WEST VIRGINIA
VIRGINIA
MARYLAND
DELAWARE
NEW JERSEY

BANKS (8,000)

JACKSON (16,000)

Wadsworth (18,000)
WASHINGTON

McDOWELL
(40,000, inc. Shields)

J.R. Anderson

Branch

J.E. JOHNSTON
(60,000)

McCLELLAN
(105,000)

Delaware Bay

Chesapeake Bay

Atlantic Ocean

Evacuated 9 May.

10   0   10   20   30 Mi.
SCALE

When McClellan finally arrived at the Chickahominy, he directed the III and IV Corps to seize bridgeheads on the south side of the river (*sketch* a). He did so believing that operations against Richmond were feasible only from the south. It was his intention to move the entire army across when McDowell arrived. For the time being, he detained the remainder of his army on the north bank to protect the communications to the base at White House. In this position the Army of the Potomac remained from 20 May until 31 May, when the isolated III and IV Corps were attacked by Johnston in the Battle of Fair Oaks (known also as the Battle of Seven Pines).

On 18 May, McClellan had been informed that he could expect McDowell's advance and that he should extend his line north of Richmond preparatory to a juncture with McDowell. McClellan later referred to this directive in defending his unusual dispositions and the selection of White House as a base. He claimed that he had wished to keep his army concentrated and to base it on the James River, but that McDowell's projected arrival had given him no choice. Whatever the merits of his contentions, McClellan had been apprised on 24 May that McDowell was being sent to the Valley, and no logical reason can be found for maintaining the army in its vulnerable position. He did, however, construct several bridges across the river to facilitate communications.

Apprehensive of McDowell's arrival, Johnston planned to attack the Union forces north of the river on 29 May. But when he was informed (on 28 May) that McDowell was en route to the Valley, he decided to direct his attack against Maj. Gen. Erasmus D. Keyes' exposed corps on 31 May. His attack plan was a good one. Maj. Gen. Ambrose P. Hill and Magruder were to contain Union forces north of the river. Longstreet, commanding the main attack, was to strike Keyes from three directions: his own division from the northwest along the Nine Mile Road;

Huger from the southwest along the Charles City Road; and D. H. Hill directly from the west along the Williamsburg Road. Brig. Gen. William H. C. Whiting (commanding G. W. Smith's division) was to take position at Old Tavern to aid Longstreet or to repulse any Union attack from the north.

A glance at the sketch will show that the execution of the plan bore little resemblance to its original conception. Longstreet took the wrong road and moved south where he confused and delayed the advance of D. H. Hill and Huger to the extent that no attack could be launched until 1:00 P.M. Then D. H. Hill attacked alone, but the Union forces had been partially alerted and withstood the assault. When reinforced by Longstreet, Hill finally drove Keyes and Kearny back (*sketch* b). While moving to Hill's assistance, Whiting was struck unexpectedly in flank. This blow was delivered by Brig. Gen. John Sedgwick's division of the II Corps, sent across the river by Brig. Gen. Edwin V. Sumner on his own initiative, just in time to prevent the rout of Keyes' IV Corps. Darkness ended the battle, which had been fought in violent weather and seas of mud.

The Confederates had bungled an excellent opportunity to gain an important victory and, Johnston having been wounded, had lost their commander. Longstreet must bear the major responsibility for this failure: he had disrupted rather than coordinated the attack, had engaged his forces piecemeal, and had employed less than half of the available forces.

G. W. Smith assumed command and directed Longstreet to attack on the next day. The attack was feeble and accomplished nothing. That day (1 June) Robert E. Lee arrived to take command. McClellan also arrived on the battlefield on 1 June, having been ill the previous day. Except for Sumner's exemplary individual action, the Union forces north of the river had remained completely inactive.

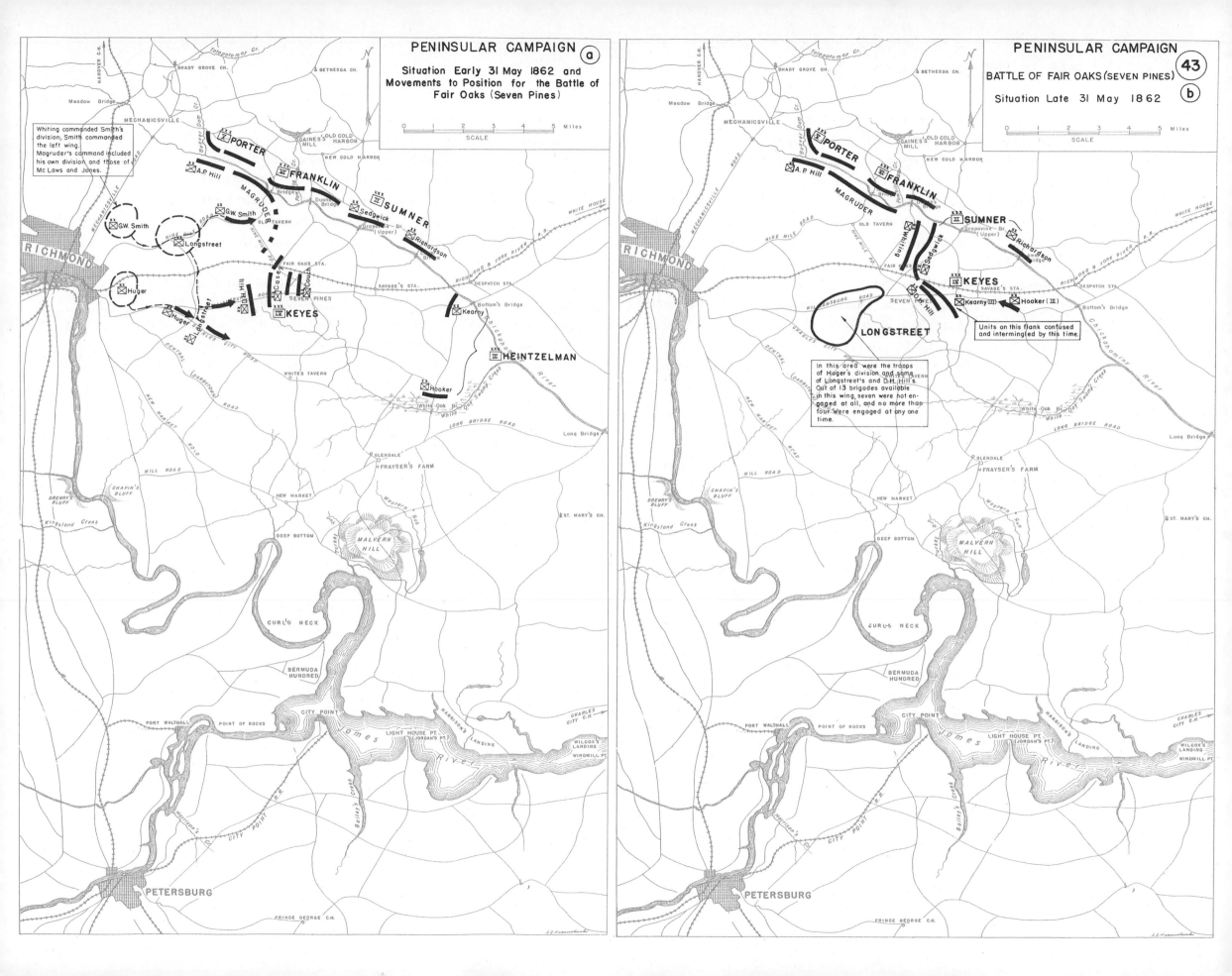

PENINSULAR CAMPAIGN (a)

Situation Early 31 May 1862 and
Movements to Position for the Battle of
Fair Oaks (Seven Pines)

SCALE
0   1   2   3   4   5 Miles

Whiting commanded Smith's
division, Smith commanded
the left wing.
Magruder's command included
his own division and those of
Mc Laws and Jones.

RICHMOND

PORTER
A.P. Hill
FRANKLIN
MAGRUDER
Sedgwick
SUMNER
Richardson
G.W. Smith
Longstreet
Huger
D.H. Hill
Casey
Couch
Huger
Longstreet
KEYES
SEVEN PINES
FAIR OAKS STA.
Kearny
HEINTZELMAN
Hooker

PETERSBURG

PENINSULAR CAMPAIGN (43)

BATTLE OF FAIR OAKS (SEVEN PINES) (b)

Situation Late 31 May 1862

SCALE
0   1   2   3   4   5 Miles

RICHMOND

PORTER
A.P. Hill
FRANKLIN
MAGRUDER
Whiting
SUMNER
Sedgwick
Richardson
KEYES
Fair Oaks
Seven Pines
D.H. Hill
Kearny
Hooker
LONGSTREET

Units on this flank confused
and intermingled by this time.

In this area were the troops
of Huger's division and some
of Longstreet's and D.H. Hill's.
Out of 13 brigades available
in this wing, seven were not engaged at all, and no more than
four were engaged at any one
time.

PETERSBURG

After the Battle of Fair Oaks, McClellan gradually shifted his forces to the south side of the Chickahominy until only Brig. Gen. Fitz-John Porter's V Corps remained on the north side to protect the communications to the White House base. For several weeks McClellan displayed no intention to undertake serious offensive operations. True, the weather was bad and rain fell intermittently until 20 June, but Johnston had found it possible to launch his attack at Fair Oaks under similar conditions even though they had been accentuated by the flooded Chickahominy, swampy areas, and muddy roads. The Union commander busied himself in emplacing siege artillery, in shifting troops, and in local attacks to force Lee back into the Richmond entrenchments—all indications that he had in mind the capture of Richmond through siege operations. As at Yorktown, he seemed to recoil from the thought of a full and determined offensive. Nor should the question of relative strengths have caused him concern, for though McDowell's main force had for a third time been restrained from movement to Richmond—this time by Jackson's victory at Port Republic on 8 June—two of McDowell's divisions and sufficient additional replacements had joined McClellan at Richmond to raise his strength almost to that which he possessed when he had first left Washington. Yet, McClellan, estimating Lee's force to be half again that of his own, abstained from seizing the initiative.

The Confederates did not lack for vigorous leadership. While his men were busy strengthening the fortifications of Richmond, Lee made plans and preparations for an offensive. To engage the imposing Union array with a reasonable chance of success, Lee needed reinforcements. His thoughts turned to the possibility of bringing Jackson down from the Valley to strike Porter on the north bank while the remainder of his army dealt with McClellan's forces on the south. On 12 June, he dispatched Stuart to gain information about the Union north flank. Stuart converted this reconnaissance into a raid encircling the Union army—the first of many cavalry raids made by both sides during the war, most of which were of dubious over-all value. He did bring Lee convincing information that the Union position could be turned on the north, but he also probably alerted McClellan, for on 18 June the latter began loading transports and advised the navy to prepare to move the base to the James River.

After consultation with President Davis and Longstreet, Lee now decided to move the bulk of his army across the Chickahominy to attack the Union north flank, leaving only Huger and Magruder to hold the line of entrenchments against McClellan's vastly superior strength. (Jackson was called south and reached Ashland Station on 25 June.) The venture was bold and risky indeed, but the rewards of success promised to be equally great. Lee needed a decisive victory. His lesser forces could not withstand a battle of attrition; nor could he remain static, for his position was becoming more and more untenable. On the other hand, the danger to Huger and Magruder was not as great as it appeared at first glance, for McClellan had repeatedly displayed the characteristics of slowness and caution.

Despite Jackson's efforts to cover his movement, both Washington and McClellan concluded on 24 June that he was en route to attack Porter. McClellan had planned a local attack for the 25th near Fair Oaks Station; now, knowing Jackson's likely intentions, he was faced with a new and difficult decision: should he reinforce Porter, or should he expand the projected local attack into a full assault on Richmond? He postponed the decision for a day; then the problem became academic, for Lee had opened the Battle of Mechanicsville.

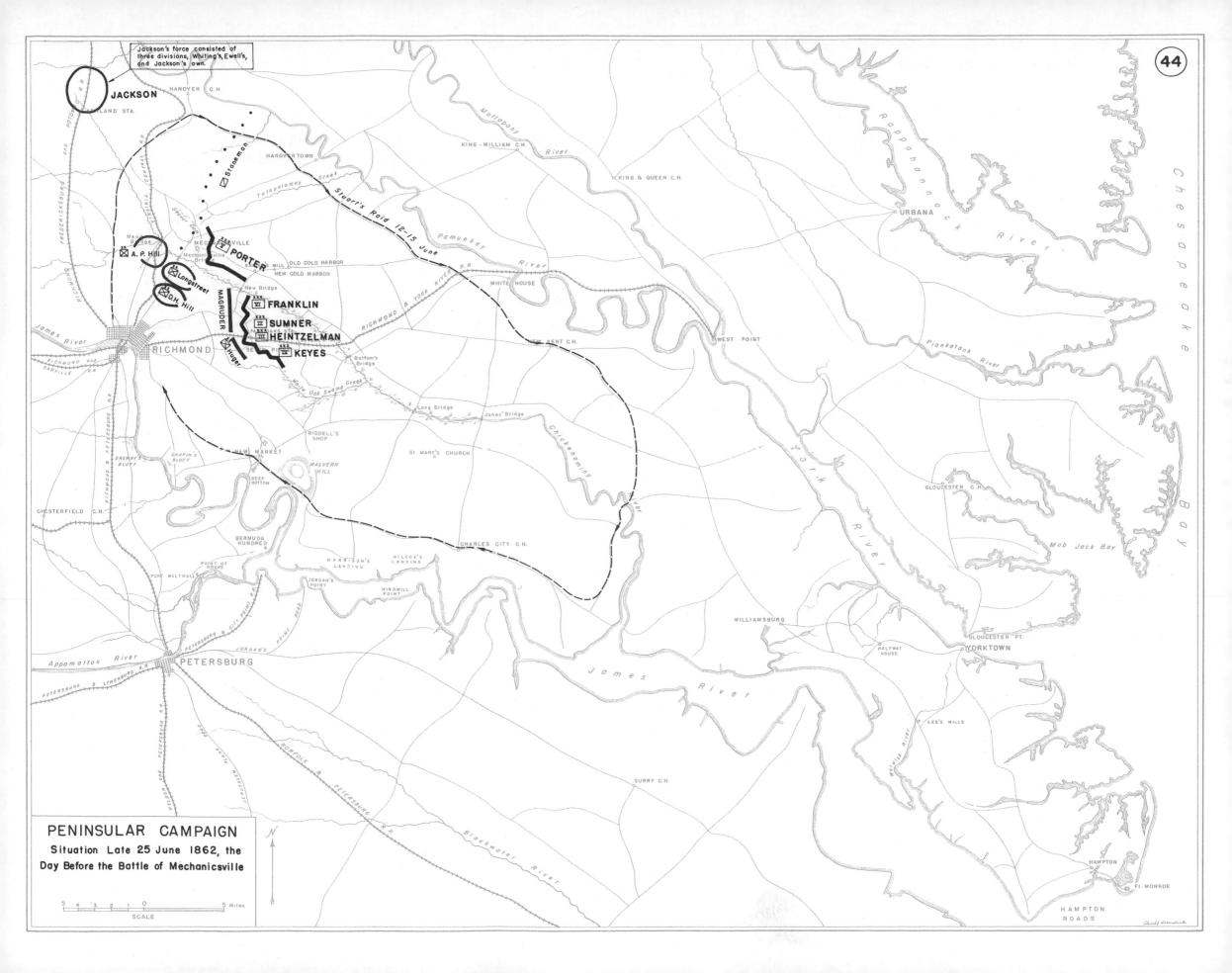

Jackson's force consisted of three divisions, Whiting's, Ewell's, and Jackson's own.

JACKSON

HANOVER C.H.

Stoneman

HANOVER TOWN

KING WILLIAM C.H.   River

KING & QUEEN C.H.

URBANA

Stuart's Raid 12-15 June

Pamunkey   River

PORTER

A. P. Hill

Longstreet

D.H. Hill

FRANKLIN
VI

SUMNER
II

HEINTZELMAN
III

KEYES
IV

MAGRUDER

Huger

RICHMOND

WHITE HOUSE

WEST POINT

Piankatank   River

NEW KENT C.H.

Bottom's Bridge

Long Bridge   Jones' Bridge

RIDDELL'S SHOP

St. Mary's Church

Chickahominy

GLOUCESTER C.H.

NEW MARKET

MALVERN HILL

CHAPIN'S BLUFF

DEEP BOTTOM

CHESTERFIELD C.H.

CHARLES CITY C.H.

Mob Jack Bay

BERMUDA HUNDRED

HARRISON'S LANDING   WILCOX'S LANDING

POINT OF ROCKS

PORT WALTHALL

JORDAN'S POINT

WINDMILL POINT

WILLIAMSBURG

GLOUCESTER PT.

YORKTOWN

Appomattox   River

PETERSBURG

HALFWAY HOUSE

James   River

SURRY C.H.

Blackwater   River

HAMPTON

FT. MONROE

HAMPTON ROADS

PENINSULAR CAMPAIGN

Situation Late 25 June 1862, the
Day Before the Battle of Mechanicsville

N

5 4 3 2 1 0   5 Miles
SCALE

Lee's dispositions for the Battle of Mechanicsville (*sketch* a) present a good illustration of the basic military precepts of concentration of combat power (or mass) and economy of force. On the north, where he expected a decision, he assembled 65,500 troops to oppose Porter's 30,000; only 25,000 were left before Richmond to contain the remainder of the Union army—60,000. His plan called for Jackson to attack Porter's north flank early on 26 June. Upon hearing Jackson's guns, A. P. Hill was to advance from Meadow Bridge (*top left*), clear Union pickets from Mechanicsville, and then move to Beaver Dam Creek, behind which lay the Union entrenchments. D. H. Hill and Longstreet were then to pass through Mechanicsville—the former to support Jackson, the latter to support A. P. Hill. Meanwhile, Magruder and Huger were to demonstrate in order to deceive the Union forces on their front. It was not anticipated that the Union entrenchments would be assaulted; rather, it was expected that Jackson's enveloping attack would force Porter to abandon them.

As the well-conceived Confederate plan at Fair Oaks went awry in its execution, so did Lee's fine concept at Mechanicsville. Instead of arriving and attacking early in the morning, Jackson did not reach Totopotomoy Creek until 5:00 P.M., and then he went into bivouac. Meanwhile, A. P. Hill, despairing of Jackson's arrival, advanced at 3:00 P.M. without orders and, supported by one of D. H. Hill's brigades, assaulted Porter's entrenched position at the creek. The result was a bloody repulse of the Confederates. To the south, Magruder and Huger achieved great success in accomplishing their mission. Energetically maneuvering and firing as if they had 50,000 troops, they convinced McClellan—though not Hooker or Kearny—that a Union assault there could not succeed.

There appears to be no valid explanation for Jackson's derelic-tion, which frustrated Lee's entire plan. This was the first of four occasions within the next seven days when Jackson would fail to display initiative, resourcefulness, or dependability—the very qualities that were later to raise him to the stature of one of the foremost military leaders.

Porter had gained a victory on the 26th; but Lee, with greatly superior strength in the north, was sure to attack again the next day. That night McClellan pondered over a course of action. His subordinates urged an attack on Magruder—but in vain, for McClellan was still obsessed with the idea that an overwhelming Confederate army confronted him. He finally decided to change his base to the James River, but the only order he issued that night was for Porter to withdraw behind Powhite Creek and to send his trains and heavy artillery south of the Chickahominy.

Porter began his withdrawal before dawn on the 27th and took up the position shown (*sketch* b). Lee again planned an envelopment of Porter's right. By 2:00 P.M., A. P. Hill was attacking vigorously. Jackson, preceded by D. H. Hill, worked his way around toward Porter's right; but again he was slow, took the wrong road, and had to backtrack. It was not until about 4:30 P.M., after urgent messages from Lee, that he finally attacked with his three divisions. Longstreet joined the assault about 4:00 P.M. After resisting repeated assaults, Porter's line broke about dark. Covered by his excellent artillery and by two brigades from Sumner's corps, he crossed the Chickahominy about 4:00 A.M., 28 June, destroying the bridges behind him.

Gaines's Mill was a victory for Lee, though not a decisive one. Jackson's slowness had been a major factor; but Lee was not without fault, for he had failed to coordinate effectively the activities of his divisions. On the Union side, Porter had fought splendidly and almost unassisted for two days, while McClellan had held the remainder of the army inactive.

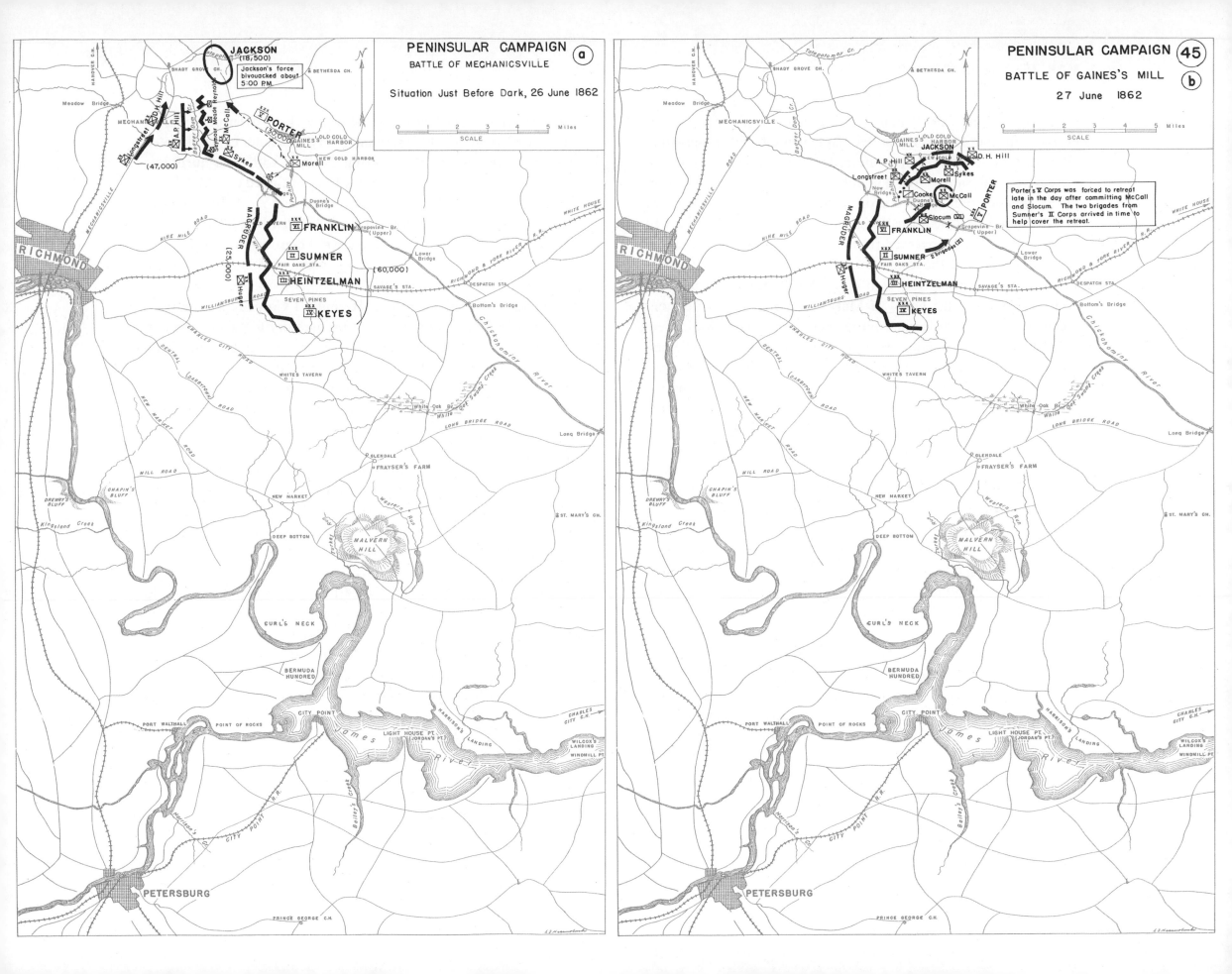

PENINSULAR CAMPAIGN (a)

BATTLE OF MECHANICSVILLE

Situation Just Before Dark, 26 June 1862

SCALE
0   1   2   3   4   5 Miles

JACKSON (18,500)

Jackson's force bivouacked about 5:00 PM

XXX PORTER (30,000)

Longstreet A.P. Hill (47,000)

Seymour Meade Reynolds McCall

Sykes

Morell

XXX FRANKLIN

XXX SUMNER

XXX HEINTZELMAN

XXX KEYES

MAGRUDER (25,000)

Huger

(60,000)

RICHMOND

PETERSBURG

PENINSULAR CAMPAIGN (45) (b)

BATTLE OF GAINES'S MILL

27 June 1862

SCALE
0   1   2   3   4   5 Miles

JACKSON

A.P. Hill

D.H. Hill

Longstreet

Morell

Sykes

Cooke

McCall

Slocum

XXX PORTER

Porter's V Corps was forced to retreat late in the day after committing McCall and Slocum. The two brigades from Sumner's II Corps arrived in time to help cover the retreat.

XXX FRANKLIN

XXX SUMNER
2 brigades

XXX HEINTZELMAN

XXX KEYES

MAGRUDER

Huger

RICHMOND

PETERSBURG

Late on 27 June, McClellan directed that the planned change of base to the James River be implemented. Then—possibly prompted by a secret panic—he ordered his entire army into a retreat to that same river (*sketch* a). It is indeed difficult to justify this decision. Only one of his five corps had been engaged in battle, and it had acquitted itself extremely well. Had he decided to stand and fight, supported from his safe base on the James, he would have placed the Confederates in a difficult position. Lee would have found himself with major Union forces to his front and rear, because the corps of McDowell, Banks, and Fremont meanwhile had been formed into a new army under Maj. Gen. John Pope, who was under orders to move south to aid McClellan. All of this McClellan knew, but the excess caution that characterized his actions during the two days of the Gaines's Mill battle, and before, persisted.

Keyes was directed to take up a position west of Glendale to protect the withdrawal. Porter's tired command was ordered to Malvern Hill to secure that key position, and the wagon trains were started south to the James. McClellan himself then rode south without designating a second in command or specifying corps routes of withdrawal. Three battles were to be fought in the next four days without benefit of the army commander's presence or direction.

Lee spent 28 June trying to ascertain McClellan's intentions. Stuart's cavalry, his best source of information, had been sent east and south to reconnoiter, but again Stuart resorted to raiding and was of little assistance for the next three days. Maj. Gen. Richard S. Ewell had been sent down the Chickahominy to watch for Union attempts to cross that river. Lee's problem was a perplexing one. Before he moved the bulk of his force from north of the Chickahominy, it was necessary to know the direction of McClellan's retreat. If McClellan moved directly south, Lee could cross the river and give chase. If he made this crossing and found

that McClellan had moved southeast to Fort Monroe, crossing the Chickahominy downstream, then he would be confronted with the arduous task of recrossing the river, with consequent loss of time in the pursuit. Late that day Lee concluded that McClellan had moved south. He ordered Longstreet and A. P. Hill to move to strike the Union columns in flank (*sketch* b) and Jackson to press directly against the Union rear. Magruder was ordered to move east along the Williamsburg Road, and Huger southeast along the Charles City Road.

Meanwhile, the Union II, III, and VI Corps had withdrawn to Savage's Station (*upper right*) preparatory to passing the narrow defiles of White Oak Swamp. On the morning of the 29th, Magruder ran into the Union forces at the station, and his advance was checked. He was slow in organizing an attack, but in mid-afternoon he launched an assault against Sumner and Smith. Magruder expected to be assisted by Jackson at any moment, but for the third time in the campaign Jackson failed, spending the entire day of the 29th resting his command and rebuilding Grapevine Bridge, though a suitable ford was available nearby. He finally crossed at 2:30 A.M., 30 June. Thus, Magruder's assaults were repulsed, and the rearmost Union corps managed to extricate themselves from a dangerous position, due principally to Jackson's procrastination.

Two incidents are indicative of the lack of higher direction in the Union army. While Sumner was engaged at Savage's Station, Maj. Gen. Samuel P. Heintzelman decided that his corps was not needed and, without authority, withdrew to the south. About the same time, Brig. Gen. Henry P. Slocum withdrew his division to the south without the knowledge or permission of Franklin, his corps commander. Slocum had met McClellan earlier in the day, and, pleading that his division had suffered covering Porter's withdrawal from Gaines's Mill, had received McClellan's permission to withdraw.

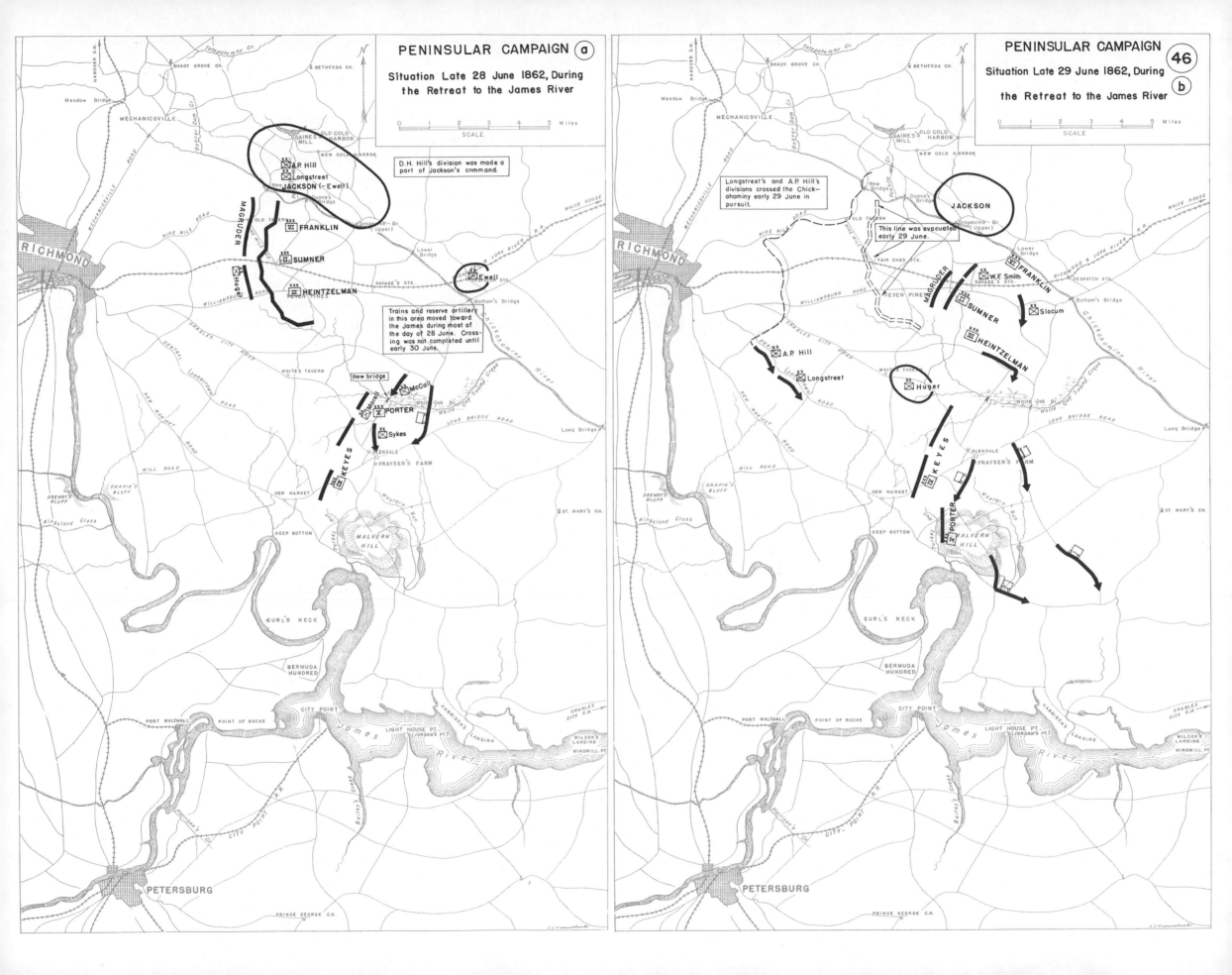

PENINSULAR CAMPAIGN (a)

Situation Late 28 June 1862, During the Retreat to the James River

SCALE
0 1 2 3 4 5 Miles

D.H. Hill's division was made a part of Jackson's command.

Trains and reserve artillery in this area moved toward the James during most of the day of 28 June. Crossing was not completed until early 30 June.

PENINSULAR CAMPAIGN 46

Situation Late 29 June 1862, During the Retreat to the James River (b)

SCALE
0 1 2 3 4 5 Miles

Longstreet's and A.P. Hill's divisions crossed the Chickahominy early 29 June in pursuit.

This line was evacuated early 29 June.

During the night following its engagement at Savage's Station, the Union rear guard withdrew southward. By noon of the next day, McClellan's trains, reserve artillery, and rear guard had cleared White Oak Swamp Creek (*sketch* a). However, because of poor reconnaissance, the trains had not made use of all available roads, and a bottleneck developed at Glendale. Thus, the troops again had to take up a position to protect the withdrawal.

Lee's divisions, less Holmes, were converging on the Union position. Holmes, recently arrived from south of the James, was ordered to seize Malvern Hill, or at least to harass the movement of the trains across it. Lee expected to employ his divisions in one concentrated effort to destroy the Union army, but such was not to be the case. Huger's timidity, Magruder's vacillation, and Jackson's lethargy—plus poor staff work and the difficulties of concentrating forces directly on the field of battle—combined to thwart his intentions. Huger, slowed by obstructions placed by Union troops along the Charles City Road, made no attempt to move by other roads and failed to participate in the battle. Magruder, undecided whether to support Holmes or Longstreet (Lee had specified the former), marched and countermarched without actually supporting either. Jackson, again dawdling, spent the entire day north of the creek, making feeble efforts to cross and attack Franklin.

As a result, only A. P. Hill and Longstreet attacked in the Battle of Frayser's Farm (and Longstreet did not assault with concentrated force, but by brigade). They succeeded in forcing back Brig. Gen. George A. McCall's division, but reinforcements soon sealed off the penetration. Fighting lasted into the night, without any advantage to the Confederates. That night the last three Union corps moved unmolested into the position on Malvern Hill that had been selected and occupied by Porter (*sketch* b).

Lee was to have one more opportunity to destroy McClellan's army, but this time the prevailing circumstances were not to be as favorable as they had been on previous occasions. The Confederate troops had been attacking and marching for five days and had lost heavily in the process, while the Union position on Malvern Hill that confronted them was the best McClellan had yet occupied. The hill offered good observation, fine artillery positions, and excellent fields of fire across an open space to the north. Beyond this space the terrain was swampy and thickly wooded. Instead of outflanking the position, Lee attacked it directly, expecting his artillery to enfilade that of McClellan and clear the way for an infantry assault. But the Union artillery proved to be superior and took a heavy toll of the Confederate guns. Lee then canceled the attack. Late in the afternoon he observed Union troop movements and, believing them to indicate a withdrawal, he again ordered an assault. It was badly mismanaged and resulted in a piecemeal attack, first by D. H. Hill, then by Jackson, and finally by Huger. A. P. Hill and Longstreet never entered the fray. The Union forces, under Porter (McClellan was at Harrison's Landing), had little difficulty in repulsing the assaults. On the following day they withdrew to the position at the landing. Lee decided not to attack and moved his army back to Richmond.

In the campaign, Lee had preserved Richmond and had put his opponent to flight. But the Union army, though somewhat demoralized, remained strong. Under a more energetic and confident commander, it could have again advanced on Richmond. Instead, it remained at Harrison's Landing until August, when it was recalled to the Washington area.

In the series of battles from Mechanicsville to Malvern Hill—known as the Seven Days' Battles—the Confederate total losses were about 20,000; the Union, about 16,000.

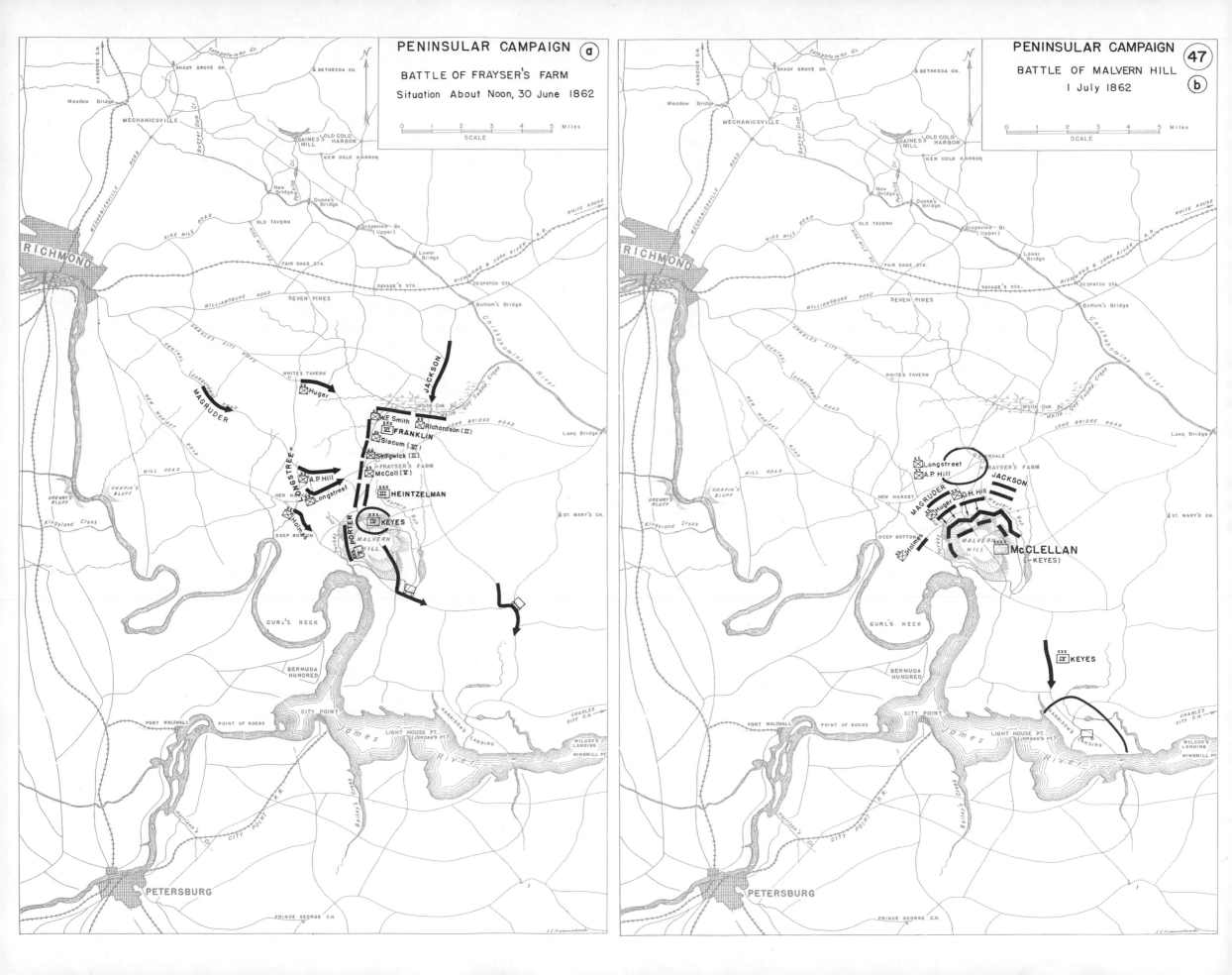

Map (a) — Battle of Frayser's Farm

RICHMOND

MECHANICSVILLE

HANOVER C.H.
SHADY GROVE CH.
BETHESDA CH.
Totopotomoy Cr.
Meadow Bridge
GAINES'S MILL
OLD COLD HARBOR
NEW COLD HARBOR
New Bridge
Duane's Bridge
Grapevine Br. (Upper)
Lower Bridge
WHITE HOUSE
OLD TAVERN
NINE MILE ROAD
FAIR OAKS STA.
RICHMOND & YORK RIVER R.R.
SAVAGE'S STA.
DESPATCH STA.
WILLIAMSBURG ROAD
SEVEN PINES
Bottom's Bridge
Chickahominy River

JACKSON
MAGRUDER
Huger
WHITES TAVERN
White Oak Br.
White Oak Swamp Creek
W.F. Smith
Richardson (II)
FRANKLIN (VI)
Slocum (VI)
Sedgwick (II)
FRAYSER'S FARM
McCall (V)
HEINTZELMAN (III)
LONGSTREET
A.P. Hill
Longstreet
Long Bridge
LONG BRIDGE ROAD
Western Run
KEYES (IV)
Holmes
PORTER
MALVERN HILL
DEEP BOTTOM
ST. MARY'S CH.

CHAPIN'S BLUFF
DREWRY'S BLUFF
Kingsland Creek
NEW MARKET
MILL ROAD
CENTRAL (DARBYTOWN) ROAD
CHARLES CITY ROAD

CURL'S NECK
BERMUDA HUNDRED

James River
PORT WALTHALL
POINT OF ROCKS
CITY POINT
LIGHT HOUSE PT.
JORDAN'S PT.
HARRISON'S LANDING
WILCOX'S LANDING
WINDMILL PT.
CHARLES CITY C.H.
Bailey's Creek
CITY POINT R.R.

PETERSBURG
PRINCE GEORGE C.H.

Map (b) — Battle of Malvern Hill

RICHMOND

MECHANICSVILLE

HANOVER C.H.
SHADY GROVE CH.
BETHESDA CH.
Totopotomoy Cr.
Meadow Bridge
GAINES'S MILL
OLD COLD HARBOR
NEW COLD HARBOR
New Bridge
Duane's Bridge
Grapevine Br. (Upper)
Lower Bridge
WHITE HOUSE
OLD TAVERN
NINE MILE ROAD
FAIR OAKS STA.
RICHMOND & YORK RIVER R.R.
SAVAGE'S STA.
DESPATCH STA.
WILLIAMSBURG ROAD
SEVEN PINES
Bottom's Bridge
Chickahominy River

WHITES TAVERN
White Oak Br.
White Oak Swamp Creek
GLENDALE
FRAYSER'S FARM
Longstreet
A.P. Hill
Magruder
Huger
D.H. Hill
JACKSON
Long Bridge
LONG BRIDGE ROAD
Western Run
Holmes
MALVERN HILL
McCLELLAN (-KEYES)
DEEP BOTTOM
ST. MARY'S CH.

CHAPIN'S BLUFF
DREWRY'S BLUFF
Kingsland Creek
NEW MARKET
MILL ROAD
CENTRAL (DARBYTOWN) ROAD
CHARLES CITY ROAD

KEYES (IV)

CURL'S NECK
BERMUDA HUNDRED

James River
PORT WALTHALL
POINT OF ROCKS
CITY POINT
LIGHT HOUSE PT.
JORDAN'S PT.
HARRISON'S LANDING
WILCOX'S LANDING
WINDMILL PT.
CHARLES CITY C.H.
Bailey's Creek
CITY POINT R.R.

PETERSBURG
PRINCE GEORGE C.H.

A study of the Peninsular campaign reveals that Jackson's activities in the Shenandoah Valley were responsible for preventing McDowell's corps from reinforcing McClellan during his operations against Richmond. But, perhaps more important, the record of Jackson's achievements in his Valley campaign has become a military classic in that it portrays the ideal military leader in action. For this reason, we now go back in time to review his operations in detail. As we read, his deficiencies during the Seven Days' Battles become less and less comprehensible.

Except for the facts that Maj. Gen. William S. Rosecrans is shown as commanding the Union forces in West Virginia (instead of Fremont, who relieved him later) and that Banks at this time was an integral part of McClellan's command, the situation shown here is the same as that which prevailed at the beginning of the Peninsular campaign (*see map 39*).

In November, 1861, "Stonewall" Jackson, then a major general, had been sent to Winchester to command the Valley District. Initially his command consisted of militia, but it was soon reinforced with the "Stonewall" Brigade, the unit he commanded at Bull Run where, because of its unyielding defense, it—as well as he—had acquired this distinctive appellation. In December, Jackson was joined by Brig. Gen. William W. Loring and 6,000 troops, but his total force was insufficient to undertake serious offensive operations. Jackson's mission, as the left wing of Johnston's army, was to watch Banks and to be prepared to return to Manassas if McClellan should advance toward that town.

While Banks remained stationary north of the Potomac, Col. Turner Ashby's cavalry reconnoitered the Union forces aggressively and raided the Chesapeake & Ohio Canal and the Baltimore & Ohio Railroad. Jackson devoted the time to intensive training of his infantry, but meanwhile grew more and more impatient for action. The two exposed Union posts at Romney and Bath (which

lay in the area where he had spent his boyhood) seem to have taunted him, for in midwinter he made a difficult march to attack them. The Union garrisons escaped, but Jackson captured some supplies. These operations had no tangible result other than a temporary severance of communications between Rosecrans and Banks. The Confederates soon withdrew, and the Union forces reoccupied the localities. However, during the campaign Jackson's troops learned something of the character of their leader and of the discipline and service he demanded.

That Jackson expected to have complete control and authority over his command also became apparent in this campaign. He had left Loring at Romney to garrison the town. Loring, dissatisfied with his post, appealed directly to the secretary of war for permission to return to Winchester. The secretary authorized this move, whereupon Jackson submitted his letter of resignation. Johnston eventually persuaded him to remain.

The part of western Virginia herein designated as the Valley (*this map, upper left*) is the area between the Allegheny and Blue Ridge Mountains, running northeast from Staunton to Harper's Ferry. It is drained by the Shenandoah River, which is formed by the North and South Forks. These branches flow on either side of Massanutten Mountain, a barrier equally as formidable as the Blue Ridge Mountains. The road net then in the Valley was good, the best route being the Valley Turnpike which ran from Staunton through Harrisonburg and along the North Fork to Winchester. The mountains could be crossed only at certain easily defensible passes (or gaps). Railroads traversed two of the passes. During the war, the Valley was valuable to the South both as an abundant granary and as a direct invasion route to the important region of Maryland and Pennsylvania. To the Union, the Valley had little military value, for its southern exit led to no objective of consequence.

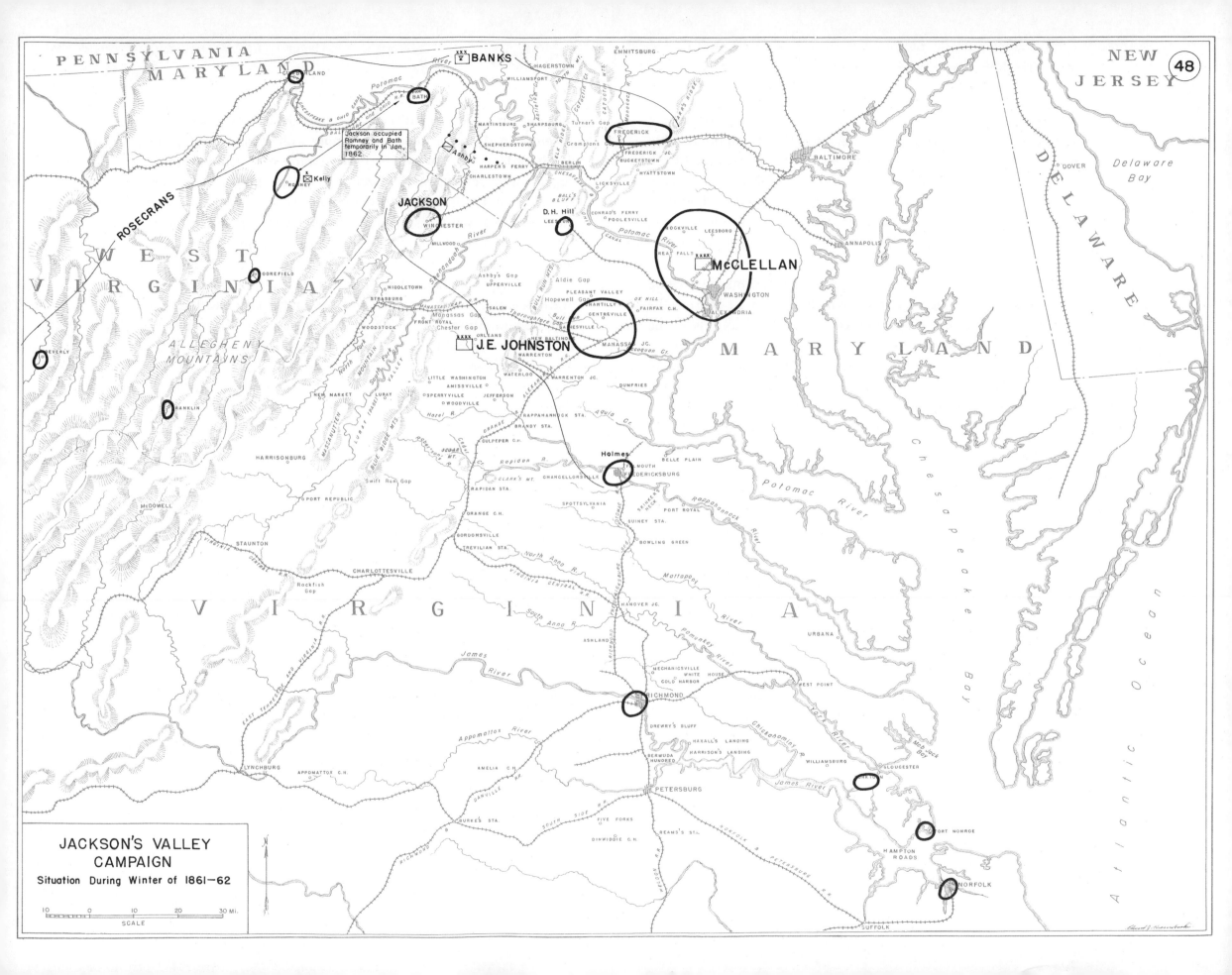

PENNSYLVANIA

MARYLAND

NEW

JERSEY

48

WEST

VIRGINIA

ROSECRANS

ALLEGHENY
MOUNTAINS

Jackson occupied
Romney and Bath
temporarily in Jan.,
1862

BANKS

Kelly

JACKSON

Winchester

D. H. Hill

McCLELLAN

Washington

J.E. JOHNSTON

DELAWARE

Delaware
Bay

BALTIMORE

ANNAPOLIS

M   A   R   Y   L   A   N   D

V   I   R   G   I   N   I   A

Holmes

Fredericksburg

RICHMOND

PETERSBURG

Norfolk

SUFFOLK

HAMPTON
ROADS

Chesapeake Bay

Potomac River

Atlantic Ocean

JACKSON'S VALLEY
CAMPAIGN

Situation During Winter of 1861-62

10   0   10   20   30 Mi.

SCALE

Banks crossed the Potomac in late February and moved south to protect the Chesapeake & Ohio Canal and the Baltimore & Ohio Railroad from Ashby's raids. This movement jeopardized D.H. Hill's command at Leesburg; therefore, on 7 March, Johnston ordered Hill's return to the main Confederate force at Manassas. When Johnston evacuated Manassas and moved to Culpeper two days later, Jackson was left in an advanced and isolated position at Winchester.

In pursuance of his orders from McClellan, Banks continued his advance south and occupied Winchester on 12 March, the day after Jackson evacuated the town. Too weak to oppose the Union forces, Jackson had withdrawn to Strasburg, above Woodstock (*left center*). Banks, independent of McClellan's command since 15 March, was directed—as part of the over-all strategy for the Peninsular campaign—to move farther south and drive Jackson from the Valley. This accomplished, he was to withdraw to a position nearer Washington. Banks began his movement south from Winchester on 17 March with a strong advance force under Brig. Gen. James Shields. At that same time McClellan began to embark at Washington for his movement to the Peninsula.

As for Jackson, his instructions from Johnston, though simple in concept, were not easy to execute. He was to avoid pitched battles and the likelihood of being overwhelmed, but at the same time he was to keep Banks so occupied that he could not detach troops to reinforce McClellan on the Peninsula. Accordingly, as Shields advanced upon his Strasburg position, Jackson withdrew to Mount Jackson, leaving Ashby behind to screen and delay. Shields followed to Woodstock and sent his cavalry beyond in a vain effort to penetrate Ashby's screen. The Union cavalry returned and reported to Shields that Jackson had fled from the Valley. Shields forsook further advance, returned to Winchester, and informed Banks of the report of his cavalry. Banks, guided by this erroneous information, concluded that the first part of his mission—the ejection of Jackson from the Valley—had been accomplished, and proceeded to comply with the second element of his orders—to move east to the vicinity of Washington. He began the movement on 20 March, leaving Shields at Winchester to guard the northern exit of the Valley. When the news of the movement reached Jackson on 21 March, he became exasperated, for Banks was now doing precisely what Jackson had been directed to prevent.

The following day Ashby skirmished with Shields' outposts at Kernstown, just south of Winchester, and reported to Jackson that the Union forces in that area were weak. Actually, Shields' force (now commanded by Kimball, Shields having been wounded in a skirmish the evening before) was more than twice as strong as Jackson's, and the Union soldiers were eager for a fight. Relying on Ashby's report, Jackson moved north from Woodstock and arrived before the Union position at Kernstown at 1:00 P. M., 23 March (*inset sketch*). He found that Ashby had been forced back and immediately reinforced him with one brigade. With the other two brigades Jackson sought to envelop the Union right by way of Sandy Ridge. But Col. Erastus B. Tyler's brigade countered this movement, and, when Col. Nathan Kimball's brigade moved to his assistance, the Confederates were driven from the field. There was no effective Union pursuit. The Stonewall Brigade had retreated without Jackson's permission, and its commander, Brig. Gen. Richard B. Garnett, was censured by Jackson and subjected to court-martial charges.

That night Jackson bivouacked within three miles of the battlefield and the next day marched toward Mount Jackson. He was furious over his failure to accomplish his mission. In reality he had succeeded, for the engagement at Kernstown was to cause the return of Banks to the Valley.

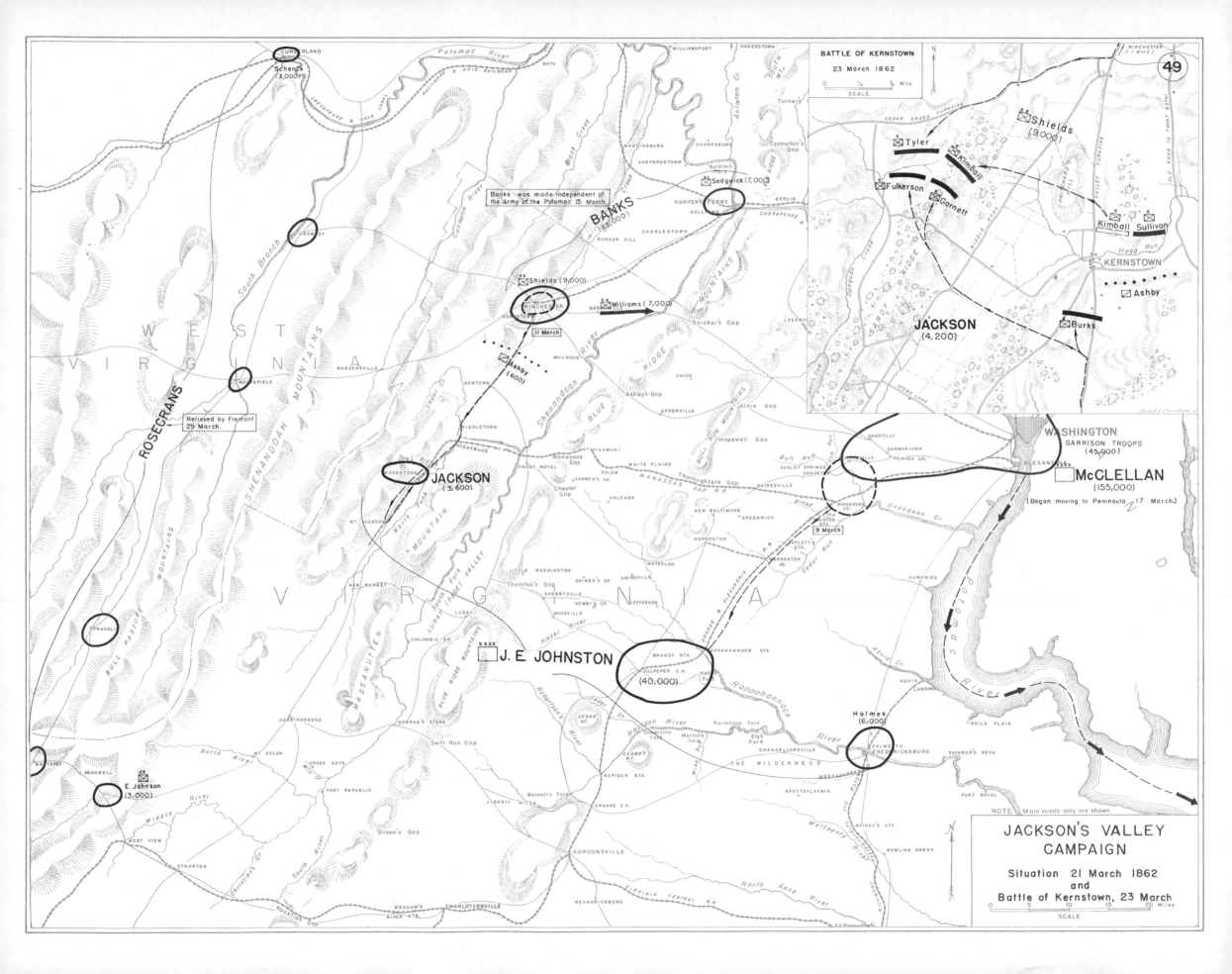

BATTLE OF KERNSTOWN
23 March 1862

0   ¼   ½ Mile
SCALE

49

Shields (9,000)

Tyler

Kimball

Fulkerson

Garnett

Kimball Sullivan

KERNSTOWN

Ashby

JACKSON
(4,200)

Burks

CUMBERLAND

Schenck
(3,000)

Potomac River

WILLIAMSPORT

HAGERSTOWN

BATH

MARTINSBURG

SHARPSBURG

Botelor's Ford

Sedgwick (7,000)

HARPERS FERRY

Banks was made independent of
the Army of the Potomac 15 March.

BANKS
(38,000)

CHARLESTOWN

BUNKER HILL

ROMNEY

Shields (9,000)

WINCHESTER

Williams (7,000)

11 March

Snicker's Gap

Ashby
(600)

MILLWOOD

Ashby's Gap

UPPERVILLE

Aldie Gap

MOOREFIELD

Relieved by Fremont
29 March.

MIDDLETOWN

STRASBURG

Hopewell Gap

WHITE PLAINS

Thoroughfare Gap

CHANTILLY

GERMANTOWN

CENTREVILLE

FAIRFAX C.H.

WASHINGTON
GARRISON TROOPS
(45,000)

WEST VIRGINIA

ROSECRANS

Tom's Brook

WOODSTOCK

JACKSON
(3,600)

MT. JACKSON

FRONT ROYAL

MANASSAS GAP

Bull Run

Sudley Springs

GROVETON

MANASSAS JC.

9 March

BRISTOE STA.

McCLELLAN
(155,000)

(Began moving to Peninsula 17 March.)

ALEXANDRIA

NEW MARKET

LITTLE WASHINGTON

GAINES' CR.

AMISSVILLE

NEW BALTIMORE

GREENWICH

WARRENTON

Occoquan Cr.

DUMFRIES

VIRGINIA

Thornton's Gap

SPERRYVILLE

WOODVILLE

WATERLOO

WARRENTON JC.

Cedar Run

XXXX J. E. JOHNSTON

BRANDY STA.

RAPPAHANNOCK STA.

CULPEPER C.H.

Kelly's Ford

(40,000)

Rappahannock River

AQUIA LANDING

BELLE PLAIN

Holmes
(6,000)

FALMOUTH
FREDERICKSBURG

Potomac River

MONTEREY

McDOWELL

E. Johnson
(3,000)

CROSS KEYS

PORT REPUBLIC

CLARK'S MT.

RAPIDAN STA.

THE WILDERNESS

CHANCELLORSVILLE

SPOTTSYLVANIA

PORT ROYAL

HARRISONBURG

MT. SOLON

SWIFT RUN GAP

Brown's Gap

Barnett's Ford

ORANGE C.H.

LIBERTY MILLS

QUINEY'S STA.

BOWLING GREEN

WEST VIEW

GORDONSVILLE

North Anna River

STAUNTON

MECHUM'S RIVER STA.

CHARLOTTESVILLE

VIRGINIA CENTRAL R.R.

MECHANICSBURG

Rockfish Gap

NOTE: Main roads only are shown.

JACKSON'S VALLEY CAMPAIGN

Situation 21 March 1862
and
Battle of Kernstown, 23 March

0   5   10   15   20 Miles
SCALE

The bold Confederate attack at Kernstown convinced Shields that Jackson had, or expected soon to have, a large force in the Valley. He asked Banks for reinforcements. Banks, mindful of his mission as it concerned Jackson, moved back to Strasburg. On 2 April, he moved forward a few miles to Woodstock (*inset sketch, center*), where he remained for two weeks. Jackson observed him from Mount Jackson. The Union cavalry had not been able to determine the Confederate strength on this front, so Banks estimated it as equal to his own. Actually, Jackson had only 6,000 men; Banks had 15,000.

The enticement of Banks back to the Valley was only one of the effects of Jackson's Kernstown attack. Lincoln, apprehensive of the defenses of Washington since McClellan had left, decided not to allow McDowell's corps to move to the assistance of McClellan on the Peninsula as had been planned, but to keep it near Washington. He also ordered Brig. Gen. Louis Blenker's division (*top center*) withheld from McClellan and sent to Fremont. Banks' delay at Woodstock was due primarily to his fear that, were he to move south, Jackson would cross Massanutten Mountain and move down the Luray Valley to attack his communications at Front Royal (*center*). It was not until 17 April that Banks realized that the obvious move to frustrate such an attack was to advance south and seize the New Market crossroads and mountain pass. When he moved with this intention, Jackson, not strong enough to meet Banks in a pitched battle, withdrew through Harrisonburg to Conrad's Store. This destination was determined by Jackson's fear that, if he remained west of Massanutten Mountain, Banks might advance up the Luray Valley east of the mountain and cut him off from Maj. Gen. Richard S. Ewell's division. (Ewell had been left behind to cooperate with Jackson when Johnston moved to the Peninsula to oppose McClellan.) By 26 April, Banks' forces had occupied Harrisonburg and New Market; Jackson had extended from Conrad's Store to Swift Run Gap. Here, Jackson occupied a classic "flanking position"—that is, if Banks moved south of Harrisonburg it would be easy for Jackson to advance and cut him off from his communications, whereas Jackson's own communications remained secure.

However, the over-all situation in the east was not favorable to the Confederates: McClellan, with superior forces, threatened Magruder's position at Yorktown on the Peninsula; McDowell was again preparing to move south toward Richmond; and Fremont, having occupied the town of McDowell (*lower left*), was preparing to advance to capture the major base at Staunton. The Confederates decided to conduct operations to prevent the loss of Staunton and, simultaneously, to prevent a juncture between Banks and Fremont in the south. It was hoped that these operations would also keep Banks' entire force in the Valley. On 30 April, Jackson, having been given over-all command of the operation, ordered Ashby to feint toward Harrisonburg and Ewell to occupy Swift Run Gap to counter any attempted advance by Banks. Meanwhile, to mystify his opponent as to his destination, he himself moved by the devious route shown to West View. Here he picked up Brig. Gen. Edward Johnson's division and continued on to McDowell, which he reached on 7 May. Brig. Gen. Robert C. Schenck moved his Union brigade south from Franklin (*lower left*) to join Brig. Gen. Robert H. Milroy's brigade at McDowell, and together they engaged Jackson in battle on 8 May (*inset sketch*).

By late that afternoon, Jackson had occupied a position on Sitlington's Hill and was searching for a route by means of which he could envelop Milroy's position across the river. However, the Union forces attacked. They were repulsed in fighting that continued until 9:00 P.M. and retreated across the river. The next day Schenck and Milroy withdrew to the town of Franklin, followed by Jackson, who was hindered by forest fires set by the Union forces. On 12 May, Jackson left Ashby before Franklin as a screen and returned to McDowell, whence he took the road toward Harrisonburg and Banks.

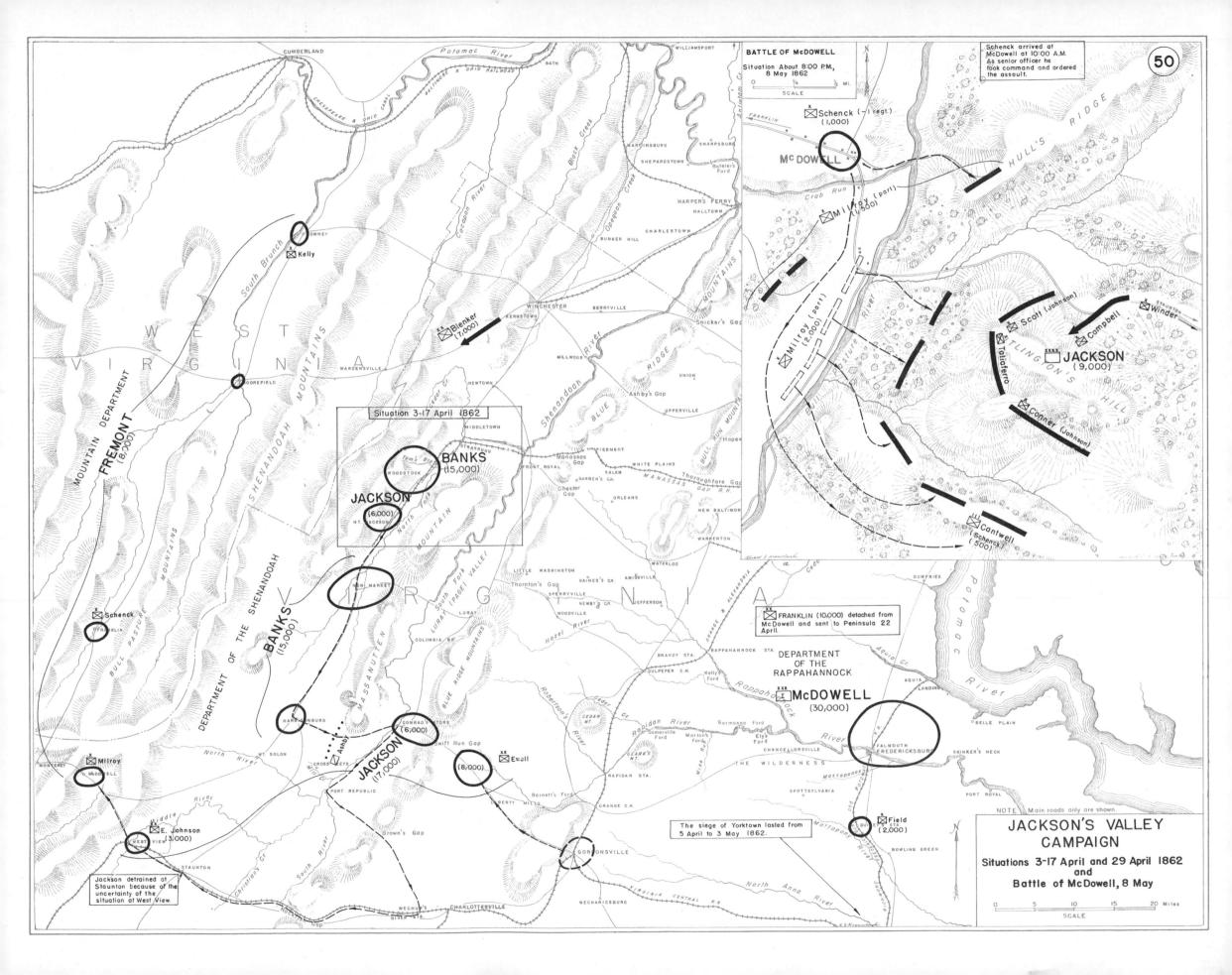

50

BATTLE OF McDOWELL
Situation About 8:00 P.M.,
8 May 1862
0   ½   1 Mi.
SCALE

Schenck arrived at
McDowell at 10:00 A.M.
As senior officer he
took command and ordered
the assault.

Schenck (-1 regt.)
(1,000)

McDOWELL

Milroy (part)
(1,500)

Milroy (part)

Milroy (part)

Milroy
(2,000)

Scott (Johnson)

Taliaferro

Campbell

Winder

JACKSON
(9,000)

Conner (Johnson)

Cantwell
(Schenck)
(500)

MOUNTAIN DEPARTMENT

FREMONT
(8,000)

WEST VIRGINIA

Kelly

Blenker
(7,000)

Situation 3-17 April 1862

BANKS
(15,000)

JACKSON
(6,000)

DEPARTMENT OF THE SHENANDOAH

BANKS
(15,000)

Schenck

VIRGINIA

Milroy

McDowell

E. Johnson
(3,000)

Jackson detrained at
Staunton because of the
uncertainty of the
situation at West View.

Harrisonburg

Ashby

CONRAD'S
STORE
(6,000)

JACKSON
(17,000)

Ewell
(8,000)

Field
(2,000)

FRANKLIN (10,000) detached from
McDowell and sent to Peninsula 22
April.

DEPARTMENT
OF THE
RAPPAHANNOCK

McDOWELL
(30,000)

FREDERICKSBURG

The siege of Yorktown lasted from
5 April to 3 May 1862.

GORDONSVILLE

NOTE: Main roads only are shown.

JACKSON'S VALLEY
CAMPAIGN

Situations 3-17 April and 29 April 1862
and
Battle of McDowell, 8 May

0   5   10   15   20 Miles
SCALE

The period from 1 May to 20 May was fraught with problems for the Confederate high command. It was not at all certain that Jackson's operations against Fremont would immobilize Banks. The possibility of Banks' force moving from the Valley to join McDowell in an advance south from Fredericksburg on Richmond, in conjunction with McClellan's advance up the Peninsula, was of paramount concern to Lee in his capacity as military advisor to Jefferson Davis. Accordingly, Lee urged Ewell, in Jackson's absence, to raid Banks' communications.

Ewell soon became perplexed as to his command status and mission. He had been subordinated to Jackson for the operations against Fremont; Jackson had ordered him to take post at Swift Run Gap and counter any advance by Banks. Now Lee urged him to take the offensive against Banks. Next, on 13 May, Johnston, irked at being bypassed, bluntly informed Lee that operations in the Valley were under his direction and issued further orders to Ewell. He sanctioned operations against Banks, providing Jackson's force was strong enough, but he added that if Banks moved east of the Blue Ridge Mountains, Ewell should move to join either Brig. Gen. Joseph R. Anderson's force at Fredericksburg or the Confederate forces on the Peninsula.

On being informed that Banks' forces at Harrisonburg and New Market appeared to be preparing to move, Ewell gave up thoughts of a raid, pending clarification of Banks' intentions, and informed Jackson of events. The receipt of this information concerning Banks, coupled with the realization that he could do little more against Fremont and the fact that his primary mission was to keep Banks in the Valley, impelled Jackson to leave Franklin and move against Banks at Harrisonburg. Actually, Banks had been preparing for a withdrawal. Shields' departure for Fredericksburg had reduced his forces to 8,000; he did not know Jackson's location and feared a surprise attack in his exposed position. Therefore, evacuating Harrisonburg and New Market, he concentrated at Strasburg, sending a detachment, under Col. John R. Kenly, to Front Royal to watch the Luray Valley.

On 17 May, Jackson was at Mount Solon; Banks was fortifying Strasburg; and Ewell, with the bulk of his forces still at Swift Run Gap, again found himself in a quandary. On 14 May, Lee had told him to forgo any movement until Jackson returned to the Valley, while Jackson had ordered him to follow Banks. Then, on the 15th, Johnston's order had arrived directing him in no uncertain terms to move east if Banks' troops did, while on the same day Jackson had ordered him to move to New Market. When, on 17 May, Ewell learned that Shields had left the Valley, it seemed that the conditions established by Johnston had materialized and that, accordingly, he should move east out of the Valley. But Ewell perceived the opportunity in the Valley for the great victory at which Jackson had hinted, and he decided to visit his immediate commander. Jackson's instructions remained unchanged.

On 20 May, Jackson was just south of New Market and Ewell was at Luray. Then Jackson's rapidly maturing plan for operations against Banks was again placed in jeopardy. Another message from Johnston directed Ewell to move east and Jackson to remain in the Valley. It also cautioned the latter against risking an attack on Banks' fortified position at Strasburg. Jackson laid the problem before Lee, who convinced Johnston that a great opportunity existed in the Valley and that Ewell should remain with Jackson.

Thus the stage was set for the decisive phase of the Valley campaign, which was to have far-reaching effects.

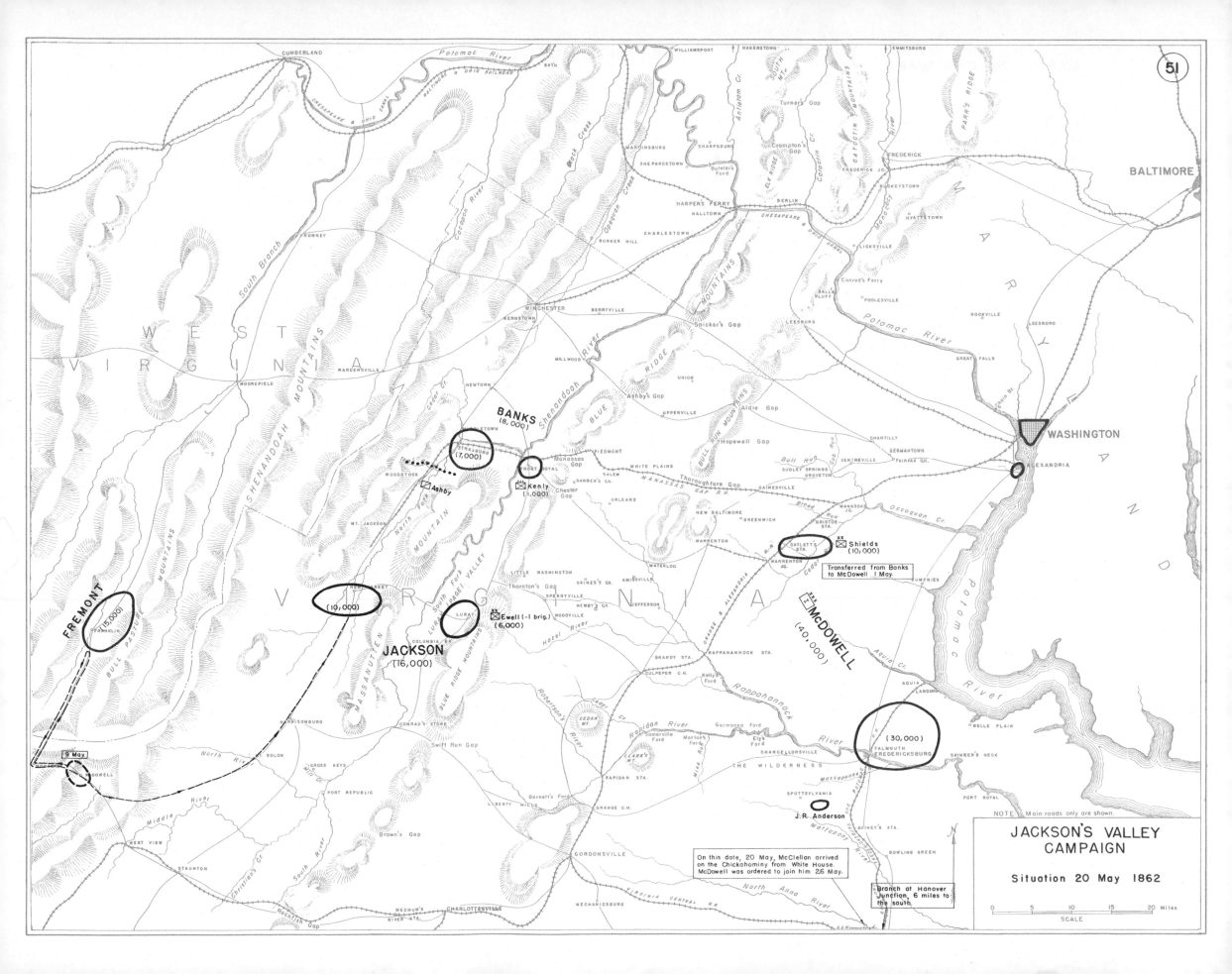

JACKSON'S VALLEY
CAMPAIGN

Situation 20 May 1862

NOTE: Main roads only are shown.

On this date, 20 May, McClellan arrived on the Chickahominy from White House. McDowell was ordered to join him 26 May.

Branch at Hanover Junction, 6 miles to the south.

Transferred from Banks to McDowell 1 May.

51

BALTIMORE

WASHINGTON

FREMONT
(15,000)

BANKS
(8,000)

STRASBURG
(7,000)

Kenly
(1,000)

Ashby

JACKSON
(16,000)

(10,000)

Ewell (-1 brig.)
(6,000)

Shields
(10,000)

McDOWELL
(40,000)

(30,000)
FALMOUTH
FREDERICKSBURG

J.R. Anderson

9 May

SCALE
0   5   10   15   20 Miles

Ashby's cavalry had screened Jackson's movements so effectively since he left Franklin on 12 May that neither Fremont nor Banks was sure of his location. Early on 21 May, Jackson's immediate command, reinforced by Brig. Gen. Richard Taylor's brigade of Ewell's division, started north. To the bewilderment of his subordinate commanders, Jackson turned east at New Market, and speculation mounted in the command as to the destination and intentions of their secretive leader. When he passed through Luray, absorbed Ewell's command, and turned north down the Luray Valley, Jackson's plan became more apparent. It was to wipe out Kenly's command at Front Royal (*see map 51*) in a lightning stroke and to move quickly on Banks' line of communications to Harper's Ferry (*upper center*), thus forcing Banks to evacuate his fortified position at Strasburg and fight in the open for his very existence.

Rapidly the Valley army moved on Front Royal as Jackson pushed his men to the utmost. Ashby had left a small detachment to watch Banks' position at Strasburg and, with his main body, had joined Jackson. At Front Royal, Kenly had neglected to picket the Luray Valley roads properly. Jackson's superior forces surprised him on 23 May, routing his little force after a short fight. Early on the 24th, Jackson moved to get behind Banks. He sent his cavalry to Middletown and Newtown while his infantry started for Winchester; but he later reconsidered and ordered his infantry to follow the cavalry to Middletown.

Meanwhile, Banks, at first incredulous that Jackson's entire force had attacked Front Royal, finally became convinced of the true situation. Early on the 24th, he began his withdrawal (*this map*). His main force had passed Middletown when Ashby's cavalry reached the road and attacked the rear elements. Jackson continued to direct his forces to Middletown, with the result that Banks' main force escaped to Winchester. Here, unwisely, Banks elected to stand; but the Confederates enveloped the Union right, whereupon Banks retired across the Potomac. Jackson pushed the pursuit which, because of the failure of his cavalry, was unsuccessful.

The ejection of Banks from the Valley had its repercussions in Washington. McDowell's orders to move to the Peninsula were canceled on 24 May, though this time not solely because Lincoln feared for the safety of Washington. Instead, Lincoln saw an opportunity to destroy the troublesome Jackson. McDowell was ordered to send 20,000 troops to Front Royal, and Fremont was ordered to move to Harrisonburg. For a variety of reasons, Fremont moved to Moorefield instead of to Harrisonburg. Lincoln now attempted to coordinate from Washington the movements of McDowell and Fremont. If both forces could converge rapidly at Strasburg, Jackson's only escape route up the Valley would be cut (*inset*).

On 29 May, Jackson learned of Fremont's move and on the 30th he heard of Shields' march. Appreciating the danger of his position, he immediately began to withdraw up the Valley. Arriving at Winchester ahead of his troops, he learned that on noon of that day, the 30th, Shields had surprised the Confederate regiment at Front Royal and seized the town. Shields had an excellent opportunity to reach Strasburg before Jackson, but he had no orders to push forward to Strasburg and made little effort to close the trap. Jackson outnumbered him and Federals were strung out badly along muddy roads. To the west, Fremont, opposed only by Ashby's cavalry, moved forward with less vigor than the occasion demanded. By day and by night, the Confederates hastened south through Strasburg. One brigade was sent east to hold off Shields, and Ewell's division turned to support Ashby against Fremont. By the night of 31 May, Jackson had escaped the trap. That same night McDowell reached Front Royal, and on the following morning he sent a cavalry force to Strasburg. It was repulsed by Ewell. Shields was then ordered to move south to Luray with instructions to keep his brigades within supporting distance.

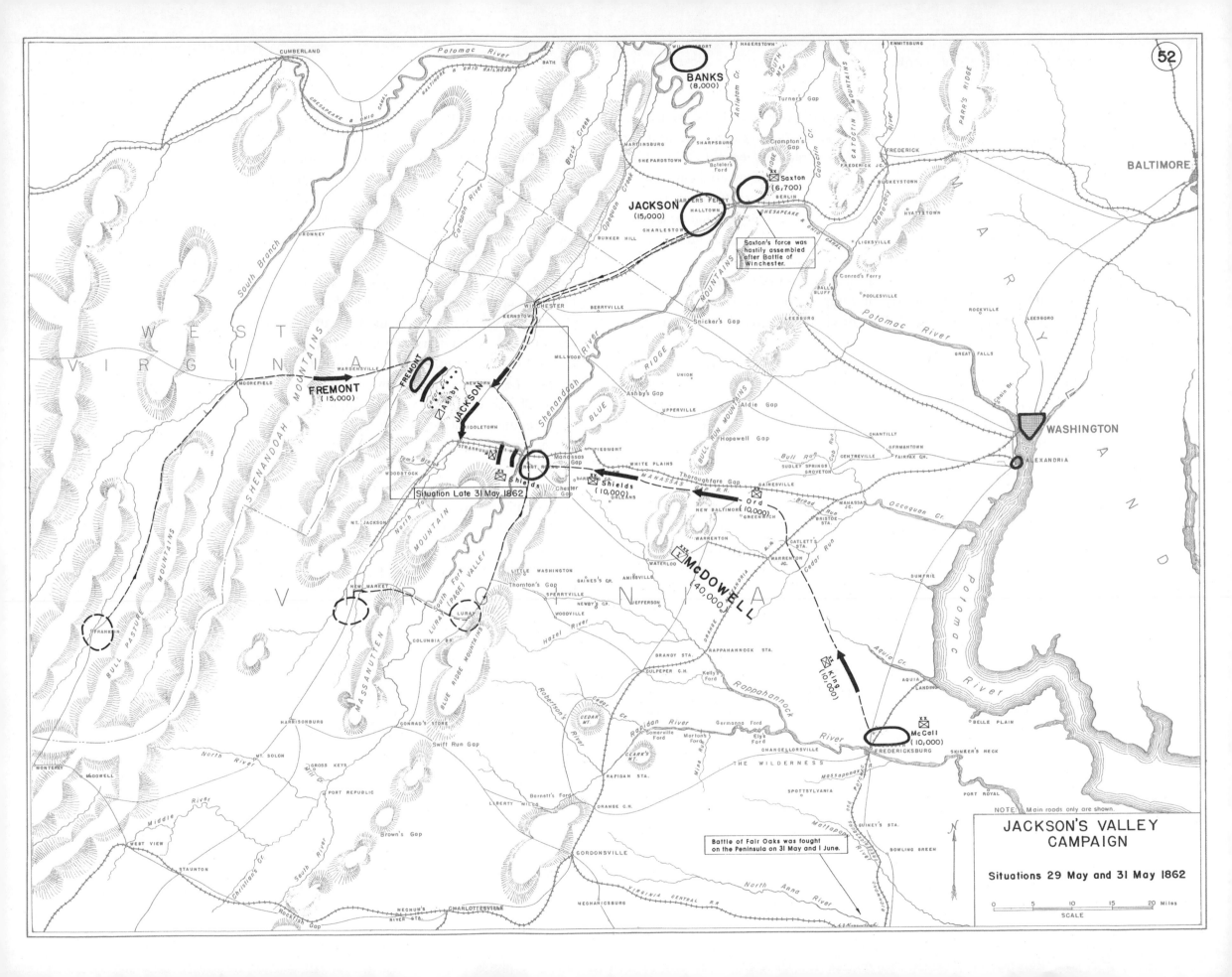

52

BANKS
(8,000)

Saxton
(6,700)

JACKSON
(15,000)

Saxton's force was
hastily assembled
after Battle of
Winchester.

FREMONT
(15,000)

FREMONT

JACKSON

Shields

Situation Late 31 May 1862

Shields
(10,000)

Ord
(10,000)

WASHINGTON

McDOWELL
(40,000)

King
(10,000)

FRANKLIN

McCall
(10,000)

Battle of Fair Oaks was fought
on the Peninsula on 31 May and 1 June.

JACKSON'S VALLEY CAMPAIGN

Situations 29 May and 31 May 1862

NOTE: Main roads only are shown.

0   5   10   15   20 Miles
SCALE

BALTIMORE

In the late afternoon of 1 June, Jackson's rear guard, the weary Stonewall Brigade, passed south through Strasburg (*center*). That night Ewell withdrew from his position facing Fremont and followed. In the morning Fremont's troops and McDowell's cavalry closed the "trap" at Strasburg—but behind, not in front of, the Confederate army. There were several reasons for Jackson's escape from his seemingly hopeless position: Jackson moved along the excellent Valley Turnpike, whereas the Union forces moved along poor roads made worse by three days of rain; he had trained his infantry to move swiftly in emergencies; the Union forces lacked unity of effort; and the Union commanders, particularly Fremont, lacked aggressiveness.

On 2 June, McDowell and Fremont moved south after Jackson. Fremont, reinforced with Brig. Gen. George Bayard's cavalry from McDowell's corps, moved up the Valley Turnpike, and Shields up the Luray Valley. Banks crossed the Potomac and also moved south. Frequent clashes occurred between the Confederate rear guard and Fremont's advance parties during the next five days. In one of these, Ashby was killed. This was a serious loss to the Confederacy, for Ashby had shown promise of becoming a fine cavalry leader. Jackson gained much time by destroying the bridges over the flooded streams, particularly those over South Fork, the destruction of which prevented Shields from establishing communications with Fremont.

By the night of the 7th, Jackson had occupied Cross Keys and Port Republic (*lower left*) and controlled the bridge between. That same day Shields moved toward Port Republic, his forces strung out along the road. The Confederates could have moved east through Brown's Gap to safety, but the separation of the Union forces invited attacks on each individually. With the Port Republic bridge and fords in his possession, Jackson could readily concentrate against either Fremont or Shields. Since Fremont was the greater threat at the moment, Jackson planned to attack him on the 7th. But Fremont, nearer Harrisonburg than Cross Keys, could not be enticed into battle that day.

Early on the 8th, a raid on Port Republic by Shields' cavalry surprised and almost captured the Confederate trains and Jackson himself. This event caused him to ponder that perhaps Shields was the greater immediate threat and should be dealt with first. Thus, when Fremont later in the day made a halfhearted attack on Ewell's fight at Cross Keys (*inset sketch*), and Ewell wanted to launch a counterattack, Jackson forbade it.

That night Jackson decided to attack Shields, meanwhile leaving a reinforced brigade under Brig. Gen. Isaac R. Trimble to hold off Fremont. Early on 9 June the attack was launched against the two brigades of Shields' division that had reached the field. The assault was not well managed. It was characterized by piecemeal attacks against a strong position; these were repulsed by vigorous Union counterattacks and excellent artillery support. Winder's Stonewall Brigade took heavy casualties and was in danger of rout until reinforced by Ewell. Finally, Taylor's envelopment on the south forced the Union brigades to withdraw. Jackson pursued almost to the Swift Run Gap road, where Shields' two rear brigades stopped him. Concluding that it was now impracticable to attack Fremont, Jackson concentrated all of his forces at Brown's Gap, where they remained until ordered to the vicinity of Richmond on 17 June.

Thus ended the Valley campaign. After Port Republic, just as after Front Royal, Jackson's victory resulted in the cancellation of McDowell's marching orders. Although one division (Brig. Gen. George A. McCall's) had already been sent to the Peninsula, McDowell's remaining force was retained in the Valley until the formation of Pope's army for the second Bull Run campaign.

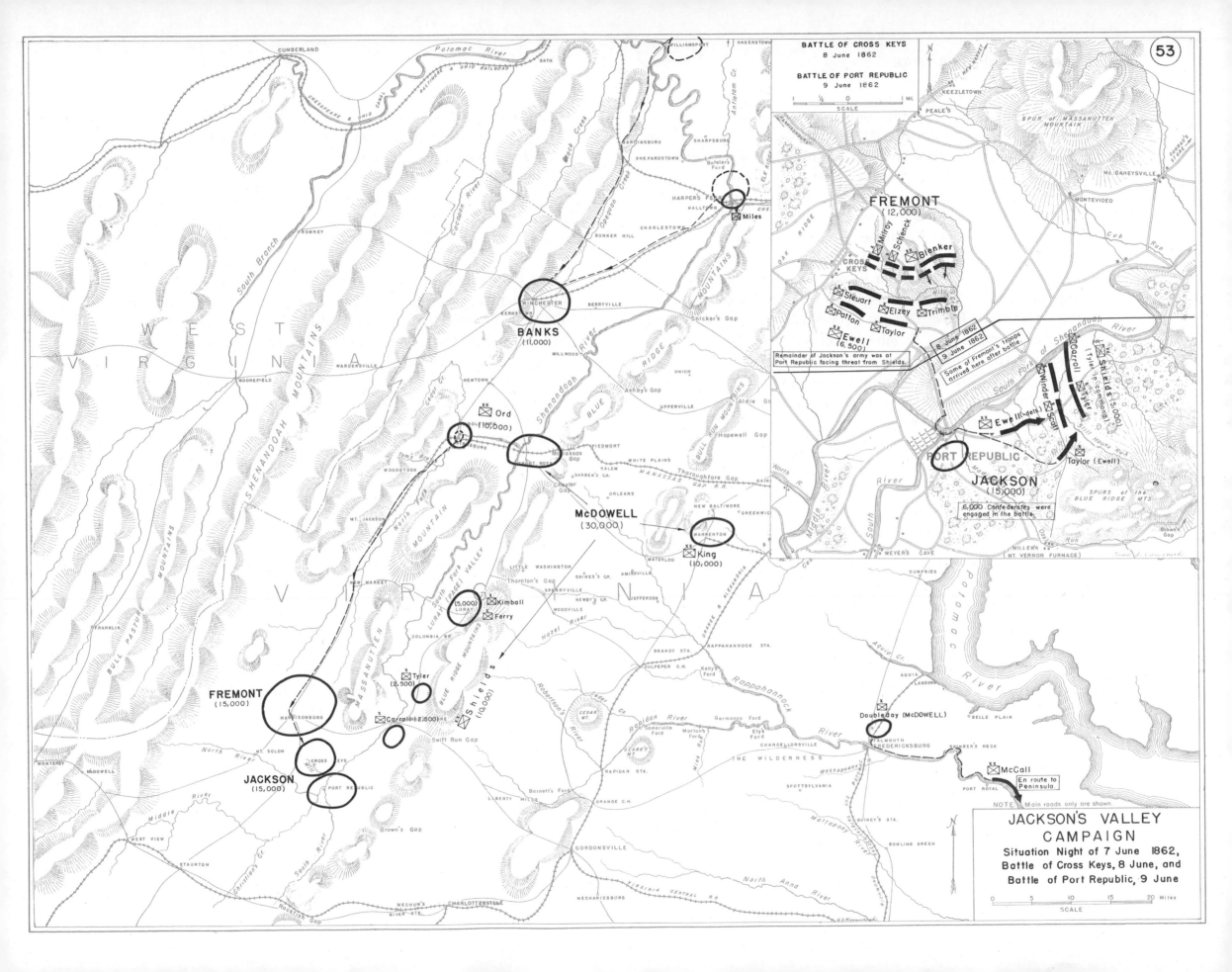

53

BATTLE OF CROSS KEYS
8 June 1862

BATTLE OF PORT REPUBLIC
9 June 1862

1   ½   0   1 MI.
SCALE

FREMONT
(12,000)

Milroy Schenck
Blenker

CROSS
KEYS

Steuart
Patton   Elzey   Trimble

Ewell
(6,500)

Remainder of Jackson's army was at
Port Republic facing threat from Shields.

8 June 1862
9 June 1862

Some of Fremont's troops
arrived here after battle.

Carroll
(Tyler in command)

Shields (5,000)
(Tyler in command)

Winder   Scott

Ewell (-det.)

Taylor (Ewell)

PORT REPUBLIC

JACKSON
(15,000)

6,000 Confederates were
engaged in the battle.

SPURS of the
BLUE RIDGE MTS.

CUMBERLAND

Potomac River
BALTIMORE & OHIO RAILROAD

WILLIAMSPORT   HAGERSTOWN

Bath

HARDINSBURG   SHARPSBURG

SHEPARDSTOWN

HARPER'S FERRY   Boteler's
Ford
HALLTOWN

Miles

CHARLESTOWN

BUNKER HILL

WINCHESTER   BERRYVILLE

Snicker's Gap

BANKS
(11,000)

MILLWOOD

Ashby's Gap

UPPERVILLE   Aldie

WEST
VIRGINIA

MOOREFIELD

WARDENSVILLE

UNION

NEWTOWN

XX
Ord
(10,000)

Manassas Gap

WHITE PLAINS   Thoroughfare Gap

McDOWELL
(30,000)

WARRENTON

XX
King
(10,000)

V   I   R   G   I   N   I   A

NEW MARKET

LITTLE WASHINGTON

(5,000)
LURAY
Kimball
Ferry

JEFFERSON

WOODVILLE

COLUMBIA BR.

BRANDY STA.   RAPPAHANNOCK STA.

CULPEPER C.H.

DUMFRIES

DOUBLEDAY
Doubleday (McDOWELL)

BELLE PLAIN

X
Tyler
(2,500)

Shields

FREMONT
(15,000)

HARRISONBURG

XX
Carroll (2,500)

XX
(10,000)

Swift Run Gap

CEDAR
MT.

Rapidan River

CHANCELLORSVILLE   THE WILDERNESS

FALMOUTH
FREDERICKSBURG

McCall

En route to
Peninsula.

CROSS
KEYS

JACKSON
(15,000)

PORT REPUBLIC

Brown's Gap

MONTEREY

McDOWELL

WEST VIEW

STAUNTON

Brown's Gap

GORDONSVILLE

VIRGINIA CENTRAL R.R.

CHARLOTTESVILLE

NOTE: Main roads only are shown.

JACKSON'S VALLEY
CAMPAIGN

Situation Night of 7 June 1862,
Battle of Cross Keys, 8 June, and
Battle of Port Republic, 9 June

0   5   10   15   20 Miles
SCALE

The Union failures in the Valley campaign, caused by the impossibility of coordinating the different Union commands from Washington, probably convinced Lincoln that the departmental organization he had set up was not sound. On 26 June, he created the Army of Virginia which incorporated the forces of Banks, Fremont, McDowell, and several lesser forces—the troops in Washington (Brig. Gen. Samuel D. Sturgis' Reserve Division), a small force at Winchester, and the division of Brig. Gen. Jacob D. Cox in West Virginia. For its commander, Lincoln selected one of the more successful generals from the western theater, Maj. Gen. John Pope. The new commander was junior to all of his corps commanders. Fremont objected to this arrangement and resigned. His corps was given to German-born Maj. Gen. Franz Sigel, whose selection may have been influenced by the fact that many of the men in the corps were of German extraction. The two cavalry brigades were assigned as organic elements of corps —Brig. Gen. John P. Hatch's to the II Corps and Bayard's to the III Corps. Hence, Pope had no cavalry directly under his control, and the consequences of this deficiency became apparent as the campaign progressed.

Shields' division, decimated in the rugged fighting in the Valley, was broken up and its units sent elsewhere. It was a general Union policy during the war not to rebuild battle-tested veteran regiments, but instead to allow them to decline to the point of ineffectiveness, after which they were often dissolved. This process was due primarily to the Union mobilization system, which was based on unit rather than individual replacement. Thus, when Jackson's operations in the Valley induced an intensified Union recruiting program, only 50,000 men were obtained as replacements for the veteran regiments while, at the same time, an additional 420,000 were formed into new units.

Pope's mission contained three principal provisions: to protect Washington against attack from the direction of Richmond; to assure the safety of the Shenandoah Valley; and, by operating toward Gordonsville, to draw Confederate troops away from Richmond, thus aiding McClellan's operations. The mission implied that some offensive operations would be necessary, but Pope was not expected, nor did he plan, to move on Richmond. It will be recalled that on 26 June, the day Pope's army was constituted, Lee attacked McClellan's north flank at Mechanicsville, thus initiating the Seven Days' Battles. Upon their conclusion, when McClellan withdrew to Harrison's Landing, Pope's future operations would of necessity have to conform to the subsequent disposition and activity of McClellan's army.

The resultant Second Battle of Bull Run was fought on substantially the same ground as the first battle. The area of preliminary maneuvering, however, bears examination, for it had an important influence on most of the campaigns in Virginia. The Rappahannock and Rapidan Rivers, though bridged at some points and fordable at others during the dry season, were nevertheless good defensive obstacles. North and west of Gordonsville (*center, left; small red circle*) the country is mountainous and was then fairly heavily wooded. The roads were primarily earthen (thus muddy in wet weather), but the Warrenton-Alexandria Turnpike was hard-surfaced. The Bull Run Mountains were another obstacle and could be crossed by large bodies of troops only at certain passes. The railroads were of great importance to both sides. Note that the Confederate railroads from the west, south, and east converge at Gordonsville. Therefore, retention of that town was a matter of primary concern to Lee.

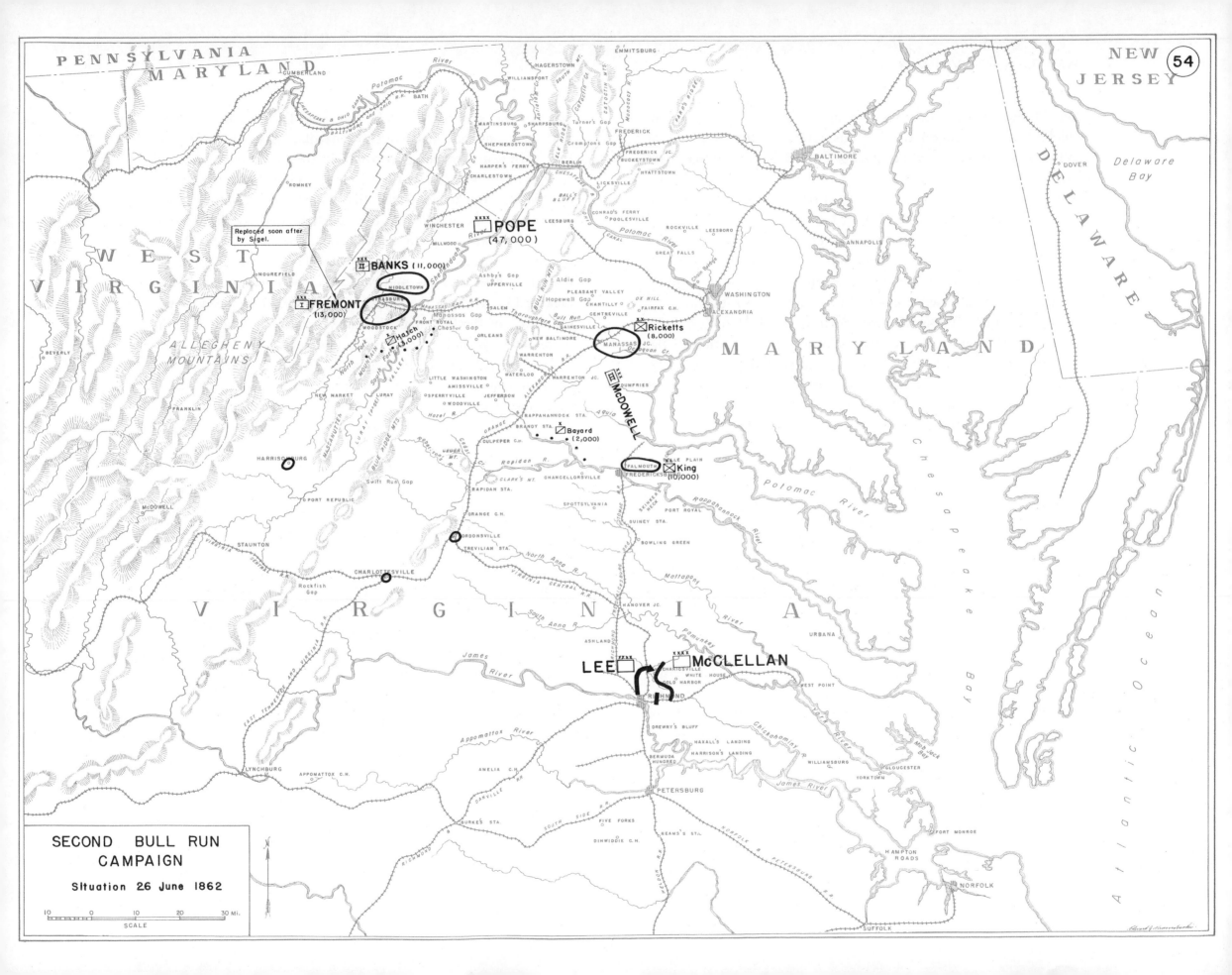

PENNSYLVANIA

MARYLAND

WEST

VIRGINIA

Replaced soon after
by Sigel.

XXXX
☐ POPE
(47,000)

XXX
☐ BANKS (11,000)

XXX
☐ FREMONT
(13,000)

XXX
☐ Hatch
(3,000)

ALLEGHENY
MOUNTAINS

XX
☒ Ricketts
(8,000)

MARYLAND

XX
☐ McDOWELL

X
☐ Bayard
(2,000)

XX
☒ King
(10,000)

DELAWARE

Delaware
Bay

Chesapeake Bay

Potomac River

V I R G I N I A

XXXX
☐
LEE

XXXX
☐ McCLELLAN

Atlantic Ocean

SECOND BULL RUN
CAMPAIGN

Situation 26 June 1862

10   0   10   20   30 Mi.
SCALE

On 11 July, 1862, Lincoln appointed Halleck as general in chief of all the Union forces, thus returning the direction of military operations to military hands. Pope was directed to remain in Washington until Halleck could assume his new duties. Meanwhile, in pursuance of his mission, Pope ordered his corps to concentrate east of the Blue Ridge Mountains. Since it was necessary to leave one division to protect the base at Falmouth (*center*), which had been established by McDowell preparatory to his previously contemplated move south, Pope had to disperse his troops over a wider front than he felt was desirable.

On the 14th, Banks was ordered to dispatch Hatch's cavalry to destroy the railroad connecting Gordonsville, Charlottesville, and Lynchburg. Instead of moving lightly and with speed as ordered, Hatch so encumbered his force with artillery and a wagon train, and moved so slowly, that it was the 19th before he reached a point ten miles from Gordonsville. Then he learned that Jackson had just occupied the town in considerable strength.

Meanwhile, Halleck pondered the employment of McClellan's army, which had been resting at Harrison's Landing since 3 July. On 27 July, he discussed the matter with McClellan at the landing. Though McClellan argued that the decision by arms should be reached in the Petersburg-Richmond area, Halleck concluded—and Lincoln approved—that the army should be moved to Aquia Creek, just north of Falmouth. Maj. Gen. Ambrose E. Burnside's IX Corps, which had arrived at Fort Monroe from North Carolina on 28 June as a reinforcement for McClellan, was also ordered to Aquia Creek.

At first glance, Halleck's decision seems open to criticism. The Army of the Potomac was in position to threaten Petersburg, the gateway to Richmond. Three years later Grant was to achieve final victory by operating through Petersburg. But Halleck had to face reality. The simple, governing fact was that McClellan was not the man to undertake this task. Even though he knew that Jackson had gone to Gordonsville, McClellan estimated Lee's army in front of Richmond at 200,000. (It was actually weaker than the Army of the Potomac.) Giving his own strength as 90,000, McClellan stated that, if he were reinforced with 20,000 men, he would *try* to take Richmond. If the disparity in strength was as great as McClellan believed—and Halleck was by no means so convinced—then the safest course dictated that the forces of Pope and McClellan be combined before attacking Lee. Perhaps the proper course would have been to leave the Army of the Potomac where it was and to provide it with a more energetic and less cautious commander.

During July and early August, Lee faced a dilemma equally as perplexing as that which confronted Halleck. He had no desire to continue operations in the Richmond area, but, as long as McClellan's army remained there posing a threat to the capital, he was powerless to employ his full force in major operations elsewhere. Nor could he sit idly by and allow Pope to advance south and sever Confederate communications with the Valley and the west. Thus, when he learned on 12 July of Pope's advance east of the Blue Ridge Mountains, Lee immediately dispatched Jackson, with two divisions, to secure Gordonsville.

Seldom, however, was Lee content to remain on the defensive if any opportunity could be found to strike a blow. Since he occupied a central position between Pope and McClellan, he might be able to concentrate against each of them in turn. There was a chance that Jackson could defeat Pope, then rejoin Lee for a new drive against McClellan. So Lee proceeded to gather reinforcements for Jackson. One means was to arrange to move at least two brigades from South Carolina to the Richmond area; another was to strengthen the fortifications at Richmond to allow the release of some troops.

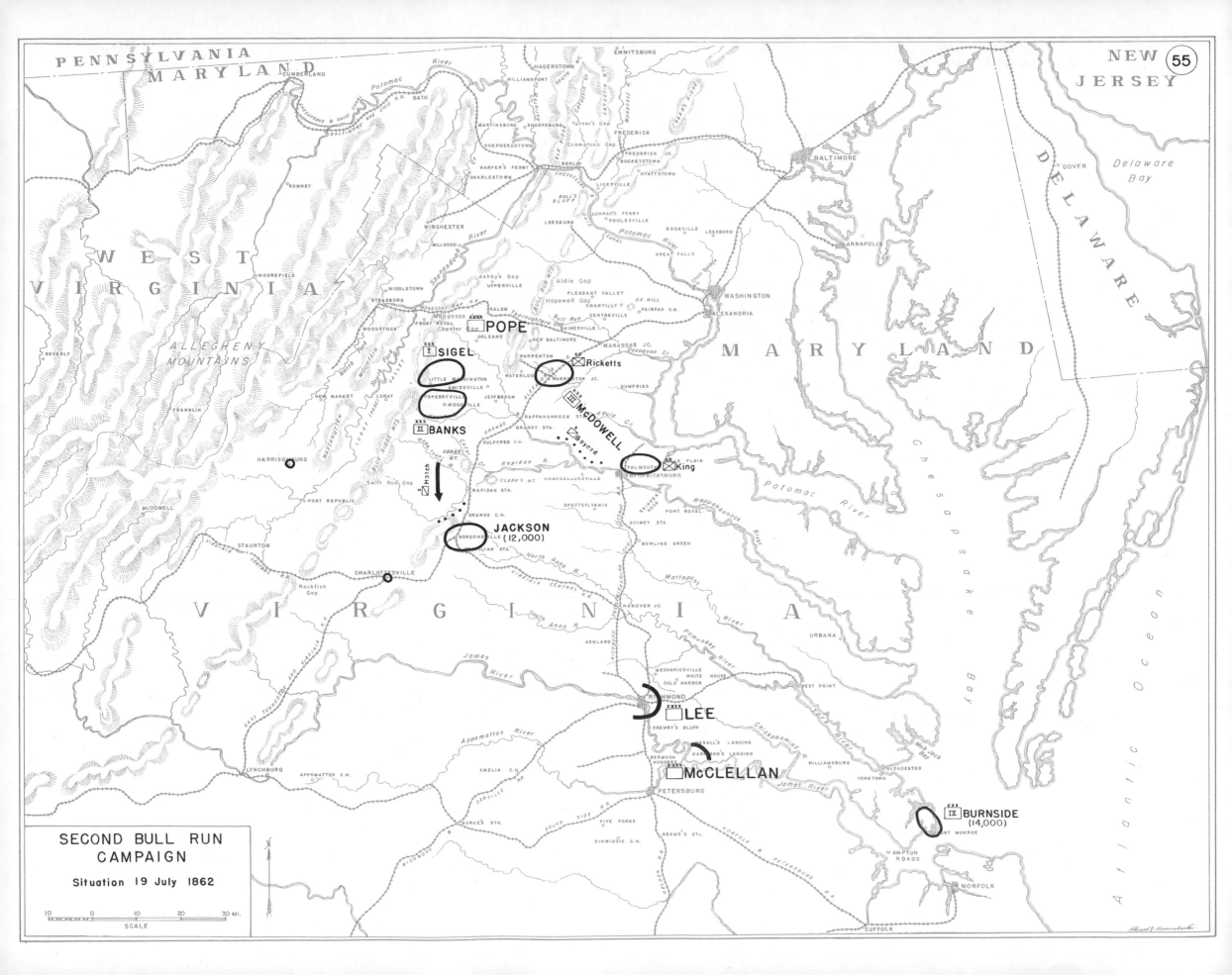

PENNSYLVANIA
MARYLAND

WEST
VIRGINIA

ALLEGHENY
MOUNTAINS

MARYLAND

DELAWARE

Delaware
Bay

POPE

SIGEL

Ricketts

McDOWELL

BANKS

Bayard

King

HICH

JACKSON
(12,000)

V I R G I N I A

LEE

McCLELLAN

BURNSIDE
(14,000)

Atlantic Ocean

Chesapeake Bay

SECOND BULL RUN
CAMPAIGN

Situation 19 July 1862

10   0   10   20   30 Mi.
SCALE

On 27 July, Lee, deciding to gamble on McClellan's continued inactivity, sent A. P. Hill, with 12,000 men, to join Jackson in operations against Pope. To mislead McClellan, he conducted diversionary operations (primarily artillery bombardments) against the Union base at Harrison's Landing. On 5 August, Burnside arrived in Fredericksburg from Fort Monroe. It now appeared that the Union strategy provided for a major effort in northern Virginia. But Lee became skeptical of this idea when, on 5 August, some of McClellan's troops moved north from Harrison's Landing to Malvern Hill. Lee moved south from Richmond to give battle. Some preliminary skirmishing and preparations for a fight ensued, but, when 7 August dawned, Lee found that the Union troops had returned to the landing. Claiming he could not move the remainder of his army up to support them in time, McClellan had ordered their withdrawal. Now in a quandary, Lee decided to grant authority to Jackson to act as he saw fit. However, Jackson, not waiting for any such authority, had begun a march on Culpeper on 7 August. He hoped to deal with Pope's corps individually before they could unite.

Pope himself had left Washington for the field on 29 July, after having been apprised by Halleck that McClellan's army was to be moved north to unite with his own. Pope should now have appreciated the fact that this movement of the Army of the Potomac invalidated part of his previously assigned mission. Once McClellan left the Peninsula, Lee was sure to join Jackson with the rest of his force, and Pope would then be confronted with a Confederate force slightly larger than his own. Thus, logic dictated that he should await a juncture with McClellan's army, falling back before Lee, if necessary. But, influenced primarily by Halleck's determination to hold the Aquia Landing base, he moved forward to a position near Cedar Mountain, from which he could launch cavalry raids against Gordonsville.

About noon on 9 August, Jackson arrived at Cedar Mountain, forcing Bayard's cavalry back before him. Banks, sent forward by Pope to delay Jackson while Pope concentrated, attacked the Confederates. In the fighting which followed, Winder was killed and his division was badly mauled by a surprise attack against its left flank. The arrival of A. P. Hill's division prevented a rout and enabled Jackson to mount a counterattack which drove Banks, badly outnumbered, back across Cedar Creek. At the end of the day, Jackson's advance was stopped by Brig. Gen. James B. Ricketts' division, which had been hurried forward by Pope. Jackson now learned that all of Pope's corps were in the vicinity and hence that his opportunity to defeat them individually had disappeared. He remained in position until 12 August, hoping that Pope would attack. On that date he fell back to Gordonsville.

The fierce afternoon battle had cost Banks 2,353 casualties and Jackson 1,338. Neither commander had acquitted himself well. It was Pope's intention that Banks would defend until Sigel's corps arrived on the field of battle. But his orders, given orally, were poor and were misunderstood by Banks. Consequently, he had attacked—without reserves—and had delayed sending back for reinforcements when the need was indicated. Jackson's orders to his units had also been unclear and had led to confusion and unwarranted delay in the advance from Gordonsville. His initial dispositions on the battlefield had not been good, and his reluctance to divulge his plans had disturbed A. P. Hill and had prevented his playing a greater part in the battle.

Jackson's withdrawal convinced Lee that Jackson alone could not defeat Pope. Again he relied on McClellan's inactivity and, on 13 August, sent Longstreet to reinforce Jackson. On 14 August, upon learning definitely that McClellan was leaving the Peninsula, he started all but two brigades of his army northward. Lee's primary concern was now to meet and defeat Pope before the latter could be joined by McClellan.

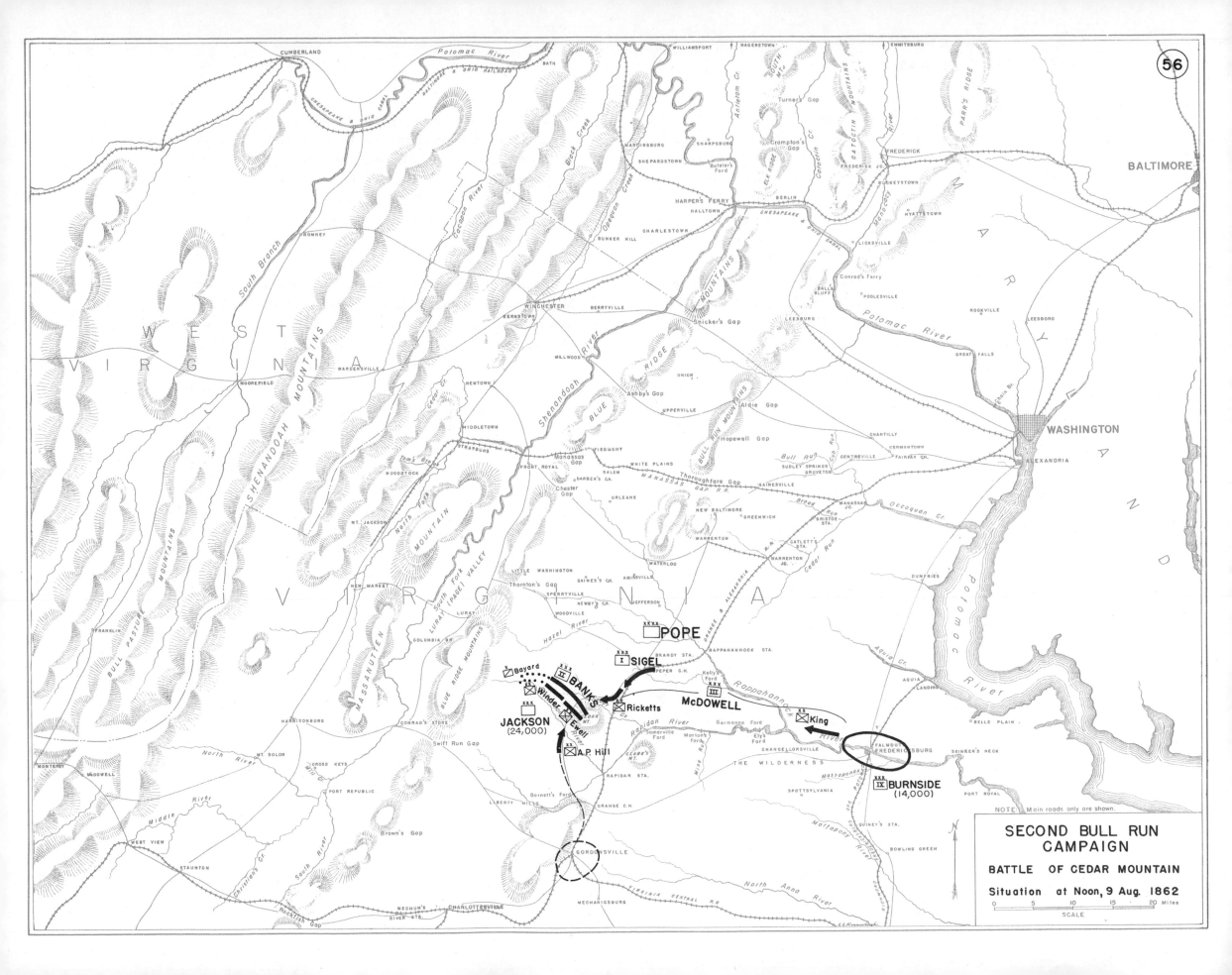

56

SECOND BULL RUN
CAMPAIGN

BATTLE OF CEDAR MOUNTAIN

Situation at Noon, 9 Aug. 1862

NOTE: Main roads only are shown.

0   5   10   15   20 Miles
SCALE

POPE

SIGEL

BANKS

Bayard

Winder

JACKSON
(24,000)

Ewell

A.P. Hill

Ricketts

McDOWELL

King

BURNSIDE
(14,000)

WEST
VIRGINIA

V I R G I N I A

M A R Y L A N D

BALTIMORE

WASHINGTON

ALEXANDRIA

When Lee arrived at Gordonsville on 15 August, he at once evolved a plan for offensive operations against Pope before the latter could be reinforced by McClellan. Should this juncture occur before Pope was defeated, the combined Union armies would so outnumber Lee as to make an attack by him unfeasible. Accordingly, Lee sought to maneuver quickly against Pope's line of communications in order to cut him off from his base of supply and then to attack and defeat him.

In pursuance of this plan, Lee massed his army behind Clark's Mountain with a view to moving to the Rapidan River, concealed from Pope's vision by the hill mass. He was to be preceded by his cavalry, under Maj. Gen. James E. B. Stuart, who would cross the Rapidan east of Somerville Ford, proceed to Rappahannock Station, and destroy the railroad bridge at that point. Lee, crossing at Somerville Ford, would then fall upon Pope's left and rear and wreak destruction upon the Union army, whose major route of withdrawal would have been severed by Stuart. Lee's plan called for crossing the Rapidan on 18 August.

Meanwhile, Pope, far from being discouraged by his repulse at Cedar Mountain, continued to act aggressively, though not in such a state of ignorance of events as has often been supposed. On 16 August, he exhorted Halleck to speed the movement of McClellan's forces, pointing out his danger should Jackson and Lee unite. But despite his fears of being cut off, Pope remained in his exposed position at Cedar Mountain. He may have been influenced by the fact that, through no fault of his own, he was receiving troops and supplies over two lines of communications— one from Aquia Landing and the other from Manassas. It was not until 22 August that Halleck began diverting McClellan's troops to Alexandria because of inadequate berthing facilities at Aquia. Then Pope's line through Manassas became his major route.

Lee's excellent plan to turn Pope's left on 18 August was never executed. Confederate logistical difficulties and the failure of Stuart's cavalry to cross the Rapidan on schedule precluded Lee's crossing at Somerville Ford until 20 August. By that time, Pope had withdrawn behind the Rappahannock. This wise move resulted from the capture by raiding Union cavalry of a copy of Lee's order for the 18 August operations. Stuart himself barely escaped capture, but his cloak and handsome plumed hat fell into Union hands. Perhaps enraged at such humiliating treatment, Stuart retaliated on 22 August with a raid on Pope's headquarters in which he made off with that general's dress coat as well as with papers which helped to establish the fact that Union reinforcements were en route.

Prior to Stuart's raid, Lee had followed Pope to the Rappahannock. He had made several attempts to turn the Union position both to the northwest and the southeast, but Pope's vigilance, plus rising waters brought on by rains on 22 and 23 August, had combined to nullify his efforts. Pope had seriously considered crossing the river to strike Lee's flank, but the flooded river prevented such a move. He had, however, ordered Sigel and Banks to attack the two Confederate brigades which, in an attempt at crossing the river at Waterloo, had been marooned by the high water. Sigel's slowness and the falling river enabled Jackson to extricate these brigades before an attack could be launched against them.

Thus, on 24 August, the two armies faced each other across the Rappahannock. A week of maneuvering by Lee had brought him nought. Aware of the reinforcements Pope was beginning to receive, Lee realized that his opportunity to strike before he was confronted with superior forces was rapidly disappearing.

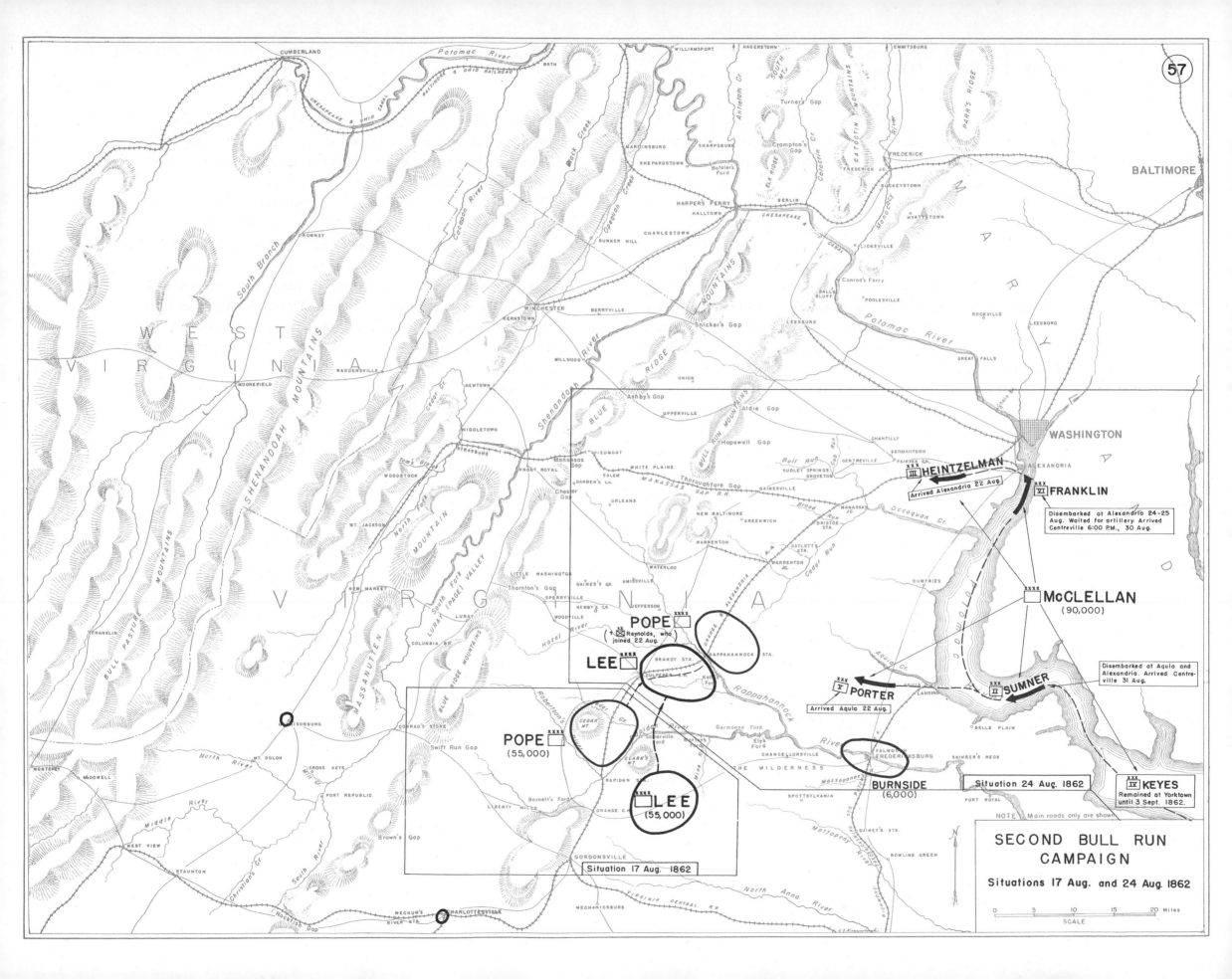

57

CUMBERLAND
Potomac River
WILLIAMSPORT
HAGERSTOWN
EMMITSBURG
BALTIMORE

BALTIMORE & OHIO RAILROAD
BATH
CHESAPEAKE & OHIO CANAL

Back Creek
MARTINSBURG
Antietam Cr.
SHARPSBURG
South Mt.
Turner's Gap
CATOCTIN MOUNTAINS
Parr's Ridge

SHEPARDSTOWN
Boteler's Ford
Crampton's Gap
FREDERICK JC.
FREDERICK

HARPERS FERRY
BERLIN
Monocacy River
BUCKEYSTOWN

ROMNEY
HALLTOWN
CHESAPEAKE & O.
HYATTSTOWN

WEST VIRGINIA
CHARLESTOWN
LICKSVILLE
M A R Y

BUNKER HILL
Conrad's Ferry
POOLESVILLE

WINCHESTER
BERRYVILLE
Shicker's Gap
ROCKVILLE
LEESBORO

KERNSTOWN
LEESBURG
LEESBURG

MILLWOOD
UNION
GREAT FALLS
Potomac River

NEWTOWN
Ashby's Gap

MIDDLETOWN
UPPERVILLE
Aldie Gap

WASHINGTON

STRASBURG
PIEDMONT
WHITE PLAINS
CHANTILLY
FAIRFAX C.H.
ALEXANDRIA

Manassas Gap
Hopewell Gap
Bull Run
GENTREVILLE
XXX III HEINTZELMAN

FRONT ROYAL
SALEM
Thoroughfare Gap
SUDLEY SPRINGS
GROVETON
Arrived Alexandria 22 Aug.

WOODSTOCK
MANASSAS GAP R.R.
GAINESVILLE
XXX VI FRANKLIN

CHESTER GAP
ORLEANS
NEW BALTIMORE
GREENWICH
MANASSAS JC.
BRISTOE STA.
Disembarked at Alexandria 24–25 Aug. Waited for artillery. Arrived Centreville 6:00 P.M., 30 Aug.

MT. JACKSON
WARRENTON
CATLETT'S STA.
WARRENTON JC.

LITTLE WASHINGTON
WATERLOO
Cedar Run
DUMFRIES
McCLELLAN
(90,000)

NEW MARKET
GAINES'S GR.
AMISSVILLE

Thornton's Gap
SPERRYVILLE
JEFFERSON
Aquia Cr.

WOODVILLE
POPE XXXX
+ Reynolds, who joined 22 Aug.
ORANGE & ALEXANDRIA
RAPPAHANNOCK STA.
Disembarked at Aquia and Alexandria. Arrived Centreville 31 Aug.

COLUMBIA BR.
BRANDY STA.
XXX V PORTER
XXX II SUMNER

LEE XXXX
CULPEPER C.H.
Kelly's Ford
Arrived Aquia 22 Aug.

Cedar Cr.
Robertson's R.
Rappahannock River

HARRISONBURG
LURAY
Hazel River

Swift Run Gap
CEDAR MT.
Germanna Ford
BELLE PLAIN

POPE XXXX
(55,000)
Robinson's R.
Rapidan River
Ely's Ford

MT. SOLON
CLARK'S MT.
CHANCELLORSVILLE
FALMOUTH FREDERICKSBURG
SKINKER'S NECK

CROSS KEYS
RAPIDAN STA.
THE WILDERNESS
Situation 24 Aug. 1862

McDOWELL
LEE XXXX
(55,000)
Massaponax Cr.
BURNSIDE
(6,000)
XXX IV KEYES
Remained at Yorktown until 3 Sept. 1862

PORT REPUBLIC
Bornett's Ford
SPOTTSYLVANIA
PORT ROYAL

WEST VIEW
GORDONSVILLE
GUINEY'S STA.
NOTE: Main roads only are shown

STAUNTON
LIBERTY MILLS
ORANGE C.H.
BOWLING GREEN

VIRGINIA CENTRAL R.R.
MECHANICSBURG
North Anna River

MECHUM'S RIVER STA.
CHARLOTTESVILLE

SECOND BULL RUN
CAMPAIGN
Situations 17 Aug. and 24 Aug. 1862

Situation 17 Aug. 1862

0   5   10   15   20 Miles
SCALE

Lee, hopeful of cutting off and defeating Pope before he could be further reinforced, conceived a new plan. On 24 August, he discussed it with Jackson and explained the part the latter was to play. The boldness of the plan stimulated Jackson, who had grown weary of futile attempts to cross the river in the face of Union resistance.

In brief, Lee prescribed that Jackson, with half of the army and Stuart's cavalry, was to move secretly up the river, cross it where feasible, and then get astride Pope's line of communications—the Orange & Alexandria Railroad. To divert attention from Jackson's movement, the remainder of the army would conduct diversionary operations against Pope and then follow Jackson. It was Lee's expectation that this maneuver would force Pope to retreat and, in so doing, would create the opportunity for the decisive Confederate attack which Lee had been seeking so desperately.

Lee's plan has been regarded by some critics as being too audacious—even foolhardy. Others contend that, under the existing circumstances, Lee was forced to take bold measures immediately or face eventual defeat by overwhelming forces. It is not likely that Lee conceived his venturous maneuver in disdain for Pope's ability, for the latter had frustrated every Confederate move during the preceding week. Rather, it was probably born of necessity and of Lee's confidence in his own ability to take advantage of any error by Pope.

Early on 25 August, Jackson moved north and, by driving his men hard all day, reached Salem that night. At dawn on the 26th, he started his cavalry for Thoroughfare Gap with instructions to seize and hold it for passage of his troops. The movement through the mountain pass was accomplished with practically no Federal opposition. That night Jackson bivouacked at Bristoe Station, on Pope's line of communications. Upon learning that the bulk of the Union supplies were at Manassas Junction, Jackson sent Stuart's cavalry and Trimble's brigade to seize the junction before it could be reinforced from Alexandria. This same night (26 August) Longstreet was at Orleans, en route to join Jackson, and McClellan himself arrived in Alexandria.

The corps of McClellan's army had debarked, some at Aquia Landing and others at Alexandria. Heintzelman's III and Porter's V Corps had already joined Pope. McClellan was under the impression that he was to command the combined forces; Pope understood that Halleck would do so. Halleck, burdened with details and concerned over the critical Union situation in Kentucky and Tennessee, had given little thought to the matter. So, on the eve of battle, the Union high-command structure was far from clear.

Meanwhile, Pope was not ignorant of Jackson's initial movements. By noon of the 25th, he had received detailed reports of Jackson's march and had accurately estimated his strength. But his cavalry, being in a run-down state, soon lost track of Jackson's force; and both Pope and McDowell first conjectured that Jackson was covering the movement of Lee's entire army to the Valley. On the 26th, some troops were sent to Waterloo in search of the Confederates; others were directed to concentrate and to be prepared to march on short notice. At 8:00 P.M. that night, the telegraph line to Manassas went dead. At 10:00 P.M., McDowell's scouts reported that Jackson had moved east on Manassas. Early the next morning, a party that had been sent to Bristoe Station to investigate the broken telegraph line returned with the news—which Pope had begun to suspect—that Jackson was at Manassas.

McDowell jubilantly pointed out to Pope that, with Lee's army now split, a golden opportunity had arisen. All depended upon the troop dispositions and movements now ordered by Pope. If judiciously made and expeditiously executed, these could well frustrate Lee's bold plan and perhaps lead to his defeat.

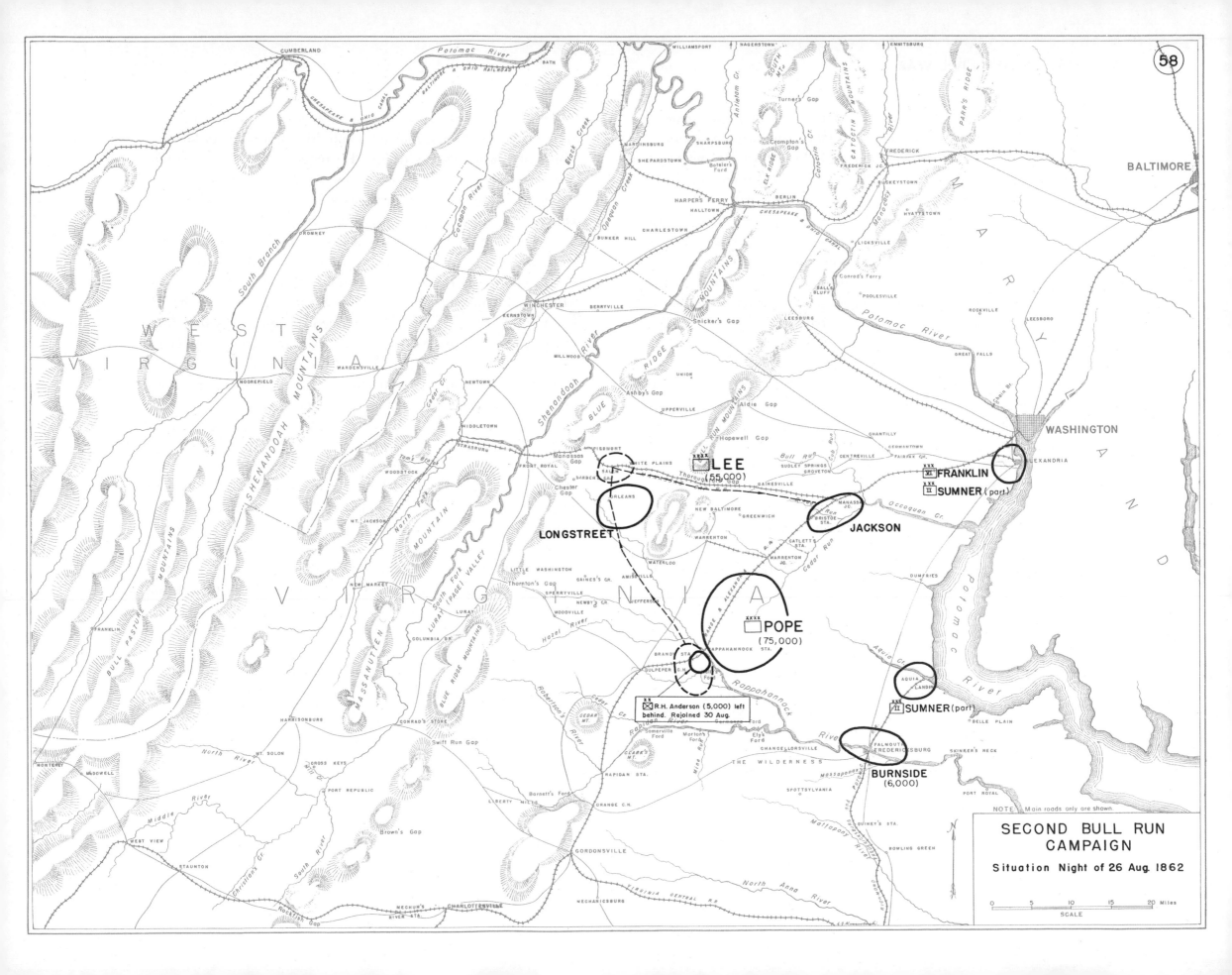

SECOND BULL RUN
CAMPAIGN

Situation Night of 26 Aug. 1862

On the morning of 27 August, General John Pope made a sound estimate of the prevailing situation and arrived at an excellent decision as to the employment of his forces. He knew that a major force of all arms was astride his line of communications at Bristoe Station and Manassas Junction. His cavalry and signal observation parties had apprised him of Longstreet's northward movement. It was clear to him that the movements of Lee's forces had made his position on the Rappahannock untenable. On the other hand, if he moved his troops promptly and properly, he had an excellent opportunity to interpose his army between Jackson and Longstreet and to defeat them separately.

By the evening of the 27th, the Union forces had reached the positions shown on the map, as prescribed in Pope's orders. Hooker had been directed to move to Bristoe Station, drive away the enemy, and reopen communications with Alexandria. He found the station occupied by Ewell who, though outnumbering Hooker, was under orders to avoid becoming heavily engaged and, accordingly, withdrew to join Jackson at Manassas Junction. That night Hooker encamped at Bristoe Station. His remaining ammunition supply was sufficient for only about five rounds per man. (The III Corps, of which he was a part, and Porter's V Corps had arrived from the Peninsula short of ammunition, artillery, and transportation.) There were several deficiencies in Pope's otherwise excellent plan. First, Hooker's division was too small a force to send on his assigned mission, especially since Pope had known that Jackson was at Manassas Junction with about 24,000 men. Secondly, he had failed to order McDowell to defend the mountain passes, particularly Thoroughfare Gap, through which Longstreet would have to move to unite with Jackson. Finally, he had assigned his cavalry to subordinate units and had none under his direct control.

At 10:00 A.M., Pope had sent a message to Halleck, via Burnside, informing him of Jackson's activities and of the orders he, Pope, had issued to his troops. He requested Halleck to send provisions and construction materials to Manassas Junction, expecting to reopen communications with Washington that night. However, Halleck already knew of Jackson's severance of the Union rail communications, having been apprised by Brig. Gen. Herman Haupt, who brilliantly supervised the railroad for Pope. Haupt, concerned for the safety of the important bridge at Union Mills, had managed to obtain the use of a brigade from the VI Corps at Alexandria and two regiments from Cox's division, recently arrived from West Virginia. This force, under Brig. Gen. George W. Taylor, moved to Union Mills by train on 27 August. Instead of taking up a position from which he could protect the bridge, Taylor foolishly advanced to attack Jackson. A. P. Hill easily repulsed the attack, drove the Federals back, and captured many of them. Then he destroyed the Union Mills bridge.

The morning of 27 August had found Jackson concentrated at Manassas Junction while three brigades under Ewell at Bristoe Station protected his rear. Except for the attacks of Hooker and Taylor, the day passed uneventfully. During the day his troops looted, plundered, and gorged themselves on the abundant stores which had been assembled at the junction to supply the two Union armies. Even Jackson's iron discipline could not restrain them. Late in the day he ordered wagons filled with ammunition, his troops to carry four days' rations, and the torch applied to what remained. He had accomplished the first part of his mission—the cutting of the railroad. Now he sought a position in which he could defend against Pope's expected attack while awaiting the arrival of Longstreet. The position he chose was Stony Ridge, near Sudley Springs.

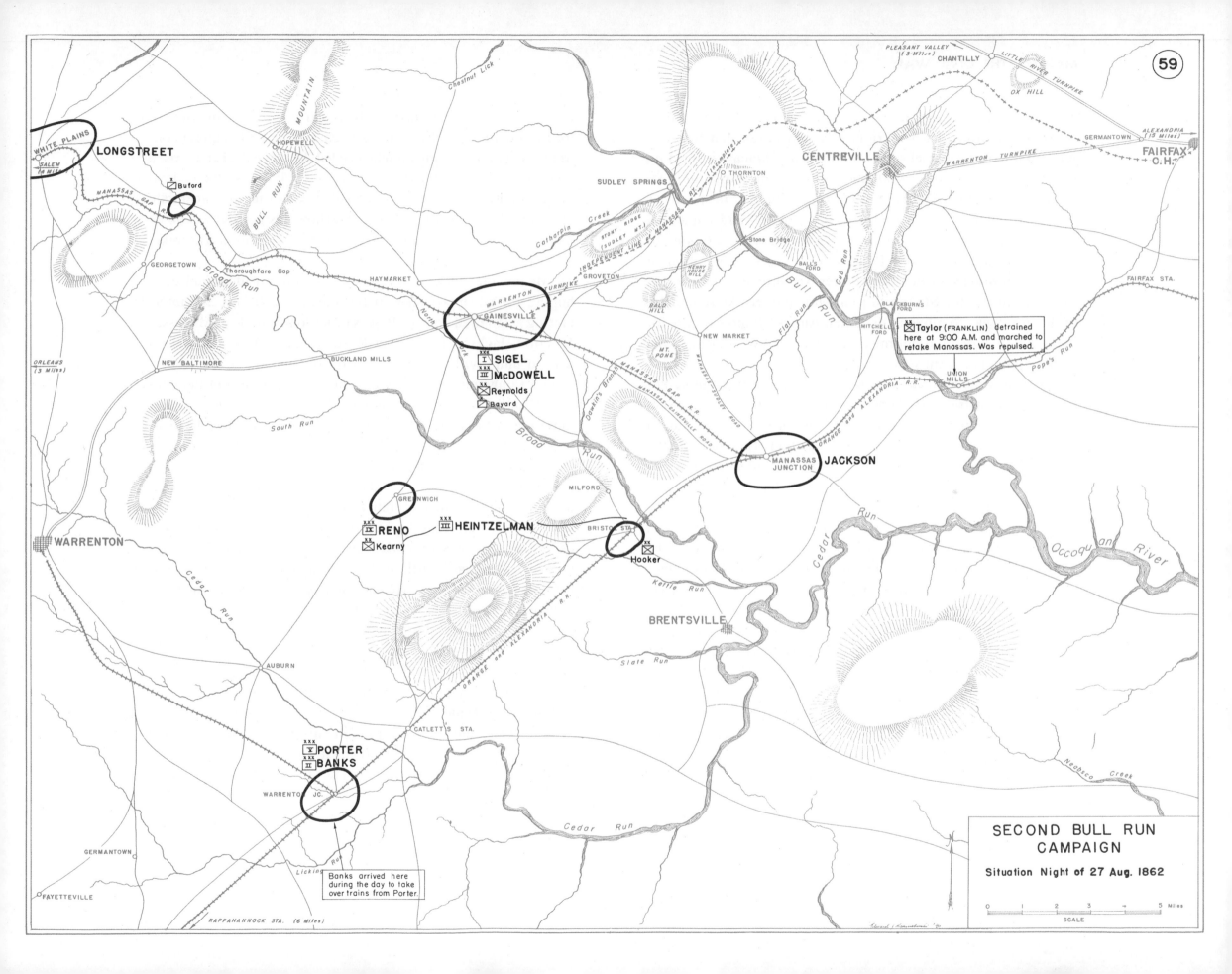

SECOND BULL RUN
CAMPAIGN

Situation Night of 27 Aug. 1862

The night of 27 August was an uneasy one for Pope, then at Bristoe Station. He was rightfully concerned that his only force in proximity to Jackson's 24,000 men at Manassas Junction was Hooker's division—4,000 men, almost out of ammunition. His apprehension probably led to a conclusion that Jackson was likely to remain in the vicinity of the junction and launch an attack on the exposed Union right flank at Bristoe Station. To forestall such a maneuver, Pope ordered the concentration of his army at Manassas Junction. Porter was directed at 1:00 A.M. to hasten to Bristoe Station to join with Hooker; the remainder of the army was to move at dawn, 28 August. Pope's orders for the move included the optimistic prediction: "We shall bag the whole crowd [Jackson's force]."

In his anxiety to destroy Jackson, Pope had either ignored or forgotten Longstreet. McDowell, on his own initiative, had sent Ricketts' division and the cavalry brigades of Bayard and Buford to hold Thoroughfare Gap against Longstreet. This, admittedly, was only a token force, but, in view of his orders to move to Manassas Junction, McDowell could not very well have dispatched a larger force.

The movements of Jackson's divisions further confused Pope. While the latter meditated at Bristoe Station on the night of the 27th, Jackson began to move his divisions to the defensive position he had selected on Stony Ridge. Because of confusing instructions issued by the secretive Jackson, Ewell and A. P. Hill took roundabout routes to the new position, and it was early afternoon before all arrived on the ridge. Meanwhile, Pope himself had entered Manassas Junction and found it abandoned. Having no information other than a report that A. P. Hill had been seen at Centreville (on his circuitous route to Stony Ridge), Pope concluded that Jackson was in that vicinity, and, at 4:15 P.M., his corps were directed to march on Centreville.

By now, Pope had lost control of the situation. Since dawn he had been marching his forces to and fro in vain attempts to locate and attack Jackson. With no cavalry under his direct control to secure the information he needed, he made decisions based on erroneous or imaginary concepts. So, at 5:30 P.M., the Federal forces, in process of executing Pope's latest order to concentrate at Centreville, were at the locations shown. Sigel and Reynolds had begun a countermarch to get on the Warrenton Turnpike, and King had turned eastward onto the pike.

Meanwhile, Jackson, in position at Stony Ridge, had been hoping for an opportunity to fall on Pope's troops. Misinterpreting a captured copy of Pope's order to assemble at Manassas Junction, Jackson feared that Pope was retreating across Bull Run to unite with the remainder of McClellan's army. He expected Longstreet momentarily and wished to prevent the concentration of the Union armies so that a decisive victory over Pope could be achieved. So, when King appeared in front of his position at 5:30 P.M., Jackson attacked, hoping to draw Pope's army upon himself and prevent the movement across Bull Run. King resisted stubbornly the attacks of the divisions of Ewell and Brig. Gen. William A. Taliaferro. Fierce but indecisive fighting continued until 9:00 P.M., with both sides sustaining heavy casualties. One of King's brigades—that of Brig. Gen. John Gibbon—here earned its title of "The Iron Brigade." On the Confederate side, Ewell was wounded and the Stonewall Brigade was reduced in strength to about 400 men.

To the west, Longstreet had arrived at Thoroughfare Gap at 3:00 P.M. Finding his way blocked, he sent troops to force the gap at Hopewell to outflank Ricketts' division. To the east, McClellan retained the corps of Franklin and Sumner at Alexandria despite Halleck's earlier instructions to send them to Pope. With his penchant for overestimating his opposition, McClellan believed that Jackson had 100,000 men—in spite of Pope's earlier message giving Jackson's strength accurately as 24,000.

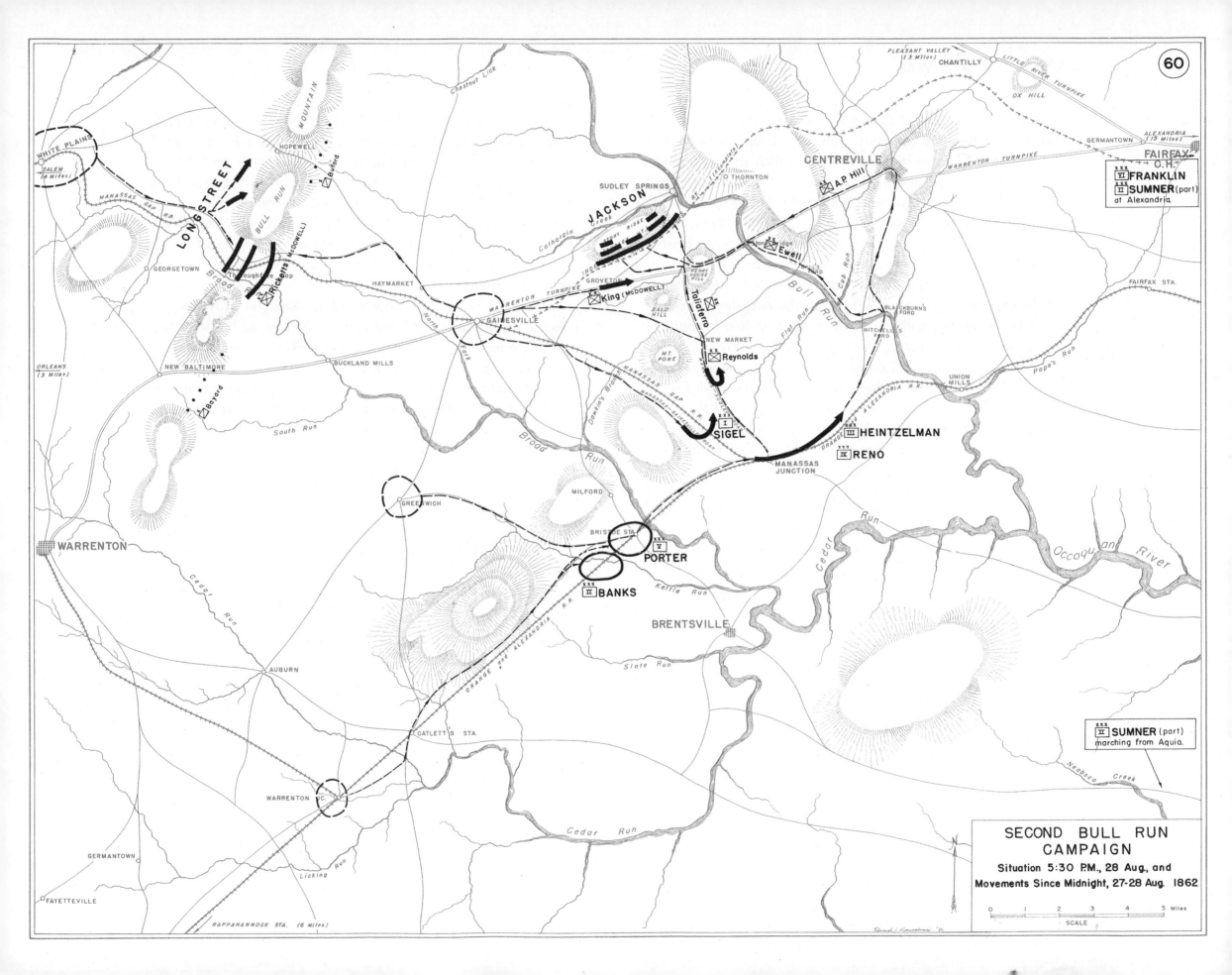

PLEASANT VALLEY
(3 Miles)
CHANTILLY
LITTLE RIVER TURNPIKE
OX HILL
GERMANTOWN
ALEXANDRIA
(15 Miles)

WHITE PLAINS
SALEM
(6 Miles)

CHESTNUT LICK

MOUNTAIN

HOPEWELL

Buford

LONGSTREET

BULL RUN

GEORGETOWN

Broad Run

MANASSAS GAP R.R.

Thoroughfare Gap

Ricketts (McDOWELL)

HAYMARKET

ORLEANS
(3 Miles)

NEW BALTIMORE

BUCKLAND MILLS

Bayard

South Run

North Fork

SUDLEY SPRINGS

JACKSON

Catharpin Creek

Stony Ridge

Ewell

WARRENTON TURNPIKE

GROVETON

King (McDOWELL)

BALD HILL

HENRY HOUSE HILL

Taliaferro

NEW MARKET

Reynolds

MT. POPE

MANASSAS GAP R.R.

Dawkins Branch

MANASSAS-GAINESVILLE

SIGEL

Dawkins Branch

Broad Run

MANASSAS JUNCTION

MILFORD

GREENWICH

BRISTOE STA.

PORTER

BANKS

Kettle Run

BRENTSVILLE

Slate Run

WARRENTON

Cedar Run

AUBURN

ORANGE and ALEXANDRIA R.R.

CATLETT'S STA.

GERMANTOWN

WARRENTON JC.

Licking Run

RAPPAHANNOCK STA.
(6 Miles)

FAYETTEVILLE

CENTREVILLE

A.P. Hill

FAIRFAX
C.H.

FRANKLIN
SUMNER (part)
at Alexandria

Cub Run

Bull Run

BLACKBURN'S FORD

MITCHELL'S FORD

UNION MILLS

Pope's Run

FAIRFAX STA.

HEINTZELMAN

RENO

Cedar Run

Occoquan River

SUMNER (part)
marching from Aquia.

Neabsco Creek

Cedar Run

SECOND BULL RUN
CAMPAIGN

Situation 5:30 P.M., 28 Aug., and
Movements Since Midnight, 27-28 Aug. 1862

0   1   2   3   4   5 Miles
SCALE

Dawn of 29 August found Pope's forces in the locations shown. The march during the previous night had been confused and fatiguing due to changes in Pope's orders, which caused counter-marching. Heintzelman and Maj. Gen. Jesse L. Reno had reached Centreville; Sigel and Reynolds, Warrenton Turnpike at Henry House Hill; Porter and Banks, Bristoe Station. Brig. Gen. Rufus King was at Manassas Junction, and Ricketts was at Bristoe Station. Two cavalry brigades opposed Longstreet's advance.

Late on the night of the 28th, Pope had issued orders for the battle he expected to wage with Jackson the next day. The contents of his orders indicate clearly that when he had formulated them he had neither correct knowledge of the activities of his own forces nor of those of Longstreet. King's fight with Jackson had given Pope the idea that Jackson was withdrawing down the pike toward Gainesville. His orders directed Sigel and Reynolds to attack the Confederates at daybreak, Heintzelman and Reno to march to Sigel's support, Porter to move to Centreville, and McDowell to march east from the Gainesville area and join in the attack. Thus, with forces converging on Jackson from east and west, Pope visualized complete victory on the 29th.

Pope's orders to McDowell make it evident that the Union commander was ignorant as to the whereabouts of two of the latter's divisions—those of King and Ricketts. Ricketts, after being forced away from Thoroughfare Gap by Longstreet's en-veloping maneuver through the pass at Hopewell, had fallen back to Gainesville. Here he had met King who, after his encounter with Jackson at Groveton, had reversed his march on the turnpike. McDowell had gone in search of Pope; in his absence, King (who was extremely ill) had, instead of waiting for orders, marched his division to Manassas. Ricketts likewise had moved to Bristoe Station. Thus, by the time McDowell learned of Pope's plan for the 29th, these two divisions were not available to carry out their assigned mission.

It will be noted that Pope's orders made no provision for possible participation by Longstreet in the coming battle. Somehow, Pope had gained the impression that Longstreet had earlier forced the gap, but had thereafter been driven back to the west of the mountains. How he had arrived at this erroneous understanding is puzzling, for at no time had he issued instructions to anyone to defend the gaps. Actually, Longstreet was east of the mountains at dawn of the 29th. His troops were less than ten miles from those of Jackson, and between them were only two worn-down brigades of Union cavalry.

Pope became aware of McDowell's actual dispositions early on the 29th. The orders he had issued for battle that day were no longer feasible; they would have to be modified to conform to realities.

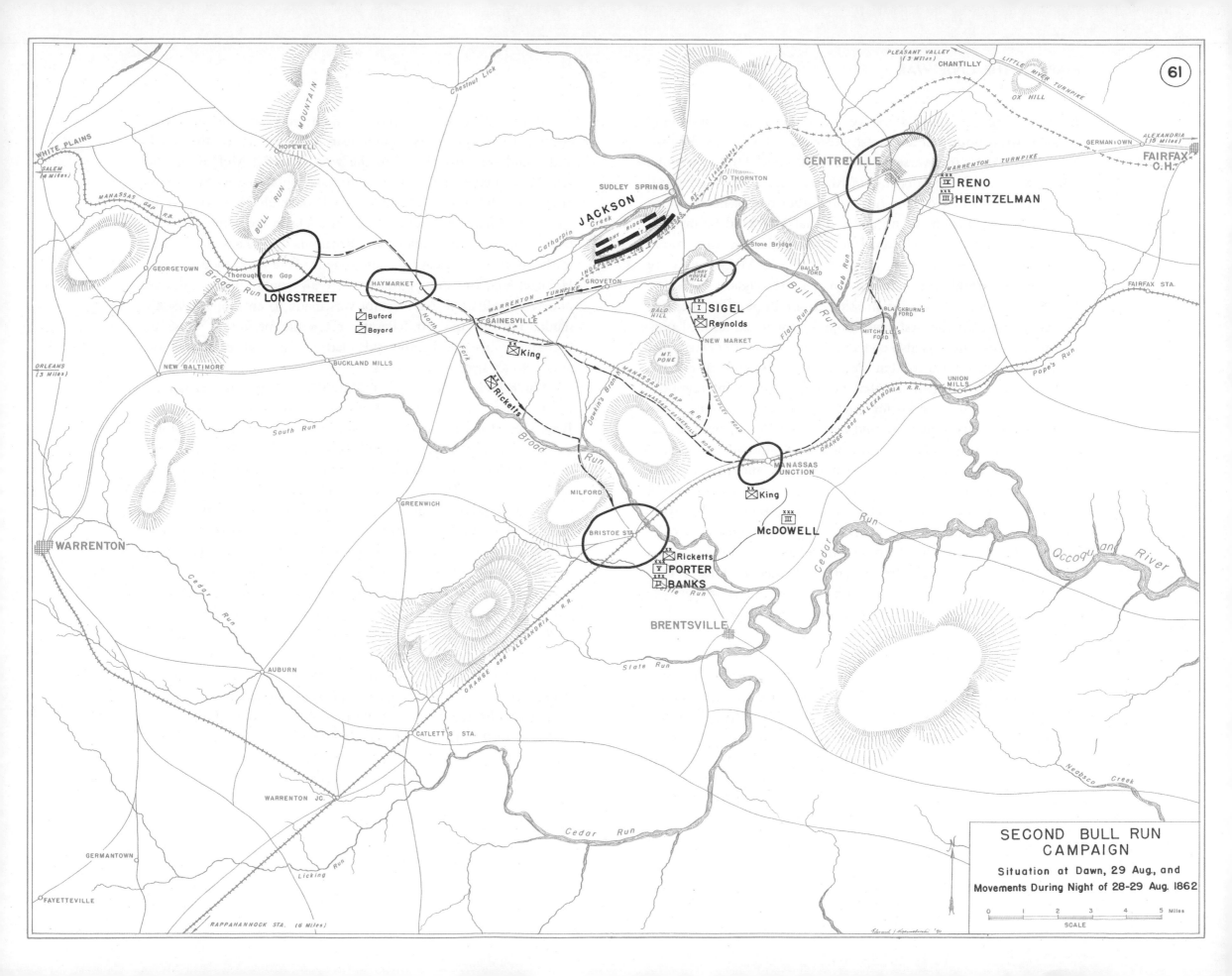

SECOND BULL RUN
CAMPAIGN

Situation at Dawn, 29 Aug., and
Movements During Night of 28-29 Aug. 1862

In modifying his plan, Pope retained the idea of attacking Jackson from both east and west. About 5:00 A.M., 29 August, he ordered Porter to reverse his march and proceed to Gainesville, taking with him King's division of McDowell's corps. McDowell had received no new orders, but, noting that one of his divisions was to go with Porter, he anticipated that he would be ordered to do likewise and so followed Porter with Ricketts' division.

About two hours later, when Porter and McDowell were approaching Bethlehem Church on the Manassas-Gainesville Road, they received a joint message from Pope. The message indicated that, for the first time, Pope was worried about Longstreet—and that he was also concerned over the matter of supply. It furthermore suggested that Pope still believed Jackson was withdrawing and recognized that he might escape interception, for it directed that, once Porter and McDowell made contact with Sigel, the entire command should halt. Then Pope would decide whether to continue the advance beyond Gainesville or to fall back east of Bull Run to replenish supplies and to await the attack of Lee's united army. The message contained no attack instructions for Porter or McDowell, but it authorized departure from its provisions "if any considerable advantages are to be gained." Presumably, the corps commanders could attack or not as they saw fit. Though the message indicated that Pope considered Longstreet a threat, it also showed that Pope grossly miscalculated the imminence of that threat, for he predicted that, if unopposed, Longstreet could not arrive at Centreville before dark of the following day.

Actually, Longstreet's four divisions had passed through Gainesville at 9:00 A.M. on the 29th and were in the positions shown before noon. At 11:00 A.M., Brig. Gen. John Buford's cavalry reported to McDowell that the Confederates had been at Gainesville at 9:00 A.M. and gave an accurate count of Longstreet's force. This report would have clarified whatever misconceptions Pope had concerning Longstreet, but McDowell failed to forward it to him.

McDowell and Porter pondered the message and discussed courses to adopt. They could hear artillery fire to the north and could see dust clouds to the west. Finally, McDowell, the senior, decided to have Porter continue his march toward Gainesville while he moved his corps north through New Market to aid Sigel. Meanwhile, the attack on Jackson from the east had been made as planned, Sigel and Reynolds having assaulted early in the morning and having been joined before noon by Reno and Heintzelman. But Pope's attacks were all frontal, piecemeal, and poorly coordinated. No attempt was made to envelop Jackson's flank. Though the Confederate left came perilously close to breaking, when the fighting subsided at sunset all of the Union assaults had been beaten back.

While Jackson struggled at Stony Ridge, Longstreet remained inactive in position nearby. Late in the evening he dispatched Brig. Gen. John B. Hood's division (his own left-flank division) forward to reconnoiter for a likely spot for an attack the next day, but Hood encountered Hatch (who had taken over King's division) and withdrew to his lines. On three different occasions Lee had wanted Longstreet to attack Pope's south flank, but each time he had reluctantly succumbed to Longstreet's pleas for postponement. Had Lee been insistent, it is very likely that the Confederates would have gained an important victory.

In the meantime, Porter had stopped at Dawkin's Branch where he had encountered Stuart's cavalry. Between 5:00 and 6:00 P.M. he received a message from Pope directing him to attack the Confederate right but at the same time to maintain contact with Reynolds. Apparently, Pope was still unaware of Longstreet's arrival and had in mind an envelopment of Jackson. Obviously, Porter could not obey both provisions of the order simultaneously. But he could have felt out Longstreet's position and informed Pope of the true state of affairs. He was later court-martialed for failing to obey Pope's order and was dismissed from the service. Twenty years later, when the real circumstances became known, his sentence was remitted.

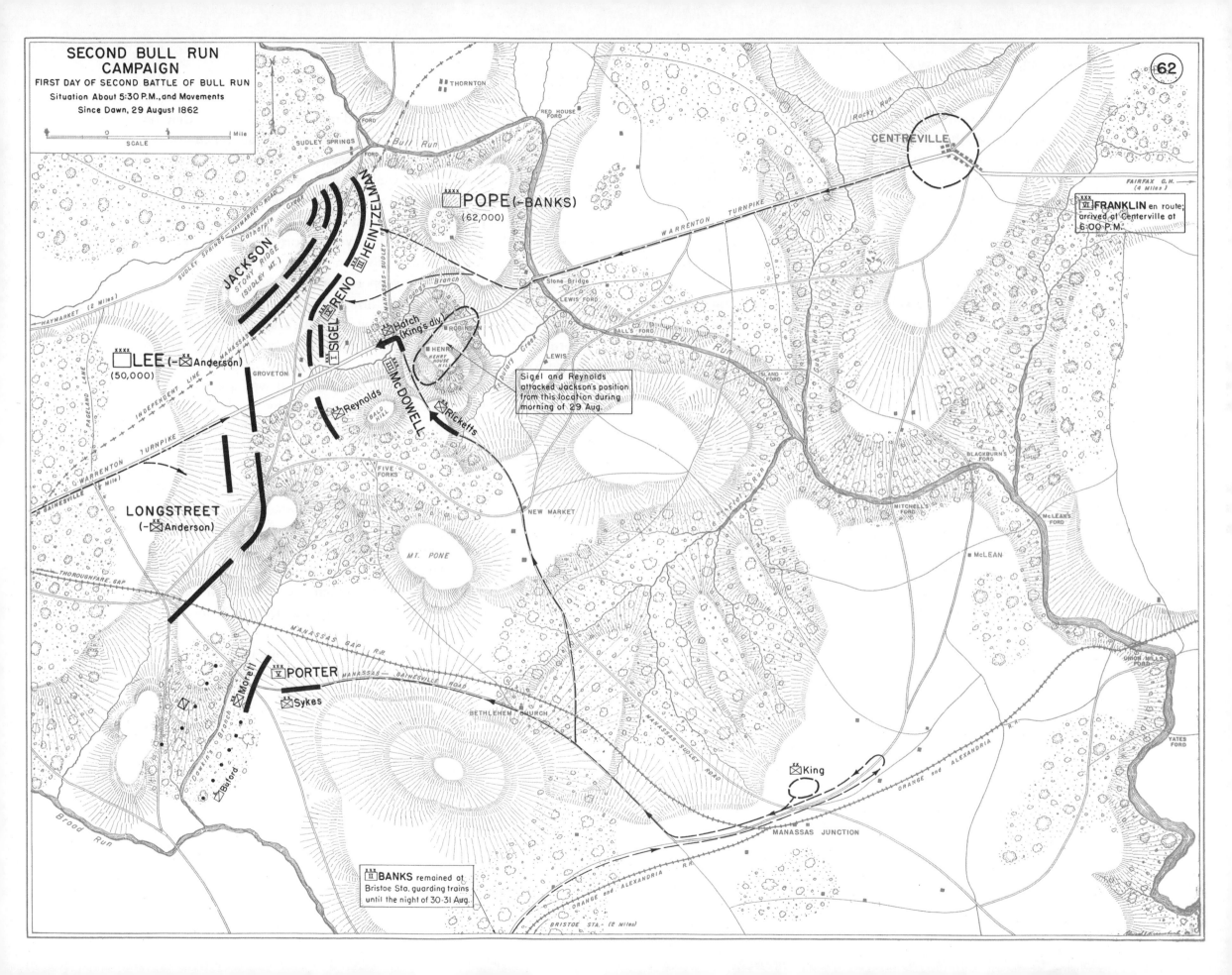

SECOND BULL RUN CAMPAIGN
FIRST DAY OF SECOND BATTLE OF BULL RUN
Situation About 5:30 P.M., and Movements
Since Dawn, 29 August 1862

62

SCALE

0   1 Mile

THORNTON

RED HOUSE FORD

FORD

CENTREVILLE

SUDLEY SPRINGS

FORD

Bull Run

Rocky Run

FAIRFAX C.H. (4 Miles)

POPE (-BANKS) (62,000)

WARRENTON TURNPIKE

VI FRANKLIN en route; arrived at Centerville at 6:00 P.M.

JACKSON STONY RIDGE (SUDLEY MT.)

SIGEL RENO III HEINTZELMAN

Stone Bridge

LEWIS FORD

LEE (-Anderson) (50,000)

GROVETON

Hatch (King's div)

ROBINSON

BALL'S FORD

Bull Run

ISLAND FORD

Reynolds

BALD HILL

HENRY HOUSE

HENRY

LEWIS

McDOWELL

Ricketts

Sigel and Reynolds attacked Jackson's position from this location during morning of 29 Aug.

FIVE FORKS

Tributary Creek

Young's Branch

NEW MARKET

BLACKBURN'S FORD

McLEAN'S FORD

LONGSTREET (-Anderson)

MT. PONE

MITCHELL'S FORD

McLEAN

MANASSAS GAP R.R.

UNION MILLS FORD

V PORTER

Morell

Sykes

MANASSAS - GAINESVILLE ROAD

BETHLEHEM CHURCH

King

YATES FORD

Buford

Broad Run

ORANGE and ALEXANDRIA R.R.

MANASSAS JUNCTION

II BANKS remained at Bristoe Sta. guarding trains until the night of 30-31 Aug.

BRISTOE STA. (2 Miles)

ORANGE and ALEXANDRIA R.R.

Hood's withdrawal on the evening of 29 August, combined with reports on the morning of the 30th from McDowell and Heintzelman, seemed to convince Pope that the Confederates were withdrawing from the field of battle. Ever sanguine in his outlook, Pope, about noon on the 30th, issued orders for McDowell to take up the pursuit with his own corps and the corps of Heintzelman and Porter. (The latter had arrived that morning from his position of the previous day at Dawkin's Branch.)

However, a withdrawal was the action least contemplated by Lee. Not desiring to assault the Union position, he was formulating plans to maneuver deep around Pope's right to interpose his army between the Union army and Alexandria. Nor had he expected Pope to resume the offensive. Thus, when Jackson came under heavy attack about 1:30 P.M. on the 30th, Lee was surprised. He immediately saw the opportunity for a Confederate counterstroke while the Union forces were out of position and in the open.

Shortly after Pope had issued his orders for the pursuit, Reynolds apprised him that the Confederates were not retreating, as Pope had believed. The Union commander then decided to renew the attack on Jackson's position. Porter's relatively fresh corps was ordered to make the main attack on Jackson's right while Heintzelman's corps and Hatch's and Ricketts' divisions of McDowell's corps attacked on the left. Reno and Sigel were placed in reserve, and Reynolds was directed to hold Bald Hill, in order to protect the south flank. Initially, Porter's assault achieved considerable success. Jackson's line, weakened from three

days of fighting, became so hard-pressed on the right that he asked for reinforcements. When Longstreet had taken up his position, most of his artillery had been placed on high ground that dominated the area over which Porter was attacking. So in response to Jackson's plea, Lee ordered Longstreet to unleash a strong artillery bombardment on Porter's troops. Surprised and taken in the flank by this artillery fire, Porter's corps broke and was forced back. Reynolds' division, except for one brigade, was rushed from Bald Hill to support Porter.

Both Lee and Longstreet now perceived the excellent opportunity to strike a decisive blow on Pope's southern flank. Lee ordered the attack, and Longstreet, already prepared, set his five divisions (Maj. Gen. Richard H. Anderson's division had arrived the previous evening) in motion. Bald Hill was quickly seized and held, despite repeated counterattacks by Sigel. Pope drew troops from his right to strengthen his left. The opposition on his north flank thus weakened, Jackson was enabled to advance there in support of Longstreet's attack. The Union army eventually was forced back to a position at Henry House Hill. Though the fighting there raged until dark, Lee was unable to dislodge the Union forces.

As the tired troops rested, Pope prepared plans for a withdrawal to Centreville. It would have been possible to bring up Franklin's fresh corps and strengthen the defenses during the night, so that by morning Lee would have been confronted with a formidable and well-manned position at Henry House Hill. But Pope, shaken over the failure of his plans during the last two days, apparently felt that a withdrawal was the wisest course.

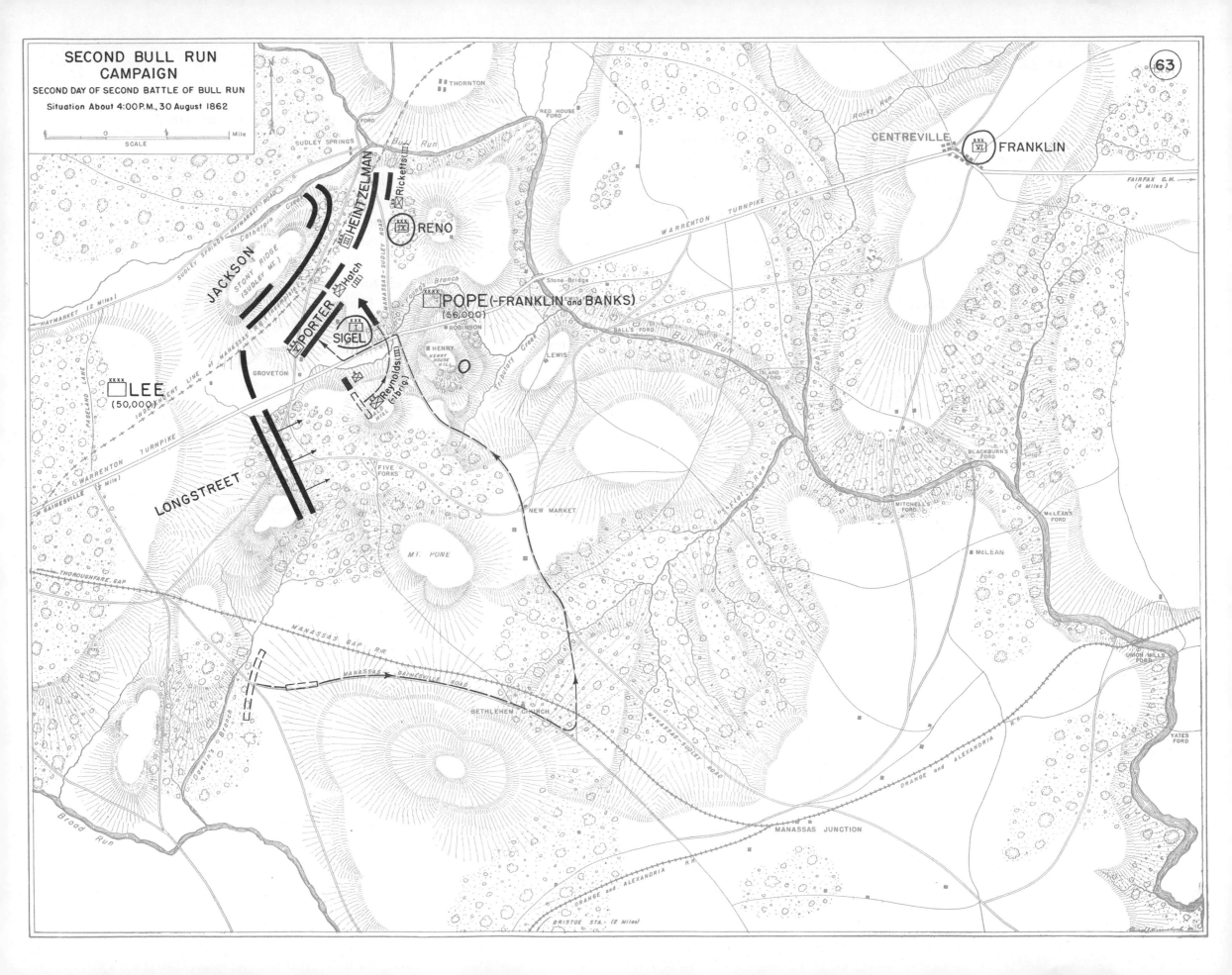

63

SECOND BULL RUN CAMPAIGN

SECOND DAY OF SECOND BATTLE OF BULL RUN

Situation About 4:00 P.M., 30 August 1862

SCALE

Mile

Pope issued his order for withdrawal to Centreville at 7:00 P.M., 30 August. The movement began after dark, with McDowell's corps acting as a covering force. Sigel's troops, the last to cross Bull Run, destroyed Stone Bridge. The march was uneventful and proceeded in a calm and orderly manner. By midnight, the bulk of the Union army was in position at Centreville. The withdrawal might have been different if Lee had followed it aggressively during the night, but his troops were extremely tired and, at this period in history, night attacks were not frequently attempted.

It will be remembered that Banks had been left at Bristoe Station to guard the army's trains. He was now ordered to rejoin the army at Centreville. Since the railroad bridge over Bull Run at Union Mills had been demolished, he was ordered to destroy much rolling stock and the many supplies which he could not take with him and to cross at Blackburn's Ford. All this he accomplished without serious interference from the Confederates.

Early on 31 August, as heavy rains fell, Pope composed a message to Halleck, introducing for the first time a note of discouragement. He intimated that if Lee should attack again, the Union army might be destroyed. Lee, however, had no intention of trying to cross the swollen Bull Run and attack frontally. Instead, he sent Jackson to the north to get behind the Union position at Centreville. Longstreet remained in position one day to deceive Pope, and then followed. Jackson bivouacked that night at Pleasant Valley, a few miles north of Centreville. Later in the day, Pope's spirits improved. In a wire to Halleck, he correctly predicted Lee's turning movement and expressed confidence in his ability to cope with it.

Meanwhile, McClellan, at Alexandria, had been badgering Halleck, in Washington, since early morning with messages reflecting fear for the safety of Washington. By noon, he had conjured up visions of Lee's already occupying Fairfax Court House and threatening to cut off Pope. Two days earlier he had harassed Halleck into allowing him to retain Franklin unnecessarily. Now, Halleck, relying on Pope's latest dispatch, would not order the army to withdraw from Centreville, much to McClellan's dissatisfaction.

Early the next morning (1 September), Pope ordered Sumner, who had arrived at Centreville, to send a brigade north to reconnoiter—his cavalry being so exhausted that it was necessary to send infantry on the mission. About 9:00 A.M., Pope's mood again changed and he wired Halleck that, though he intended to fight, he believed the army should be recalled to Washington. At noon he sent McDowell to occupy Germantown. Then he sent two brigades of the IX Corps, under Maj. Gen. Isaac I. Stevens, to Chantilly to block Jackson. Kearny's division joined Stevens later in the afternoon.

That same morning Jackson had started from Pleasant Valley toward Fairfax Court House. But his troops were hungry—not having received rations the previous evening—and almost exhausted from seven days of marching and fighting. By the middle of the afternoon, they had advanced only three miles—and then encountered Stevens' troops. The Battle of Chantilly (*inset, top right*) followed and continued until dark. The Confederates attacked several times, but, though outnumbering the defenders, they were repulsed. Both Stevens and Kearny were killed. That night Longstreet arrived to relieve Jackson's troops, and the Union force retired to Germantown and Fairfax Court House. In the morning, Pope again wired Halleck, recommending withdrawal. At noon he received authority to move into the fortifications of Washington.

So ended the second Bull Run campaign. Lee, bold to the extreme, had outmaneuvered his opponents and won a notable victory. The Union, plagued with divided command problems and Pope's misconceptions at critical times, found its army practically besieged in Washington and the country threatened with invasion. Lee's victory, however, had not been without cost—he had suffered about 9,197 casualties while inflicting some 16,054 on the Federals.

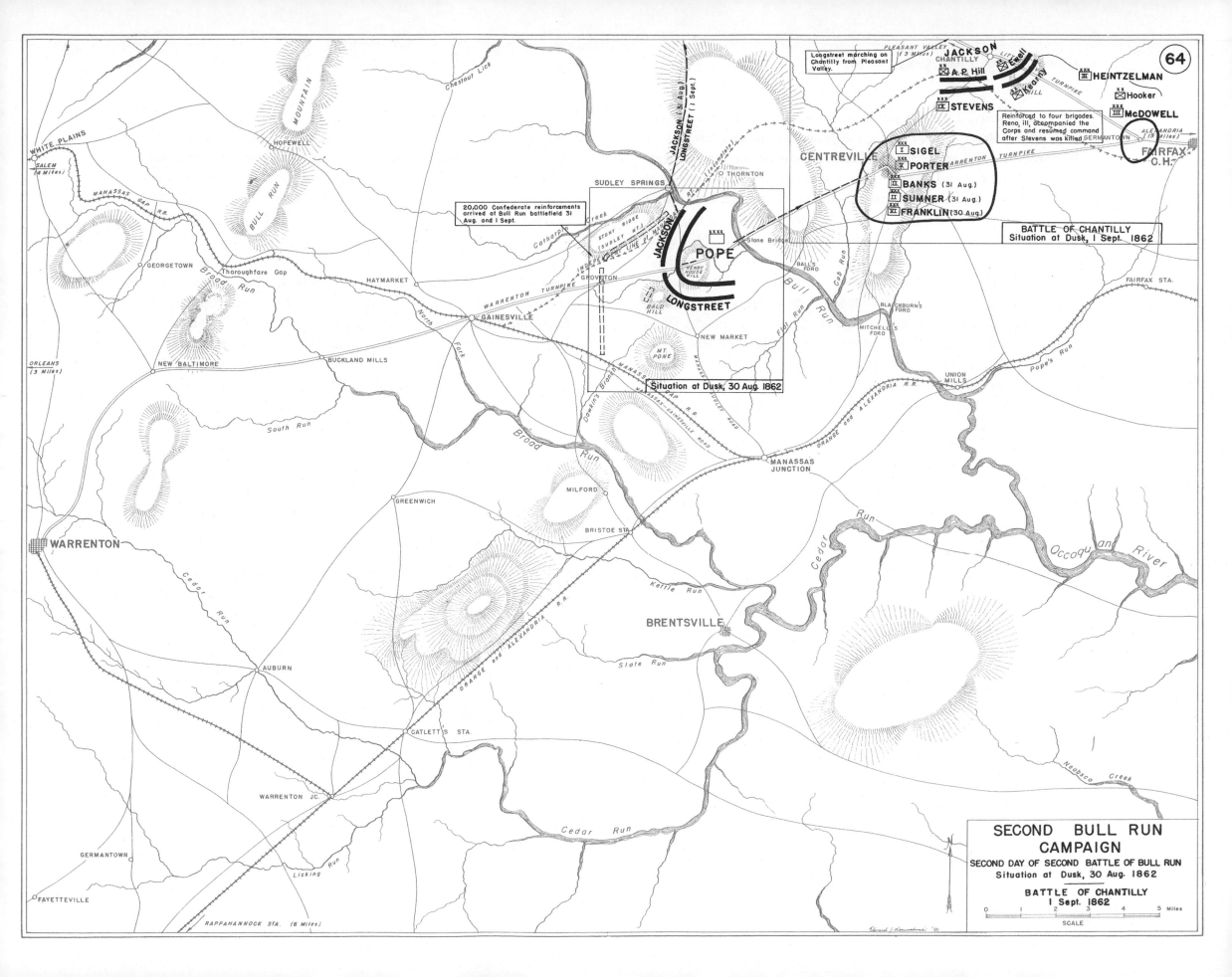

64

Longstreet marching on Chantilly from Pleasant Valley.

PLEASANT VALLEY (3 Miles)

JACKSON
CHANTILLY

☒ A.P. Hill

⊠ Ewell

☒ Hill

Branell

IX STEVENS

III HEINTZELMAN

☒ Hooker

III McDOWELL

ALEXANDRIA (15 Miles)

GERMANTOWN

FAIRFAX C.H.

Reinforced to four brigades. Reno, ill, accompanied the Corps and resumed command after Stevens was killed.

CENTREVILLE

I SIGEL

V PORTER

II BANKS (31 Aug.)

II SUMNER (31 Aug.)

VI FRANKLIN (30 Aug.)

BATTLE OF CHANTILLY
Situation at Dusk, 1 Sept. 1862

WARRENTON TURNPIKE

JACKSON (31 Aug.)
LONGSTREET (1 Sept.)

SUDLEY SPRINGS

THORNTON

20,000 Confederate reinforcements arrived at Bull Run battlefield 31 Aug. and 1 Sept.

STONY RIDGE (SUDLEY MT.)

JACKSON

LINE BY NOON

XXXX POPE

Stone Bridge

BALL'S FORD

Cub Run

INDEPENDENT LINE

GROVETON

HENRY HOUSE HILL

LONGSTREET

BALD HILL

NEW MARKET

Flat Run

Bull Run

BLACKBURN'S FORD

MITCHELL'S FORD

Situation at Dusk, 30 Aug. 1862

MT. PONE

GAINESVILLE

HAYMARKET

MANASSAS GAP R.R.

WHITE PLAINS

SALEM (6 Miles)

HOPEWELL

MOUNTAIN

Chestnut Lick

BULL RUN

Catharpin Creek

MANASSAS GAP R.R.

Thoroughfare Gap

GEORGETOWN

Broad Run

North Fork

Dawkin's Branch

MANASSAS GAP R.R.

MANASSAS-GAINESVILLE ROAD

SUDLEY ROAD

ORANGE AND ALEXANDRIA R.R.

UNION MILLS

FAIRFAX STA.

Pope's Run

ORLEANS (3 Miles)

NEW BALTIMORE

BUCKLAND MILLS

South Run

Broad Run

MILFORD

MANASSAS JUNCTION

GREENWICH

BRISTOE STA.

Kettle Run

Cedar Run

Occoquan River

WARRENTON

Cedar Run

BRENTSVILLE

Slate Run

AUBURN

ORANGE AND ALEXANDRIA R.R.

CATLETT'S STA.

Licking Run

WARRENTON JC.

GERMANTOWN

Naobsco Creek

FAYETTEVILLE

RAPPAHANNOCK STA. (6 Miles)

Cedar Run

**SECOND BULL RUN
CAMPAIGN**

SECOND DAY OF SECOND BATTLE OF BULL RUN
Situation at Dusk, 30 Aug. 1862

BATTLE OF CHANTILLY
1 Sept. 1862

Edward J Krasnoborski '80

0   1   2   3   4   5 Miles
SCALE

After Chantilly, Lee did not pursue the Union forces, which, on 3 September, withdrew in good order within the defenses of Washington. For two days confusion reigned over the reorganization of the Federal forces. Halleck refused to accept any actual responsibility; Pope wanted to reorganize, move out again, and fight; McClellan did "not despair of saving the capital," but thought it wise to send his wife's silver elsewhere. However, McClellan still had the confidence of the officers and men who had served under him, and Lincoln therefore decided that he was the best commander available. Pope's Army of Virginia consequently was integrated into the Army of the Potomac, Pope going to St. Paul to command the Northwest Department.

McClellan worked hard at reorganizing his army—indeed, this short period shows him probably at his best. The army contained a good nucleus of fresh troops, for the major part of the corps of Franklin and Sumner had not fought in the recent campaign. Also, thirty-five new regiments arrived and were distributed to fill out depleted divisions. Brig. Gen. Alfred Pleasonton's cavalry, just returned from the Peninsula, was sent forward to contend with Stuart.

Meanwhile, screened to the east by Stuart's cavalry, Lee began crossing the Potomac on 4 September and on the 7th was concentrated around Frederick, Maryland (sketch a). A number of reasons led him to risk this invasion: the need to retain the initiative; the chance that the invasion would win foreign recognition for the Confederacy; the hope of sparking a revolt in Maryland; and the desire to free his beloved Virginia from ravagement by contending armies. His over-all plan was opportunistic and vague —he would strike toward Harrisburg, Pennsylvania (top right), and cut the North's major east-west railroads, then consider operations against Philadelphia, Baltimore, or Washington. A quick estimate of his meager logistical capabilities should have tempered his optimism.

From Frederick, Longstreet was ordered to Boonsboro, where he was to await the return of Jackson, who meanwhile was to capture Harper's Ferry. However, a rumor that Pennsylvania militia (actually some twenty men) were mustering at Chambersburg (top left) caused Lee to push Longstreet on to Hagerstown (sketch b). This left only Stuart and D. H. Hill's division directly in front of McClellan. As a result, when the Union army finally approached, Lee's army was badly scattered.

The invasion produced new problems for the Confederates. Marylanders were polite but would not heed Lee's appeal to rise and regain their rights. The hard northern roads crippled the many men and horses without shoes. Supplies of all sorts were lacking; men lived on green corn and developed diarrhea. Only in morale and leadership was Lee's army formidable. But Lee knew McClellan well and counted on reaching the Susquehanna River before the Union commander would react.

Lee's crossing of the Potomac soon became known in Washington and, on 6 September, McClellan began to move slowly to the northwest. Now he was again bedeviled by one of his major weaknesses—the inability to obtain and logically evaluate military intelligence. Even in friendly territory, where accurate information was relatively easy to obtain, he was haunted by a vision of "not less than 120,000" Confederates lying in wait for him. Actually, his army was half again as large as Lee's. Also, concern for the safety of Washington was now reversed—Halleck badgered McClellan, who was already worried enough.

On 13 September, McClellan reached Frederick. There, he was handed a document which one of his soldiers had found in D. H. Hill's abandoned camp site. It was a copy of "Special Order No. 191," issued by Lee on 9 September, containing the entire Confederate plan of operations. McClellan delayed sixteen hours before putting his troops into motion. Then, on the night of the 13th, Burnside was directed to move toward Turner's Gap and Franklin toward Crampton's Gap.

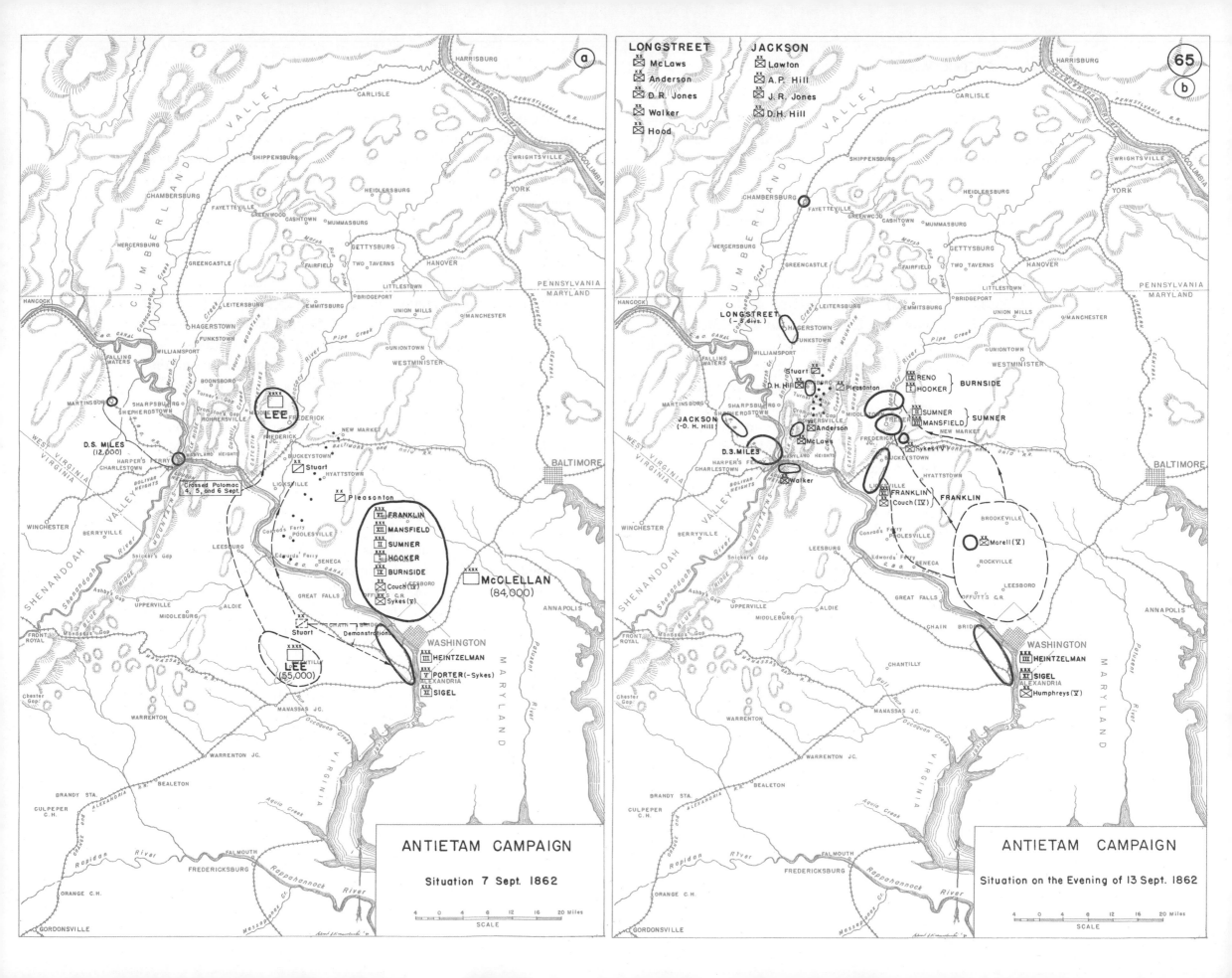

65

ANTIETAM CAMPAIGN

Situation 7 Sept. 1862

ANTIETAM CAMPAIGN

Situation on the Evening of 13 Sept. 1862

LONGSTREET
McLaws
Anderson
D.R. Jones
Walker
Hood

JACKSON
Lawton
A.P. Hill
J.R. Jones
D.H. Hill

McClellan made the mistake of allowing a local Confederate sympathizer to be present when Lee's captured order was being discussed. Consequently, by 10:00 A.M. the next day (14 September), Lee was warned; he started D. H. Hill and Longstreet to block Turner's Gap, which was then defended only by two of Hill's brigades (sketch a). It will be recalled that, though McClellan had received Lee's order by noon of the 13th, he did not advance his forces until daybreak of the 14th.

D. H. Hill was slow moving up the remainder of his division to defend Turner's Gap. However, he arrived in time to oppose Burnside, who finally concentrated at the gap about noon. The Union attack in the ensuing engagement (the Battle of South Mountain) was conducted cautiously, because of McClellan's exaggerated estimates of Confederate strength. Longstreet arrived to support Hill, and heavy fighting continued into the night. Finally, the Confederates, roughly handled and enveloped on both flanks, withdrew, leaving Turner's Gap in Union possession. General Reno was killed in the battle.

Meanwhile, to the south, Franklin proceeded on his mission to seize Crampton's Gap (sketch b); to cut off, destroy, or capture Maj. Gen. Lafayette McLaws' command; and to relieve Harper's Ferry. He reached the gap about noon and encountered part of McLaws' force, which had just taken up a defensive position. Attacking after a leisurely deployment, he swept the Confederates aside and began moving down Pleasant Valley toward Harper's Ferry. But McLaws, by dint of getting every man he could spare into a line across the valley, bluffed Franklin into thinking himself outnumbered. Franklin paused to consider the situation. He was still considering it when Harper's Ferry surrendered.

According to Lee's order, Harper's Ferry was to be surrounded by 12 September, but it was not until late the next day that the three commands assigned this mission reached their initial positions (sketch c). Why Lee decided on a dangerous dispersal of his army to capture Harper's Ferry is somewhat obscure. He may have felt that its garrison was a threat to his new line of communications down the Shenandoah Valley, or it may simply have offered too tempting a target. The Confederates spent most of 14 September establishing communications between their different forces, though McLaws and Maj. Gen. John C. Walker began bombarding the Federal position.

The town of Harper's Ferry itself was indefensible. It was dominated by high ground on all sides, especially by Maryland Heights just across the Potomac. McClellan had wanted to add the Harper's Ferry garrison to his field army, but Halleck had refused, saying that the movement would be too difficult and that Miles must defend himself until McClellan could relieve him. Halleck was probably wrong, but he undoubtedly expected Miles to show some military knowledge and courage. Instead, though reinforced by the Federal garrison from Martinsburg which had eluded Jackson (Jackson's attempt to bag it was responsible for most of his delay in reaching Harper's Ferry), Miles insisted on keeping most of the troops near the town instead of taking up a commanding position on Maryland Heights. Once the detachment he had left on the heights was driven in, he was hopelessly trapped by Confederates on higher ground on all sides.

During the night of 14 September, Col. Benjamin F. Davis and Col. Amos Voss led their 1,200 cavalrymen out of Harper's Ferry through McLaws' lines, capturing Longstreet's ammunition train en route. Miles made no effort to follow with his infantry. He had not been informed of Franklin's movement to relieve him. Whether this knowledge would have encouraged him to resist further is problematical. At 9:00 A.M. the next morning, 15 September, the garrison, bombarded from all sides, surrendered. Miles himself had been mortally wounded.

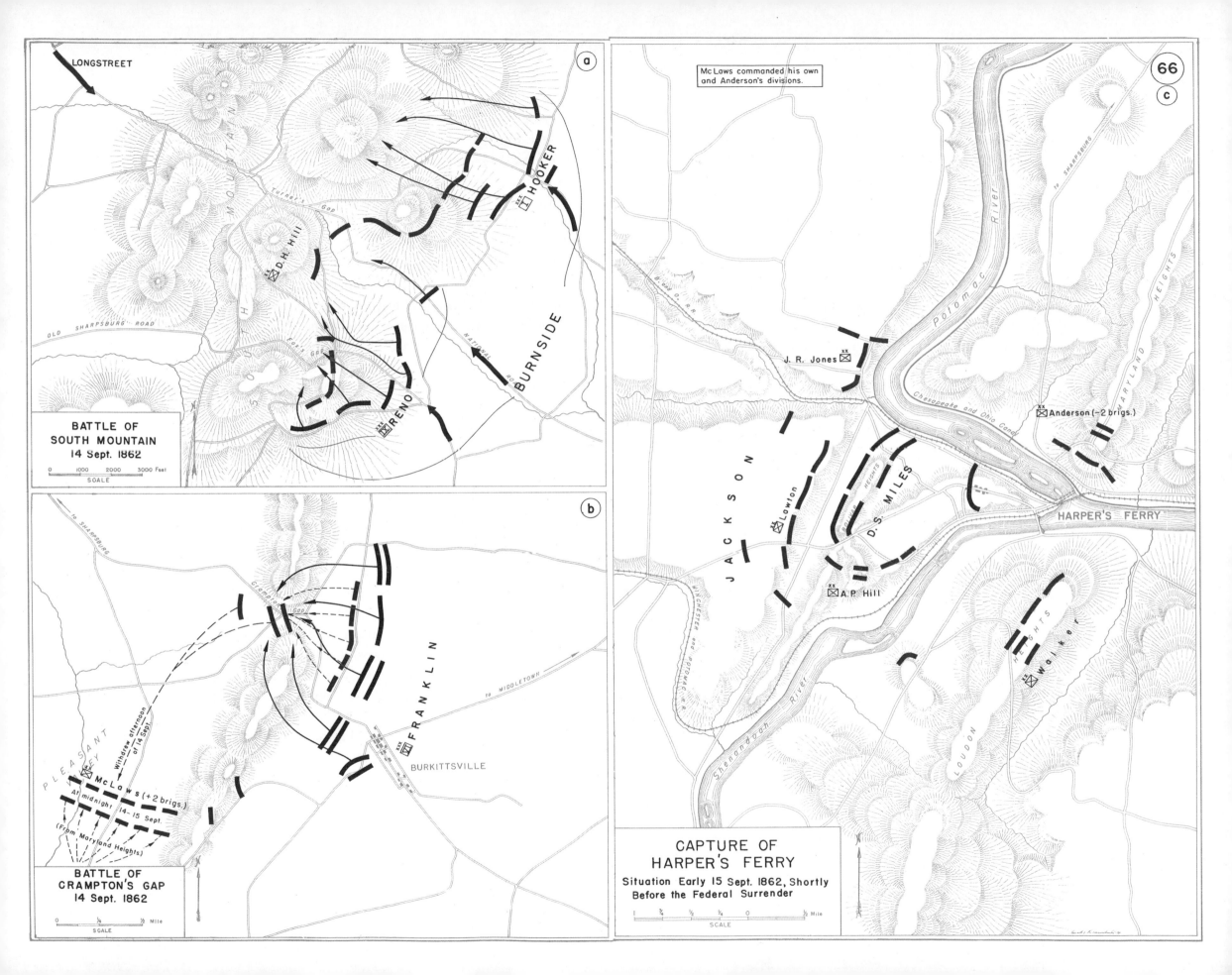

a

LONGSTREET

Turner's Gap

D.H. Hill

HOOKER

OLD SHARPSBURG ROAD

Fox's Gap

NATIONAL ROAD

RENO

BURNSIDE

BATTLE OF
SOUTH MOUNTAIN
14 Sept. 1862

0 1000 2000 3000 Feet
SCALE

b

to SHARPSBURG

Crampton's Gap

FRANKLIN

to MIDDLETOWN

PLEASANT VALLEY

Withdrew afternoon of 14 Sept.

McLaws (+2 brigs.)

At midnight 14–15 Sept.

(From Maryland Heights)

BURKITTSVILLE

BATTLE OF
CRAMPTON'S GAP
14 Sept. 1862

0 ¼ ½ Mile
SCALE

c

66

McLaws commanded his own
and Anderson's divisions.

B. and O. R.R.

Potomac River

to SHARPSBURG

MARYLAND HEIGHTS

J. R. Jones

Chesapeake and Ohio Canal

Anderson (~2 brigs.)

JACKSON

Lawton

Bolivar Heights

D. S. MILES

HARPER'S FERRY

WINCHESTER and POTOMAC R.R.

A.P. Hill

Shenandoah River

B. and O. R.R.

LOUDON HEIGHTS

Walker

CAPTURE OF
HARPER'S FERRY
Situation Early 15 Sept. 1862, Shortly
Before the Federal Surrender

1 ¾ ½ ¼ 0 ½ Mile
SCALE

Having lost the South Mountain passes, Lee planned to withdraw through Sharpsburg (*sketch* a) to the south bank of the Potomac and concentrate his forces before McClellan could crush them in detail. McLaws was instructed to abandon Maryland Heights and likewise move south of the river. But when Jackson reported that Harper's Ferry might soon fall, Lee decided to halt temporarily at Sharpsburg. Then, once he learned that Jackson had captured Harper's Ferry and was moving to rejoin him, Lee's innate combativeness reasserted itself. He immediately took up a defensive position behind Antietam Creek and awaited McClellan.

The position was shallow and only moderately strong. Probably its weakest point was that Lee could retreat or receive reinforcements only by way of Boteler's Ford—deep, rocky, and in rear of the extreme right of the Confederate line. Another major weakness of the position was that high ground along the east bank of Antietam Creek provided excellent positions from which Union artillery could dominate most of the Confederate position. Antietam Creek was of limited value as an obstacle, except below the Middle Bridge where its west bank was steep and rugged. In addition to the four bridges across it, there were several regular fords and, at this season, it could be waded in many other places. Lee failed to strengthen his line with field fortifications, but numerous irregularities in the ground and several small woods gave his troops considerable shelter.

McClellan's main body (Franklin had been left at Rohrersville to cover Harper's Ferry) arrived at the position shown during the early afternoon of 15 September. McClellan, however, judged it too late in the day to begin an attack. He spent 16 September in skirmishing and formulating plans. A determined attack that morning with his superior numbers would have crushed the little force Lee then had with him. Later in the day, Jackson and Walker rejoined Lee. Anderson and McLaws were preparing to follow. A. P. Hill remained at Harper's Ferry to complete the paroling of the Union garrison there.

Eventually, McClellan formed a plan. He decided, in words that reveal his innate lack of decision and clarity, "to make the main attack upon the enemy's left—at least to create a diversion in favor of the main attack, with the hope of something more, by assailing the enemy's right—and, as soon as one or both of the flank movements were fully successful, to attack their center with any reserve I might then have in hand." Nebulous as this conception was, his numerical superiority ensured success, if the various attacks were properly coordinated. McClellan, however, issued no written general order for the attack, made no effective reconnaissance to discover Lee's exact position or the points at which Antietam Creek could be forded, and rearranged his forces so as to thoroughly break up the existing organization of his army (*compare sketches* a and b). Finally, it was not until midnight of the 16th that he ordered Franklin to rejoin him.

In accordance with his plan, McClellan sent Hooker's corps across the Upper Bridge and a nearby ford (*sketch* a) on the afternoon of the 16th to get into position for the attack the next morning on the Confederate left. Naturally, the movement was discovered, and Hood was sent out to dispute it. After some brisk skirmishing, Hood was withdrawn and Hooker went into bivouac. Maj. Gen. Joseph K. F. Mansfield, who was to support Hooker, did not receive his orders until about midnight, and consequently had no chance to reconnoiter.

As soon as there was enough light on the morning of the 17th, Hooker delivered a powerful assault on Lee's left (*sketch* b). Here, Jackson's line gave way in heavy fighting but did not break. A savage counterattack by Hood and enfilading fire from Stuart's artillery helped to check the Union attack; however, Confederate losses were heavy. Mansfield brought the XII Corps forward, but was killed almost instantly. Shortly thereafter, Hooker was wounded.

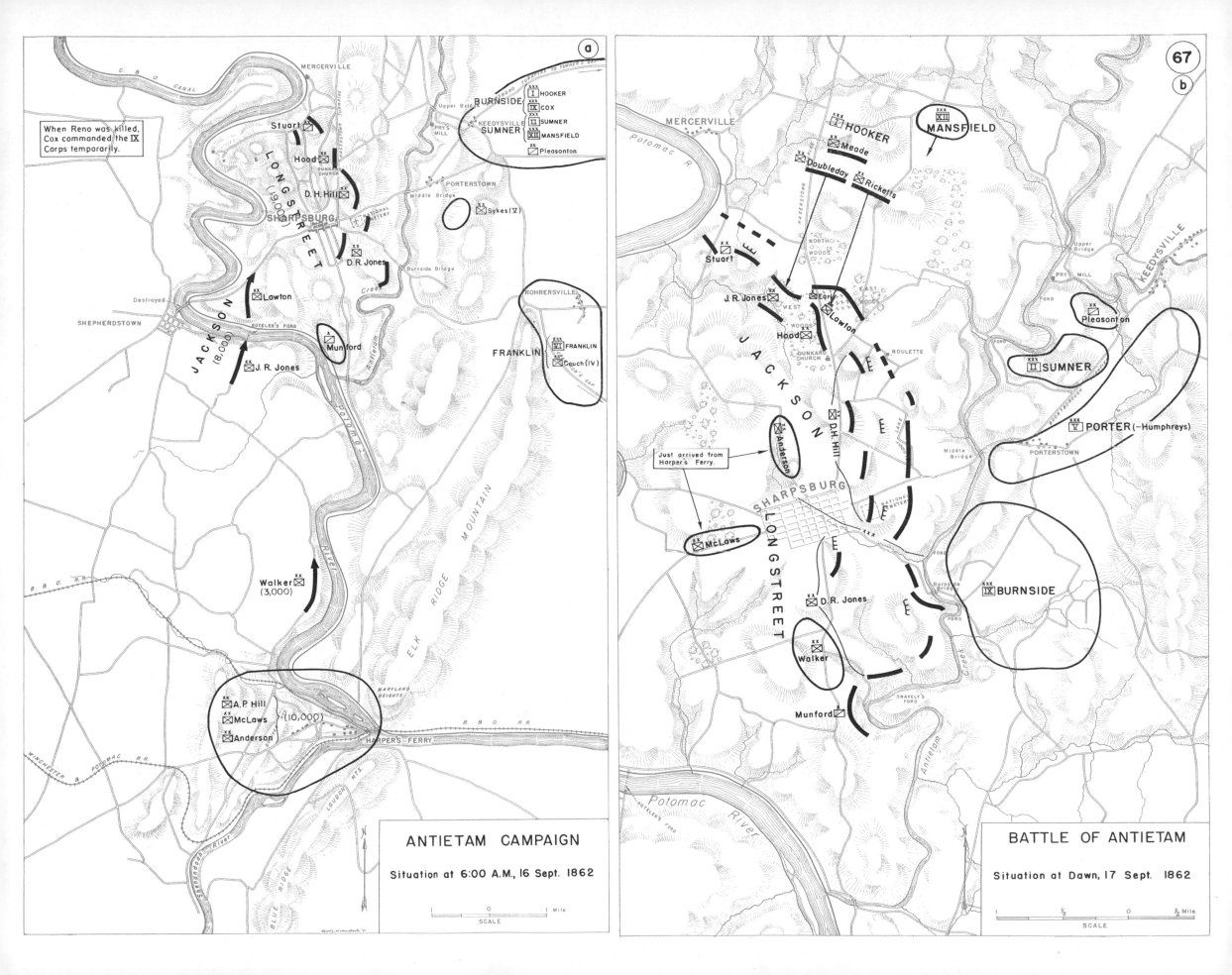

Map (a) — Antietam Campaign

When Reno was killed, Cox commanded the IX Corps temporarily.

MERCERVILLE

C. & O. CANAL

Upper Brid'ge
PRY'S MILL
KEEDYSVILLE

Stuart

Hood

LONGSTREET
(19,000)

D. H. Hill

SHARPSBURG

PORTERSTOWN

Middle Bridge

Sykes (V)

D. R. Jones

Burnside Bridge

Antietam Creek

BURNSIDE
I HOOKER
IX COX
SUMNER
II SUMNER
XII MANSFIELD
Pleasonton

Lawton

JACKSON
(8,000)

Munford

J. R. Jones

Destroyed

SHEPHERDSTOWN

Potomac River

BOTELER'S FORD

ROHRERSVILLE

FRANKLIN

VI FRANKLIN
Couch (IV)
CRAMPTON'S GAP

ELK RIDGE MOUNTAIN

Walker
(3,000)

B. & O. R. R.

MARYLAND HEIGHTS

B. & O. R. R.

A. P. Hill
McLaws
(10,000)
Anderson

HARPER'S FERRY

WINCHESTER & POTOMAC R.R.

LOUDON MTS.

Shenandoah River

BLUE RIDGE

ANTIETAM CAMPAIGN

Situation at 6:00 A.M., 16 Sept. 1862

0   Mile
SCALE

Map (b) — Battle of Antietam

MERCERVILLE

Potomac R.

HOOKER

Meade

MANSFIELD

Doubleday   Ricketts

HAGERSTOWN

NORTH WOODS

Stuart

EAST WOODS

Upper Bridge

PRY'S MILL

FORD

J. R. Jones   Early

WEST WOODS

Lawton

Hood

DUNKARD CHURCH

ROULETTE

Pleasonton

JACKSON

D. H. Hill

II SUMNER

Anderson

Just arrived from Harper's Ferry.

SHARPSBURG

LONGSTREET

Middle Bridge

V PORTER (–Humphreys)

PORTERSTOWN

McLaws

NATIONAL CEMETERY

Burnside Bridge

IX BURNSIDE

D. R. Jones

FORD

Walker

SNAVELY'S FORD

Antietam Creek

Munford

Potomac River

BOTELER'S FORD

BATTLE OF ANTIETAM

Situation at Dawn, 17 Sept. 1862

1/2   0   1/2 Mile
SCALE

The loss of two fighting corps commanders, Hooker and Mansfield, left no one in over-all control of McClellan's "main attack" on the Confederate left (*sketch* a). Meade rallied the remnants of the I Corps near North Woods (*top left*), while the XII Corps' division commanders, Brig. Gen. Alpheus Williams and Brig. Gen. George S. Greene, pressed the attack. They completed the shattering of the Confederate left and forced it back beyond the Dunkard Church and West Woods. Soon Williams had to withdraw his division to rest and replenish ammunition, but Greene clung to the Dunkard Church and part of the woods around it.

Sumner had been alerted the previous evening to be ready for action early the next morning. Though eager to advance to the sound of the guns, he was held at McClellan's headquarters until 7:20 A.M. Finally securing orders to advance, he moved out with his II Corps, he himself riding with the leading division, that of Maj. Gen. John Sedgwick. Sumner, a reckless old cavalryman, brought Sedgwick's division forward in mass without pausing for reconnaissance. Flung into the action in column formation (*map* b), it was soon trapped by Confederate troops sent forward by Jackson in a hasty counterattack from three directions. With the advantage of position and surprise, the outnumbered Confederates drove Sedgwick back in disorder, the Federals losing about 2,200 men. The Confederates pressed the pursuit and almost regained the ground lost earlier in the morning, but they were finally stopped by strong Union artillery fire. When Sedgwick's division left the field, Greene, now exposed on his right, was also forced to withdraw.

The second division of Sumner's corps, that of Brig. Gen. William H. French, had somehow missed the road taken by Sedgwick. It came into line farther south against the left of Lee's center, where it became engaged in a savage fight with D. H. Hill. Sumner's last division, that of Maj. Gen. Israel B. Richardson, arrived later on French's left, after having been delayed for an hour by McClellan. Together, the two divisions forced the Confederates back into Bloody Lane (a sunken road which formed a natural trench). Here the battle reached the extreme of viciousness and frightful carnage. Finally, the Union forces gained enfilade fire on the lane. One Confederate commander, seeking to get his troops out of the line of fire, ordered them to face about and march to the rear. This suggestion of retreat affected the other troops in the lane. They broke and fled, leaving the lane to the Union forces.

The last Confederate regiment north of Sharpsburg had been committed. Lee's artillery, though still fighting back gamely, had been overwhelmed by the mass of expertly handled Federal guns. Sharpsburg was filled with demoralized soldiers; famous commands, like Hood's Texans, were completely shattered; most of the left and center was held only by devoted handfuls, hanging on out of sheer courage. One more vigorous Federal attack and the Army of Northern Virginia would face destruction.

Meanwhile, on the Union left flank, Burnside was to execute that part of McClellan's plan "to create a diversion in favor of the main attack, with the hope of something more, by assailing the enemy's right." He had started his deployment at about 7:00 A.M. It was apparently 10:00 A.M. before he received the order to attack. By that time, the main attack on the Confederate left and center was in its last stage and about to subside.

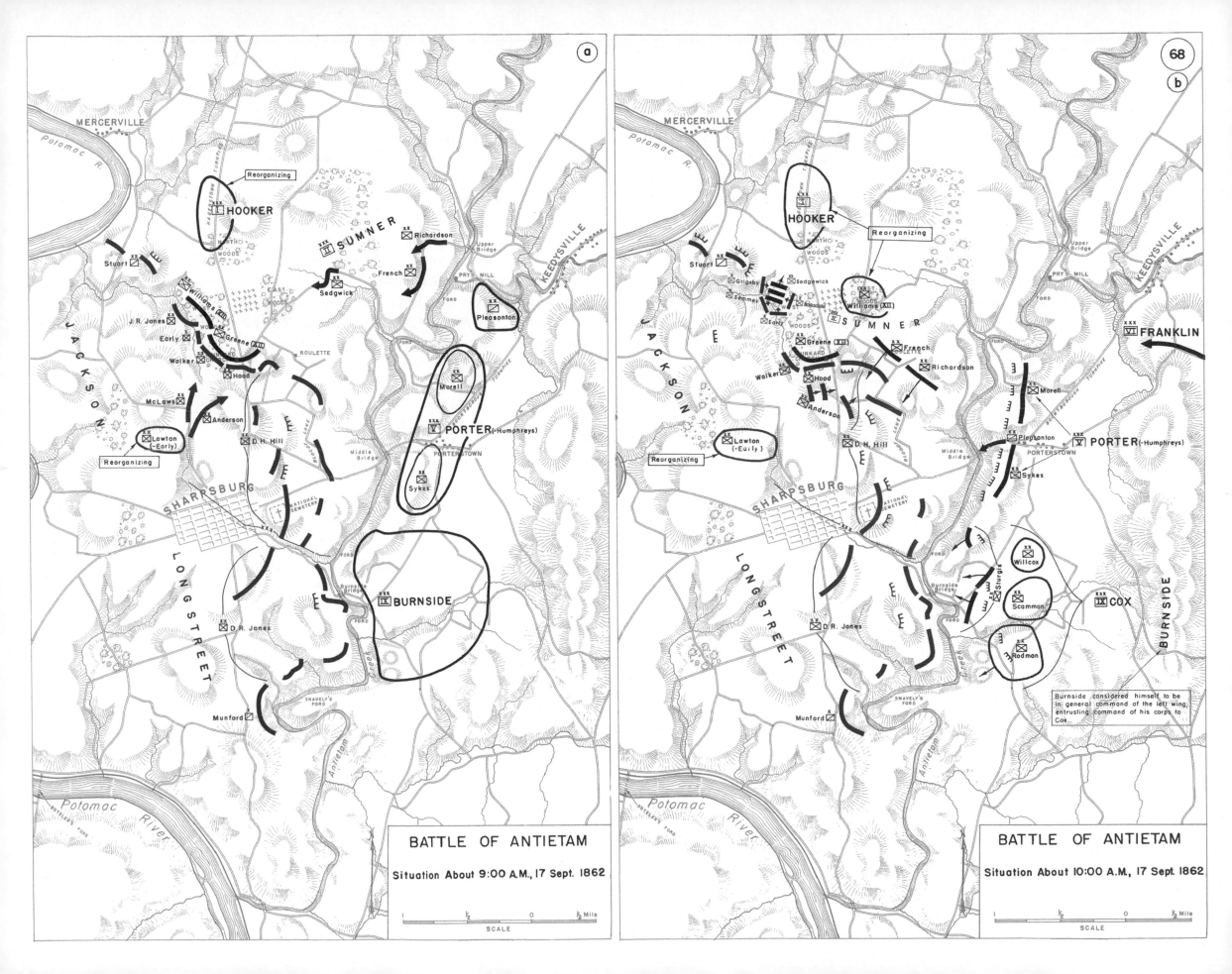

(a) Reorganizing · HOOKER · SUMNER · Richardson · Upper Bridge · KEEDYSVILLE · JACKSON · Stuart · Williams · French · PRY'S MILL · Sedgwick · J. R. Jones · EAST WOODS · FORD · Early · Greene (XII) · Pleasonton · Walker · ROULETTE · Hood · McLaws · Morell · Anderson · Lawton (-Early) · Reorganizing · D. H. Hill · Middle Bridge · PORTERSTOWN · V PORTER (-Humphreys) · Sykes · SHARPSBURG · NATIONAL CEMETERY · LONGSTREET · Burnside Bridge · IX BURNSIDE · FORD · D. R. Jones · SNAVELY'S FORD · Munford · Antietam · Potomac River · BOTELER'S FORD · MERCERVILLE · Potomac R.

BATTLE OF ANTIETAM
Situation About 9:00 A.M., 17 Sept. 1862

SCALE · 1 · ½ · 0 · ½ Mile

(b) 68 · MERCERVILLE · Potomac R. · HOOKER · Reorganizing · Upper Bridge · PRY'S MILL · KEEDYSVILLE · Stuart · Grigsby · Sedgwick · Semmes · Williams (XII) · Early · SUMNER · VI FRANKLIN · Greene (XII) · French · JACKSON · Walker · Hood · Richardson · Anderson · Morell · Lawton (-Early) · Reorganizing · D. H. Hill · Pleasonton · Middle Bridge · PORTERSTOWN · V PORTER (-Humphreys) · Sykes · SHARPSBURG · NATIONAL CEMETERY · LONGSTREET · Willcox · Burnside Bridge · Sturgis · Scammon · IX COX · D. R. Jones · Rodman · BURNSIDE · SNAVELY'S FORD · Munford · Antietam · Potomac River

Burnside considered himself to be in general command of the left wing, entrusting command of his corps to Cox.

BATTLE OF ANTIETAM
Situation About 10:00 A.M., 17 Sept. 1862

SCALE · 1 · ½ · 0 · ½ Mile

Following the capture of Bloody Lane, Richardson drove the Confederates from the hills to the south of it, completely wrecking Lee's center (*sketch* a). Richardson was seriously wounded while regrouping for a final assault, but Franklin was now on the field and was eager to make the decisive attack. Sumner, however, thoroughly shaken by his recent repulse, asserted his rank as senior corps commander present and forbade another advance. Franklin appealed to McClellan, whereupon McClellan upheld Sumner.

There still remained Burnside's effort on the south. He had forgotten to have the creek scouted for possible crossings; consequently, his main effort was made against the bridge now known by his name. However, he did send Brig. Gen. Isaac P. Rodman to cross at a ford (Snavely's) reported to exist some distance downstream. Two attacks on the bridge were repulsed, but a third rush at about 1:00 P.M. carried it. About that same time, Rodman finally located his ford while, ironically, other elements of Burnside's command discovered that the creek could be waded at many places along their front. Still, it was 3:00 P.M. before the IX Corps was deployed across the creek (*sketch* b). Initially, the IX Corps' renewed attack was highly successful. By 4:00 P.M., it had gained almost all of the high ground to the east and south of Sharpsburg, though Lee moved every available man and gun to resist it.

Meanwhile, in the center, Pleasonton's cavalry and Sykes' infantry had pushed across the Middle Bridge and detected the weakness of the Confederate line before Sharpsburg. They urged an attack, but again McClellan declined to exploit the opportunity. Then, as Burnside's men drove to the edge of Sharpsburg, A. P. Hill's command came panting uphill from Boteler's Ford after a strenuous forced march and crashed into the Union flank. Burnside had not foreseen such an attack, and McClellan had not spared any cavalry to cover the Union left. To add to the confusion, many of Hill's men wore blue uniforms captured at Harper's Ferry. Their charges drove the IX Corps back to the ridges along the creek, where it held. There the battle ended.

As though in open contempt of McClellan, Lee remained in his precarious position throughout 18 September, wringing a moral victory out of a lost battle and a mismanaged campaign. Early on the 18th, McClellan received reinforcements which, added to the two corps and the cavalry not used in the battle, gave him fresh troops probably exceeding in number Lee's remaining army. One determined drive by this force toward Boteler's Ford could hardly have been stopped, and Lee's army would have been helplessly pinned against the unfordable Potomac to its rear. Yet McClellan remained idle all day, and, during the night, Lee made a skillful and unmolested withdrawal via his only avenue of retreat—Boteler's Ford. Porter timidly crossed after Lee on 19 September but soon withdrew; he crossed again the next day and was forced back by A. P. Hill.

The failure of the Union army to gain a decisive victory under the prevailing favorable circumstances can be attributed directly to McClellan. The Union troops had fought well; most of the subordinate commanders had led well; and the artillery support had been superb. But there had been lacking a leader with imagination, initiative, and determination. Early in the campaign, through slowness and overcaution, McClellan had allowed the badly dispersed Confederates to unite. He had fought the battle by bits, committing single corps after single corps, which usually had run against superior numbers of Confederates—for Lee had been left free to shift his troops to meet each attack in turn. On the several occasions when opportunity for a decisive assault had arisen, McClellan had refused to act. Throughout the battle he had neither led nor inspired, but remained little more than a spectator.

Lee had available for the battle some 38,000 troops; McClellan, some 75,500. Total Confederate casualties were about 10,318; Union, 12,410.

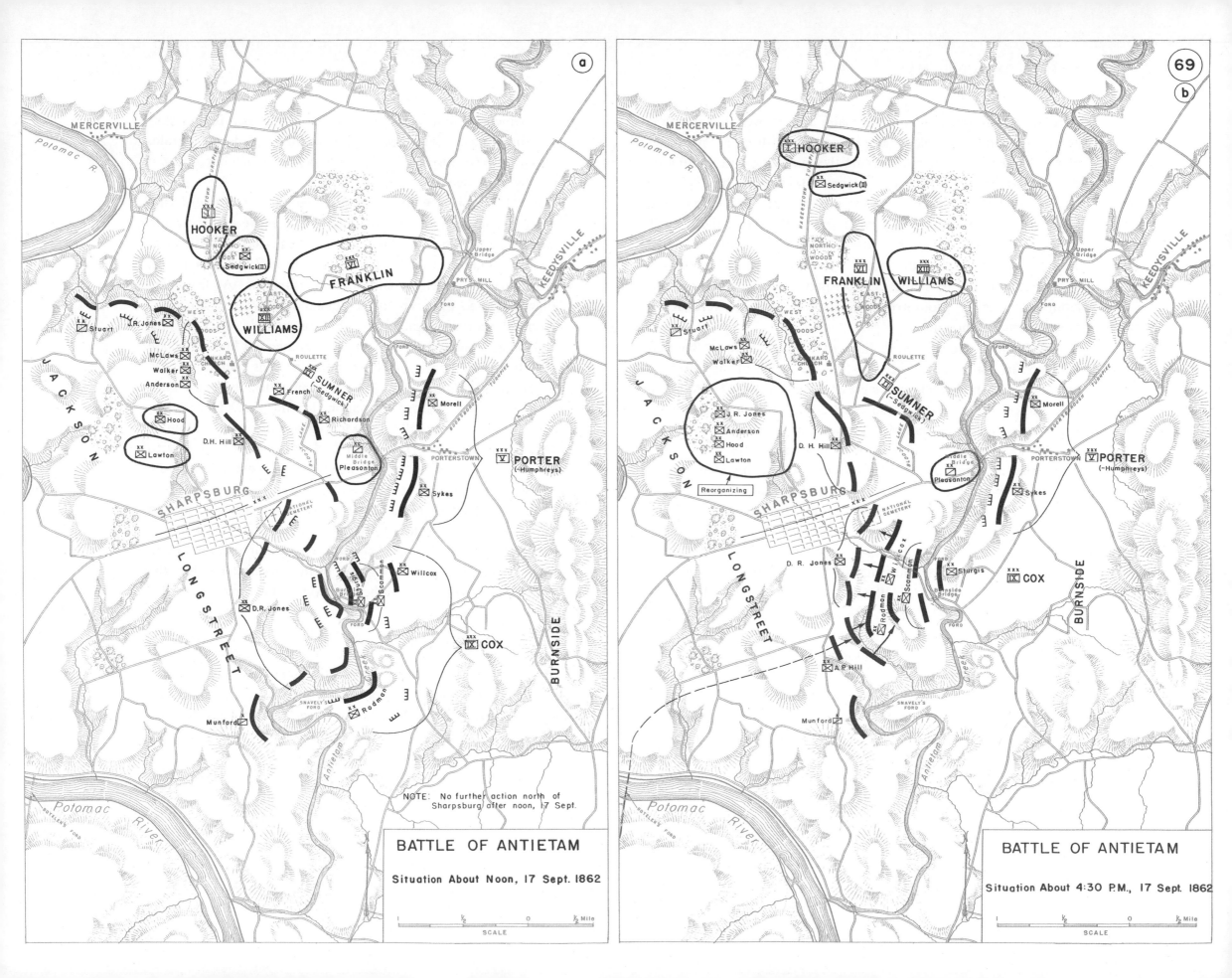

a

MERCERVILLE

Potomac R.

HOOKER

Sedgwick(II)

FRANKLIN

VI

WILLIAMS

XII

Upper Bridge

KEEDYSVILLE

PRY'S MILL

Stuart

J.R. Jones

WEST WOODS

EAST WOODS

FORD

McLaws

Walker

Anderson

DUNKARD CHURCH

ROULETTE

FORD

French

SUMNER
(Sedgwick)

Morell

JACKSON

Hood

Richardson

Lane

Lawton

D.H. Hill

Middle Bridge
Pleasonton

PORTERSTOWN

PORTER
(-Humphreys)
V

SHARPSBURG

NATIONAL CEMETERY

Sykes

LONGSTREET

Scammon

Willcox

D.R. Jones

Burnside Bridge

FORD

COX
IX

BURNSIDE

Munford

SNAVELY'S FORD

Rodman

NOTE: No further action north of
Sharpsburg after noon, 17 Sept.

Potomac River

BOTELER'S FORD

BATTLE OF ANTIETAM

Situation About Noon, 17 Sept. 1862

1 ½ 0 ½ Mile

SCALE

b

MERCERVILLE

Potomac R.

HOOKER
I

Sedgwick(II)

NORTH WOODS

FRANKLIN
VI

WILLIAMS
XII

Upper Bridge

KEEDYSVILLE

PRY'S MILL

Stuart

WEST WOODS

EAST WOODS

FORD

McLaws

Walker

DUNKARD CHURCH

ROULETTE

FORD

JACKSON

J.R. Jones

Anderson

Hood

Lawton

Reorganizing

SUMNER
(Sedgwick)
II

D.H. Hill

Morell

Middle Bridge
Pleasonton

PORTERSTOWN

PORTER
(-Humphreys)
V

SHARPSBURG

NATIONAL CEMETERY

Sykes

LONGSTREET

D.R. Jones

Willcox

Scammon

Rodman

Sturgis

Burnside Bridge

COX
IX

BURNSIDE

A.P. Hill

Munford

SNAVELY'S FORD

Potomac River

BOTELER'S FORD

BATTLE OF ANTIETAM

Situation About 4:30 P.M., 17 Sept. 1862

1 ½ 0 ½ Mile

SCALE

After his withdrawal from Antietam, Lee moved his battered army to Opequan Creek, where he could find food for it. Stragglers who had fallen behind during the marching and fighting of the second Bull Run campaign (and others who had left the ranks rather than take part in the invasion of the North) were rounded up and returned to their units. By November, Lee's strength had risen to 85,000. (McClellan, also reinforced, had 120,000.) Confederate discipline tightened, and the army was organized for the first time into permanent corps. Jackson and Longstreet, newly promoted to lieutenant general, were designated corps commanders.

Meanwhile, McClellan, feeling "that I have done all that can be asked in twice saving the country," sat north of the Potomac and feuded with Halleck by telegraph. The Army of the Potomac had earned some rest and did need some re-equipping and re-organizing, but in matters of supply discipline neither McClellan nor his staff were particularly adept. It seemed impossible to get his command clothed, armed, and equipped to his satisfaction. And so, in the east, the good October campaigning weather passed away quietly, while in the west, Bragg's invasion of Kentucky made a brief sensation before it ebbed, and Rosecrans gained successes at Iuka and Corinth.

There were minor interruptions of the peace along the Potomac. On 6 October, Halleck, acting on President Lincoln's instructions, wired McClellan "to cross the Potomac and give battle to the enemy, or drive him south." McClellan reacted with customary passive resistance. Another interruption disturbed his equanimity: the irrepressible Stuart, between 10 and 13 October, led some 1,500 picked cavalrymen entirely around McClellan's army. As a military operation, this was rather pointless: Stuart's only tangible objective—a railroad bridge north of Chambersburg which Lee wanted destroyed—was left undamaged because of a rainstorm. (Actually, Civil War cavalrymen in general displayed a chronic inability to carry out any major demoli-

tion in which burning was impracticable.) But, as a feat of skill and daring, Stuart's exploit was excellent for Confederate morale. It may also have inspired Stuart to undertake a similar raid the following June, with less happy results.

On 21 October, Halleck telegraphed once more, ordering McClellan to report the date he proposed to move and the route he would follow. The President and Halleck preferred an advance southward along the eastern slopes of the Blue Ridge Mountains, since such a movement would cover Washington. At first, McClellan proposed to move up the Shenandoah Valley, fearing—since the Potomac was then low—that Lee would cross back into Maryland as soon as the Army of the Potomac left his immediate front. By late October, however, autumn rains had raised the river, flooding the fords, and McClellan now decided to advance east of the mountains on Warrenton, leaving the XII Corps at Harper's Ferry and Morell's division to guard the upper Potomac. It took from 26 October through 2 November for his army to cross the river; then he moved slowly south, complaining continuously about his unpreparedness.

Lee countered by dividing his army, again leaving Jackson in the Shenandoah Valley, while he himself retired deliberately before McClellan's advance. There was considerable cavalry fighting during the movement, with most of the successes going to the Union cavalry. By 6 November, the opposing forces were disposed as shown on the map.

Apparently, McClellan had no specific plan. In his subsequent writings, he mentioned an intention to turn westward toward Little Washington to get between the separated Confederate forces and defeat them in detail, but none of his actions at that time support this claim. And, in any event, Jackson still hung on the Federal right rear, while Lee had plenty of maneuver room.

In the late evening of 7 November, McClellan received a War Department order directing that he turn over his command to Maj. Gen. Ambrose E. Burnside.

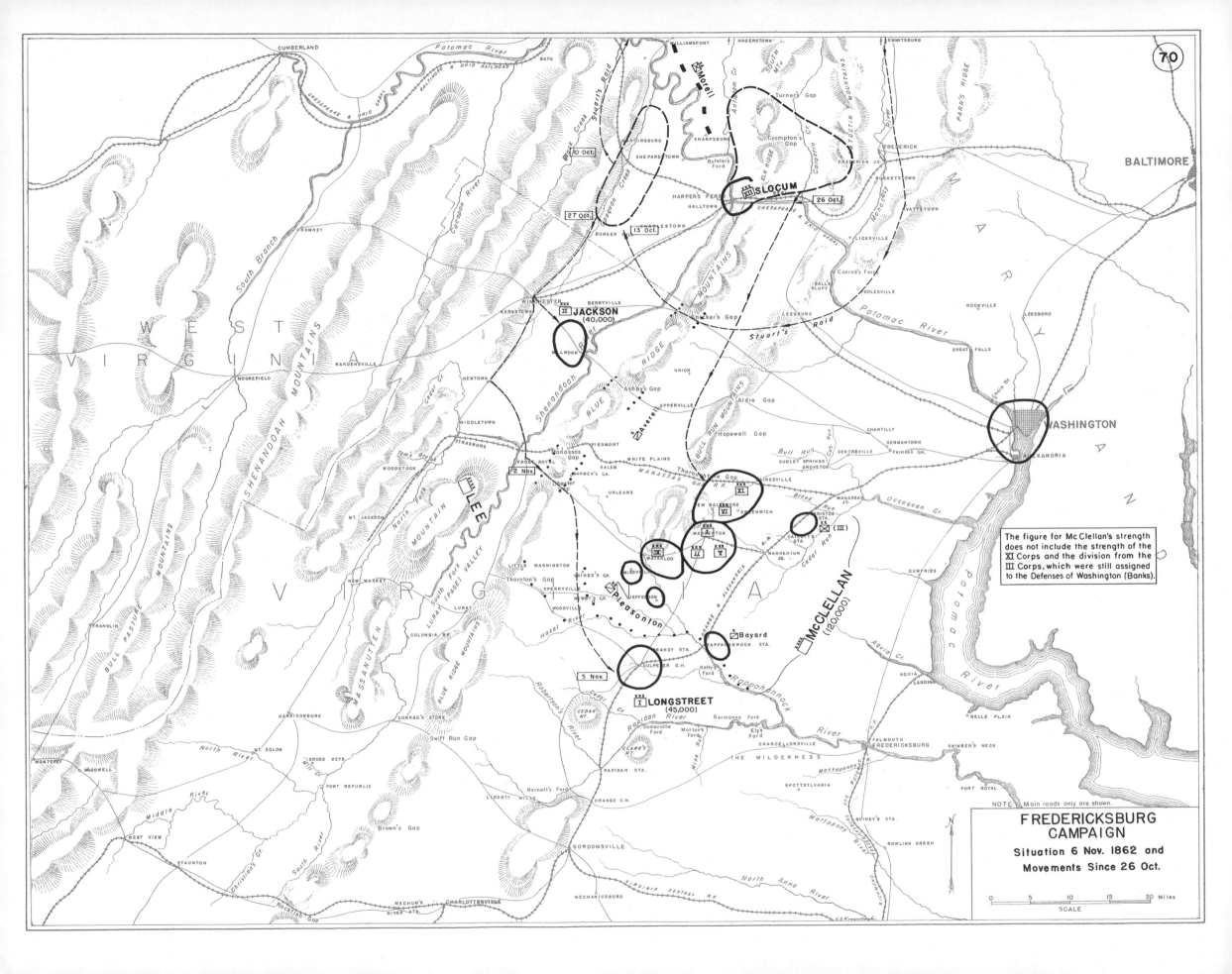

70

The figure for McClellan's strength
does not include the strength of the
XI Corps and the division from the
III Corps, which were still assigned
to the Defenses of Washington (Banks).

NOTE: Main roads only are shown.

FREDERICKSBURG
CAMPAIGN

Situation 6 Nov. 1862 and

Movements Since 26 Oct.

0   5   10   15   20 Miles

SCALE

President Lincoln's selection of Burnside as commander of the Army of the Potomac may require some explanation. The generals of best reputation—McClellan, McDowell, and Pope—had failed him. None of the others had so far particularly distinguished themselves. However, Lincoln knew that Burnside had proved himself as an independent commander in early 1862, by organizing and executing a successful amphibious operation along the North Carolina coast. During the second Bull Run campaign, he had supported Pope loyally and efficiently. And at Antietam he had not done noticeably worse than the other corps commanders. Finally, Burnside was a loyal and dedicated soldier who, unlike McClellan, had no interest in politics. But he did not feel qualified to command the Army of the Potomac and did not desire the post.

On 9 November, Burnside transmitted his proposed plan of operations to Halleck. This was to concentrate near Warrenton, as if for an attack on either Culpeper or Gordonsville; to accumulate four or five days' supplies; then to shift to Fredericksburg "with a view to a move upon Richmond from that point." He felt that his communications (the Orange & Alexandria Railroad) were exposed to a sudden stroke by Jackson, and that the risk of such an attack would steadily increase as he moved directly south from Warrenton. Also, the railroad was single-tracked and rickety, with doubtful capacity to supply his large army without interruption. An advance through Fredericksburg, though it would have wider rivers to cross, would be easier to support logistically, since Burnside could use Aquia Creek (*lower right*) —at the end of a secure line of water transportation from Washington—as a base. More important, such an advance would be a direct threat to Richmond, and Lee would have to rush to its defense. In so doing, Lee's forces might conceivably be caught separated and vulnerable to defeat in detail by a concentrated Union army. To support his plan, Burnside wanted prompt dispatch of a ponton train from Alexandria to Falmouth, and assembly of supplies at Falmouth, Aquia Creek, and Belle Plain (*all lower right*).

Halleck managed to avoid any responsibility for deciding on the plan, but Lincoln reluctantly approved it on 14 November, adding "it will succeed if you move very rapidly, otherwise not." On 15 November, Burnside moved out; on 17 November, his leading element, under Sumner, entered Falmouth. The Aquia Landing–Falmouth section of railroad was being restored to serviceable condition, and supplies were beginning to arrive. But there were no pontons on hand. In addition, the weather turned bad. Sumner wanted to ford the Rappahannock at once, drive off the handful of Confederates near Fredericksburg, and occupy the hills behind the town. However, Burnside, feeling the weight of his new responsibility, feared that the rains would make the fords impassable behind Sumner who, thus isolated, would be at the mercy of Lee.

On 25 November—a week late—the first pontons arrived; the Washington engineer supply authorities had refused to respond to the urgency of Burnside's need. But the opportunity for an unopposed crossing had now disappeared. On 21 November, Longstreet's corps had arrived at Fredericksburg; Jackson was to arrive on the 30th. Lee had not overlooked the possibility of Burnside's march to Fredericksburg, but he had been surprised by the speed with which it had been carried out. At first, he thought it would be necessary to take a stand behind the North Anna River (*lower right*), but when Burnside delayed his crossing, Lee moved directly to Fredericksburg.

Still, Burnside had one more opportunity. Longstreet was at Fredericksburg, but Jackson could not possibly join him for several days. A swift march back up the Rappahannock would have enabled Burnside to place his entire army between the two Confederate corps. But Burnside's thoughts were focused on Richmond, rather than on his true objective—Lee's army.

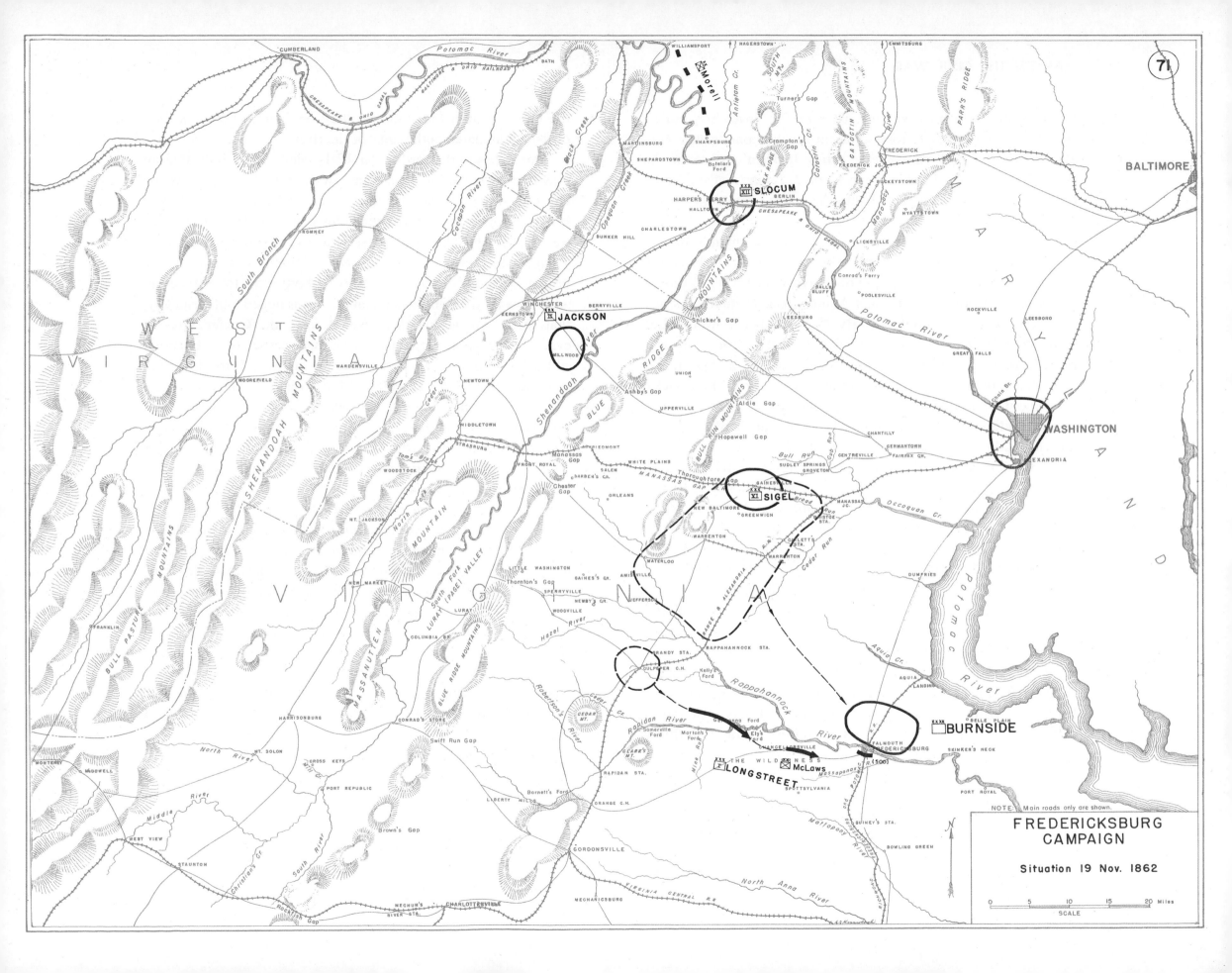

71

CUMBERLAND

Potomac River

BATH

WILLIAMSPORT HAGERSTOWN

⊠ Morell

EMMITSBURG

BALTIMORE

SHARPSBURG

XXX
XII SLOCUM

HARPER'S FERRY
BERLIN

FREDERICK

WINCHESTER
BERRYVILLE

XXX
II JACKSON

MILLWOOD

LEESBURG

Potomac River

WASHINGTON

ALEXANDRIA

XXX
XI SIGEL

WARRENTON

XXXX
BURNSIDE

BELLE PLAIN

CULPEPER C.H.

Rappahannock River

FALMOUTH
FREDERICKSBURG

⊡ (500)

XXX
I LONGSTREET
THE WILDERNESS
XXX McLAWS

PORT ROYAL

NOTE: Main roads only are shown.

FREDERICKSBURG
CAMPAIGN

Situation 19 Nov. 1862

0   5   10   15   20 Miles
SCALE

W E S T   V I R G I N I A

V I R G I N I A

M A R Y L A N D

Burnside had hoped to cross the river on 26 November, but by then he had received pontons sufficient for only one bridge. Had all needed pontons been available before Jackson's arrival on the 30th, he might still have overwhelmed Longstreet's isolated corps. Now he was confronted with the entire Confederate army (*sketch* a).

Meanwhile, Lee had feared that Burnside might suddenly embark his army for an amphibious operation south of the James River. This suspicion was revived on 22 November when Burnside moved some troops back toward Aquia Creek (actually, merely to relieve his supply problems). By 25 November, however, Lee seems to have deduced the general Union plan. His army was posted along the river, with Early at Skinker's Neck and D. H. Hill near Port Royal (*neither shown*), downstream from Fredericksburg about ten and twenty miles, respectively.

Burnside had originally planned to cross at Skinker's Neck, but changed his mind after Early's arrival there. He now planned to cross at Fredericksburg, under the impression that "a large force of the enemy is concentrated in the vicinity of Port Royal, its left resting near Fredericksburg." Again, as at Antietam, Burnside had failed to scout Lee's position aggressively. Instead, he depended largely on balloon observation, which was ineffective in such wooded country.

Shortly after taking command, Burnside had reorganized his army into three "grand divisions" of two corps each—under Sumner, Franklin, and Hooker—and a reserve corps, under Sigel. This reorganization greatly reduced his command problems.

The crossings began on the night of 10 December. On the Union left, Franklin met little opposition. At Fredericksburg, Brig. Gen. William Barksdale's Mississippians, firing from houses along the river, repeatedly stopped the bridge building. Artillery fire failed to dislodge these snipers. Eventually, Union volunteers crossed in boats and cleared the town. By then, it was almost dark, and Burnside suspended operations for the day. The crossing was completed on 12 December under cover of a heavy fog. Lee had chosen not to offer greater resistance at the river because

the concentration of Union artillery on Stafford Heights (*top center*) dominated both banks of the river.

Burnside's verbal orders on 12 December had indicated an intention to make his main attack with Franklin, supported by Hooker, while Sumner made a secondary attack on Marye's Heights (*top left*). Unfortunately, his written orders for the 13th were vague. Franklin was to send a division to seize the high ground near Hamilton (*lower right*); Sumner was to push one up the Telegraph Road (*left center*); both were to be ready to advance with their entire commands. It was hoped, optimistically, that these two weak attacks would force the Confederates to evacuate the whole ridge. This order made sense only if Burnside still believed that only a part of Lee's army was confronting him. Early on the 13th, D. H. Hill and Early rejoined Jackson.

The prescribed attack on Franklin's front toward Hamilton was made by Meade's division, supported by those of Brig. Gen. Abner Doubleday and Brig. Gen. John Gibbon (*sketch* b). Major John Pelham's horse artillery delayed Meade initially, but, once Pelham was forced to withdraw, Meade drove forward through a weak spot and surprised and routed Brig. Gen. Maxcy Gregg's brigade in the Confederate second line. Gibbon, advancing on Meade's right, was initially successful. However, the two divisions lost contact in the dense woods and were counterattacked furiously about 1:30 P.M. by the Confederates. Badly battered, they were driven into the open and hotly pursued. Franklin had so thoroughly deployed his grand division that he had no reinforcements available. Sickles and Birney of Hooker's command advanced and drove back the Confederates. Later, Jackson attempted a major counterattack, but halted it when his first movements brought down an overwhelming storm of Federal artillery fire.

On Sumner's front the attack was made at 11:00 A.M. by French's division, followed in quick succession by those of Hancock, Howard, and Sturgis. By 1:30 P.M., these had all been beaten back with heavy losses.

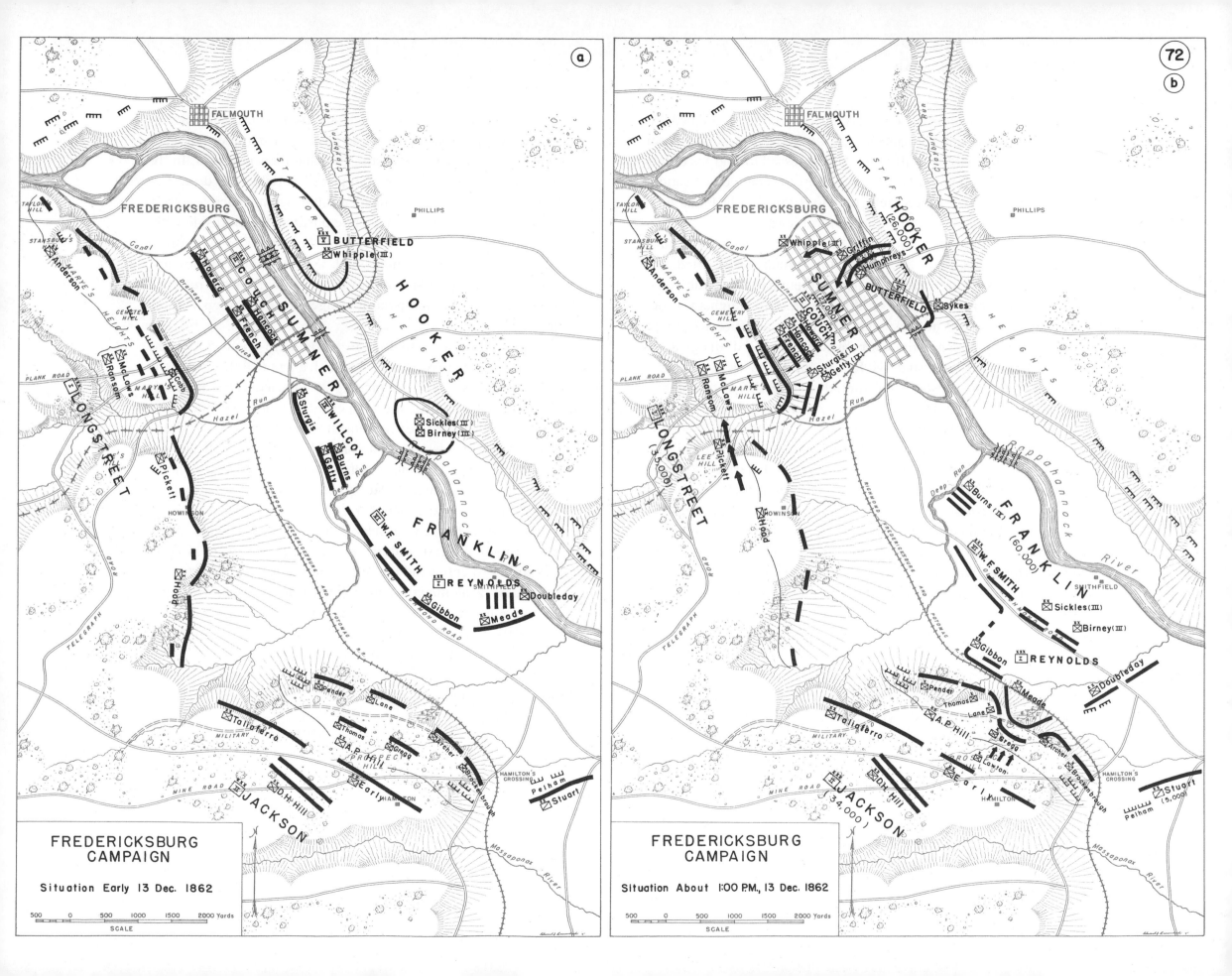

(a)

FALMOUTH

FREDERICKSBURG

PHILLIPS

TAYLOR'S HILL

STAFFORD HEIGHTS

STANSBURY'S HILL

Anderson

BUTTERFIELD
Whipple (III)

MARYE'S HEIGHTS

CEMETERY HILL

Howard

COUCH SUMNER

Hancock

French

HOOKER HEIGHTS

McLaws

Ransom

PLANK ROAD

Cobb

Sturgis

WILLCOX

Getty

Burns

Sickles (III)
Birney (III)

LONGSTREET

Pickett

HOWISON

Hood

FRANKLIN

W.F. SMITH

REYNOLDS

SMITHFIELD

TELEGRAPH

Gibbon
Meade

Doubleday

Pender

Lane

Taliaferro

Thomas

Gregg

Archer

A.P. HILL

A.P. PROSPECT HILL

Brockenbrough

HAMILTON'S CROSSING

Pelham

Stuart

MILITARY

D.H. Hill

Early

JACKSON

MINE ROAD

HAMILTON

Massaponax River

FREDERICKSBURG CAMPAIGN

Situation Early 13 Dec. 1862

500   0   500   1000   1500   2000 Yards
SCALE

(72)

(b)

FALMOUTH

FREDERICKSBURG

PHILLIPS

TAYLOR'S HILL

STAFFORD HEIGHTS

HOOKER (26,000)

STANSBURY'S HILL

Anderson

Whipple (III)

Griffin

Humphreys

MARYE'S HEIGHTS

CEMETERY HILL

COUCH

Howard

Hancock

French

SUMNER

BUTTERFIELD

Sykes

PLANK ROAD

McLaws

Ransom

Sturgis

Getty (IX)

LONGSTREET (35,000)

Pickett

LEE HILL

Hood

HOWISON

Burns (IX)

FRANKLIN (60,000)

W.F. SMITH

SMITHFIELD

Sickles (III)

Birney (III)

TELEGRAPH

Gibbon

REYNOLDS

Meade

Doubleday

Pender

Thomas

Lane

Taliaferro

A.P. HILL

Gregg

Bragg

Lawton

Archer

Brockenbrough

HAMILTON'S CROSSING

MILITARY

Early

Stuart (5,000)

D.H. Hill

JACKSON (34,000)

MINE ROAD

HAMILTON

Pelham

Massaponax River

FREDERICKSBURG CAMPAIGN

Situation About 1:00 P.M., 13 Dec. 1862

500   0   500   1000   1500   2000 Yards
SCALE

After Jackson's abortive counterattack, Franklin remained inactive along the line shown (*sketch* a), despite at least one direct order to attack with his full force. He professed to find his orders obscure, but he apparently made no effort to secure clarification, even though he had a direct telegraph to Burnside's headquarters. His one activity was to plead for reinforcements.

On the Union right, the initial attack had been delayed until 11:00 A.M., principally because of fog. When it had lifted, the Union troops in the Fredericksburg streets had been subjected to heavy artillery fire. Union artillery on Stafford Heights was out of range and could not respond. The Union advance had to be made across an open plain, cut by a steep-banked drainage ditch some thirty feet wide and six feet deep. There were only two bridges over this obstacle, so the advancing Union troops had been forced to remain in columns until across, thus presenting a massed target to the Confederates on the heights above. At the foot of Marye's Hill, a sunken road with stone retaining walls on either side formed a natural trench for Confederate riflemen. Attempts to shift the attack farther to the right had been halted by swampy ground.

Burnside now called upon Hooker to resume the assault on Marye's Hill, and upon Franklin to attack on his front. Franklin remained inactive, as we have seen, and Hooker complied reluctantly, meanwhile protesting against sacrificing his command. Lee had already taken advantage of Franklin's lethargy to shift Pickett's division and one of Hood's brigades to Marye's Hill. Griffin's division renewed the attack at 3:30 P.M., followed by Humphreys' division about 4:00 P.M. Both met the fate of the divisions that preceded them in attacks against the hill. Toward dark, Getty assaulted Marye's Hill from the east, and was repulsed. Hooker now suspended the assault and withdrew his forces from contact (*sketch* b).

Burnside wished to renew the attack the next morning but was dissuaded by his grand division commanders. Both sides remained on the field during the 14th, strengthening their positions. In the afternoon a truce was arranged to permit burial of the dead. Lee hoped that on the 15th Burnside would again batter his army against the impregnable Confederate position, but Burnside withdrew across the river on the night of the 14th. The withdrawal was accomplished with great skill. All the Union troops and supplies (down to the last foot of telegraph wire) were returned across the river, and the ponton bridges were taken up without detection.

The Confederate casualties in battle were about 5,580; the Federal casualties exceeded 12,600 with about 6,300 occurring at the foot of Marye's Hill. Beginning 20 January, 1863, Burnside moved up the Rappahannock in an effort to turn Lee's left. Heavy rains, however, halted this movement—"the mud march." Union morale was at a low ebb, and Burnside found himself at odds with most of his subordinates. On 25 January, President Lincoln relieved Burnside, Sumner, and Franklin, giving command of the Army of the Potomac to Hooker.

Burnside had failed, as had all former commanders of the Union army in the east, and for substantially the same reasons—the inability to command the army and to direct its efforts with decisiveness, zeal, initiative, and imagination. In fairness to Burnside, one must remember that he accepted the command of the Army of the Potomac humbly and reluctantly, for he doubted his qualifications for the post. If he had feared he was lacking in those attributes essential for high command, events had proved his fears well-founded.

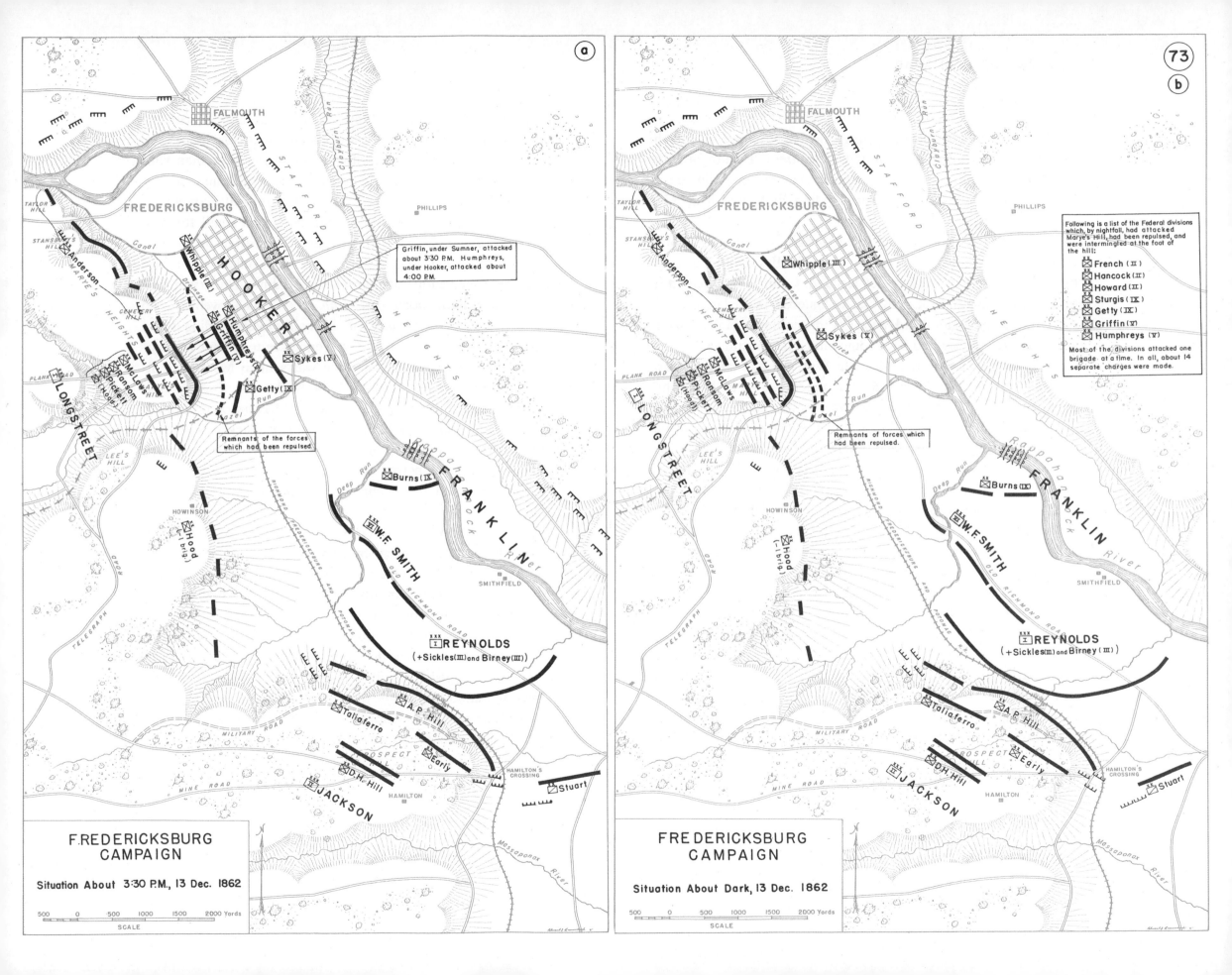

a

FALMOUTH

PHILLIPS

FREDERICKSBURG

TAYLOR HILL

STANSBURY'S HILL

Anderson

Lee's Hill

MARYE'S HEIGHTS

Whipple (III)

HOOKER

Humphreys

Griffin (V)

Sykes (V)

Griffin, under Sumner, attacked about 3:30 P.M. Humphreys, under Hooker, attacked about 4:00 P.M.

McLaws

Ransom

Pickett (Hood)

Getty (IX)

CEMETERY HILL

PLANK ROAD

LONGSTREET

LEE'S HILL

Remnants of the forces which had been repulsed

HOWINSON

Hood (1 brig.)

TELEGRAPH ROAD

Burns (IX)

FRANKLIN

W.F. SMITH

SMITHFIELD

REYNOLDS

(+Sickles(III) and Birney(III))

Taliaferro

A.P. Hill

MILITARY ROAD

PROSPECT HILL

D.H. Hill

Early

JACKSON

HAMILTON

HAMILTON'S CROSSING

Stuart

MINE ROAD

Massaponax River

F. FREDERICKSBURG CAMPAIGN

Situation About 3:30 P.M., 13 Dec. 1862

500   0   500   1000   1500   2000 Yards

SCALE

---

b

FALMOUTH

PHILLIPS

FREDERICKSBURG

TAYLOR HILL

STANSBURY'S HILL

Anderson

Whipple (III)

Sykes (V)

McLaws

Ransom

Pickett (Hood)

CEMETERY HILL

PLANK ROAD

LONGSTREET

LEE'S HILL

Remnants of forces which had been repulsed.

HOWINSON

Hood (1 brig.)

TELEGRAPH ROAD

Burns (IX)

FRANKLIN

W.F. SMITH

SMITHFIELD

REYNOLDS

(+Sickles(III) and Birney(III))

Taliaferro

A.P. Hill

MILITARY ROAD

PROSPECT HILL

D.H. Hill

Early

JACKSON

HAMILTON

HAMILTON'S CROSSING

Stuart

MINE ROAD

Massaponax River

Following is a list of the Federal divisions which, by nightfall, had attacked Marye's Hill, had been repulsed, and were intermingled at the foot of the hill:

French (II)
Hancock (II)
Howard (II)
Sturgis (IX)
Getty (IX)
Griffin (V)
Humphreys (V)

Most of the divisions attacked one brigade at a time. In all, about 14 separate charges were made.

FREDERICKSBURG CAMPAIGN

Situation About Dark, 13 Dec. 1862

500   0   500   1000   1500   2000 Yards

SCALE

After the Battle of Shiloh (6-7 April, 1862), Halleck moved his headquarters to Pittsburg Landing and began concentrating his forces. To the south, at Corinth (*left center*), Beauregard likewise was summoning all available reinforcements, including troops from Arkansas under Maj. Gen. Sterling Price and Maj. Gen. Earl Van Dorn.

Halleck reorganized his army into a right wing, under Thomas (now a major general); a center, under Buell; a left wing, under Pope; and a reserve, under McClernand. Grant he appointed his second in command, and thereafter ignored him. Then, on 30 April, his army began its advance in three columns. Halleck's only previous field service had been some minor skirmishing as a junior engineer officer during the Mexican War. He had studied European authorities on the art of war extensively but apparently retained little except a predilection for the eighteenth-century theory of "strategic points." Consequently, he made the railroad center of Corinth—rather than Beauregard's army—his objective. His advance was deliberate and cautious; also, it was further slowed by bad roads and Buell's timidity. Halleck took four weeks to cover the approximately twenty miles from Shiloh to Corinth, corduroying miles of roads and entrenching securely at every halt. But his advance was also inexorable; Beauregard could never catch him at a disadvantage.

Corinth was heavily fortified and formed a strong defensive position. Nevertheless, Beauregard wisely chose not to risk a battle that was likely to lead to his being shut up in the city. Covering his actions with an elaborate program of deception designed to convince the Federals that he was being constantly reinforced and would fight to hold Corinth, he steadily evacuated his troops and supplies. Even during the night of 29 May, as the last of the Confederates left the town, constant railroad activity and cheering convinced Pope that he might be attacked in the morning. Beauregard marched safely to Tupelo (*lower left*),

justly proud of his skillful withdrawal. But here he met with the displeasure and wrath of Jefferson Davis, who was more concerned over the Confederate withdrawals in the west than with the skill of their execution. Beauregard resigned command, for reasons of health; Bragg took over the Confederate command.

After the capture of Corinth, Halleck sent a small force in a short, ineffective pursuit of Beauregard. Thereafter, he gave no thought to following up and destroying the Confederate army. Instead, he dispersed his own army. On 10 June, Buell was sent east to take Chattanooga (*see map 75*). This movement, no doubt, was made in conformity with Lincoln's long-standing desire to introduce Union troops into east Tennessee to bolster the pro-Union element of the state. Sherman was sent to Memphis (already captured by naval forces); Pope held a covering position south of Corinth; and one division was sent to reinforce the Federal troops in Arkansas. What further plans Halleck was pondering remain uncertain. His summons to Washington to serve as general in chief came before he had announced a decision. Halleck's departure left the command divided between Buell and Grant.

Buell's move to Decatur (*this map, right center*) was easy enough. Thereafter, logistical troubles plagued him. Because of the summer heat, rivers were low, throwing the whole burden of supply on the battered railroads. At first, following Halleck's instructions, Buell based himself on Corinth, using the Memphis & Charleston Railroad as his supply line. On his arrival at Athens (*right center*), he had expected to find supplies sent from Nashville via the damaged Nashville & Decatur Railroad, but learned that his staff had failed to issue the necessary orders. Guerrillas began raiding the rail line to Corinth. To add to his troubles, Buell—like McClellan—believed in a "soft" war and was unwilling to feed his army off the countryside or to use a hard hand against guerrillas.

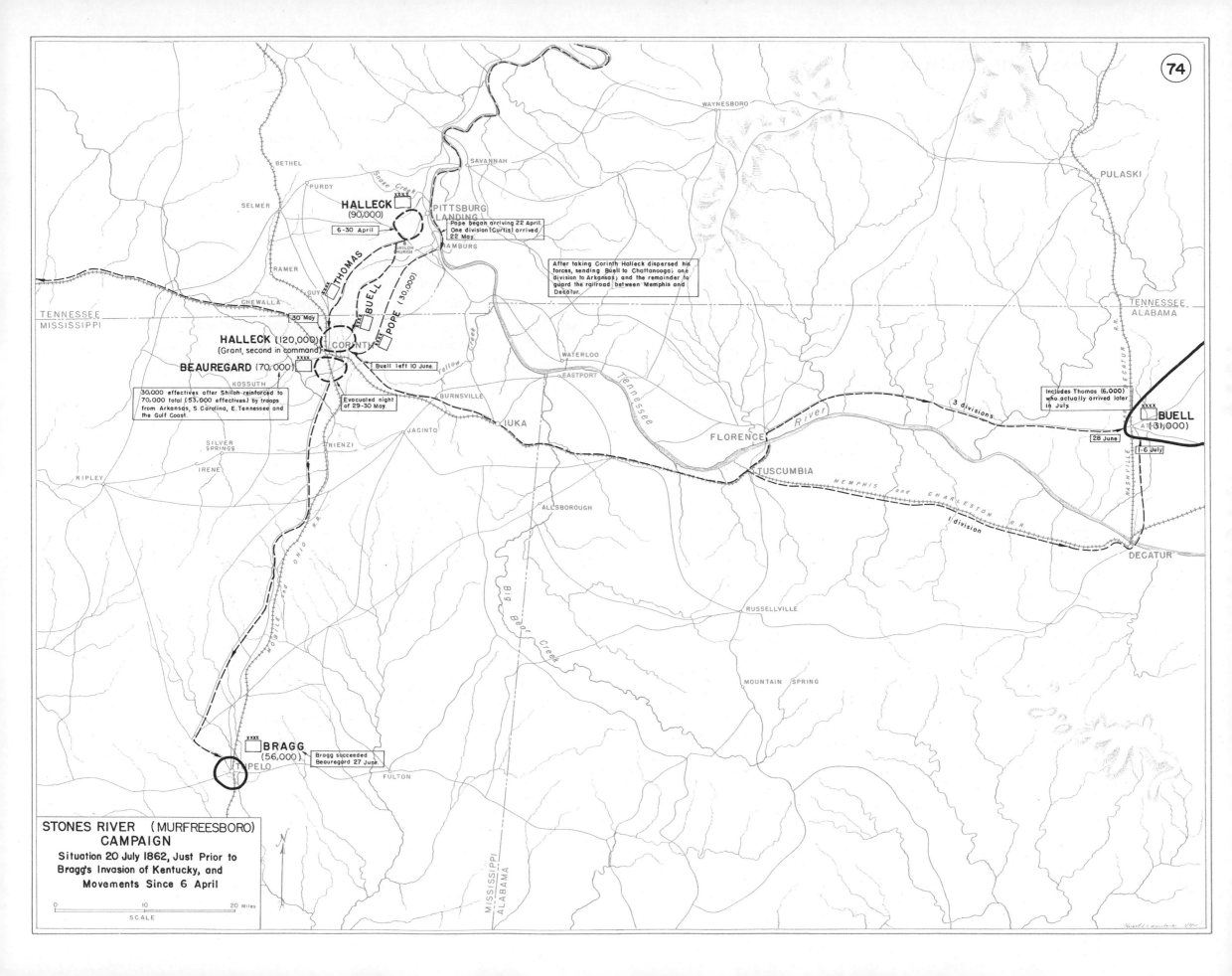

74

WAYNESBORO

PULASKI

BETHEL

PURDY

SELMER

HALLECK
(90,000)

PITTSBURG
LANDING

6-30 April

Pope began arriving 22 April.
One division (Curtis) arrived
22 May.

SAVANNAH

SHILOH
CHURCH

HAMBURG

After taking Corinth Halleck dispersed his
forces, sending Buell to Chattanooga; one
division to Arkansas; and the remainder to
guard the railroad between Memphis and
Decatur.

THOMAS

RAMER

CHEWALLA

GUY

BUELL

POPE (30,000)

TENNESSEE
MISSISSIPPI

30 May

HALLECK (120,000)
(Grant, second in command)

BEAUREGARD (70,000)

CORINTH

Buell left 10 June

WATERLOO

TENNESSEE
ALABAMA

Includes Thomas (6,000)
who actually arrived later
in July.

BUELL
(31,000)

KOSSUTH

30,000 effectives after Shiloh reinforced to
70,000 total (53,000 effectives) by troops
from Arkansas, S. Carolina, E. Tennessee and
the Gulf Coast.

Evacuated night
of 29-30 May.

BURNSVILLE

EASTPORT

3 divisions

28 June

1-6 July

SILVER
SPRINGS

JACINTO

IUKA

FLORENCE

TUSCUMBIA

1 division

DEGATUR

RIPLEY

IRENE

TRIENZI

ALLSBOROUGH

RUSSELLVILLE

MOUNTAIN SPRING

BRAGG
(56,000)

TUPELO

Bragg succeeded
Beauregard 27 June.

FULTON

STONES RIVER (MURFREESBORO)
CAMPAIGN

Situation 20 July 1862, Just Prior to
Bragg's Invasion of Kentucky, and
Movements Since 6 April

0   10   20 Miles
SCALE

MISSISSIPPI
ALABAMA

Repair work was finally completed on the Nashville & Chattanooga Railroad, and Buell now had an excellent rail line of supply to Nashville (*center*) and Louisville (*top center*). But on 13 July, Forrest raided Murfreesboro (*south of Nashville*) and so damaged the railroad there that it was not repaired until the 28th. The Union advance on Chattanooga was stopped temporarily. When it was resumed, Buell sent his divisions to the locations shown by broken circles. But, on 12 August, Brig. Gen. John H. Morgan's cavalry again disrupted communications by destroying a railroad tunnel near Gallatin, northeast of Nashville. Buell lacked the cavalry necessary to deal with such raiders. Infantry could seldom intercept them, and the poor discipline and security measures of isolated garrisons frequently made them easy prey for small raiding parties which they should have easily repulsed.

Bragg meanwhile had decided that an advance north from Tupelo (*bottom left*) was not practicable. He therefore left Price and Van Dorn to fix Grant, and shifted 35,000 men from Tupelo to Chattanooga by way of Mobile, Alabama. Though he did not leave Tupelo until 21 July, he reached Chattanooga before Buell could do so. Bragg's general plan was to invade Kentucky in a joint operation with Kirby Smith, hoping to cut Buell's line of communications, defeat him, and then turn on Grant.

Kirby Smith left Knoxville (*right center*) on 14 August and forced Brig. Gen. George W. Morgan to evacuate Cumberland Gap. Continuing his advance, he overwhelmed a small force of raw, hastily assembled Union troops at Richmond, and continued to Lexington (*upper right*).

Bragg left Chattanooga as Kirby Smith approached Lexington. Marching along the Sequatchie River valley, his initial advance was hidden from Buell by the plateau of the Cumberland Mountains. But Union scouts soon determined the Confederate route and numbers. Thomas urged Buell to concentrate at McMinnville (*near Murfreesboro*) and to strike Bragg as he emerged from the valley, near Sparta. Instead, Buell, somewhat confused,

withdrew to Murfreesboro. Grant sent the divisions of R. B. Mitchell and Paine to assist, but Buell continued his retreat to Nashville. There he left a garrison and moved back to his supply depot at Bowling Green.

Bragg reached Glasgow (*right center*) the day before Buell arrived at Bowling Green. He then continued on to Munfordville. His advance guard was sharply repulsed by the Federal garrison there, but, with the arrival of Bragg's main army, the garrison surrendered. The Confederates were now squarely across Buell's supply line to Louisville. In this crisis Buell shied from an attack on Bragg's position. Louisville and Cincinnati, alarmed by the Confederate advance, were preparing as best they could against attack. Grant now sent Brig. Gen. Gordon Granger's division to Louisville to assist Buell. By aggressive marching and maneuvering, Bragg had forced Buell back almost to the Ohio River.

The boxed note at Huntsville (*bottom center*) refers to Mitchel having been in that area for some time. Actually, while the armies were concentrating at Corinth early in April, one of Buell's division commanders, Brig. Gen. Ormsby M. Mitchel, had undertaken a campaign of his own. From his position at Shelbyville (*bottom center*), he had advanced and seized Huntsville. From there, he had sent troops in captured trains east and west along the railroad to capture Decatur and Stevenson, and dispatched a small group of volunteers to burn the railroad bridges south of Chattanooga. However, this raid—popularly known as "the great locomotive chase"—failed. Mitchel operated in the area independently until Buell's arrival; at one time, one of his detachments shelled Chattanooga from across the Tennessee. His independent exploits gained Buell's displeasure, but Lincoln was highly pleased and promoted Mitchel to major general. The friction between Buell and Mitchel caused the latter to request a transfer. He was placed in command of the Department of the South, but died shortly thereafter.

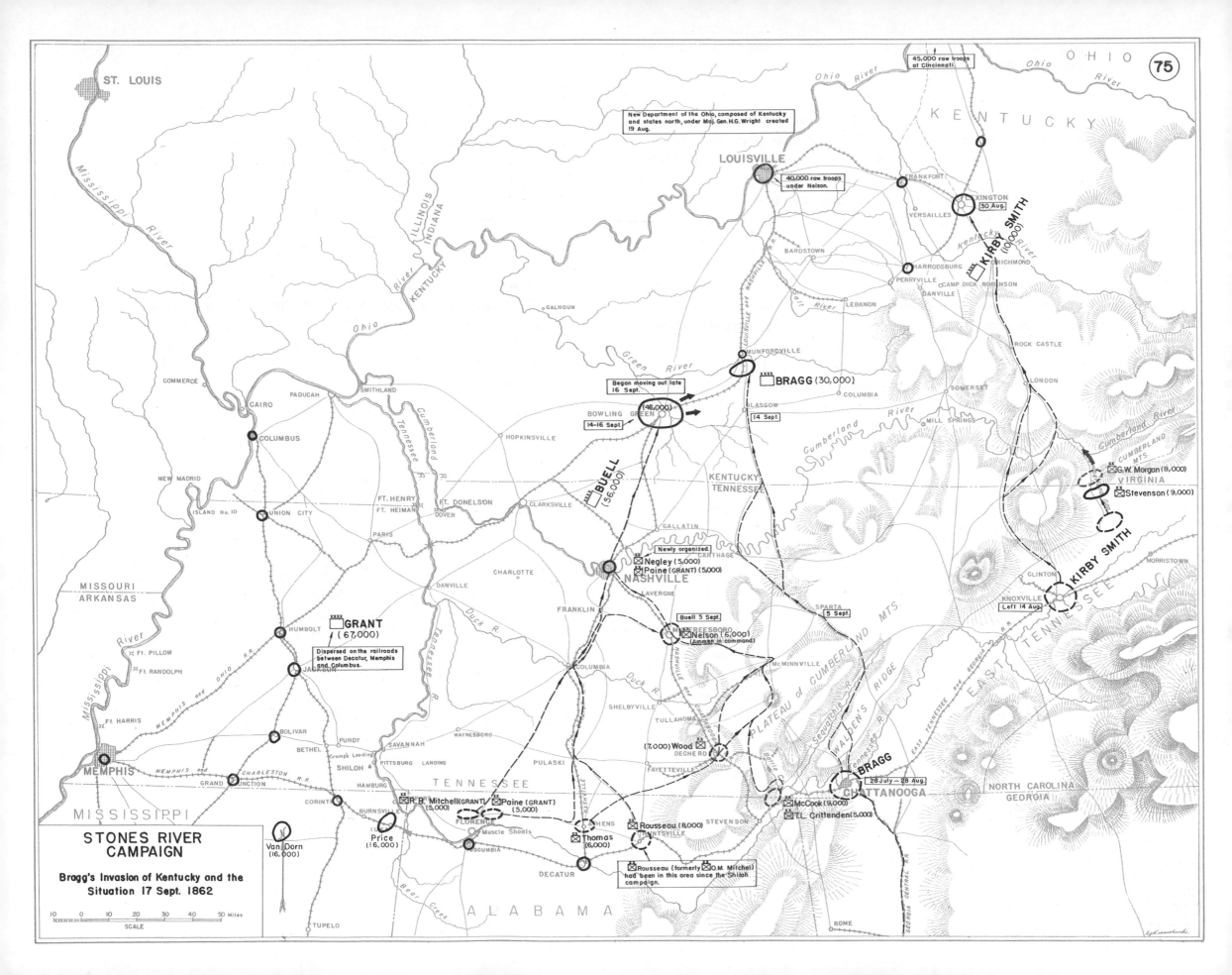

STONES RIVER
CAMPAIGN

Bragg's Invasion of Kentucky and the
Situation 17 Sept. 1862

The Confederate success in occupying Munfordville, on Buell's line of communications, was to prove of little advantage. Bragg felt that his army was too small to attack Buell, but he hoped to lure Buell into an assault on the strong Confederate position at Munfordville. Failing in this, and running short of supplies, he moved north to Bardstown, on the road to Lexington. Buell then moved rapidly to Louisville.

Had Kirby Smith moved to join Bragg, the combined forces would have equaled the strength of the Union force. But Bragg and Kirby Smith were independent commanders, and the latter, though normally cooperative, believed in this instance that Bragg could easily capture Louisville alone. He therefore devoted his own energy to collecting stores at Lexington and to unsuccessfully attempting to intercept G. W. Morgan's division (*off map, right*), which was moving through the mountains toward the Ohio River. Meanwhile, the Confederate invasion was not achieving the results expected—few Kentuckians joined the Confederate forces, and an attempt at conscription in eastern Tennessee failed completely.

By now, the Union administration was thoroughly dissatisfied with Buell. He was ordered relieved by Thomas—unless he had fought, or was about to fight, a battle. Thomas, however, refused to accept the command, stating that Buell had completed his preparations to move against Bragg and therefore should be retained. On 1 October, Buell advanced slowly on Bardstown, sending two detached divisions toward Frankfort in an attempt to confuse the Confederates. On 7 October, the Union advance approached Perryville and found Confederate forces present in some strength. Buell thereupon began concentrating his army, the columns of which had become somewhat separated in their search for water. His intentions are not clear; apparently he intended to attack, if conditions seemed favorable.

Bragg, meanwhile, had left his isolated army and was in Frankfort for the rather amazing purpose of formally inaugurating a Confederate governor of Kentucky. Polk had been left in command at Bardstown. Believing Buell's feint toward Frankfort to be the main Federal army, Bragg ordered Polk to move north and strike its flank. But Polk, painfully aware of the actual situation, had already abandoned Bardstown and was retreating to the southeast. Bragg now ordered a concentration at Harrodsburg; then he ordered Polk back to Perryville to attack the Federals there, apparently under the misconception that they were only a small part of Buell's army.

On the morning of 8 October, fighting began around Perryville over possession of water. Sheridan's division of Brig. Gen. Charles C. Gilbert's corps forced the Confederates away from one creek and dug in. Early in the afternoon, Maj. Gen. Alexander M. McCook's corps arrived and began forming into line. At this moment, Polk attacked. McCook was pushed back about a mile with heavy losses, but Sheridan held his ground. Col. William P. Carlin's brigade counterattacked and drove the Confederates out of Perryville. Maj. Gen. Thomas L. Crittenden allowed his corps to be bluffed by Wheeler's handful of cavalry and did not get into action. Buell, who had not left his headquarters, was unaware of the battle until it was half over.

That night Bragg, realizing that he faced Buell's main army, ordered a retreat to Harrodsburg. Kirby Smith joined him there on 10 October. Bragg now had a strong force of veteran troops, but made no effort to regain the initiative. Equally passive, Buell refused to attack Bragg's position. Bragg—reportedly completely disheartened—retreated through Cumberland Gap, eventually regaining Murfreesboro.

Buell failed to make even a pretense of pursuit. He likewise ignored the Federal administration's urgings that he occupy eastern Tennessee, insisting that he must return to Nashville and refit his troops. Consequently, he was replaced by Rosecrans. Buell had served loyally according to his conception of his duties and had done excellent work in organizing his army. However, he completely lacked any sense of urgency or any desire to close with his opponent and destroy him.

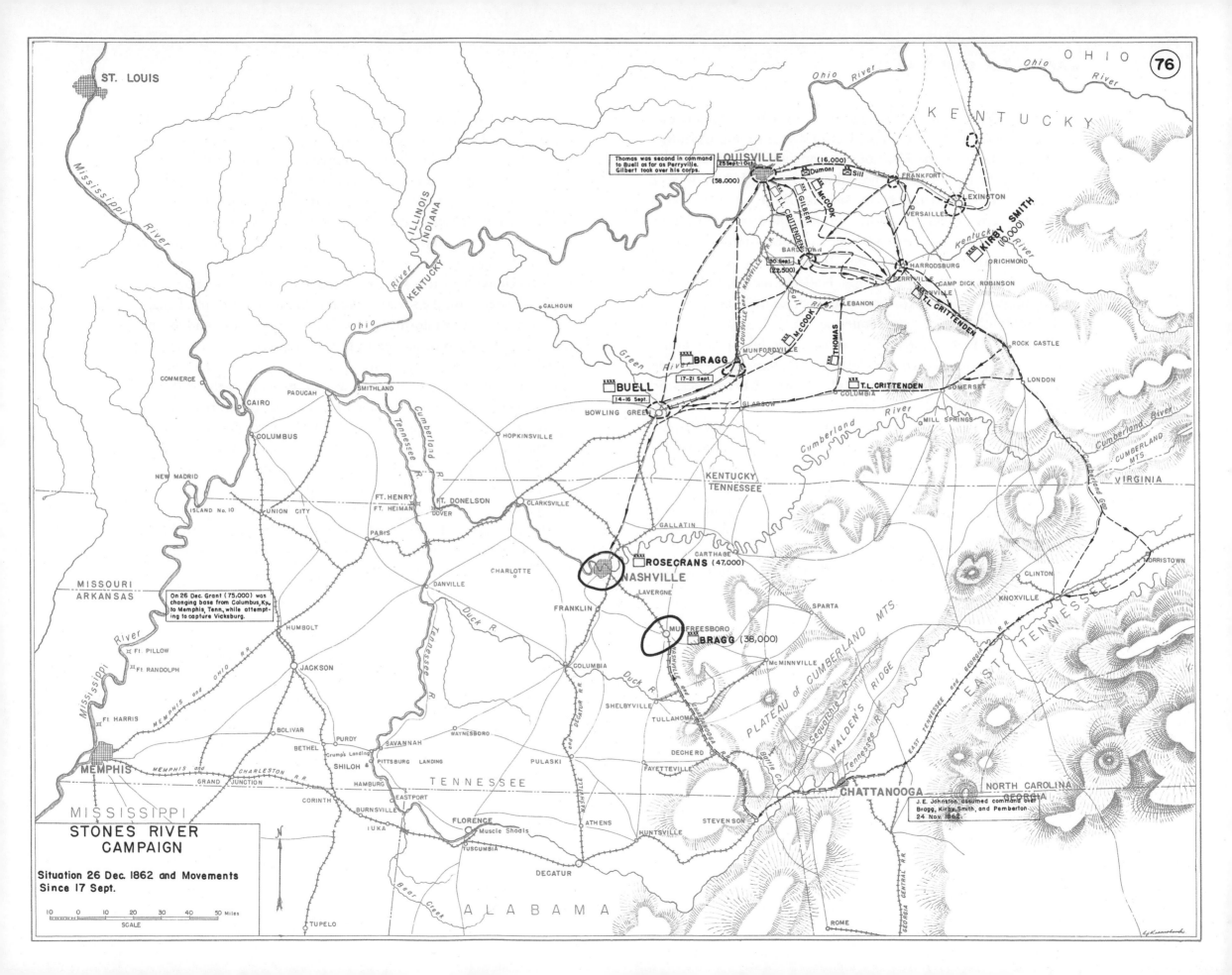

OHIO

76

KENTUCKY

Thomas was second in command to Buell as far as Perryville. Gilbert took over his corps.

LOUISVILLE
25 Sept-1 Oct.
(58,000)
(16,000)

Dumont   Sill

FRANKFORT

LEXINGTON

McCOOK

VERSAILLES

T.L. GILBERT
CRITTENDEN

KIRBY SMITH
(10,000)

KENTUCKY
River

BARDSTOWN
(30 Sept.)
(22,500)

HARRODSBURG

RICHMOND

PERRYVILLE   Camp Dick Robinson

DANVILLE

T.L. CRITTENDEN

BRAGG
17-21 Sept.

MUNFORDVILLE

McCOOK

THOMAS

LEBANON

ROCK CASTLE

BUELL
14-16 Sept.

GLASGOW

BOWLING GREEN

COLUMBIA

SOMERSET

LONDON

T.L. CRITTENDEN

HOPKINSVILLE

Green   River

Cumberland   River

MILL SPRINGS

CUMBERLAND
MTS.

ST. LOUIS

Mississippi   River

Ohio   River

COMMERCE

CAIRO

PADUCAH

SMITHLAND

Cumberland R.

Tennessee R.

KENTUCKY

VIRGINIA

COLUMBUS

KENTUCKY
TENNESSEE

NEW MADRID

ISLAND No. 10

UNION CITY

FT. HENRY
FT. HEIMAN

FT. DONELSON
DOVER

CLARKSVILLE

GALLATIN

CARTHAGE

SPARTA

Cumberland Gap

On 26 Dec. Grant (75,000) was changing base from Columbus, Ky. to Memphis, Tenn, while attempting to capture Vicksburg.

PARIS

CHARLOTTE

ROSECRANS (47,000)

NASHVILLE

KNOXVILLE

MISSOURI
ARKANSAS

DANVILLE

LAVERGNE

CLINTON

MORRISTOWN

FRANKLIN

MURFREESBORO

BRAGG (38,000)

McMINNVILLE

EAST
TENNESSEE

Mississippi   River

FT. PILLOW

HUMBOLT

Tennessee R.

COLUMBIA

Duck R.

PLATEAU OF CUMBERLAND MTS.

WALDEN'S RIDGE

FT. RANDOLPH

JACKSON

SHELBYVILLE

TULLAHOMA

Sequatchie R.

FT. HARRIS

BOLIVAR

PURDY

SAVANNAH

WAYNESBORO

DECHERD

FAYETTEVILLE

PULASKI

Tennessee River

NORTH CAROLINA

MEMPHIS

BETHEL

Crump's Landing

SHILOH

PITTSBURG Landing

HAMBURG

EASTPORT

TENNESSEE

CHATTANOOGA

GEORGIA

J. E. Johnston assumed command over Bragg, Kirby Smith, and Pemberton 24 Nov. 1862

MISSISSIPPI

GRAND JUNCTION

CORINTH

BURNSVILLE

IUKA

FLORENCE
Muscle Shoals

ATHENS

HUNTSVILLE

STEVENSON

STONES RIVER
CAMPAIGN

Situation 26 Dec. 1862 and Movements
Since 17 Sept.

N

DECATUR

ALABAMA

TUPELO

Bear Creek

ROME

GEORGIA CENTRAL R.R.

10   0   10   20   30   40   50 Miles
SCALE

Maj. Gen. William S. Rosecrans, the new Union commander, had received credit for the recent victories at Iuka and Corinth—the initial phases of the Vicksburg campaign. He was a skillful strategist, personally brave, and willing to fight; but he was extremely excitable and too easily satisfied with his own accomplishments. His orders placed him in command of the recreated Department of the Cumberland, which included all of Tennessee east of the Cumberland River and such parts of Alabama and Georgia as his troops might occupy. Halleck, the general in chief in Washington, defined Rosecrans' immediate mission, generally, as the occupation of eastern Tennessee.

Rosecrans' first actions were to reorganize his cavalry and to begin concentrating his army at Nashville. The city had been under sporadic attack, usually unsuccessful, by two of Bragg's cavalry leaders, Forrest and Morgan. Halleck urged Rosecrans forward, but the latter delayed in Nashville accumulating supplies and organizing his communications. Meanwhile, Bragg massed at Murfreesboro, and Morgan's cavalry surprised and captured a brigade of Union infantry at Hartsville, some thirty-five miles northeast of Nashville. Bragg now detached part of his cavalry under Morgan and Forrest—the first to operate against Rosecrans' communications, the other against Grant's along the Mississippi.

On 26 December, Rosecrans finally marched south. A small column of Union cavalry moved across the mountains east of Cumberland Gap to break up Bragg's rail communications. This raid was successful, but had no appreciable effect on the course of the campaign. From the beginning, Rosecrans' march was slowed by the effective delaying tactics of Bragg's remaining cavalry under Wheeler. In fact, the advance was a constant skirmish, the Confederate cavalry forcing the Union infantry to deploy at every piece of strong defensive terrain. Meanwhile, the weaker Union cavalry was employed on flank protection and other missions with the several Union columns. As a result, Bragg was kept accurately informed of the Union dispositions and movements, whereas Rosecrans had little information of the Confederate forces. The Union army was further delayed by steady rains and constant fogs, so that it was the evening of the 29th before its leading corps—Crittenden's—approached Murfreesboro.

Rosecrans' march from Nashville had been conducted in three columns. Initially, one of Bragg's corps—Hardee's—had been at Triune (*lower left*), fifteen miles west of Murfreesboro. Thomas and McCook were therefore directed along routes which would enable them to turn this flank of the Confederate army—the former, by way of Franklin. But Bragg recalled Hardee to Murfreesboro, and the Union forces converged on the town as shown. Here Bragg proposed to stand and fight.

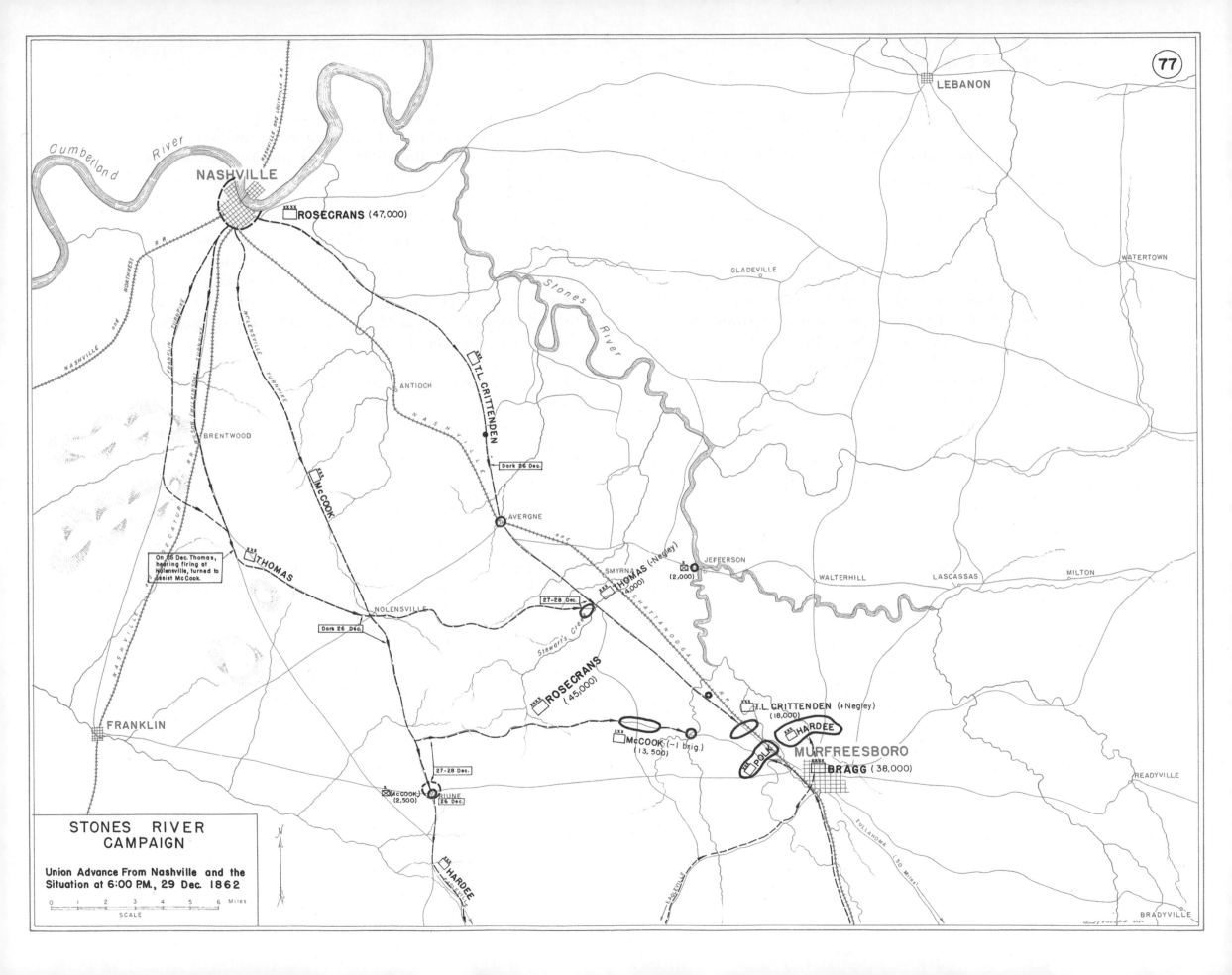

77

LEBANON

Cumberland River

NASHVILLE

WATERTOWN

Nashville and Louisville R.R.

GLADEVILLE

Stones River

ROSECRANS (47,000)

ANTIOCH

T.L. CRITTENDEN

Dark 26 Dec.

BRENTWOOD

NASHVILLE

McCOOK

Avergne

On 26 Dec. Thomas, hearing firing at Nolensville, turned to assist McCook.

THOMAS

THOMAS (-Negley) (4,000)

SMYRNA

JEFFERSON

(2,000)

WALTERHILL

LASCASSAS

MILTON

NOLENSVILLE

27-28 Dec.

Dark 26 Dec.

Stewart's Creek

ROSECRANS (45,000)

T.L. CRITTENDEN (+Negley) (18,000)

FRANKLIN

HARDEE

McCOOK (-1 brig.) (13,500)

POLK

MURFREESBORO

BRAGG (38,000)

READYVILLE

27-28 Dec.

McCOOK (2,500)

RIUNE 26 Dec.

TULLAHOMA 50 Miles

STONES RIVER CAMPAIGN

Union Advance From Nashville and the Situation at 6:00 P.M., 29 Dec. 1862

HARDEE

0 1 2 3 4 5 6 Miles
SCALE

BRADYVILLE

Bragg had taken up a defensive position astride the West Fork of Stones River (referred to as Stones River hereafter), his front strengthened in places by light entrenchments. The river was not a major obstacle at this time, for it could be crossed by several bridges and numerous fords. However, if rains caused the river to rise appreciably, Polk's corps would be dangerously isolated. The ground between the river and Overall Creek to the west was generally level; there were many clearings, but most of the area was covered with scrub cedar which limited visibility yet was no great obstacle to troop movements. The dominating terrain was the group of hills east of the river and north of Murfreesboro, held by the division of Maj. Gen. John C. Breckinridge. It is conjectural whether Bragg selected this awkward position to spare Murfreesboro the ravages of battle or to maintain a Confederate foothold on the west bank as a springboard if an opportunity for offensive action arose.

On the evening of 30 December, the opposing forces were disposed as shown. Polk occupied the west bank and Hardee the east. On that day the Confederate cavalry had ridden completely around the Union army, doing considerable damage to its supply trains. Bragg apparently had anticipated a Union attack, but, since it did not materialize, he himself issued orders for an attack early on 31 December. Hardee's corps (less Breckinridge's division) was to move to the south, cross Stones River—and, with the aid of Brig. Gen. John A. Wharton's cavalry, envelop the Union right flank. Polk would then join the attack, pivoting on his own right flank. The over-all object was to drive Rosecrans off his communications and pin him against the river. Bragg had no fear that Breckinridge, on the east bank, would be attacked; rather, he considered him as a reserve.

At about the same time, Rosecrans was issuing oral orders for an enveloping attack against the Confederate right flank. Crittenden was to send two divisions across the river to seize the high ground held by Breckinridge, from which the artillery of these two divisions could dominate the whole Confederate front. McCook was to engage the Confederates on his front (by offensive or defensive action as necessary) to hold them on the west bank of the river. Apparently, Thomas' corps and Brig. Gen. John M. Palmer's division were to make limited attacks in the center until Crittenden's envelopment was completed; then they were to join in a general Union assault. To deceive the Confederates, Rosecrans ordered McCook to build a line of campfires beyond his right flank to simulate the presence there of large bodies of troops. Successfully executed, this plan would drive Bragg off his line of communications and entrap most of his army between the victorious Federal army and the river.

Since the two plans were basically identical—each designed to envelop the opponent's right flank—victory would probably go to the commander who struck first and harder. Bragg issued his orders on the 30th, and Cleburne's division shifted to the opposite flank during that night. On the Union side, though pioneer troops moved up to the fords during the night to prepare them for crossing, Brig. Gen. Horatio P. Van Cleve and Brig. Gen. Thomas J. Wood did not receive their orders to advance until the morning of the 31st. One of Wood's brigade commanders somehow learned of Cleburne's shift. This information went at least as far as Crittenden, but no action was taken. McCook and Brig. Gen. Richard W. Johnson, his right-flank division commander, appear to have been content with routine local security measures and made no effort to reconnoiter aggressively along their front. Finally, Rosecrans failed to inspect McCook's position to learn if his troops were properly posted to resist an attack.

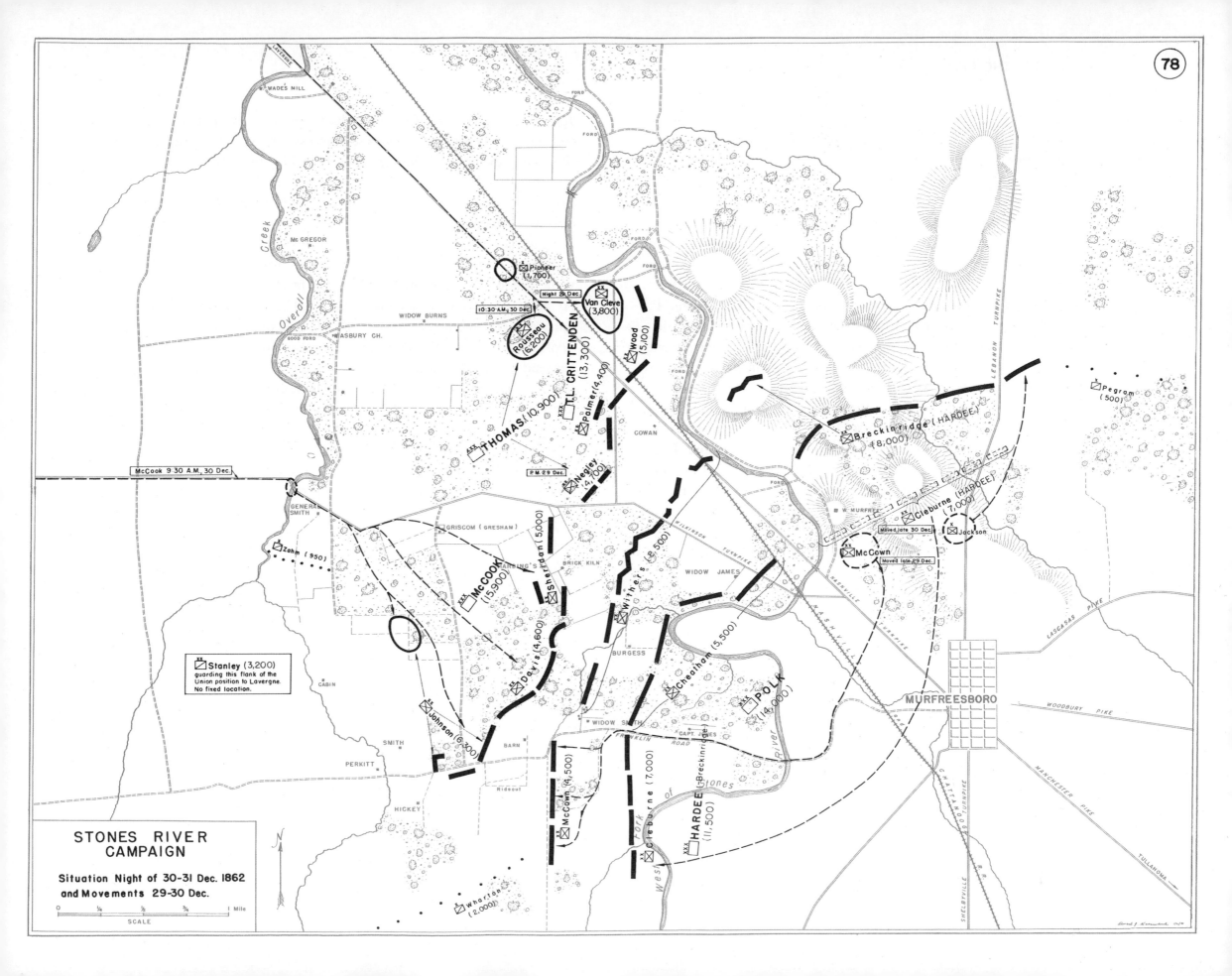

78

STONES RIVER
CAMPAIGN

Situation Night of 30-31 Dec. 1862
and Movements 29-30 Dec.

0   ¼   ½   ¾   1 Mile
SCALE

Stanley (3,200)
guarding this flank of the
Union position to Lavergne.
No fixed location.

At dawn (approximately 6:00 A.M.), Hardee and Wharton drove suddenly against the Union right flank. Apparently, McCook's extra campfires in prolongation of the right of his line failed to deceive the Confederates. Union outposts were quickly driven in; Johnson's division, caught preparing breakfast, was quickly broken up and forced back. Johnson eventually rallied his command along the railroad some three miles to the rear. His initial resistance, however, gave Brig. Gen. Jefferson C. Davis' division on his left time to pull back its right flank and to get into line. The leading Confederate division, that of Maj. Gen. John P. McCown, met stubborn resistance—despite the advantage of surprise—and was forced off somewhat to the left. This movement created a gap which Cleburne promptly filled, but Davis held his position against both McCown and Cleburne.

Polk now joined the attack, sending in his first line, Maj. Gen. Jones M. Withers' division, against Davis' left and Sheridan's right in a strong, but unsuccessful, attack. Following this repulse, Polk sent in his reserve division (that of Maj. Gen. B. Franklin Cheatham), but the Confederates were still unable to break the Union line. To add further weight to Polk's assault, Brig. Gen.

John K. Jackson's brigade—which had been temporarily attached to Breckinridge's division—was sent across the river. In the meantime, the advance of Wharton's cavalry had caused considerable alarm in the Union rear, for Col. Lewis Zahm's small cavalry brigade, outnumbered two to one, had been unable to offer effective resistance.

On the Federal left flank, Van Cleve—after receiving his orders to advance at 7:00 A.M.—had begun crossing Stones River, while Wood was preparing to cross at the ford directly to his front. At about this time, Rosecrans, convinced that his army was in danger, directed Thomas to shift Maj. Gen. Lovell H. Rousseau's division to Sheridan's right rear. He also ordered that Wood suspend his preparations for crossing the river, and that Van Cleve withdraw such of his troops as had already crossed, leave a brigade to guard the fords, and move the rest of his command to the vicinity of the railroad.

Meanwhile, Breckinridge had learned of the start of Van Cleve's advance across the river, and had concluded that he was about to be attacked by strong Union forces.

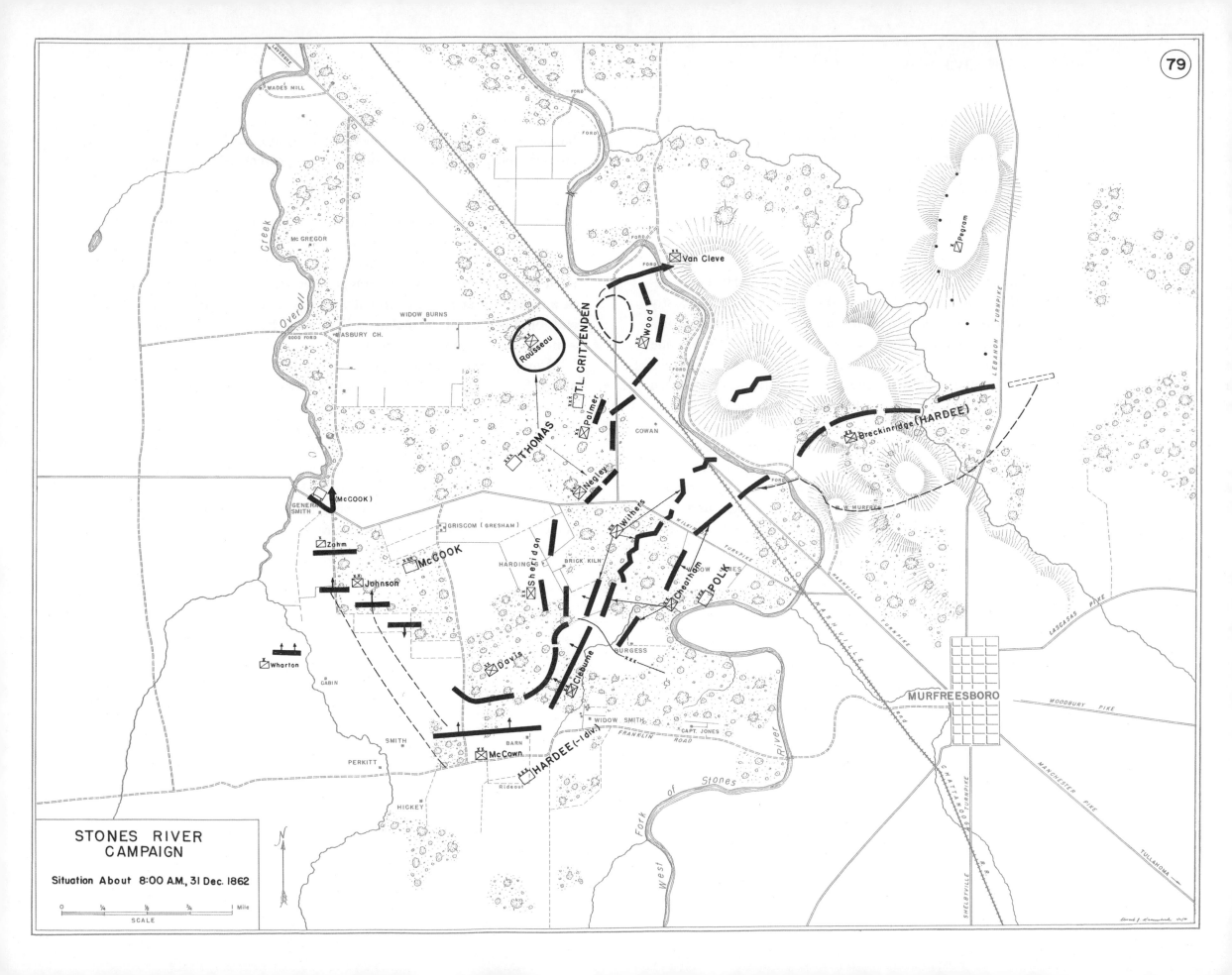

STONES RIVER
CAMPAIGN

Situation About 8:00 A.M., 31 Dec. 1862

0   1/4   1/2   3/4   1 Mile
SCALE

Persistent Confederate pressure on Davis' right flank eventually made his position (*left center*) untenable. Also, Wharton's cavalry had driven Zahm's brigade off the field and was deep in the Union rear. Consequently, Davis had to withdraw, some of his units doing so in considerable disorder.

The full force of Hardee's ably handled attack thus fell upon Sheridan's division, which proved to be the toughest opponent yet encountered. Sheridan's outposts had been alert during the night and had reported considerable enemy activity. He had therefore placed his command in line by 4:00 A.M. Repeated and costly attacks by Polk had not dislodged him. Now, his right flank uncovered by Davis' retreat, Sheridan moved his extreme left brigade across the rear of his position and launched it in a vigorous counterattack against Hardee, checking the latter's advance. In the time thus gained, Sheridan fell back to a position parallel to the Nashville Turnpike.

Rousseau's division came into action on the right of Sheridan's position, and a new line, perpendicular to the original front, was thus established on the Union right. Rosecrans rapidly extended this line by adding a brigade from each of Wood's and Van Cleve's divisions. In the center, Brig. Gen. James S. Negley's division continued to hold off Polk's assaults. By now, however, Sheridan's men were almost out of ammunition, since McCook's ammunition train had to be withdrawn to prevent its capture by Wharton.

Wharton had gotten deep into the Union rear, creating considerable confusion, but his attempt to capture McCook's ammunition train was defeated by one of Zahm's regiments which had held firm when the other three fled. Wharton, however, gathered in hundreds of fugitives and stragglers and claimed the capture of a battery of artillery. Eventually he was checked by odds and ends of Union cavalry—including Rosecrans' headquarters escort—in a series of confused actions.

Van Cleve had already gotten his artillery and two brigades across Stones River when he received Rosecrans' orders to halt his advance and recross the river. His withdrawal was rapidly and efficiently executed. Breckinridge, poorly served by Pegram's cavalry, was not aware of this movement.

Temporarily, the battle had been stabilized. Hardee's and Polk's units had become badly intermingled, and their men were beginning to tire. Rosecrans, displaying inspiring personal courage and energy, was working furiously to regain control of the action.

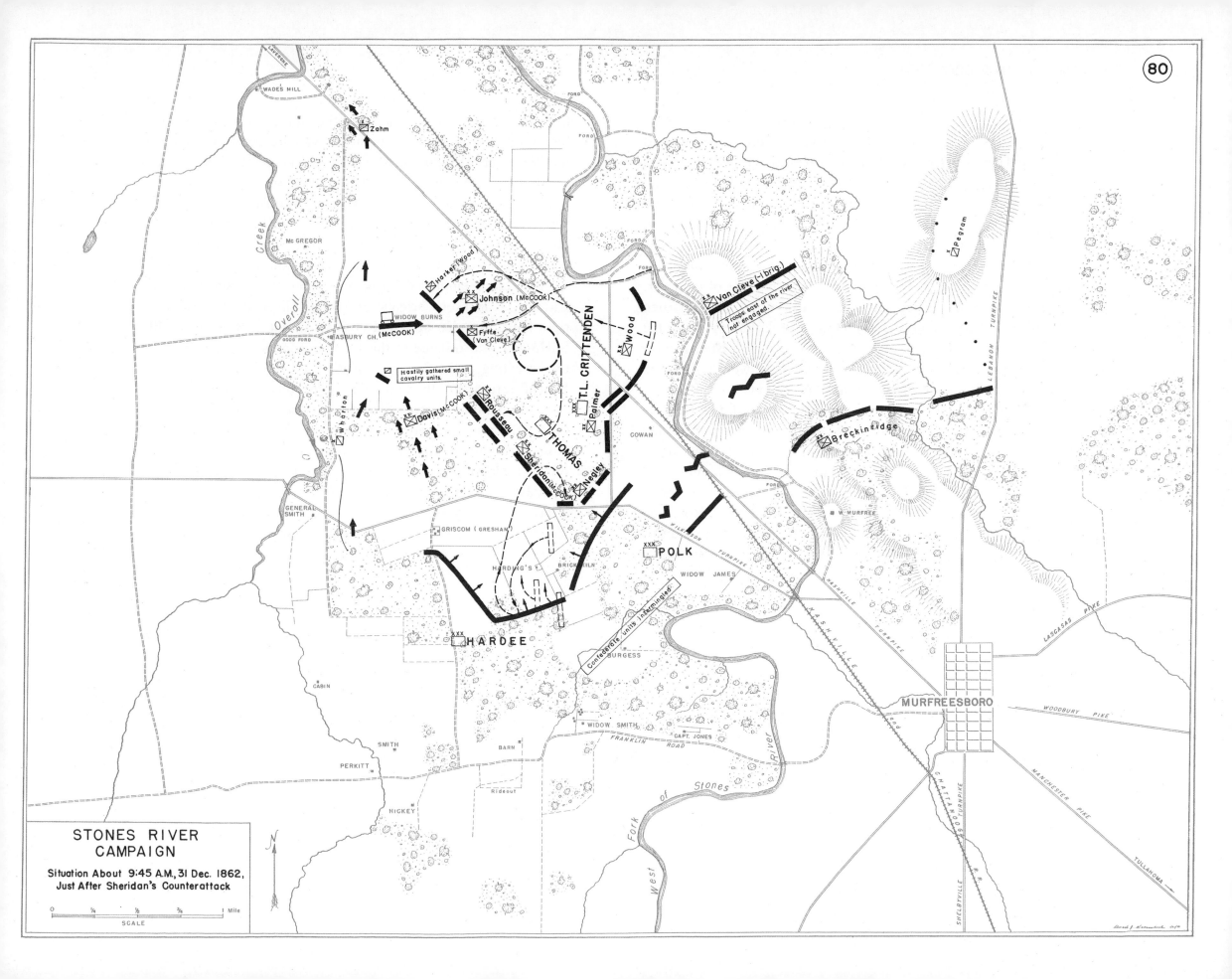

80

Zahm

WADES MILL

McGREGOR

Harker (Wood)

Johnson (McCOOK)

WIDOW BURNS

ASBURY CH.(McCOOK)

Fyffe (Van Cleve)

Van Cleve (-1 brig.)

Troops east of the river not engaged.

Pegram

Wood

T.L. CRITTENDEN

Hastily gathered small cavalry units.

Wharton

Rousseau

Davis (McCOOK)

THOMAS

Palmer

Breckinridge

COWAN

Sheridan(McCook)

Negley

W. MURFREE

GENERAL SMITH

GRISCOM (GRESHAM)

POLK

HARDING'S

BRICK KILN

WIDOW JAMES

HARDEE

BURGESS

Confederate units intermingled

CABIN

WIDOW SMITH

CAPT. JONES

MURFREESBORO

SMITH

BARN

FRANKLIN ROAD

PERKITT

RIDEOUT

HICKEY

STONES RIVER CAMPAIGN

Situation About 9:45 A.M., 31 Dec. 1862,
Just After Sheridan's Counterattack

N

0   ¼   ½   ¾   1 Mile

SCALE

By 10:00 A.M., Bragg, aware that his attack was slackening, ordered Breckinridge to send two brigades across the river to reinforce Hardee. Breckinridge, unaware of Van Cleve's withdrawal, replied that he himself expected to be attacked at any moment and could not spare any troops. Bragg thereupon ordered him to advance and attack any Union forces east of Stones River, instead of standing passively on the defensive. Breckinridge accordingly moved forward, only to make the embarrassing discovery that there were no Federal troops on his side of the river. At about this time, Bragg received a false report that a strong Union force was moving south along the Lebanon Turnpike (*upper right*). This led him to cancel his orders that Breckinridge send the two brigades across the river. These two Confederate blunders may have saved Rosecrans from defeat.

At about 11:00 A.M., however, after several Confederate attacks on the new Union line had been beaten off, Sheridan warned Thomas that his men were out of ammunition and would have to withdraw from their position between Thomas' two divisions (Rousseau and Negley). Hardee immediately thrust forward into the gap created by Sheridan's withdrawal. Rousseau fell back in good order; Negley—already under attack by Polk— had to fight front, flank, and rear, beating off Polk's pursuit while he broke through Hardee's advancing forces. Thomas reunited his two divisions on some slightly elevated ground just south of the Nashville Turnpike, where they had good fields of fire, and repulsed all subsequent Confederate attacks in that sector.

Negley's withdrawal forced Palmer, in turn, to pull back the right of his line. His left-flank brigade (Col. William B. Hazen), posted on high ground astride the railroad, held tenaciously to its position—the only part of the original Union line attacked to do so. Rosecrans employed all of Van Cleve's division, plus Col. Charles G. Harker's brigade of Wood's division, to rebuild his right flank. Another of Wood's brigades, that of Brig. Gen. Milo S. Hascall, was ordered to that flank but found the road blocked by retreating units. Receiving a plea for support from Palmer, Hascall returned to the battle line on his own initiative.

Considerable disorder existed in places immediately behind the hastily reestablished Union front, but the vigorous efforts of Rosecrans and his subordinate commanders kept practically all of the Federal units intact. Also, both Johnson and Davis had rallied their men. Farther to the rear, Wharton had made several efforts to destroy portions of the Union trains between Overall Creek and the front, but was finally outfought by hastily assembled detachments of Union cavalry.

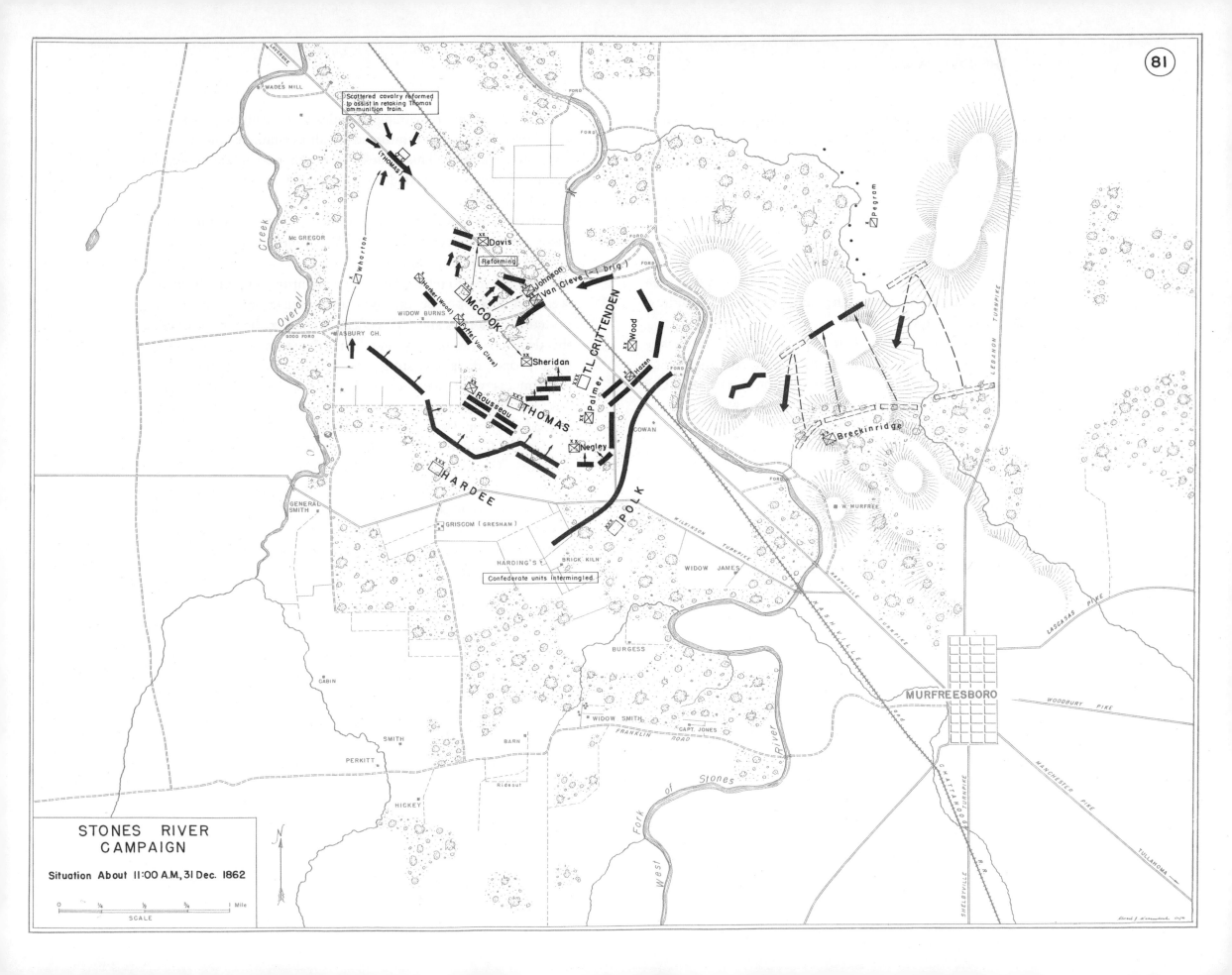

81

Scattered cavalry reformed
to assist in retaking Thomas
ammunition train.

[THOMAS]

Wharton

McGREGOR

Creek

Overall

GOOD FORD

WADES MILL

LAVERGNE

FORD

FORD

FORD

FORD

Pegram

Davis

Reforming

Johnson

Van Cleve (- brig.)

Harker (Wood)

McCOOK

WIDOW BURNS

Roberts (Van Cleve)

ASBURY CH.

Sheridan

Wood

T.L. CRITTENDEN

Palmer

Hazen

FORD

Rousseau

THOMAS

Cowan

Breckinridge

Negley

HARDEE

W. MURFREE

GENERAL
SMITH

POLK

GRISCOM (GRESHAM)

Confederate units intermingled.

HARDING'S

BRICK KILN

WILKINSON

TURNPIKE

WIDOW JAMES

LEBANON TURNPIKE

NASHVILLE

TURNPIKE

LASCASAS PIKE

CABIN

BURGESS

SMITH

WIDOW SMITH

CAPT. JONES

MURFREESBORO

WOODBURY PIKE

PERKITT

BARN

FRANKLIN ROAD

Stones

West Fork of Stones River

HICKEY

Rideout

CHATTANOOGA R.R.

SHELBYVILLE & TULLAHOMA TURNPIKE

MANCHESTER PIKE

TULLAHOMA

STONES RIVER
CAMPAIGN

Situation About 11:00 A.M., 31 Dec. 1862

N

0   ¼   ½   ¾   1 Mile

SCALE

By noon, Rosecrans had completed the organization of his new line, which ran almost at right angles to his original one. Confederate assaults against it continued, but these were uniformly unsuccessful.

Earlier in the morning, Rosecrans had ordered his chief of cavalry, Brig. Gen. David S. Stanley, who had been guarding his line of communications, to come forward and cover the Union right flank. Both Stanley and the ubiquitous Wheeler arrived about noon and continued the indecisive cavalry fight in that area until about nightfall. Both claimed the victory, and both withdrew comparatively undamaged.

Bragg now decided that his best hope for a decisive victory lay in an overwhelming attack against the Union left flank, which he felt had been weakened to bolster the Union right flank. The only fresh troops available for such an assault were those of Breckinridge. Bragg ordered him across the river, but Breckinridge moved unwillingly and slowly. Meanwhile, by 2:00 P.M., Hardee had been fought to a standstill and had even been pushed back in places, chiefly by Van Cleve and the "Pioneer" brigade of engineer troops.

It was almost 4:00 P.M. before Breckinridge's first two brigades came into line opposite Hazen. Polk immediately committed them to battle and suffered a heavy repulse. As soon as Breckinridge's two remaining brigades were available, Polk likewise committed them, reinforced by all available elements of his own battered corps. This attack was another complete and costly failure. Thomas responded with a limited counterattack which cleared his front.

That night Rosecrans held a council of war, concerning which there are a number of accounts. Apparently, some of the commanders present felt that the army had been defeated and that it would be wise to retreat before it was entirely cut off. Rosecrans seems to have opposed this view and to have been strongly supported by Thomas and Crittenden. Whatever the circumstances, the decision was to stay and fight. Brigades were returned to their proper divisions, stragglers were rounded up, and minor adjustments were made to straighten the front. Union morale rose. As Rosecrans expressed it after the battle was over, "Bragg's a good dog, but Hold Fast's a better."

On the Confederate side, Bragg was certain that he had won a victory. His troops, less optimistic, began digging in.

At 3:00 A.M. on the morning of 1 January, 1863, Rosecrans—reverting to his original plan—ordered Van Cleve's division (now under Col. Samuel Beatty, Van Cleve having been wounded) to cross the river and occupy the hill which commanded the two fords nearest the Union right.

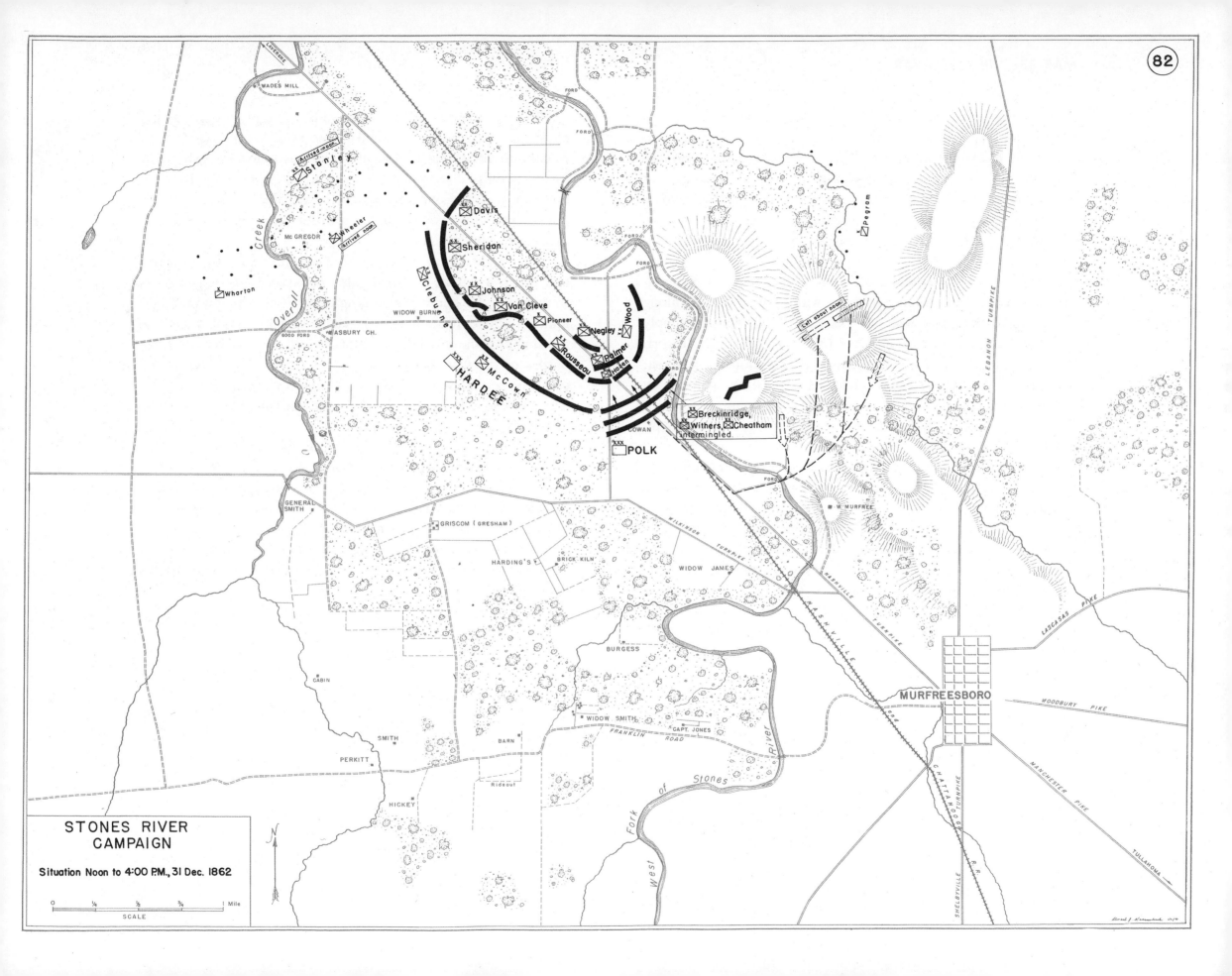

82

Arrived at noon
Stanley

Davis

McGREGOR
Wheeler
Arrived noon

Wharton

Sheridan

Johnson

Cleburne

Van Cleve

WIDOW BURNE

Pioneer

Wood

Negley

Rousseau
Palmer
Hazen

McCown

HARDEE

Pegram

Left about noon

Breckinridge,
Withers, Cheatham
intermingled.

COWAN

POLK

LaVERGNE

WADE'S MILL

Creek

Overall

FORD

FORD

FORD

FORD

FORD

FORD

GOOD FORD

ASBURY CH.

GENERAL
SMITH

GRISCOM (GRESHAM)

HARDING'S
BRICK KILN

WIDOW JAMES

WILKINSON
TURNPIKE

W. MURFREE

TURNPIKE

LEBANON
TURNPIKE

NASHVILLE

CABIN

BURGESS

West

Fork

of

Stones

River

WIDOW SMITH
CAPT. JONES

SMITH

BARN

FRANKLIN
ROAD

MURFREESBORO

WOODBURY PIKE

PERKITT

HICKEY

Rideout

Road

CHATTAN

TURNPIKE

MANCHESTER PIKE

LASCASAS PIKE

SHELBVILLE R.R.

TULLAHOMA

STONES RIVER
CAMPAIGN

Situation Noon to 4:00 P.M., 31 Dec. 1862

N

0   ¼   ½   ¾   Mile
SCALE

New Year's Day was relatively quiet. Polk closed on the new Union line, occupying ground relinquished by Rosecrans to straighten his front, and made several efforts to test Thomas' position. This brought him nothing but more casualties. An attack that afternoon on Sheridan met the same fate. Meanwhile, Beatty, with Van Cleve's division, completed the occupation of the hill east of the river, confronting Breckinridge, who had also returned to the far bank.

Wheeler's cavalry continued to harass the Federal rear, bringing on a series of minor engagements, with varying success, along the turnpike back to Nashville. Because of his raiding, supply trains and convoys of wounded had to travel under heavy escort. Wheeler interpreted such movements as preparations for a retreat and reported them to Bragg as such. His hopes thus confirmed by this supposedly firsthand source, Bragg was content to wait for Rosecrans to retire, meanwhile resting his men and collecting all available booty.

The morning of 2 January revealed Rosecrans still in position. Abruptly, Bragg sent Breckinridge with four brigades to drive the Federal left wing back across Stones River. Breckinridge protested that the mission was suicidal, yet he attacked with determination. Van Cleve's division (under Beatty), the only Federal unit east of the river at the time, was dislodged, but massed Union artillery, firing across the river into the Confederate flank, stopped Breckinridge's division. Union infantry in force rushed across the river and counterattacked, driving the Confederates back to their line of departure.

Early on the morning of the 3d, a large supply train, escorted by a reinforced brigade, reached Rosecrans. Wheeler attempted to capture an ammunition train which was following it, but was forced to retire after some fighting. Late in the evening, Thomas, apparently on his own initiative, attacked the center of the opposing line with two brigades and drove the Confederates from their entrenchments at that point.

That night Bragg withdrew skillfully through Murfreesboro and began a retreat to Tullahoma (*not shown*), thirty-six miles to the south. He had fought courageously, if not capably, and had inflicted heavier losses than he had suffered. Perhaps his army was too small for the attack he attempted. Still, more than most other battles of the war, this was a conflict between the wills of the opposing commanders. Rosecrans, powerfully supported by Thomas and others, would not admit himself beaten and so— in the end—won a victory of sorts.

Rosecrans occupied Murfreesboro but made no effort to pursue Bragg. Murfreesboro had also been one of the bloodiest battles of the war, each army suffering about 12,000 casualties— the Union forces somewhat more, the Confederates slightly less. Officers and men of both armies performed splendidly. In an engagement much like the Battle of Shiloh, neither side exhibited the loss of control or the mass straggling that had characterized that battle.

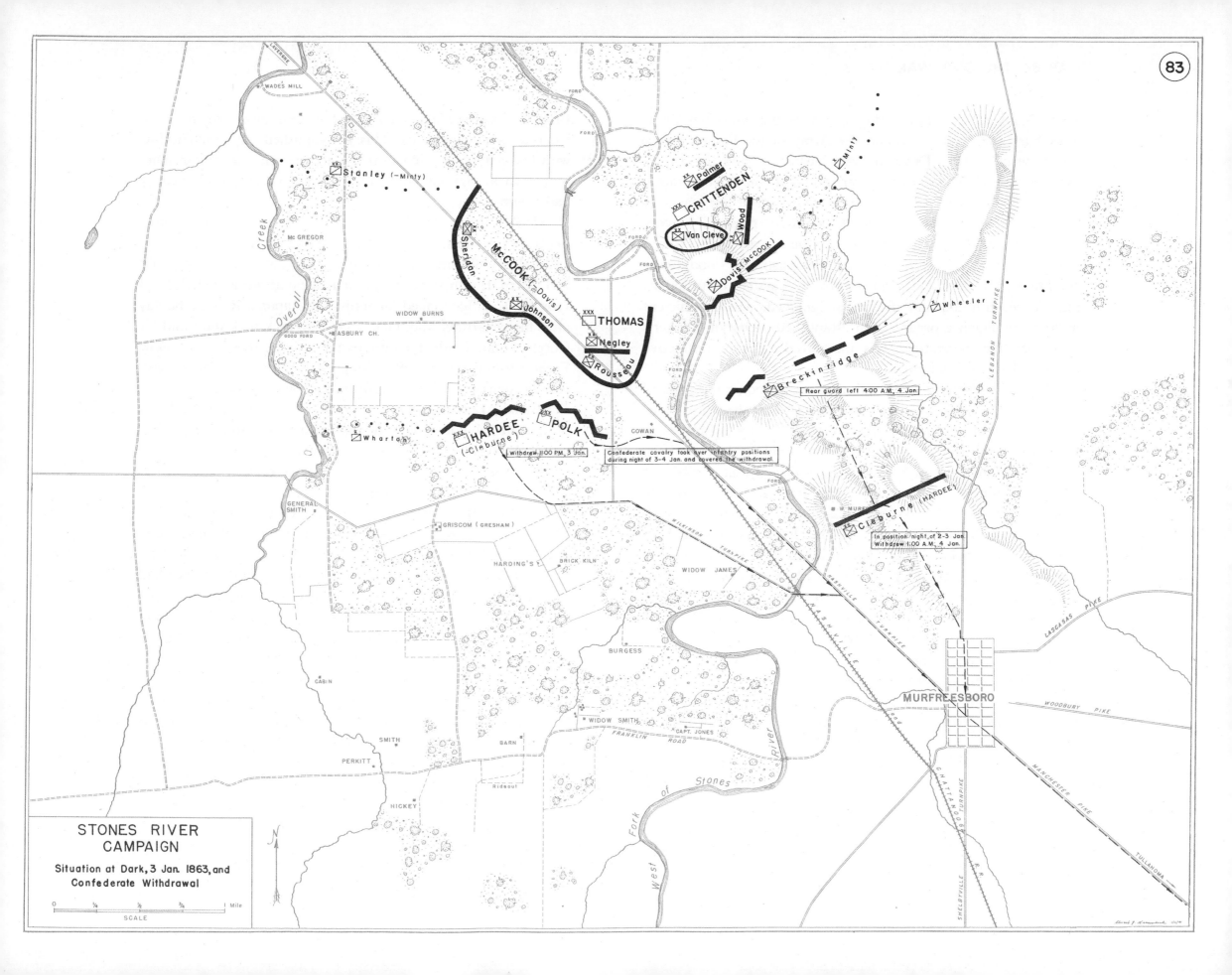

83

STANLEY (-Minty)

Minty

Palmer

CRITTENDEN

Wood

Van Cleve

Davis (McCOOK)

McCOOK (-Davis)

Sheridan

Johnson

THOMAS

Negley

Rousseau

Wheeler

Breckinridge

Rear guard left 4:00 A.M., 4 Jan.

Wharton

HARDEE
(-Cleburne)

POLK

GOWAN

Withdrew 11:00 PM, 3 Jan.

Confederate cavalry took over infantry positions
during night of 3-4 Jan. and covered the withdrawal.

W. MURFF

Cleburne (HARDEE)

In position night of 2-3 Jan.
Withdrew 1:00 A.M., 4 Jan.

GENERAL
SMITH

GRISCOM (GRESHAM)

BRICK KILN

HARDING'S

WIDOW JAMES

BURGESS

CABIN

MURFREESBORO

WOODBURY PIKE

SMITH

WIDOW SMITH

CAPT. JONES

PERKITT

BARN

HICKEY

Rideout

WADES MILL

Mc GREGOR

WIDOW BURNS

ASBURY CH.

GOOD FORD

FORD

FORD

FORD

FORD

FORD

FORD

FORD

Creek

Overall

West Fork of Stones River

Stones River

LAVERGNE

WILKINSON TURNPIKE

FRANKLIN ROAD

NASHVILLE TURNPIKE

LEBANON TURNPIKE

LASCASAS PIKE

MANCHESTER PIKE

SHELBYVILLE

CHATTANOOGA TURNPIKE

TULLAHOMA R. R.

STONES RIVER
CAMPAIGN

Situation at Dark, 3 Jan. 1863, and
Confederate Withdrawal

N

0   ¼   ½   ¾   1 Mile
SCALE

When Hooker had relieved Burnside after the disastrous Fredericksburg campaign, he found the Army of the Potomac in a low state of morale. Desertion was increasing, and the army's own interior administration—never too good—had deteriorated.

Hooker was a boastful, ambitious man, apt at intrigue—yet a commander who had set a high record for personal bravery and aggressive combat leadership. Now he unexpectedly showed himself an outstanding organizer and administrator. Food, living conditions, and hospitals were improved, a system of furloughs introduced, training and discipline tightened, and an efficient military intelligence organization established. (One of Hooker's most effective innovations was the introduction of distinctive corps and division insignia.)

Abolishing Burnside's "grand divisions," Hooker reorganized his forces into seven infantry corps and one cavalry corps. This consolidation of the cavalry—much of which had previously been attached to infantry corps and divisions—rapidly increased the efficiency of the Federal horsemen. Stuart's constant harassment of Union outposts had irritated them all winter; on 17 March, Brig. Gen. William W. Averell crossed the Rappahannock with his cavalry division at Kelly's Ford and drove back—though he failed to overwhelm—Brig. Gen. Fitzhugh Lee's smaller command. On the other hand, Hooker made a serious mistake in decentralizing tactical control of his artillery to his corps commanders. As a result, Federal artillery in the coming Battle of Chancellorsville was not properly massed.

In planning his offensive, Hooker had the problem of crossing the Rappahannock against a dangerous opponent. Lee had carefully fortified the south bank, from Port Royal to Banks's Ford, with detached works guarding United States Ford farther upstream. Hooker knew, however, that he possessed a decided numerical superiority, since he had learned that Lee—alarmed by reports that the Federal IX Corps was aboard transports at Hampton Roads—had sent Longstreet south with two divisions to guard the Virginia-Carolina coast.

Hooker's decision was to move up the Rappahannock and turn Lee's left flank. His first plan was to try to force Lee to retreat from Fredericksburg by sending the Federal cavalry, under Brig. Gen. George Stoneman, ahead on a raid to destroy the Confederate communications. This accomplished, he would follow with his infantry, hoping to trap Lee between it and Stoneman. Stoneman moved out slowly on that mission, but was halted by bad weather.

Hooker then recast his plan into the better one shown here. Following demonstrations at Kelly's Ford and Port Royal, Maj. Gen. Henry Slocum marched on 27 April with the V, XI, and XII Corps. He surprised the Confederate outposts at Kelly's Ford (*top left*) and continued on across the Rapidan River. The day after his departure, Maj. Gen. John Sedgwick took the I and VI Corps ostentatiously forward to the river, crossing just below Fredericksburg on the 29th. Maj. Gen. Darius N. Couch, with two divisions of his II Corps, went into concealed positions opposite Banks's Ford (his third division—Brig. Gen. John Gibbon's—was left behind, since its original camp was visible to Confederate observers). The III Corps, under Brig. Gen. Daniel E. Sickles, was alerted but left temporarily in reserve. The cavalry was to destroy Lee's communications.

Lee himself had been planning an offensive movement in the Shenandoah Valley. Now the extent of Hooker's movements temporarily baffled him; he concluded that Slocum might be striking at Gordonsville (*off map, southwest*). The Federal advance had gotten between him and Stuart, so that it took considerable time for the latter's dispatches to reach him (though Stuart had soon detected Slocum's march). On 29 April, Lee moved the three divisions on his right flank closer to Fredericksburg and sent Anderson to occupy a position near Chancellorsville. Once there, Anderson soon decided a withdrawal was necessary. Stuart, meanwhile, detaching one brigade to watch Stoneman, clung to Slocum's flank.

By 3:00 P.M., Hooker had three corps in Lee's rear near Chancellorsville, and Couch's two divisions (called forward from Banks's Ford) were close behind. A prompt advance would have gotten this force into more open ground, cleared Banks's Ford, and halved the distance between it and Sedgwick. Hooker, however, halted the three corps to await reinforcements.

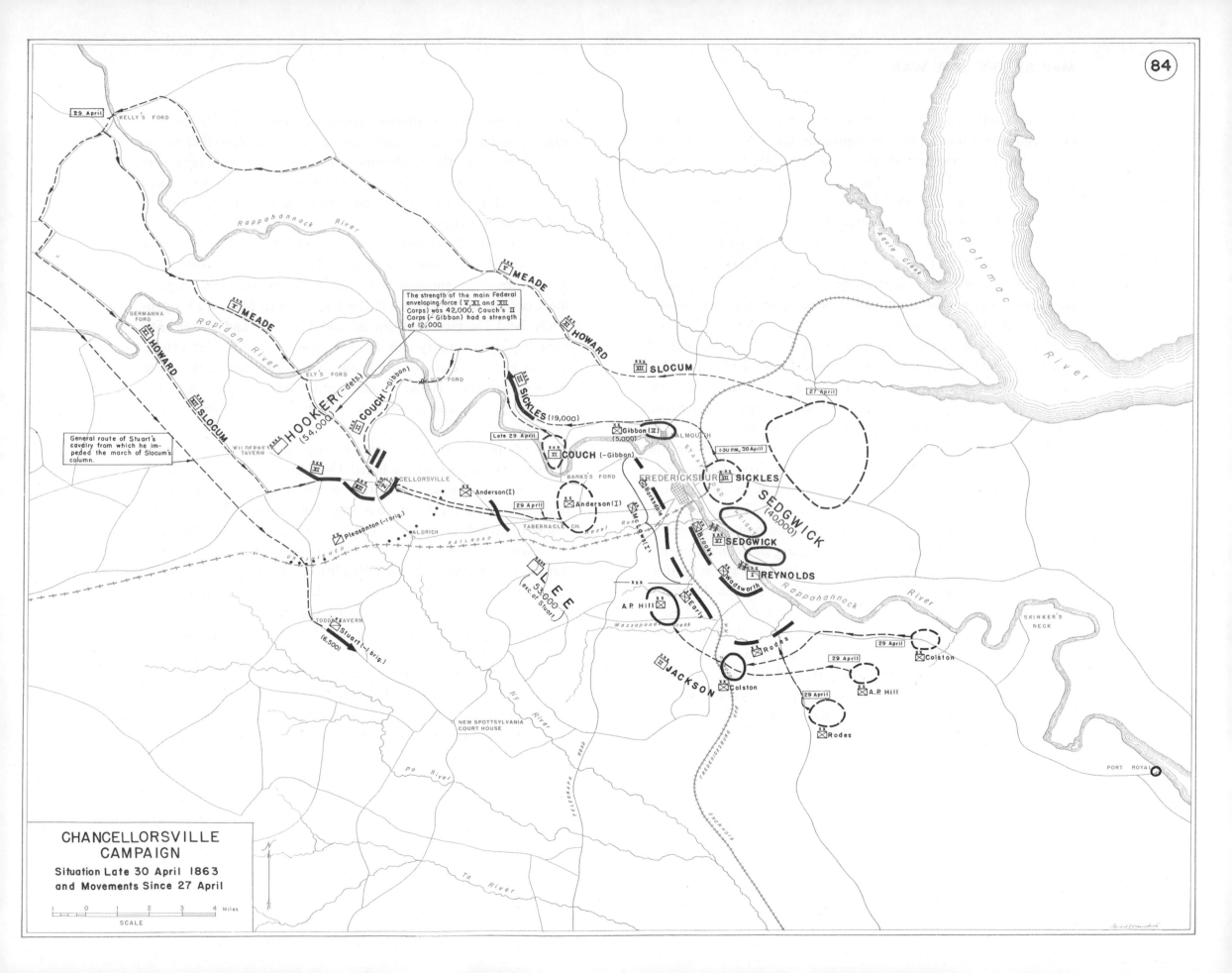

84

29 April — KELLY'S FORD

Rappahannock River

GERMANNA FORD

Rapidan River

XXX MEADE Ⅴ

XXX MEADE Ⅴ

ELY'S FORD

XXX HOWARD Ⅺ

XXX SLOCUM Ⅻ

General route of Stuart's cavalry from which he impeded the march of Slocum's column.

WILDERNESS TAVERN

XXXXX HOOKER (54,000) (~dets.)

XXX COUCH (~Gibbon) Ⅱ

XXX HOWARD Ⅺ

XXX SLOCUM Ⅻ

The strength of the main Federal enveloping force (Ⅴ, Ⅺ and Ⅻ Corps) was 42,000. Couch's Ⅱ Corps (~ Gibbon) had a strength of 12,000

XXX SICKLES (19,000) Ⅲ

Late 29 April

Gibbon (Ⅱ) (5,000)

FALMOUTH

27 April

U.S. FORD

XXX COUCH (~Gibbon) Ⅱ

BANKS'S FORD

CHANCELLORSVILLE

Anderson (Ⅰ)

29 April

Anderson (Ⅰ)

Barksdale

1:30 P.M., 30 April

FREDERICKSBURG

XXX SICKLES Ⅲ

SEDGWICK (40,000)

MARYE'S HEIGHTS

XXX SEDGWICK Ⅵ

Brooks

Pleasonton (~1 brig.)

ALDRICH

RAILROAD

TABERNACLE CH.

Hazel Run

McLaws (Ⅰ)

UNFINISHED

XXXXX LEE 52,000 (exc. of Stuart)

Wadsworth

XXX REYNOLDS Ⅰ

XXX

Rappahannock River

TODD'S TAVERN

Stuart (~1 brig.) (6,500)

A.P. Hill

Early

Massaponax Creek

SKINKER'S NECK

XXX JACKSON Ⅱ

Rodes

Colston

Colston

29 April

A.P. Hill

29 April

Ny River

NEW SPOTTSYLVANIA COURT HOUSE

29 April

Rodes

Po River

Po River

PORT ROYAL

To River

TELEGRAPH ROAD

FREDERICKSBURG AND R.R.

Ta River

FREDERICKSBURG AND POTOMAC R.R.

Aquia Creek

Potomac River

CHANCELLORSVILLE CAMPAIGN

Situation Late 30 April 1863 and Movements Since 27 April

N

1 0 1 2 3 4 Miles
SCALE

Chancellorsville (*left center*) was a lone brick house at a minor crossroads in a waste area appropriately known as "the Wilderness." Thick second-growth pine and oak, tangled with undergrowth, severely limited visibility and made movement off the few roads difficult for individuals and next to impossible for formed bodies of troops. The area was further cut up by many swampy little streams. The dominating terrain, such as it was, was the hill at Hazel Grove. In such an area, artillery and cavalry could seldom operate except along the roads; the full force of numbers could not be employed because there was little opportunity to deploy or maneuver.

Nevertheless, Hooker delayed in the area and did not advance from Chancellorsville until about 11:00 A.M. on 1 May. Apparently he had given up the idea of promptly seizing Banks's Ford when, late on 29 April, he had ordered Couch to move from his position opposite the ford to Chancellorsville.

Meanwhile, Lee had faced a series of problems. Even after he had learned that Anderson had retreated from Chancellorsville, he was still uncertain as to which wing of the Union army he could more profitably attack. As usual, it did not occur to him to stand on the defensive. He and Jackson first reconnoitered Sedgwick's bridgehead below Fredericksburg but concluded that the Union position—supported as it was by artillery on Stafford Heights—offered no real chance for victory. Lee then decided to leave Early's division, reinforced by one brigade, to hold Sedgwick while he moved the rest of his army against Hooker. During 30 April, Anderson had begun entrenching a position between Tabernacle Church and Duerson's Mill (*both center*). When Jackson arrived early the next morning, he stopped the work on Anderson's position and moved all the troops forward to meet Hooker.

So far, except for delay due to bad weather, Hooker had experienced only one major difficulty. Having no cavalry with him except one of Pleasonton's brigades, which could seldom penetrate Stuart's counterreconnaissance screen, he had to advance blindly for the greater part of the time. Nevertheless, he came forward in three columns as shown. French's division was to turn off to the right later and occupy Todd's Tavern (*lower left*). Sickles' corps, which had arrived that morning, covered the rear of the army.

The initial clashes were indecisive. Sykes forced McLaws back until Confederate reinforcements outflanked him and drove him, in his turn, back through Hancock's division; Hancock stopped the Confederate advance. On the Union right, Slocum also generally held his ground. Both he and Hancock had gotten into relatively open country and reached strong positions. Meanwhile, Meade met no resistance and was soon across the flank of the Confederate line. Hooker's observation balloons had detected Lee's movement and the weakness of Early's forces on Marye's Heights.

And then—with every opportunity at hand for a decisive victory—Hooker's courage failed. Over the indignant protests of his corps commanders, he ordered the troops back into their positions of the night before around Chancellorsville. Later, he countermanded this order, but by then his troops had withdrawn. Meanwhile, Sedgwick received several conflicting orders, and so did nothing aggressive. It is difficult to explain Hooker's unwarranted surrender of the initiative under such favorable circumstances. He was personally brave; he had built up a splendid army; and he had planned skillfully. It may have been that it was difficult for him to visualize and assess properly a military operation on such a large scale that many of its phases were beyond the range of his direct control. Possibly it was the inward knowledge of this inadequacy which, at this critical moment, weakened his determination. Later, as a corps commander in more restricted operations, he again proved to be a fine leader.

When the Union forces withdrew, the Confederates followed carefully, puzzled and suspicious of such an easy victory.

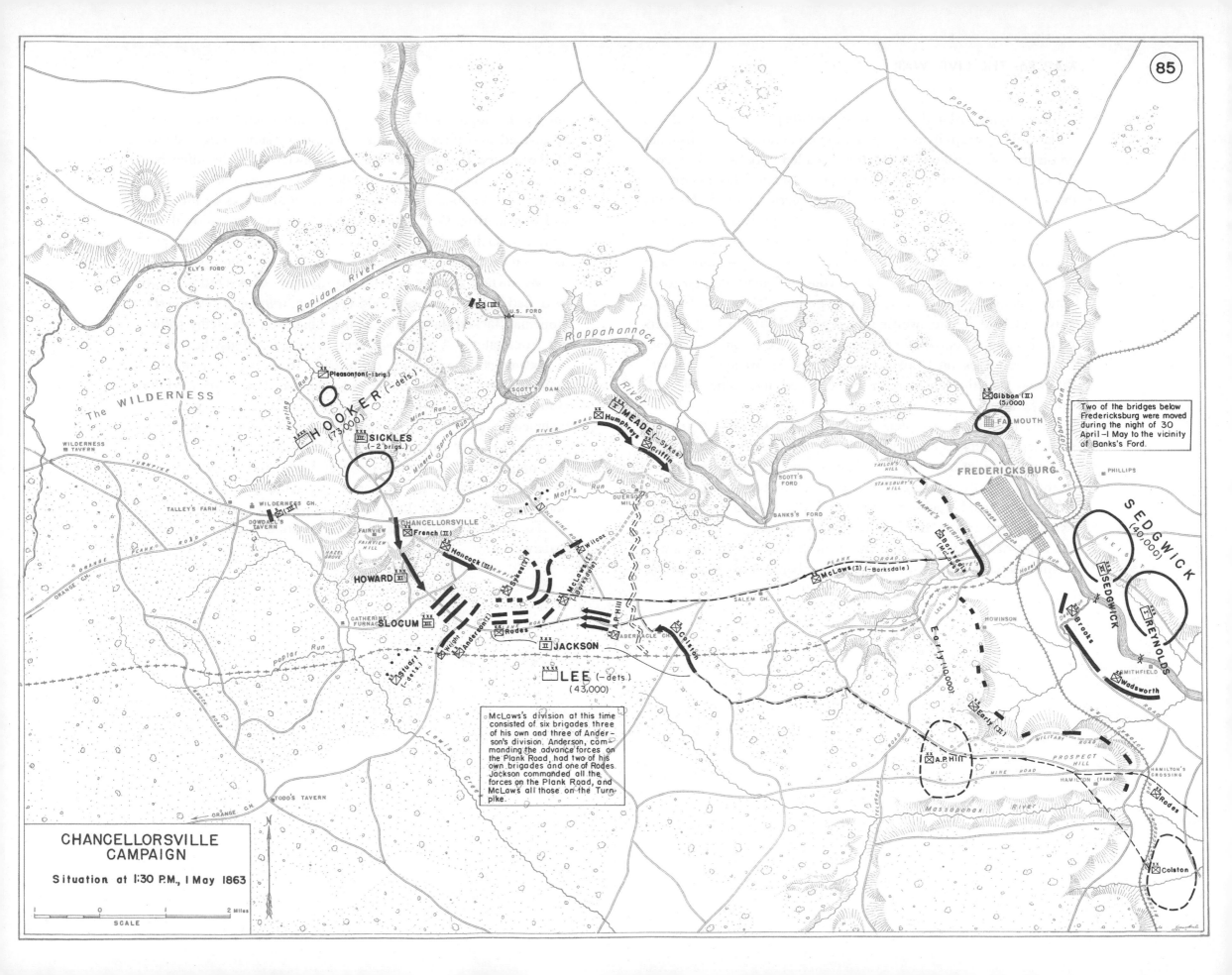

85

Two of the bridges below
Fredericksburg were moved
during the night of 30
April-1 May to the vicinity
of Banks's Ford.

McLaws's division at this time
consisted of six brigades three
of his own and three of Anderson's division. Anderson, commanding the advance forces on
the Plank Road, had two of his
own brigades and one of Rodes.
Jackson commanded all the
forces on the Plank Road, and
McLaws all those on the Turnpike.

CHANCELLORSVILLE
CAMPAIGN

Situation at 1:30 P.M., 1 May 1863

1   0   1   2 Miles
SCALE

Hooker having ordered the Chancellorsville position fortified, the Federal troops rapidly constructed log breastworks and obstacles consisting of interlaced felled trees (called "abatis"). Lee considered these defenses formidable and confined his operations during the afternoon to skirmishing and reconnaissance. He fully appreciated the extreme seriousness of the prevailing situation. He could not hope to assault Hooker's position east and south of Chancellorsville successfully; and Early would not be able to stop Sedgwick if the latter attacked vigorously. Something had to be done quickly; consequently, a weak point in Hooker's defenses must be found. While awaiting the reports of various staff officers he had sent to scout the Federal position, Lee began to consider a possible attack on Hooker's right. Then Stuart appeared with the news that the Union right was exposed and vulnerable to a surprise attack.

Lee now made his plans. Jackson, with some 26,000 men, screened by Stuart's cavalry, would circle around the Union position and attack it from the west; Lee, meanwhile, with the approximately 17,000 remaining men, would keep Hooker engaged on the present front. Jackson's maneuver was a dangerous one, for he would have to march fourteen miles by narrow roads across the front of the Union army. But even more risky was the entire Confederate enterprise. Already outnumbered more than two to one by the opposing Union forces, the Confederate army would be divided into three segments, each out of supporting distance of the others. If either Hooker or Sedgwick took the offensive, the army might be destroyed in detail. There was also the possibility that Gibbon might cross suddenly at Banks's Ford, and so Lee sent Brig. Gen. Cadmus M. Wilcox to take station there. Only two such commanders as Lee and Jackson, possessing perfect confidence in one another, could carry off such a stroke.

Meanwhile, Stoneman, with the divisions of Averell and Buford, had begun his cavalry raid (*off map, south and southwest*). Stoneman lacked dash (and, at this time, was reportedly suffering from piles). Averell was sent toward Gordonsville, where he became involved chasing the brigade Stuart had left behind to maintain contact with Stoneman. He was finally recalled by Hooker. Stoneman broke up Buford's division into several detachments and sent them raiding deep into Virginia. In so doing, he failed to carry out Hooker's instructions and missed an excellent opportunity to destroy most of Lee's trains and supplies, which were concentrated under a very small guard at Guiney's Station, approximately fifteen miles south of Fredericksburg.

To the east, Sedgwick, lacking definite orders, remained inactive.

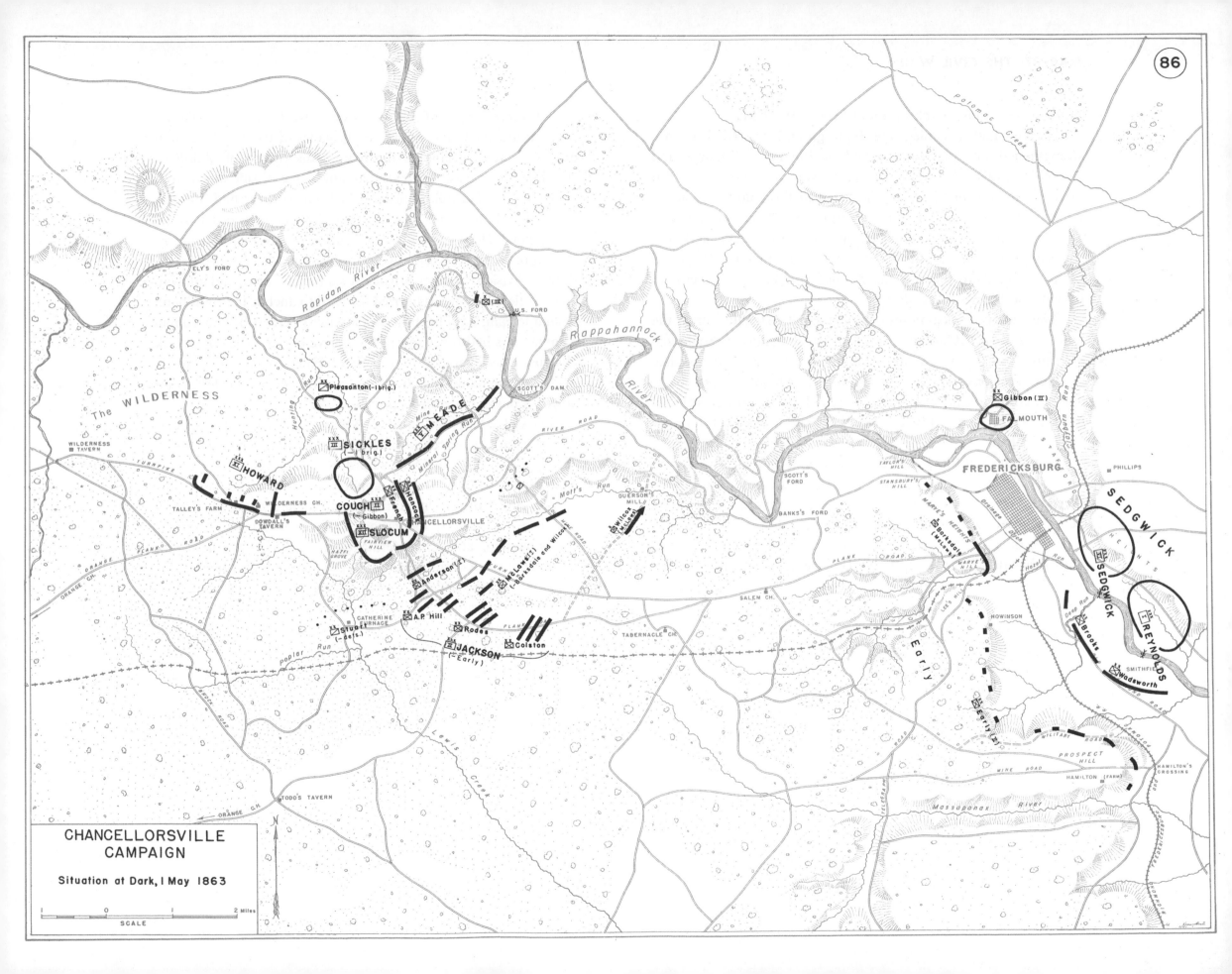

86

The WILDERNESS

WILDERNESS
TAVERN

ELY'S FORD

Rapidan River

Hunting Run

Pleasonton(-1 brig.)

SCOTT'S DAM

U.S. FORD

Rappahannock

River

SCOTT'S
FORD

MEADE

SICKLES
(-1 brig.)

Mine Spring Run

RIVER ROAD

Gibbon (II)

FALMOUTH

HOWARD

TALLEY'S FARM

WILDERNESS CH.

COUCH
(-Gibbon)

Hancock

Mott's Run

DUERSON'S
MILL

BANKS'S FORD

TAYLOR'S
HILL

STANSBURY'S
HILL

FREDERICKSBURG

PHILLIPS

TURNPIKE

DOWDALL'S
TAVERN

CHANCELLORSVILLE

SLOCUM

FAIRVIEW
HILL

Wilcox (McLaws)

SCOTT'S
HILL

MARYE'S HEIGHTS

Barksdale
(McLaws)

MARYE
HILL

SEDGWICK

ORANGE

PLANK

ROAD

HAZEL
GROVE

Anderson (-)

McLaws(-)
(-Barksdale and Wilcox)

SALEM CH.

PLANK ROAD

LEE'S HILL

SEDGWICK

ORANGE CH.

Poplar Run

CATHERINE
FURNACE

Stuart
(-dets.)

A.P. Hill

Rodes

PLANK ROAD

TABERNACLE CH.

HOWISON

Brooks

REYNOLDS

Colston

JACKSON
(-Early)

Lewis Creek

Early

SMITHFIELD

Wadsworth

ORANGE GH.

TODD'S TAVERN

Early (-)

Poplar Run

MILITARY

PROSPECT
HILL

HAMILTON'S
CROSSING

HAMILTON [FARM]

MINE ROAD

Massaponax River

CHANCELLORSVILLE
CAMPAIGN

Situation at Dark, 1 May 1863

1   0   1   2 Miles

SCALE

N

Jackson began his march at about 6:00 A.M., 2 May.

Hooker had occupied the high ground at Hazel Grove, strengthened his lines, and called in Reynolds' I Corps and Averell's cavalry division. His troops were in good spirits, but his behavior the previous day had shaken the confidence of his corps commanders. Advised about 9:00 A.M. of Jackson's march, he immediately suspected an attempt to turn his right flank and warned Maj. Gen. Oliver O. Howard, who commanded the XI Corps there. Unfortunately, he did not visit Howard's sector to inspect the latter's dispositions.

The sight of Jackson's long parade passing steadily across the Union front caused Sickles to urge an attack against it. Sometime after noon, Sickles finally got permission to make a reconnaissance in force. He converted this into an attack, which did some damage but could not halt Jackson's march. This action pulled Howard's reserve brigade (Brig. Gen. Francis C. Barlow) forward to cover Sickles' flank.

For some unfathomable reason, Sickles' slight success convinced Hooker that Jackson was actually retreating toward Gordonsville. He gave orders to prepare for a pursuit and ordered Sedgwick and Gibbon to attack on their fronts.

Jackson had completed his movement and had begun forming for his attack about 2:30 P.M. But the heavy brush made this slow work, and it was some three hours later before he was satisfied with his deployment. His activities had been no secret to a large number of XI Corps officers. One patrol after another reported the impending attack. But Howard was not troubled. A brave and devoted soldier, he was also an opinionated individual and so ignored repeated warnings. Nor was Hooker's headquarters any more receptive to such reports.

At approximately 6:00 P.M.—only two hours before dark—Jackson attacked. The right-flank brigades of the XI Corps were quickly routed, fleeing to the rear in disorder. Col. Adolphus Buschbeck's brigade, however, holding a line of rifle pits at right angles to the Turnpike, checked Jackson for over half an hour. Then, with both flanks turned, it withdrew in good order. In the time gained, Howard and Hooker built a new line comprising the hard core of the XI Corps, two brigades from Maj. Gen. Hiram G. Berry's division, another brigade from the II Corps, and all available artillery. Reynolds hurried forward to anchor the right flank. Rough terrain, hard fighting, and a series of errors by subordinate commanders had taken most of the drive out of Jackson's attack. His rush was finally stopped west of Fairview Hill. Lee, meanwhile, was making limited attacks against the Union left to pin down as many Federals as possible.

Darkness fell, but Jackson, seeking to exploit his success, went forward in search of a route that would enable him to cut Hooker off from United States Ford. Returning, he was shot down by his own men, who were apparently jumpy from an earlier chance clash with a Union cavalry regiment moving north from Hazel Grove. Shortly thereafter, A. P. Hill, next in command, was wounded, and Confederate operations against the Union right came to a confused halt. (Jackson died on 10 May.)

Hooker later ordered Sickles to make a night attack from Hazel Grove against the right flank of Jackson's command. This attack lost its way, got involved in a fire fight with other Union troops around Fairview, and fell back to Hazel Grove. Thus, Hooker's one aggressive move during the battle came to nought.

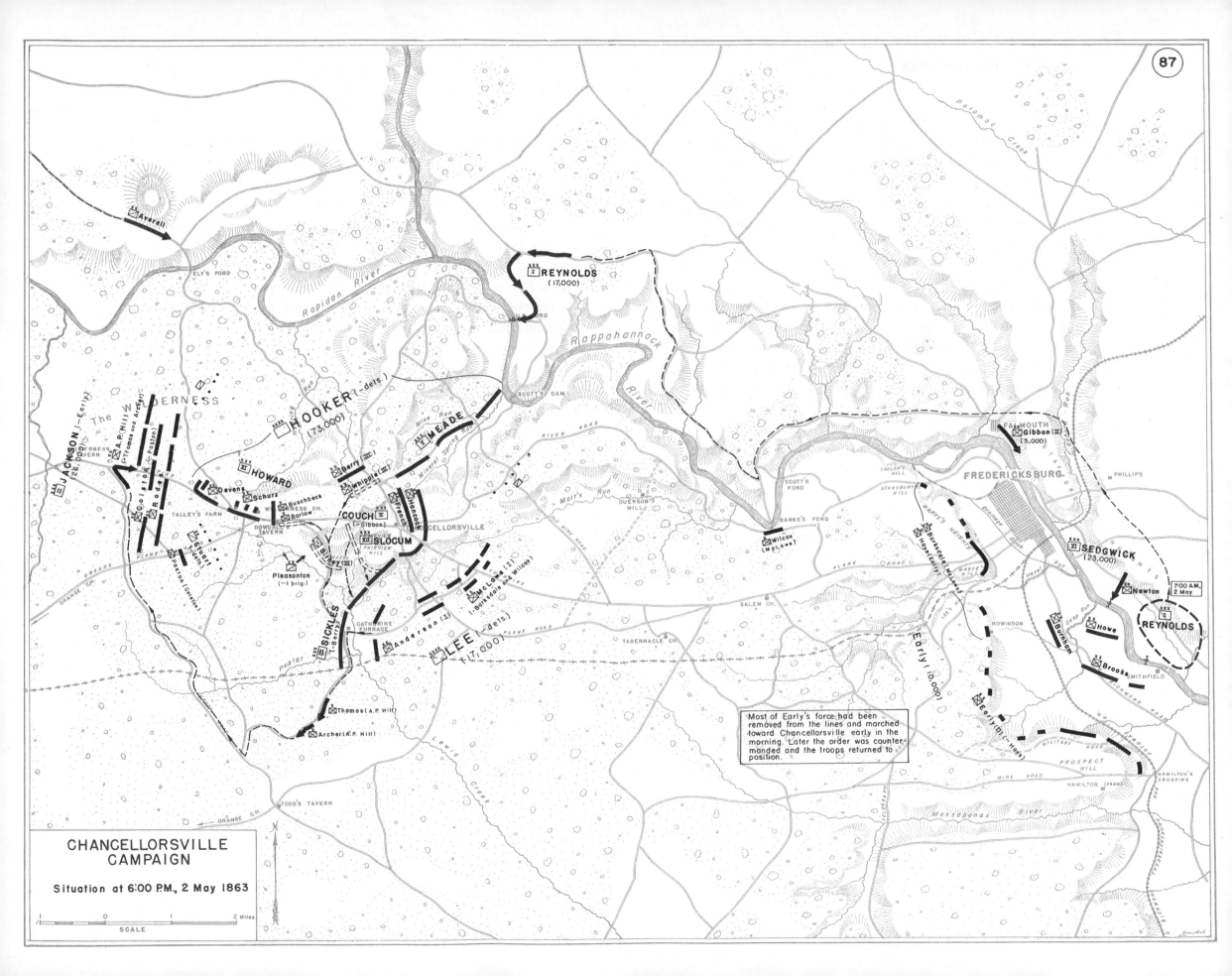

87

CHANCELLORSVILLE
CAMPAIGN

Situation at 6:00 P.M., 2 May 1863

SCALE

Most of Early's force had been
removed from the lines and marched
toward Chancellorsville early in the
morning. Later the order was countermanded and the troops returned to
position.

On the morning of 3 May, Hooker again had a splendid opportunity to defeat Lee. The Confederate army around Chancellorsville was completely split, with its two halves almost a day's march apart. Furthermore, the arrival of Reynolds' I Corps and the relatively prompt rally of most of Howard's XI Corps gave Hooker an approximately two-to-one numerical superiority in the area. Nevertheless, he made no effort to regain the initiative. Instead, he ordered a secondary line of defense prepared north of Chancellorsville.

The night before, after Jackson's attack had been stopped just west of Fairview Hill, Sickles had returned from Catherine Furnace and had taken up a position which included the high ground at Hazel Grove (about the same as that now occupied by the right half of Heth's division on the map). This high ground dominated that at Fairview Hill and the surrounding area. Hooker visited Hazel Grove early on the 3d, and should have perceived that a Federal attack from Hazel Grove could strike the flank of either half of Lee's army. Nevertheless, he ordered the Hazel Grove position abandoned, and Sickles fell back to Fairview, taking up the position shown.

This withdrawal was probably the greatest of Hooker's blunders. It left the Confederates free to use the Dowdall's Tavern–Catherine Furnace road, thus reuniting their separated army. It also gave up the dominating terrain in the area. Stuart (who had taken over Jackson's command) advanced at daybreak on the 3d, rapidly got thirty-one guns—later increased to fifty—on the abandoned hilltop, and opened a destructive enfilade fire against the lines of both Sickles and Slocum. At the same time, the Confederates attacked both sides of the Union perimeter, especially from the west, where Stuart sent in charge after charge against the Federal earthworks. After several hours of furious fighting, Federal ammunition began to run short, and the Confederate attacks slowly gained ground.

Hooker had been little more than a passive spectator. Now, at the height of the Confederate assault, he was leaning against one of the front-porch pillars of the Chancellor house. As if in ironic justice, a Confederate shell fired from the battery at Hazel Grove struck the pillar and knocked him unconscious. When revived, he was in great pain and partially paralyzed. Couch, a stark fighter, was next in command; the I and V Corps were fresh and ready to attack; the XI Corps was only lightly engaged. Lee's forces, on the other hand, were almost completely committed and had taken heavy losses. But Hooker did not relinquish the command, and the Union medical director, Surgeon Jonathan Letterman, would not take the responsibility of ruling him too disabled to exercise it. At about 9:30 A.M., Hooker ordered Couch to pull the army back to the prepared line north of Chancellorsville. Lee, on his part, pushed his tired troops forward in an attempt to complete his success.

To the east, Sedgwick had received Hooker's order to attack about midnight of 2-3 May. Pushing back some light Confederate outposts, he occupied Fredericksburg by 5:00 A.M. Another ponton bridge was thrown into position to enable Gibbon to join him there. At daybreak, the Federals attacked the thinly held Confederate position (which had been strongly fortified since Burnside's attack) behind the town. The first three Union assaults were repulsed. Then Wilcox arrived from Banks's Ford to strengthen the left of the Confederate defenses. He had moved to the sound of the cannon on his own initiative, upon noticing that the Union troops opposite Banks's Ford were decreasing in numbers and that those who remained were wearing their full equipment, as if in readiness to move off. But in spite of Wilcox's arrival, Sedgwick's fourth effort—a combined penetration and envelopment—carried Marye's Heights and overran part of the Confederate artillery there.

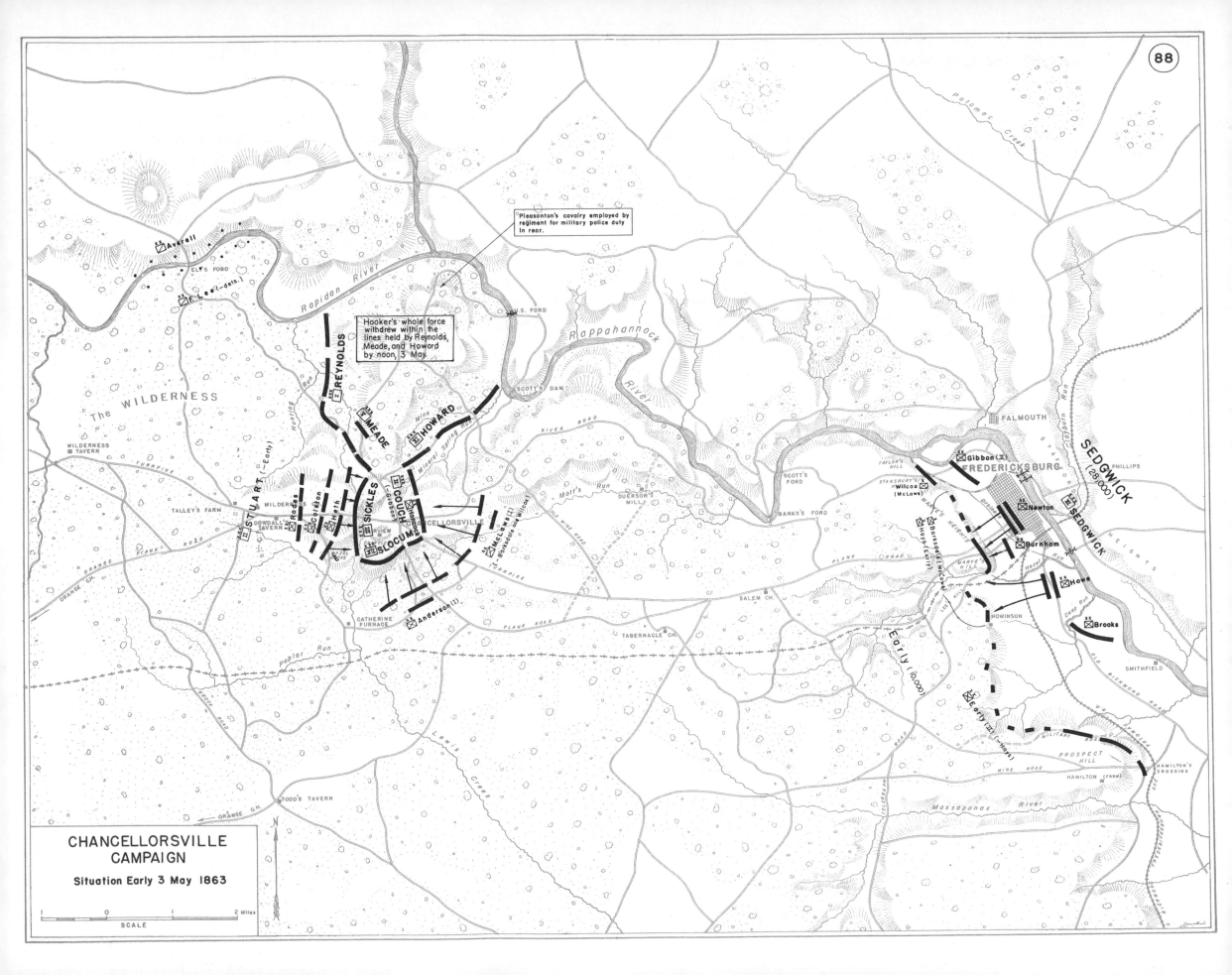

88

Pleasonton's cavalry employed by regiment for military police duty in rear.

Hooker's whole force withdrew within the lines held by Reynolds, Meade, and Howard by noon, 3 May.

Averell

EL'S FORD

F. Lee (-dets.)

Rapidan River

Rappahannock

U.S. FORD

SCOTT'S DAM

The WILDERNESS

RIVER ROAD

SCOTT'S FORD

FALMOUTH

REYNOLDS

MEADE

HOWARD

Mineral Spring Run

Mott's Run

Hunting Run

DUERSON'S MILL

BANKS'S FORD

TAYLOR'S HILL

Gibbon (II)

FREDERICKSBURG

SEDGWICK (28,000)

WILDERNESS TAVERN

STUART (-Early)

TURNPIKE

WILDERNESS

Colston

Rodes

Gordon

Heth

SICKLES

COUCH (-Gibbon)

CHANCELLORSVILLE

McLaws (-)

-Barksdale and Wilcox

STANSBURY'S HILL

Wilcox

(McLaws)

MARYE'S HEIGHTS

Newton

SEDGWICK

TALLEY'S FARM

DOWDALL'S TAVERN

SLOCUM

Barksdale (McLaws)

Burnham

Hoye's (Early)

MARYE HILL

HOWISON

Howe

PLANK ROAD

ORANGE CH.

PLANK ROAD

McLaws (-)

Anderson (-)

SALEM CH.

TABERNACLE CH.

LEE MILL

Brooks

Deep Run

SMITHFIELD

CATHERINE FURNACE

Early (10,000)

Poplar Run

Lewis Creek

Early (III -Hoye's)

MILITARY

PROSPECT HILL

HAMILTON'S CROSSING

HAMILTON (FARM)

TODD'S TAVERN

ORANGE CH.

Massaponax River

MINE ROAD

OLD RICHMOND ROAD

PHILLIPS

STAFFORD HEIGHTS

SEDGWICK

CHANCELLORSVILLE CAMPAIGN

Situation Early 3 May 1863

1   0   1   2 Miles

SCALE

Hooker's withdrawal enabled Lee to occupy the ruins of Chancellorsville and reunite his army along the line of the Turnpike. Though the new Union position was naturally strong, and was further strengthened by field fortifications, Lee moved aggressively against it—only to be stopped by a report that Sedgwick was on Marye's Heights. He immediately sent McLaws with four brigades to meet this new threat.

Under the sudden surge of Sedgwick's assault, Early retreated southward along Telegraph Road. Wilcox, however, fell back toward Chancellorsville, seeking to delay the Union advance. Sedgwick followed along Plank Road about 2:00 P.M., leaving Gibbon's division to hold Marye's Heights in his rear but requesting that an alternate line of communications be established by way of Banks's Ford, in the event that he was cut off from Fredericksburg.

McLaws reached Salem Church before 3:00 P.M. and took up position there; Wilcox joined him shortly thereafter. Approximately an hour later, Sedgwick came up and—probably concluding logically that Hooker was engaging practically all of Lee's army, so that the force in front of him could not be large—attacked immediately with his leading division, directly from his column of march. Initially successful, the attacking Union division was finally checked and thrown back by superior numbers. Sedgwick's second division, in turn, checked McLaws. As darkness approached, both forces bivouacked on the battlefield.

During the day, Hooker had ordered Averell to come forward on the Union right, but Averell soon returned, reporting the country impassable for cavalry. Hooker thereupon relieved him. Pleasonton was then given command of Averell's division, in addition to his own.

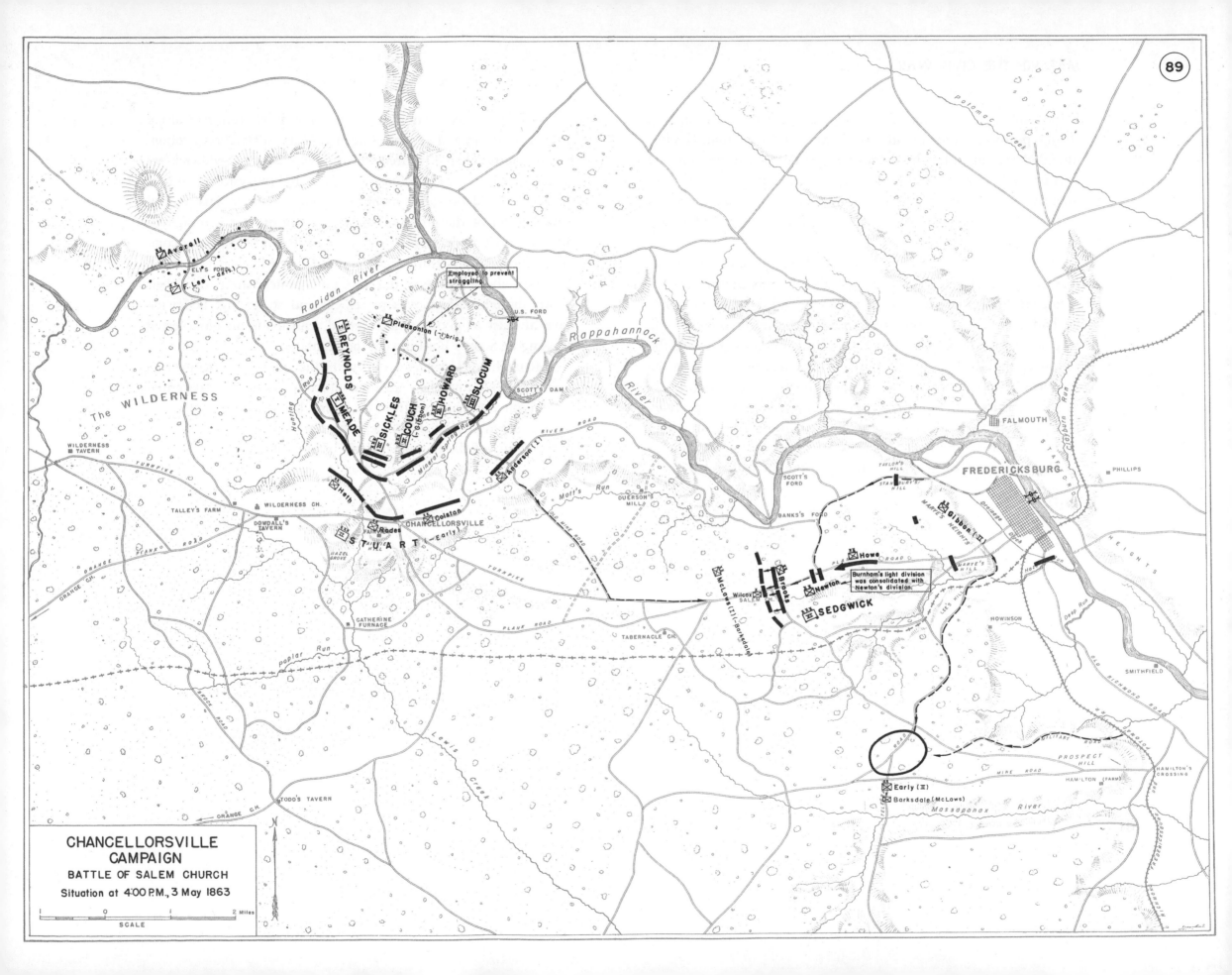

89

Averell

ELY'S FORD

F. Lee (-det.)

Rapidan River

Employed to prevent straggling.

U.S. FORD

Pleasonton (-1 brig.)

REYNOLDS

The WILDERNESS

Rappahannock River

SCOTT'S DAM

MEADE

SICKLES

COUCH
(-Gibbon)

HOWARD

SLOCUM

River

FALMOUTH

WILDERNESS TAVERN

Hunting Run

RIVER ROAD

TAYLOR'S HILL

FREDERICKSBURG

PHILLIPS

Anderson [1]

Mott's Run

SCOTT'S FORD

STANBURY'S HILL

Gibbon [1] II

Heth

Mineral Spring Run

DUERSON'S MILL

BIG MINE ROAD

BANKS'S FORD

HEIGHTS

TALLEY'S FARM

WILDERNESS CH.

TURNPIKE

Colston

Rodes

MARYE'S HEIGHTS

DOWDALL'S TAVERN

Fairview

CHANCELLORSVILLE

Howe

PLANK ROAD

MARYE'S HILL

PLANK ROAD

ORANGE

STUART (-Early)

Burnham's light division was consolidated with Newton's division.

ORANGE CH.

HAZEL GROVE

TURNPIKE

McLaws [2] -Barksdale

Brooks

Wilcox
SALEM CH.

Newton

SEDGWICK

HOWINSON

CATHERINE FURNACE

PLANK ROAD

TABERNACLE CH.

Poplar Run

SMITHFIELD

OLD RICHMOND ROAD

BROCK ROAD

Lewis Creek

Early (II)

PROSPECT HILL

TODD'S TAVERN

MINE ROAD

Barksdale (McLaws)

HAMILTON (FARM)

HAMILTON'S CROSSING

ORANGE CH.

Massaponax River

CHANCELLORSVILLE CAMPAIGN
BATTLE OF SALEM CHURCH
Situation at 4:00 P.M., 3 May 1863

SCALE

0   1   2 Miles

During the night, Hooker's troops had strengthened their already strong position. Judging this to be an indication that Hooker intended to remain on the defensive, Lee decided to concentrate against Sedgwick, in the hope of destroying his corps. Consequently, he left Stuart with 25,000 men to contain Hooker's 75,000, while he moved with 21,000 men against Sedgwick's 19,000.

Sedgwick was a slow and conscientious general; he might lack the necessary dash and imagination for his present assignment, but he would take care of his command. During the night, he had established communication with the north bank of the Rappahannock by means of a ponton bridge laid by Army of the Potomac engineers at Scott's Ford. A detached brigade from the II Corps set up a protective bridgehead on the south bank. Early in the morning of the 4th, Sedgwick received a message from Hooker stating that Hooker intended to await Lee's attack in his new position and that Sedgwick had permission to go either to Banks's Ford or Fredericksburg, if the safety of his corps required it.

As Lee's concentration got under way, Early returned along Telegraph Road and advanced against Marye's Heights. Gibbon, heavily outnumbered, retired into Fredericksburg. Sedgwick set up a horseshoe-shaped defense and prepared hasty fortifications, hoping to hold out until night and then withdraw. His skillful organization of the ground, which—among other advantages—denied the Confederates the use of Plank Road to maintain communication among their units, greatly delayed Lee's deployment. Not until about 5:30 P.M. did the Confederates attack; then their effort, though gallant, was piecemeal and straggling. Sedgwick gave at least as good as he received, and made an unmolested crossing at Scott's Ford during the night.

Meanwhile, Hooker—even with the sound of Sedgwick's cannon plainly audible—made no effort to advance. Apparently, he had not yet recovered from his injury, but—lacking any action by a competent medical officer—he remained in full command of the Army of the Potomac, if not of himself.

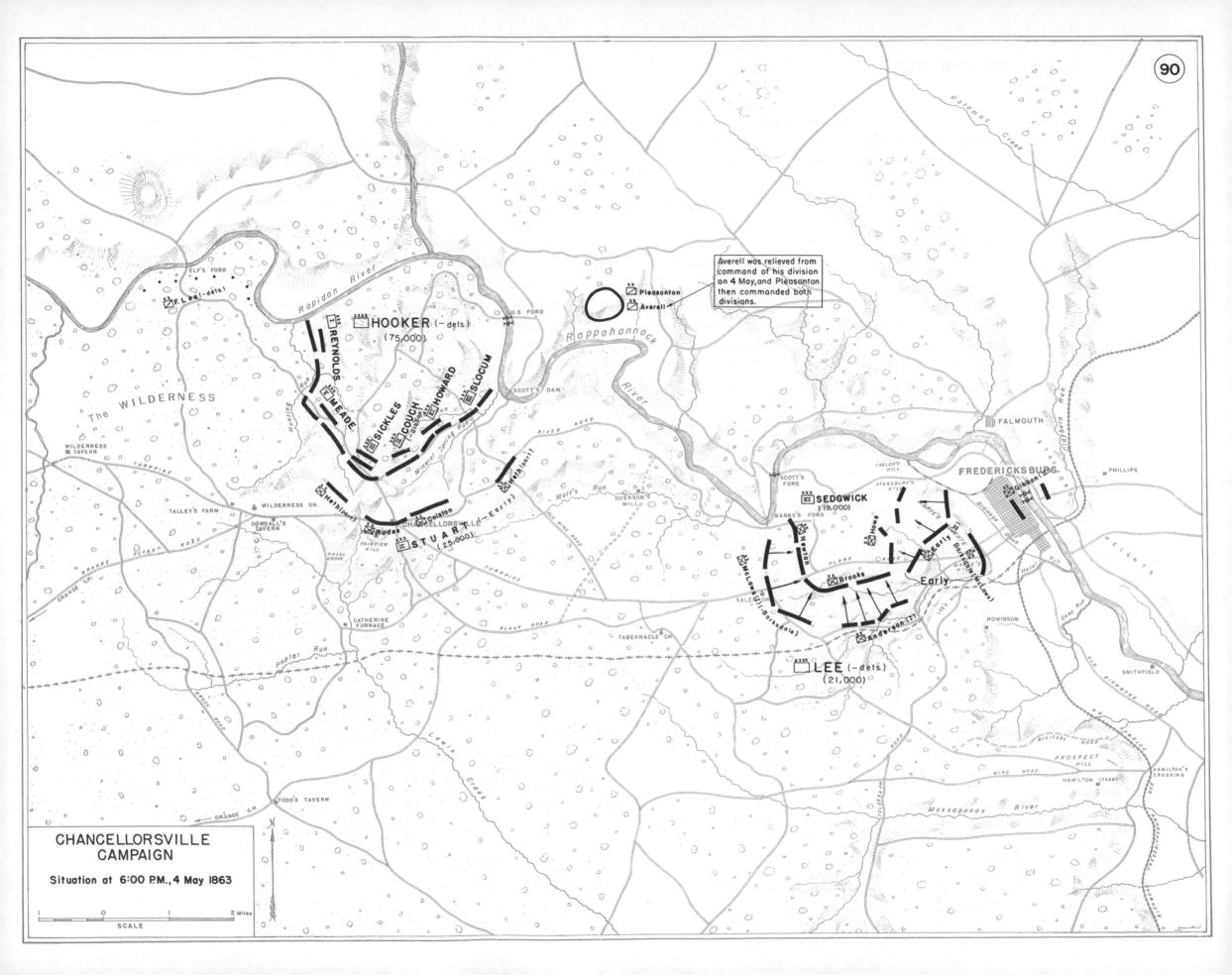

90

Averell was relieved from command of his division on 4 May, and Pleasonton then commanded both divisions.

Pleasonton

Averell

Rapidan River

ELY'S FORD

F. Lee (-dets.)

U.S. FORD

HOOKER (-dets.) (75,000)

REYNOLDS

Rappahannock River

The WILDERNESS

Hunting Run

MEADE

SICKLES

COUCH (-Gibbon)

HOWARD

SLOCUM

Mineral Spring Run

Scott's Dam

SCOTT'S FORD

River

RIVER ROAD

WILDERNESS TAVERN

WILDERNESS CH.

Heth (port.)

Heth (port.)

BANKS'S FORD

FALMOUTH

TAYLOR'S HILL

STANSBURY'S HILL

FREDERICKSBURG

PHILLIPS

Gibbon

TURNPIKE

TALLEY'S FARM

DOWDALL'S TAVERN

Rodes

CHANCELLORSVILLE (-Early)

Colston

STUART (25,000)

FAIRVIEW HILL

Mott's Run

QUERSON'S MILL

OLD MINE ROAD

SEDGWICK (19,000)

Newton

Early

Barksdale (McLaws)

HEIGHTS

MARYE'S

HOWISON

HAZEL RUN

LEE'S HILL

PLANK ROAD

CATHERINE FURNACE

TABERNACLE CH.

Poplar Run

ORANGE CH.

ORANGE PLANK ROAD

McLaws (-Barksdale)

SALEM CH.

Brooks

Howe

Early

Anderson (?)

LEE (-dets.) (21,000)

SMITHFIELD

Lewis Creek

BROCK ROAD

ORANGE CH.

TODD'S TAVERN

MINE ROAD

PROSPECT HILL

HAMILTON (FARM)

HAMILTON'S CROSSING

Massaponax River

MILITARY ROAD

OLD RICHMOND ROAD

N

CHANCELLORSVILLE CAMPAIGN

Situation at 6:00 P.M., 4 May 1863

0   1   2 Miles

SCALE

During the early morning of 5 May, Gibbon skillfully recrossed to the north bank of the Rappahannock, and all ponton bridges downstream from United States Ford were taken up.

Lee determined to crush Hooker. The latter's position was by now a formidable mass of field fortifications, yet Lee—with that same stubborn aggressiveness that had cost him dearly at Malvern Hill, and would cost him even more at Gettysburg—concentrated every available man for an assault at sunrise on the 6th.

Hooker, however, had lost all his former combativeness. About midnight of 5-6 May, he called his corps commanders to a council of war to determine whether to advance or withdraw. Meade, Reynolds, and Howard voted to advance; Sickles, stating that he was an amateur soldier and could not speak with authority, voted for a retreat; Couch bitterly chose to retreat because Hooker intended to continue in command; Slocum was absent. Hooker then took upon himself the responsibility of ordering the withdrawal.

Meade's V Corps received the mission of serving as a rear guard to cover the withdrawal. The rest of the army was massed near the river, and the difficult operation began. Hooker crossed with the artillery during the night. His infantry began to cross at 5:00 A.M., 6 May. Then the river rose as a result of continual rains and threatened to break the ponton bridges, which rapidly became too short as the river widened. Couch had been left in command on the south bank. He proposed that there might still be a chance to fight a real battle. However, Hooker, possibly guessing his second in command's intent, sent an emphatic order to withdraw. The two bridges were made into one, and the crossing continued during the morning.

This movement took Lee completely by surprise. Only a few of his advance scouts even made contact with the withdrawing Federals.

Stoneman's raiding parties gradually returned to the army, some by way of the Federal posts along the western shore of Chesapeake Bay, after riding close to Richmond and creating a scare in the Confederate capital. They did some damage to railroads and supply depots but had no effect on the outcome of the campaign.

Confederate losses were approximately 13,000; Federal, 17,000. Proportionately, Lee suffered by far the worse damage—even without considering the loss of the irreplaceable Jackson. Actually, his brilliant and daring maneuvers had defeated only one man—"Fighting Joe" Hooker. Few battles have ever more clearly exemplified Napoleon's maxim: "The General is the head, the whole of the army." The Army of the Potomac was much more humiliated than hurt.

Hooker's plan—except for his employment of his cavalry as a raiding force—had been excellent up to that moment when he fell back into the Wilderness and went on the defensive. Even then, with Lee forced to gamble on securing a quick victory, Hooker had every chance of repulsing Lee's attack and then crushing the Confederates with a counterattack. The first, Hooker's troops accomplished; the second, he could not nerve himself to order.

Other factors contributing to his defeat were Howard's stubborn carelessness, Hooker's own inexplicable blunder in giving up Hazel Grove, and his failure to coordinate properly the two wings of his army so that their attacks would be mutually supporting. Finally, in spite of Lincoln's injunction to "this time, put in *all* your men," Hooker allowed nearly one-third of his army to stand idle during the heaviest fighting. Consequently, Lee was able to mass superior forces against Howard and, later, Sedgwick.

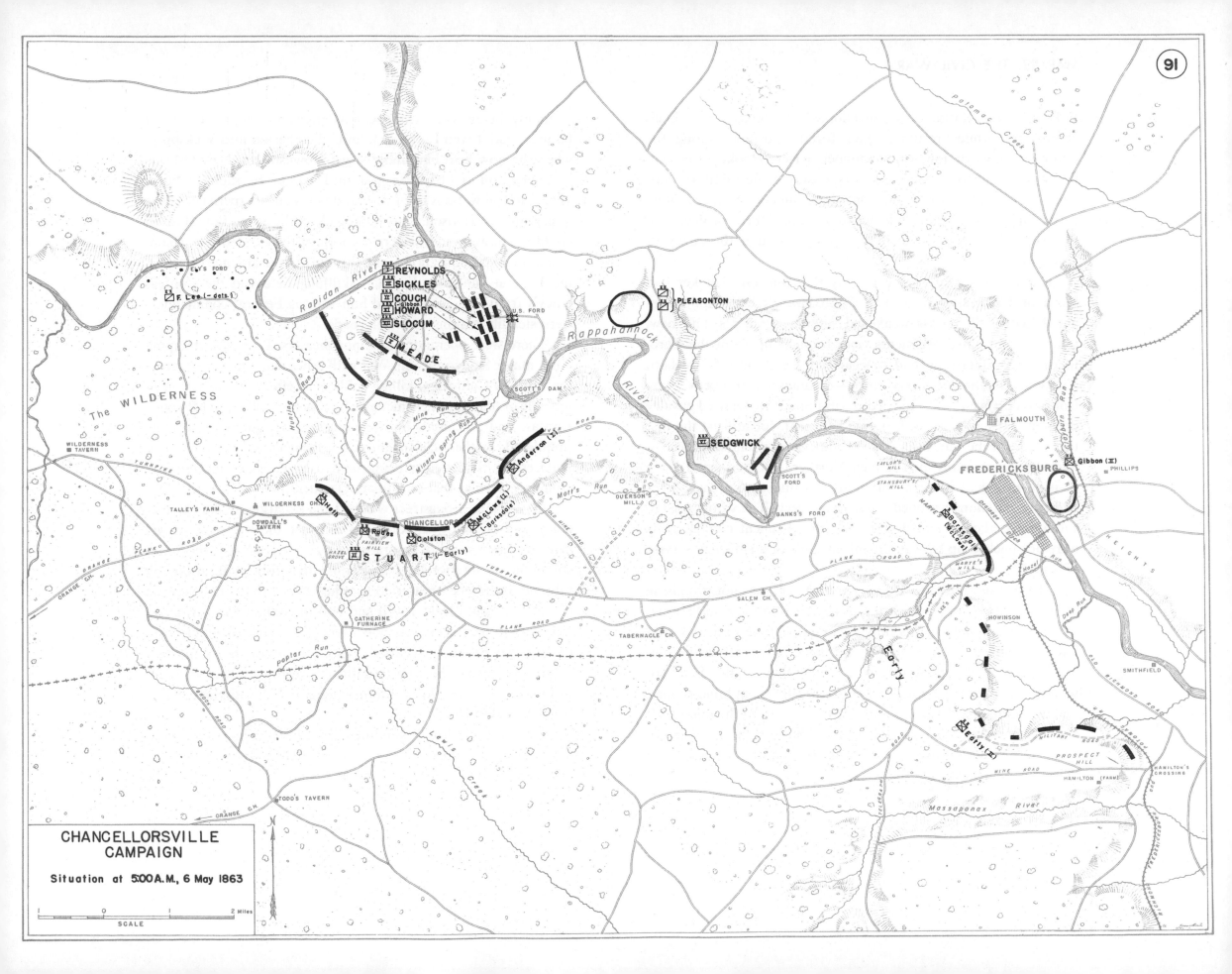

91

REYNOLDS
SICKLES
COUCH
(-Gibbon)
HOWARD
SLOCUM
MEADE

F. Lee (- dets.)

ELY'S FORD

Rapidan River

Rappahannock River

U.S. FORD

PLEASONTON

The WILDERNESS

WILDERNESS TAVERN

SCOTT'S DAM

SEDGWICK

FALMOUTH

Gibbon (II)

PHILLIPS

Anderson (5)

FREDERICKSBURG

TALLEY'S FARM

WILDERNESS CH.

Heth

DOWDALL'S TAVERN

McLaws (2)
(-Barksdale)

CHANCELLORSVILLE

Rodes

Colston

STUART (-Early)

FAIRVIEW HILL

HAZEL GROVE

CATHERINE FURNACE

SCOTT'S FORD

BANKS'S FORD

OUERSON'S MILL

Moff's Run

TAYLOR'S HILL

STANSBURY'S HILL

Barksdale
(McLaws)

MARYE'S HILL

LEE'S HILL

HOWINSON

SMITHFIELD

Early

Early (II)

PROSPECT HILL

HAMILTON (FARM)

HAMILTON'S CROSSING

TODD'S TAVERN

ORANGE CH.

Lewis Creek

Poplar Run

Massaponax River

CHANCELLORSVILLE CAMPAIGN

Situation at 5:00 A.M., 6 May 1863

SCALE

2 Miles

Following the Battle of Chancellorsville, Hooker's and Lee's contending armies resumed their former positions along the opposite banks of the Rappahannock River. Hooker was temporarily restricted to the mission of ensuring the safety of Harper's Ferry and Washington. On the Confederate side, morale was at its highest pitch. Chancellorsville had been a deceptive victory; a feeling of invincibility spread through the Army of Northern Virginia.

It was now a far stronger army than the one Hooker had faced at Chancellorsville. The Confederacy's conscription enabled Lee to fill up his weakened veteran regiments, and new, relatively untrained regiments were brought up from the Carolinas. Accordingly, he had reorganized the Army of Northern Virginia into three infantry corps—commanded respectively by Longstreet, Ewell, and A. P. Hill—and Stuart's oversized cavalry division. (It might be well to note here that, for at least the first three years of the war, the average Southern corps and division had almost twice as many men as their Northern counterparts.) Each division now had its own battalion of artillery, and each corps had two battalions assigned as corps artillery. The whole organization was efficient and flexible, but the excellent combat units were not backed up by well-organized staffs or an efficient service of supply.

The over-all military situation shown here was not promising for the Confederacy. The Army of the Potomac was still strong, and Lee knew that it was only a matter of time until it would launch a new offensive. The Federal naval blockade was becoming increasingly tight, and one after another of the Southern seaports was being occupied in a series of minor amphibious operations. Though such expeditions drew troops from the main Federal armies, they also pinned down almost equal numbers of Confederates and provided beachheads from which attacks inland might be launched.

In the center, Rosecrans and Bragg neutralized one another for the time being, but the war along the Mississippi River was definitely being lost by the Confederacy. Grant, after several failures, had driven Lt. Gen. John C. Pemberton into Vicksburg, where he now held him under siege. Downstream, New Orleans had been captured by Rear Admiral David G. Farragut in April, 1862, and now Banks (of Shenandoah Valley experience) was besieging Port Hudson. Only between Vicksburg and Port Hudson could the eastern and western sections of the Confederacy maintain a tenuous connection—and this only in the absence of prowling Federal gunboats. Lee had skillfully defended the Confederacy's front door, but behind him various Federal commanders were steadily making serious inroads.

There were operations in minor theaters. Pope was stamping out a major Sioux uprising. War with other tribes flickered across the trails to California, killing soldiers as effectively as Chancellorsville or Shiloh (and sometimes far more brutally). In Missouri, Kansas, and Arkansas, an even more savage guerrilla struggle smoldered; neither side fought a "gentlemen's war," the Confederate effort in particular being tainted by gangs of professional criminals, such as that of William Quantrill.

In Virginia, Longstreet weighed the situation of the Confederacy and offered a solution—to consider the war as a whole, instead of as a series of separate theaters. He reasoned: the South still retained interior lines and could therefore shift troops by railroad from one theater to another faster than the Federals could; Lee could leave Ewell and Hill to contain Hooker, move west with Longstreet's corps and all other available eastern troops, incorporate Bragg's, Buckner's, and Johnston's forces into his army, and throw the whole against Rosecrans; a victory there would paralyze the North; Grant undoubtedly would be recalled from Vicksburg.

This proposal had possibilities, though it overrated the capabilities of the Confederate railroads. But Lee had gone to war primarily to defend Virginia, and he hesitated to concern himself with matters outside the area of his command.

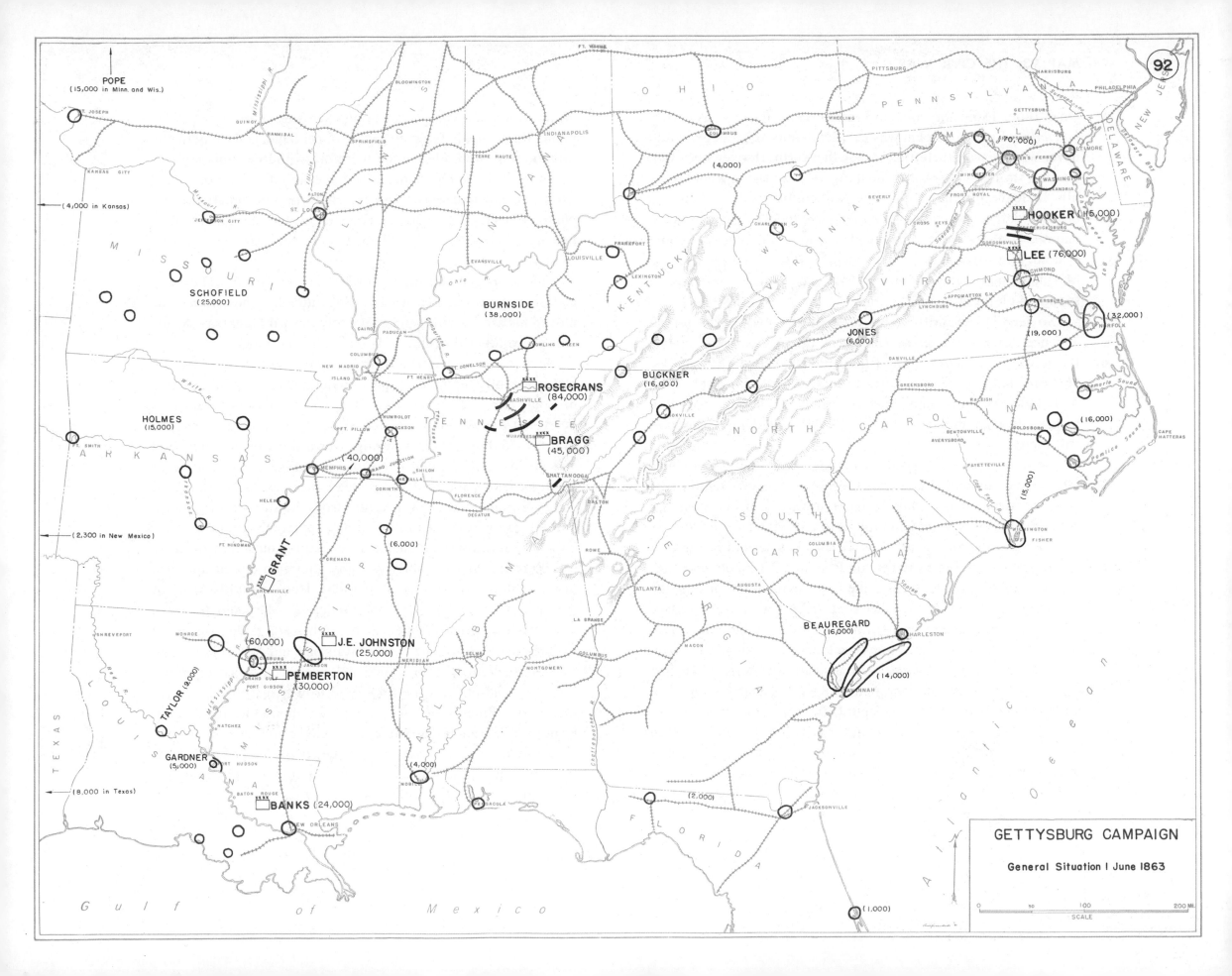

92

POPE
(15,000 in Minn. and Wis.)

(4,000)

(4,000 in Kansas)

SCHOFIELD
(25,000)

BURNSIDE
(38,000)

HOLMES
(15,000)

(40,000)

(2,300 in New Mexico)

(6,000)

GRANT

(60,000)

J.E. JOHNSTON
(25,000)

PEMBERTON
(30,000)

TAYLOR (9,000)

GARDNER
(5,000)

(8,000 in Texas)

BANKS (24,000)

(4,000)

ROSECRANS
(84,000)

BUCKNER
(16,000)

BRAGG
(45,000)

JONES
(6,000)

HOOKER (115,000)

LEE (76,000)

(32,000)

(19,000)

(16,000)

(15,000)

BEAUREGARD
(16,000)

(14,000)

(2,000)

(1,000)

GETTYSBURG CAMPAIGN

General Situation 1 June 1863

0   50   100   200 MI.
SCALE

On 9 June, 1863, the opposing forces were disposed as shown (*sketch* a). Lee's own plan was simple: defensive strategy would never win the war; therefore, invade the North. Hooker's position was too strong to attack, but the threat of an invasion would force him to leave it. That done, Lee was confident of inflicting a decisive defeat upon him which might end the war. Also, between natural shortages and chronic ineptness of the Confederate supply system, Lee's troops were in constant want. Across the river, in Maryland and Pennsylvania, there were ample resources of food and clothing.

So Lee began shifting his army quietly westward for an advance down the Shenandoah and up the Cumberland Valleys. By holding the passes in the Blue Ridge and South Mountains, he could both screen his advance and protect his supply line. A. P. Hill's corps remained around Fredericksburg, spread thin to keep Hooker thinking that the whole Confederate army was still there.

Hooker's nerve might fail in a crisis, but he had the instincts of a good commander, and his staff included an efficient intelligence section. By late May, he had indications of Lee's general plan. His first reaction (5 June) was to cross the river as soon as Lee moved west and to attack A. P. Hill. His second inspiration (10 June) was to move directly on Richmond. Lincoln and Halleck vetoed both plans, stating that Lee's main army must be the objective. On 5-6 June, Hooker sent Sedgwick across the river to test the Confederate strength in the Fredericksburg area. Hill reacted aggressively and convinced Sedgwick that the main Confederate army was still there. Dissatisfied with this report, Hooker ordered Pleasonton (now commanding the Cavalry Corps) on a reconnaissance toward Culpeper (*inset, bottom left*).

Stuart's cavalry division lay at Brandy Station with orders to march west on 10 June. Early on 9 June, Pleasonton suddenly arrived, taking Stuart completely by surprise. This started the biggest cavalry fight in American history—a highly confused affair with some 10,000 sabers on each side. Late in the afternoon, Stuart slowly began to get the upper hand, and Confederate infantry appeared. Pleasonton therefore withdrew—his mission accomplished—to report that large forces of infantry were around Culpeper and that Stuart had marching orders. Stuart did not pursue. This fight encouraged Federal cavalrymen. Though they had frequently done as well, or better, this was their biggest fight yet.

Hooker began shifting his forces farther west. On the 13th, at last certain that Lee was moving into the Shenandoah, he moved his army swiftly and efficiently toward Manassas. As his rear guard left Falmouth, A. P. Hill followed Lee.

Maj. Gen. Robert H. Milroy, at Winchester (*left center*), had innocently reported a big Confederate "raid" building up to his south. On 10 June, he received orders to withdraw to Harper's Ferry, but was slow to obey. Consequently, Ewell almost bagged him (12-15 June), Milroy losing over a third of his command and all his guns (*action not shown*). The survivors and other small Federal garrisons in the area concentrated on Maryland Heights. Stanton called for militia from the surrounding states, but only New York could furnish any appreciable number.

By 17 June, the Confederates were strung out over a distance of 100 miles, as shown. By 24 June, they had closed up north of the Potomac (*sketch* b); on that day, Hooker set his Army of the Potomac in motion toward Frederick, Maryland (*center*). Brig. Gen. John D. Imboden's cavalry brigade raided westward to damage the Baltimore & Ohio Railroad and collect livestock. Stuart screened the right flank of Lee's advance as far as the Potomac, and at the same time tried to watch Hooker's movements. But Pleasonton, in a series of fights along the eastern slopes of the Blue Ridge Mountains, prevented him from obtaining information. Lee, therefore, remained in ignorance of Hooker's whereabouts, while Hooker's scouts north of the Potomac had little trouble determining Lee's numbers and line of march.

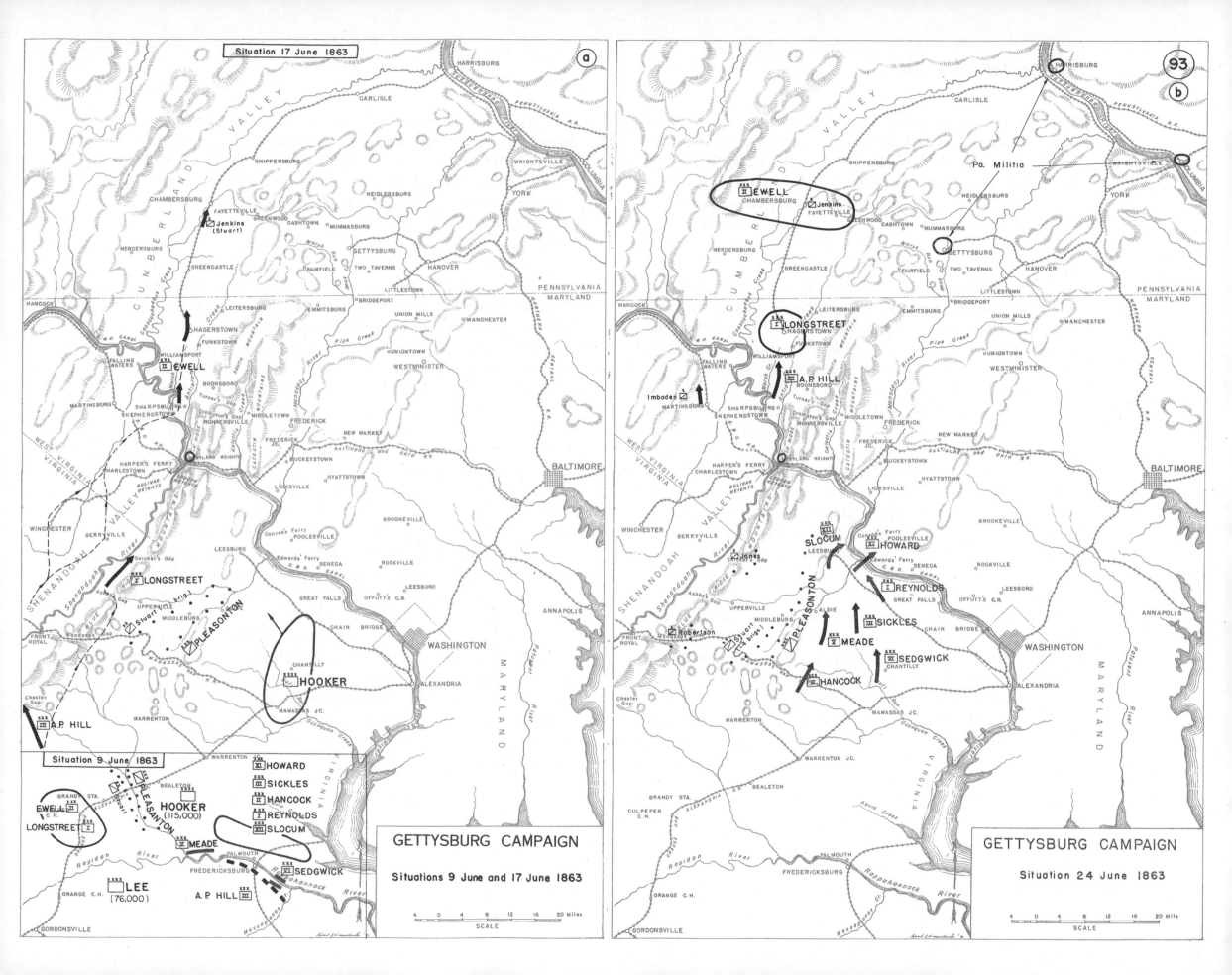

Situation 17 June 1863

(a)

93

(b)

Pa. Militia

GETTYSBURG CAMPAIGN

Situation 24 June 1863

XXX Ⅱ EWELL
Jenkins

XXX Ⅰ LONGSTREET

XXX Ⅲ A.P. HILL

Imboden

Jones

SLOCUM XXX Ⅻ

HOWARD XXX Ⅺ

Robertson

Stuart (3 brig.)

P. PLEASONTON

REYNOLDS XXX Ⅰ

SICKLES XXX Ⅲ

MEADE XXX Ⅴ

SEDGWICK XXX Ⅵ

HANCOCK XXX Ⅱ

BALTIMORE

WASHINGTON

Situation 9 June 1863

Jenkins (Stuart)

XXX Ⅱ EWELL

XXX Ⅰ LONGSTREET

Stuart

PLEASONTON

HOOKER XXXX

XXX Ⅲ A.P. HILL

WARRENTON

HOWARD XXX Ⅺ

SICKLES XXX Ⅲ

HANCOCK XXX Ⅱ

REYNOLDS XXX Ⅰ

SLOCUM XXX Ⅻ

HOOKER (115,000)

EWELL Ⅱ

LONGSTREET Ⅰ

PLEASONTON

MEADE XXX Ⅴ

SEDGWICK XXX Ⅵ

LEE XXXX (76,000)

A.P. HILL XXX Ⅲ

GETTYSBURG CAMPAIGN

Situations 9 June and 17 June 1863

4 0 4 8 12 16 20 Miles
SCALE

On 27 June, Hooker had the Army of the Potomac concentrated between Frederick and South Mountain and had ordered cavalry sent forward toward Emmitsburg (*center, left*) and Gettysburg. He appears to have been planning an operation against Lee's line of communications but had issued no definite orders. So far, he had handled his army expertly, but his relations with Halleck—and even with Lincoln—were becoming increasingly tense. The President and his general in chief have been frequently criticized for being so nervous about the safety of Washington that they hampered Hooker; actually, their principal worry at this time must have been Hooker's psychological fitness as an army commander. The United States could not afford another Chancellorsville—especially one fought on Northern soil. They had given Hooker all available reinforcements, including a large part of the Washington garrison, yet Hooker was beginning to complain loudly that Lee's army outnumbered his own! Matters came to a climax over Hooker's desire to evacuate the garrison of Maryland Heights. Piqued at Halleck's insistence on leaving them there as a threat to Lee's communications, Hooker asked to be relieved. Lincoln hastily acquiesced. At about 3:00 A.M., 28 June, a special courier from Washington awoke Maj. Gen. George G. Meade and told him that he was the new commander of the Army of the Potomac.

Meanwhile, by 28 June, the Confederate forces had reached the scattered positions shown. Their marches had been easy and uneventful. There had been no opposition, except for a handful of Pennsylvania militia, which Early had scattered just west of Gettysburg on the 26th during his march to York. Another militia unit had withdrawn hastily across the Susquehanna at Wrightsville, burning the bridge there behind it. The town caught fire, and Brig. Gen. John B. Gordon's men helped to save it from the flames. Lee was feeding and supplying his troops off the country-side, taking what he needed by forced purchase (with Confederate money) or formal requisitions on local authorities. Early demanded $100,000 in United States currency from the town of York, but compromised for the $28,000 immediately available. Ewell, especially, was collecting food; but he was authorized to take Harrisburg, if he could. Under such favorable conditions, Confederate morale and discipline were excellent.

But, below the Potomac, "Jeb" Stuart was brewing trouble for Lee. On the 23d, when Lee's army was safely across the Potomac, Stuart had received his orders. They were so vague and allowed such latitude that he could interpret them to suit himself. Stuart still smarted under the thorough lashing he had received from the Southern press for having been taken by surprise by Pleasonton at Brandy Station, and his ego had been severely irritated. He now planned a campaign of his own to restore his reputation. Detaching the commands of Brig. Gens. Beverly H. Robertson and William E. Jones to guard the gaps of the Blue Ridge Mountains, he took his three favorite brigades and rode east. Almost immediately, Stuart found himself entangled among Union columns that had not yet crossed the Potomac, and in a countryside that was stripped bare of forage for his hard-worked horses. Not until late on the 27th could he find a ford across the Potomac. The next day, he resumed his march, heading for Hanover (*upper center*). During the day, he captured a 125-wagon Federal supply train, which he took with him.

Meanwhile, Lee had no information concerning the Army of the Potomac; he proceeded, therefore, under the very optimistic assumption that it was still sitting south of the Potomac. Now, late in the evening of the 28th, Longstreet's personal spy reached Chambersburg (*upper left*) from Washington, and made his report: the Army of the Potomac was around Frederick, and General Meade was in command.

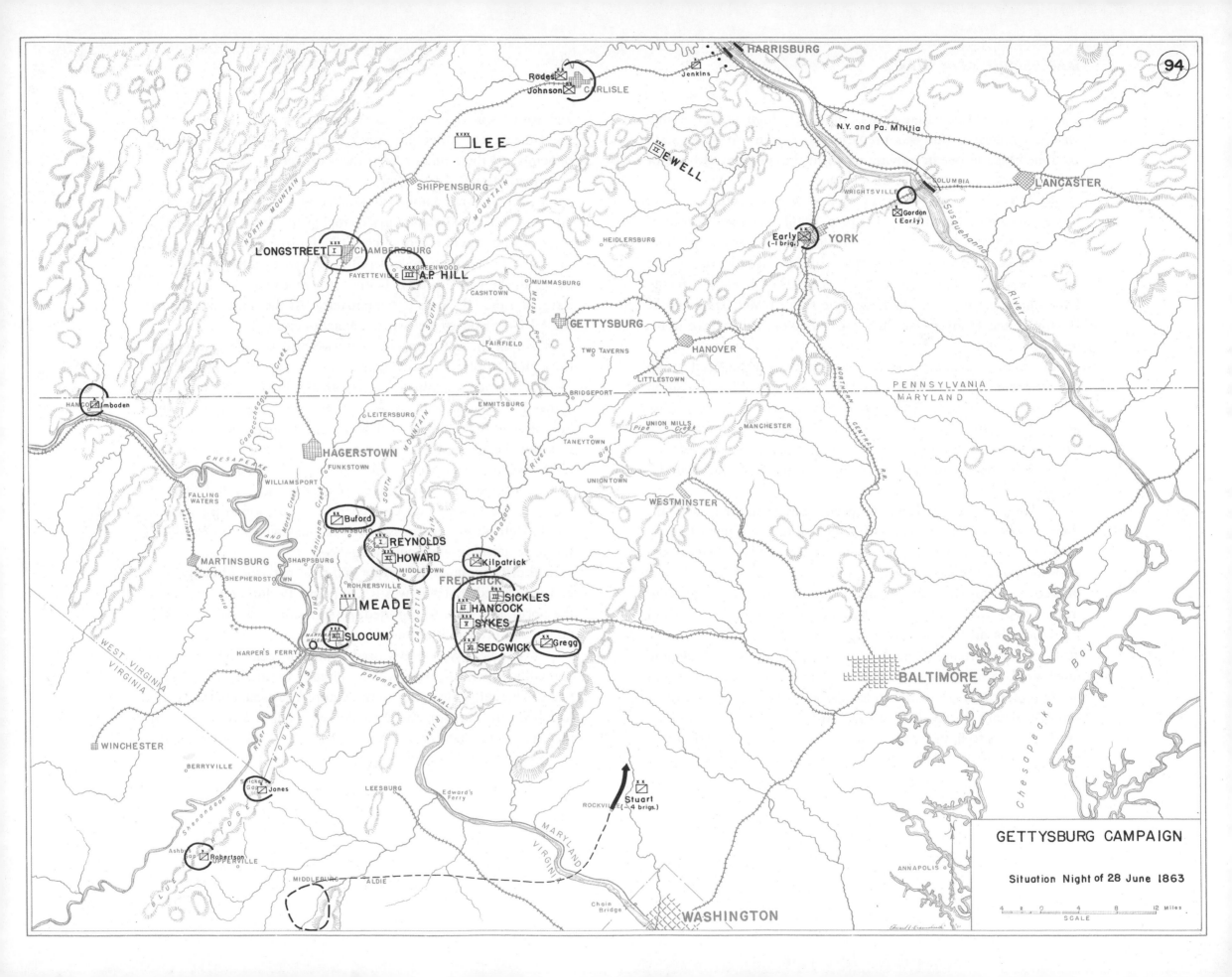

94

HARRISBURG

Rodes
Johnson CARLISLE
Jenkins

N.Y. and Pa. Militia

LEE

EWELL

SHIPPENSBURG

Columbia
LANCASTER

WRIGHTSVILLE

Gordon
(Early)

LONGSTREET
CHAMBERSBURG

FAYETTEVILLE

GREENWOOD
A.P. HILL

CASHTOWN

MUMMASBURG

HEIDLERSBURG

Early
(–1 brig.)
YORK

GETTYSBURG

FAIRFIELD

TWO TAVERNS

HANOVER

LITTLESTOWN

BRIDGEPORT

PENNSYLVANIA

MARYLAND

HANCOCK Imboden

LEITERSBURG

EMMITSBURG

UNION MILLS

Pipe Creek

MANCHESTER

HAGERSTOWN

FUNKSTOWN

TANEYTOWN

Big

WESTMINSTER

WILLIAMSPORT

FALLING
WATERS

UNION TOWN

Buford

REYNOLDS
HOWARD

Kilpatrick

MARTINSBURG

SHARPSBURG

MIDDLETOWN

FREDERICK

SICKLES
HANCOCK
SYKES

SHEPHERDSTOWN

ROHRERSVILLE

MEADE

SLOCUM

SEDGWICK

Gregg

HARPER'S FERRY

BALTIMORE

WEST
VIRGINIA
VIRGINIA

Chesapeake Bay

WINCHESTER

BERRYVILLE

Snicker's
Gap
Jones

LEESBURG

Edward's
Ferry

Stuart
(–4 brigs.)

ROCKVILLE

Ashby's Gap Robertson
UPPERVILLE

MIDDLEBURG
ALDIE

MARYLAND
VIRGINIA

ANNAPOLIS

Chain
Bridge

WASHINGTON

GETTYSBURG CAMPAIGN

Situation Night of 28 June 1863

4 2 0   4   8   12 Miles
SCALE

The spy's news was actually out of date; the Union army not only was at Frederick, but was preparing to march. At 4:00 A.M., 29 June, Meade began moving north in the announced hope of catching Lee's army at a disadvantage.

Maj. Gen. George Gordon Meade was a cautious, canny fighter, nervous and irritable. The responsibility suddenly dropped upon him was crushing; he knew little about the over-all situation, since Hooker had been as secretive with his subordinates as the late Stonewall Jackson had been with his. Also, Meade was facing Lee—the champion who had been the ruin of McClellan, Pope, Burnside, and Hooker—while Stuart was loose somewhere in his rear.

His major advantages were the support of a seasoned group of corps commanders and an excellent knowledge of Lee's position and actual strength. Halleck gave him no instructions except that he was to "maneuver and fight in such a manner as to cover the capital, and also Baltimore, as far as circumstances will admit." All Federal troops in the area of operations were placed under his command.

The night of 28-29 June had been a busy one for Lee's staff; orders went out on the gallop for all Confederate units to concentrate at Cashtown (*upper center*). Lee's exact plan is unknown—probably he had not yet formulated one—but Cashtown offered a strong defensive position, and a Confederate concentration there would be on the flank of any Union advance from Frederick. In all this, it must be remembered that Lee was operating blindly. Stuart, "The Eyes of the Army," was struggling northward toward Hanover, fighting a few petty skirmishes and doing minor damage to the railroads he crossed. Even so, there was still plenty of cavalry with the Army of Northern Virginia, but Lee seems to have forgotten it. Jenkins' activities are obscure; Imboden was still collecting livestock; below the Potomac, Jones

and Robertson were left watching the empty landscape west of the Blue Ridge Mountains until 29 June, when Lee suddenly remembered them and ordered them forward.

Meade's earlier determination to find and fight Lee was weakening. He suffered under his new responsibility—losing sleep, missing meals, and frequently changing his mind. On the 30th, while his engineers reconnoitered a defensive position along Big Pipe Creek (*center*), he ordered Reynolds to advance the next day with the I, XI, and III Corps—the first two corps to Gettysburg, and the III Corps to Emmitsburg. At the same time, he left the VI Corps far to the rear at Manchester.

Also on the 30th, Buford, with two brigades of cavalry, rode through Gettysburg toward the Cashtown gap. West of the town, his leading riders clashed briefly with the brigade of Brig. Gen. James J. Pettigrew, which was en route from Cashtown to Gettysburg in search of a supply of shoes reported there. Lacking cavalry to scout the Union force confronting him, Pettigrew fell back to Cashtown and reported its presence to his division commander, Maj. Gen. Henry Heth, and his corps commander, A. P. Hill. Both men were certain that all the Federal infantry was still far to the south; Heth secured permission to take his division to Gettysburg the next morning and "get those shoes."

Buford examined the terrain and road net around Gettysburg and concluded that this was a key point. Pushing out patrols to the north and west, he reported the situation to Meade and Reynolds, and prepared to hold the town.

This same day, Stuart's tired command came into Hanover and collided with Kilpatrick in a mutually unsatisfactory engagement. Thereafter, learning from captured newspapers that Early had been in York on the 28th, Stuart made a strenuous night march toward that town, his men sleeping in their saddles. But he took those 125 wagons.

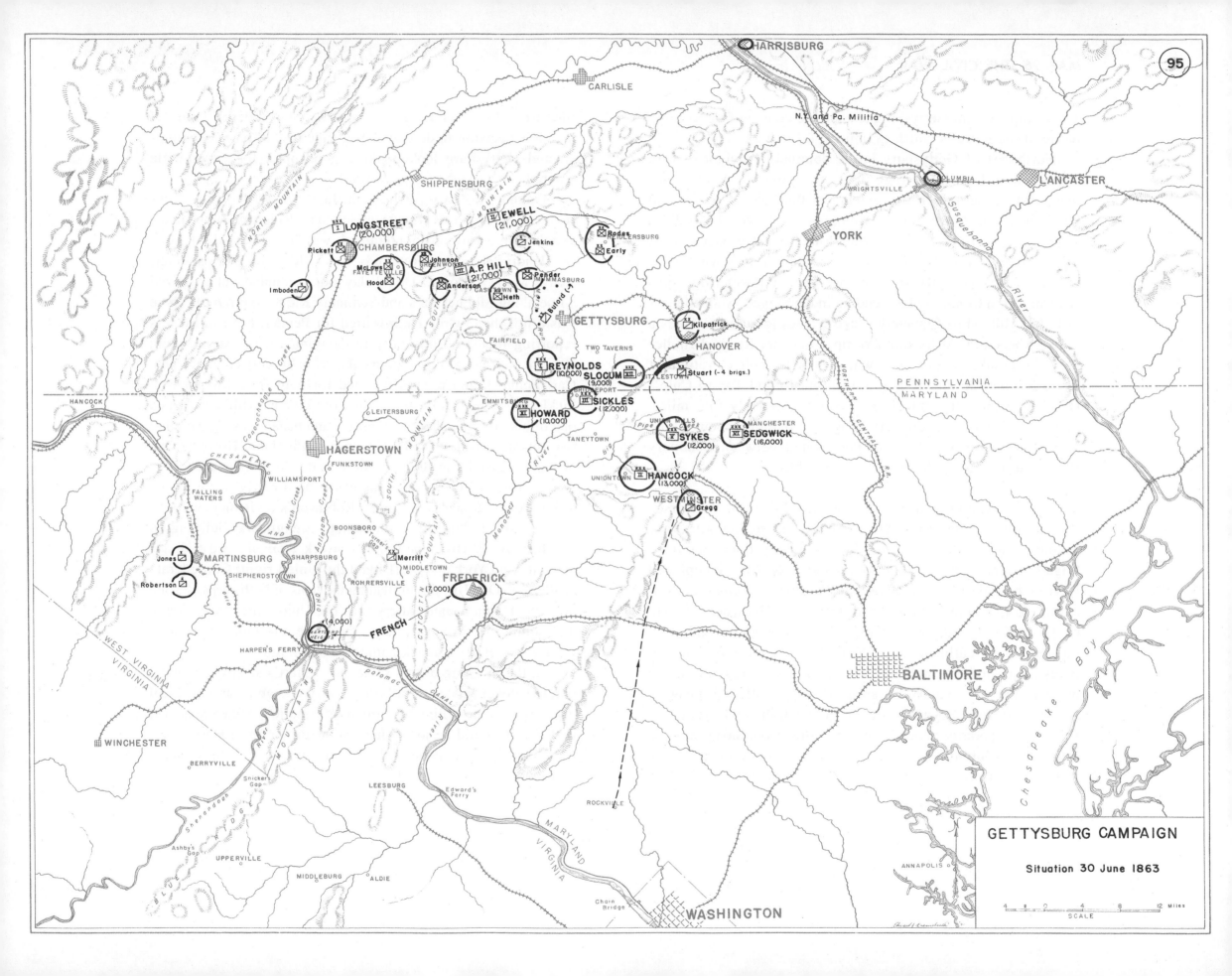

95

HARRISBURG

CARLISLE

SHIPPENSBURG

N.Y. and Pa. Militia

COLUMBIA

WRIGHTSVILLE

LANCASTER

YORK

LONGSTREET
(20,000)

EWELL
(21,000)

Rodes

Pickett CHAMBERSBURG

Jenkins

Early

McLaws FAYETTEVILLE

Johnson GREENWOOD

A.P. HILL
(21,000)

Imboden

Hood

Anderson

Pender

Heth

Buford (-)

GETTYSBURG

Kilpatrick

FAIRFIELD

TWO TAVERNS

HANOVER

REYNOLDS
(10,000)

SLOCUM
(9,000)

Stuart (- 4 brigs.)

PENNSYLVANIA
MARYLAND

HANCOCK

EMMITSBURG

SICKLES
(12,000)

LEITERSBURG

HOWARD
(10,000)

TANEYTOWN

SYKES
(12,000)

MANCHESTER

SEDGWICK
(16,000)

HAGERSTOWN

FUNKSTOWN

WILLIAMSPORT

FALLING
WATERS

CHESAPEAKE AND OHIO CANAL

UNIONTOWN

HANCOCK
(13,000)

WESTMINSTER

Gregg

BOONSBORO

Turner's Gap

Merritt

Jones

MARTINSBURG

SHARPSBURG

MIDDLETOWN

FREDERICK
(7,000)

SHEPHERDSTOWN

Robertson

ROHRERSVILLE

(4,000)

MARYLAND
HEIGHTS

FRENCH

HARPER'S FERRY

WEST VIRGINIA
VIRGINIA

WINCHESTER

BERRYVILLE

LEESBURG

EDWARD'S
FERRY

ROCKVILLE

BALTIMORE

Chesapeake Bay

Snicker's
Gap

UPPERVILLE

MIDDLEBURG

ALDIE

MARYLAND
VIRGINIA

Chain
Bridge

ANNAPOLIS

WASHINGTON

GETTYSBURG CAMPAIGN

Situation 30 June 1863

4 2 0 4 8 12 Miles
SCALE

The terrain around Gettysburg shaped the course of the coming battle; it therefore is worth examining (*sketch* a).

Northwest of Gettysburg is the dominating height of Oak Hill. From Oak Hill, two high ridges run generally south: Seminary Ridge, the longer one, extends to the Peach Orchard and along the Emmitsburg Road beyond; just to the west is McPherson's Ridge (*not labeled*), wider but lower. North of Gettysburg, the ground is relatively open and level; south of the town, Cemetery Hill rises abruptly some eighty feet. A lower ridge runs eastward from Cemetery Hill, ending in the rugged, wooded mass of Culp's Hill, while Cemetery Ridge extends for approximately a mile to the south. At its southern tip, Cemetery Ridge dwindles into a low, timbered area, after which come the bold elevations of Little Round Top and Round Top. From Round Top to Culp's Hill, along this "fish hook" line, is approximately four miles. Seminary Ridge and Cemetery Ridge run parallel, about a mile apart, across open fields, but the ground between Seminary Ridge and the Round Tops is rough and broken.

Heth's division, followed by that of Maj. Gen. W. Dorsey Pender, left Cashtown at 5:00 A.M., 1 July; about 8:00 A.M., they encountered Buford's outposts. Buford deployed a dismounted brigade under Gamble along McPherson's Ridge; he deployed Devin's brigade across the Carlisle Road (*top center*), considerably north of Gettysburg, awaiting Ewell. His troopers were badly outnumbered, but their position was good, and their breechloading carbines gave them the firepower of several times their number of infantry. For almost two hours, this single brigade and one battery of artillery stopped Heth's advance. About 9:30 A.M., Reynolds was on the field, the divisions of his I Corps (temporarily under Doubleday) strung out along the road behind him. Buford's line had been pushed back to Seminary Ridge, and his brigade on the Carlisle Road was reporting pressure from Ewell at Heidlersburg. Reynolds did not know of Meade's decision to defend at Big Pipe Creek; he was a fighter, and Gettysburg looked like a good place for a battle. He ordered Howard's XI Corps forward.

Around 11:00 A.M., Brig. Gen. James S. Wadsworth's division relieved Buford's brigade on Seminary Ridge, meeting Heth's attack with a furious counterattack which wrecked the latter's two leading brigades. Reynolds was killed by a sharpshooter; stodgy Maj. Gen. Abner Doubleday took command and organized a line along McPherson's and Seminary Ridges (*sketch* b). There was a lull then, while Heth waited for Pender, but Buford was reporting increased difficulty in delaying Ewell. About noon, Howard arrived and took command (giving his corps to Brig. Gen. Carl Schurz), and promptly called for help from Slocum and Sickles. Recognizing the importance of Cemetery Hill, he dropped one of his divisions there as a reserve and began moving the other two toward Oak Hill on Doubleday's right flank. However, the arrival of Ewell's leading division, under Maj. Gen. Robert E. Rodes, forced him to form them in line directly north of the town. Rodes' first attack against Robinson's division developed into a costly failure. But Confederate strength was building up too fast. A. P. Hill renewed his attack from the west; Early arrived from York and outflanked the Union right; Confederate artillery on Oak Hill was enfilading the lines of both corps, despite effective Union counterbattery fire. The Union lines gave, slowly and stubbornly in most places, but more and more rapidly on the right as Early's attack gathered momentum.

On the morning of this same day, Stuart's sleepy command entered Dover (just west of York). Early was gone, and the local citizens were unwilling to furnish information. Stuart reasoned that Ewell should be somewhere in the direction of Harrisburg, if the invasion were going well. Halting only to water his mounts, he took the road to Carlisle.

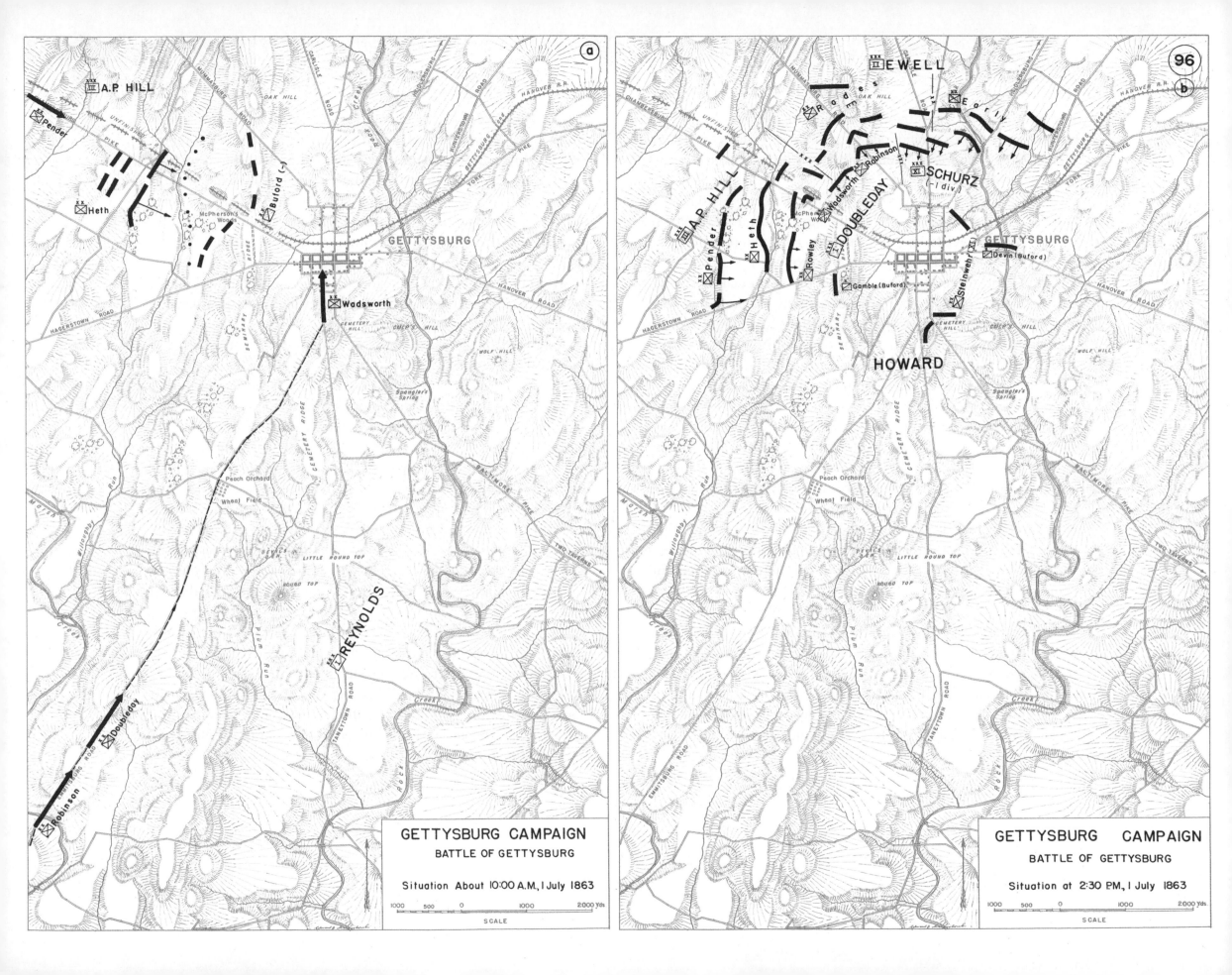

a

96

b

XXX A.P. HILL

☒ Pender

☒ Heth

McPherson's Woods

☒ Buford (-)

GETTYSBURG

☒ Wadsworth

CARLISLE ROAD

OAK HILL

CHAMBERSBURG PIKE

MUMMASBURG ROAD

GETTYSBURG PIKE

YORK PIKE

HANOVER R.R.

UNFINISHED R.R.

HERR RIDGE

SEMINARY RIDGE

CEMETERY HILL

CULP'S HILL

WOLF HILL

Spangler's Spring

HAGERSTOWN ROAD

HANOVER ROAD

BALTIMORE PIKE

WILLOUGHBY Run

PLUM Run

Peach Orchard

Wheat Field

DEVIL'S DEN

LITTLE ROUND TOP

ROUND TOP

TANEYTOWN ROAD

EMMITSBURG ROAD

☒ REYNOLDS

☒ Doubleday

☒ Robinson

TWO TAVERNS

Creek

MOTTER Creek

GETTYSBURG CAMPAIGN

BATTLE OF GETTYSBURG

Situation About 10:00 A.M., 1 July 1863

1000 500 0 1000 2000 Yds

SCALE

XXXX EWELL

XXX Rodes

XXX Early

XXX A.P. HILL

☒ Pender

☒ Heth

☒ Robinson

☒ Wadsworth

McPherson's Woods

☒ Rowley

XXX DOUBLEDAY

XXX SCHURZ (1 div)

☒ Devin (Buford)

GETTYSBURG

☒ Gamble (Buford)

☒ Steinwehr

HOWARD

CHAMBERSBURG PIKE

UNFINISHED R.R.

MUMMASBURG ROAD

OAK HILL

CARLISLE ROAD

HARRISBURG ROAD

YORK PIKE

HANOVER R.R.

HERR RIDGE

SEMINARY RIDGE

CEMETERY HILL

CULP'S HILL

WOLF HILL

Spangler's Spring

HAGERSTOWN ROAD

HANOVER ROAD

BALTIMORE PIKE

WILLOUGHBY Run

PLUM Run

Peach Orchard

Wheat Field

DEVIL'S DEN

LITTLE ROUND TOP

ROUND TOP

TANEYTOWN ROAD

EMMITSBURG ROAD

TWO TAVERNS

Creek

MOTTER Creek

GETTYSBURG CAMPAIGN

BATTLE OF GETTYSBURG

Situation at 2:30 P.M., 1 July 1863

1000 500 0 1000 2000 Yds

SCALE

The XI Corps became disorganized during its retreat through Gettysburg, losing a considerable number of prisoners (*sketch* a). The I Corps withdrew in relatively good order, covered on its left by Buford.

A. P. Hill was content to halt on Seminary Ridge, but Ewell's advance flowed into Gettysburg. Howard rallied the remnants of the XI Corps on Cemetery Hill, where Brig. Gen. Adolph von Steinwehr, the commander of the division he had left there, had turned the cemetery on the north end of the hill into a strong point. Both Union corps had suffered losses of over 50 per cent, but most of their artillery had fought its way clear. Cemetery Hill and Cemetery Ridge soon bristled with guns.

Shortly after 4:00 P.M., Hancock arrived on the field, under orders from Meade to take command. Howard was senior to Hancock, and stood stiffly on that seniority, but he cooperated. They rapidly organized the position; Hancock grasped the importance of Culp's Hill and browbeat Doubleday into sending the survivors of the Iron Brigade (of Wadsworth's division) to occupy it. The XII Corps began arriving shortly after 5:00 P.M.; and elements of the III Corps, an hour later.

Robert E. Lee had become enmeshed in a trap of his own making. He had invaded the North in the hope of winning a decisive battle, yet he had scattered his infantry across south-central Pennsylvania and had lost control of his cavalry. Now, with his army half concentrated, aggressive subordinates had plunged him into a major battle. He had won a partial success against a weaker enemy, but he did not know where the rest of the Union army might be. Now, eager to destroy the withdrawing Union forces, he ordered Ewell to take Cemetery Hill "if practicable."

Ewell studied the battered condition of his troops, the emplaced artillery on the hill above him, and a false report that a Federal column was advancing down the York Pike, and did not consider it "practicable" to take the hill. Johnson arrived at 7:30 P.M. with Ewell's last division, but by then it was almost dark. Ewell, despite the mutters of his staff and Lee's gentle hints, still would not risk an attack. Later, he received a report that Culp's Hill was unoccupied, and ordered Johnson to seize it. Johnson's patrols found the Iron Brigade in possession and withdrew hurriedly. Ewell needed cavalry badly. Jenkins' whereabouts were obscure; Stuart was at Carlisle, unsuccessfully trying to bluff a newly arrived militia garrison into surrendering.

That night and the next morning, both armies massed around Gettysburg (*sketch* b). Lee's numerical superiority grew slimmer. Meade had arrived at midnight and somewhat regretfully decided to fight there.

Lee's plan for 2 July was for Longstreet to get around the Federal left (which Lee mistakenly thought extended south from Cemetery Hill, along Cemetery Road) and attack north. Anderson's division would then join the assault; Ewell would attack when he heard Longstreet's guns. Lee had wanted an early attack, but it was 11:00 A.M. before his orders were issued.

Longstreet did not approve. He had strongly favored taking up a defensive position and letting Meade attack, and he had thought that Lee had accepted his ideas. Now, disgruntled, he advanced over strange ground, trying to avoid detection by the Federal signal station on Little Round Top. Sharpshooters of the III Corps ambushed his advance guard; the Federal line was not where Lee had expected it; Hood and McLaws had trouble forming for the attack. At 3:00 P.M., Longstreet's artillery opened.

There were three flaws in the Federal position: the Round Tops were not occupied; Pleasonton had ordered Buford from the south flank back to Westminster and had forgotten to replace him; and Sickles had moved his corps forward from the ground just north of the Round Tops without permission from Meade. Sickles' new position was on higher ground, but its salient shape permitted Confederate artillery to take it under fire from two directions; also, it was too extensive for his one corps.

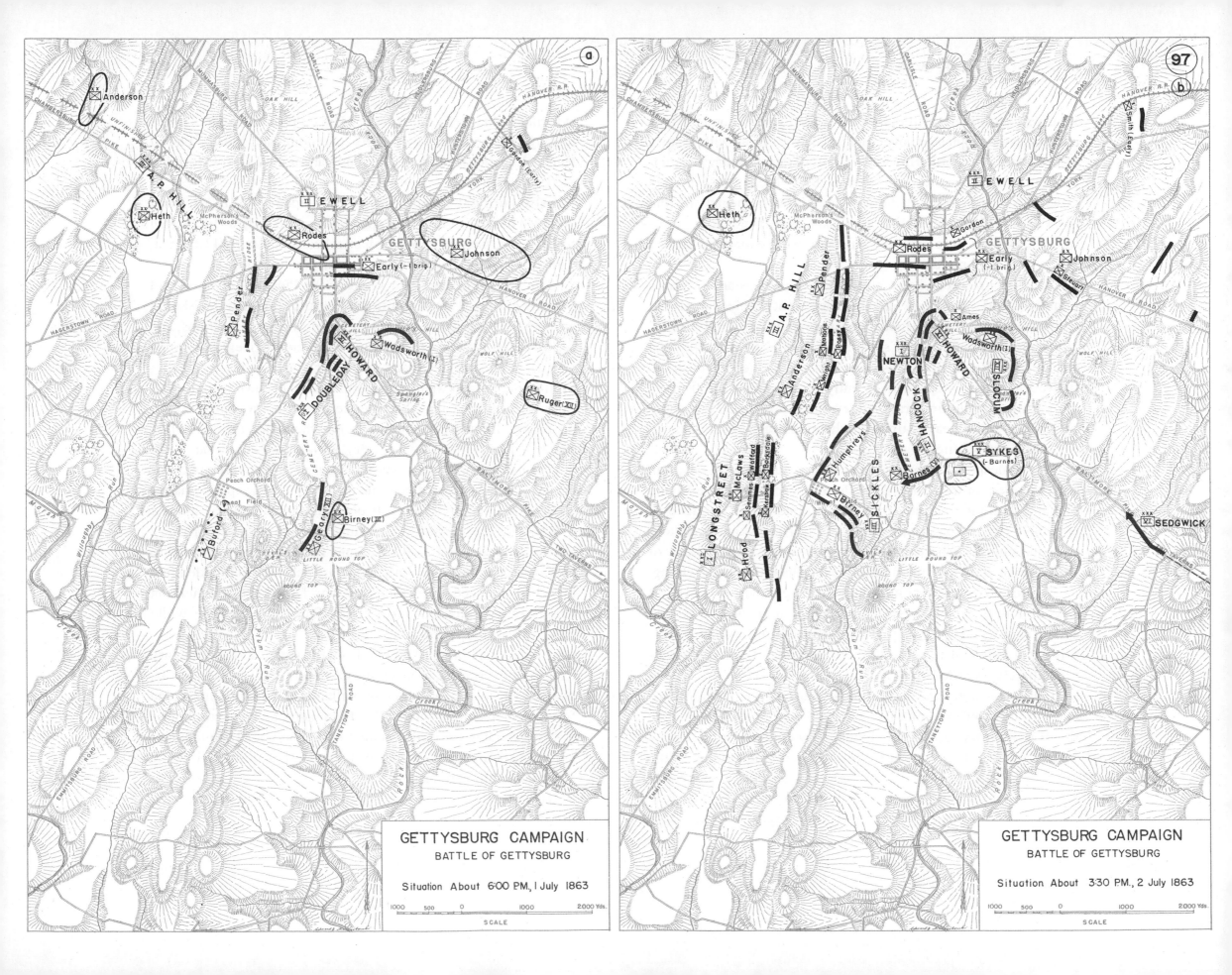

97

GETTYSBURG CAMPAIGN

BATTLE OF GETTYSBURG

Situation About 6:00 P.M., 1 July 1863

1000 500 0 1000 2000 Yds.

SCALE

GETTYSBURG CAMPAIGN

BATTLE OF GETTYSBURG

Situation About 3:30 P.M., 2 July 1863

1000 500 0 1000 2000 Yds.

SCALE

Hearing Longstreet's artillery, Meade rode to the Union left flank and expressed displeasure over Sickles' new position, with its apex at the Peach Orchard. However, Confederate infantry was advancing, and it was too late to withdraw. Meade had already ordered Sykes to support the left flank; now he began shifting most of the XII Corps to this area (*sketch* a). The leading units of the VI Corps were arriving, but these were exhausted from a thirty-four-mile march.

At 4:00 P.M. Longstreet attacked. From the start, it was a jumbled effort. Divisions and brigades went in piecemeal, but with savage enthusiasm. Hood's division rapidly smashed Sickles' left flank, overran the Devil's Den; and went clawing up the west side of Little Round Top. This was the key to the Federal position. Its west and north slopes had recently been cleared, and from its crest artillery could fire straight down the Union line. (Round Top was higher, but so heavily timbered that it offered neither observation nor fields of fire.)

At this desperate moment, Brig. Gen, Gouverneur K. Warren, chief engineer of the Army of the Potomac, reached Little Round Top and found it held only by a small signal detail. On his own responsibility, he ordered two V Corps brigades and a battery onto its summit. These units got there a few yards ahead of Hood's men and drove them off in furious hand-to-hand fighting.

Sickles' center and right flank held longer, but were eventually driven back as shown. Anderson's division joined the assault, but its advance also was poorly coordinated. One of its brigades momentarily broke through the Federal center, but was immediately expelled.

Ewell's artillery opened at the sound of Longstreet's guns, but Union batteries soon silenced it. It was almost dark when Ewell's infantry attacked. Johnson occupied some empty entrenchments at the foot of Culp's Hill, but could not carry the bill itself. Attacking the eastern side of Cemetery Hill, two of Early's brigades got to the top. Only their dead stayed there.

That night, Meade called a council of war: should the army stay and fight, or should it retire? His corps commanders voted to stay. In the interest of unity of command, Meade placed Hancock in charge of the II, III, and part of the I Corps, forming the Union center.

Also during the night, Slocum regrouped his XII Corps and prepared to recover his former position around Culp's Hill (*sketch* b). Johnson, heavily reinforced, attacked first but. by 11:00 A.M. 3 July, had been driven back to his original position.

Lee's last uncommitted forces were Pickett's division and Stuart's cavalry. Longstreet urged that the Confederates should envelop the Federal left, get across Meade's communications, and so force him to attack them. But a blind combativeness gripped Lee. He could not delay and maneuver, for his army was living off the country and would soon strip it bare; his own communications were highly vulnerable; the enemy was before him. He gave his orders: Longstreet would penetrate the Federal center, while Stuart, with all the army's cavalry, struck the Union rear.

Longstreet protested, but made the necessary preparations. He had 159 guns massed opposite the Union center; approximately 15,000 infantry under Pickett concentrated for the assault At 1:00 P.M., the Confederate guns opened; Union artillery answered until about 2:00 P.M., when their firing was stopped to conserve ammunition. Confederate artillerymen concluded that they had silenced the Union cannon. Their own ammunition being almost exhausted, they urged Pickett to advance while they still could support him.

Confederate infantry poured from the woods along Seminary Ridge. Converging Union artillery fire tore gaps in their ranks, but they closed up and came on gallantly. Union infantry came forward against their flanks. Yet, for a moment, the central mass of Confederates stormed into the first Union line. Then the Federals closed in, and the attack of Pickett's men collapsed. Some quit, more ran, and many died.

Behind this fight, Brig. Gen. David M. Gregg intercepted Stuart (*off map, upper right*) and drove him back.

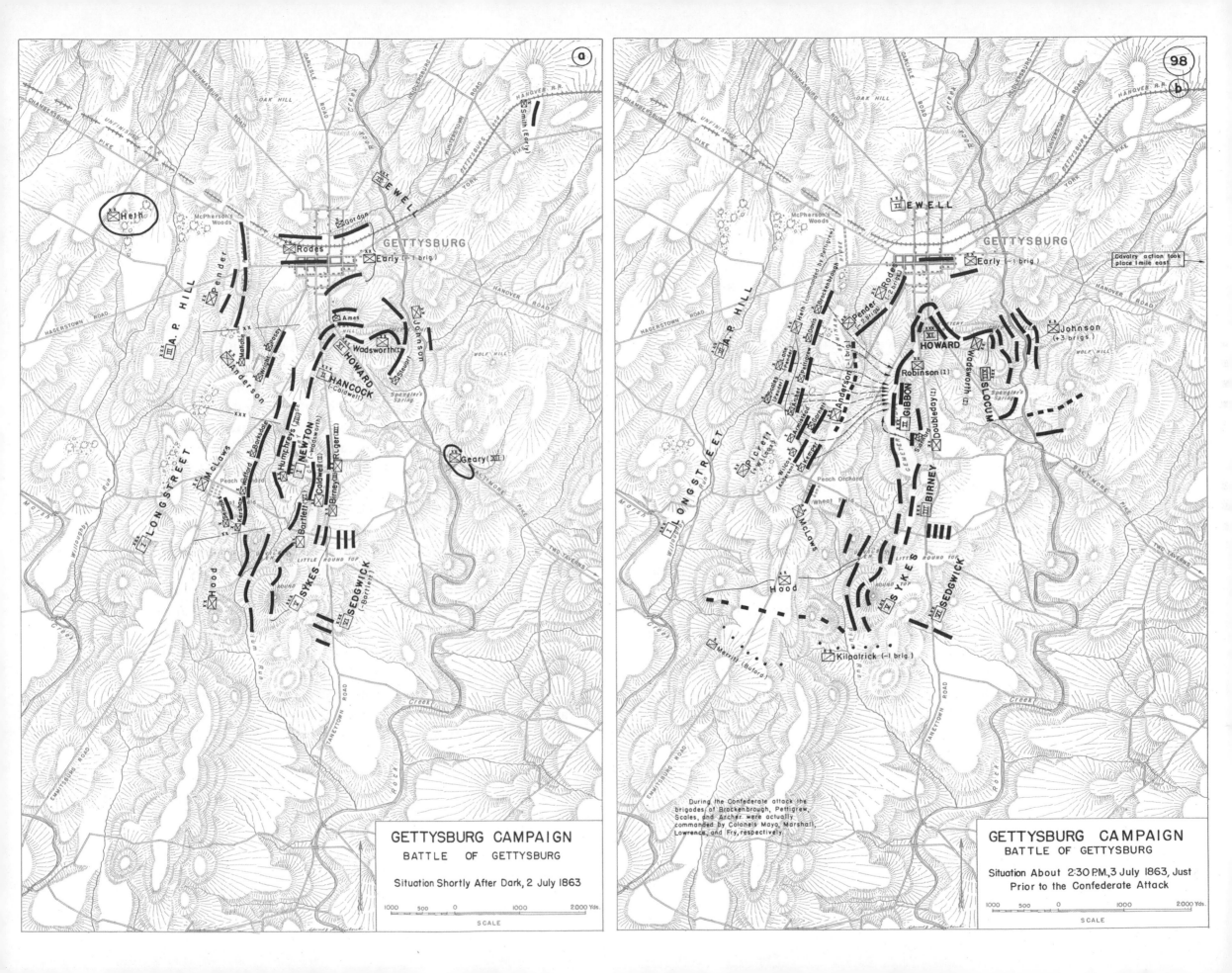

98

GETTYSBURG CAMPAIGN
BATTLE OF GETTYSBURG

Situation Shortly After Dark, 2 July 1863

1000 500 0 1000 2000 Yds.

SCALE

GETTYSBURG CAMPAIGN
BATTLE OF GETTYSBURG

Situation About 2:30 P.M., 3 July 1863, Just
Prior to the Confederate Attack

1000 500 0 1000 2000 Yds.

SCALE

During the Confederate attack the
brigades of Brockenbrough, Pettigrew,
Scales, and Archer were actually
commanded by Colonels Mayo, Marshall,
Lowrence, and Fry, respectively.

Cavalry action took
place 1 mile east.

Hancock, wounded in Pickett's final assault, urged an immediate counterattack by the V and VI Corps. The VI Corps was fresh—it had hardly fired a shot—and Slocum had already offered one or two brigades from the XII Corps.

Meade, however, had contented himself with fighting a purely defensive battle and had made no plans to seize the initiative from Lee. Instead of keeping the VI Corps concentrated for a decisive counterstroke at the critical time, he had scattered it behind his lines to form local reserves. In so doing, he lost his chance to destroy Lee's army.

Lee took the blame for Pickett's repulse: "It's all my fault," he told the throng of fugitives that straggled back to Seminary Ridge, still mercilessly hammered by the Union guns. Aided by Longstreet, he hastily rallied them to meet the counterattack which he expected, but which never came. That night, he pulled his army together and dug in on a line running from Oak Hill to the Peach Orchard (*broken red box*).

Both armies were badly mauled. The Federals had lost 23,049 killed, wounded, or missing—approximately one man out of every four. The Confederates reported losses totaling 20,451, but their returns are incomplete; their actual casualties appear to have been nearer 28,000, or one-third of their force.

Undoubtedly, Gettysburg was the lowest point of Lee's generalship. He was careless; his orders were vague; he suggested when he should have commanded; and he sacrificed the pick of his infantry in a foredoomed attempt to win a battle he had already lost. But, on 4 July, he reasserted himself. All day—as he had the year before at Antietam—he held his army in position, defying Meade to attack and so reestablishing something of the old tradition of invincibility. Meanwhile, his long convoy of wounded started to the rear. That night, in a driving rain, the rest of the Army of Northern Virginia followed.

Meade spent the 4th reorganizing. He had already begun to talk about the need for resting and resupplying his army. All through the day, his observation stations reported Confederate trains assembling or moving to the rear, but he remained cautious and passive, planning a reconnaissance in force for the 5th. On the 5th, Lee was gone.

During this campaign, a relatively small Federal force under French had remained in the vicinity of Frederick. On 3 July, French had sent a cavalry raid against Lee's ponton bridge over the Potomac at Falling Waters (*left center*); the guard there was surprised, and the bridge destroyed. Constant rains had the river running bankfull. Without a bridge, Lee would be trapped on the north bank.

Meanwhile, Lee's retreat and Meade's slow pursuit went on, along the routes shown. The Union cavalry harried the Confederate trains aggressively, but they were outnumbered by Stuart.

Meade now began to exaggerate Confederate strength and to worry that Lee would try to fight another pitched battle. Actually, Lee had arrived at Williamsport on the 7th. He was almost out of ammunition, and straggling and desertion had further thinned his forces to about 35,000. In desperation, he entrenched with his back to the river and began improvising a bridge, tearing down warehouses to build pontons. On the 12th, Meade, with over 85,000 men, carefully approached this position. Then he called a council of war. The aggressive corps commanders —Reynolds, Hancock, Sickles—were dead or wounded; a majority of the council voted not to attack. Lee got his command across the river during the night of 13-14 July, catching Meade completely unaware. Buford detected the last phases of the movement early on the 14th and drove Lee's rear guard into the river, capturing over 500 prisoners. But Lee and the Army of Northern Virginia had escaped.

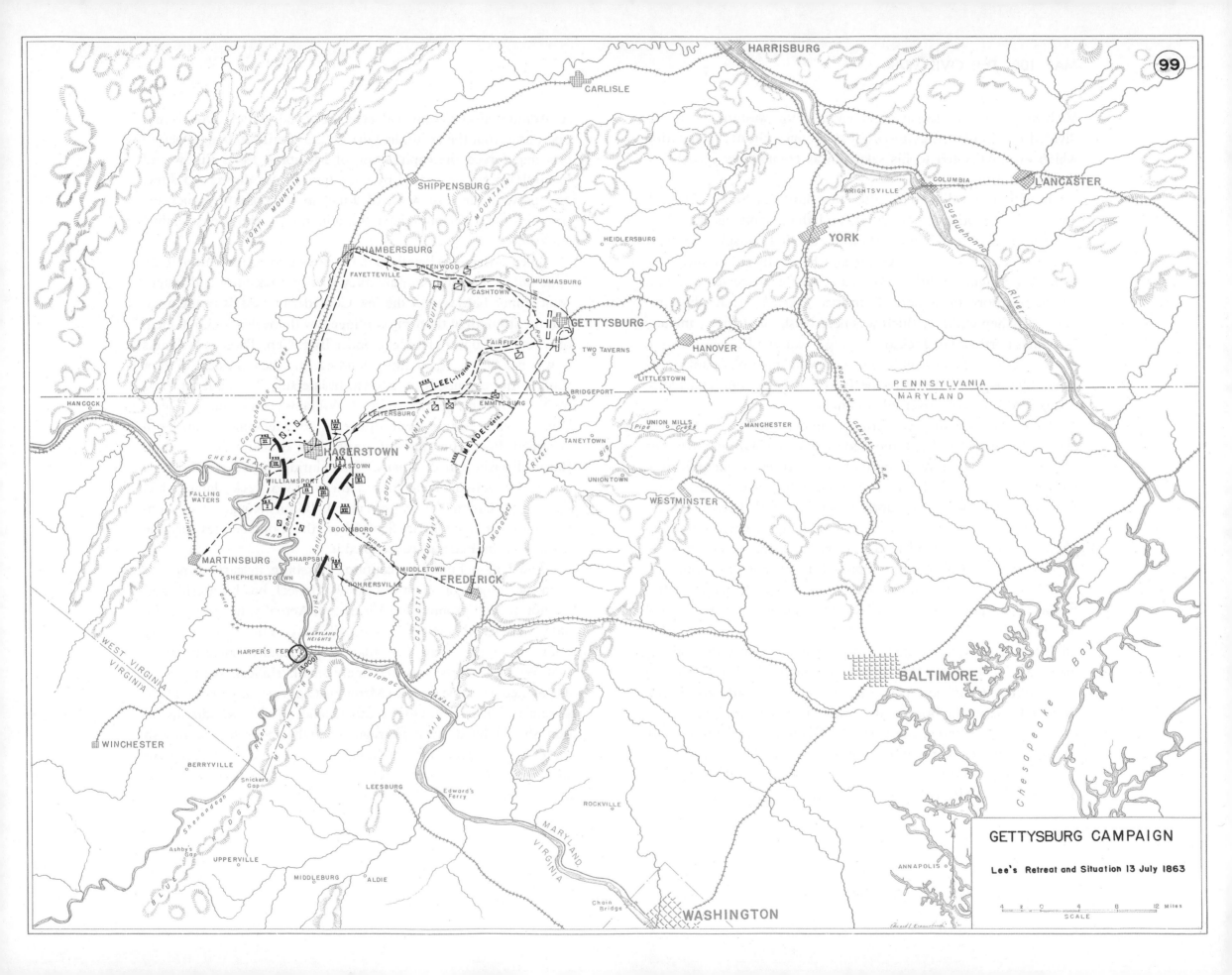

99

HARRISBURG

CARLISLE

SHIPPENSBURG

HEIDLERSBURG

COLUMBIA

LANCASTER

CHAMBERSBURG

FAYETTEVILLE

GREENWOOD

MUMMASBURG

CASHTOWN

GETTYSBURG

YORK

WRIGHTSVILLE

FAIRFIELD

TWO TAVERNS

HANOVER

LEE (-trains)

BRIDGEPORT

LITTLESTOWN

PENNSYLVANIA

MARYLAND

HANCOCK

LEITERSBURG

EMMITTSBURG

UNION MILLS

MANCHESTER

TANEYTOWN

MEADE (-dets.)

HAGERSTOWN

FUNKSTOWN

WILLIAMSPORT

UNIONTOWN

WESTMINSTER

FALLING WATERS

BOONSBORO

Turner's

MARTINSBURG

SHARPSBURG

MIDDLETOWN

FREDERICK

SHEPHERDSTOWN

ROHRERSVILLE

WEST VIRGINIA

MARYLAND HEIGHTS

HARPER'S FERRY

(3000)

VIRGINIA

WINCHESTER

BERRYVILLE

Snicker's Gap

ROCKVILLE

Edward's Ferry

LEESBURG

MARYLAND

VIRGINIA

Ashby's Gap

UPPERVILLE

ANNAPOLIS

MIDDLEBURG

ALDIE

Chain Bridge

WASHINGTON

BALTIMORE

CHESAPEAKE BAY

GETTYSBURG CAMPAIGN

Lee's Retreat and Situation 13 July 1863

4 2 0 4 8 12 Miles

SCALE

Vicksburg was the decisive campaign in the western theater. It divided the Confederacy in two and brought Grant a reputation which eventually led to his selection as commander in chief of the Union armies.

It will be recalled that, after the Battle of Shiloh, Halleck advanced to Corinth (*sketch* a), and that, upon his departure for Washington on 17 July, 1862, he divided his splendid army into two commands under Grant and Buell. In accordance with Halleck's design, Grant's army was thereafter dispersed to guard communications in western Tennessee (*sketch* b). At this time (about 12 September), Buell was near Nashville (approximately 140 miles northeast of Jackson) trying to counter Bragg's invasion of Kentucky. He had been reinforced with three of Grant's divisions. Opposing Grant were the forces of Price and Van Dorn, acting under Bragg's over-all command.

Vicksburg was of great strategic importance to the Confederates. In their hands, it blocked Union navigation down the Mississippi and—more important—it allowed communication with the states west of the river, upon which the Confederates depended extensively for supplies. The natural defenses of the city were ideal for warfare of that period. It is located on a high bluff overlooking a bend in the river; the maze of swamps and bayous to the north hamper approach from that direction.

The city had been under Union naval attack before. After Farragut's brilliant capture of New Orleans on 25 April, he had moved up the river capturing the principal cities en route. On 18 May, his advance elements had reached Vicksburg and demanded its surrender. The Confederates had refused, and, because Farragut had insufficient troops for a landing, he had moved back to New Orleans. In June, under orders to try again, he returned to Vicksburg. By now, however, the Confederates had not only strengthened the defensive batteries but had reinforced Van Dorn with about 15,000 men (3,000 were in the immediate vicinity of Vicksburg). Meanwhile, Captain Charles H. Davis (successor

to Admiral Foote, who had been wounded at Fort Donelson), operating from the north, had driven the Confederate fleet before him and forced the capitulation of Memphis. Forts Pillow and Randolph were evacuated by the Confederates during 4-5 June, and now, in the last week of June, in response to a message from Farragut, Davis joined the admiral in operations against Vicksburg.

Their attempt to bombard the fortress into surrender on 26-28 June failed. Throughout July, they shelled Vicksburg and fought some minor battles with the few Confederate vessels in the area. But the strength of the army contingent with the fleet—3,300 men, of whom 1,200 were laborers, under Brig. Gen. Thomas Williams—was insufficient to attempt a landing, and the navy despaired of forcing the surrender of the town. In late July, Farragut returned to New Orleans, leaving part of Williams' command at Baton Rouge, while Davis went upstream to Memphis. Van Dorn occupied Port Hudson and dispatched Breckinridge to seize Baton Rouge. On 5 August, Breckinridge attacked Williams but was repulsed (*action not shown*). Two weeks later, when the weak Union forces evacuated Baton Rouge, the Confederates occupied it; in September, the Confederates left the town, and the Federals reoccupied it.

The Union failure to capture Vicksburg in early June has been the subject of much discussion. Halleck has been criticized for not moving promptly on Vicksburg. Actually, he expected the navy to seize the town without difficulty. This was an overly optimistic appraisal of the situation, particularly since he knew that Williams' force was extremely small. Halleck should have dispatched a sizable force to Memphis to accompany Davis downstream to Vicksburg. On the other hand, the Union administration should have given Farragut enough troops to accomplish the task it assigned him. In June, such an operation might have succeeded; in December, Vicksburg was heavily garrisoned and able to withstand anything but a major offensive.

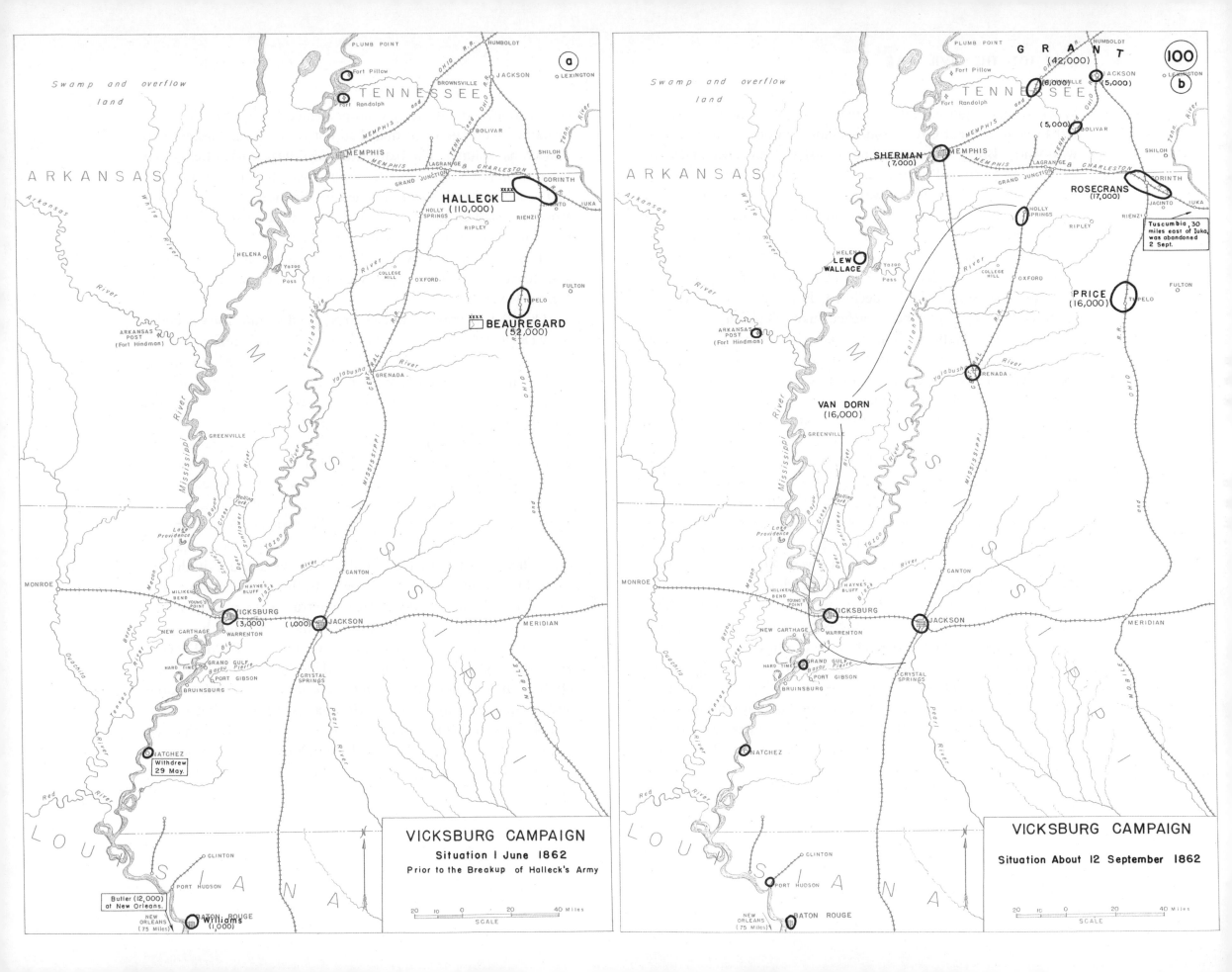

100

VICKSBURG CAMPAIGN

Situation 1 June 1862

Prior to the Breakup of Halleck's Army

SCALE
20 10 0 20 40 Miles

VICKSBURG CAMPAIGN

Situation About 12 September 1862

SCALE
20 10 0 20 40 Miles

Map a (left):

Swamp and overflow land

TENNESSEE

ARKANSAS

PLUMB POINT
Fort Pillow
HUMBOLDT
JACKSON
LEXINGTON
Fort Randolph
BROWNSVILLE
BOLIVAR
SHILOH
MEMPHIS
LAGRANGE
GRAND JUNCTION
CHARLESTON
CORINTH
IUKA

HALLECK
(110,000)

HOLLY SPRINGS
RIENZI
RIPLEY

HELENA
Yazoo Pass
COLLEGE HILL
OXFORD
FULTON

ARKANSAS POST
(Fort Hindman)

BEAUREGARD
(52,000)

TUPELO

GREENVILLE

Lake Providence

CANTON

MONROE

HAYNES' BLUFF
MILIKEN'S BEND
YOUNG'S POINT
VICKSBURG (3,000)
(1,000) JACKSON
WARRENTON
MERIDIAN

NEW CARTHAGE
HARD TIMES
GRAND GULF
PORT GIBSON
BRUINSBURG
CRYSTAL SPRINGS

MISSISSIPPI

LOUISIANA

NATCHEZ
Withdrew 29 May.

CLINTON
PORT HUDSON

Butler (12,000) at New Orleans.

NEW ORLEANS (75 Miles)
BATON ROUGE
Williams (1,000)

Map b (right):

Swamp and overflow land

TENNESSEE

ARKANSAS

PLUMB POINT
Fort Pillow
HUMBOLDT

GRANT
(42,000)

(6,000)
JACKSON (5,000)
LEXINGTON
Fort Randolph
(5,000)
BOLIVAR
SHILOH

SHERMAN
(7,000)
MEMPHIS
LAGRANGE
GRAND JUNCTION
CHARLESTON
CORINTH

ROSECRANS
(17,000)
JACINTO
IUKA

HOLLY SPRINGS
RIENZI
RIPLEY

Tuscumbia, 30 miles east of Iuka, was abandoned 2 Sept.

HELENA
LEW WALLACE
Yazoo Pass
COLLEGE HILL
OXFORD
FULTON

PRICE
(16,000)
TUPELO

ARKANSAS POST
(Fort Hindman)

VAN DORN
(16,000)

GREENVILLE

Lake Providence

CANTON

MONROE

HAYNES' BLUFF
MILIKEN'S BEND
YOUNG'S POINT
VICKSBURG
JACKSON
WARRENTON
MERIDIAN

NEW CARTHAGE
HARD TIMES
GRAND GULF
PORT GIBSON
BRUINSBURG
CRYSTAL SPRINGS
GRENADA

MISSISSIPPI

LOUISIANA

NATCHEZ

CLINTON
PORT HUDSON

NEW ORLEANS (75 Miles)
BATON ROUGE

When Bragg departed with his main army for Chattanooga, he left Price to prevent Grant from sending reinforcements to Buell, with whom Bragg was to contend in eastern Tennessee and Kentucky. Van Dorn had the primary mission of guarding Vicksburg. But, by 2 September, Bragg was under the erroneous impression that Rosecrans had evacuated Corinth and had marched to join Buell. Accordingly, he urged Price to move with all speed to Nashville to balance the scales. Price attempted to persuade Van Dorn to accompany him, but Van Dorn's interests lay in operations in Mississippi, and he declined. Price therefore advanced alone and, on 14 September, reached Iuka (*sketch a*).

Meanwhile, Halleck wanted Grant to send more reinforcements to Buell. Grant replied that his mission to protect the railroads had already caused an overdispersion of his forces. Halleck then authorized the abandonment of the railroad east of Corinth, thus allowing Grant to shift his forces and to send a third division to Buell.

When Price reached Iuka, he learned that Rosecrans had not left Corinth to join Buell, as Bragg had thought. He therefore decided to abandon his move to Nashville and to cooperate with Van Dorn in a strike against Corinth. At the same time, Grant decided to attack Price at Iuka to prevent his joining Bragg. Grant's plan called for Maj. Gen. Edward O. Ord to advance from Corinth southeast along the railroad, while Rosecrans moved south and then east through Jacinto to cut off Price. Meanwhile, Hurlbut (*not shown*) was to demonstrate south of Bolivar and watch Van Dorn, known to be at Holly Springs.

As frequently occurs in such efforts to converge on the battlefield, the plan went awry. Rosecrans was delayed by an unexpected rain and by the fact that one of his divisions took the wrong road. Instead of attacking the Confederates early in the morning of 19 September, he did not attack until 4:00 P.M. By then, Price, aware of the Federal march, had moved part of his force to repulse the attack. Ord took no part in the fight because he had halted, as directed, three miles from Iuka to await Rose-

crans' attack. The westerly wind prevented his hearing the noise of battle, and communications had not yet been established with Rosecrans' column. The battle continued until dark, after which Price withdrew south along the Fulton Road—which Rosecrans had failed to block—and marched to Ripley to join Van Dorn. Rosecrans and Ord returned to Corinth, the latter shortly moving north to Jackson (*off map, north*). Grant, at Halleck's urging, spent most of the next week unsuccessfully trying to work out a plan to destroy Confederate ironclads under construction on the Yazoo River.

On 30 September, the combined Confederate forces, under Van Dorn, moved on Corinth by way of Pocahontas (*center*). Union cavalry scouted the Confederates and warned Rosecrans of the impending attack. Early on 3 October, Van Dorn launched his assault against the Union forces occupying the entrenchments around Corinth previously built by Beauregard (*sketch c*). Rosecrans' two center divisions bore the brunt of the onslaught and were forced back; troops from the Union left were moved to bolster the line. Late in the afternoon, Rosecrans' rightmost division launched an attack against Van Dorn's left flank and brought the fighting to a close for the day. The next day, Van Dorn renewed the attack (*sketch d*); but, by noon, he had been repulsed everywhere. Acknowledging failure, he began a withdrawal toward Chewalla (*sketch b*). Rosecrans, though he had two relatively fresh divisions, postponed pursuit until the next morning.

In the meantime, Grant, aware of the battle and hoping to trap Van Dorn, had dispatched Brig. Gen. James B. McPherson with four regiments to Corinth and Hurlbut's division to Pocahontas, where it blocked Van Dorn. The latter retraced his march and escaped by way of Ripley. Rosecrans followed, but Grant, troubled by reports that approximately 9,000 recently exchanged Confederate prisoners had joined Van Dorn, halted the pursuit.

The Battle of Corinth cost the Confederates 4,838 casualties; the Federals, 3,090.

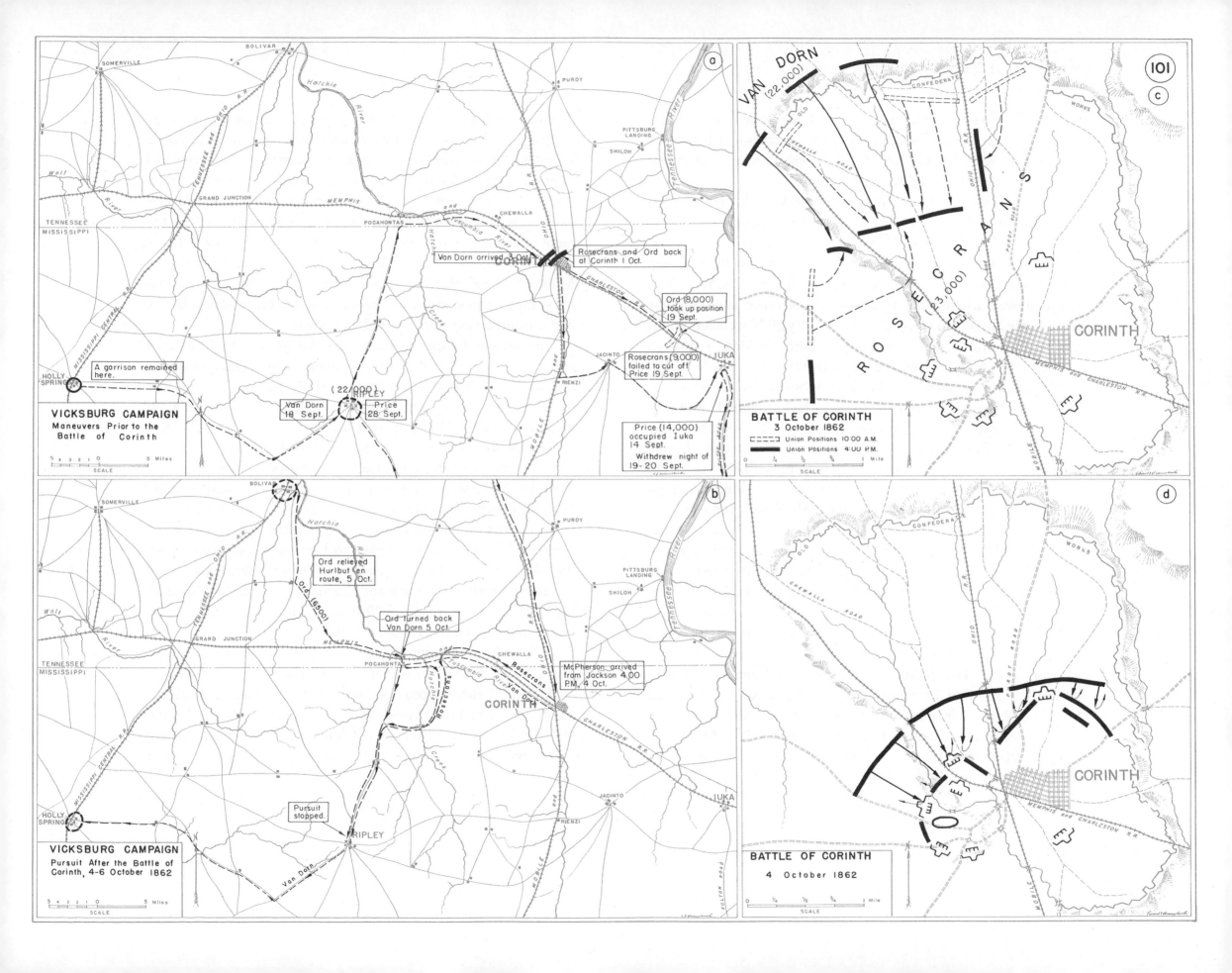

(a)

SOMERVILLE

BOLIVAR

PURDY

Hatchie River

PITTSBURG LANDING

SHILOH

Tennessee River

GRAND JUNCTION

MEMPHIS

CHEWALLA

POCAHONTAS

TENNESSEE
MISSISSIPPI

Wolf River

CORINTH

Van Dorn arrived 3 Oct.

Rosecrans and Ord back at Corinth 1 Oct.

Ord (8,000) took up position 19 Sept.

A garrison remained here.

HOLLY SPRINGS

(22,000)

RIPLEY

Van Dorn 18 Sept.

Price 28 Sept.

JACINTO

RIENZI

IUKA

Rosecrans (9,000) failed to cut off Price 19 Sept.

Price (14,000) occupied Iuka 14 Sept.

Withdrew night of 19-20 Sept.

VICKSBURG CAMPAIGN
Maneuvers Prior to the Battle of Corinth

5 4 3 2 1 0   5 Miles
SCALE

(b)

SOMERVILLE

BOLIVAR

PURDY

Hatchie River

PITTSBURG LANDING

SHILOH

Tennessee River

Ord relieved Hurlbut en route, 5 Oct.

Ord (6500)

Ord turned back Van Dorn 5 Oct.

GRAND JUNCTION

MEMPHIS

POCAHONTAS

CHEWALLA

Rosecrans

TENNESSEE
MISSISSIPPI

Wolf River

CORINTH

Van Dorn

McPherson arrived from Jackson 4:00 P.M., 4 Oct.

CHARLESTON R.R.

HOLLY SPRINGS

Pursuit stopped.

RIPLEY

Van Dorn

JACINTO

RIENZI

IUKA

VICKSBURG CAMPAIGN
Pursuit After the Battle of Corinth, 4-6 October 1862

5 4 3 2 1 0   5 Miles
SCALE

(c) ⑩⑪ 101

VAN DORN (22,000)

CONFEDERATE

WORKS

OLD

NEWALLA ROAD

ROSECRANS (23,000)

OHIO R.R.

CORINTH

MEMPHIS and CHARLESTON R.R.

BATTLE OF CORINTH
3 October 1862

▭▭▭▭ Union Positions 10:00 A.M.
▬▬▬▬ Union Positions 4:00 P.M.

0   ½   1 Mile
SCALE

(d)

CONFEDERATE

WORKS

OLD

CHEWALLA ROAD

PURDY ROAD

OHIO R.R.

CORINTH

MEMPHIS and CHARLESTON R.R.

MOBILE and OHIO R.R.

FULTON ROAD

BATTLE OF CORINTH
4 October 1862

0   ¼   ½   ¾   1 Mile
SCALE

A period of watchful waiting followed the Battle of Corinth. Meanwhile, Rosecrans, selected as Buell's successor, left Grant's department, and Lt. Gen. John C. Pemberton assumed command of all Confederate forces in Mississippi.

During October, Grant pressed Halleck to let him get on with the war and finally received the response: "Fight the enemy when you please." On 2 November, he advanced south from Bolivar (*sketch* a, *top right*) with five divisions on the first step of a prospective overland drive (*not shown*) to Vicksburg. Van Dorn showed a reluctance to oppose the advance and withdrew from Holly Springs to Grenada (*center*). By 20 November, Grant had reached Holly Springs and, on the 24th, decided to move to Grenada. On 5 December, the Federals were fifteen miles south of Oxford, but, by now, Van Dorn's opposition had stiffened.

Earlier—on 23 November—Halleck had intimated his preference for a major move down the Mississippi to Vicksburg. By 5 December, Grant, too, seems to have concluded that an advance by water with part of his army was desirable. With Halleck's concurrence, he ordered Sherman on 9 December to return to Memphis to prepare for the river advance. Sherman's force was to consist of four divisions (*top left*). Grant himself, with the remainder of the army, was to advance a short distance and attack when he perceived an opportunity. Just as Grant's reversal of strategy may have been influenced by Halleck, so Halleck's desire for a river campaign may have been prompted by pressure from Lincoln. The President had made known his wish to repeat the two-pronged naval drive on Vicksburg, but this time with strong ground forces. The politically minded McClernand had convinced Lincoln that he could lead an army down the river and take Vicksburg. Lincoln enthusiastically approved the proposal and decided to have Banks—Butler's successor in New Orleans—advance upstream at the same time. Of these grandiose plans, Halleck knew little and Grant nothing.

Sherman's force left Memphis on 20 December, and arrived opposite Vicksburg on 26 December. The next two days, his debarked divisions worked their way through the difficult swamps and bayous to a position from which Chickasaw Bluffs could be assaulted (*inset, sketch* a). Pemberton, warned of the move, had reinforced the Vicksburg garrison. So, when Sherman attacked on 29 December, though he had superior numbers, the Confederates easily repulsed the attack from well-prepared positions. On the night of 31 December, an attempt to move up the Yazoo River and attack Hayne's Bluff also failed. Sherman then withdrew to Miliken's Bend (*sketch* a, *opposite Vicksburg*), where, on 2 January, McClernand arrived to take command. In the south, Banks had advanced only as far as Baton Rouge.

Meanwhile, Grant had been subjected to raids by Van Dorn and Forrest which had seriously disrupted his communications and destroyed his advanced base at Holly Springs, forcing him to live off the country. This reversal, coupled with the information he received on 18 December that McClernand—in whom he had no confidence—was to command the river force, caused him to abandon the overland route. He now prepared to move his army down the Mississippi to reinforce the troops at Vicksburg, leaving Hurlbut's corps to secure the rear (*sketch* b). But McClernand, seeking a victory and personal glory, moved from Miliken's Bend to attack Fort Hindman at Arkansas Post on the Arkansas River (*top left*) and, on 11 January, captured the fort. Grant considered this move a serious diversion and summarily ordered McClernand back to the bend. Arriving on 29 January, Grant assumed personal command of operations against Vicksburg the next day.

Primarily to placate discontented politicians and a critical press, Grant made four attempts to reach high ground east of Vicksburg. (These appear on the map as the Lake Providence Route, the canal to bypass Vicksburg, Steele's Bayou Route, and the Yazoo Pass Route.) All four attempts were uniformly unsuccessful, either because of Confederate resistance or natural obstacles.

The route of Grierson's famous raid is also shown on sketch b. Its relation to the campaign is discussed on the next map.

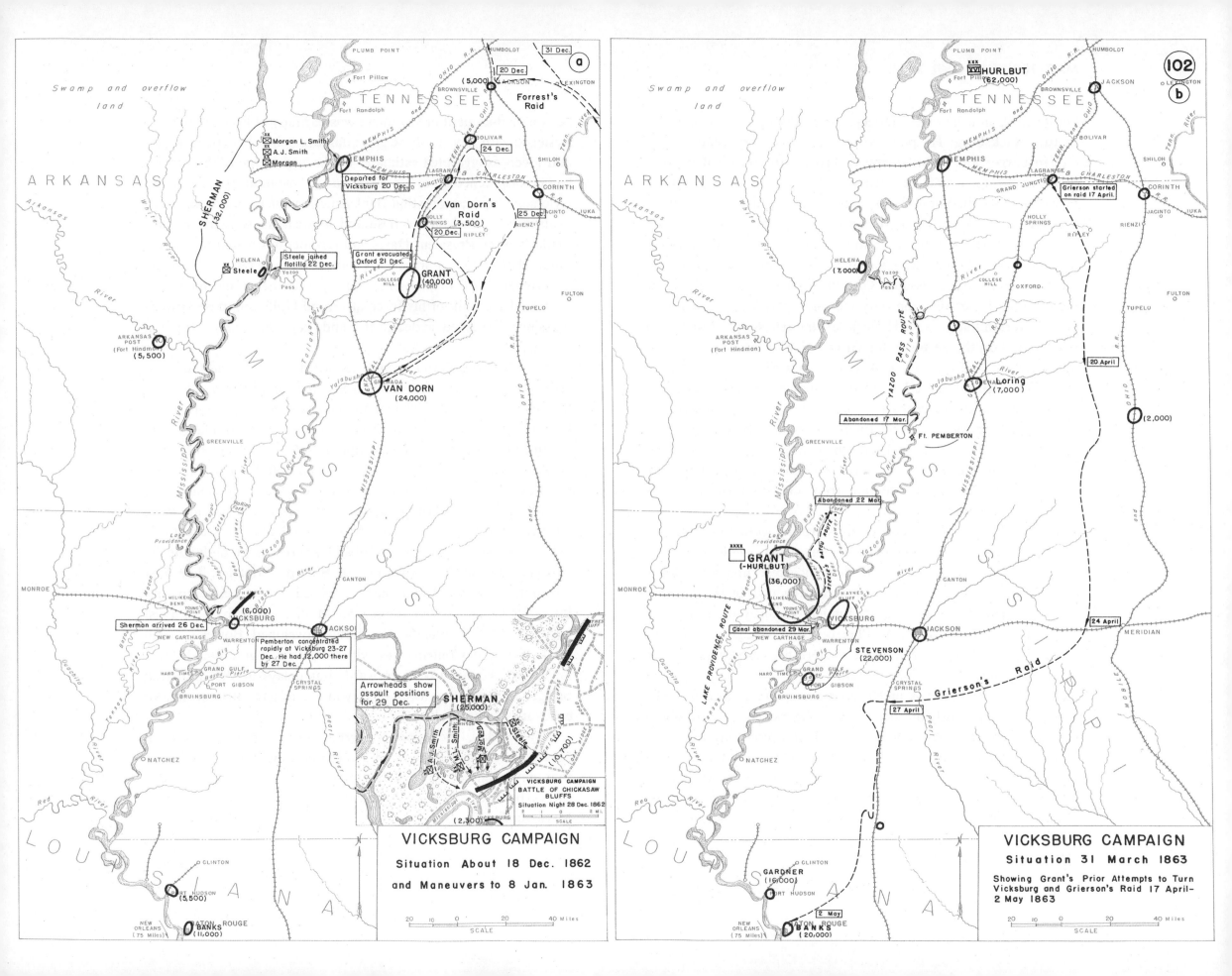

Map (a) — left panel labels:

Swamp and overflow land

31 Dec.

ⓐ

PLUMB POINT
HUMBOLDT
Fort Pillow
BROWNSVILLE
Fort Randolph
TENNESSEE
20 Dec.
(5,000)
JACKSON
LEXINGTON
Forrest's Raid

ARKANSAS

Morgan L. Smith
A. J. Smith
Morgan

MEMPHIS
SHERMAN (32,000)
Departed for Vicksburg 20 Dec.
LAGRANGE JUNCTION
CHARLESTON
CORINTH
SHILOH
BOLIVAR
24 Dec.

HELENA
Steele joined flotilla 22 Dec.
Steele
Yazoo Pass
HOLLY SPRINGS
Van Dorn's Raid (3,500)
20 Dec.
RIPLEY
JACINTO
IUKA
25 Dec.
RIENZI

Grant evacuated Oxford 21 Dec.
COLLEGE HILL
OXFORD
GRANT (40,000)

ARKANSAS POST (Fort Hindman) (5,500)

TUPELO
FULTON

GRENADA
VAN DORN (24,000)

GREENVILLE

Lake Providence

MONROE

Sherman arrived 26 Dec.
VICKSBURG (6,000)
HAYNES BLUFF
JACKSON
CANTON

Pemberton concentrated rapidly at Vicksburg 23-27 Dec. He had 12,000 there by 27 Dec.

NEW CARTHAGE
WARRENTON
GRAND GULF
PORT GIBSON
BRUINSBURG
HARD TIMES
CRYSTAL SPRINGS

Arrowheads show assault positions for 29 Dec.

Inset:
VICKSBURG CAMPAIGN
BATTLE OF CHICKASAW BLUFFS
Situation Night 28 Dec. 1862
SHERMAN (25,000)
A. J. Smith
M. L. Smith
Morgan
Steele
(10,700)
(2,300)

NATCHEZ

LOUISIANA

CLINTON
PORT HUDSON (5,500)
BATON ROUGE
NEW ORLEANS (75 Miles)
BANKS (11,000)

VICKSBURG CAMPAIGN

Situation About 18 Dec. 1862
and Maneuvers to 8 Jan. 1863

20 10 0 20 40 Miles
SCALE

Map (b) — right panel labels:

ⓑ
102

Swamp and overflow land

PLUMB POINT
Fort Pillow
HURLBUT (62,000)
BROWNSVILLE
JACKSON
HUMBOLDT
LEXINGTON

TENNESSEE

ARKANSAS

MEMPHIS
Grierson started on raid 17 April.
GRAND JUNCTION
LAGRANGE
CHARLESTON
CORINTH
SHILOH
BOLIVAR

HELENA (7,000)
Yazoo Pass
HOLLY SPRINGS
COLLEGE HILL
OXFORD
RIPLEY
RIENZI
JACINTO
IUKA

YAZOO PASS ROUTE

Abandoned 17 Mar.
Ft. PEMBERTON
LORING (7,000)

20 April

(2,000)

GREENVILLE

Abandoned 22 Mar.

Lake Providence
GRANT (-HURLBUT) (36,000)
Steele's Bayou Route

MONROE

LAKE PROVIDENCE ROUTE

Canal abandoned 29 Mar.
HAYNES BLUFF
VICKSBURG
STEVENSON (22,000)
JACKSON
CANTON
MERIDIAN
24 April

NEW CARTHAGE
WARRENTON
GRAND GULF
PORT GIBSON
BRUINSBURG
HARD TIMES
CRYSTAL SPRINGS
Grierson's Raid
27 April

NATCHEZ

LOUISIANA

GARDNER (16,000)
CLINTON
PORT HUDSON
BATON ROUGE
2 May
NEW ORLEANS (75 Miles)
BANKS (20,000)

VICKSBURG CAMPAIGN

Situation 31 March 1863

Showing Grant's Prior Attempts to Turn
Vicksburg and Grierson's Raid 17 April-
2 May 1863

20 10 0 20 40 Miles
SCALE

On 4 April, in a letter to Halleck, Grant divulged his latest plan to turn Vicksburg. He planned to move his army south of the city in barges and small steamers through the series of bayous. Some marching would be necessary, but drier weather was approaching, so this should not present too difficult a problem. Concurrently, Porter's gunboats and large transports would run past the Vicksburg batteries, and transport the troops across the river below Vicksburg. McClernand was willing, but both Porter and Sherman tried to dissuade Grant from undertaking this movement in the belief that the only feasible operation was a return to the overland approach; Halleck left the decision to Grant, but commented on the necessity for Grant to aid Banks in operations against Port Hudson (*off map, south*) before moving on Vicksburg. When Grant replied on 11 April that, once across the river, he planned to send a corps to aid Banks, Halleck was satisfied. Grant's plan provided that Sherman would initially remain before Vicksburg and confuse Pemberton by demonstrations and a false move back up the river. Also, Grierson's raid was timed to coincide with and to divert attention from Grant's crossing below Vicksburg.

The area through which Grant's troops were to travel was wide bottom land, cut by many streams which frequently made new channels in the soft soil, leaving crescent-shaped lakes (bayous) of stagnant water. Road construction in the swampy expanse was difficult and required much corduroy work. But, by 29 April, Grant had moved McPherson's and McClernand's corps to Hard Times (*lower left*), where Porter's fleet, which had passed Vicksburg successfully, joined them.

Though the Federals had been moving south since 5 April, Pemberton apparently did not learn of the movement until about 17 April. On the 28th, aware of the Union concentration near Hard Times, he correctly predicted an attack on Grand Gulf (*lower left*); but he sent only 5,000 reinforcements to Brig. Gen. John S. Bowen, his commander in that area, thus raising Bowen's strength to 9,000—Grant's force was still vastly superior. Pem-

berton's subsequent predicament was partially of his own making. Besieged with reports of the great damage being done by Grierson and given exaggerated estimates of the size of the raiding force, he had dispatched all of his cavalry and some infantry to intercept Grierson. Again, aware that Banks might move from Baton Rouge against Port Hudson, he hesitated to weaken its garrison, particularly since President Davis had repeatedly stressed the importance of the town. Further, a Union force was reported moving on Grenada (*off map, north*). Thus, when he should have concentrated the bulk of his force at Grand Gulf to oppose Grant's crossing, he acted indecisively and kept his forces far too dispersed.

On 29 April, Porter's gunboats attacked the Grand Gulf batteries, but the position was so strong that Grant decided to land farther downstream. His first thought was to cross at Rodney, but, being informed by a Negro that a good road led inland from Bruinsburg, he crossed McClernand and McPherson there, on 30 April, without Confederate opposition. On that day, Sherman was advised to bring the bulk of his force south. Maj. Gen. Frank Blair's division and Brig. Gen. John McArthur's brigade were left behind to guard the depots. McClernand, after an inexcusable delay, marched toward Port Gibson where, about midnight, he engaged in a skirmish with one of Bowen's brigades. The next morning (1 May), McClernand attacked. Bowen came up with his other brigade about noon, and McPherson arrived to assist McClernand. Eventually, the latter enveloped Bowen's north flank, and the Confederates withdrew that night. On 2 May, Grant pushed his troops forward, but delays at the destroyed bridges over the two forks of Bayou Pierre gave Bowen time to evacuate Grand Gulf.

By 7 May, the opposing forces were disposed as shown. Sherman had arrived at Hard Times and crossed to Grand Gulf that day. Pemberton now began assembling at Vicksburg the forces he had scattered throughout the length and breadth of Mississippi.

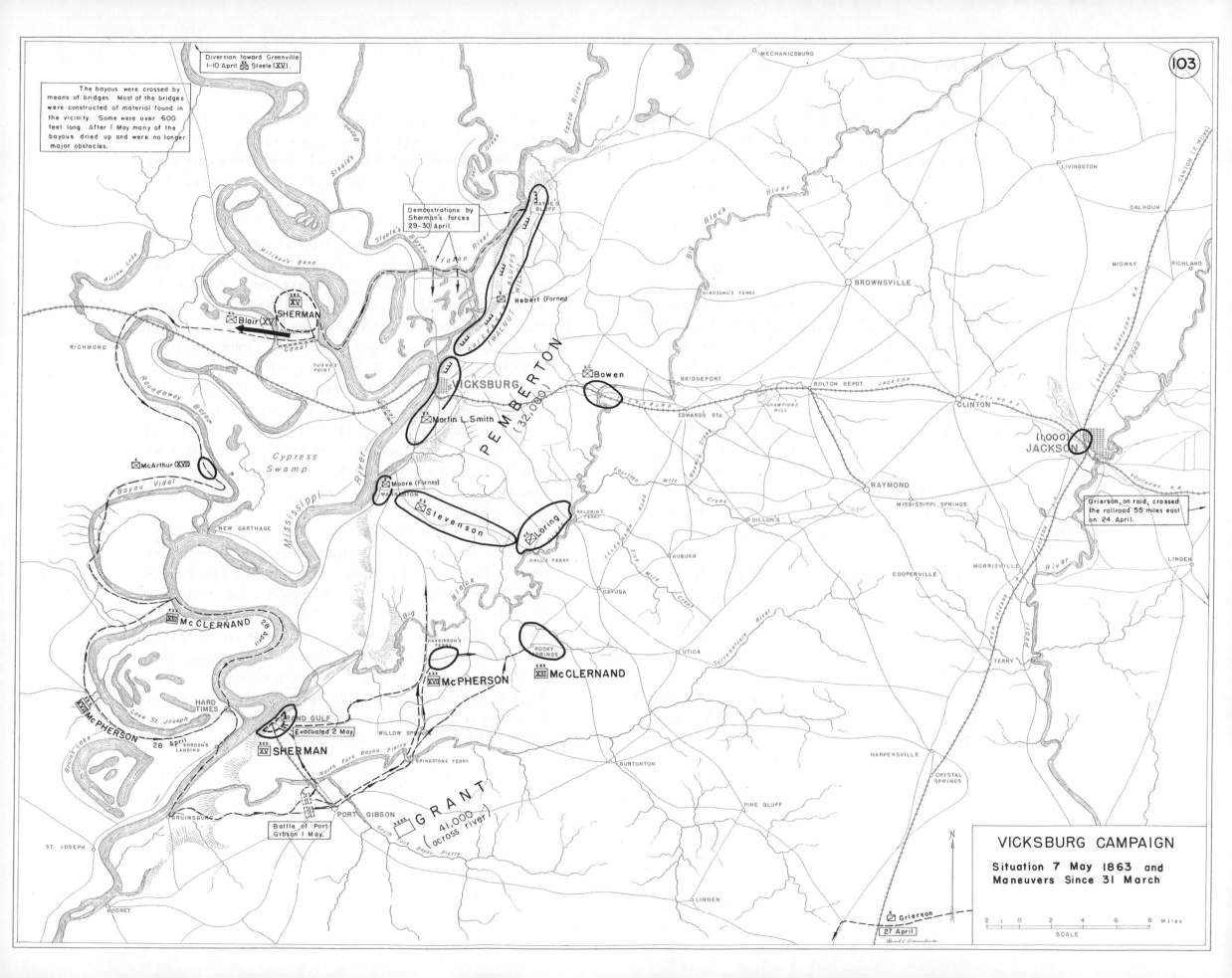

103

Diversion toward Greenville
1–10 April ⊠ Steele (XV).

The bayous were crossed by means of bridges. Most of the bridges were constructed of material found in the vicinity. Some were over 600 feet long. After 1 May many of the bayous dried up and were no longer major obstacles.

Demonstrations by Sherman's forces 29–30 April.

MECHANICSBURG

Yazoo River

HAYNE'S BLUFF

Deer Creek

Black River

LIVINGSTON

CALHOUN

Steele's Bayou

Steele's Bayou

Willow Lake

Milliken's Bend

SHERMAN ⦻ XV

⊠ Blair (XV)

Yazoo River

⊠ Hebert (Forney)

CHICKASAW BLUFFS

WALNUT HILLS

MIDWAY

RICHLAND

RICHMOND

Young's Point

Canal

⊠ Martin L. Smith

VICKSBURG

PEMBERTON (32,000)

×C ⊠ Bowen

BRIDGEPORT

Big Black River

BIRDSONG'S FERRY

BROWNSVILLE

BOLTON DEPOT

JACKSON

VICKSBURG RAILROAD

EDWARDS STA.

CHAMPIONS HILL

CLINTON

Cypress Swamp

Mississippi River

⊠ McArthur (XVII)

Bayou Vidal

Roundaway Bayou

⊠ Moore (Forney)
WARRENTON

⊠ Stevenson

⊠ Loring

HALL'S FERRY

BALDWIN'S FERRY

Fourteen Mile Creek

Baker's Creek

RAYMOND

MISSISSIPPI SPRINGS

(1,000) JACKSON

SOUTHERN R.R.

Grierson, on raid, crossed the railroad 55 miles east on 24 April.

NEW CARTHAGE

Lake St. Joseph

XIII McCLERNAND 28 April

Telegraph Road

Five Mile Creek

DILLON'S

AUBURN

COOPERVILLE

MORRISVILLE

LINDEN

CAYUGA

UTICA

Tallahatchie River

HARD TIMES

Big Black River

HANKINSON'S FERRY

ROCKY SPRINGS

XVII ⊠ McPHERSON

XIII ⊠ McCLERNAND

XVII McPHERSON 28 April

Bruin's Lake

SHROON'S LANDING

GRAND GULF
Evacuated 2 May.

XV SHERMAN

WILLOW SPRINGS

North Fork Bayou Pierre

GRINDSTONE FERRY

BURTONTON

HARPERSVILLE

CRYSTAL SPRINGS

Pearl River

TERRY

PINE BLUFF

BRUINSBURG

PORT GIBSON

GRANT 41,000 (across river)

South Fork Bayou Pierre

Battle of Port Gibson 1 May.

ST. JOSEPH

RODNEY

LINDEN

⊠ Grierson
27 April

VICKSBURG CAMPAIGN

Situation 7 May 1863 and Maneuvers Since 31 March

2 1 0   2   4   6   8 Miles

SCALE

It will be recalled Grant had promised Halleck that, once across the river, he would send a corps south to assist Banks in operations against Port Hudson. Apparently, it was Grant's intention to hold most of his army near Grand Gulf while McClernand's corps assisted Banks. Then both armies could be united for the final operation against Vicksburg. Now, on 2 May, he learned that Banks, having been on a wild-goose chase up the Red River (*off map, southwest*), would not be ready until 10 May, and then with only 15,000 men.

This turn of events had disastrous implications. The reward for which Grant had labored so long and desperately could well elude his grasp, for celerity of action was now of paramount importance. If he waited for Banks, Pemberton might be reinforced to a strength superior to that of the Union army. Further, Grant's long and tenuous supply line might be cut. On the other hand, if he advanced at once, his supply line would lengthen and become even more susceptible to interruption. Grant decided to sever connections with his base and to operate without a supply line—one of the boldest decisions made in the war. He calculated that the troops could live primarily off the land, but ammunition supply was a different matter. All available wagons (two per regiment) were crossed at Bruinsburg and loaded exclusively with ammunition, as were all animals and vehicles that could be requisitioned in the surrounding countryside. On 30 April, three days' rations were issued to the men, and Sherman was ordered to bring forward 120 wagons loaded with salt, sugar, coffee, and hardtack.

Grant now had to decide how to attack the Confederates. McPherson's reconnaissance north of the Big Black River had revealed Pemberton's concentration around Vicksburg, as shown on map 103. Grant also knew that a force was building up at Jackson. He therefore adopted a favorite Napoleonic maneuver and advanced so as to get between the two forces and destroy the one at Jackson.

Meanwhile, Pemberton, under orders from Davis to hold Vicksburg and simultaneously directed to concentrate and attack Grant by Joseph E. Johnston (who, on 24 November, 1862, had assumed over-all command in the west), decided to compromise. Believing that Grant might raid Jackson but could not long remain away from the river and his supplies, Pemberton concentrated his forces along the Big Black River (*center*).

On 11 May, Grant began his advance from Rocky Springs, and by nightfall his three corps were abreast as shown. That day, Pemberton sent Bowen to occupy Edward's Station (*center*). On the 12th, McClernand and Sherman encountered pickets along Fourteen Mile Creek, and McPherson had a stiff skirmish with troops at Raymond (*center, right*). That night, Grant appreciated that Pemberton now was building up Confederate strength at Edward's Station. By the 14th, Sherman and McPherson had reached Jackson, and McClernand, at Raymond and Clinton, blocked any Confederate advance from the west. That day, Johnston, who had arrived at Jackson (*right center*) on the 13th, made a stand there (*inset sketch*). Unable to stop the vigorous Union attacks, particularly that of McPherson, he evacuated the town late in the afternoon.

That night, Grant received from McPherson a copy of a message Johnston had dispatched to Pemberton the previous day. McPherson had received it from a Union agent. The message ordered Pemberton to move toward Clinton (*right center*) on Grant's rear, in order that the two Confederate forces might unite. Realizing that time was all-important and expecting that Pemberton was already complying with the order, Grant made plans to advance to the west and strike Pemberton at once.

The Confederate situation on the night of the 14th approached the ludicrous. Johnston was retreating to the northeast, and Pemberton, as will be seen, was preparing to advance to the southeast in search of a nonexistent Union supply line. Grant, well concentrated, was squarely between them.

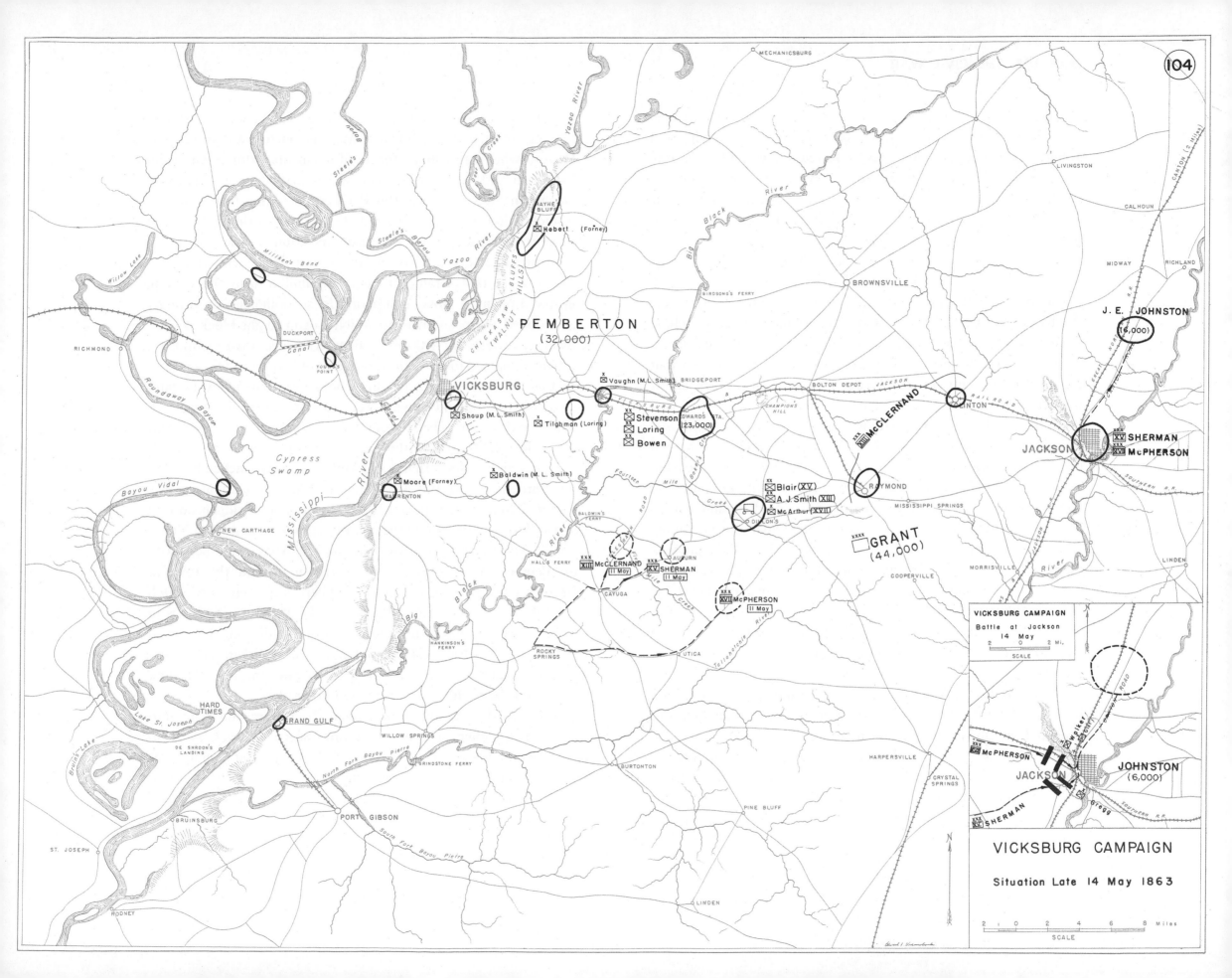

104

PEMBERTON
(32,000)

Hebert (Forney)

Vaughn (M.L. Smith)

Shoup (M.L. Smith)

Tilghman (Loring)

Stevenson
Loring
Bowen

EDWARDS
(23,000)

Moore (Forney)

Baldwin (M.L. Smith)

McCLERNAND

Blair (XV)
A.J. Smith (XIII)
McArthur (XVII)

GRANT
(44,000)

J. E. JOHNSTON
(6,000)

SHERMAN
McPHERSON
JACKSON

McCLERNAND
(11 May)

SHERMAN
(11 May)

McPHERSON
(11 May)

GRAND GULF

PORT GIBSON

VICKSBURG CAMPAIGN

Battle at Jackson
14 May

2   0   2 Mi.

SCALE

McPHERSON
JACKSON
JOHNSTON
(6,000)

Walker

Gregg

SHERMAN

VICKSBURG CAMPAIGN

Situation Late 14 May 1863

2 1 0   2   4   6   8 Miles

SCALE

Upon receipt of Johnston's order on 14 May, Pemberton called a council of war. The majority opinion favored carrying out Johnston's strategy; the minority preferred to attack Grant's communications. Pemberton hesitated to move away from Vicksburg, but adopted the minority plan. However, he decided to postpone until the 15th the movement toward Raymond designed to cut the imagined Union supply line.

By the night of the 15th, he had advanced from Edward's Station only as far as Champion's Hill, having been delayed by a not too diligent search for fords across the intervening creek. At the same time, McPherson and McClernand were approaching Champion's Hill (*right inset*), and Sherman was in Jackson destroying railroads and any industry of war value. Thus, on that night, the opposing armies bivouacked but four miles apart, neither aware of the presence of the other.

Early on 16 May, Confederate pickets skirmished with, and thus located, Grant's army. Now Pemberton received a second order from Johnston, written after the latter had evacuated Jackson but still directing that the two forces unite at Clinton— Johnston apparently expected that Grant would remain quietly at Jackson for a few days. Realizing that under the prevailing circumstances he could neither strike at Grant's "communications" nor move to Clinton, Pemberton elected to return to Edward's Station, whence he could either move northeast via Brownsville to unite with Johnston or return to Vicksburg. But, by 7:30 A.M., he was engaged with the Federal forces and had no choice but to stay at Champion's Hill and fight (*left inset sketches*).

Maj. Gen. Carter L. Stevenson's division occupied Champion's Hill (*not labeled*), and Pemberton's two other divisions occupied the ridge extending to the south. A ravine ran along the front of the position, and the hillsides were covered with dense forest and undergrowth. Brig. Gen. Alvin P. Hovey's division was the first to become engaged, and, by 11:00 A.M., had wrested part of the ridge from Stevenson. Meanwhile, McClernand kept his other two divisions in light contact with Bowen and Loring while

he sent a message to Grant asking what he should do. Attack, replied Grant and then hurried McPherson forward to support Hovey, who was calling for reinforcements. Maj. Gen. John Logan moved to Hovey's right and actually got a brigade in Stevenson's left and rear. But Pemberton, noting McClernand's disinclination to attack, ordered Bowen and Loring to move to support Stevenson in his precarious position on the left. Thus, such pressure was exerted on Hovey and Brig. Gen. Marcellus M. Crocker that Grant, probably unfamiliar with the terrain, moved Logan to Hovey's support. In so doing, he unwittingly abandoned the position from which Logan might block a Confederate retreat. By 4:00 P.M., Pemberton decided to withdraw. Loring remained to cover the movement of Bowen and Stevenson's remnants (*lower inset*), but his troops were cut off by Logan's aggressive action and he was forced to withdraw to the southeast. The next day, he reached Crystal Springs (*main map, lower right*). Grant lost 2,441 men in the engagement, and Pemberton 3,851.

That night, McClernand and McPherson bivouacked between the battlefield and Edward's Station, and Sherman at Bolton Depot. Pemberton, with 5,000 men, occupied a bridgehead east of Big Black River, while the rest of his force retreated to Vicksburg. The next morning, McClernand and McPherson advanced on Pemberton's position, while Sherman crossed the river at Bridgeport to attempt to cut off Pemberton as well as to watch for Johnston on that flank. Part of the Confederate force was in a trench on the east bank awaiting Loring; the remainder had been moved to the west bank that morning. When the Union forces stormed the trenches, the Confederates on the west bank destroyed the bridge, sacrificing their comrades.

On 18 May, Grant pushed on to Vicksburg and went into position as shown. The next morning, Sherman's cavalry occupied the abandoned Hayne's Bluff forts (*upper left*) and, after eighteen days, reopened communications along the Mississippi. On the 19th, Grant, believing that a prompt assault might win the town, attacked, but without success.

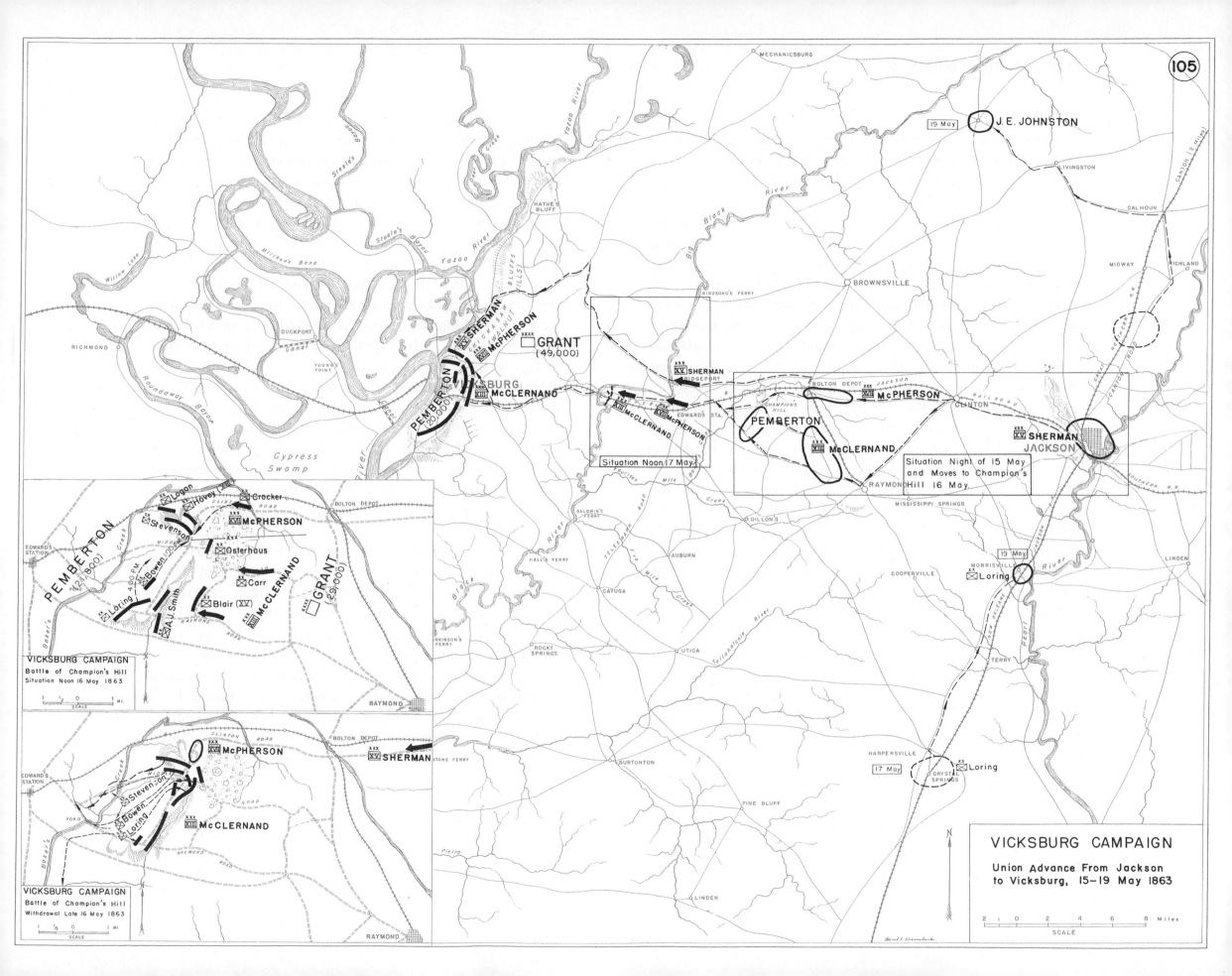

105

MECHANICSBURG

19 May J. E. JOHNSTON

LIVINGSTON

CANTON (2 MILES)

CALHOUN

MIDWAY

RICHLAND

BROWNSVILLE

Yazoo River

Black River

HAYNE'S
BLUFF

BIRDSONG'S FERRY

xxx
SHERMAN
Bridgeport

Big Black River

BOLTON DEPOT

xxx JACKSON
XVII McPHERSON

RAILROAD

CLINTON

SOUTHERN R. R.

xxx
SHERMAN
Steele's Bayou

GRANT
(49,000)

xx
SHERMAN
XV
XVII McPHERSON
Chickasaw
WALNUT HILLS

XIII
McCLERNAND

VICKSBURG

PEMBERTON
(20,000)

Situation Noon 17 May

CHAMPION'S HILL

PEMBERTON

xxx
XIII McCLERNAND

Situation Night of 15 May
and Moves to Champion's
Hill 16 May

RAYMOND

MISSISSIPPI SPRINGS

xxx
SHERMAN
JACKSON

Milliken's Bend

DUCKPORT
Canal

YOUNG'S
POINT

RICHMOND

Roundaway Bayou

Bayou

Cypress
Swamp

River

BALDWIN'S FERRY

Fourteen Mile Creek

Telegraph Road

HALL'S FERRY

AUBURN

O DILLON'S

Five Mile Creek

19 May

River

Loring

LINDEN

MORRISVILLE

COOPERVILLE

Loring

Battle of Champion's Hill inset:

Logan
Hovey
Crocker
BOLTON DEPOT

CLINTON ROAD

Stevenson
xxx
XVII McPHERSON

PEMBERTON
(21,800)

Osterhaus

Bowen
4:00 PM
MIDDLE ROAD

Carr

GRANT
(29,000)

Loring
A. J. Smith
RAYMOND ROAD

Blair (XV)

xxx
XIII McCLERNAND

EDWARD'S
STATION

Baker's Creek FORD

VICKSBURG CAMPAIGN
Battle of Champion's Hill
Situation Noon 16 May 1863

1 1/2 0 1 MI.
SCALE

Black River

JENKINSON'S FERRY

ROCKY SPRINGS

GAYUGA

UTICA

Tallahatchie River

River

TERRY

HARPERSVILLE

BURTONTON

17 May
CRYSTAL
SPRINGS

xx
Loring

PINE BLUFF

Second Champion's Hill inset:

CLINTON ROAD

xxx
XVII McPHERSON

BOLTON DEPOT
STONE FERRY

xxx
XV SHERMAN

Stevenson
MIDDLE ROAD

Bowen
Loring

xxx
XIII McCLERNAND

EDWARD'S
STATION

FORD

RAYMOND ROAD

VICKSBURG CAMPAIGN
Battle of Champion's Hill
Withdrawal Late 16 May 1863

1/2 0 1
SCALE

Pierre

OLINDEN

NEW ORLEANS JACKSON R.R.

VICKSBURG CAMPAIGN

Union Advance From Jackson
to Vicksburg, 15-19 May 1863

N

2 1 0 2 4 6 8 Miles
SCALE

Before resorting to a siege, Grant was determined to try one more assault (*sketch* a). The attack of 19 May had been hastily organized, but this one would be better coordinated. Porter's gunboats could aid in hammering the enemy batteries, Union artillery ammunition could be replenished, and the positions won on 19 May offered some advantage. Grant had good reasons for attempting the assault. If he could take Vicksburg now, Johnston's small force could be easily disposed of before it could be reinforced; then Grant could aid Banks in taking Port Hudson. The temper of his men encouraged an assault; a dull, dreary siege in the hot summer months was not enticing. Furthermore, an investment would require many more troops than Grant now had, and, while it was in progress, his long supply line down the Mississippi might be interdicted. Hence, at 10:00 A.M., 22 May, the assault was launched. The confident Union troops advanced gallantly, but only at a few points were they able to reach the parapet of the strong Confederate fortifications. Not all the Confederates had suffered the demoralization of defeat at Champion's Hill and Big Black River, and those who had had regained their confidence, once they were within the fortifications. Hence, the resistance was spirited. By 11:30 A.M., Grant was convinced that the assault had failed, but now he began to receive optimistic messages from McClernand. The last of these arrived about 1:00 P.M. and indicated that two forts were in Union hands (actually, only one fort had been occupied temporarily). Grant therefore decided to continue the attack, ordering Sherman and McPherson to renew the assault and instructing the latter to reinforce McClernand with one division. By dark, it was obvious that McClernand had not properly assessed the situation, for the Federals were repulsed everywhere. The attack cost Grant 3,200 casualties, half of which he attributed to the prolongation of the battle.

Before considering the siege which was now necessary, it would be well to examine Johnston's final order to Pemberton, given on 17 May. That day, after the defeat at Big Black River, Pemberton had advised Johnston that he was withdrawing to Vicksburg. Immediately, the latter had wired him to evacuate that city, if it were not too late, and save his army from surrender. Again Pemberton resorted to a council of war, which concluded that it was impossible to withdraw; thus he ignored not only Johnston's good advice but his positive order as well. Johnston, when informed of the situation, exhibited remarkable self-restraint in advising Pemberton to hold out while he attempted to gather a relief force. Indeed, he did labor to gather a force, but, considering Bragg's and Lee's situations at the time, reinforcements were not easily obtained. When he finally began an advance to relieve the fortress, only 31,000 troops were present for duty, although he had 55,000 on paper.

Meanwhile, Grant methodically went about laying siege to the city (*sketch* b). He brought down reinforcements from Hurlbut's corps and completely invested the fortress. At the same time, Sherman carefully watched for any advance by Johnston. Approaches were dug, and mines and countermines were employed as the ring closed ever tighter. The monotonous siege dragged on, with men dying daily from the mining, sniping, and artillery fire.

For McClernand, though, things were livelier. On 30 May, he issued a congratulatory order to his troops, claiming most of the credit for the success of the campaign. Sherman and McPherson were furious, the former pointing out that if McClernand had led, it was usually in the wrong direction. On 18 June, Grant relieved McClernand, finally weary of his troublemaking.

Eventually, Pemberton's force was reduced to a state of starvation, and orders were issued by Grant for a final assault. But it was unnecessary, for, on 4 July, the Confederates surrendered. Immediately, Sherman, who was aware of Johnston's approach and had been making preparations, was ordered to move to attack that general.

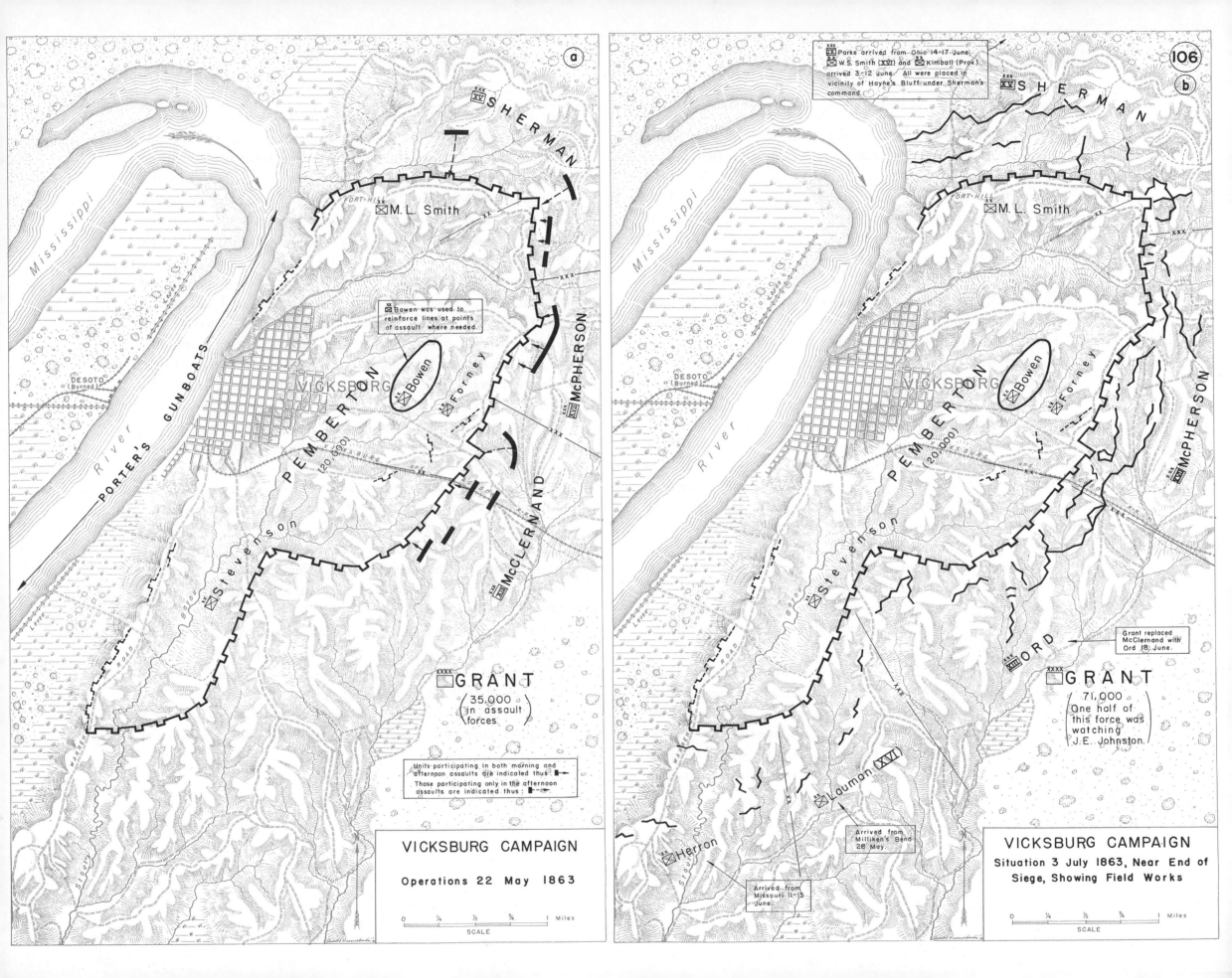

106

Map a (left):

XXX
XV SHERMAN

FORT HILL

M. L. Smith

XXX

Bowen was used to
reinforce lines at points
of assault where needed.

Bowen

Forney

VICKSBURG

PEMBERTON
(20,000)

Stevenson

McCLERNAND

McPHERSON

XVII

XIII

River

Mississippi

PORTER'S GUNBOATS

DESOTO
(Burned)

WARREN ROAD

XXXX
GRANT
(35,000
in assault
forces)

Units participating in both morning and
afternoon assaults are indicated thus:

Those participating only in the afternoon
assaults are indicated thus:

VICKSBURG CAMPAIGN

Operations 22 May 1863

0   ¼   ½   ¾   1 Miles
SCALE

Map b (right):

XXX Parke arrived from Ohio 14-17 June;
IX W.S. Smith XVI and Kimball (Prov.)
arrived 3-12 June. All were placed in
vicinity of Hayne's Bluff under Sherman's
command.

XXX
XV SHERMAN

FORT HILL

M. L. Smith

XXX

Bowen

Forney

VICKSBURG

PEMBERTON
(20,000)

Stevenson

McPHERSON

XVII

ORD
XIII

Grant replaced
McClernand with
Ord 18 June.

River

Mississippi

DESOTO
(Burned)

WARREN ROAD

Lauman XVI

Herron

Arrived from
Milliken's Bend
28 May.

Arrived from
Missouri 11-15
June.

XXXX
GRANT
(71,000
One half of
this force was
watching
J.E. Johnston.)

VICKSBURG CAMPAIGN

**Situation 3 July 1863, Near End of
Siege, Showing Field Works**

0   ¼   ½   ¾   1 Miles
SCALE

Even while Grant invested Vicksburg, he kept a wary eye on Johnston. As the Federal forces were built up, Grant formed a covering force (*not shown*) to the east and north of his main army. One division was stationed in the vicinity of the Big Black River railroad bridge; another reconnoitered as far north as Mechanicsburg; spies and scouts were sent into Confederate-held territory. Johnston, it was learned, was at Canton (*just off map, northeast*) gathering his forces. By 10 June, the greater part of Burnside's IX Corps—moved to Cincinnati after the Battle of Fredericksburg—was transferred to Grant under the command of Maj. Gen. John G. Parke. This corps now formed the nucleus of a special task force with the sole mission of preventing Johnston from interfering with the siege. Grant placed Sherman in command of this force on 22 June; Steele took over Sherman's former corps. Shortly thereafter, Sherman had the force disposed from Hayne's Bluff to the Big Black River (*dashed blue oval*) with cavalry pickets out to the north and east. Ord picketed the Big Black River to the south of the railroad. Nor did Grant ignore the area across the river from Vicksburg. Kirby Smith's forces made half-hearted efforts to advance to Vicksburg, but Porter's gunboats, plus troops from Hurlbut's corps (*not shown*), repulsed the only serious effort—that made at Miliken's Bend on 7 June.

On 28 June, Johnston advanced to Pemberton's relief and, by 1 July, he had reached the Big Black River, as shown. He spent the next three days reconnoitering. In all likelihood, had he advanced on 2 or 3 July, he would have been rebuffed, for the vigilant Sherman was well advised of his actions and well disposed to counter any attack. But he did not advance and, on 4 July, upon learning of Pemberton's capitulation, countermarched to Jackson. Sherman, advised by Grant as early as 22 June to be ready to move against Johnston's army on short notice, was on the heels of the Confederates by nightfall of the 4th. Reinforced with Ord's corps, he closed in upon Johnston, who had entered the defensive works around Jackson. To Johnston's dismay, Sherman refrained from an attack on the strong Confederate position and prepared to invest the city. The former, accordingly, withdrew before the trap could be closed. Thus, the Vicksburg campaign came to an end. With the fall of Vicksburg, Port Hudson, under siege by Banks since 24 May, could no longer resist, and on 9 July this fortress, accepting the inevitable, likewise surrendered.

Grant's casualties from 1 May until Vicksburg surrendered totaled 9,362, exceeding by only one man the total suffered by Grant (but not including Buell) at Shiloh. It was indeed a cheap price to pay for the strategic results achieved—the splitting of the Confederacy and the control of the Mississippi River. In the eighteen days from the time he had crossed the river at Bruinsburg until he arrived at Vicksburg, Grant had marched almost 200 miles, keeping his army concentrated, and had defeated the Confederates in four separate engagements. Well could Sherman say, as he looked down on the Mississippi River on 19 May, that until then he had not been certain the operation would succeed, but that, even if Vicksburg were never taken, it had nevertheless been a successful campaign.

The turning point in the war had been reached, for as Grant tended to the business of feeding Pemberton's starved troops on 4 July, Lee's shattered army was retreating from Gettysburg.

Grierson's raid, one of the war's most successful, had helped Grant immensely. With 1,000 men, he marched 600 miles in seventeen days, captured 500 men and 1,000 horses, destroyed fifty miles of railroad, fought four engagements, and—most important of all—diverted Pemberton's attention from Grant and drew the Confederate cavalry away from the critical Vicksburg area.

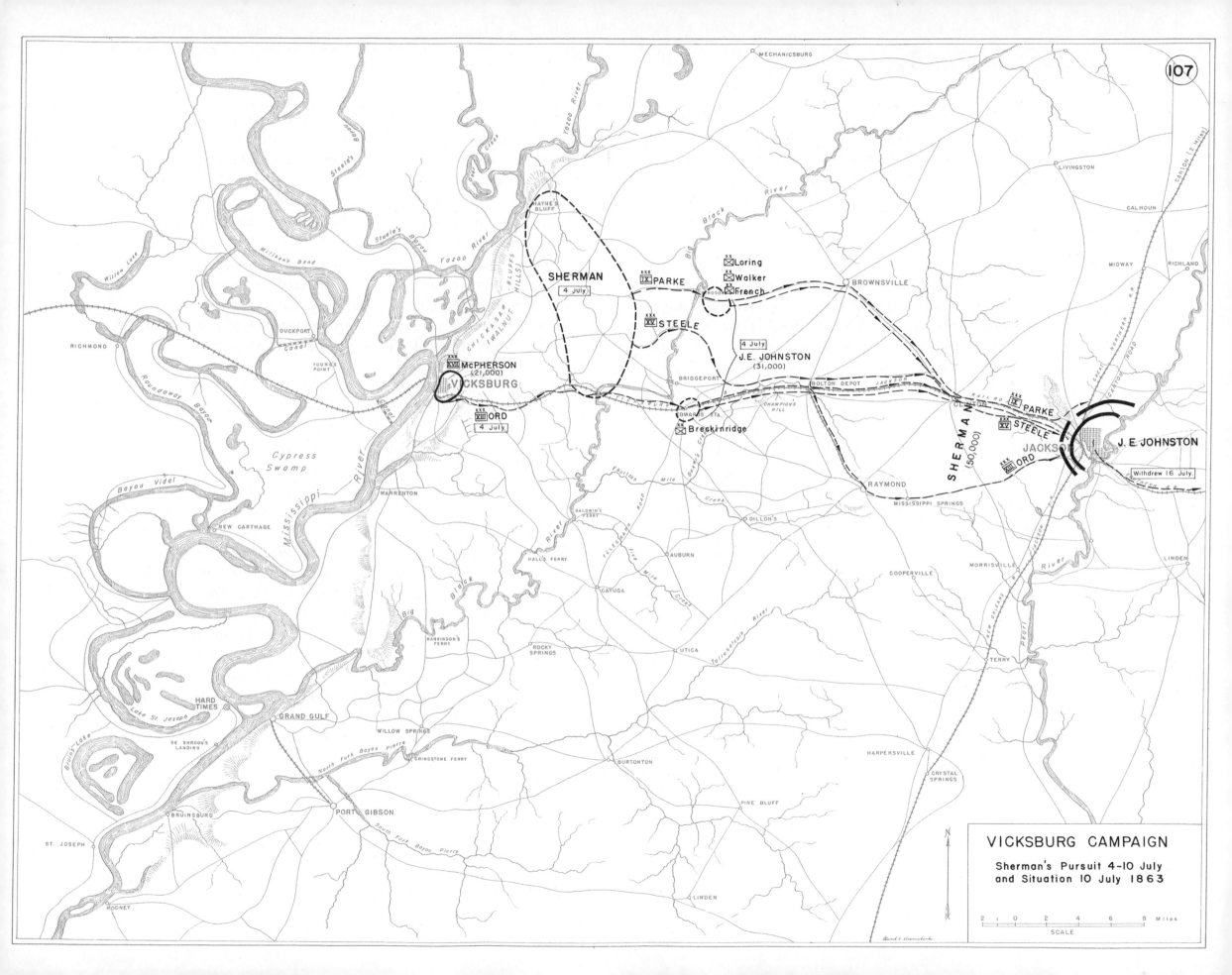

107

SHERMAN
4 July

XXX IX PARKE

XX Loring
XX Walker
XX French

XXX XV STEELE

4 July
J.E. JOHNSTON
(31,000)

XXX XVII McPHERSON
(21,000)

VICKSBURG

XXX XIII ORD
4 July

XX Breckinridge

BROWNSVILLE

BRIDGEPORT
BOLTON DEPOT   JACKSON
CLINTON
EDWARDS STA.   CHAMPION'S
                    HILL

XXX IX PARKE
XXX XV STEELE

SHERMAN
(50,000)

JACKSON   J. E. JOHNSTON

XXX XIII ORD
Withdrew 16 July.

RAYMOND

MISSISSIPPI SPRINGS

VICKSBURG CAMPAIGN

Sherman's Pursuit 4-10 July
and Situation 10 July 1863

2 1 0   2   4   6   8 Miles
SCALE

After the Battle of Stones River in January, 1863, Bragg withdrew and took position south of Murfreesboro. One corps was stationed at Shelbyville and the other at Wartrace, both in strong positions. His cavalry screened both flanks, and infantry pickets controlled the mountain gaps to the north, through which ran the likely Union routes of advance. Rosecrans occupied the area around Murfreesboro and seemed to be content to remain there.

Outnumbered as he was, and with Vicksburg receiving priority for troops, Bragg had to remain on the defensive, making every effort to prevent Union seizure of Chattanooga. This city was of great strategic importance to the Confederacy. It was an important railroad junction, the loss of which would throttle one of the South's east-west routes. Also, the city, in Union hands, would turn the Allegheny barrier on the south and simplify a drive into Georgia or an advance to Knoxville (*just off map, northeast*). Thus, the Federals might well achieve Lincoln's long-cherished plan of liberating the pro-Union inhabitants of eastern Tennessee and northern Georgia.

If these considerations gave meaning to Bragg's mission, they also acted as a spur to the authorities in Washington. Halleck constantly prodded Rosecrans during the winter, urging him to begin an advance. But the latter obstinately refused to do so, offering as his principal reason the ridiculous theory that such an advance might cause Bragg to join with Pemberton and thus complicate Grant's problem. The bickering continued to the point of Rosecrans' being threatened with relief if he did not advance. The grace period came and went, but Rosecrans stayed on and icily informed Washington that he would not be browbeaten and would do his duty for the sake of his country. Halleck, instead of relieving him, merely protested "against the expense to which [Rosecrans] put the government for telegrams."

Both Bragg and Rosecrans occupied themselves with the favorite—and generally profitless—practice of sending cavalry on raids. In February, Wheeler went after Fort Donelson (*off map, northwest*), and failed dismally; in March, Rosecrans sent a detachment to cut Bragg's communications, and lost it; Forrest bungled a raid on Rosecrans' communications; and Morgan made his famous trek into Ohio and Pennsylvania, which ended in his capture. In all, the Confederates lost 4,000 cavalrymen, but did cause Rosecrans some concern over his supply lines. The Union lost 3,300 men and received little in return.

Finally, on 26 June, Rosecrans was ready to move. His strategy was sound: Maj. Gen. David S. Stanley's cavalry corps and the Reserve Corps were to move around the generally open flank toward Shelbyville to deceive Bragg into believing that this was the main effort; meanwhile, the infantry corps would traverse the gaps and the rugged country to the east and turn the Confederate right flank. Despite the pouring rain, which made all movements over the ·muddy roads extremely difficult, the maneuver deceived Bragg and was highly successful. By 30 June, after some small but stiff fights at the gaps, Rosecrans had reached Manchester, and Bragg had withdrawn to Tullahoma.

Once under way, Rosecrans could move rapidly, as he now demonstrated. He immediately sought to seize the crossings over Elk River behind the Confederates and thus isolate them from their base. Bragg, however, managed to evade the trap, though only after leaving some supplies and guns behind. The Federals followed so rapidly that he could not take up another position behind Elk River. Presumably because the mountain range between Salem and Tracy City (which formed the next natural defensive position) had the Tennessee River close to its rear, Bragg withdrew all the way to Chattanooga, arriving there on 4 July.

Thus, in nine days of very skillful maneuvering, Rosecrans had forced Bragg across the Tennessee and, in so doing, had suffered only 560 casualties.

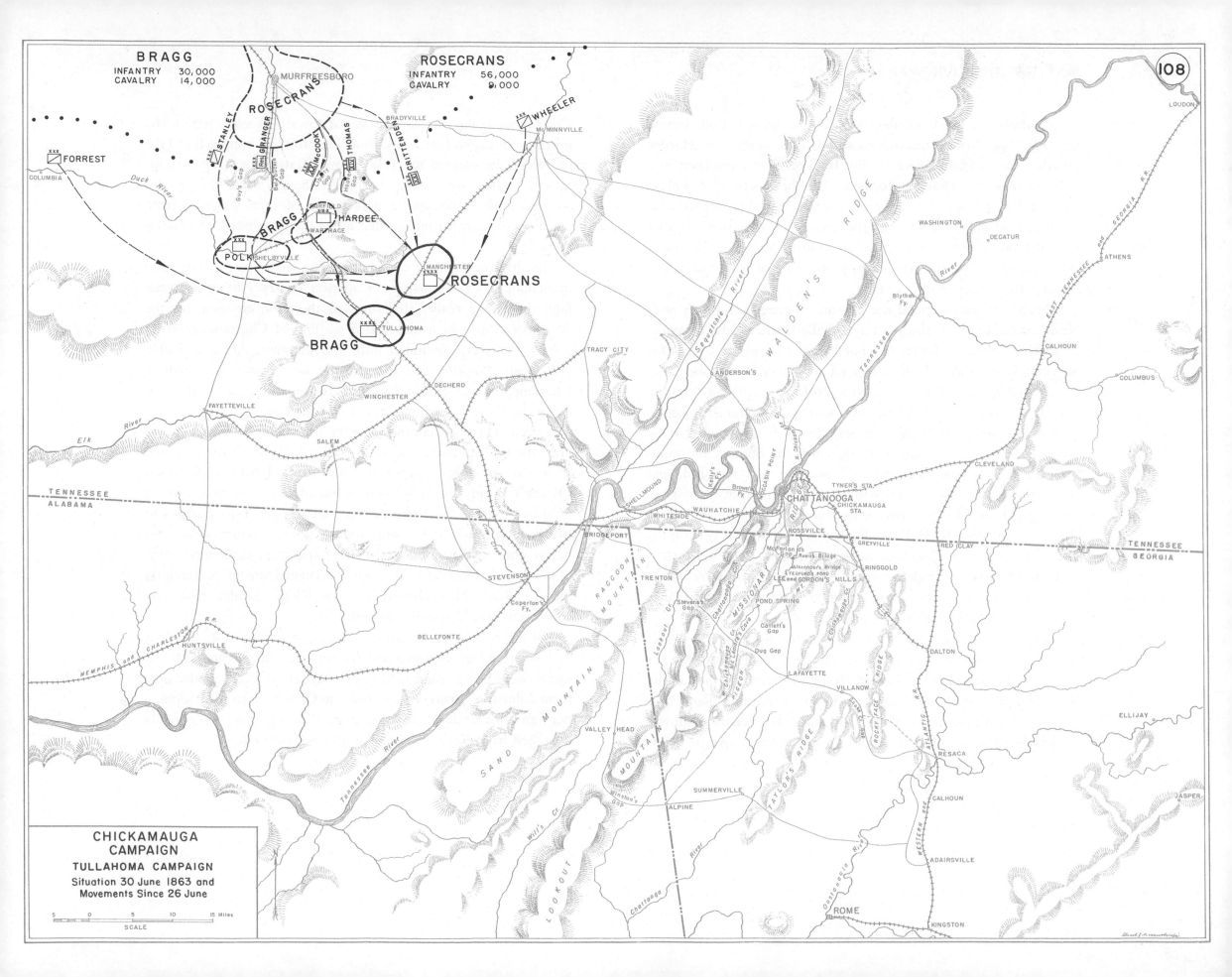

108

BRAGG
INFANTRY 30,000
CAVALRY 14,000

ROSECRANS
INFANTRY 56,000
CAVALRY 9,000

FORREST

MURFREESBORO

ROSECRANS

STANLEY

GRANGER

McCOOK

THOMAS

BRADYVILLE

WHEELER
McMINNVILLE

CRITTENDEN

HARDEE

FAIRFIELD

WARTRACE

BRAGG

POLK SHELBYVILLE

MANCHESTER

ROSECRANS

TULLAHOMA

BRAGG

LOUDON

WASHINGTON

DECATUR

ATHENS

BLYTHE Fy.

CALHOUN

COLUMBUS

TRACY CITY

ANDERSON'S

WALDEN'S RIDGE

CLEVELAND

WINCHESTER

DECHERD

FAYETTEVILLE

SALEM

Elk River

TENNESSEE
ALABAMA

HUNTSVILLE

BELLEFONTE

STEVENSON

BRIDGEPORT

SHELLMOUND

WHITESIDE

WAUHATCHIE

CHATTANOOGA

CHICKAMAUGA STA.

ROSSVILLE

GREYVILLE

RINGGOLD

FRED CLAY

TENNESSEE
GEORGIA

TRENTON

COPERTON'S Fy.

RACCOON MOUNTAIN

LEE and GORDON'S MILLS

DALTON

VALLEY HEAD

SAND MOUNTAIN

LAFAYETTE

VILLANOW

RESACA

ELLIJAY

LOOKOUT MOUNTAIN

SUMMERVILLE

ALPINE

TAYLOR'S RIDGE

CALHOUN

JASPER

ADAIRSVILLE

CHICKAMAUGA
CAMPAIGN

TULLAHOMA CAMPAIGN

Situation 30 June 1863 and
Movements Since 26 June

ROME

KINGSTON

SCALE

Bragg stationed his Confederate forces as shown. Polk busied himself strengthening the defenses of Chattanooga, and Hardee guarded the railroad to Knoxville. Buckner (now returned in a prisoner-of-war exchange program) had his corps of 9,000 in the vicinity of Knoxville (*off map, northwest*). One brigade held a bridgehead at Bridgeport, and the cavalry was disposed on either side of Chattanooga, ostensibly for security purposes. However, being on the east bank, the cavalry could be of little aid in discerning Rosecrans' movements.

Rosecrans had stopped the pursuit of Bragg on 4 July with his advanced corps on the line Fayetteville-Decherd-McMinnville, as shown. There his forces remained until 15 August, except for Sheridan's division, which advanced to Stevenson. During this month and a half, Halleck fumed at Rosecrans' procrastination. The latter resisted all efforts of the Union administration to coerce him into advancing. He steadfastly maintained that he could not successfully attack Bragg until the corn in the fields ripened, the railroad forward to Stevenson was repaired, and support was provided for his flanks—by Grant from Mississippi on his right, and by an advance by Burnside from Cincinnati to Knoxville on his left. Halleck did not believe such a preponderance of force was necessary, considering Bragg's strength. Further, he feared the excessive delay would enable Johnston to reinforce Bragg. Finally, Rosecrans was peremptorily ordered to advance on 4 August; twelve days later, he obeyed.

Note that not until he began his advance did Rosecrans close to the river with his entire army. This was probably wise, for such a move would have enabled Bragg to ascertain more easily the principal point of crossing, or would have required Rosecrans to make a flank march in the face of his foe. His general plan was to turn Bragg's position. He could do this either above or below Chattanooga, but, since an advance toward Washington in the north would take him away from his principal supply line (the railroad), he elected to cross below Chattanooga. The troops moved to the river, using the routes shown, while the cavalry covered both flanks, and a detachment of three brigades from Crittenden's corps demonstrated along the river north of Chattanooga.

By 20 August, the Federal army had closed to the river, and immediately began crossing at Caperton's Ferry. Not until a week later did Bragg realize that this was the main crossing, for the demonstration, which included a shelling of Chattanooga from across the river, continued until 1 September. Also, he had a preconceived notion that the crossing would be made north of Chattanooga—to enable Burnside to cooperate, as well as to avoid the difficult terrain southwest of the city.

Indeed, the mountainous country that confronted Rosecrans after the river crossing was formidable. A glance at the map will show that, in order to reach the Western and Atlantic Railroad (Bragg's supply line), Rosecrans would have to cross a series of ridges, valleys, and streams, all running generally parallel to the Tennessee River. The only roads—poor, country ones—connected the small towns in the valleys and crossed the mountains at the few gaps indicated. It was in this rugged terrain, particularly the Lookout Mountain–Missionary Ridge locale, that two campaigns would soon be fought.

Bragg had been preparing for the impending test. Buckner had been alerted to move to Chattanooga, and other reinforcements were being readied. Maj. Gen. W. H. T. Walker's division, from Johnston's army, was en route to Chattanooga by 4 September, and three days later Longstreet's corps was temporarily detached from Lee's army and started westward.

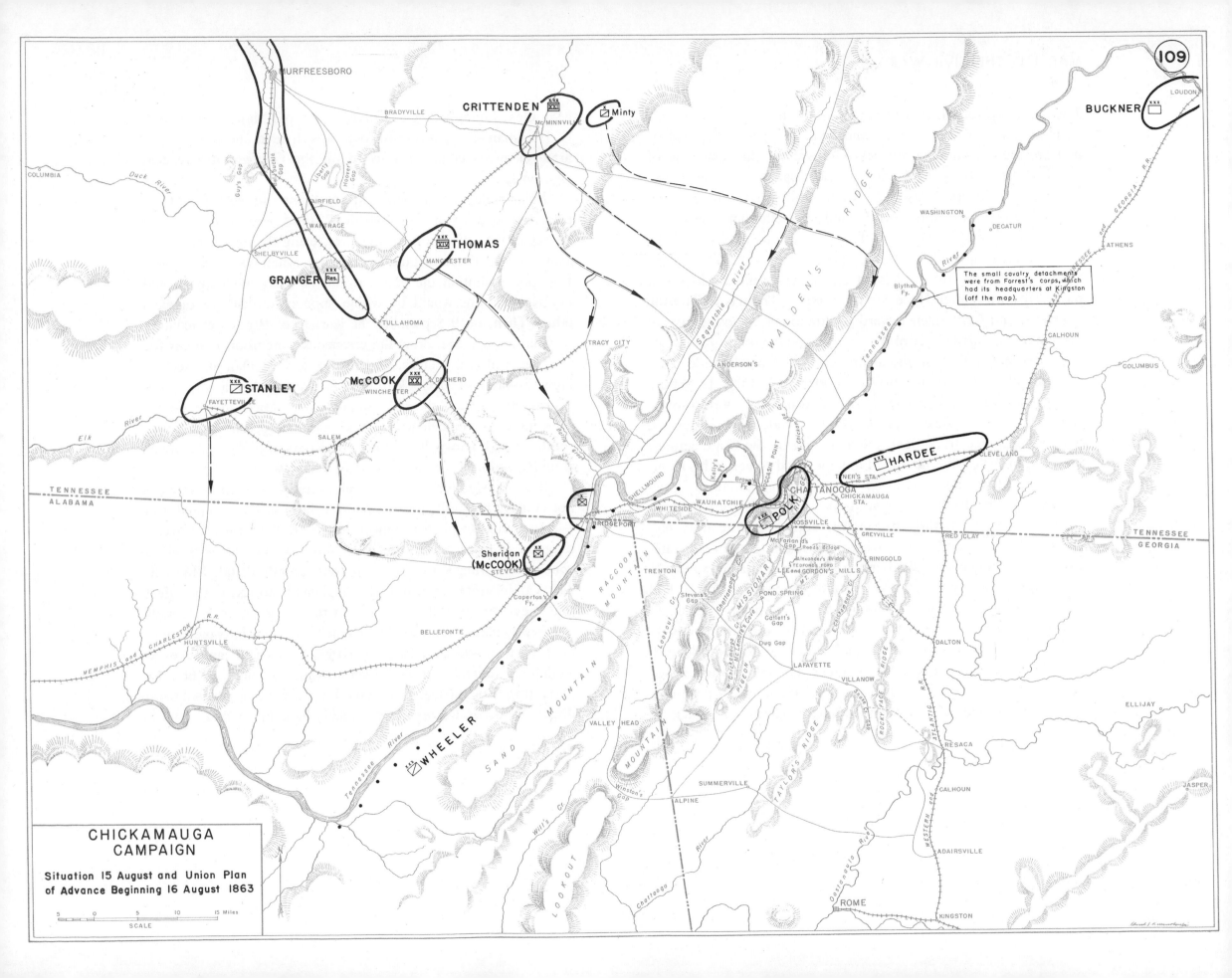

COLUMBIA

MURFREESBORO

BRADYVILLE

Duck River

Guy's Gap

Bell Buckle Gap

Liberty Gap

Hoover's Gap

AIRFIELD

WARTRACE

SHELBYVILLE

CRITTENDEN XXX XXI

McMINNVILLE

X Minty

LOUDON

BUCKNER XXX

WASHINGTON

DECATUR

ATHENS

THOMAS XXX XIV

MANCHESTER

GRANGER XXX Res.

TULLAHOMA

TRACY CITY

ANDERSON'S

Saguatchie River

WALDEN'S RIDGE

Tennessee River

Blythe's Fy.

The small cavalry detachments
were from Forrest's corps, which
had its headquarters at Kingston
(off the map).

CALHOUN

COLUMBUS

STANLEY XXX

FAYETTEVILLE

McCOOK XXX XX

DECHERD

WINCHESTER

SALEM

Elk River

TENNESSEE
ALABAMA

SHELLMOUND

WHITESIDE

WAUHATCHIE

Kelly's Fy.

Brown's Fy.

MOCCASIN POINT

N. Chickamauga Cr.

CHATTANOOGA

CHICKAMAUGA STA.

HARDEE XXX

TINER'S STA.

CLEVELAND

BRIDGEPORT

POLK XXX

ROSSVILLE

GREYVILLE

RED CLAY

TENNESSEE
GEORGIA

Sheridan
(McCOOK) XX

STEVENSON

McFarland's Gap

Reed's Bridge

Alexander's Bridge

Tedford's Ford

LEE and GORDON'S MILLS

RINGGOLD

RACCOON MOUNTAIN

TRENTON

Caperton's Fy.

Stevens's Gap

POND SPRING

Catlett's Gap

Dug Gap

MISSIONARY RIDGE

LAFAYETTE

DALTON

BELLEFONTE

Memphis and Charleston R.R.

HUNTSVILLE

W. Chickamauga Cr.

Pigeon Mt.

McLemore's Cove

E. Chickamauga Cr.

VILLANOW

Rocky Face

Western and Atlantic R.R.

RESACA

VALLEY HEAD

LOOKOUT MOUNTAIN

SUMMERVILLE

TAYLOR'S RIDGE

CALHOUN

ELLIJAY

WHEELER XXX

SAND MOUNTAIN

Tennessee River

Winston's Gap

ALPINE

Will's Cr.

Chattooga River

LOOKOUT MT.

ROME

Oostanola River

Coosawatee River

ADAIRSVILLE

JASPER

KINGSTON

CHICKAMAUGA
CAMPAIGN

Situation 15 August and Union Plan
of Advance Beginning 16 August 1863

5   0   5   10   15 Miles
SCALE

Though Rosecrans had sufficient pontons for only one bridge, he made judicious use of rafts and boats, and, by 4 September, had crossed his entire army, less Granger, to the east bank of the Tennessee River. McCook, less Sheridan (*not shown*) who crossed at Bridgeport, used the Caperton's Ferry crossing site; Thomas crossed at both of these and at Shellmound; and Crittenden also used the last site. Then, in accordance with Rosecrans' plan to sever Bragg's supply line, the corps marched to the east on the only three roads traversing the mountains. McCook moved toward Valley Head (*lower center*), Thomas to Trenton (*center*), and Crittenden toward Chattanooga. Apprehensive of his flanks and particularly of the open one on the south, Rosecrans allocated McCook all of his cavalry, except for one brigade. That brigade, plus an infantry brigade under Col. John T. Wilder which Rosecrans had previously mounted in an attempt to overcome his cavalry deficiency, rode with Crittenden. Thus Thomas, who was destined to be dealt the first blow by the Confederates, marched in the center, devoid of any mounted screen to his front.

While Rosecrans advanced across the mountains, Bragg concentrated his forces in preparation for a battle. On 8 September, he learned conclusively that the entire Federal army had crossed the river and was moving against his rear. Forrest and Buckner having been called in by this time, Bragg evacuated Chattanooga and moved his army south to Lafayette. D. H. Hill (*not shown*), who had just been transferred from Virginia to replace Hardee, used one division to hold the mountain gaps on Thomas' front, while Wheeler and Forrest scouted and delayed the advance of McCook and Crittenden. The information Bragg had of his foe was a true depiction of Rosecrans' dispositions, for on the evening of 9 September, when ordering an attack on Maj. Gen. James S. Negley's division, he told Maj. Gen. Thomas C. Hindman that Rosecrans' force was divided and that its separate elements could be crushed—if the Confederates reacted vigorously.

Meanwhile, how and why had Rosecrans allowed himself to be placed in such a vulnerable position? It has been mentioned that he began the advance from the river, using the only three roads available. He thus accepted the fact that when his corps reached Lookout Mountain the flanks would be forty miles apart, and no two columns would be within supporting distance of each other. Then, on 9 September, he learned of Bragg's evacuation of Chattanooga and drew the erroneous conclusion that his foe was demoralized, hungry, and fleeing toward Dalton. Accordingly, he ordered McCook to push forward to Alpine and to use his cavalry to break the railroad at Resaca (*lower right*). At the same time, Crittenden was to take Chattanooga and then turn south through Ringgold, supposedly in pursuit of Bragg. Thomas would continue his advance toward Lafayette.

Rosecrans' failure to have cavalry screening his entire front—not entirely his fault since he had too little of the mounted arm—contributed to his being misinformed. But he was also overly sanguine in his interpretation of such information as he received concerning Bragg's activities and consequently deluded himself. The Confederates appear to have planted stories to the effect that they were in full flight, and in this information Rosecrans apparently placed considerable reliance. Thus, misinformed about his foe's dispositions, Rosecrans, after his brilliant maneuver at Tullahoma and his successful river crossing, was about to blunder into a trap. But whether Bragg could take advantage of the Union dispersion depended upon how quickly he could strike.

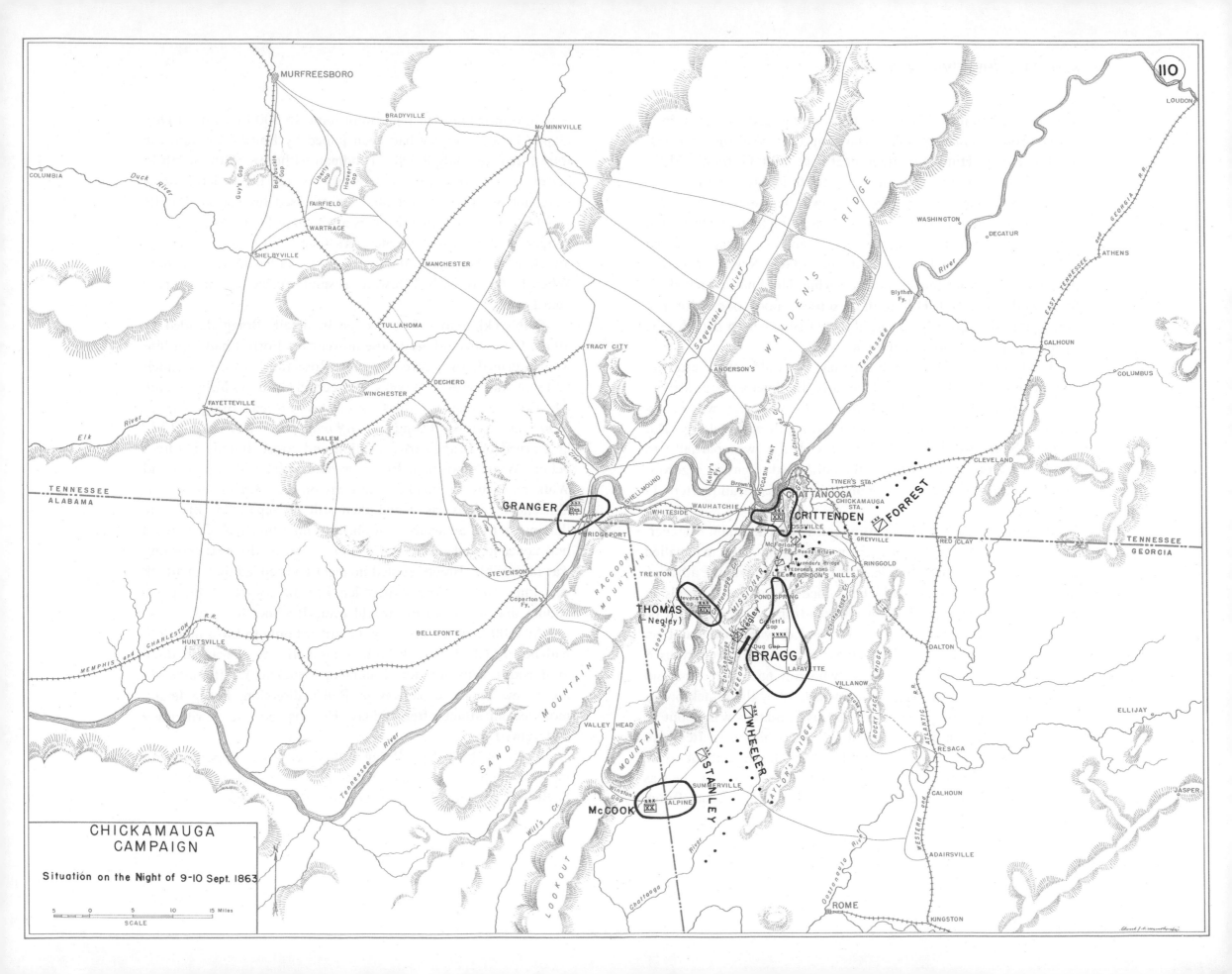

CHICKAMAUGA
CAMPAIGN

Situation on the Night of 9-10 Sept. 1863

5 0 5 10 15 Miles
SCALE

Late on 9 September, Negley's division emerged from Stevens's Gap en route to his position at Dug Gap (*sketch* a, *right center*). That evening, Hindman, then near Lee and Gordon's Mills, received orders from Bragg to move south in McLemore's Cove and attack Negley. Starting before dawn, he moved timidly and only to Pond Spring (*right center*), encamping there while a small force went forward to reconnoiter. Meanwhile, Bragg ordered Hill to move through Dug Gap and attack Negley frontally, presumably to hold him in position while Hindman attacked his flank and rear. But Hill found excuses—poor ones—for not attacking; consequently, Bragg directed Buckner to detach part of his troops to support Hindman.

By 1:30 P.M., Hill concluded that he could attack after all and moved to Dug Gap. Simultaneously, Buckner's troops arrived to join Hindman below Pond Spring. Now Negley was neatly entrapped—providing Hindman moved south with celerity. But nothing happened that day. For this, Bragg was partially to blame: instead of appearing on the battlefield to ensure vigorous execution of his orders, he remained at his headquarters in Lafayette.

That night, 10 September, Bragg ordered Hindman, Buckner, and Hill to attack Negley early the next morning. Hindman called a council of war at which it was decided to postpone the advance until more information could be gained about the Federals at Stevens's Gap. Should they appear too strong, or should Hill be unable to attack, Hindman recommended withdrawal and an attack on Crittenden instead. But the intransigent Bragg refused and summarily ordered Hindman, who still had part command of Buckner's troops as well as his own, to obey the attack order.

The next morning, however, just as Hindman was about to march, Bragg made the mistake of informing him of Crittenden's and McCook's whereabouts. Hindman felt himself about to be surrounded and advanced very cautiously. By 11:00 A.M., he was still two miles north of the Dug Gap–Stevens's Gap road. Bragg now informed him that there were some 15,000 Federals at Dug Gap. (Though Negley had been joined by Baird's division, the total force was only 8,000.) Hindman withdrew to the north in alarm. Later, upon learning from scouts that the Federal forces were not as large as estimated, he reversed his march. But he was too late—the Federal forces at the gap, finally aware of the danger, had retreated to Stevens's Gap. Hill, under orders to attack when he heard Hindman's guns, waited in vain all day. When he finally pushed forward at sundown, he met only a rear guard.

Still seeking to defeat his foe in detail, Bragg decided to attack Crittenden, about whose movements Forrest had kept him well informed. In accordance with Rosecrans' plan, Crittenden had sent one division (Wood's) to Lee and Gordon's Mills (*sketch* b), while his other two divisions moved to Reed's Bridge (*upper right*) and on toward Ringgold (*off map, east*). But, on the 12th, he learned of Bragg's true location and concentrated his forces behind Wood's position. Bragg ordered Polk, with his own and Walker's corps, to attack Wood early on the 13th, believing that Crittenden's divisions would then still be separated. But, late that night (12 September), Polk informed him that Crittenden had concentrated and that for him to attack the next morning was impossible. Bragg erupted in anger and replied that an attack was imperative before Crittenden became aware of his peril, adding that he personally would bring Buckner forward.

At 9:00 A.M. the next day, he arrived only to learn that Polk had not attacked, though he had a superiority of four to three in divisions, with two more coming up (Buckner). After unleashing a few choice expletives in Polk's direction, Bragg finally mounted an attack after midday. He was too late—Crittenden had retired.

Twice in three days, Bragg had missed a fine opportunity to inflict a serious reverse upon Rosecrans. The latter, at last aware of Bragg's true dispositions, began to concentrate his forces.

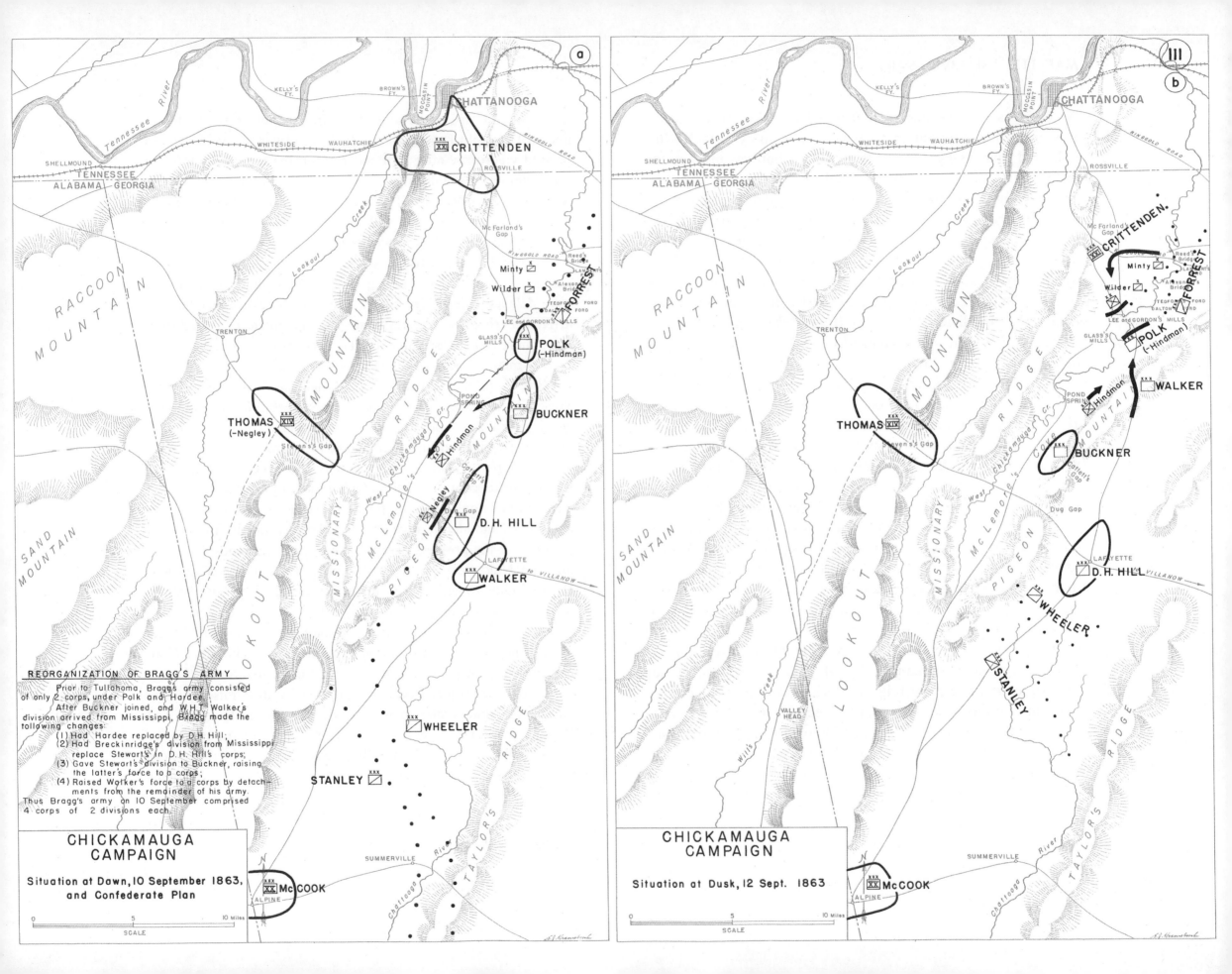

a

CHATTANOOGA

XXX
XX CRITTENDEN

Minty X

Wilder X

FORREST

XXX
XX POLK
(-Hindman)

XXX
XX BUCKNER

Hindman

THOMAS XXX
XIV
(-Negley)

Negley

XXX
XX D.H. HILL

XXX
XX WALKER

to VILLANOW

RACCOON MOUNTAIN

FORREST

SAND MOUNTAIN

LOOKOUT MOUNTAIN

MISSIONARY RIDGE

PIGEON MOUNTAIN

TAYLORS RIDGE

XXX
XX WHEELER

XXX
XX STANLEY

REORGANIZATION OF BRAGG'S ARMY

Prior to Tullahoma, Bragg's army consisted of only 2 corps, under Polk and Hardee.
After Buckner joined, and W.H.T. Walker's division arrived from Mississippi, Bragg made the following changes:
(1) Had Hardee replaced by D.H. Hill;
(2) Had Breckinridge's division from Mississippi replace Stewart's in D.H. Hill's corps;
(3) Gave Stewart's division to Buckner, raising the latter's force to a corps;
(4) Raised Walker's force to a corps by detachments from the remainder of his army.
Thus Bragg's army on 10 September comprised 4 corps of 2 divisions each.

CHICKAMAUGA CAMPAIGN

Situation at Dawn, 10 September 1863, and Confederate Plan

0   5   10 Miles
SCALE

XXX
XX McCOOK

III

b

CHATTANOOGA

XXX
XX CRITTENDEN

Minty X

Wilder X

FORREST

XXX
XX POLK
(-Hindman)

XXX
XX WALKER

Hindman

XXX
XX BUCKNER

THOMAS XXX
XIV

XXX
XX D.H. HILL

VILLANOW

RACCOON MOUNTAIN

SAND MOUNTAIN

LOOKOUT MOUNTAIN

MISSIONARY RIDGE

PIGEON MOUNTAIN

TAYLORS RIDGE

XXX
XX WHEELER

XXX
XX STANLEY

CHICKAMAUGA CAMPAIGN

Situation at Dusk, 12 Sept. 1863

0   5   10 Miles
SCALE

XXX
XX McCOOK

As early as the evening of 10 September, Wood had warned Rosecrans that information obtained at Lee and Gordon's Mills indicated that Bragg was not withdrawing but was massing for an attack. Rosecrans rightly insisted on verification, since the original source of the information was of dubious reliability. Negley's near-disaster convinced Thomas of the truth of the rumor, but not Rosecrans. However, when Crittenden just managed to evade Bragg's attack, Rosecrans was finally swayed and . at once ordered McCook north to Stevens's Gap. By 17 September, the Union corps had closed up, so that they were much less vulnerable to individual defeat by Bragg (*sketch* a). Brig. Gen. Robert B. Mitchell now commanded the cavalry corps in place of Stanley, who had become ill.

Bragg, having moved most of his army north to launch the abortive attack of the 13th on Crittenden, had later called up Hill's corps. If he moved quickly and resolutely, he might still be able to defeat a portion of Rosecrans' army before the remainder could interfere. Such was the situation on the eve of the Battle of Chickamauga. Either commander, if willing to expose his communications, could turn the other's flank. But Bragg, proving to be the more determined and the bolder, refused to relinquish the initiative gained on 12-13 September and decided to attack. Rosecrans would probably have been more foolhardy than bold to attempt an attack under the conditions that existed on 18 September; and after that time, Bragg did not give him the opportunity to go on the offensive.

Early on 18 September, Longstreet's first three brigades from Virginia arrived, commanded by Maj. Gen. John B. Hood. Longstreet and two more brigades were due on the 19th, but his last four and the artillery were not expected until about the 21st. Bragg, having also received some additional troops from Mississippi (under Brig. Gen. Bushrod R. Johnson) decided on the morning of the 18th to advance on Crittenden's left, sever the routes to McFarland's Gap and Rossville, and thus cut off the three Union corps to the south from their supply base at Chattanooga. He might have accomplished this object sooner if he had pressed vigorously after Crittenden when the latter withdrew on 13 September. At that time, he would have had to contend only with the XXI Corps, for Thomas was at Stevens's Gap, eighteen miles away, and McCook still farther south. By now, five days later, Rosecrans had feverishly closed up his forces, so that Thomas was at Pond Spring, five miles south of Crittenden, and McCook was at Stevens's Gap. Having delayed this long, Bragg might have delayed a few days longer until all his reinforcements had arrived. Perhaps he underestimated his opponent, or feared that, given more time, Rosecrans would reinforce Granger's weak corps (6,000 men) at Rossville, and thus frustrate his plan.

Bragg's plan called for Hood, Walker, and Buckner to cross West Chickamauga Creek where shown (*sketch* b), while the cavalry protected both flanks (Wheeler was off map, to south); Hill was to guard the northern exit of McClemore's Cove (*sketch* a; *center, right*) and prevent Thomas and McCook from using that route to come to Crittenden's relief; Polk was to cross at Lee and Gordon's Mills, or farther north if met by strong resistance. The Confederate advance got under way shortly after Hood's arrival, but the progress over the poor mountain roads was slow, and the Union cavalry resisted stoutly. Late in the afternoon, Hood finally forced a crossing at Reed's Bridge, but Walker, unable to seize Alexander's Bridge, had to cross at Lambert's Ford. That night, Walker and Hood managed to cross all of their troops and bivouacked to the west of the creek. The other Confederate corps had just reached the stream by nightfall.

In the meantime, Rosecrans, alerted by dust raised by the marching Confederates in the morning, seems to have guessed Bragg's plan. He ordered Thomas and McCook to march to Crittenden's support. That night, while the Confederates were crossing the creek, Thomas began to arrive in rear of Crittenden's position.

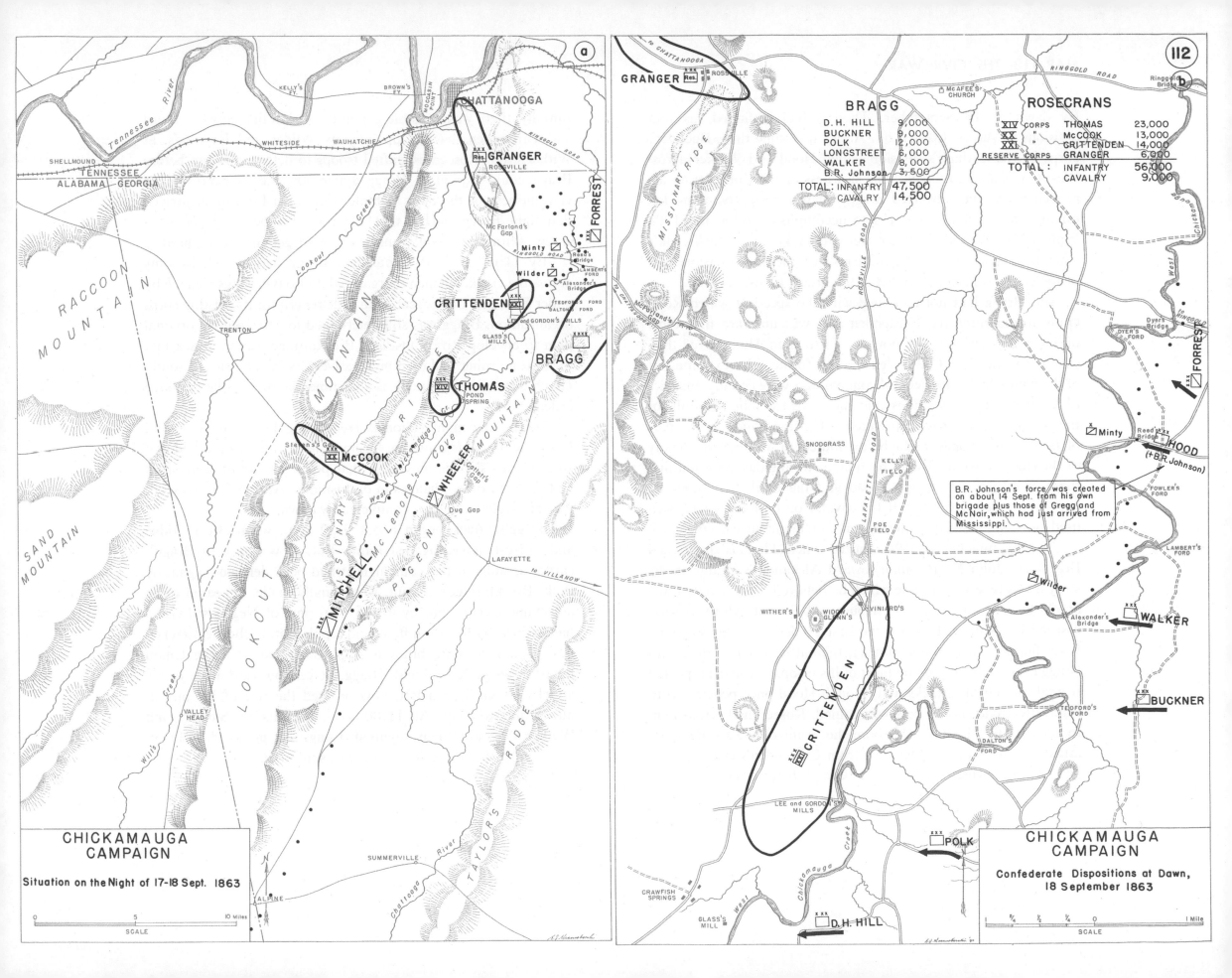

CHICKAMAUGA CAMPAIGN

Situation on the Night of 17-18 Sept. 1863

0 ___ 5 ___ 10 Miles
SCALE

BRAGG

D.H. HILL	9,000
BUCKNER	9,000
POLK	12,000
LONGSTREET	6,000
WALKER	8,000
B.R. Johnson	3,500

TOTAL: INFANTRY 47,500
CAVALRY 14,500

ROSECRANS

XIV CORPS	THOMAS	23,000
XX "	McCOOK	13,000
XXI "	CRITTENDEN	14,000
RESERVE CORPS	GRANGER	6,000

TOTAL: INFANTRY 56,000
CAVALRY 9,000

B.R. Johnson's force was created on about 14 Sept. from his own brigade plus those of Gregg and McNair, which had just arrived from Mississippi.

CHICKAMAUGA CAMPAIGN

Confederate Dispositions at Dawn, 18 September 1863

1 ... 3/4 ... 1/2 ... 1/4 ... 0 ... 1 Mile
SCALE

By dawn of 19 September, Thomas had stationed his four divisions as shown (*sketch* a). About this same time, Buckner's corps and Cheatham's division joined Hood and Walker across West Chickamauga Creek. The slowness of the Confederate approach march had thwarted Bragg's plan to turn Rosecrans' left on the 18th, but he expected to accomplish this on the 19th. Walker, Hood, and Buckner were to make this attack, while Cheatham acted as the immediate reserve; the three divisions east of the creek were not included in the attack plans.

But Bragg had not reckoned with the speed at which Rosecrans would reinforce Crittenden and was unaware that three of Thomas' divisions were north of Crittenden. He believed that, except for cavalry, Crittenden's corps formed the extreme left of the Union line. The Federal commanders were equally unaware of Confederate dispositions and had no idea that the bulk of Bragg's army had crossed the creek. This ignorance on the part of both commanders might be attributed to the fact that many of the troop movements had been made during darkness and that the area between Lafayette Road and the creek was generally heavily wooded. However, if the cavalry on both sides had been used more aggressively, some information might have been gained.

The fighting on the 19th started when Thomas dispatched Brig. Gen. John M. Brannan toward Alexander's Bridge to destroy a Confederate brigade which he believed was the only force across the stream. Brannan encountered Forrest, who was soon assisted by Walker. In what can best be described as very confused fighting (*action not shown*), the battle raged all day, with Bragg eventually employing most of his troops. He made repeated frontal, piecemeal attacks and, though Hood once penetrated to Lafayette Road, no success was gained. Rosecrans hurried reinforcements to Thomas, who bore the brunt of the Confederate attacks; these included elements from Crittenden's corps as well as McCook's, which had arrived at Crawfish Springs before noon.

Initially, there was a sizable gap in the Union line between Baird and Crittenden, backed up only by Wilder and Reynolds, at Wither's, but Rosecrans shifted troops to defend this gap before Bragg could exploit it. Bragg apparently was unaware of the vigorousness of the day's fighting, for, when Longstreet arrived that night, Bragg told him that "the troops had been engaged in . . . severe skirmishing while endeavoring to get in line of battle."

By 11:00 P.M., 19 September, Bragg had his whole army across the creek. He then reorganized it into two wings (*sketch* b) under Polk and Longstreet, with little regard for its existing corps organization. Bragg was still determined to carry out his original plan to envelop Rosecrans' left. Breckinridge was to attack first the next morning, followed progressively by the units to the south. (Such a progressive attack is sometimes known as the "oblique order.")

During the night, Thomas erected log breastworks around Kelly Field and, fearing that his north flank was weak, asked that Negley's division be moved to that point. Rosecrans concurred and directed other changes in dispositions. All the moves except that of Negley had been completed by dawn.

Bragg's attack began about 9:30 A.M., when Breckinridge and Forrest moved against Baird. But, as was true of Bragg's earlier assaults in this campaign, it had been delayed—again by Polk. Breckinridge's assault, when finally made, appeared to be achieving success, but by 10:15 A.M. part of Negley's division had arrived on the north flank and repulsed it. Cleburne attacked next, at 10:00 A.M., but was stopped by fire from the Union breastworks at Kelly Field. Bragg, perceiving the failure of his attacks on the Union left, now ordered the rest of his line to attack immediately. At 11:00 A.M., assaults by Stewart and Walker were eventually repulsed. Longstreet attacked at 11:30 A.M. and began to achieve some measure of success.

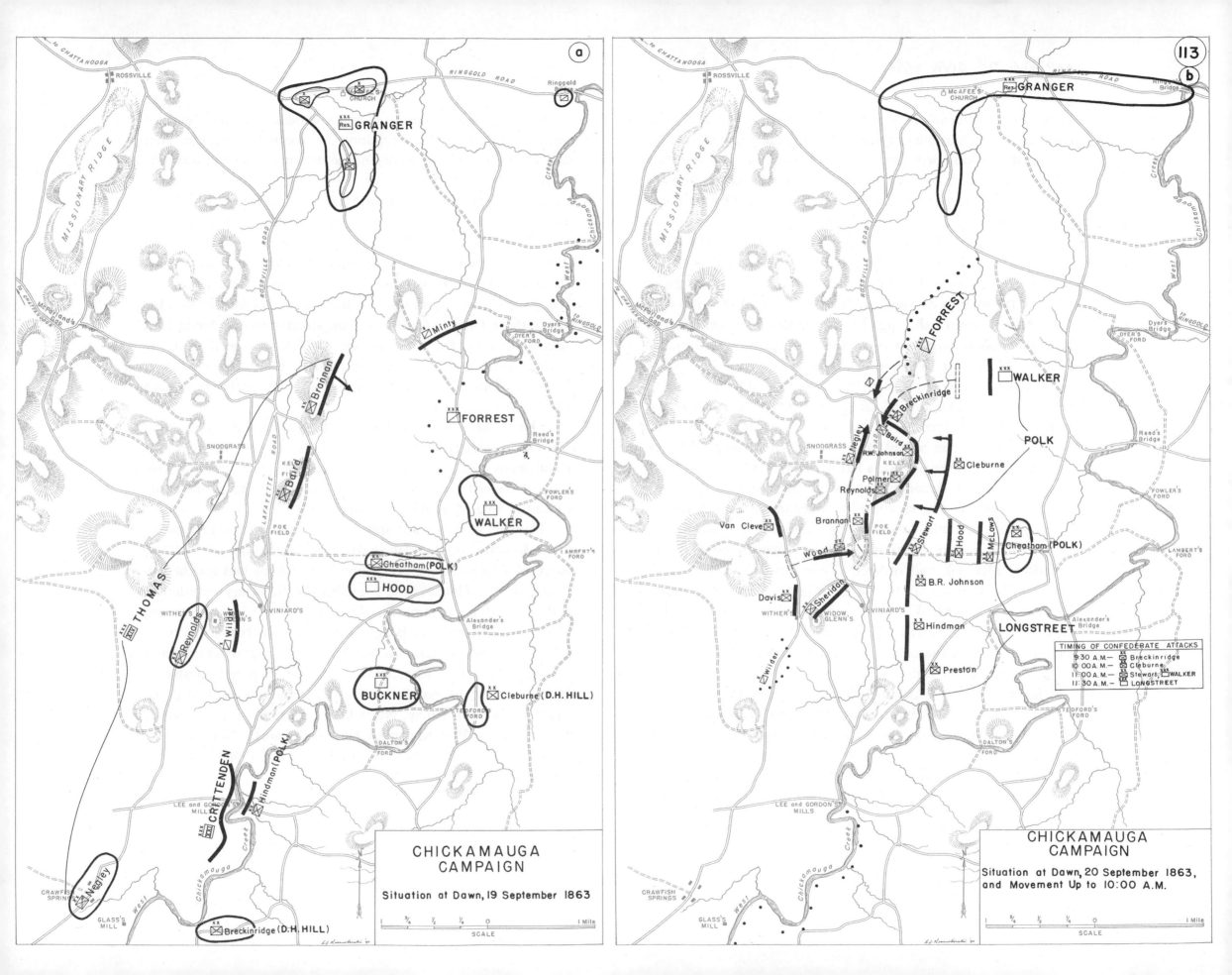

(a)

to CHATTANOOGA

ROSSVILLE

RINGGOLD ROAD

Ringgold
Bridge

McAFEE'S
CHURCH

XXX
Res. GRANGER

MISSIONARY RIDGE

McFarland's
Gap

West Chickamauga Creek

ROSSVILLE ROAD

☒ Minty

Dyer's
Bridge

Dyer's
Ford

to RINGGOLD

XX ☒ Brannan

☒ FORREST

Reed's
Bridge

SNODGRASS

KELLY
FIELD

Baird

POE
FIELD

FOWLER'S
FORD

XXX
☒ WALKER

THOMAS

LAFAYETTE ROAD

WITHER'S

WIDOW
GLENN'S

XX ☒ Reynolds

☒ Wilder

LAMBERT'S
FORD

XX ☒ Cheatham (POLK)

☒ HOOD

Alexander's
Bridge

VINIARD'S

☒ BUCKNER

XX ☒ Cleburne (D.H. HILL)

TEDFORD'S
FORD

CRITTENDEN

LEE and GORDON'S
MILLS

Hindman (POLK)

DALTON'S
FORD

XXX ☒ Negley

CRAWFISH
SPRINGS

West Chickamauga Creek

GLASS'S
MILL

XX ☒ Breckinridge (D.H. HILL)

**CHICKAMAUGA
CAMPAIGN**

Situation at Dawn, 19 September 1863

3/4 1/2 1/4 0   1 Mile
SCALE

(b)

113

to CHATTANOOGA

ROSSVILLE

RINGGOLD ROAD

Ringgold
Bridge

McAFEE'S
CHURCH

XXX
Res. GRANGER

MISSIONARY RIDGE

McFarland's
Gap

West Chickamauga Creek

ROSSVILLE ROAD

Dyer's
Bridge

Dyer's
Ford

to RINGGOLD

☒ FORREST

XXX
☒ WALKER

Breckinridge

Negley

R.W. Johnson

Baird

POLK

SNODGRASS

KELLY
FIELD

☒ Cleburne

Palmer

Reynolds

Reed's
Bridge

FOWLER'S
FORD

Van Cleve ☒

Brannan ☒

POE
FIELD

Stewart

☒ Hood

McLaws

Cheatham (POLK)

LAMBERT'S
FORD

Wood

XX ☒ B.R. Johnson

Davis ☒

Sheridan

WITHER'S

WIDOW
GLENN'S

VINIARD'S

LONGSTREET

Alexander's
Bridge

XX ☒ Hindman

Wilder

XX ☒ Preston

TEDFORD'S
FORD

DALTON'S
FORD

LEE and GORDON'S
MILLS

CRAWFISH
SPRINGS

West Chickamauga Creek

GLASS'S
MILL

TIMING OF CONFEDERATE ATTACKS	
9:30 A.M.— ☒ Breckinridge	
10:00 A.M.— ☒ Cleburne	
11:00 A.M.— ☒ Stewart, ☐ WALKER	
11:30 A.M.— ☐ LONGSTREET	

**CHICKAMAUGA
CAMPAIGN**

Situation at Dawn, 20 September 1863,
and Movement Up to 10:00 A.M.

3/4 1/2 1/4 0   1 Mile
SCALE

When, after Cleburne's failure, Bragg ordered the rest of his line to attack, he obviously had given up his original plan for envelopment of the Union north flank and, in desperation, was resorting to frontal attacks. Longstreet, the last to attack, moved forward about 11:30 A.M. with his entire wing, except for Preston's division, which he held in reserve (sketch a).

On the Union side, Thomas, under heavy attack and with an exposed left flank, persistently asked for reinforcements. Rosecrans finally issued orders to Crittenden and McCook to move troops to the support of Thomas. Thus, between 10:00 and 11:30 A.M., there was much shifting of Union forces. The remainder of Negley's division and most of Van Cleve's division had moved north by 11:30 A.M. At about 11:00 A.M., Wood pulled out of line to carry out an order given by Rosecrans' aide "to close on Reynolds." The facts behind this fateful move are clouded, but it appears that Rosecrans, misinformed about Brannan's exact location, believed that he had either withdrawn or had pulled back his right, thus exposing Wood's left flank. Wood knew this to be untrue, for he was in contact with Brannan's right on the battle line. However, when he received the order to close on Reynolds, the only way he could do so was by withdrawing from the line and moving in rear of Brannan, which he proceeded to do. In the meantime, McCook had ordered Davis forward on Sheridan's left, and Sheridan started two of his brigades north to reinforce Thomas. Hence, when Longstreet's heavy columns arrived, they entered the void in the Union line created by Wood's withdrawal and struck in flank the columns of Davis, Wood, and Sheridan's two brigades—all of which were in motion.

The result was a resounding success for Longstreet. Sheridan and Davis, separated from the rest of the army and heavily outnumbered, withdrew from the field via McFarland's Gap (sketch b, upper left). Rosecrans, carried along in the hurried retreat, apparently was convinced that the battle was lost. McCook and Crittenden soon followed. Thus, by 1:00 P.M., Thomas, by de-

fault, was left in sole command on the battlefield. Soon he received word from Rosecrans to withdraw the troops to Rossville. That day Rosecrans displayed none of the determination and fortitude he had shown at Stones River.

Meanwhile, Granger, at McAfee's Church (top right), heard the firing to the south and, on his own initiative, sent Brig. Gen. James B. Steedman to Thomas' support. Steedman arrived about 2:30 P.M., just in time to stop Longstreet's attempt to envelop Brannan's right. (Previously, Thomas had sent the remnants of Wood's division [not shown] to Brannan's front to help stop the attack there.) About 4:00 P.M., Longstreet made one final effort, spearheaded by Preston's division (which had been guarding against Wilder), but could not break the stubborn Union defense. Likewise, Thomas repulsed Bragg's final effort with Cheatham's division on the north flank.

That night, Thomas withdrew to Rossville, aided by Sheridan and Davis, who had returned to the battlefield via the Rossville Road about 7:00 P.M. The Confederates failed to pursue—a grave error perceived only by Forrest at the time. The Confederate casualties totaled 18,454; the Union, 16,170.

Thomas' sterling leadership was a decisive factor in preventing a disastrous Union defeat. Here he earned the title of "The Rock of Chickamauga," for, though all troops had fought valiantly, it was Thomas who provided the necessary determined and inspired leadership. On the Confederate side, the troops fought equally well, but Bragg's conduct of the battle was poor. He kept no reserve under his own control—a reserve which could well have been used to maintain the momentum of Longstreet's initially highly successful attack. Even Cheatham, sent to Longstreet at the proper time, might have turned the scales; instead, Bragg directed Polk to employ him on the north. Nor would he strip Polk of his reserves to bolster Longstreet, though Polk was stalemated.

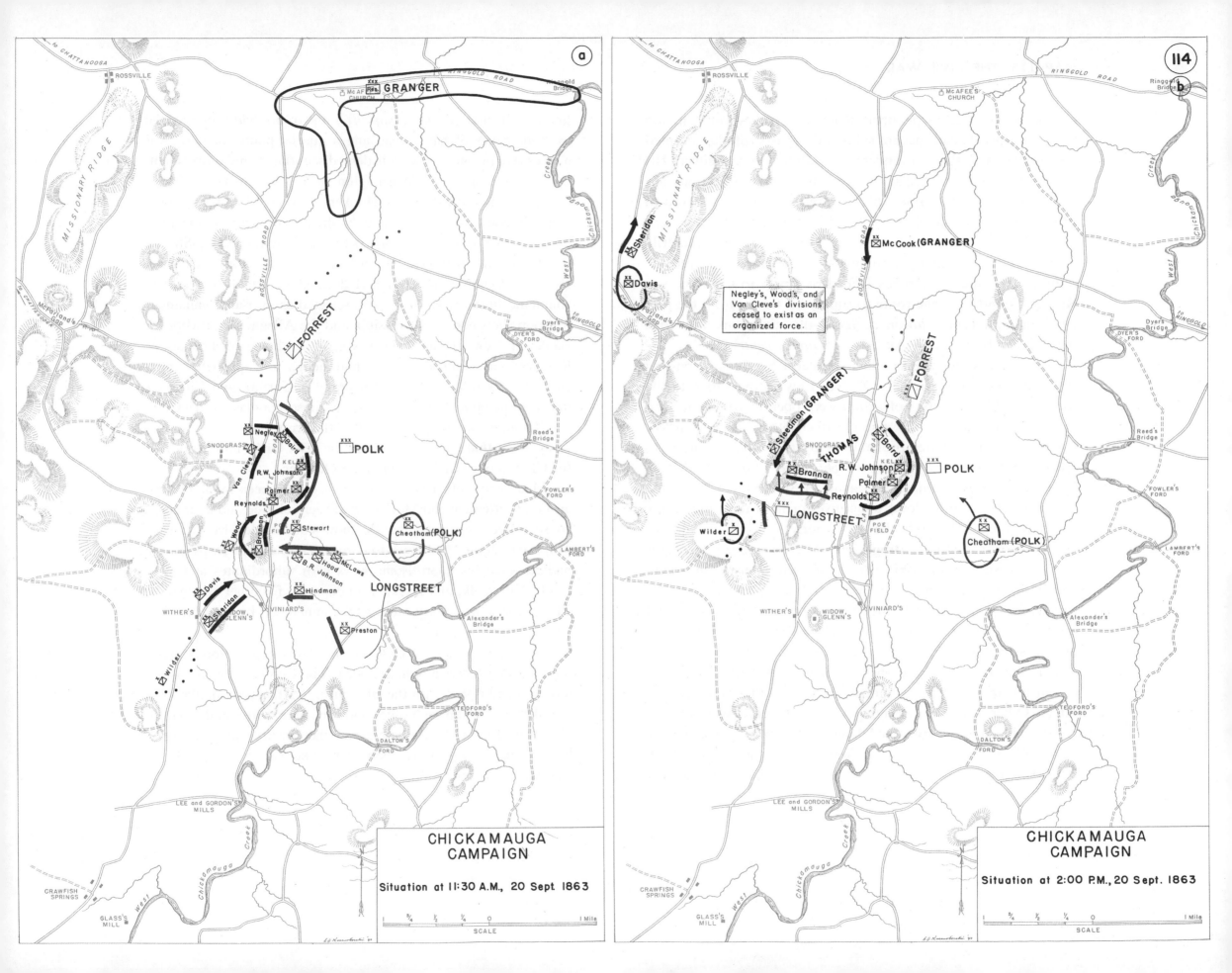

Map (a) — left panel

CHICKAMAUGA CAMPAIGN

Situation at 11:30 A.M., 20 Sept. 1863

Labels: To CHATTANOOGA, ROSSVILLE, RINGGOLD ROAD, McAFEE'S CHURCH, GRANGER, Ringgold Bridge, MISSIONARY RIDGE, ROSSVILLE ROAD, FORREST, POLK, SNODGRASS, Negley, Baird, Van Cleve, R.W. Johnson, KELL, Palmer, Reynolds, Wood, Brannan, Stewart, Cheatham (POLK), Reed's Bridge, Dyer's Bridge, DYER'S FORD, FOWLER'S FORD, To RINGGOLD, McFARLAND'S GAP, POE FIELD, Hood, McLaws, B.R. Johnson, LONGSTREET, Hindman, LAMBERT'S FORD, Davis, Sheridan, WIDOW GLENN'S, Preston, WITHER'S, VINIARD'S, Wilder, Alexander's Bridge, TEDFORD'S FORD, DALTON'S FORD, LEE and GORDON'S MILLS, CRAWFISH SPRINGS, GLASS'S MILL, West Chickamauga Creek

Scale: 3/4 1/2 1/4 0 1 Mile SCALE

Map (b) — right panel

114

CHICKAMAUGA CAMPAIGN

Situation at 2:00 P.M., 20 Sept. 1863

Labels: To CHATTANOOGA, ROSSVILLE, RINGGOLD ROAD, McAFEE'S CHURCH, Ringgold Bridge, MISSIONARY RIDGE, Sheridan, McCook (GRANGER), Davis, McFARLAND'S GAP, ROSSVILLE ROAD, Negley's, Wood's, and Van Cleve's divisions ceased to exist as an organized force., FORREST, Steedman (GRANGER), SNODGRASS, THOMAS, Baird, Brannan, R.W. Johnson, KELL, Palmer, POLK, Reynolds, LONGSTREET, POE FIELD, Wilder, Cheatham (POLK), Reed's Bridge, Dyer's Bridge, DYER'S FORD, FOWLER'S FORD, To RINGGOLD, LAMBERT'S FORD, WITHER'S, WIDOW GLENN'S, VINIARD'S, Alexander's Bridge, TEDFORD'S FORD, DALTON'S FORD, LEE and GORDON'S MILLS, CRAWFISH SPRINGS, GLASS'S MILL, West Chickamauga Creek

Scale: 3/4 1/2 1/4 0 1 Mile SCALE

By the night of 21 September, Rosecrans had withdrawn into Chattanooga. He had succumbed to a defeatist attitude, accepted investment, and thus surrendered his ability to maneuver. His troops occupied and began to strengthen the fortifications left earlier by the Confederates; his cavalry was posted as shown to protect his line of supply from Bridgeport (*center*) and to warn of Confederate attempts to cross the river. Having voluntarily given up to Bragg the high ground that dominated the river, the railroad, and the short roads from Bridgeport to Chattanooga, Rosecrans had only one route to supply his troops from the railhead at Stevenson (*lower center*)—the circuitous hill road through Bridgeport and Anderson's (*upper center*).

By the same night, Bragg had invested Chattanooga, posting the brigade of Brig. Gen. E. McIver Law in the valley to the southwest. Three courses of action were open to Bragg: to turn Rosecrans' position by crossing the river either above or below Chattanooga (the latter probably being the better choice); to move to Knoxville (*just off upper right corner of map*) to destroy Burnside's corps, meanwhile leaving a small force to watch Rosecrans; or to settle down to an investment of the Union army at Chattanooga. He chose the third course.

Now, on 1 October, Bragg sent Wheeler's cavalry to sever Rosecrans' supply line. Wheeler crossed the river on his front, advanced to Anderson's, and burned 300 Federal wagons while capturing 1,800 mules. He then moved toward the railroad and the Union base at Murfreesboro. But Rosecrans' cavalry was on his heels and so pressed him that he was unable to do further serious damage. On 8 October, through good fortune, his disorganized and depleted command recrossed the Tennessee to safety. Other attempts at raiding proved even less successful.

But the rainy weather and long haul over poor roads took heavy toll of Union animals and wagons. Soon Rosecrans' artillery horses died of starvation. By 27 October, when a short supply line was opened (*see text, map 116*), the troops had been reduced to "four cakes of hard bread and a quarter-pound of pork" for a three-day ration, and were listless, discouraged, and despondent.

The authorities in Washington meanwhile dispatched reinforcements to aid Rosecrans. Hooker, with the XI and XII Corps from Meade's army, arrived at Nashville (*off map, upper left*) on 4 October and received orders to guard the railroad to Stevenson. Grant was instructed to send reinforcements from Vicksburg. By early October, Lincoln had decided to establish a unified command in the west. Grant was selected as over-all commander of troops between the Mississippi and the Alleghenies, except for Banks at New Orleans. He was given a choice of Thomas or Rosecrans as commander at Chattanooga and, probably influenced by his relations with Rosecrans at Corinth and Lincoln's unfavorable opinion of Rosecrans, he chose Thomas. On 19 October, Thomas took over command of the army and received orders from Grant that Chattanooga must be held. Grant himself started for Chattanooga and arrived on 23 October.

Meanwhile, other command changes had been made in both armies. Crittenden and McCook had been relieved and their corps consolidated into one: the IV, now commanded by Granger. Maj. Gen. John M. Palmer took over Thomas' old corps. Bragg had resumed his quarrelsome ways with subordinates and, as a result, Hill, Polk, and Buckner all departed for other commands. Their reorganized corps were now commanded by Breckinridge, Hardee, and Longstreet.

During the month of October, there was little action between the opposing forces at Chattanooga. The Confederates occasionally dropped a shell into the city, but the outposts along the lines did little but watch each other and exchange stories and tobacco. However, Law's sharpshooters and the cavalry along the river below Chattanooga were soon to be unpleasantly surprised by Thomas' first move.

BATTLES AROUND CHATTANOOGA

Situation 1 October 1863

5 0 5 10 15 Miles
SCALE

The long supply route through Anderson's having proved unsatisfactory, Thomas decided to open the short route between Bridgeport and Chattanooga by driving away the Confederate troops and artillery which now controlled it (*sketch* a). W. F. Smith, Thomas' chief engineer, devised a splendid plan to accomplish this purpose. On the night of 26 October, under cover of heavy fog, Hazen, with 1,500 men, moved downstream in bridge pontons to Brown's Ferry (*upper right*), while the remainder of his brigade and Turchin's brigade moved overland as shown. Hazen's water-borne force landed at dawn at Brown's Ferry, surprised and routed Law's men, and established a beachhead. The overland force was quickly ferried across and a bridge built. Meanwhile, Hooker, leaving most of the XII Corps to guard the railroad, advanced as shown with the remainder of his force. Palmer's division moved to protect Hooker's rear. By the evening of 28 October, the short route to Bridgeport was open, under Hooker's protection. Bragg failed to appreciate the importance of this Union coup, for his only reaction was some feeble shelling of Brown's Ferry and an unsuccessful four-brigade night attack. Instead, he apparently felt secure enough to dispatch Longstreet to attack Burnside at Knoxville.

Sherman had left Vicksburg with the XV and XVII Corps in late September, but, under orders from Halleck to repair the Memphis-Decatur railroad en route, he progressed slowly. Finally, Grant countermanded Halleck's order, and Sherman arrived at Bridgeport on 15 November. Grant ordered him to move from Bridgeport to Brown's Ferry, cross there, and move northeast into position (*sketch* b, *top center, dashed oval*). Early on the 21st, he was to cross the river and seize Tunnel Hill (*top right*). Meanwhile, Thomas would advance, initially bearing left, and together they would then drive south along Missionary Ridge. Hooker would guard Lookout Valley, and Howard would act as a reserve. But heavy rains delayed Sherman's crossing at Brown's Ferry, and he did not reach his attack position (*oval*) until the night of the 23d. The Brown's Ferry bridge broke before his last division (Osterhaus) could cross. Grant sent Osterhaus to Hooker and changed the latter's role from defense to attack. Meanwhile, Longstreet's move against Burnside at Knoxville had caused

considerable concern in Washington, and Grant had been hardpressed to do something. On the 23d, he suddenly ordered Thomas forward in a limited attack. Made in broad daylight and in full view of the Confederates, the attack was surprisingly successful, and Thomas occupied the line shown through Orchard Knob and Indian Hill (*center*). Bragg then moved Walker's division from Lookout Mountain to strengthen his right.

Early on 24 November, Hooker and Sherman attacked as planned. By noon, Hooker had driven the Confederates from the defile—which they had failed to entrench—between Lookout Mountain and the river. About 3:00 P.M., Hooker halted because of ammunition shortage and a blinding fog. That night, Bragg withdrew his southernmost forces across Chattanooga Creek (*sketch* c), burning the bridges en route. To the north, Sherman's crossing was successful, but he delayed in order to concentrate his forces and was not ready to advance to Tunnel Hill until afternoon. By then, Cleburne, entraining to join Longstreet, had been rushed up and entrenched on the hill. Sherman then halted for the night.

Grant now changed his plan for 25 November to a double envelopment by Sherman and Hooker; Thomas was to advance when Hooker reached Missionary Ridge. Sherman's attack, though eventually reinforced by Howard, could not break Cleburne's line (*sketch* d, *top right*). Hooker's march was slow and delayed by the destroyed bridges. By 3:30 P.M., Grant, puzzled by Hooker's delay and possibly concerned for Sherman, against whom Bragg seemed to be sending more troops, ordered Thomas to seize the lowest of the three lines of Confederate trenches along Missionary Ridge. This was soon done, but the troops, exposed to fire from the upper lines, continued upward and, to the surprise of all Union commanders, carried them also. By 4:30 P.M., Bragg's troops had broken and fled in panic.

Grant erred in failing to pursue the fleeing Confederates, but he had shown great flexibility in modifying his plans to meet changing conditions and, above all, had provided forceful leadership. Bragg, from the beginning, failed badly as a leader and tactician.

Union losses were 5,824; Confederate, 6,667.

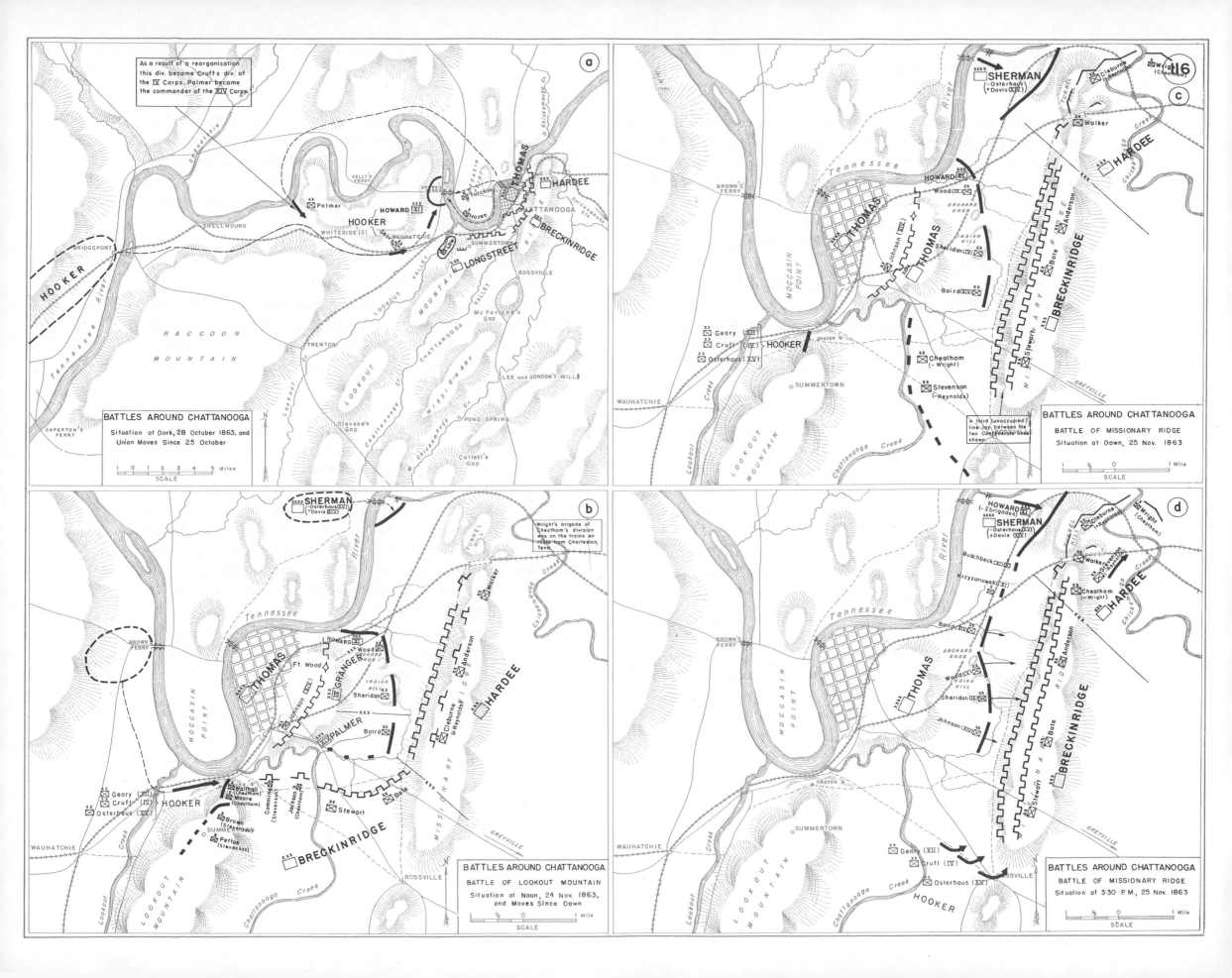

(a)

As a result of a reorganization this div. became Cruft's div. of the IV Corps. Palmer became the commander of the XIV Corps.

BATTLES AROUND CHATTANOOGA

Situation at Dark, 28 October 1863, and Union Moves Since 25 October

1 0 1 2 3 4 5 Miles
SCALE

(b)

Wright's brigade of Cheatham's division was on the trains en route from Charleston, Tenn.

BATTLES AROUND CHATTANOOGA

BATTLE OF LOOKOUT MOUNTAIN

Situation at Noon, 24 Nov. 1863, and Moves Since Dawn

½ 0 1 Mile
SCALE

(c) 116

Geary (XII)
Cruft (IV) HOOKER
Osterhaus (XV)

A third (unoccupied) line lay between the two Confederate lines shown.

BATTLES AROUND CHATTANOOGA

BATTLE OF MISSIONARY RIDGE

Situation at Dawn, 25 Nov. 1863

½ 0 1 Mile
SCALE

(d)

BATTLES AROUND CHATTANOOGA

BATTLE OF MISSIONARY RIDGE

Situation at 3:30 P.M., 25 Nov. 1863

½ 0 1 Mile
SCALE

On 14 July, once more south of the Potomac, the Army of Northern Virginia limped slowly up the Shenandoah Valley. Too many irreplaceable officers had been killed or disabled; morale was low in a good many regiments; and there was a continuing run of desertions.

Three days later, Meade began crossing the Potomac farther downstream. He was displeased and grumbling, claiming that Lee's army was almost as strong as his own and that it might be reinforced by part of Bragg's forces. At times, he sounded very much like McClellan.

Yet, once across the Potomac, he came rapidly down the eastern slope of the Blue Ridge Mountains, completely outmarching Lee. On the 22d, he was opposite Manassas Gap (*center*), while Lee's army was still moving past it on the western side of the mountains. Meade immediately drove through the gap, the III Corps leading, for an attack (*not shown*) against the flank of Lee's retreating column. It was a bold, skillful maneuver—but the wrong man led the III Corps. Sickles, its former commander, had lost a leg at Gettysburg; his successor, the undistinguished French, now fell victim to an exaggerated case of caution. He failed to push vigorously that evening and sparred lackadaisically with Lee's rear guard for most of the 23d. Late in the day, the Federals finally forced the rear guard aside and located Lee's main body—in line of battle near Front Royal (*center, left*). Meade planned to attack on the 24th, but once more Lee slipped away expertly during the night.

Thereafter, Lee took up a position around Culpeper (*bottom center*), while Meade's army watched him from across the Rappahannock. Both armies rested and reorganized. When furloughs and an amnesty for deserters who returned to the ranks failed to stop the constant sapping of his army's strength through desertion, Lee grimly used the firing squad—as did Meade on occasion. On 8 August, Lee wrote Davis, suggesting that Gettysburg and the subsequent retreat might have resulted in a loss of public confidence and that it therefore might be well to appoint a new commander for the Army of Northern Virginia. Davis naturally refused his offer.

The leaders of the Confederacy now faced a major dilemma. The Federals were victorious on all fronts: in the west, they held the Mississippi; in the center, Rosecrans had maneuvered Bragg out of his Tullahoma defenses; in the east, Lee had been defeated; along the coast, the blockade tightened ruthlessly, with a Federal expeditionary force attacking the coastal defenses of Charleston, South Carolina. Most of them felt that it was essential that the Southern forces regain the initiative; the only question was: On which front? Lee, always the Virginian, wished his army reinforced for a new offensive. Other commanders, Longstreet among them, urged that units of the Army of Northern Virginia be sent to reinforce Bragg before Grant and Rosecrans exploited their successes by a drive across Georgia. Davis would have preferred to have Lee take over the general command of the forces of both Johnston and Bragg, but accepted Lee's refusal. In the end, Longstreet took his corps—less two brigades sent to Charleston—to reinforce Bragg.

Such a movement could not be kept secret in Richmond for long, though Halleck originally felt that the whole of Longstreet's corps had gone to the Carolinas.

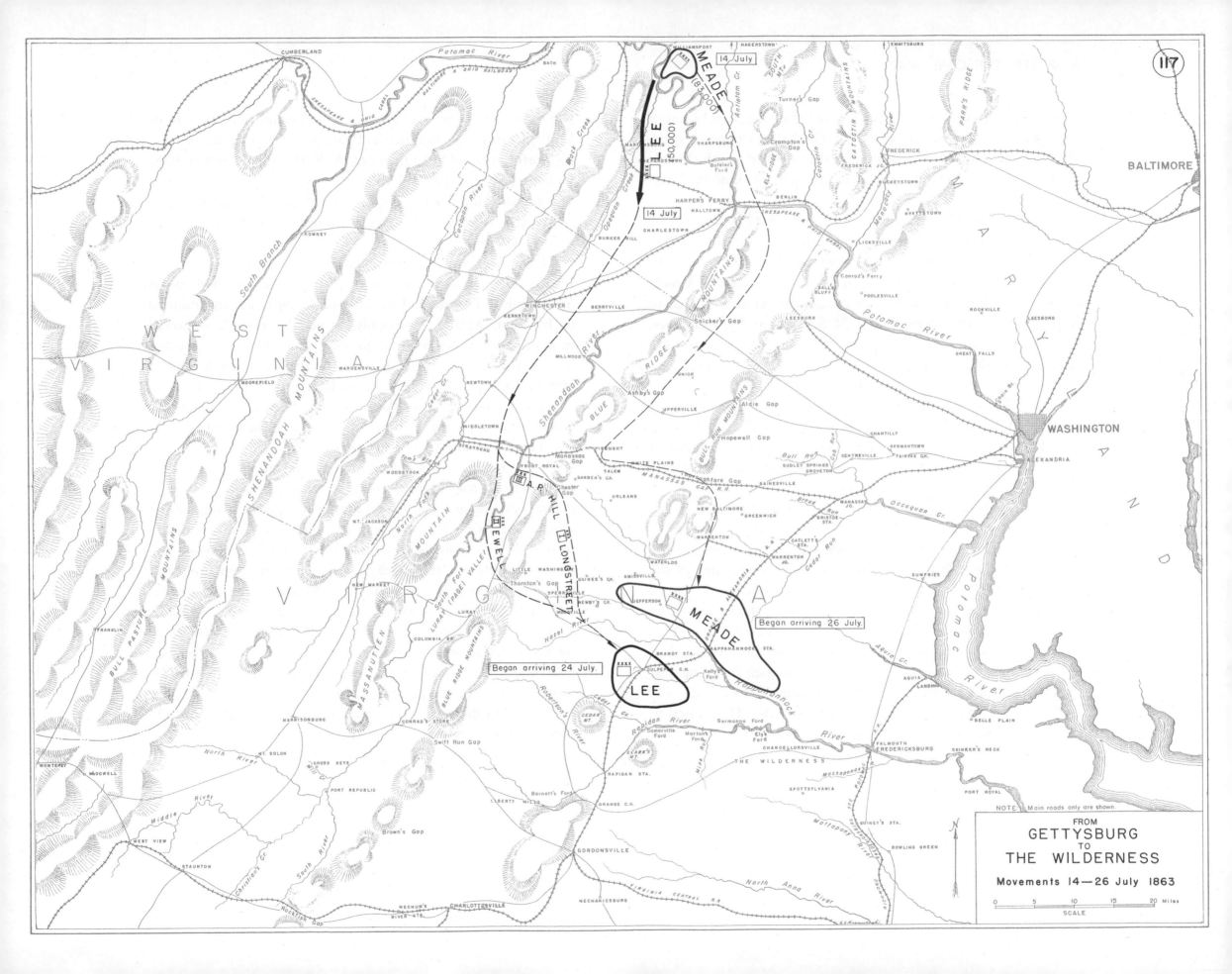

FROM
GETTYSBURG
TO
THE WILDERNESS

Movements 14—26 July 1863

NOTE: Main roads only are shown.

0   5   10   15   20 Miles
SCALE

Aware that Lee's army had been weakened by the detachment of Longstreet's corps, Meade advanced. On 13 September, his cavalry crossed the Rappahannock and drove Stuart south. Meade followed, occupying Culpeper, while Lee retired behind the Rapidan (*lower center*).

Meade now planned to exploit his numerical superiority by executing a turning movement—much like the one Hooker had planned for Chancellorsville—against the Confederates. This, however, was abruptly thwarted by Rosecrans' defeat at Chickamauga, which made it necessary to rush the XI and XII Corps to his relief. These corps left on 24 September. By 1 October, Lee was fully aware of their departure; on the 9th, he moved out around Cedar Mountain in an attempt to turn Meade's right flank and get between him and Washington.

The Federals had intercepted Confederate signals indicating a major movement, so Meade was not surprised. Nevertheless, unwilling to risk a battle which did not offer a good chance of success, Meade retreated—even though his remaining forces were somewhat stronger than those of Lee.

Neither commander displayed outstanding brilliance in the operations that followed. Both cavalry forces seem to have put far more energy into a series of minor actions against each other than into keeping their respective commanders informed of the opponent's whereabouts. Stuart's addiction to chasing wagon trains led him unsuspectingly into the midst of the retreating Union forces near Warrenton. Ewell was sent to rescue him; however, by hiding all night and making a bold dash for freedom in the morning, Stuart managed to extricate himself from amongst the amazed Federals, with only slight assistance from Ewell.

Meade's withdrawal proceeded in good order. He refused to halt at any position where there was any danger of his west flank being enveloped (as had happened to Pope and Hooker), but he kept his army well together and gave Lee no opportunity for a successful attack. On 14 October, A. P. Hill finally overtook the Union rear guard, under Warren, near Bristoe Station, just south of Manassas Junction (*center, right*). Hill attacked with headlong fury, only to thrust his leading division into a clever trap where it was shattered.

This check took the remaining drive out of Lee's pursuit. Meade was now well entrenched at Centreville; Lee had outrun his supplies. Therefore, Lee fell back, destroying the railroad as he went. Meade, thoroughly nagged by Halleck, followed promptly; but it took a month to re-lay the railroad track behind his army. The one major incident of this period was Stuart's attempt to trap Kilpatrick at Broad Run, just south of Manassas Junction. Stuart's plan worked perfectly, but the Union cavalry was now better mounted. A quick retreat (the "Buckland Races") got them clear with only light losses.

Lee returned to his old position behind the Rappahannock, but retained a fortified bridgehead on the north bank at the Rappahannock bridge where the Orange & Alexandria Railroad had crossed the river. This was held to enable the Confederates to recross the river rapidly and attack the flank of any Union command attempting to force Kelly's Ford, the weakest point in Lee's defensive position. On 7 November, Meade began crossing at Kelly's Ford, where some of the defending Confederate units made an unexpectedly poor showing. Early rapidly reinforced the Confederate bridgehead, but, just after dark, Sedgwick made a skillful surprise attack, capturing almost all of the two brigades which formed the bridgehead garrison.

This twin defeat sent Lee back below the Rapidan, his officers embittered by their lack of success.

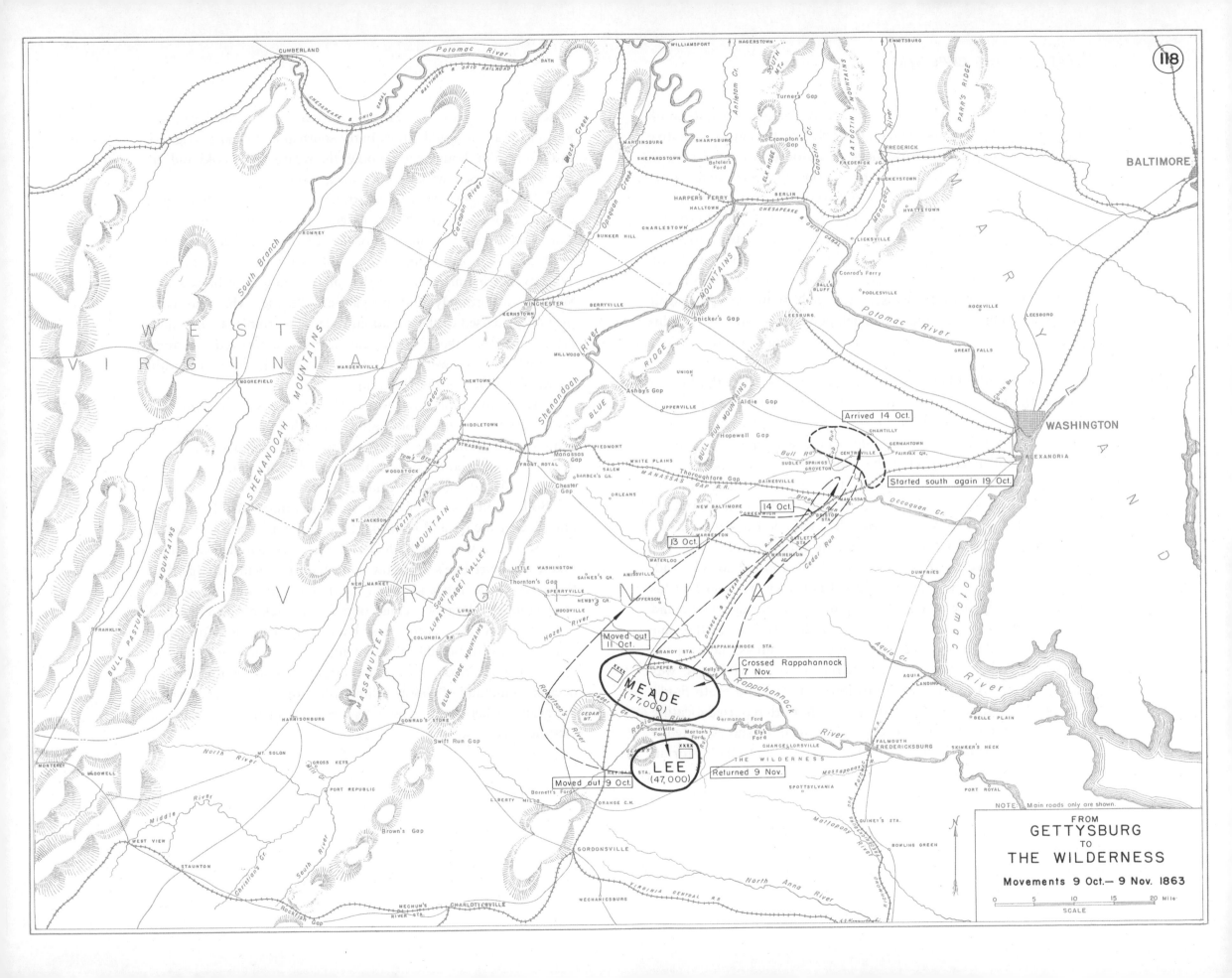

118

Arrived 14 Oct.

Started south again 19 Oct.

14 Oct.

13 Oct.

Moved out 11 Oct.

Crossed Rappahannock 7 Nov.

MEADE (77,000)

LEE (47,000)

Moved out 9 Oct.

Returned 9 Nov.

NOTE: Main roads only are shown.

FROM
GETTYSBURG
TO
THE WILDERNESS

Movements 9 Oct.—9 Nov. 1863

0   5   10   15   20 Mile
SCALE

By late November, the Confederate army was building huts south of the Rapidan for its winter quarters. Lee had made tentative plans, including the defense lines to be occupied, to deal with any renewed Federal advance. His troops, however, were rather widely scattered, and Meade conceived the plan of marching rapidly downstream, crossing at Germanna and Ely's Fords beyond Stuart's cavalry screen. Once across, he would turn west to penetrate between Hill and Ewell and destroy them in detail.

This movement was worked out with great care. Meade calculated the exact time necessary for each of his corps to cover the required distances and issued detailed orders. No supply trains were to be taken along, each soldier carrying ten days' rations instead.

Actually, the plan was too detailed; it neglected the human factor and allowed no latitude for the unexpected, which habitually plagues the conduct of military operations. French marched slowly and got to his crossing site behind schedule. The Federal engineers had miscalculated the width of the river and had not brought enough pontons forward; temporary extensions had to be improvised. One day had been lost before Meade could put the Rapidan behind him. Once across, the ineffable French promptly took the wrong road, further delaying the initial attack.

By this time, Confederate scouts had reported Meade's advance. Lee pulled Ewell back, called Hill forward, and had his whole army digging in along a steep north-south ridgeline behind Mine Run Creek (*lower center*). Meade came up to this line early on the 28th and began a series of reconnaissances in the hope of finding a weak point. Warren, with the II Corps, was shifted south to see if it were possible to turn Lee's south flank; Sedgwick examined the Confederate north. Both reported locating points which could be attacked with a chance for success. Meade therefore spent the 29th massing his troops on both flanks for an attack the next morning. There was to be a heavy artillery preparation; Warren would attack in the south at 8:00 A.M.; Sedgwick in the north an hour later. Though the weather was cold and the terrain rough, Sedgwick's troops were eager.

With daylight, the Union artillery on the north flank and center opened fire, but Warren's guns in the south were silent. The Confederate lines in front of the II Corps had been strengthened and reinforced during the night to a point where both Warren and his men realized that an assault would be suicidal. Warren, accordingly, did not attack. Meade, who had been promptly advised of the situation, rode to Warren's position and, after inspecting the Confederate defenses, approved Warren's decision. Supplies were running low, so Meade ordered a withdrawal back across the Rapidan.

At the same time, unknown to Meade, Lee was concentrating his troops for an enveloping attack, which would emulate Jackson's blow at Chancellorsville, against the Federal south flank. The attack jumped off on the morning of 2 December, but it hit only air—Meade had retired undetected.

Both armies now went into winter quarters. Meade had disappointed Lincoln and Halleck. True, he had been successful in a conservative way, for he had kept his head, avoided rash mistakes, and hurt Lee's army far more than Lee had hurt his. But there was little fire and much caution in the man; he missed opportunities—largely because of a certain lack of flexibility and a poor choice of subordinates. Eventually, he would probably wear Lee down, but the nation could not wait for him.

President Lincoln now called Grant to Washington to take over-all command of Union military operations; Congress revived the grade of lieutenant general as a reward for his long string of victories in the west.

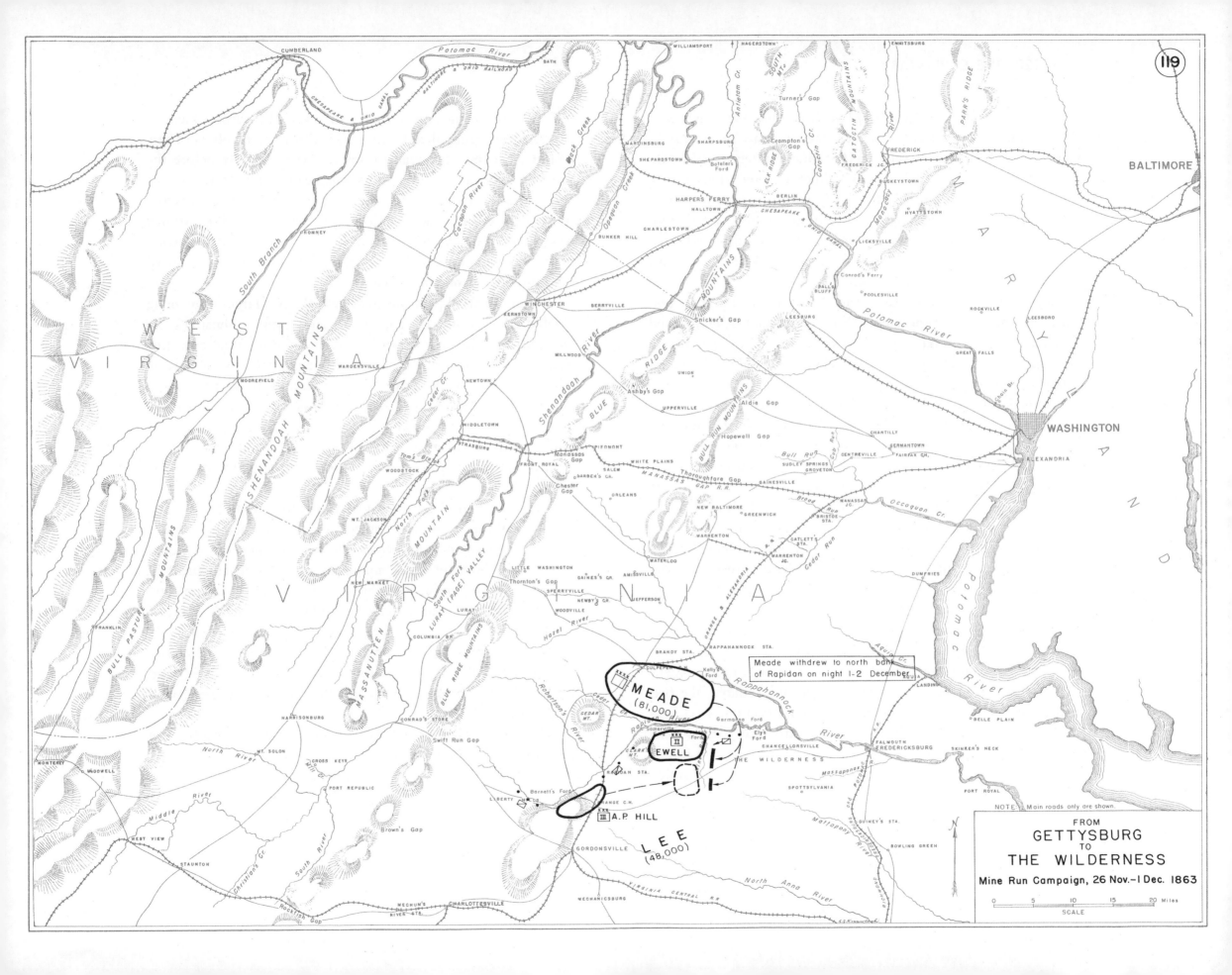

119

MEADE
(81,000)

Meade withdrew to north bank
of Rapidan on night 1-2 December

EWELL

A.P. HILL

LEE
(48,000)

NOTE: Main roads only are shown.

FROM
GETTYSBURG
TO
THE WILDERNESS

Mine Run Campaign, 26 Nov.–1 Dec. 1863

0   5   10   15   20 Miles
SCALE

For some five months after the Mine Run campaign, there was little action in the Virginia theater, the only sizable operation there being Kilpatrick's raid on Richmond (February-March, 1864, *not shown*), made in hopes of liberating the thousands of Union prisoners of war held there. By hard and skillful riding, Kilpatrick reached the city's fortifications, found them more heavily garrisoned than he had anticipated, and had to withdraw down the Peninsula to Fort Monroe. Part of his advance guard was cut off and its commander killed.

Winter was hard on Lee's army. Clothing was scarce, and horses and men alike went hungry. Early in December, Davis tried to persuade Lee to take over the command of Bragg's defeated army in Georgia, but once more Lee chose to remain in Virginia. Johnston then replaced Bragg.

Early in March, Lieutenant General Ulysses S. Grant took command as general in chief of all the Union armies—approximately 533,000 men in seventeen different commands. Halleck, though replaced by Grant, remained in Washington in the newly created position of chief of staff, in which capacity he took care of the mass of operational and administrative details and served as a communications link between Grant and Lincoln. Grant himself decided to accompany the Army of the Potomac, since it confronted the strongest remaining Confederate army and also because it would be easier for him to maintain communication with Washington from its headquarters than from that of a western army. Meade retained command of the Army of the Potomac. Generally speaking, Grant gave him only broad strategic missions, leaving to him the tactical decisions necessary to implement them. This arrangement was awkward but unavoidable; the two men managed it with a minimum of personal friction.

Meade had reorganized his infantry into three corps. This made the army as a whole somewhat easier to handle, but it also had an adverse effect upon its morale. Men from the disbanded I and III Corps had been proud of their organizations and therefore resented being transferred. Moreover, the corps which received them, being already burdened with large numbers of raw recruits, had not had time to absorb them properly before the campaign began. All the cavalry was again concentrated in one corps under Sheridan, who also had recently been transferred from the west. Burnside's IX Corps, just returned from Knoxville, was at first directly under Grant, but became part of the Army of the Potomac on 24 May. Initially, it was employed to guard the railroads in the army's rear.

Grant's over-all plan was to destroy the two largest remaining Confederate armies—Lee's, in Virginia, and Johnston's, in Georgia. Meade was to operate against Lee—"Wherever Lee goes, there you will go also"; Sherman, against Johnston. Several minor offensives (*not shown*) were organized to assist these two major ones. Butler, with 33,000 men, was to move against Richmond along the south bank of the James River; Sigel would advance up the Shenandoah Valley to destroy the Virginia & Tennessee Railroad; and Banks was to conduct operations against Mobile.

Lee's position along the Rapidan was too strong to be taken by a frontal attack. An envelopment of his left flank would have the advantage of moving across favorable terrain, but it would expose the Union line of communications. An envelopment of Lee's right flank, on the other hand, would cover the Union communications and threaten Lee's. It would also place the Army of the Potomac and Butler's Army of the James in better position for mutual support. Its major drawback would be the necessity of advancing through the same Wilderness that had blinded Hooker the year before. Grant chose the Wilderness route around Lee's right flank.

During the night of 3 May, the Union forces moved to the fords across the Rapidan as shown; on the 4th, Lee put his forces in motion as indicated to counter the Union move.

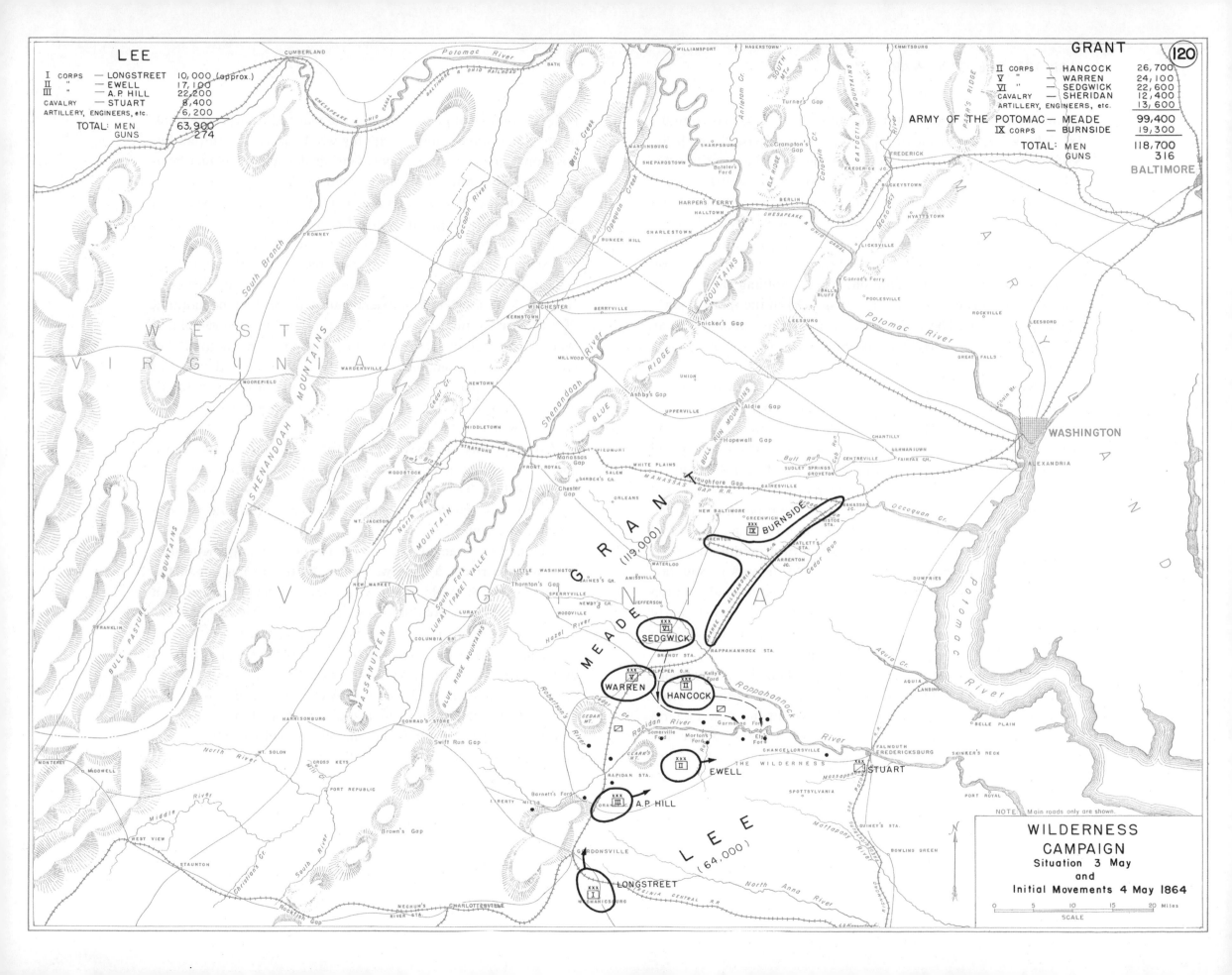

LEE

I CORPS	— LONGSTREET	10,000 (approx.)
II "	— EWELL	17,100
III "	— A.P. HILL	22,200
CAVALRY	— STUART	8,400
ARTILLERY, ENGINEERS, etc.		6,200

TOTAL: MEN 63,900
GUNS 274

GRANT

II CORPS	— HANCOCK	26,700
V "	— WARREN	24,100
VI "	— SEDGWICK	22,600
CAVALRY	— SHERIDAN	12,400
ARTILLERY, ENGINEERS, etc.		13,600

ARMY OF THE POTOMAC — MEADE 99,400
IX CORPS — BURNSIDE 19,300

TOTAL: MEN 118,700
GUNS 316

BALTIMORE

WEST VIRGINIA

VIRGINIA

WASHINGTON

G R A N T
(119,000)

M E A D E

BURNSIDE

SEDGWICK

WARREN

HANCOCK

EWELL

A.P. HILL

STUART

THE WILDERNESS

L E E
(64,000)

LONGSTREET

NOTE: Main roads only are shown.

WILDERNESS CAMPAIGN
Situation 3 May
and
Initial Movements 4 May 1864

| 0 | 5 | 10 | 15 | 20 Miles |
SCALE

Grant began his advance at midnight on 3 May in two columns (*sketch* a), hoping to move rapidly enough to pass through the Wilderness before Lee could concentrate enough troops to offer effective opposition. In order to move more swiftly, Grant resorted to leaving artillery behind and taking only essential supplies as the campaign developed. Even so, these filled a wagon train between sixty and seventy miles long. The cavalry corps was again divided, with Meade sending one division ahead of each infantry column, while holding Brig. Gen. Alfred T. A. Torbert's division (*not shown*) in the rear to guard the lagging trains. Therefore, no cavalry was available to screen the exposed Federal right flank during the move through the Wilderness.

By virtue of hindsight, it now appears that Grant and Meade might have done better to send the whole of their cavalry corps ahead to seize the southern and western exits from the Wilderness and protect the passage of the rest of the army. The infantry and artillery could have moved in three columns, the third one using one or more of the fords farther downstream. The trains could have followed this eastern column, under the protection of some of Burnside's infantry. By thus advancing on a wider front, and by starting at nightfall on 3 May instead of at midnight, Grant probably could have gotten through the Wilderness in one day. As it actually happened, the trains soon lagged behind, and the II and V Corps were halted in the Wilderness, as shown, early in the afternoon of 4 May to let them close up. Here, the two corps provided Lee with an excellent target.

Lee had been seeking an opportunity to launch another major offensive against the Army of the Potomac. Now, with that army reported on the march, he was in hopes that the new Federal commander would move through the Wilderness, where the superior numbers of the Union troops and their splendid artillery would be nullified by the tangled, unfamiliar terrain. Once the Federals were well into that region, he planned to strike the flank of their marching columns with his whole army. His initial dispositions, however, were poor. During the winter, it had been necessary to scatter the Army of Northern Virginia somewhat widely to make the task of feeding it a little easier. But, even with the Federals pouring southward, Lee was slow to concentrate. Stuart, who should have been scouting the line of the Rapidan, was still near Fredericksburg; Longstreet was at Gordonsville, some forty-two miles away, and thus out of supporting distance. Had Lee had the whole Confederate army in hand on the morning of 5 May, it is quite possible that he might have overwhelmed Warren's and Hancock's corps. One explanation for his delay may be that the Confederate intelligence service had failed to convince Lee that the Army of the Potomac was much larger than his own. Actually, as we have seen (*see text, map 120*), it was almost twice as large.

Consequently, the first clash on the morning of 5 May was a chance encounter. Ewell, advancing eastward along the Orange-Fredericksburg Turnpike at about 7:00 A.M., collided with Warren, who was marching toward Parker's Store (*sketch* b). The surprise was mutual.

Lee had not wanted to bring on a general engagement until Longstreet arrived. Meade was only anxious to get out of the green maze of the Wilderness. So poorly had the cavalry of both armies done their work that neither commander had any conception of the other's location and strength. Meade apparently thought that Warren had met a division-size delaying force, left behind by Lee to cover a Confederate concentration farther south along the North Anna River. He ordered Warren to attack these Confederates and determine their actual strength. Hancock was to halt at Todd's Tavern until this matter was settled, one way or another. Sedgwick was to cover Warren's right flank.

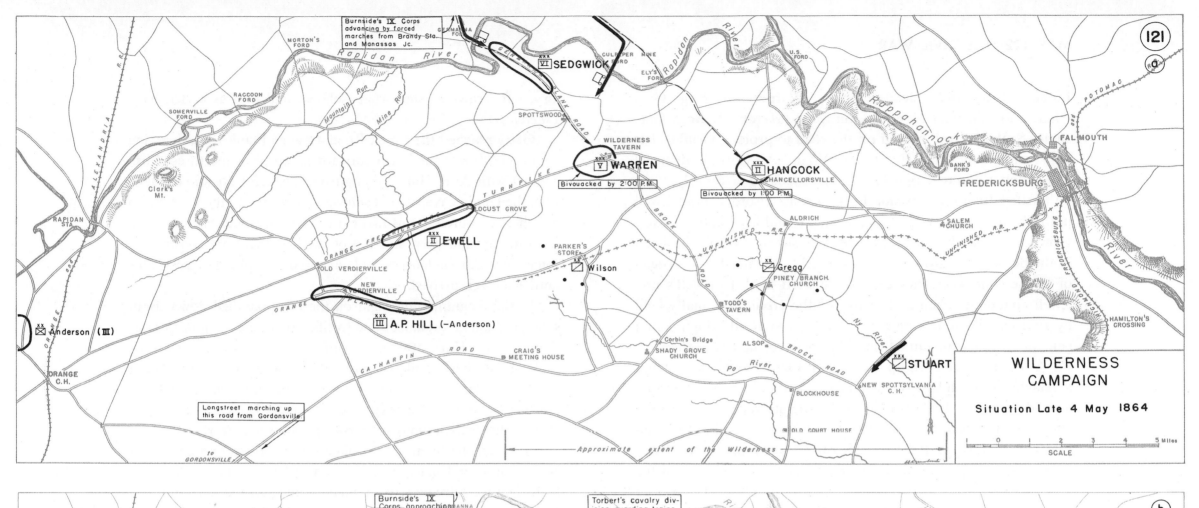

Burnside's IX Corps advancing by forced marches from Brandy Sta. and Manassas Jc.

MORTON'S FORD

Rapidan River

SOMERVILLE FORD

RACCOON FORD

Mountain Run

Mine Run

VI SEDGWICK

CULPEPER MINE FORD

ELY'S FORD

U.S. FORD

Rapidan River

Rappahannock River

POTOMAC R.R.

FALMOUTH

SPOTTSWOOD

Clark's Mt.

WILDERNESS TAVERN

V WARREN

Bivouacked by 2:00 P.M.

II HANCOCK

CHANCELLORSVILLE

FREDERICKSBURG

BANK'S FORD

SALEM CHURCH

ALDRICH

RAPIDAN STA.

TURNPIKE

LOCUST GROVE

II EWELL

ORANGE-FREDERICKSBURG

BROCK ROAD

UNFINISHED R.R.

UNFINISHED R.R.

PARKER'S STORE

Wilson

Gregg

PINEY BRANCH CHURCH

HAMILTON'S CROSSING

OLD VERDIERVILLE

NEW VERDIERVILLE

ORANGE PLANK RD

III A.P. HILL (-Anderson)

TODD'S TAVERN

Anderson (III)

ORANGE C.H.

CATHARPIN ROAD

CRAIG'S MEETING HOUSE

Corbin's Bridge

SHADY GROVE CHURCH

Po River

ALSOP

BROCK ROAD

NEW SPOTTSYLVANIA C.H.

Ny River

STUART

WILDERNESS CAMPAIGN

Situation Late 4 May 1864

Longstreet marching up this road from Gordonsville

BLOCKHOUSE

OLD COURT HOUSE

to GORDONSVILLE

Approximate extent of the Wilderness

1 0 1 2 3 4 5 Miles

SCALE

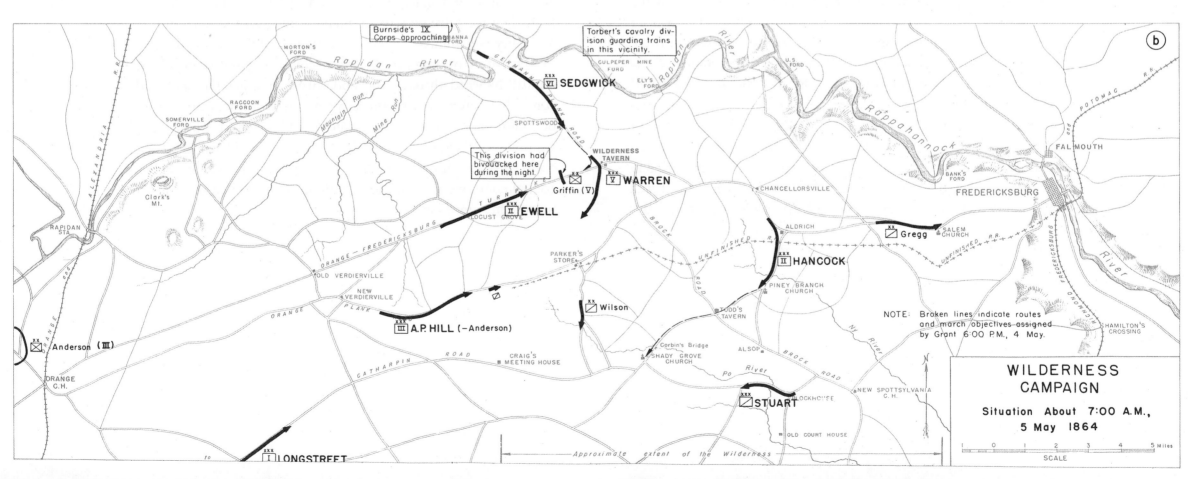

b

Burnside's IX Corps approaching

Torbert's cavalry division guarding trains in this vicinity.

MORTON'S FORD

Rapidan River

SOMERVILLE FORD

RACCOON FORD

Mountain Run

Mine Run

VI SEDGWICK

GERMANNA PLANK ROAD

CULPEPER MINE FORD

ELY'S FORD

U.S. FORD

Rapidan River

Rappahannock River

POTOMAC R.R.

FALMOUTH

SPOTTSWOOD

Clark's Mt.

This division had bivouacked here during the night

WILDERNESS TAVERN

Griffin (V)

V WARREN

CHANCELLORSVILLE

FREDERICKSBURG

BANK'S FORD

RAPIDAN STA.

TURNPIKE

LOCUST GROVE

II EWELL

ORANGE-FREDERICKSBURG

BROCK ROAD

ALDRICH

Gregg

SALEM CHURCH

UNFINISHED R.R.

UNFINISHED R.R.

PARKER'S STORE

OLD VERDIERVILLE

NEW VERDIERVILLE

ORANGE PLANK RD

III A.P. HILL (-Anderson)

II HANCOCK

PINEY BRANCH CHURCH

Wilson

TODD'S TAVERN

HAMILTON'S CROSSING

Anderson (III)

ORANGE C.H.

CATHARPIN ROAD

CRAIG'S MEETING HOUSE

Corbin's Bridge

SHADY GROVE CHURCH

Po River

ALSOP

BROCK ROAD

NEW SPOTTSYLVANIA C.H.

Ny River

STUART

NOTE: Broken lines indicate routes and march objectives assigned by Grant 6:00 P.M., 4 May.

WILDERNESS CAMPAIGN

Situation About 7:00 A.M., 5 May 1864

BLOCKHOUSE

OLD COURT HOUSE

to I LONGSTREET

Approximate extent of the Wilderness

1 0 1 2 3 4 5 Miles

SCALE

In accordance with Meade's orders, Warren sent Brig. Gen. Charles Griffin west along the turnpike (*sketch* a). Brig. Gen. James S. Wadsworth moved off the road to prolong Griffin's left flank, while Brig. Gen. Horatio G. Wright (VI Corps) advanced from Spottswood to support his right. Attacking vigorously, Griffin hustled Johnson's division back in some disorder, until Ewell put in his reserves. Wright, meanwhile, found his "road" so overgrown as to be almost impassable; Wadsworth lost his direction in the dense undergrowth and advanced to the northwest instead of to the southwest, thus exposing his left flank to Ewell's fire. Ewell counterattacked and recovered the ground originally held by Johnson. Then, having received orders to avoid bringing on a general engagement until Longstreet arrived, he entrenched.

A. P. Hill's advance up the Orange Plank Road encountered a detachment from Brig. Gen. James H. Wilson's cavalry division. This detachment fell back slowly, using its repeating carbines effectively to check Hill's march. Meade at once realized the importance of holding the Brock Road (*lower right*), the loss of which would separate Hancock and Wilson from the rest of the army. He therefore ordered Brig. Gen. George W. Getty (VI Corps) to move to the Orange Plank Road and, if possible, drive the Confederates there back beyond Parker's Store. Hancock was ordered to countermarch to the Brock Road–Orange Plank Road junction and support Getty. In the meantime, Brig. Gen. Samuel W. Crawford had thrown out a skirmish line to support the Union cavalry on the Orange Plank Road. Shortly thereafter, he received orders to send a brigade to support Griffin's attack. This brigade (*not shown*) became lost, blundered into Ewell's line, and was badly mauled. Its defeat, and the gradual withdrawal of the cav-

alry, left Crawford somewhat isolated, and he was pulled back (*sketch* b).

Getty reached the Brock Road–Orange Plank Road junction about 11:00 A.M. and sent forward a skirmish line to establish contact with A. P. Hill's leading troops, which were still engaged with the Union cavalry (*not shown*) a half-mile to the west. From prisoners captured in this first clash, Getty learned that two Confederate divisions were in front of him. He therefore constructed some light entrenchments and prepared to hold the crossroads until Hancock arrived.

In the meantime, the fight on the turnpike died down. Both sides gradually reorganized and fortified their lines. On the Orange Plank Road, Hill—also under orders to wait for Longstreet—took up the best available position and awaited orders. About 2:00 P.M., Hancock's corps began coming into line on Getty's left flank. Getty said he expected an attack. Hancock thereupon ordered his leading units to throw up light breastworks.

Already, the fighting had taken on the frustrating characteristics that would mark it to the end. Numbers meant little—in fact, they were frequently an encumbrance on the narrow trails. Visibility was limited, making it extremely difficult for officers to exercise effective control. Attackers could only thrash noisily and blindly forward through the underbrush, perfect targets for the concealed defenders. In attack or retreat, formations could rarely be maintained. In this near-jungle, the Confederates had the advantages of being, on the whole, better woodsmen than their opponents and of being far more familiar with the terrain. Federal commanders were forced to rely upon maps, which soon proved thoroughly unreliable.

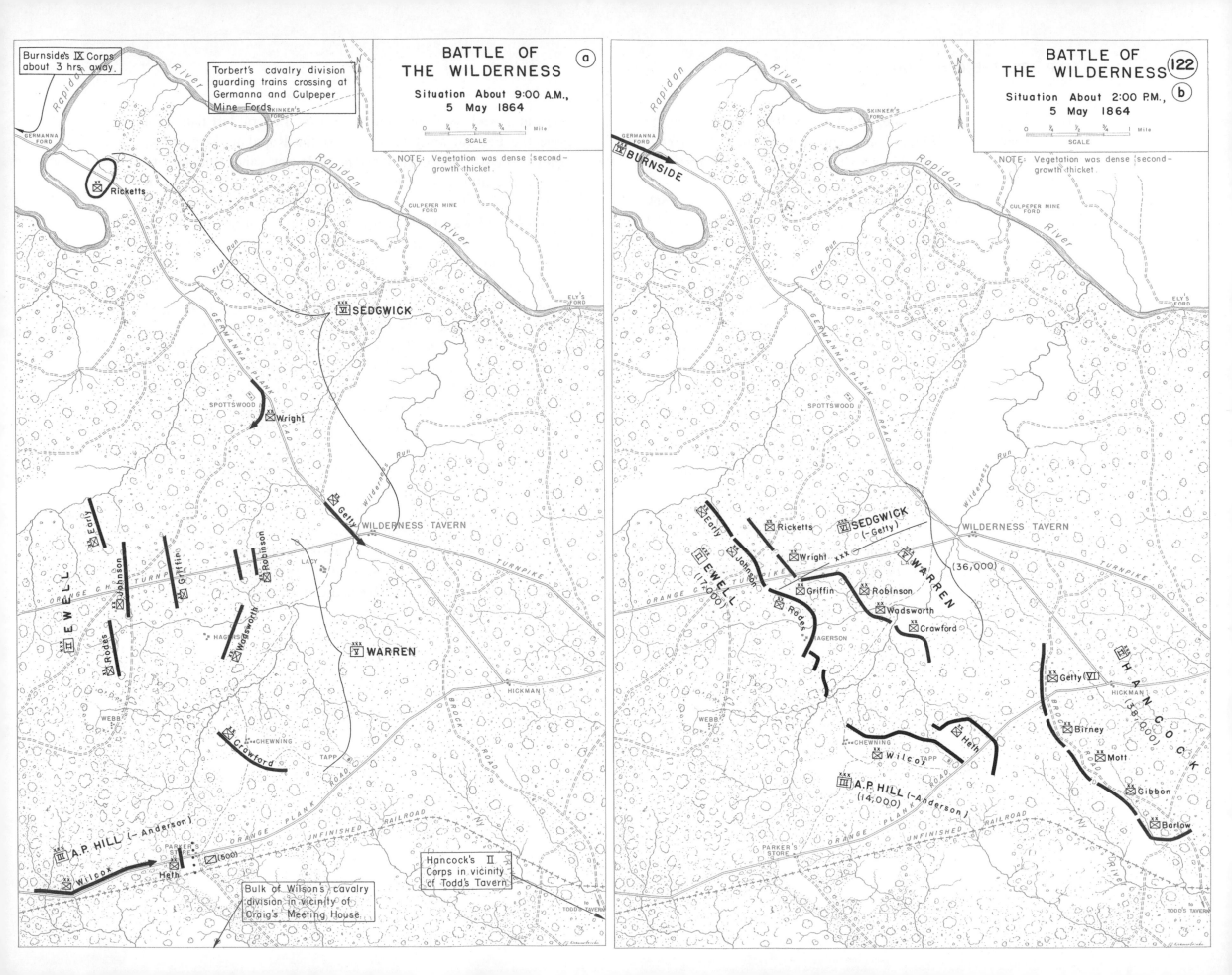

BATTLE OF
THE WILDERNESS ⓐ

Situation About 9:00 A.M.,
5 May 1864

SCALE

NOTE: Vegetation was dense second-growth thicket.

Burnside's IX Corps about 3 hrs. away.

Torbert's cavalry division guarding trains crossing at Germanna and Culpeper Mine Fords

Hancock's II Corps in vicinity of Todd's Tavern

Bulk of Wilson's cavalry division in vicinity of Craig's Meeting House

BATTLE OF
THE WILDERNESS (122)

Situation About 2:00 P.M.,
5 May 1864 ⓑ

SCALE

NOTE: Vegetation was dense second-growth thicket.

By 3:00 P.M., Lee was debating the possibility of seizing the Brock Road without bringing on a general engagement (*sketch* a). Heth was dubious, but willing to try if so ordered. Before Lee could reach a decision, the Federals attacked.

Sometime after 3:15 P.M., Getty received orders to attack at once. Hancock's divisions were to support him. Meade wanted the attack made immediately, to take advantage of Longstreet's absence. Hancock, however, delayed to complete the line of hasty breastworks he had begun along his front. (This undoubtedly was an error, since it likewise gave Hill time to strengthen his position.) At 4:15 P.M., Getty went forward and quickly met savage resistance. Hancock at once reinforced Getty; Wilcox moved to support Heth. Fighting raged desperately until dark, the Confederates barely managing to hold their general line after repeated attacks and counterattacks. Despite their valiant defense, night found Hill's men shaken and somewhat scattered; their ammunition almost exhausted; and their right flank forced back by Barlow's last attack. Hill was too sick to exercise command; consequently, his position was not properly reorganized.

During the late afternoon, Meade sent Wadsworth across country to reinforce Hancock's right flank, and also ordered renewed attacks on Ewell's line. These attacks were costly and futile. Wadsworth found the woods almost impassable and was unable to get into action before dark.

Both armies planned to attack the next day (6 May). Lee sent word to Longstreet to hurry forward, planning to use his corps and Anderson's division to turn the Federal left flank and drive the Federal army back against the Rapidan. Meanwhile, Grant ordered Hancock, Warren, Sedgwick, and Burnside to resume the attack at 5:00 A.M. (Burnside was to advance at 2:00 A.M. with two divisions to fill the gap between Warren and Hancock, and was to have them in position to attack at the required hour.) Since Hancock's line was too long for effective personal leadership in such terrain, he divided it into two commands—Gibbon on the left flank and Birney astride the Orange Plank Road (*sketch* b). Prisoners had revealed that Longstreet was expected to attack the Union right that morning.

At 5:00 A.M., the Federal attack jumped off—except for Burnside, who was still trying to find his way forward through the roadless tangle of undergrowth between the Turnpike and the Orange Plank Road. On the north, Ewell repulsed Sedgwick and Warren with heavy loss; on the south, Hill's men, struck in front and flank by Hancock's massive assault, broke and fled to the rear. Confederate artillery, firing across the open fields of the Tapp farm in Hill's rear, slowed the Union rush, but could not stop it. Except for the guns, Lee's entire right flank had crumbled.

But, shouldering through the rearward-bound wreck of Heth's and Wilcox's divisions, came Longstreet—his men remarking that the spectacle reminded them of Bragg's army. Lee was unusually excited; his subordinates had considerable trouble getting him to move farther to the rear.

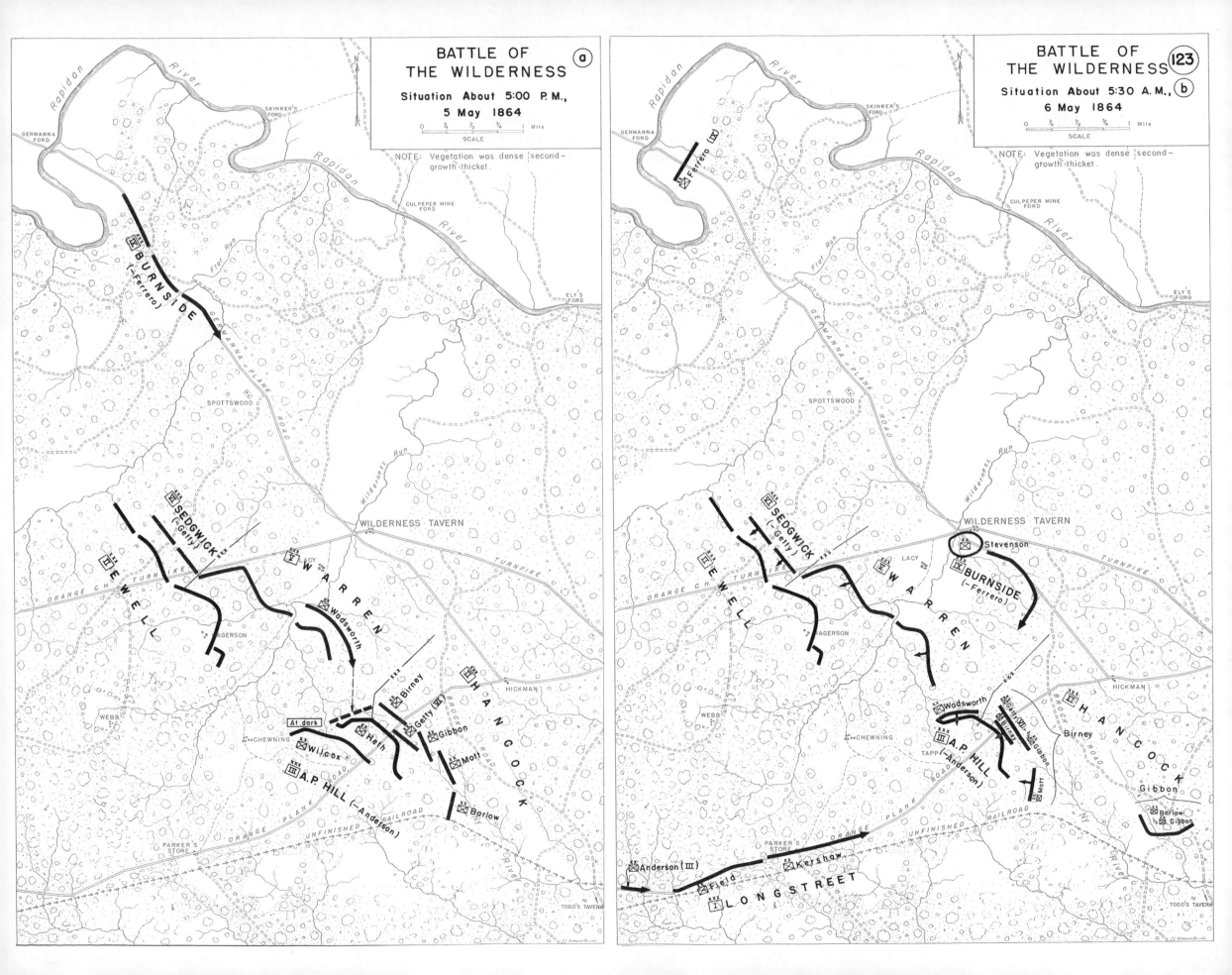

BATTLE OF THE WILDERNESS (a)

Situation About 5:00 P.M.,
5 May 1864

SCALE
0   ¼   ½   ¾   Mile

NOTE: Vegetation was dense second-
growth thicket.

BATTLE OF THE WILDERNESS (123)(b)

Situation About 5:30 A.M.,
6 May 1864

SCALE
0   ¼   ½   ¾   Mile

NOTE: Vegetation was dense second-
growth thicket.

Longstreet went directly into action, stopping Birney, but meeting stubborn resistance as he attacked in his turn (*sketch a*). A succession of assaults by both armies surged back and forth between the Brock Road and the Tapp farm. About 8:00 A.M., Meade sent Brig. Gen. Thomas G. Stevenson (IX Corps), who had been held in reserve at Wilderness Tavern, to reinforce Hancock; ordered Warren and Sedgwick to renew their offensive; and sent Sheridan's cavalry (*not shown*) against Longstreet's right rear.

At 7:00 A.M., Hancock had ordered Gibbon to send Barlow's division against the Confederate right flank, but only one brigade was ever dispatched, because of a series of apparent threats to the Federal left. The Federal command mistakenly believed that Pickett's division was with Longstreet, whereas he had, in fact, been detached for garrison duty in the Richmond area. When prisoners captured on the Orange Plank Road did not include any of Pickett's men, it was thought that his division was being held in reserve for a decisive attack. Consequently, a detachment of Federal convalescents, who had become lost while attempting to rejoin their army, were at first mistaken for Confederate infantry—as was Stuart's cavalry when it appeared dismounted near Todd's Tavern (*off map, bottom right*). The result was that Barlow was held out of action during a critical period.

By 11:00 A.M., both sides were temporarily fought out. Birney had fallen back somewhat toward his original line. Sheridan, completely neglecting to cover the exposed flanks of the Union army, was engaged in a noisy and inconsequential brawl with Stuart around Todd's Tavern. Meade had ordered Sedgwick and Warren to stop their attacks, entrench, and assemble troops to reinforce Hancock.

The lull was deceptive. Longstreet, with Lee's approval, had prepared a Chancellorsville-style flank attack to roll up the Union line. A reconnaissance by Maj. Gen. Martin L. Smith, Lee's chief engineer, had discovered that Birney's south flank was unprotected and could be easily turned by an advance along the bed of an unfinished railroad which ran parallel to the Orange Plank Road. Longstreet directed one of his staff officers, Lt. Col. G. Moxley Sorrel, to assemble four brigades and carry out this attack, while he himself led an advance along the Orange Plank Road. (Apparently, he considered using some of the troops he had concentrated there for a second, deeper envelopment to get behind the Brock Road.)

The flank attack by the troops which Sorrel had collected (apparently actually commanded by Mahone) was immediately successful, Birney's line collapsing from left to right. (*Subsequent action not shown.*) Only Hancock's dominating leadership rallied it behind the entrenchments he had ordered built the day before along the Brock Road (*sketch b*). Longstreet, pushing the Confederate drive forward, was accidentally wounded by his own men. Lee took over the direction of the attack, but found the troops too disordered by their advance through the underbrush to continue. It was 4:15 P.M. before they could be reorganized; then their attack collapsed in front of Hancock's defenses.

In the center, Burnside did not attack until 2:00 P.M.; Hill's divisions repulsed him.

To the north, Gordon had spent a thwarted day. During the previous night, his scouts had discovered that the Union right flank was unprotected and that the Confederate left flank overlapped it (*sketch a*). However, Early, supported by Ewell, refused him permission to attack. Finally, about 5:30 P.M., Lee visited Ewell's headquarters; Gordon stated his plan and secured Lee's approval. Though launched too late in the day to affect the outcome of the battle, his attack scored a handsome little success until darkness and Sedgwick's calm leadership halted it.

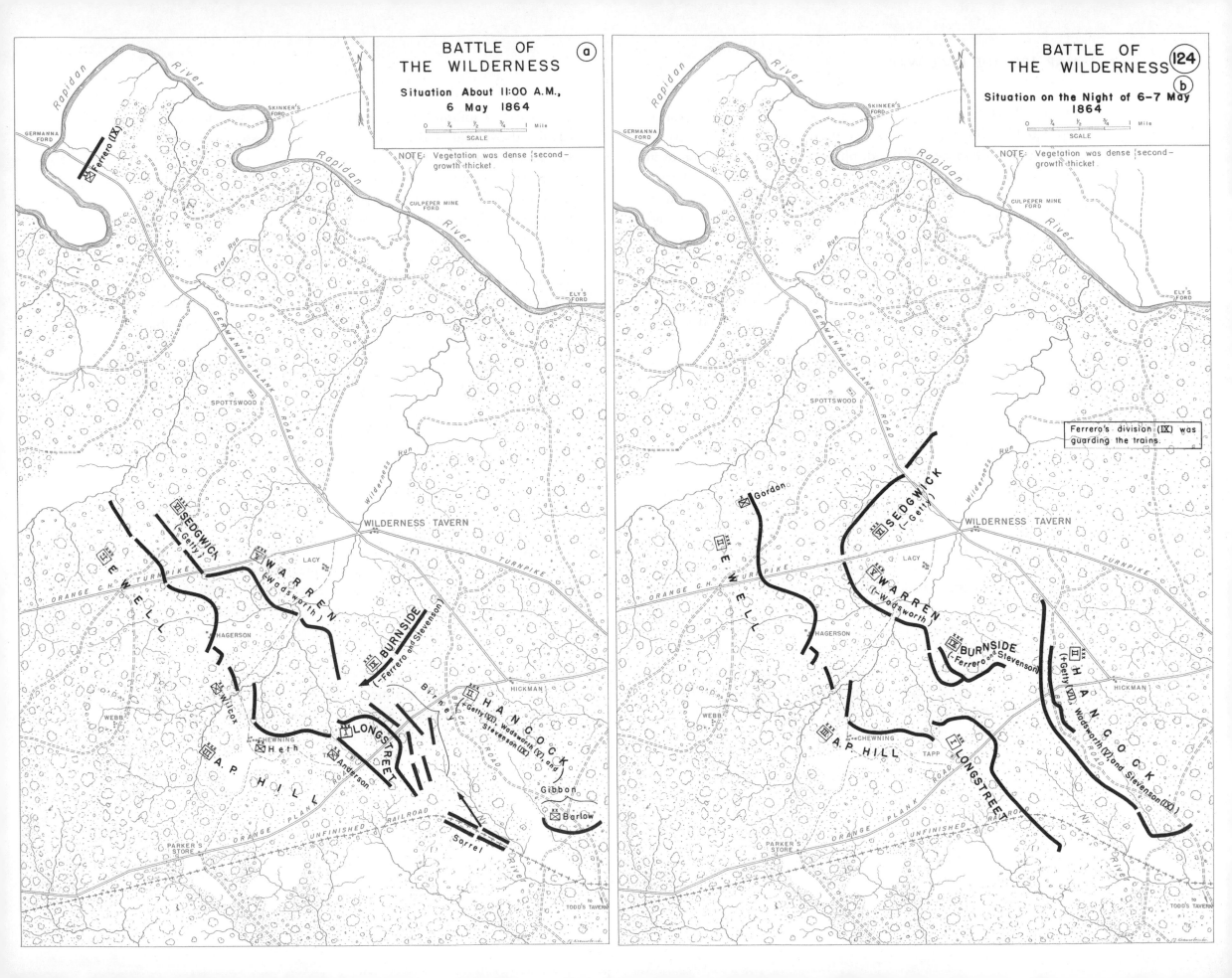

BATTLE OF
THE WILDERNESS
(a)

Situation About 11:00 A.M.,
6 May 1864

SCALE

NOTE: Vegetation was dense second-growth thicket.

BATTLE OF
THE WILDERNESS
124
(b)

Situation on the Night of 6–7 May
1864

SCALE

NOTE: Vegetation was dense second-growth thicket.

Ferrero's division (IX) was guarding the trains.

During 7 May, the two armies lay behind their breastworks, separated by three-quarters of a mile of smoldering Wilderness (*sketch* a). It had been a blind, blundering battle in which even the casualties inflicted remain in doubt: Union losses had been between 15,000 and 18,000; Confederate records are fragmentary, estimates varying from 7,750 to 11,400. Both Grant and Lee had shown great determination but no particular skill. Grant, especially, seems to have ignored the limitations which the terrain would impose upon his attacks, and neither he, Meade, nor Sheridan had employed his strong cavalry corps properly.

Lee, too, had failed to use his cavalry properly, and so had created a situation in which he had to commit his forces piecemeal as they came onto the field. He had failed in his attempt to seize the Brock Road, but had succeeded in turning both flanks of the larger Union army.

A year before, Hooker, commanding another Union army—just as large, and no more badly hurt—had accepted defeat and fallen back across the Rapidan. But now, as the day passed, indications multiplied that this time the Federal commander intended to shift to the southeast instead of retiring. To Lee, that meant that it would be necessary to hold the important road junction at New Spottsylvania Court House (*lower right*).

At 8:30 P.M., 7 May, the Army of the Potomac began to move as shown. Grant had studied the Confederate positions and concluded that they were too strong for a frontal attack. Warren and Sedgwick pulled out of line and marched for Spottsylvania; Burnside started for Aldrich; Hancock remained in position until the rest of the army had passed behind him, then moved to Todd's Tavern. It was a black night; roads were poor and hard to follow; and the march of some units was not well handled. Along the Brock Road, Fitzhugh Lee's cavalry fought a skillful delaying action (*not shown*) against Brig. Gen. Wesley Merritt's cavalry

and Warren's infantry. Farther to the southeast, Wilson's Union cavalry drove that of Brig. Gen. Thomas L. Rosser out of Spottsylvania (*action not shown*).

It was around 8:30 A.M. of the 8th before Warren's leading infantry came out into the open ground near Alsop, pushing Fitzhugh Lee's cavalry slowly before them. Here, they were suddenly checked by Confederate infantry and artillery (*sketch* b).

These Confederates were Longstreet's corps, now under Anderson, and their presence here was due to a combination of hard marching and good luck. Lee had ordered Anderson to withdraw from his position on the Orange Plank Road as soon as possible after dark, assemble his men in some quiet rear area where they could rest, and start before 3:00 A.M. the next morning for Spottsylvania. Anderson began his withdrawal at 11:00 P.M., but could find no suitable area in which to halt his command (much of the woods along the Orange Plank Road having caught fire during the battle), and so continued on toward Spottsylvania. En route the next morning, he halted for an hour to permit his men to cook breakfast. Shortly thereafter, he received a message from Stuart asking for help, and immediately pushed forward, arriving just in time to block Warren.

Wilson had held Spottsylvania for two hours. Now, the Confederate cavalry concentrated against him, and Sheridan ordered him to withdraw. At 1:00 P.M., Meade ordered Sedgwick to support an attack by Warren. Time was required to get the tired troops into position on strange ground and to coordinate Sedgwick's and Warren's efforts. As a result, the attack was not launched until late in the afternoon, and then it was rather half-hearted. Ewell arrived in time to protect Anderson's flank. On the Federal right, Hancock sent Col. Nelson A. Miles on a reconnaissance in force to Corbin's Bridge, just southwest of Todd's Tavern.

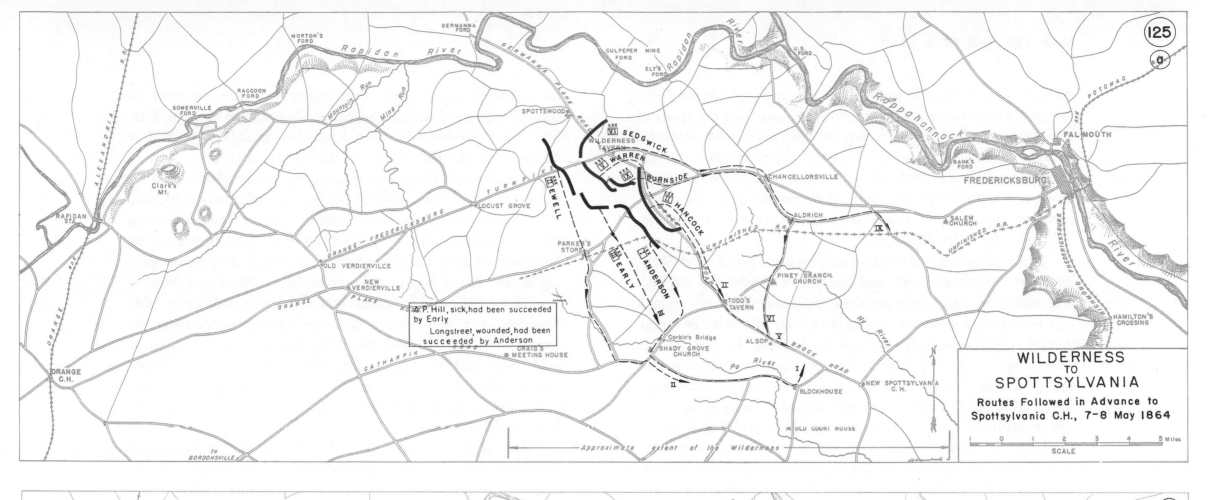

A.P. Hill, sick, had been succeeded by Early.
Longstreet, wounded, had been succeeded by Anderson

**WILDERNESS
TO
SPOTTSYLVANIA**

Routes Followed in Advance to
Spottsylvania C.H., 7-8 May 1864

0   1   2   3   4   5 Miles
SCALE

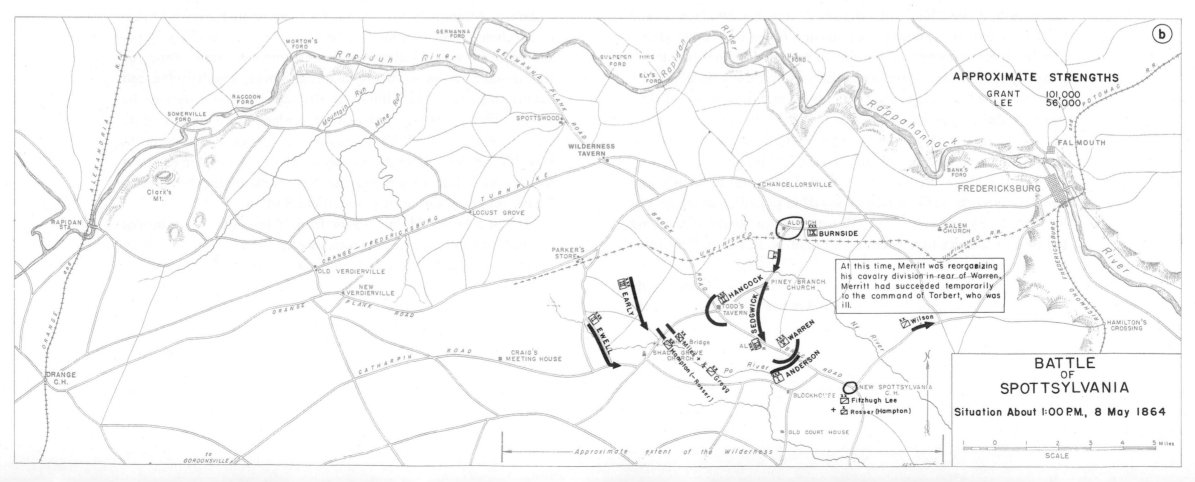

b

APPROXIMATE STRENGTHS

GRANT   101,000
LEE   56,000

At this time, Merritt was reorganizing
his cavalry division in rear of Warren.
Merritt had succeeded temporarily
to the command of Torbert, who was
ill.

Fitzhugh Lee

Rosser (Hampton)

**BATTLE
OF
SPOTTSYLVANIA**

Situation About 1:00 P.M., 8 May 1864

0   1   2   3   4   5 Miles
SCALE

At 1:00 P.M., 8 May, as both armies concentrated around Spottsylvania, Grant ordered Sheridan to "cut loose from the Army of the Potomac, pass round the left of Lee's army and attack his cavalry." That done, Sheridan was to cut the railroads in the rear of the Confederate army; if circumstances required, he could move to the James River, south of Richmond (*bottom right*), and draw supplies from Butler at Haxall's Landing before rejoining the Army of the Potomac.

This mission sprang from a clash between Meade and Sheridan over the latter's feeble and amateurish handling of the Federal horsemen. Sheridan's previous experience as a cavalryman had been only a short but creditable period of service as a regimental commander under Halleck in the west. He had not yet learned how to handle a corps—a condition not helped by the fact that, of his division commanders, Torbert had just been transferred from the infantry, while Wilson had recently been a very junior engineer officer. As noted, Sheridan had failed in the fundamental mission of screening the army's flanks. During the night march to Spottsylvania, his orders to his division commanders had been late, with the result that his cavalry blocked the advance of the infantry columns and failed to clear Fitzhugh Lee from Warren's line of march. On the other hand, Sheridan—whose great military virtue was a furious and undying pugnacity—was completely exasperated with his recent missions of guarding supply trains and protecting the flanks of the main army. Instead, he saw his task as that of first defeating the Confederate cavalry. It was on his offer to do this that Grant let him go.

The Cavalry Corps moved out on the 9th, riding slowly and confidently at the walk. Stuart followed in pursuit, leaving part of his force to cover Lee's flanks. The strength of Sheridan's column led him to suspect that Richmond might be the actual objective of this raid.

Sheridan rode deliberately south, destroying Confederate supply depots along his line of march. On the 10th, Stuart divided his command, leaving Brig. Gen. James B. Gordon to maintain contact with the Federal rear guard, while he himself took Fitzhugh Lee's division on a long detour that brought it to Yellow Tavern, between Richmond and the Federal column.

In Richmond, Bragg (who, having been relieved after Chattanooga, was now Davis' military advisor) could muster only some 4,000 home guards and convalescents—barely enough to man the city's fortifications, though he had ordered additional troops brought back from the James River front, where they were opposing Butler. Stuart may have hoped to fall on Sheridan's flank or rear if the Union commander attacked Richmond, or to hold Sheridan at Yellow Tavern until the reinforcements from the James arrived. The Union force, however, was too heavy to be held back, and Stuart's cavalry—not Richmond—was its objective. After a short, gallant defense, the Confederates broke. Stuart was mortally wounded. Gordon attacked the Federal rear, but was defeated and killed.

Sheridan then passed through the outer defenses of Richmond, but found the inner ones strongly held, and accordingly turned eastward. Attempting to cross the Chickahominy River just south of Mechanicsville, he found the bridges destroyed and the opposite bank held by Confederate infantry and artillery, while the Richmond garrison and the remnants of Stuart's cavalry advanced against his rear. The Union cavalry, however, was not to be cowed. Fighting front and rear, it bridged the Chickahominy under fire, drove back both Confederate forces, and rode on to Haxall's Landing. After a brief stay with Butler, Sheridan returned by way of White House and the west bank of the Mattapony River, rejoining Grant at Chesterfield Station.

It was a bold raid, but—aside from killing Stuart—it did not seriously cripple the Confederate cavalry. And while it was in progress, Grant, like Lee at Gettysburg, was left moving blindly in hostile territory.

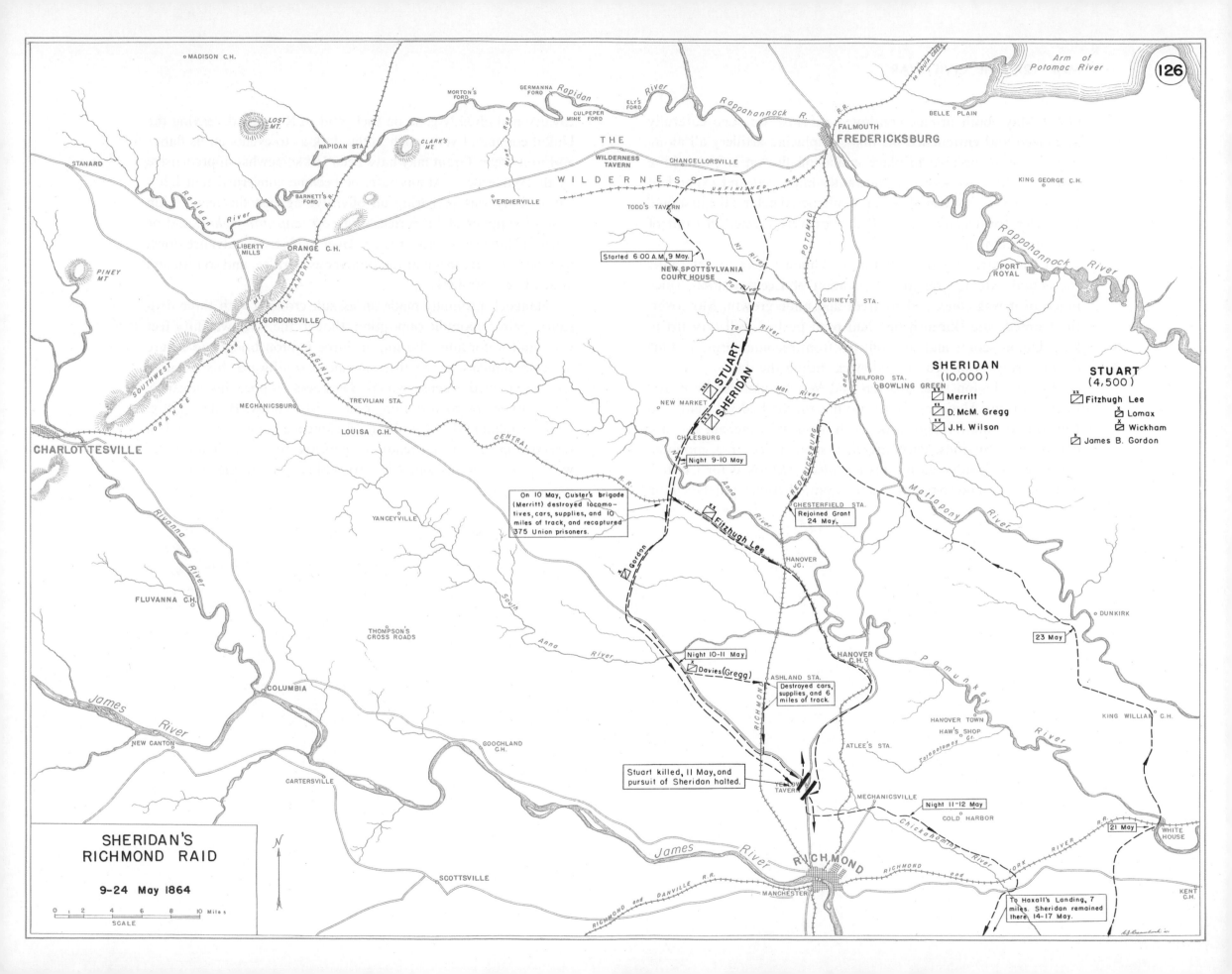

126

Arm of Potomac River

MADISON C.H.

LOST MT.

Rapidan River

RAPIDAN STA.

CLARK'S MT.

Germanna Ford
MORTON'S FORD
CULPEPER MINE FORD
ELY'S FORD

Mine Run

Rappahannock R.

to AQUIA CREEK R.R.

BELLE PLAIN

FALMOUTH
FREDERICKSBURG

STANARD

THE WILDERNESS
WILDERNESS TAVERN
CHANCELLORSVILLE

KING GEORGE C.H.

BARNETT'S FORD
PINEY MT.

LIBERTY MILLS

ORANGE C.H.

MT. ALEXANDRIA

VERDIERVILLE

TODD'S TAVERN

UNFINISHED R.R.

Started 6:00 A.M., 9 May.

NEW SPOTTSYLVANIA COURT HOUSE

Po River

GUINEY'S STA.

PORT ROYAL

Rappahannock River

GORDONSVILLE

VIRGINIA

Ta River

Mat River

MILFORD STA.

BOWLING GREEN

SOUTHWEST MT.

ORANGE and

TREVILIAN STA.

NEW MARKET

STUART
SHERIDAN

SHERIDAN
(10,000)
Merritt
D. McM. Gregg
J.H. Wilson

STUART
(4,500)
Fitzhugh Lee
Lomax
Wickham
James B. Gordon

MECHANICSBURG

LOUISA C.H.

CENTRAL

R.R.

CHARLESBURG

CHARLOTTESVILLE

Night 9-10 May

FREDERICKSBURG

Mattapony River

On 10 May, Custer's brigade (Merritt) destroyed locomotives, cars, supplies, and 10 miles of track, and recaptured 375 Union prisoners.

YANCEYVILLE

Anna River

Fitzhugh Lee

Gordon

CHESTERFIELD STA.

Rejoined Grant 24 May.

Rivanna River

HANOVER JC.

FLUVANNA C.H.

THOMPSON'S CROSS ROADS

South Anna River

Night 10-11 May

Davies (Gregg)

ASHLAND STA.

Destroyed cars, supplies, and 6 miles of track.

HANOVER C.H.

23 May

DUNKIRK

Pamunkey River

COLUMBIA

RICHMOND

HANOVER TOWN
HAW'S SHOP Gr.

KING WILLIAM C.H.

NEW CANTON

James River

GOOCHLAND C.H.

ATLEE'S STA.

Totopotomoy Cr.

CARTERSVILLE

Stuart killed, 11 May, and pursuit of Sheridan halted.

YELLOW TAVERN

MECHANICSVILLE

Night 11-12 May

COLD HARBOR

Chickahominy River

21 May

WHITE HOUSE

SHERIDAN'S RICHMOND RAID

9-24 May 1864

N

SCOTTSVILLE

James River

MANCHESTER

RICHMOND and

RICHMOND and DANVILLE R.R.

RICHMOND and

York River R.R.

KENT C.H.

To Haxall's Landing, 7 miles. Sheridan remained there 14-17 May.

0 2 4 6 8 10 Miles
SCALE

On 9 May, both armies continued to close up. Lee carefully organized and entrenched his lines, emplacing artillery all along them so as to be able to place enfilading fire on any attacking column. These works were constantly improved and expanded; in many places, a second line was constructed behind the first one. Obstacles constructed from felled trees were erected in front of the entrenchments.

It was extremely difficult for the Union forces to determine the actual extent, strength, or location of Lee's position, since much of it was concealed by trees and undergrowth. Moreover, the Confederate skirmish line had been pushed well forward to keep Union scouts and staff officers from reconnoitering it. One of these snipers picked off Sedgwick during the day.

On the Union side, Warren and Wright likewise improved their positions. Hancock came into line on the Federal right, and Burnside on the left. Burnside, with his usual penchant for misconstruing situations, encountered a small force of dismounted Confederate cavalry during his advance, mistook it for Confederate infantry, and so reported it to Grant. Sheridan and the Union cavalry had already gone on their raid to Richmond, leaving the Union command very much in the dark as to events on its flanks and to its rear. Grant may have been left somewhat apprehensive by the Wilderness. At any rate, he became concerned that Lee's entire army was preparing an offensive against the new Union base of supplies at Fredericksburg (*off map, top right*), and he ordered Hancock to cross the Po River to his front, advance down its west bank, recross it at the Blockhouse Bridge, and so turn and attack Lee's left flank.

Hancock promptly made an assault crossing with three divisions against sporadic opposition, though the river was fifty feet wide and unfordable. Putting in three ponton bridges to assure his communications, he then advanced southward, his progress hampered by the dense woods. Darkness stopped his advance, still short of the road running east to Blockhouse Bridge. (Brig. Gen. Gershom Mott's division of Hancock's corps was held in reserve [*upper center*], ready to reinforce Burnside, if the latter were attacked in his somewhat isolated position to the east.)

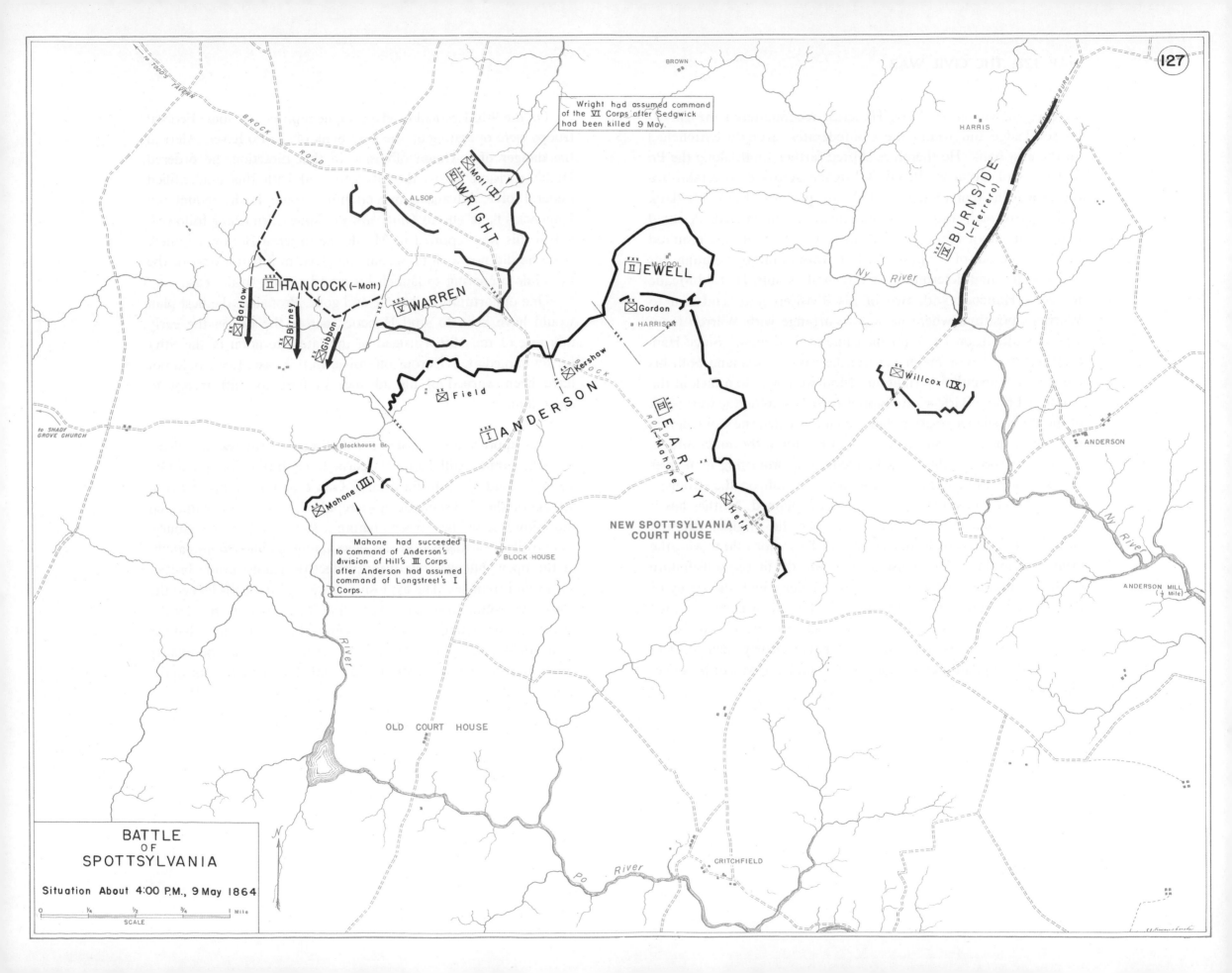

127

Wright had assumed command
of the VI Corps after Sedgwick
had been killed 9 May.

to TODD'S TAVERN

BROWN

HARRIS

to FREDERICKSBURG

BROCK ROAD

ALSOP

Mott (II)

WRIGHT

Ny River

BURNSIDE
(−Ferrero)

II EWELL

McCOOL

IX

II HANCOCK (−Mott)

Barlow

Birney

Gibbon

V WARREN

Gordon

HARRISON

Field

Kershaw

BROCK ROAD

Willcox (IX)

ANDERSON

I

EARLY
(Mahone)

ANDERSON

to SHADY
GROVE CHURCH

Blockhouse Br

Heth

NEW SPOTTSYLVANIA
COURT HOUSE

ANDERSON MILL
(½ Mile)

Mahone (III)

Mahone had succeeded
to command of Anderson's
division of Hill's III Corps
after Anderson had assumed
command of Longstreet's I
Corps.

BLOCK HOUSE

Ny RIVER

River

OLD COURT HOUSE

Po River

CRITCHFIELD

N

BATTLE
OF
SPOTTSYLVANIA

Situation About 4:00 P.M., 9 May 1864

0   ¼   ½   ¾   1 Mile
SCALE

At early dawn on 10 May, Hancock reconnoitered the Blockhouse Bridge but found the Confederates strongly entrenched on the east bank. He therefore shifted farther south along the Po and got Col. John R. Brooke's brigade across it to establish a bridgehead in rear of the Confederate position. Lee's left flank was thus turned, and his communications threatened. A rapid reinforcement of Hancock's advance was all that was required to force Lee out of his position. But Grant, not appreciating this opportunity, had determined on a frontal assault. He told Meade to recall Hancock with two of his divisions and send him to Warren's position, where he was to arrange with Warren for a vigorous attack on Lee's fortified line at 5:00 P.M. (Since Hancock was the senior major general, he would command both his corps and Warren's.) Wright and Mott were also to attack at the appointed hour. Barlow's division was to remain on the west bank of the Po, in such a position that it could threaten the Confederate left, yet withdraw easily if needed to reinforce the main attack.

The reason for this abandonment of a promising maneuver in favor of a Fredericksburg-type direct assault on the strongest sector of Lee's position has never been explained. Neither has it ever been positively determined whether the original decision was Meade's or Grant's; but Grant, as the senior officer with the army, was in the end responsible. This was the first serious failure of the anomalous system of command under which the Army of the Potomac had to finish the war. In effect, it was commanded by two generals—each with his own, occasionally jealous, staff; their respective responsibilities were never clearly defined. The result was frequently confusion; occasionally, it was to be something worse.

On the 9th, Lee had received vague reports that some Federal troops were operating on the west bank of the Po River. Alert to the danger of a Union offensive in that direction, he ordered Heth's division across the river to deal with this unidentified Federal force. Advancing by a circuitous route, Heth encountered Hancock's flank guards (*not shown*). Some skirmishing followed. When this was reported to Meade, he ordered Barlow recalled, since he did not wish to become involved in a battle west of the Po while preparing to launch his grand assault to the east.

One opportunity had come and gone. Probably, the best plan would have been to send Hancock across the Po on the early morning of the 10th (instead of the late afternoon of the 9th) for an immediate, vigorous offensive. In this case, Lee would not have been warned of his advance in time to shift troops to meet him.

It is appropriate to note here that most of the senior officers of both armies still had not learned the futility of assaulting strongly held field fortifications. Grant had seen his heaviest attacks on the Vicksburg defenses repulsed, and Lee had witnessed the failure of his best troops before a stone wall at Gettysburg. The artillery of this period was devastating against troops caught in the open, but was relatively ineffective against crude breastworks and trenches. The explosive charges of its shells lacked the power necessary to destroy them, and its fuzes were too erratic to enable the gunners to place accurate fire on the men behind them. Before many more battles, however, it became abundantly clear that one man well entrenched equaled three men in the open.

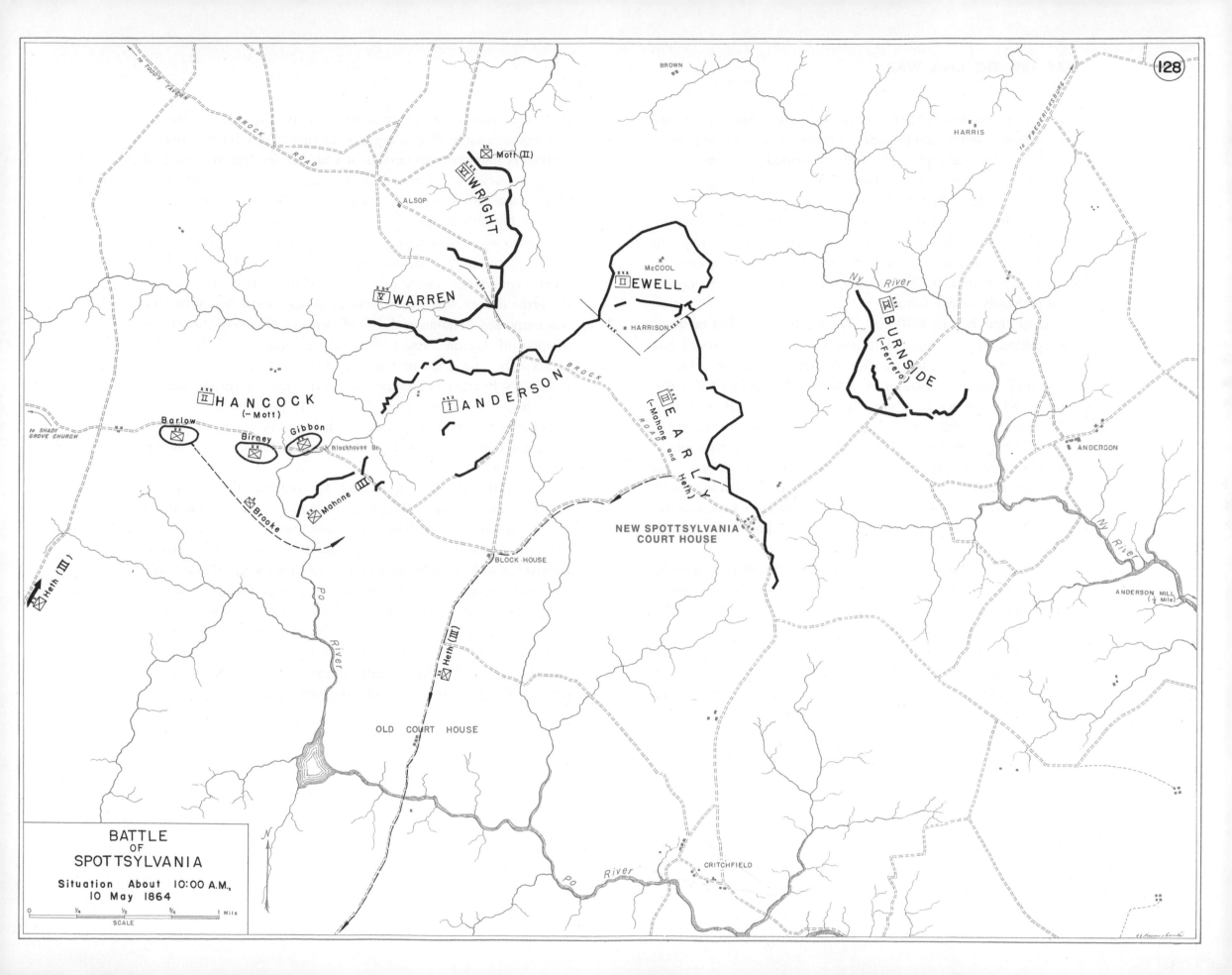

128

BROWN

HARRIS

to TODD'S TAVERN

BROCK

ROAD

to FREDERICKSBURG

Mott (II)

WRIGHT

ALSOP

McCOOL

II EWELL

Ny River

WARREN

V WARREN

Harrison

IX BURNSIDE
(-Ferrero)

II HANCOCK
(-Mott)

I ANDERSON

BROCK

EARLY
(-Mahone and Heth)

ROAD

Barlow

Birney

Gibbon

Blockhouse Br.

ANDERSON

to SHADY
GROVE CHURCH

Mahone (III)

NEW SPOTTSYLVANIA
COURT HOUSE

Brooke

Heth (III)

BLOCK-HOUSE

Po River

ANDERSON MILL
(½ Mile)

Heth (III)

OLD COURT HOUSE

Ny River

BATTLE
OF
SPOTTSYLVANIA

Situation About 10:00 A.M.,
10 May 1864

CRITCHFIELD

Po River

N

0   ¼   ½   ¾   1 Mile
SCALE

West of the Po River, Heth pushed his attack. The Union force now opposing him—two brigades, forming Barlow's rear guard—beat him off twice and successfully recrossed the river. (Heth, under the misapprehension that he had been dealing with an attempted Union offensive, flattered himself over his "victory." Actually, his isolated division had been extremely fortunate in that the last elements of the II Corps were withdrawing by the time he launched his attack.) The Confederates then extended their entrenchments westward for approximately a mile along the road to Shady Grove Church.

Some time before 3:30 P.M., Warren reported that he was of the opinion that an immediate attack on his front would have an excellent chance of success. Meade therefore authorized it, and Warren advanced at about 4:00 P.M. with Wright's VI Corps on his left and Gibbon's division of the II Corps on his right. Warren led the attack in his full-dress uniform, but his courage proved better than his judgment. Some of his men broke through the tangles of underbrush and felled trees in front of the Confederate lines; a few even got into the first Confederate entrenchments, but all of these were killed or driven out. Raked by the carefully planned Confederate crossfires, the whole attacking force streamed back into its own lines.

Farther to the east, there was more intelligent planning. Wright, after careful reconnaissance of the Confederate position on his front, had decided that its weakest point was the west face of the salient (called the "Mule Shoe" by the Confederate troops) enclosing the McCool house. The entrenchments here were strong, and were backed up by a partially completed second line, but the position could be enfiladed by Union artillery. Also, there was a belt of timber, which would conceal Union troops forming for the attack, some 200 yards in front of the Confederate works. For this operation, Wright organized a special task force of twelve regiments under the command of Col. Emory Upton, who had led the attack that surprised Lee's bridgehead at Rappahannock Station the year before. Mott's division of the II Corps was to support Upton's attack.

Upton was a born soldier and a keen student of his profession. His plans for the assault were careful and detailed. All the regimental commanders were taken forward under cover to examine the ground over which they were to attack, and a heavy battery was emplaced to hammer the Confederate works until the charge jumped off. Upton formed his troops in four lines of three regiments each: when the first line reached the Confederate works, it was to split right and left and widen the penetration; the second line was to carry the second Confederate position; the last two lines formed the reserve and were to halt and lie down just outside the Confederate breastworks until needed. There was to be no halting to fire.

At 6:10 P.M., Upton charged. Confederate fire was heavy and accurate, but the yelling Union advance went through it and over both lines of entrenchments, beating down determined Confederate opposition and capturing about 1,000 prisoners. Mott, however, had formed his men in the open; they were an unreliable lot, and Confederate artillery fire soon scattered them. Upton was left isolated, with a large part of the Confederate army concentrating against him. To support him, Hancock renewed the attack on the Federal right, but was repulsed. Upton hung on until dark, and then withdrew. Meanwhile, Burnside got his IX Corps up near the Confederate right flank and entrenched there.

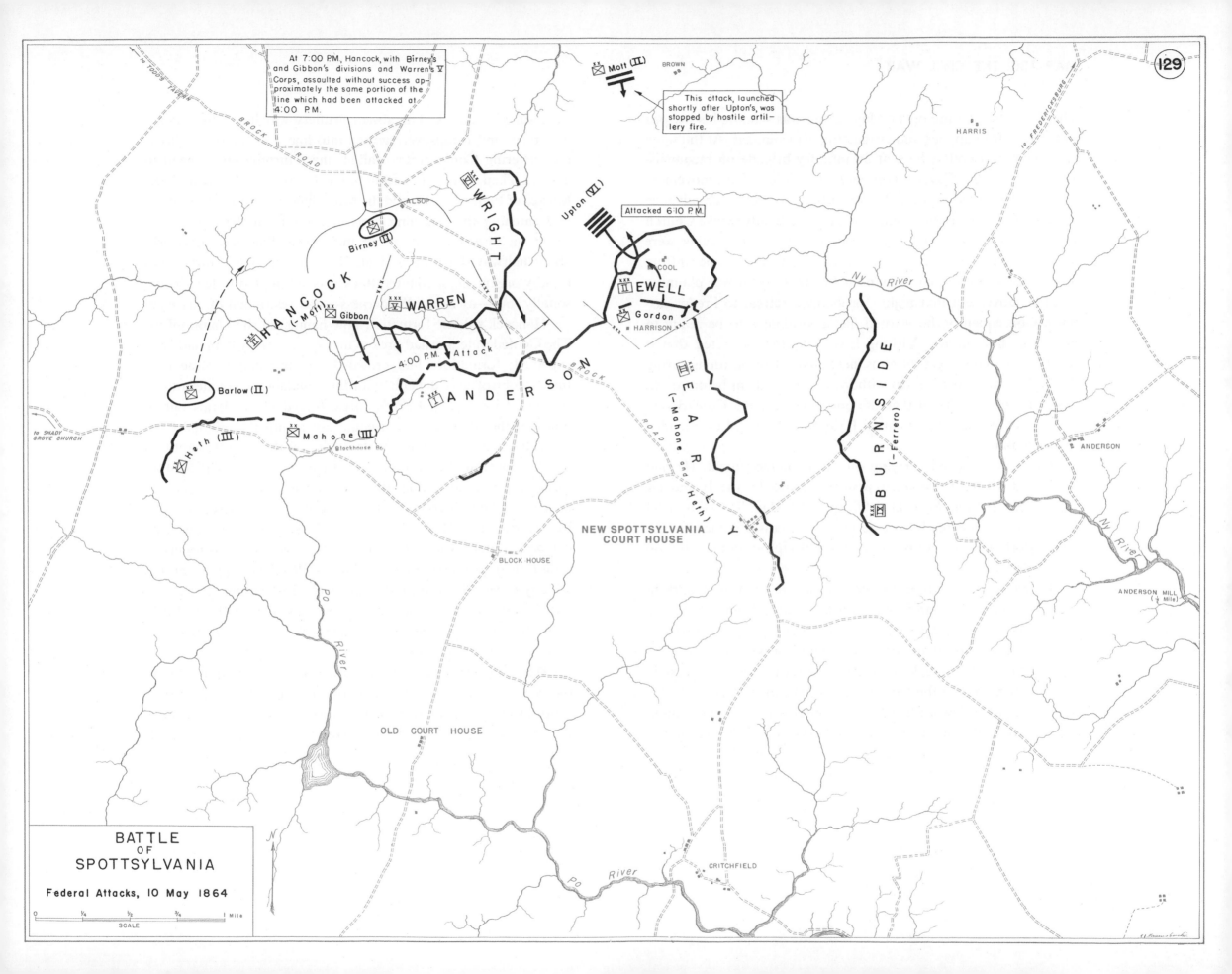

129

At 7:00 P.M., Hancock, with Birney's and Gibbon's divisions and Warren's V Corps, assaulted without success approximately the same portion of the line which had been attacked at 4:00 P.M.

Mott (II)

BROWN

HARRIS

This attack, launched shortly after Upton's, was stopped by hostile artillery fire.

WRIGHT

VI

ALSOP

Upton (VI)

Attacked 6:10 P.M.

McCOOL

Birney (II)

HANCOCK (-Mott)

WARREN
V

Gibbon

EWELL
II

Gordon

HARRISON

4:00 P.M. Attack

Ny River

Brock Road

ANDERSON

EARLY (-Mahone and Heth)

Barlow (II)

BURNSIDE (-Ferrero)

to SHADY GROVE CHURCH

Mahone (III)

Heth (III)

Blockhouse Rn.

Po River

ANDERSON

ANDERSON MILL (¼ Mile)

BLOCK HOUSE

NEW SPOTTSYLVANIA COURT HOUSE

Ny River

OLD COURT HOUSE

Po River

CRITCHFIELD

N

BATTLE
OF
SPOTTSYLVANIA

Federal Attacks, 10 May 1864

0   ¼   ½   ¾   1 Mile
SCALE

There was no fighting on 11 May. Grant was sending his wagons to the rear for supplies and evacuating his wounded. At the same time, lacking cavalry, he sent an infantry brigade on reconnaissance to Todd's Tavern (*off map, top left*). This movement alarmed Lee, who suspected a repetition of Hancock's advance on the 9th, and so pushed out troops toward Shady Grove Church (*off map, left center*). Later reports that Federal trains were moving to the rear and that Union troops appeared to be shifting to the east seem to have convinced Lee that Grant was planning a major movement that night—probably a retreat to Fredericksburg. Consequently, he warned his subordinates to be ready to move on short notice. Visiting Ewell's sector, he noted that it would be difficult to get the guns there out of their positions during the night, and told Ewell to withdraw most of them before dark. Lee was still convinced that the only chance for a Confederate victory lay in a successful battle. If Grant retreated, Lee intended to attack him.

Grant was indeed carrying out a major movement. He had instructed Meade to organize a strong attack by the II and IX Corps on the Mule Shoe at 4:00 A.M., 12 May. The V and VI Corps were to be ready to exploit any successes gained by the main effort. This was to be a repetition of Upton's attack, but on a decisive scale.

Hancock moved from his position on the right after dark in a steady rain, and began forming for his attack. Then a heavy fog set in, and it was 4:35 A.M. before it was light enough to advance. Hancock had massed his corps in heavy formations, to obtain better control in the dark and fog and to get the greatest possible number of men into the Confederate works in the first rush. He was, naturally, unaware that Lee had ordered most of the cannon withdrawn from the salient, and so expected heavy casualties until the Confederate batteries could be overrun.

In the Mule Shoe, the Confederate outposts heard sounds suggesting an attack. The absent artillery was hurriedly ordered to return, and troops were gotten into line. For almost an hour, the shivering Confederates waited; the returning guns began to appear. Then, out of the lifting fog and dark, came a great cheer. Masses of Federals swamped the Mule Shoe, capturing its garrison and catching the returning guns in column on the road. They swept on until checked by an incomplete line of breastworks about halfway down the salient. Here, the capable Gordon was rapidly organizing a counterattack. Lee attempted to lead it personally, but—as in the Wilderness—was restrained by his men.

Hancock's dense formation now hampered the Union effort. The Confederate line had broken much more easily than had been expected; formations had crowded together and become confused; control was difficult. Gordon's audacious counterattack, supported by part of Early's corps, forced the Federals out of much of the Mule Shoe, but could not regain the original Confederate position. Even where driven out of the recently captured fortifications, the Federals clung to their outer edge. The fighting raged savagely throughout the day and into the night, especially at the so-called "Bloody Angle" where Wright—ordered forward by Meade when Hancock was stalled—struck the Confederate defenses. Later, Warren was ordered to attack, but was repulsed. Grant then proposed to shift him to Wright's support at the already crowded salient, but later revoked this order. Burnside's attack had some initial success, but was soon driven back. Early then attempted a counterattack against Burnside's left flank, but was checked at the outset.

While the two armies fought stubbornly, Lee was hastening the construction of a new line across the base of the Mule Shoe south of Harrison. Work was slow; not until after midnight were the Confederates in the salient ordered to disengage and fall back to it.

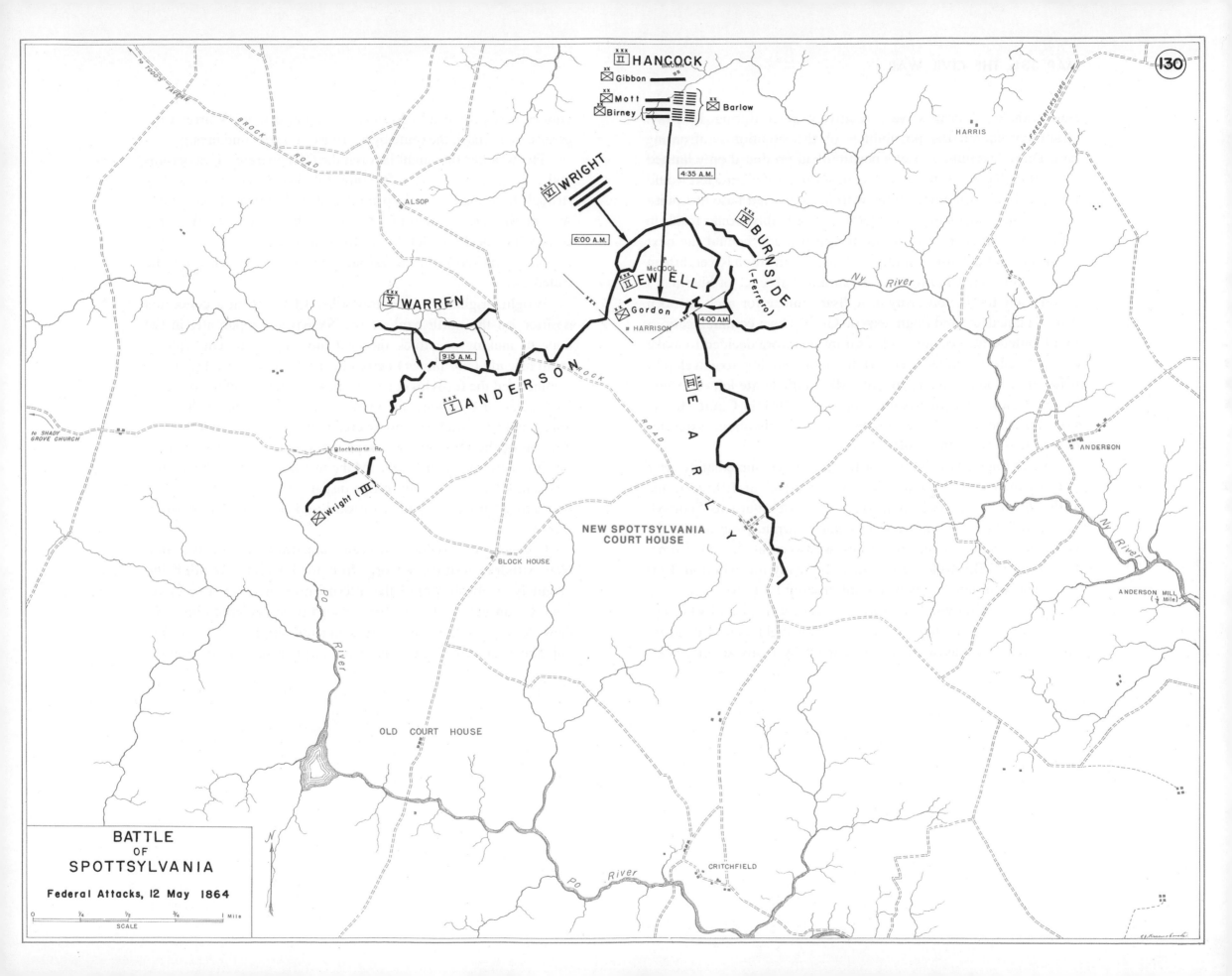

130

XXX
II HANCOCK

XX
⊠ Gibbon

XX
⊠ Mott

XX
⊠ Birney

XX
⊠ Barlow

4:35 A.M.

XXX
VI WRIGHT

XXX
IX BURNSIDE
(-Ferrero)

6:00 A.M.

McCOOL

XXX
II EWELL

XXX
V WARREN

⊠ Gordon

HARRISON

4:00 AM.

9:15 A.M.

XXX
I ANDERSON

Rock Road

Ny River

to TODD'S TAVERN

BROCK ROAD

ALSOP

HARRIS

to FREDERICKSBURG

XXX
E A R L Y

Blockhouse Br.

to SHADY GROVE CHURCH

ANDERSON

XX
⊠ Wright (III)

NEW SPOTTSYLVANIA
COURT HOUSE

BLOCK HOUSE

Ny River

ANDERSON MILL
(¼ Mile)

Po River

OLD COURT HOUSE

Po River

CRITCHFIELD

**BATTLE
OF
SPOTTSYLVANIA**

Federal Attacks, 12 May 1864

N

0   ¼   ½   ¾   1 Mile
SCALE

Both exhausted armies were relatively quiet during 13 May. Grant considered the possibilities of the situation confronting him. Direct assaults on Lee's position had produced only limited gains at high cost. A movement against the Confederate left would threaten Lee's communications with his advanced base at Louisa Court House (*off map, lower left*) and probably would result in a prompt Confederate withdrawal to a position behind the next natural line of defense—in this case, the North Anna River, fifteen miles to the south. However, the continued absence of Sheridan's cavalry left the Union army at a disadvantage for such an open war of maneuver, and might expose Grant's own communications to a Confederate counterstroke. Grant therefore decided to make his next effort against Lee's right flank, hoping to envelop it before Lee could shift troops from the Confederate left or extend his fortifications farther south from Spottsylvania Court House. (At this time, these fortifications extended only about a quarter of a mile south of the court house.)

Accordingly, Warren was ordered to move immediately after dark by the route shown and form for an attack at 4:00 A.M., the 14th, down the road leading from Fredericksburg to Spottsylvania. Wright was to move out behind Warren, form across the next road to the south, and attack westward at the same time. Hancock and Burnside were both to be ready for action at 4:00 A.M., but were not to advance until ordered to do so.

As the map shows, there were no roads for the V and VI Corps to follow. Instead, they had to move by night across country, much of which was wooded and cut up by many small creeks.

Guides were provided by Meade's headquarters, and Warren took great care to mark the route by a string of sentries and fires.

The weather that night favored the Confederates. Heavy rains and fog put out Warren's fires and blinded his columns as they struggled through knee-deep mud and underbrush. Every creek was an obstacle. Not until 6:00 A.M. did the head of the V Corps come onto the Fredericksburg Road; it took the rest of the day to collect and reorganize its exhausted men. The attack had to be called off.

Wright originally concentrated his VI Corps in a concealed position on the north bank of the Ny River—apparently in the hope of making an attack the next morning—but sent Upton's small brigade (*not shown*) across the river to occupy a hill which commanded the fords his corps must use in such an offensive. *(Following action not shown.)* Confederate cavalry—one of the units Stuart had left with Lee—discovered Upton's force, and Mahone's division of the III Corps was sent out to determine the extent of Federal activity in this area. Mahone forced Upton back, but was himself driven off by troops dispatched by Warren. Wright then moved his entire corps forward and occupied the position shown.

Confederate reaction had been comparatively slow, the complete withdrawal of the V Corps from the Federal right not being definitely established until the afternoon of the 14th. Lee thereupon began deliberately shifting troops from his left to his right flank and prolonging his entrenchments southward. Probably only the weather had saved him from surprise and serious trouble.

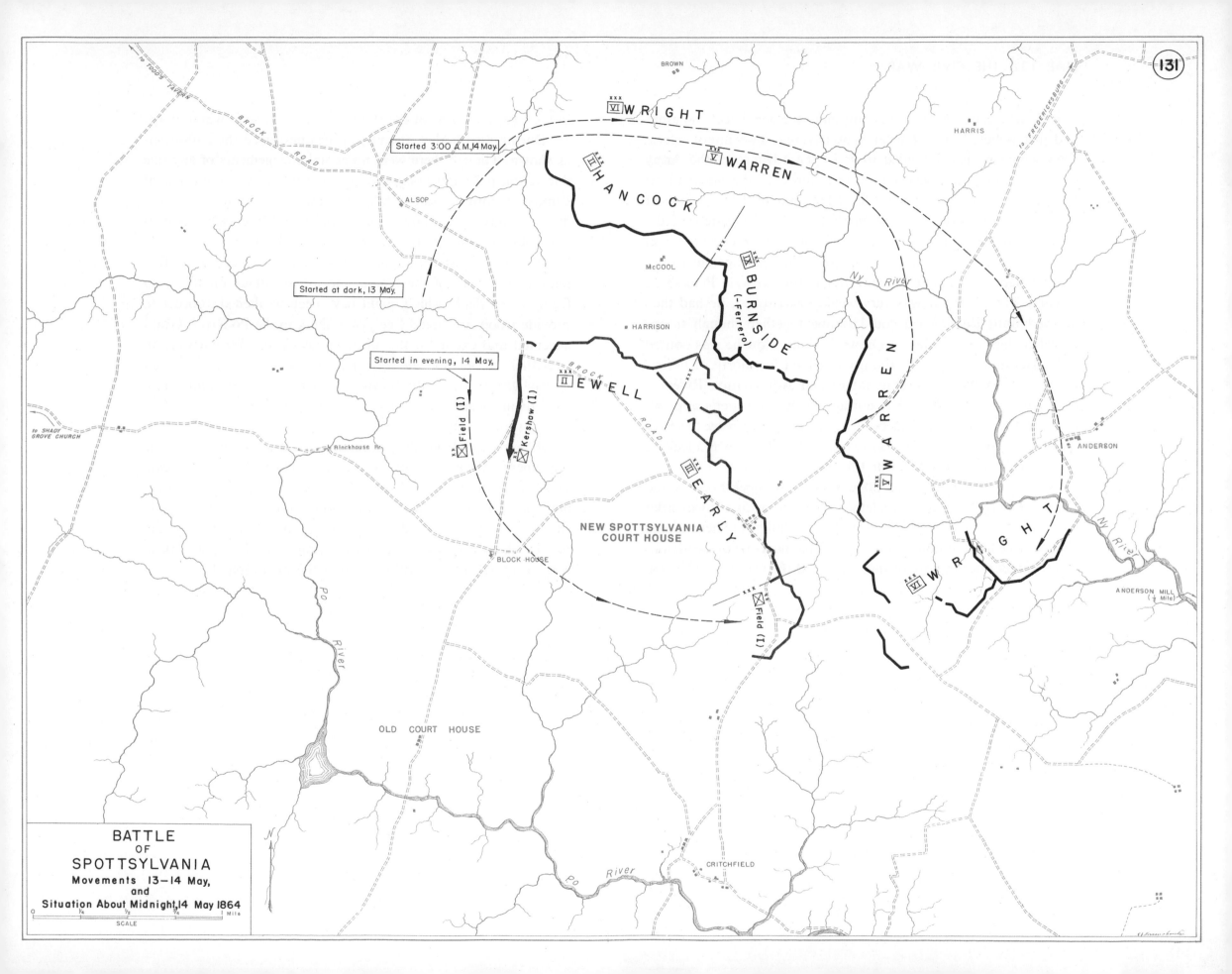

131

Started 3:00 A.M. 14 May.

Started at dark, 13 May.

Started in evening, 14 May,

xxx
VI WRIGHT

xxx
V WARREN

xxx
II HANCOCK

xxx
IX BURNSIDE
(-Ferrero)

xxx
II EWELL

xx
Field (I)

xx
Kershaw (I)

xxx
III EARLY

xxx
V WARREN

xxx
VI WRIGHT

xxx
Field (I)

NEW SPOTTSYLVANIA
COURT HOUSE

McCOOL

Harrison

BROWN

HARRIS

Ny River

ALSOP

Blackhouse Br.

BLOCK HOUSE

OLD COURT HOUSE

ANDERSON

ANDERSON MILL
(Mile)

to TODD'S TAVERN

to FREDERICKSBURG

to SHADY
GROVE CHURCH

BROCK   ROAD

BROCK   ROAD

Po   River

Po   River

Ny   River

CRITCHFIELD

BATTLE
OF
SPOTTSYLVANIA
Movements 13-14 May,
and
Situation About Midnight, 14 May 1864

SCALE
0   1/4   1/2   3/4   1 Mile

Grant had disappointments in addition to the one that the weather had just inflicted upon him at Spottsylvania. Two minor operations which he had intended to assist the advance of the Army of the Potomac had been complete failures. In the Shenandoah Valley, the patriotic but inept Sigel had managed to get himself defeated on 15 May at New Market, where the cadets of the Virginia Military Institute formed part of the Confederate force. On the James River front, the energetic but incompetent Butler had brought on another fiasco. After failing to seize Petersburg in early May, when it was very weakly garrisoned, he had then delayed until Beauregard could scrape together enough troops to defeat him on 10 May at Drewry's Bluff. Now he was bottled up at Bermuda Hundred—the neck of land just north of Petersburg between the converging James and Appomattox Rivers— where he possessed little but nuisance value. (Butler's appointment to this command had been forced on Lincoln by the hard facts that 1864 was an election year and that Butler was a leading Northern Democrat with a thirst for military glory.)

Grant could no longer hope that these operations would weaken Lee by forcing him to detach troops from his army in order to defend Richmond and Petersburg, or to hold the Shenandoah. Indeed, Lee himself now received reinforcements from the victorious Confederates in both of those areas. If the war was to be won in the east, the Army of the Potomac would have to win it alone.

During 14-17 May, the two armies improved their positions as shown. Though there were no actual engagements of any size during this period, the opposing troops were in close and constant contact. Continual skirmishing, sniping, and artillery fire produced steady losses. Grant pulled most of Hancock's II Corps out of line in order to rest it for his next offensive.

Wright suggested that his corps might suddenly be shifted back to the right of the Union line for an attack on the Confederate left flank, which might have been weakened in order to provide troops to extend Lee's right flank to the Po River. Grant accepted and expanded this idea: Hancock and Wright were to shift their troops into the former Mule Shoe area for an assault at daylight on the 18th; Burnside was to attack in conjunction with them; Warren was to support the attack with his artillery and to stand ready to advance.

Apparently, Confederate scouts and patrols detected the movement. At any rate, no surprise was achieved: the advancing Federals found the Confederates ready and waiting. The Union attacks were made with gallantry and energy, but were rapidly shot to pieces by Confederate artillery; only in a few cases did the attackers get close to the Confederate line. By about 10:00 A.M., even Grant was willing to halt the operation.

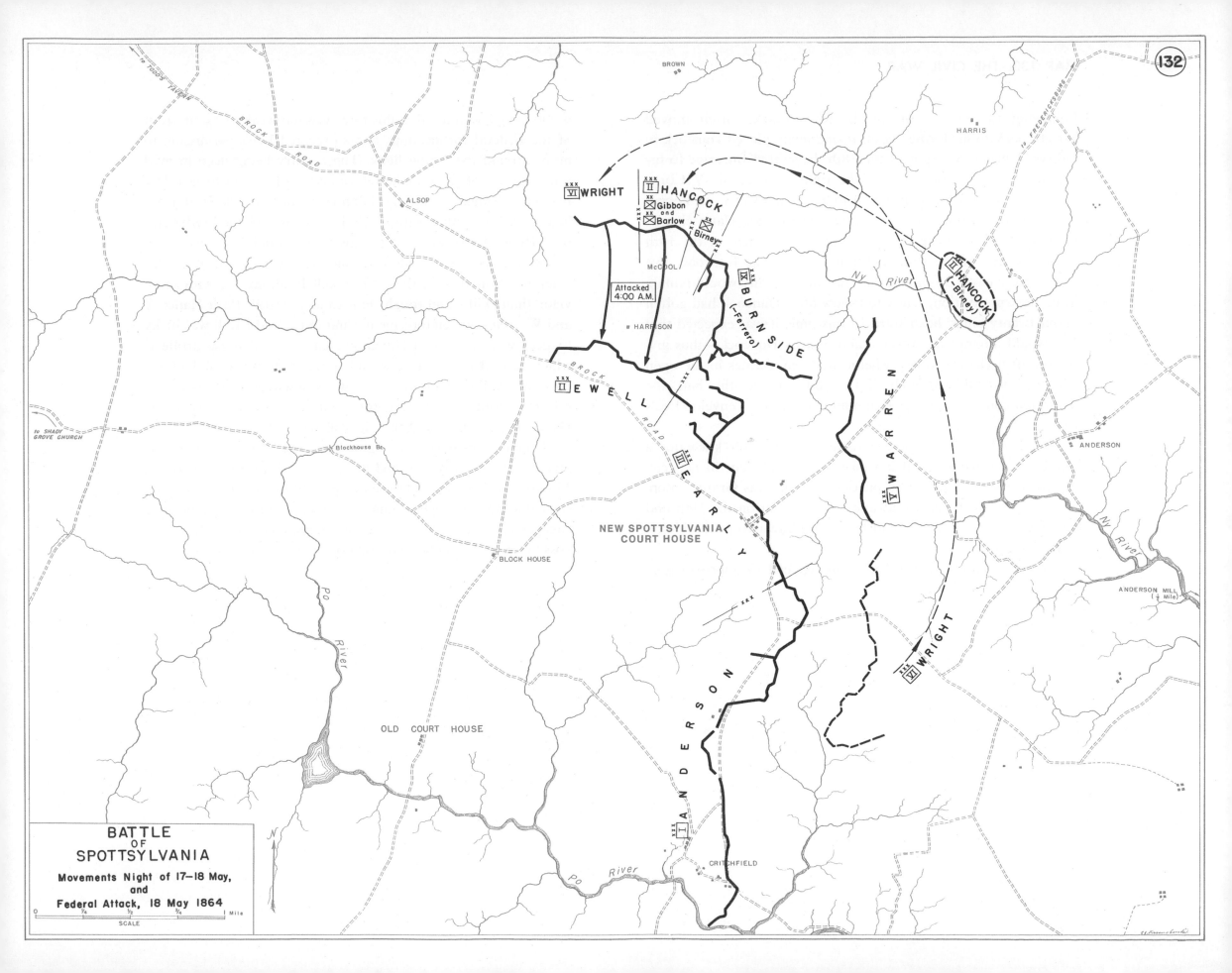

132

BROWN

HARRIS

to TODDS TAVERN

BROCK ROAD

to FREDERICKSBURG

ALSOP

XXX
VI WRIGHT

XXX
II HANCOCK

XX
Gibbon and Barlow

XX
Birney

McCOOL

Ny River

XXX
II HANCOCK
(-Birney)

Attacked 4:00 A.M.

XXX
IX BURNSIDE
(-Ferrero)

HARRISON

XXX
II EWELL

XXX
III EARLY

BROCK ROAD

to SHADY GROVE CHURCH

Blockhouse Br.

NEW SPOTTSYLVANIA
COURT HOUSE

XXX
V WARREN

ANDERSON

Ny River

BLOCK HOUSE

XXX
I ANDERSON

ANDERSON MILL
(¼ Mile)

XXX
VI WRIGHT

OLD COURT HOUSE

Po River

CRITCHFIELD

Po River

BATTLE
OF
SPOTTSYLVANIA

Movements Night of 17–18 May,
and
Federal Attack, 18 May 1864

N

0   ¼   ½   ¾   1 Mile
SCALE

Following the repulse of the 18 May attack, Grant moved Wright back to his former position and again placed Hancock in reserve. During the night of the 18th, he shifted Burnside to his extreme left. Warren extended the right flank of his V Corps across the Ny River. Grant now formed a plan which, he hoped, would lure Lee out from behind his earthworks. Hancock was ordered to advance rapidly southward on the night of the 19th along the line of the Fredericksburg & Potomac Railroad, five miles to the east (*off map*). The rest of the army would remain in its present position, ready to follow after Hancock had gotten about twenty miles' head start. In this time, it was expected that Lee would attempt to overtake and destroy Hancock—thus giving Grant a chance to overwhelm the Confederates in the open before they could entrench. If Lee did not take this bait, the operation could be converted into another effort to envelop Lee's right flank.

Some indications of these shifts reached Lee, who knew that a rapid, undetected Federal advance south might cut in between his army and Richmond. Suspicious that this was Grant's intention, he ordered Ewell to advance on his front on the 19th and determine whether troops had been withdrawn from the Union right flank.

By now, Ewell's corps had been reduced to approximately 6,000 men. Ewell felt that this force was too weak to risk in front of the Federal fortifications and so secured Lee's permission to move around the Union flank. The country being deep in mud after a series of showers, he felt obliged to leave all his artillery behind, advancing with his infantry alone. About 3:00 P.M., he established contact with Federal units covering the Fredericksburg Road. These were mostly raw troops which had never been in action before and should have had little chance against Ewell's veterans. Nonetheless, they met Ewell headlong—if with more vigor than skill—and fought him to a standstill. Both Hancock and Warren sent reinforcements, and in the end Ewell was lucky to get away, thanks to Hampton's cavalry and horse artillery, which arrived in time to cover his retreat. However, he had discovered that the Union right flank was still strong, and—as a more positive result of his adventure—Grant was led to postpone Hancock's advance until the night of the 20th.

Union losses during the fighting around Spottsylvania Court House are variously reported but appear to have been between 17,000 and 18,000. Confederate casualties are unknown, but since their forces fought behind fortifications during most of these engagements, their losses must have been considerably less—possibly between 9,000 and 10,000.

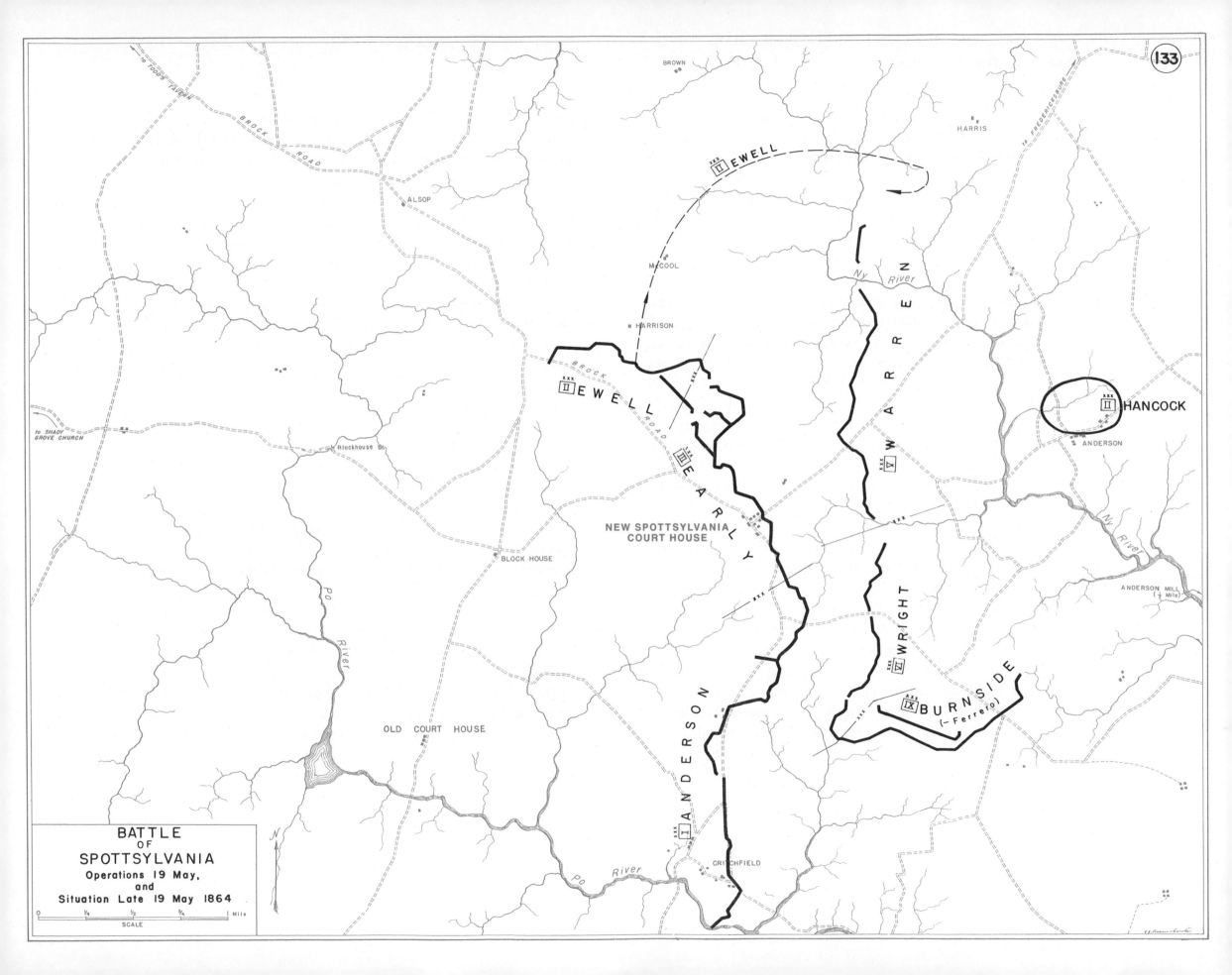

133

BROWN

HARRIS

to FREDERICKSBURG

to TODD'S TAVERN

BROCK ROAD

ALSOP

[II] EWELL

Ny River

McCOOL

WARREN

[V]

HARRISON

[II] EWELL

BROCK ROAD

[III] HANCOCK

[II] EARLY

ANDERSON

to SHADY GROVE CHURCH

Blockhouse Br.

ANDERSON MILL (½ Mile)

NEW SPOTTSYLVANIA COURT HOUSE

BLOCK HOUSE

Po River

WRIGHT [VI]

Ny River

OLD COURT HOUSE

BURNSIDE [IX] (-Ferrero)

ANDERSON [I]

CRITCHFIELD

Po River

BATTLE
OF
SPOTTSYLVANIA
Operations 19 May,
and
Situation Late 19 May 1864

0   ¼   ½   ¾   Mile
SCALE

N

This map shows the progressive movements of the opposing forces from their first engagement in the Wilderness in early May to their meeting at Cold Harbor in early June.

During the night of 20 May, Hancock began his march from Spottsylvania to Milford Station by way of Guiney's Station. His orders were to take a position near Milford Station—on the west bank of the Mattapony River, if possible; to attack the Confederates wherever he encountered them; and to keep Grant constantly informed of his progress. All available detachments of cavalry still with the army were grouped under Torbert (just returned from the hospital) to scout for him.

Hancock reached Guiney's Station at dawn and passed through it after a skirmish with some of Hampton's cavalry. About 10:00 A.M., Torbert rode into Milford Station, to find a small force of Confederate infantry dug in across his line of march. A quick assault drove this detachment across the Mattapony and captured both the wagon-road and railroad bridges. By noon, the leading division of the II Corps had set up a fortified bridgehead on the west bank to cover the crossing of the rest of the corps.

Hampton's cavalry soon warned Lee of this movement. To Lee, it represented merely the beginning of another Federal attempt to turn his right flank and get between his army and Richmond. He therefore began shifting his troops to the south bank of the Po River. When Warren, Burnside, and Wright successively withdrew from Spottsylvania during the 21st, Lee ordered a retreat to the North Anna River. It would appear that Grant, after having pushed Hancock out as bait, suddenly became apprehensive and hurried the rest of the Army of the Potomac forward prematurely, without giving Lee a chance to consider a blow at the isolated II Corps. The two armies collided at the North Anna on the 23d. (For operations there, see text, map 135.)

The Federal army left the North Anna area immediately after dark on 26 May, and once more moved south, crossing the Pamunkey River at Hanover Town. Meanwhile, Wilson's cavalry (*not shown*) had moved west along the Virginia Central Railroad in an attempt to distract Lee, but, by the 28th, the latter had his army in another naturally strong position behind the Totopotomoy Creek where it covered all the direct approaches to Richmond from the Pamunkey River crossings. In order to determine whether Federal infantry had already crossed that stream in strength, Lee then sent Hampton east to Haw's Shop near the river, where he collided with Sheridan. After a hard, day-long fight, Hampton was defeated, but not until he had established the presence of Union infantry around Hanover Town.

On the 29th, Grant came up to Lee's new position. After some skirmishing, he decided that an attack would be futile. The next day, Early attacked Warren, but was roughly repulsed. Five miles eastward, Torbert drove Fitzhugh Lee back on Cold Harbor.

On 22 May, after learning the results of Butler's blunderings, Grant had ordered that commander to group all of his troops—except a minimum garrison for Bermuda Hundred—under W. F. Smith and to send them to the Army of the Potomac. This force (approximately 12,500) moved by boat to White House (*bottom right*) on the Pamunkey River. Learning of this transfer, Lee literally wrung Maj. Gen. Robert F. Hoke's division (7,000) from Beauregard (below Richmond) as a reinforcement for the Army of Northern Virginia.

Smith reached White House on 30 May, only to find practically no facilities for disembarking his troops. On the 31st, Sheridan—who had been ordered to maintain contact with Smith, lest Lee attempt to overwhelm the latter in his isolated position—drove Fitzhugh Lee out of Cold Harbor. Hoke's leading brigade came up in support of the Confederate cavalry, but was itself beaten off. Sheridan, noting that more Confederate infantry was concentrating against him, began to withdraw, but was halted by Meade, who ordered him to hold Cold Harbor at all hazards. (Cold Harbor is discussed in the text of map 136a.)

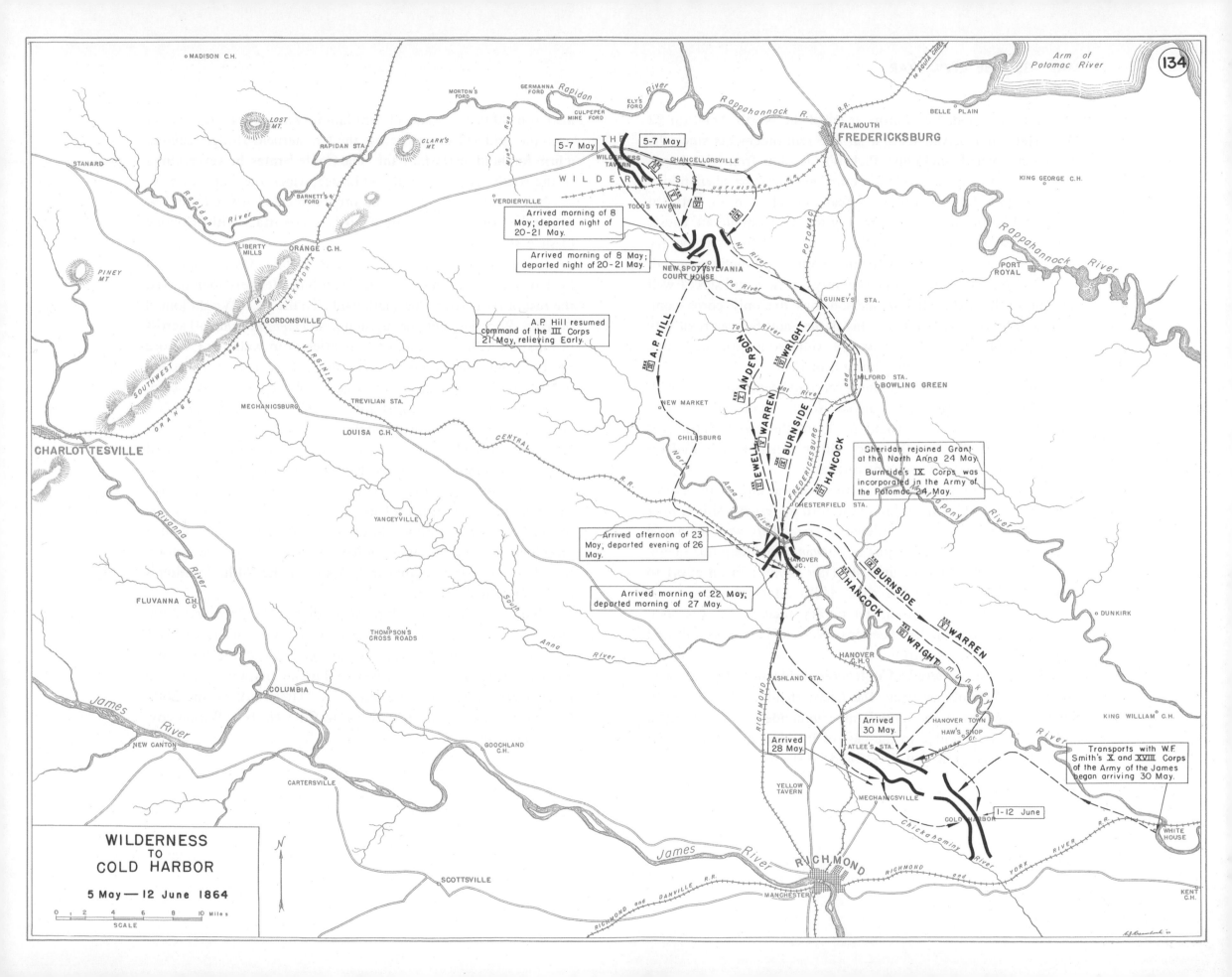

134

WILDERNESS
TO
COLD HARBOR

5 May — 12 June 1864

N

0 2 4 6 8 10 Miles
SCALE

5-7 May

5-7 May

Arrived morning of 8
May; departed night of
20-21 May.

Arrived morning of 8 May;
departed night of 20-21 May.

A.P. Hill resumed
command of the III Corps
21 May, relieving Early.

Sheridan rejoined Grant
at the North Anna 24 May.

Burnside's IX Corps was
incorporated in the Army of
the Potomac 24 May.

Arrived afternoon of 23
May, departed evening of 26
May.

Arrived morning of 22 May;
departed morning of 27 May.

Arrived
30 May.

Arrived
28 May.

Transports with W.F.
Smith's X and XVIII Corps
of the Army of the James
began arriving 30 May.

1-12 June

As has been noted, Lee's army reached the North Anna on 22 May. Here, it received its first sizable reinforcements since the campaign opened, including Pickett's division from the James River front and Breckinridge's command from the Shenandoah Valley (where he had recently defeated Sigel)—in all, between 8,000 and 9,000 men. Unfortunately for the Confederate cause, this increase in combat strength was nullified by a temporary near-collapse of the Army of Northern Virginia's high command. A. P. Hill had recently returned to duty, but was still sick; Ewell was physically exhausted; Anderson was the only corps commander fully able to discharge his duties, and he was relatively inexperienced. Then, as a climax, Lee suffered a crippling attack of diarrhea, leaving his army almost leaderless.

The Confederate position, however, had been established with great skill behind the steep-banked North Anna and carefully fortified. Its "V" shape would facilitate the rapid shifting of troops from one flank to the other, either to help repel a Federal assault or to mass for a counterattack.

The Army of the Potomac arrived at the line of the North Anna on the 23d. Warren found the ford at Jericho Mill (*upper left*) undefended, and was ordered to cross there with his whole corps. At about 6:00 P.M., just as he was completing this operation, A. P. Hill attacked furiously (*not shown*) in an effort to drive the V Corps into the river. Hill's attack, however, was clumsily made; despite some temporary success, he was soon forced to return to his fortifications. Warren thereupon followed and entrenched as shown.

Hancock encountered a Confederate bridgehead (*not shown*) on the north bank, covering the Chesterfield Bridge (*center*). Supporting works on the south bank commanded both that bridge and the railroad bridge to the east of it. After examining these outworks, Birney felt that they could be stormed; accordingly—

also at 6:00 P.M.—Hancock sent him forward. This attack swept over the bridgehead and across the Chesterfield Bridge, gaining a firm foothold on the far bank. The Confederates, however, clung to the south end of the railroad bridge, which they later burned.

In the center, Burnside had orders to cross at Ox Ford, but found the Confederate position too strong to attack with any hope of success.

Early on the 24th, Hancock found that the Confederates on his front had withdrawn to their main line. He thereupon moved the rest of his corps to the south bank. To the west, Wright joined Warren. Burnside sent one division (*movement not shown*) across at Quarle's Mill (*left center*) in an attempt to flank the Ox Ford position, but again found it too strong. This division remained on the south bank, and later extended Warren's left as shown.

Grant now, for the first time, realized the shape of Lee's position—and the awkward implications of his own. His aggressive advance had broken his army into three widely separated parts. Troops moving from one flank to reinforce the other would have to cross the North Anna twice. Had Lee not been too sick to direct an attack, it is probable that he would have thrown the whole weight of his army against Hancock. (The results of such an offensive might or might not have been a Confederate victory, for Hancock was well dug in.) Also, on the 24th, Sheridan's cavalry rejoined the army.

There was only light skirmishing during the 25th and 26th, Grant having decided against attacking. Stretches of the railroads were destroyed, while Wilson's cavalry crossed the river and moved westward to deceive Lee into thinking that Grant intended to envelop the Confederate left flank. After dark on the 26th, Grant withdrew to move southeast to Cold Harbor, Wilson covering his rear.

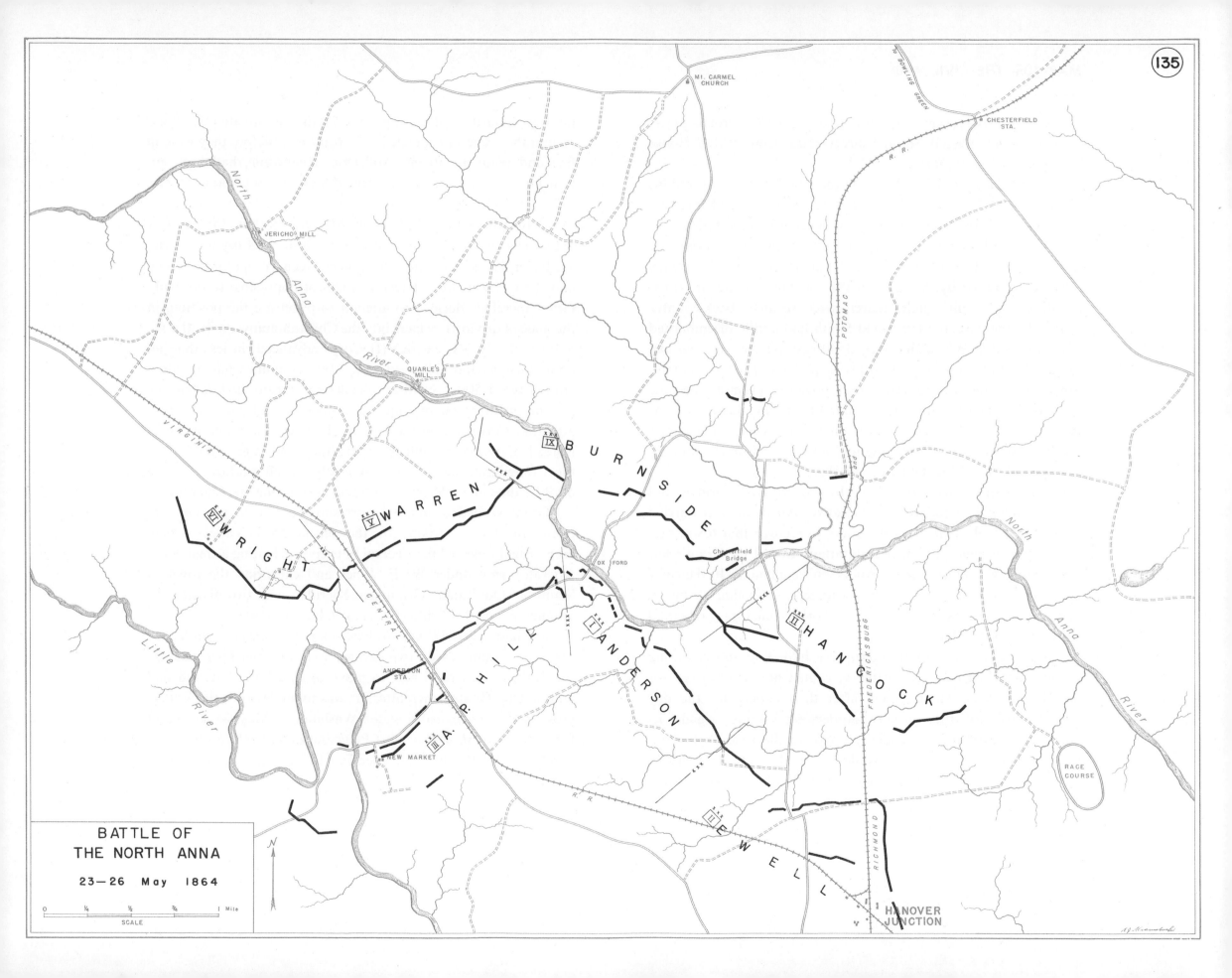

BATTLE OF
THE NORTH ANNA

23—26 May 1864

Old Cold Harbor (*sketch* a) was another little crossroads place, through which passed Smith's direct route from White House (*off map, upper right*).

During the night of 31 May–1 June, Sheridan reorganized his position at Old Cold Harbor, throwing up hasty field fortifications and preparing to hold the town, in accordance with Meade's orders, until the Union infantry arrived. (*Subsequent action not shown.*) Grant had ordered Wright to make every effort to reach Old Cold Harbor by daylight on the 1st, but this meant an exhausting fifteen-mile night march over strange, back-country roads. To the east, the frustrated Smith had finally disembarked his command at White House by 3:00 P.M. on the 31st and had marched without waiting for all his wagons and reserve ammunition to be gotten ashore. His march, however, promptly became a wild-goose chase: either Grant himself or Maj. Gen. John A. Rawlins, the chief of Grant's personal staff, twice made idiotic errors in Smith's orders, sending him hiking north to the Pamunkey instead of west to Old Cold Harbor.

Lee—with his army reinforced by Pickett, Breckinridge, and Hoke—planned to recover the initiative. Anderson was hurried toward Old Cold Harbor with orders to recover that town, preparatory to a general Confederate attack to roll up Grant's left flank. Hoke was placed under Anderson's command. In the early morning of 1 June, their combined force came rolling down on Sheridan's two slim cavalry divisions (Torbert and Gregg), behind their makeshift defenses.

Once more, as at Gettysburg, breech-loading and repeating carbines, backed by horse artillery, gained fire superiority over infantry muskets. Hoke's men, after their experience the day before, displayed little ferocity; Anderson's leading brigade, its commander shot down, suddenly broke to the rear. A Federal counterattack at this moment would have had an excellent chance of wrecking Lee's entire right flank, but Wright was still feeling

his way toward Cold Harbor, and Smith was impatiently trying to find the scene of conflict. It was 6:00 P.M. before they were in line and ready to attack. Anderson, meanwhile, had been entrenching. The Federal attack dented his line, but could not break it.

Both armies now shifted toward Cold Harbor. (*Subsequent action shown.*) On 2 June, Early tried unsuccessfully to overrun the Federal right. Lee's new position between Totopotomoy Creek and the Chickahominy River was almost impossible to outflank. Grant therefore decided to attempt to penetrate the position, in the hope of driving Lee back into the Chickahominy. At 4:30 A.M., 3 June, the II, VI, and XVIII Corps advanced; in less than an hour, their assault collapsed with 7,000 casualties (the Confederates lost 1,500). Neither Meade nor Grant had taken the precaution of reconnoitering Lee's lines or had paid particular attention to organizing the attack. However, the repulsed units, instead of retreating, dug in where they had been halted, near the Confederate breastworks. A costly trench warfare went on until 12 June, the soldiers of both armies suffering great privations.

Grant wished to maintain pressure on Lee to prevent him from transferring troops to the Shenandoah Valley—where Hunter had renewed the Federal offensive, defeating a small Confederate army under W. E. Jones and capturing the town of Staunton. On 7 June, Grant sent Sheridan with two divisions to attempt a junction with Hunter at Charlottesville.

Lee had ordered Breckinridge back to the Shenandoah Valley and sent Hampton with two cavalry divisions after Sheridan. On the 12th, he ordered Early to move to Charlottesville and find and destroy Hunter; thereafter, he was to move down the Valley, cross the Potomac, and threaten Washington. Meanwhile, except for a raid (*not shown*) against Petersburg (*sketch* b, *bottom left*) on 9 June, Butler had remained inactive at Bermuda Hundred.

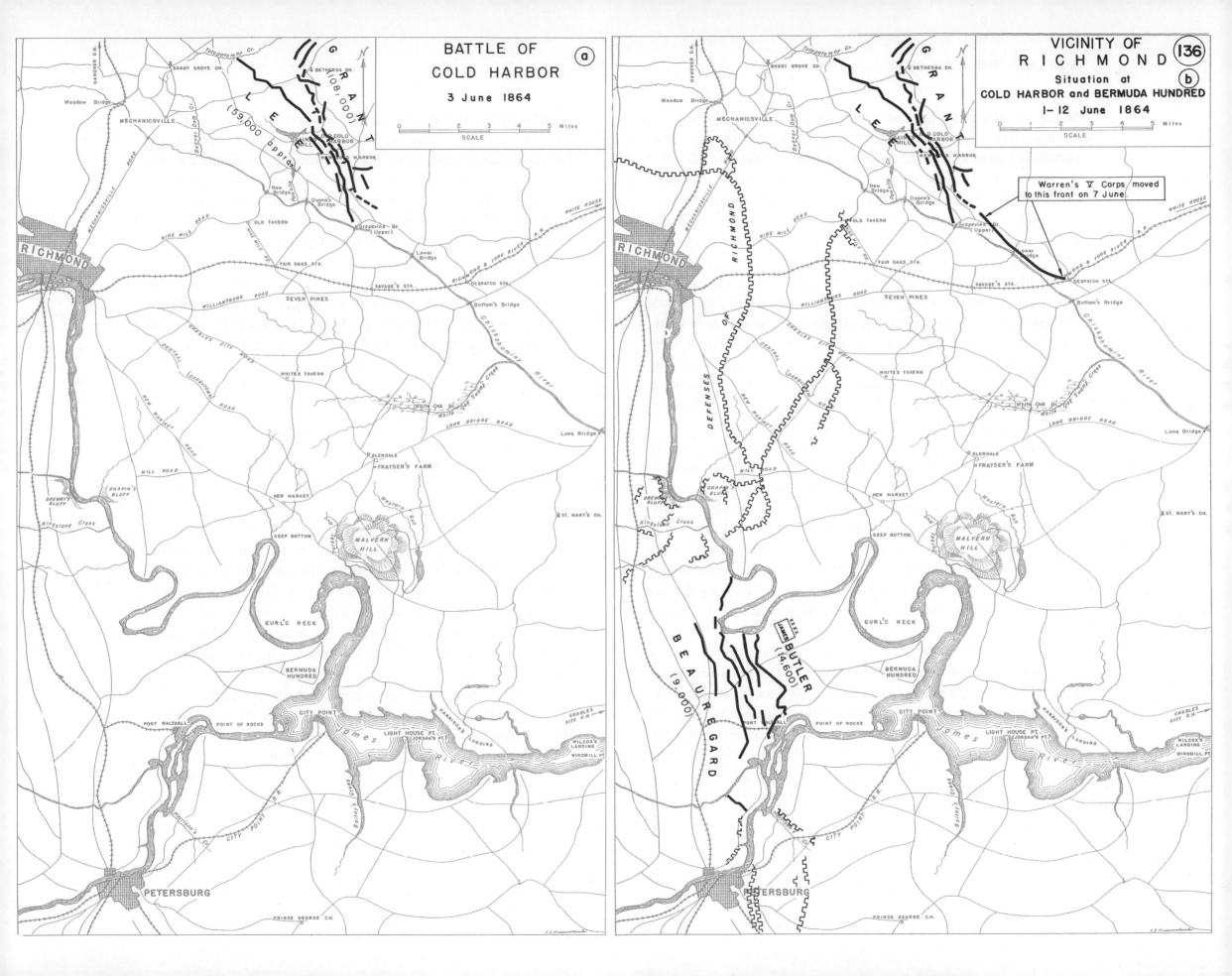

BATTLE OF COLD HARBOR
3 June 1864

SCALE
0 1 2 3 4 5 Miles

GRANT
(108,000)

LEE
(59,000 approx.)

VICINITY OF RICHMOND
136
Situation at
COLD HARBOR and BERMUDA HUNDRED
1-12 June 1864

SCALE
0 1 2 3 4 5 Miles

Warren's V Corps moved
to this front on 7 June

GRANT

LEE

BEAUREGARD
(9,000)

BUTLER
(14,600)

So far, Grant's campaign had been remarkable only for persistence —and some 55,000 casualties. (Lee's losses during the same period are estimated at anywhere between 20,000 and 40,000.)

Now, however, out of the stubborn and cold-blooded Grant of Cold Harbor emerged the farsighted and imaginative Grant of Vicksburg. All but one of the major railroads supplying Richmond—and the Army of Northern Virginia—passed through Petersburg (*lower left*). Grant decided to transfer his army to the south bank of the James River, seize Petersburg, outflank Beauregard (thus releasing Butler), then turn north and operate against the remaining rail line into Richmond. Success here would force Lee either to stand siege in the Confederate capital or to abandon it and retire westward. Grant seems to have been considering such a plan for some time. As of 26 May, he had ordered all available bridging equipment concentrated at Fort Monroe (*bottom right corner*), ready to move into the James River.

This projected movement involved several major problems. In a hostile countryside, where every inhabitant was a potential Confederate spy, the whole Army of the Potomac had to be silently extricated from its trenches under Lee's very nose, and then gotten across both the Chickahominy and James Rivers. If Lee were to detect this movement and strike the Federal columns while they were astride either river, a disastrous defeat could hardly be avoided. As a final risk, the Confederates had a strong flotilla, including several ironclads, on the upper reaches of the James River.

On 9 June, Meade had his engineers begin the preparation of a second line of fortifications (*not shown*) behind his position at Cold Harbor (*upper left*). On 12 June, as soon as it was dark, the movement began. Hancock and Wright occupied the rearward line, ready to meet any sudden Confederate attack, until the roads behind their corps were clear. Smith moved off first, heading for White House where he reembarked. Wilson rode south across the Chickahominy, then turned and pushed boldly westward.

Warren followed him and took up a good position just east of Riddell's Shop, holding it until the rest of the Army of the Potomac passed behind him. Hancock formed the advance guard, being ferried across the James on the 14th and early 15th. While he crossed, Butler's engineers were preparing a bridge site. At 4:00 P.M., 14 June, a battalion of regular engineer troops began building a ponton bridge; they had it finished by midnight. (This is one of the greatest bridges in military history—2,100 feet long, built to hold against a strong tidal current and to adjust to a four-foot tidal rise and fall.) Once it was completed, the rest of the army crossed as shown. W. F. Smith continued to Bermuda Hundred, where Butler transmitted to him Grant's orders to cross the Appomattox River and advance on Petersburg at daylight on 15 June.

On the morning of 13 June, Lee found the trenches opposite him empty. His cavalry to the south in the New Market area (*left center*) promptly began to report aggressive Union cavalry in large numbers, solidly backed by infantry. Thereupon, Grant's new movement became perfectly clear to Robert E. Lee (or so he thought); it was merely another one of those short-range attempts to envelop his right flank that the Federal commander had been trying ever since the Wilderness. Lee promptly shifted southward and dug in from Malvern Hill to White Oak Swamp Creek. By that time, there was nothing in front of him except Wilson's single cavalry division, which reconnoitered aggressively all along his front and blocked every Confederate effort to discover the dispositions of the Union infantry, which Lee felt certain was massed behind it.

To the south, Beauregard was beginning to clamor about increasing Union strength on the Petersburg front. Lee released Hoke to reinforce him, but otherwise was unconcerned.

Grant had done the near-impossible and had completely outwitted Lee. The Federal movement had been complicated and dangerous, and had been handled with rare skill.

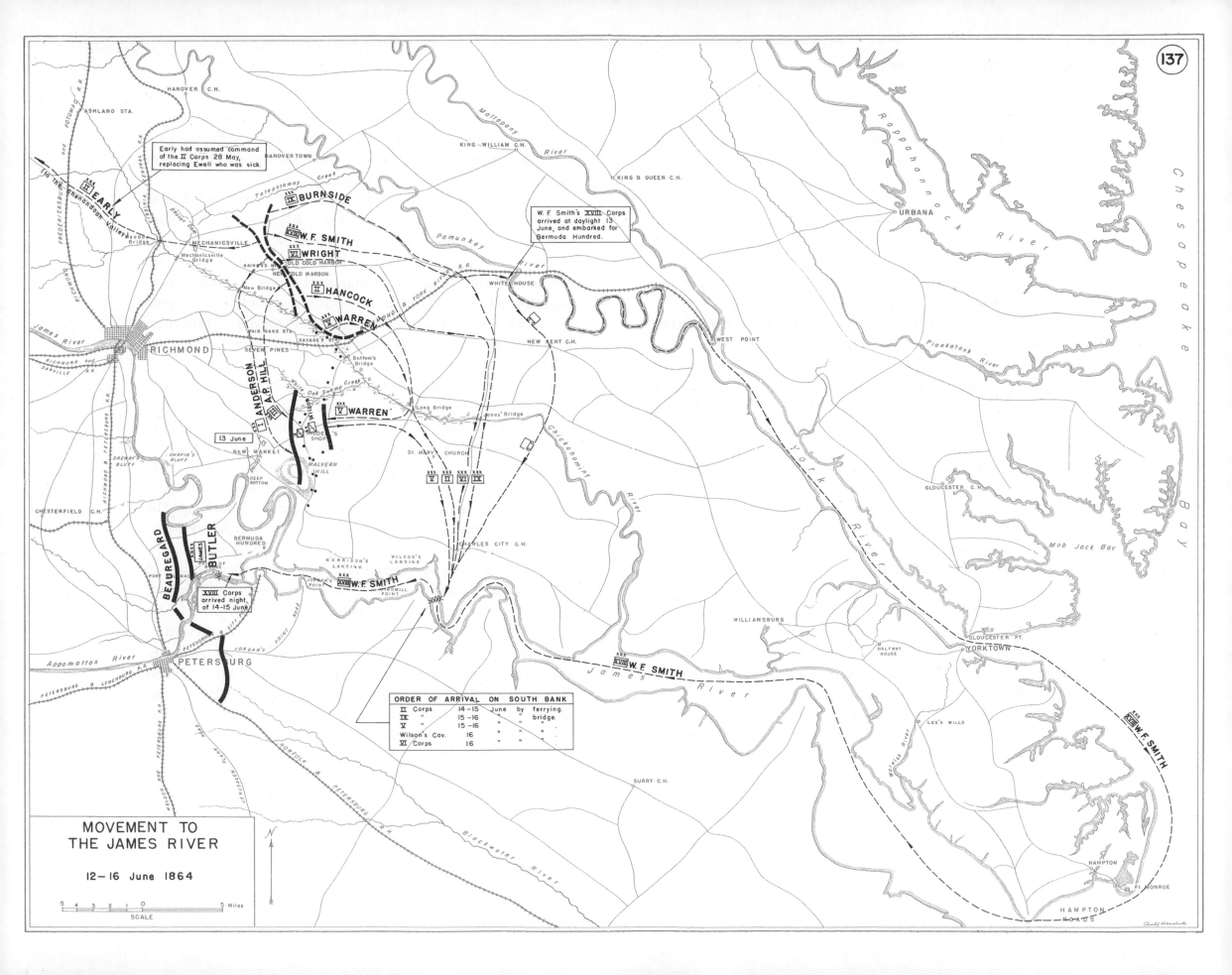

137

Early had assumed command of the II Corps 28 May, replacing Ewell who was sick.

W. F. Smith's XVIII Corps arrived at daylight 13 June, and embarked for Bermuda Hundred.

XX II EARLY

(To the Shenandoah Valley)

HANOVER C.H.

ASHLAND STA.

HANOVER TOWN

KING WILLIAM C.H.

KING & QUEEN C.H.

URBANA

IX BURNSIDE

XXX XVIII W. F. SMITH

XXX VI WRIGHT

MECHANICSVILLE

GAINES'S MILL OLD COLD HARBOR

NEW COLD HARBOR

XXX II HANCOCK

New Bridge

XXX V WARREN

WHITE HOUSE

NEW KENT C.H.

WEST POINT

RICHMOND

FAIR OAKS STA.

SEVEN PINES

SAVAGE'S STA.

Bottom's Bridge

I ANDERSON A.P. HILL

White Oak Swamp Creek

XXX V WARREN

Long Bridge

Jones' Bridge

13 June

NEW MARKET

Riddell's Shop

MALVERN HILL

St. MARY CHURCH

XXX XXX XXX XXX V II VI IX

CHESTERFIELD C.H.

DREWRY'S BLUFF

CHAPIN'S BLUFF

DEEP BOTTOM

BEAUREGARD

XXX BUTLER

BERMUDA HUNDRED

CHARLES CITY C.H.

HARRISON'S LANDING

WILCOX'S LANDING

GLOUCESTER C.H.

Mob Jack Bay

XVIII Corps arrived night of 14-15 June

JORDAN'S POINT

XXX XVIII W. F. SMITH

WINDMILL POINT

WILLIAMSBURG

GLOUCESTER PT.

YORKTOWN

PETERSBURG

Appomattox River

JORDAN'S

XXX XVIII W. F. SMITH

James River

HALFWAY HOUSE

LEE'S MILLS

ORDER OF ARRIVAL ON SOUTH BANK

II Corps	14-15	June by ferrying.
IX "	15-16	" " bridge.
V "	15-16	" "
Wilson's Cav.	16	" "
VI Corps	16	

SURRY C.H.

Blackwater River

XXX XVIII W. F. SMITH

HAMPTON

FT. MONROE

HAMPTON ROADS

MOVEMENT TO
THE JAMES RIVER

12-16 June 1864

N

5 4 3 2 1 0   5 Miles
SCALE

For his attack on Petersburg, Smith was reinforced with Brig. Gen. Edward W. Hinks's division of Negro troops and Brig. Gen. August V. Kautz's cavalry division (*sketch* a). Nevertheless, he advanced cautiously, allowing Beauregard's outposts to delay his march.

The Petersburg defenses consisted of a chain of strong redans (artillery positions designed for both flanking and frontal fire) connected by entrenchments; all approaches were obstructed by ditches and tangles of felled trees. Beauregard had plenty of guns in position, but barely enough troops to man them.

Smith remembered the disastrous, hasty attack at Cold Harbor. Therefore, he now made an exhaustive reconnaissance. About 5:00 P.M., deciding that the Confederate works were defended largely by artillery, he ordered an attack, only to be delayed by the incapacity of his own artillery commander. The attack finally jumped off about 7:00 P.M. against redans 5 and 6. Both fell quickly; Hink's division swarmed down the Confederate line as far as redan 11, opening a mile-wide gap in the Confederate fortifications. Petersburg lay open.

But Smith had picked up a rumor that Lee was arriving. He accordingly chose to stand on his laurels until Hancock could join him. Meanwhile, Beauregard brought Bushrod Johnson down from Bermuda Hundred, and Hoke's troops began arriving from Lee's army.

After crossing the James, Hancock had waited, as ordered, to draw rations which never arrived. At 10:30 A.M., he marched without them. His orders had omitted the primary fact that he was to take part in an assault on Petersburg, Grant having failed to take Meade (who issued them) into his confidence in that regard. Instead, these orders—based on an inaccurate map—merely misdirected him to a nonexistent locality near Petersburg. About 5:30 P.M., after hours of countermarching, Hancock learned from both Grant and Smith that he was supposed to be attacking that city. When he reached Smith, the latter said the Confederates had been reinforced, that it was too late to attack, and that it would be best if Hancock's corps relieved Smith's own exhausted men. Hancock—possibly weakened somewhat by his unhealed Gettysburg wound—concurred.

The next day, Grant and Meade arrived with the IX Corps. At 6:00 P.M., all three corps attacked (*sketch* b). By now, however, Beauregard had moved almost all his troops from Bermuda Hundred to Petersburg. The Union advance captured four more redans, but suffered heavily. Beauregard counterattacked unsuccessfully. At Bermuda Hundred, Butler's subordinates overran the weakly held Confederate lines, but Butler recalled them when Lee hurriedly dispatched Pickett from north of the James (*not shown*).

A surprise attack at first light on the 17th by one of Burnside's divisions took the Shand house ridge, but other attacks failed. At 4:00 A.M. on the 18th, Grant launched a major assault, only to discover that Beauregard had withdrawn almost a mile during the night and had hastily improvised a new line of works (*sketch* c). Time was needed to regroup for an attack against this line, and, in the meantime, Lee's troops were finally arriving. The last Union assault was hasty and uncoordinated; heavy losses brought minor gains.

Grant's strategy had been brilliant, but his earlier tactics had left his officers and men alike reluctant to assault fortifications. This attitude, compounded by poor staff work, caused a bright opportunity to win the war to miscarry. Grant now decided to suspend his assaults and operate against Lee's communications. He therefore entrenched his line and, on 22 June, sent the II and VI Corps to extend it south of Petersburg (*sketch* d). In so doing, the two corps lost contact in the heavily wooded terrain. Seizing the opportunity, A. P. Hill checked Wright with one division, threw two more against the left flank of the II Corps, and drove it back in confusion. Afterward, the Federal front was reestablished (*solid blue lines*).

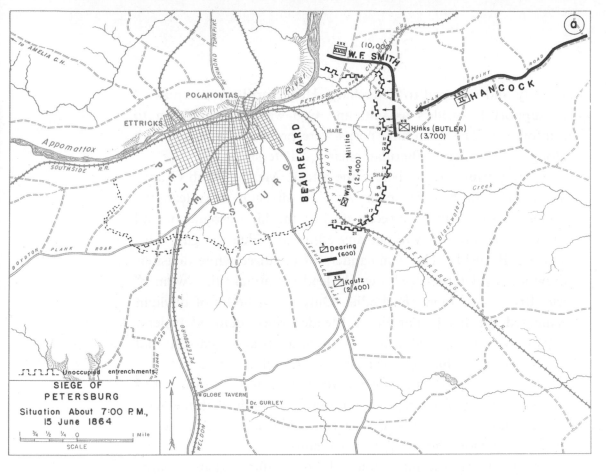

SIEGE OF PETERSBURG

Situation About 7:00 P.M., 15 June 1864

W. F. SMITH (10,000)

XVIII HANCOCK

Hinks (BUTLER) (3,700)

Wise and Militia (2,400)

Dearing (600)

Kautz (2,400)

BEAUREGARD

Unoccupied entrenchments

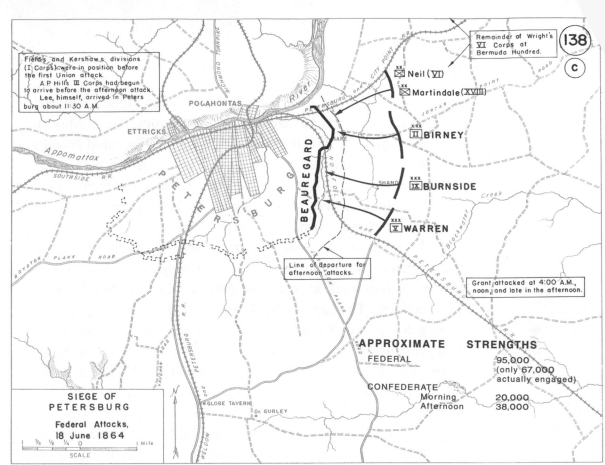

138

Field's and Kershaw's divisions (I Corps) were in position before the first Union attack.

A.P. Hill's III Corps had begun to arrive before the afternoon attack.

Lee, himself, arrived in Petersburg about 11:30 A.M.

Remainder of Wright's VI Corps at Bermuda Hundred.

Neil (VI)

Martindale (XVIII)

II BIRNEY

IX BURNSIDE

V WARREN

BEAUREGARD

Line of departure for afternoon attacks.

Grant attacked at 4:00 A.M., noon, and late in the afternoon.

APPROXIMATE STRENGTHS

FEDERAL	95,000 (only 67,000 actually engaged)
CONFEDERATE	
Morning	20,000
Afternoon	38,000

SIEGE OF PETERSBURG

Federal Attacks, 18 June 1864

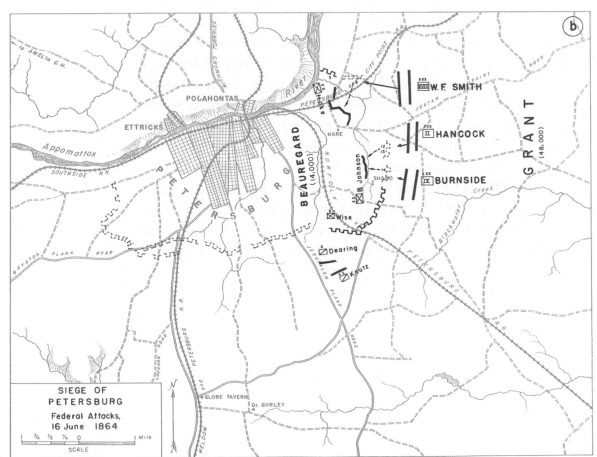

SIEGE OF PETERSBURG

Federal Attacks, 16 June 1864

W. F. SMITH XVIII

II HANCOCK

IX BURNSIDE

GRANT (48,000)

BEAUREGARD (14,000)

B. Johnson

Wise

Dearing

Kautz

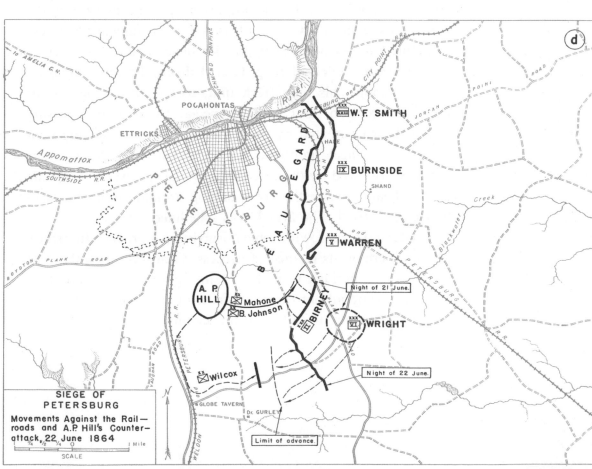

SIEGE OF PETERSBURG

Movements Against the Railroads and A.P. Hill's Counterattack, 22 June 1864

W. F. SMITH XVIII

IX BURNSIDE

V WARREN

BEAUREGARD

A. P. HILL

Mahone

B. Johnson

II BIRNEY

Night of 21 June.

VI WRIGHT

Wilcox

Night of 22 June.

Limit of advance.

The Petersburg front now subsided into static trench warfare. Both armies were exhausted—especially Grant's. Since May, it had been fighting by day and marching by night. Repeated assaults upon strong Confederate positions had killed or disabled many of the most courageous officers and men. Their replacements were sometimes dubious. The poor behavior of the II Corps—once the army's finest—on 22 June was symptomatic.

Minor operations continued in the theater in June, July, and August. Sheridan's move to meet Hunter came to nought; Hampton turned him back at Trevilian Station, sixty miles northwest of Petersburg. Farther south, Wilson wrecked the railroads at Burke's Station (*off map, left center*), but was intercepted by Hampton during his return and lost heavily before escaping. Early drove Hunter westward from the Shenandoah Valley and advanced on lightly garrisoned Washington. Grant sent the VI Corps by water to the capital; it arrived just in time to thwart Early.

At Petersburg, Lt. Col. Henry Pleasants—commander of the 48th Pennsylvania Infantry Regiment (a unit containing many miners)—proposed, and Burnside approved, the mining of the redan opposite the IX Corps. Pleasants' men tunneled 511 feet and planted 8,000 pounds of powder beneath the Confederate works. Burnside selected Brig. Gen. Edward Ferrero's division of Negro troops, his only fresh unit, to spearhead the assault after the explosion, and gave it special training. On passing through the gap created by the mine explosion, its leading regiments would wheel right and left to widen the gap; its other regiments, followed by the rest of the IX Corps, would continue straight ahead to seize the commanding ground along the Jerusalem Plank Road. The attack was scheduled for 30 July.

Meade and Grant, with some misgivings, approved Burnside's plan. To increase its chance of success, Grant, on 26 July, sent Hancock and Sheridan to make a feint against Richmond. This worked, drawing all but three Confederate divisions north of the James. On the night of 29 July, Hancock and Sheridan disengaged secretly and returned to Petersburg. Heavy artillery was massed to support Burnside's assault, and Ord was brought down to reinforce it. The remaining corps were prepared to advance all along the line, while Sheridan encircled Petersburg.

Barely twelve hours before the attack, Meade—with Grant's approval—modified this plan. A white division must lead the attack; it would move directly against the high ground behind the Confederate line without any effort to widen the gap. This stunned Burnside. The commanders of his three white divisions drew lots to determine who would lead the attack; the "winner" was Brig. Gen. James H. Ledlie. Only a few hours of daylight remained for his preparations. Meade issued detailed orders: gaps were to be opened in the Union parapets and abatis, so that the assaulting columns could advance rapidly; engineer parties would head each column. But everyone seems to have overlooked the problems involved in getting troops forward through the maze of trenches. Burnside failed to execute Meade's orders; the engineers somehow did not get into position.

At 4:40 A.M., the mine exploded; bodies, dirt, and guns soared into the air. The defenders on either side of the crater fled in terror, leaving 500 yards of the Confederate works deserted. But Ledlie hid in a dugout and plied himself with rum; Ferrero joined him. Unable to leave their trenches easily, the troops emerged slowly as individuals or in small groups. Control was lost; there was no organized attack. The first troops, passing through gaps created in the Confederate abatis by the explosion, went into the crater, only to find that they could not climb the thirty-foot bank at its far side. Others followed, jamming the pit with confused, milling soldiers. It took two hours to start another, piecemeal advance— then it was too late. The Confederates had reoccupied the flank of the crater, and now launched a furious counterattack; mortars rained shells among the mass of hapless Federal troops. Meade called off the attack—but 4,400 men had been lost.

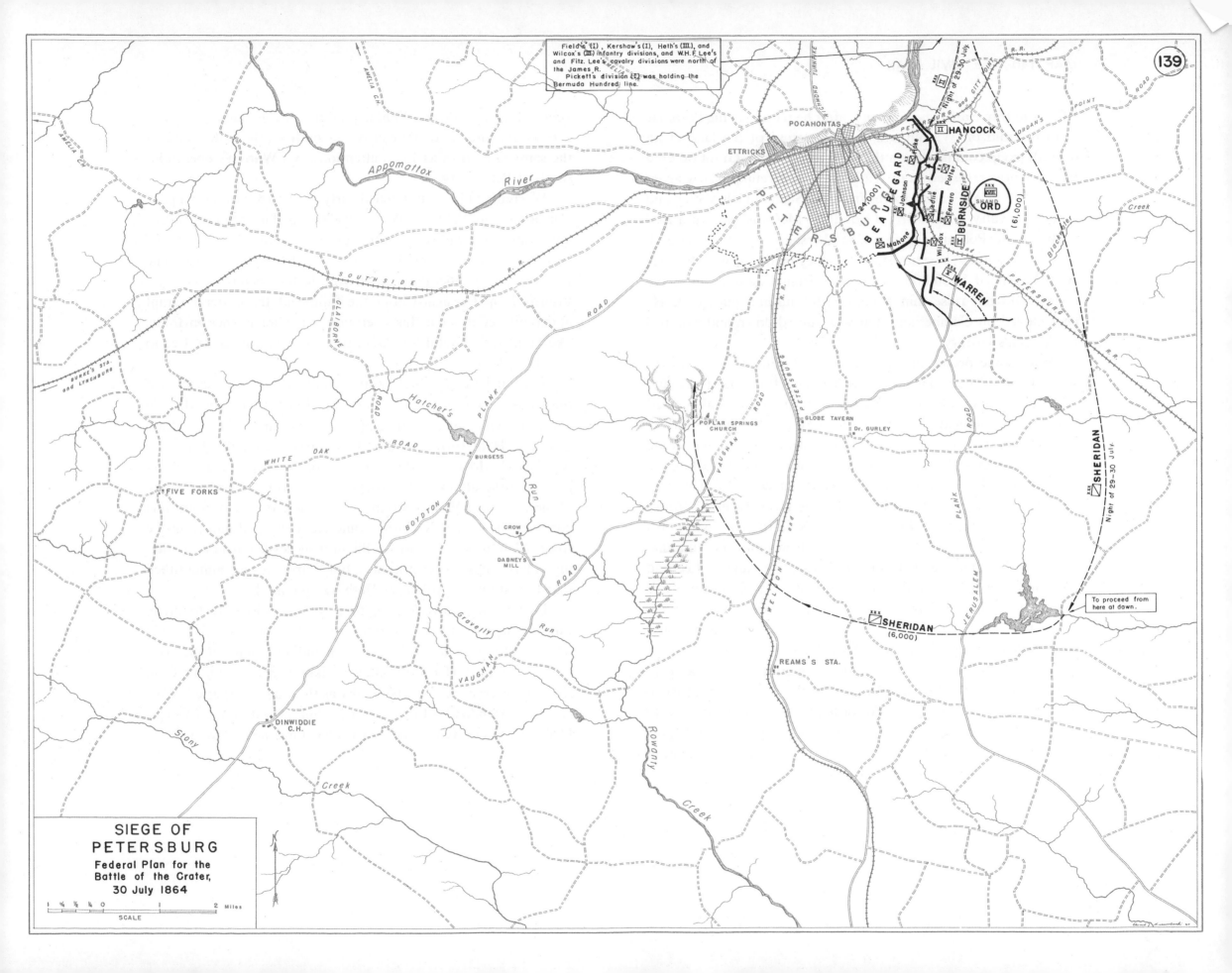

139

Field's (I), Kershaw's (I), Heth's (III), and Wilcox's (III) infantry divisions, and W.H.F. Lee's and Fitz. Lee's cavalry divisions were north of the James R.
Pickett's division (I) was holding the Bermuda Hundred line.

POCAHONTAS

ETTRICKS

Appomattox   River

HANCOCK

BEAUREGARD

Johnson

Potter

Ledlie   Ferrero

BURNSIDE

ORD
(6,000)

Mahone

Wilcox

WARREN

(24,000)

SOUTHSIDE   R. R.

CLAIBORNE   ROAD

BURKE'S STA.
and LYNCHBURG

Hatcher's

PLANK

Run

POPLAR SPRINGS
CHURCH

Globe Tavern

Dr. Gurley

BURGESS

WHITE   OAK   ROAD

FIVE FORKS

BOYDTON

CROW

DABNEY'S
MILL

ROAD

Gravelly

Run

VAUGHAN

REAM'S STA.

DINWIDDIE
C.H.

Stony

Creek

Rowanty

Creek

SHERIDAN
Night of 29-30 July.

To proceed from
here at dawn.

SHERIDAN
(6,000)

SIEGE OF PETERSBURG

Federal Plan for the
Battle of the Crater,
30 July 1864

SCALE
2 Miles

Efforts to trap Early (*not shown*), after he recrossed the Potomac from his raid on Washington, failed because of the lack of an over-all troop commander in the Washington area. Grant ordered the VI Corps returned from Washington, whereupon Early again cleared the local Federal forces from the Shenandoah Valley and sent his cavalry, under Brig. Gen. John McCausland, on a raid north of the Potomac against Chambersburg and Cumberland. These towns were to be burned unless they paid ransom. McCausland demanded $500,000 in currency from Chambersburg; the town could not raise that amount; McCausland burned it. He next moved on Cumberland, but was hunted down and whipped by Averell's cavalry.

With some prompting from Lincoln, Grant now decided to settle the problem of the Shenandoah Valley. Early must be either crushed or driven out of the Valley. After that, the Valley itself must be systematically devastated to prevent it from either feeding Lee's army or supporting a Confederate force that could constantly distract Federal operations by threatening Washington —as both Jackson and Early had done so successfully. This mission was entrusted to Sheridan, who was given Hunter's troops at Harper's Ferry, the VI Corps, the XIX Corps (brought north from Louisiana), and Torbert's and Wilson's cavalry. Initially, however, Sheridan was held in check. In early August, Lee had sent Anderson with one division of infantry and Fitzhugh Lee's cavalry to reinforce Early. Federal intelligence incorrectly believed that Anderson had taken his entire corps, which would give Early a stronger force than Sheridan's.

Acting on this belief that Anderson's entire corps was with Early, Grant decided that Lee's lines north of the James at Richmond might be weakly held. Accordingly, he sent Hancock with the II and X Corps and Gregg's cavalry against them on 13 August (*not shown*). Hancock found Lee's works strongly held, but Grant kept him there until the 20th, hoping that his threatening maneuvers would force Lee to recall Anderson from the Valley and, at the same time, distract Lee's attention from Warren's operations south of Petersburg.

Warren had been dispatched early on the 18th to seize a position across the Weldon & Petersburg Railroad near Globe Tavern and destroy the railroad as far south as possible. In addition, he was to exploit any Confederate weakness he might discover. The IX Corps, now under Parke, took over the lines before Petersburg. (Burnside had resigned after the failure at the crater.) Grant apparently considered this operation a reconnaissance in force, like Hancock's, useful for the pressure it would place on Lee to recall Anderson.

Warren had no difficulty in getting to the railroad (*dashed blue lines*) and began his work of destruction. The densely wooded country made it difficult for him to outpost his command properly. Heth surprised one of his divisions on the 18th, but was quickly driven off. At 4:30 P.M. on the 19th, A. P. Hill returned to the attack with a considerably stronger force, sending Mahone against Warren's right flank, where only a skirmish line connected it to the IX Corps, while Heth engaged him from the front. Mahone's attack was brilliantly successful at first, gathering in large numbers of prisoners, but Warren led a counterattack that forced him to withdraw. Heth was repulsed.

Feeling that to remain in that position was only to invite further surprise attacks, Warren fell back approximately a mile on the 20th and entrenched on commanding ground in the open (*solid blue line*). Here, Hill attacked him with all available Confederate reserves on the 21st, and was thoroughly repulsed. Warren now extended his fortifications to link up with the IX Corps. Hancock was moved to the Federal left for a new offensive.

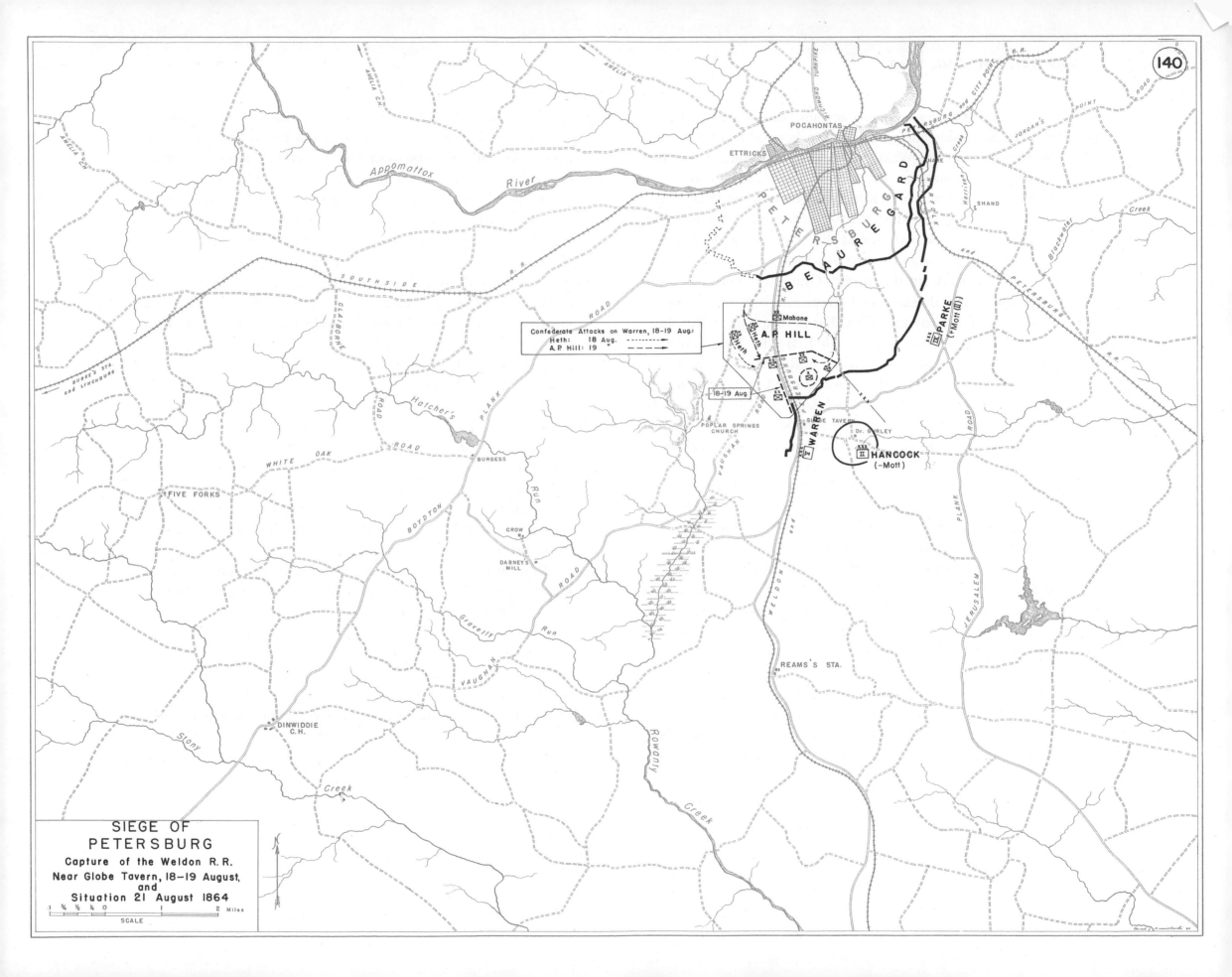

140

Confederate Attacks on Warren, 18-19 Aug.:
Heth: 18 Aug. — — — — —
A.P. Hill: 19 " – – – – –

18-19 Aug.

Mahone

A.P. HILL

Heth

PARKE
(+Mott(II))

WARREN

HANCOCK
(-Mott)

Dr. Gurley

GLOBE TAVERN

POPLAR SPRINGS
CHURCH

PETERSBURG BEAUREGARD

POCAHONTAS

ETTRICKS

Appomattox   River

SOUTHSIDE   R.R.

CLAIBORNE   ROAD

Hatcher's   PLANK

BURGESS

WHITE   OAK   ROAD

FIVE FORKS

BOYDTON

CROW N?

DABNEY'S
MILL

Gravelly   Run

VAUGHAN   ROAD

VAUGHAN

Run

DINWIDDIE
C.H.

Stony

Creek

Creek

Rowanty   Creek

REAMS'S STA.

WELDON   and   PETERSBURG   R.R.

JERUSALEM   PLANK   ROAD

BURKE'S STA.
and LYNCHBURG

AMELIA CH.

AMELIA CH.

RICHMOND TURNPIKE

PETERSBURG and CITY POINT   R.R.

JORDAN'S
POINT

SHAND

Blackwater   Creek

Harrison   Creek

Hare

NORFOLK   and   PETERSBURG   R.R.

SIEGE OF
PETERSBURG
Capture of the Weldon R.R.
Near Globe Tavern, 18-19 August,
and
Situation 21 August 1864

1 ¾ ½ ¼ 0   1   2 Miles
SCALE

Of events related in the following account, only Grant's attempt to seize the Southside Railroad is shown here in detail.

Warren had cut the Weldon & Petersburg Railroad, but the Confederates continued to use it below the break. Trains were run to a point about one day's haul by wagon south of Petersburg; there, supplies were transferred to wagons and taken into the city by roads which passed around the west end of the Federal lines, then in the vicinity of Globe Tavern.

Anxious to break up this traffic, Grant sent Hancock with Gibbon's and Miles' divisions and Gregg's cavalry (*not shown*), on 22 August, to destroy the railroad as far south as its Rowanty Creek crossing (*off map, bottom right*). By the 24th, Hancock had progressed about three miles south of Reams's Station (*lower right*). Here, he was warned that considerable Confederate forces were moving against him from Petersburg, and quickly occupied some abandoned entrenchments at Reams's Station. Hill struck him there the next morning. The first Confederate attacks were repelled, but Gibbon's division suddenly panicked, and a flank attack by Hampton's dismounted cavalry swept them away in disorder. Even Hancock could not make them stand, and he had to retire with heavy losses. Meade had started reinforcements to Hancock, but sent them by a circuitous route, so that they failed to arrive in time. (In fairness to Gibbon's division, it should be noted that, since crossing the Rapidan, its three brigades had lost nine brigade commanders and forty regimental commanders, besides the pick of its company commanders and enlisted men.) The Confederates now held Reams's Station and continued their supply operations.

Grant kept hammering—now north of the James, now south of it. Lee's lines were constantly stretched thinner. On 14 September, Anderson left the Shenandoah Valley to rejoin Lee. Sheridan immediately attacked in the Valley, defeating Early four times within a month; concurrently, he devastated the entire Valley.

On 29 September, Ord captured Fort Harrison on the James, thirteen miles north of Petersburg. South of the James, Warren fought on both 30 September and 1 October, advancing from his position along the Weldon & Petersburg Railroad and establishing the deep salient around Poplar Springs Church (*center*).

Grant, determined to cut the Southside Railroad (*upper left*) before winter put an end to campaigning, sent elements of the II, V, and IX Corps against it on 27 October (*inset sketch*). Parke was to attempt to surprise the Confederate defenses east of Hatcher's Run; if unsuccessful, he was to threaten an attack to divert attention from Hancock and Warren, who were to turn the south end of the Confederate line and strike the railroad. Hancock reached the Boydton Plank Road, but was ordered to halt there, since Warren had been unable to keep up in the heavily wooded country, and Parke had found the Confederate entrenchments too strong to attack. While Hancock was thus isolated, Hill and Hampton attacked him, front and flanks. Gregg stopped Hampton; after confused fighting, Hancock drove Hill off in disorder. That night, almost out of ammunition, Hancock withdrew. Meanwhile, Warren, on orders from Grant, had turned in to his right to envelop the Hatcher's Run defenses, but had been unable to get his men across that creek.

Both armies now went into winter quarters. Supply of the Union forces was greatly aided by the construction of a military railway behind their position.

Lee had waged an effective war of attrition. Only once—when Grant made his surprise crossing of the James—had Lee failed seriously. The casualties he had inflicted had left much of the North weary of war. But attrition worked both ways, and—though Lee might hold at Petersburg—the Shenandoah Valley was lost, Mobile was gone, Sherman was moving freely across the South, and the Army of Northern Virginia was worn out.

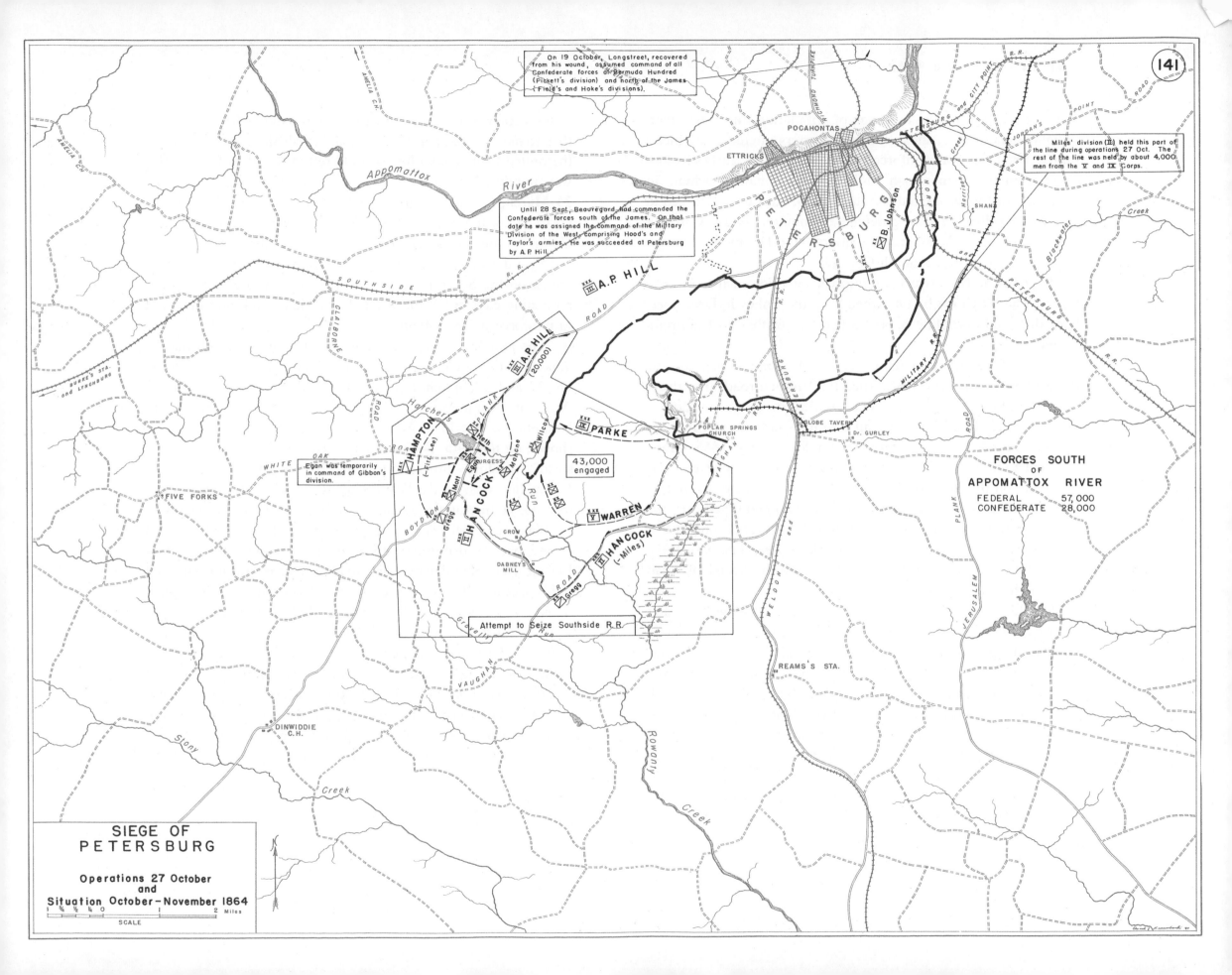

141

On 19 October, Longstreet, recovered from his wound, assumed command of all Confederate forces at Bermuda Hundred (Pickett's division) and north of the James (Field's and Hoke's divisions).

Miles' division (II) held this part of the line during operations 27 Oct. The rest of the line was held by about 4,000 men from the V and IX Corps.

Until 28 Sept. Beauregard had commanded the Confederate forces south of the James. On that date he was assigned the command of the Military Division of the West, comprising Hood's and Taylor's armies. He was succeeded at Petersburg by A.P. Hill

XXX A.P. HILL

XXX A.P. HILL (20,000)

XXX IX PARKE

XXX HAMPTON (-Fitz Lee)

Egan was temporarily in command of Gibbon's division.

43,000 engaged

XXX V WARREN

XX HANCOCK

XX HANCOCK (-Miles)

Attempt to Seize Southside R.R.

FORCES SOUTH
OF
APPOMATTOX RIVER

FEDERAL 57,000
CONFEDERATE 28,000

B. Johnson

PETERSBURG
POCAHONTAS
ETTRICKS

Appomattox River

GLOBE TAVERN
Dr. GURLEY
POPLAR SPRINGS CHURCH
REAMS'S STA.
DINWIDDIE C.H.
FIVE FORKS
BURKE'S STA. and LYNCHBURG
AMELIA C.H.
DABNEY'S MILL

SIEGE OF PETERSBURG

Operations 27 October
and
Situation October-November 1864

SCALE
2 Miles

For Lee's army, it was a winter of tribulation and discontent, somehow endured by most, though deserters filtered away incessantly. The army was reinforced by the remains of Early's former corps from the Shenandoah Valley (Early remained behind, in command of the local Confederate forces), but Lee was forced to send Hoke's division to help defend Wilmington, North Carolina —the Confederacy's last major seaport—and Hampton took one division of cavalry into South Carolina.

Beyond the breastworks, reinforcements flowed into Grant's forces. The VI Corps had returned from the Valley in December; hard drill and discipline made soldiers out of the most unpromising conscripts.

There were only two actions of any size (*not shown*) during the winter, for the rains had turned the Virginia roads into rivers of mud. During December, Warren destroyed the Weldon & Petersburg Railroad for forty miles to the south, greatly increasing the Confederate supply problem. On 5 February, 1865, Gregg was sent to break up the Confederate wagon trains believed to be operating on the Boydton Plank Road, his rear being covered by infantry under Warren and Humphreys (who had taken over the II Corps from the invalided Hancock). Gregg found only a few wagons; the infantry repulsed an attack by Lee. Thereafter, the Union line was extended to the point where the Vaughan Road crossed Hatcher's Run.

On 23 January, popular resentment against Davis' conduct of the South's war effort resulted in the Confederate Congress creating the post of commander in chief of all Confederate forces. Lee was naturally so designated, but—beyond somewhat improving the supply situation of his own forces—he did little. Indeed, there was little that any man could do: Thomas had smashed Hood at Nashville, Sherman was in Savannah, a strong Federal beachhead was building up at Wilmington, and Sheridan was hunting down Early's tiny remaining force in the Valley. But, out of desperation, the Confederate high command evolved a plan. A surprise attack was to cripple Grant's army, making it possible to hold Richmond and Petersburg with a reduced force. Lee was then to move south, join Johnston, and crush Sherman. That done, the united Confederate forces could return to defeat Grant. This was purely chimerical, but it was attempted. At 4:00 P.M., 25 March, Gordon surprised and stormed Fort Stedman at the north end of the Union's Petersburg line. There his attack stalled. Union counterattacks drove him back, with 5,000 casualties.

Two days later, Sheridan joined Grant. Foreseeing a prompt attack on the Southside Railroad, Lee concentrated most of his remaining cavalry on the Confederate right flank and prepared to reinforce it with infantry.

The attack Lee expected came swiftly, for Grant felt that he must take the offensive quickly before Lee evacuated Petersburg. On 27 and 28 March, Ord secretly brought a large part of the Army of the James to the Petersburg front, freeing Warren and Humphreys. Sheridan, Warren, and Humphreys advanced, as shown, on the 29th. For three days, the two infantry corps made steady—if slow—progress; by the 31st, they had extended the Union line west to the White Oak Road. On that day, a Confederate counterattack against Warren's left flank was repulsed.

Sheridan, meanwhile, advanced beyond Dinwiddie Court House, but was driven back to the court house during the 31st by Pickett. Here Sheridan managed to hold. Warren was now ordered to his support. It was a night of rain and poor signal communications. Bridges were out. Warren struggled forward toward Dinwiddie Court House, while Pickett, learning of his advance, retired to Five Forks and entrenched. Sheridan found him there the next morning and called Warren forward. Sheridan's staff had failed to reconnoiter the Confederate position properly and committed Warren incorrectly. However, Warren managed to swing his corps against Pickett's left flank and rear, just as Sheridan hit Pickett's front and Mackenzie circled his left. The Confederate force collapsed, 4,500 being captured. Sheridan—a bombastic fighter with no confidence in calmer generals—celebrated his victory by relieving Warren from command of the V Corps.

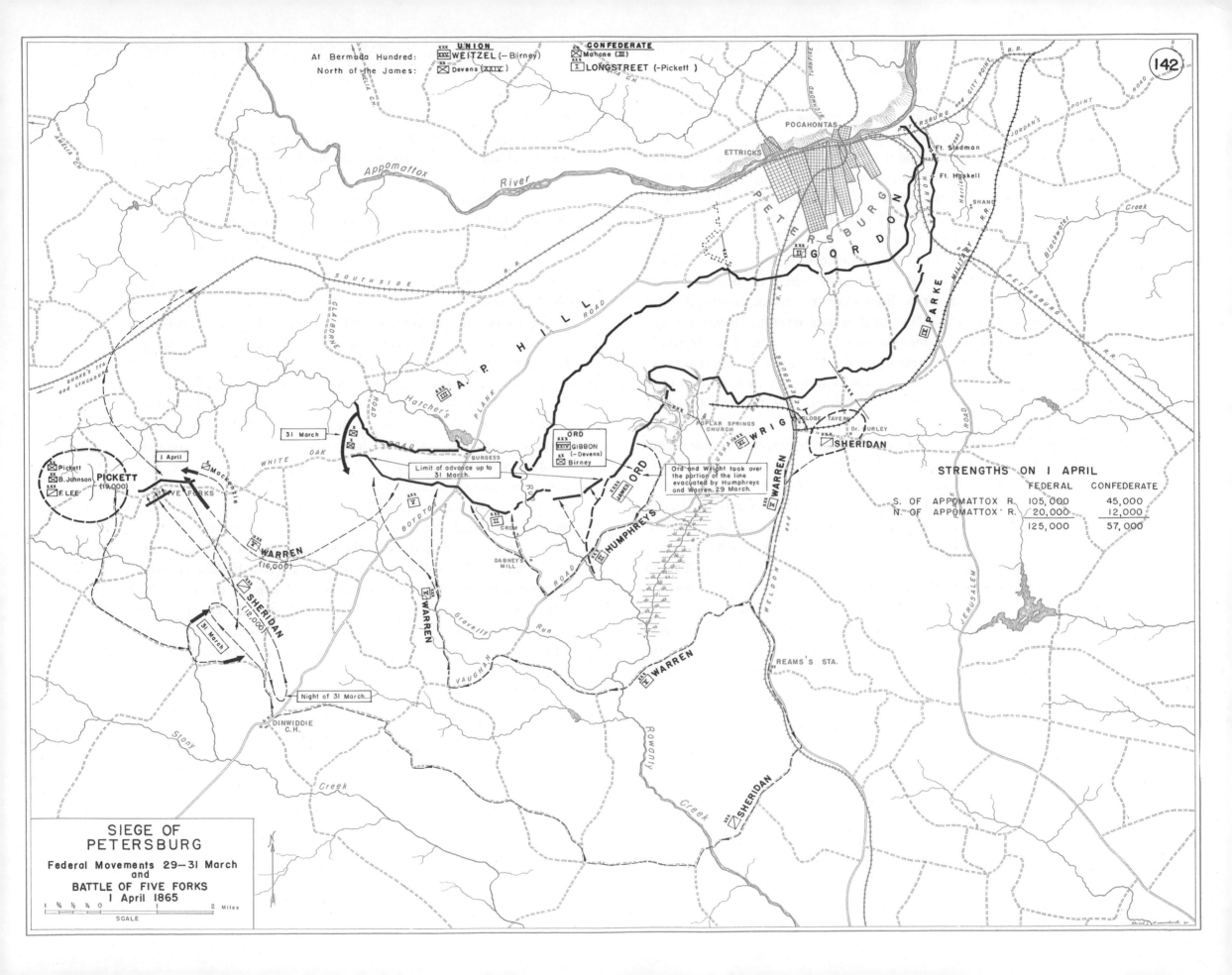

142

At Bermuda Hundred:
North of the James:

UNION
WEITZEL (-Birney)
Devens (XXIV)

CONFEDERATE
Mahone (III)
LONGSTREET (-Pickett)

POCAHONTAS

ETTRICKS

Appomattox River

Ft. Sledman

Ft. Haskell

PETERSBURG

GORDON

PARKE

A. P. HILL

31 March

Limit of advance up to 31 March.

ORD
GIBBON
(-Devens)
Birney

POPLAR SPRINGS CHURCH

WRIGHT

Globe Tavern

Dr. Gurley

SHERIDAN

Ord and Wright took over the portion of the line evacuated by Humphreys and Warren, 29 March.

BURGESS

Pickett
B. Johnson
F. Lee
PICKETT
(19,000)

1 April

FIVE FORKS

Mackenzie

WHITE OAK

WARREN
(16,000)

SHERIDAN
(12,000)

31 March

ORD
JAMES

HUMPHREYS

WARREN

DABNEY'S MILL

BOYDTON

Gravelly Run

VAUGHAN

DINWIDDIE C.H.

Night of 31 March.

Stony

Creek

Rowanty Creek

REAMS'S STA.

MELDON and PETERSBURG

JERUSALEM

SHERIDAN

STRENGTHS ON I APRIL

	FEDERAL	CONFEDERATE
S. OF APPOMATTOX R.	105,000	45,000
N. OF APPOMATTOX R.	20,000	12,000
	125,000	57,000

SIEGE OF PETERSBURG

Federal Movements 29–31 March
and
BATTLE OF FIVE FORKS
1 April 1865

SCALE
2 Miles

The defeat at Five Forks cost Lee the use of the Southside Railroad and most of his meager reserves.

On 2 April, the Federals renewed their attack against the Confederate right flank. All through the preceding night, their artillery had pounded the Confederate defenses. Now, at 4:00 A.M., their infantry went forward all along the line, while Sheridan and the V Corps covered their west flank.

Wright had carefully reconnoitered the Confederate works to his front and noticed that several gaps existed in their protective abatis. These Confederate lines were tremendously strong, built in large part by slave labor, but Lee had never had troops enough to man the whole of them properly; now—after Fort Stedman and Five Forks—the remaining defenders were spread far too thin. Even so, Wright lost 1,100 men in the fifteen minutes it took him to obtain a decisive breakthrough. On his left, Ord and Humphreys also overran the Confederate fortifications; to his right, Parke took the first line of defenses, but was unable to get through a second line. Shortly after Wright's successful attack, A. P. Hill was killed when he rode into the Federal advance.

Humphreys' left-flank division (Miles) encountered Heth's division, hastily entrenched just below the Southside Railroad, and defeated it after being twice repulsed. The main Federal attack swept ahead, up to the line of Confederate earthworks protecting the western face of Petersburg. Two detached forts—Whitworth and Gregg—checked the advance here. Both were stormed, but it was now late, and most units were exhausted and more or less disorganized. A pause to regroup was necessary. Furthermore, the gallant stand of the garrisons of these two forts had given Longstreet time to bring troops south across the James River to reinforce the Petersburg defenses. Grant issued orders for an attack on both Richmond and Petersburg early on the morning of 3 April.

Lee had immediately realized that the situation was hopeless. All he could do was to hold out as best he could until dark, then evacuate Petersburg and Richmond, and retreat to the south and west—the sole escape routes still open to him. Thereafter, he could attempt to join Johnston, who was opposing Sherman in North Carolina.

The Confederate Government was warned of the situation, and Mr. Davis (possibly mindful of the refrain "Oh, we'll hang Jeff Davis to a sour apple tree! As we go marching on!") began an attempt to get the archives, treasure, and essential officials of the Confederate Government out of Richmond. Shortly after 3:00 P.M., the various scattered units of the Army of Northern Virginia were instructed to withdraw and assemble at Amelia Court House (off map, top left). At 8:00 P.M., the retreat began, along the routes indicated.

The evacuation was excellently handled, but the Richmond mob soon formed and began looting warehouses and stores. The confusion was increased when the Confederate provost marshal set the city's tobacco warehouses afire to prevent Federal seizure of their contents. These fires spread to much of the city. By 3:00 A.M., Grant was aware that Lee had gone. Petersburg was quickly occupied; Richmond was formally surrendered by its mayor at 8:15 A.M. Federal troops soon had both fires and mobs under control.

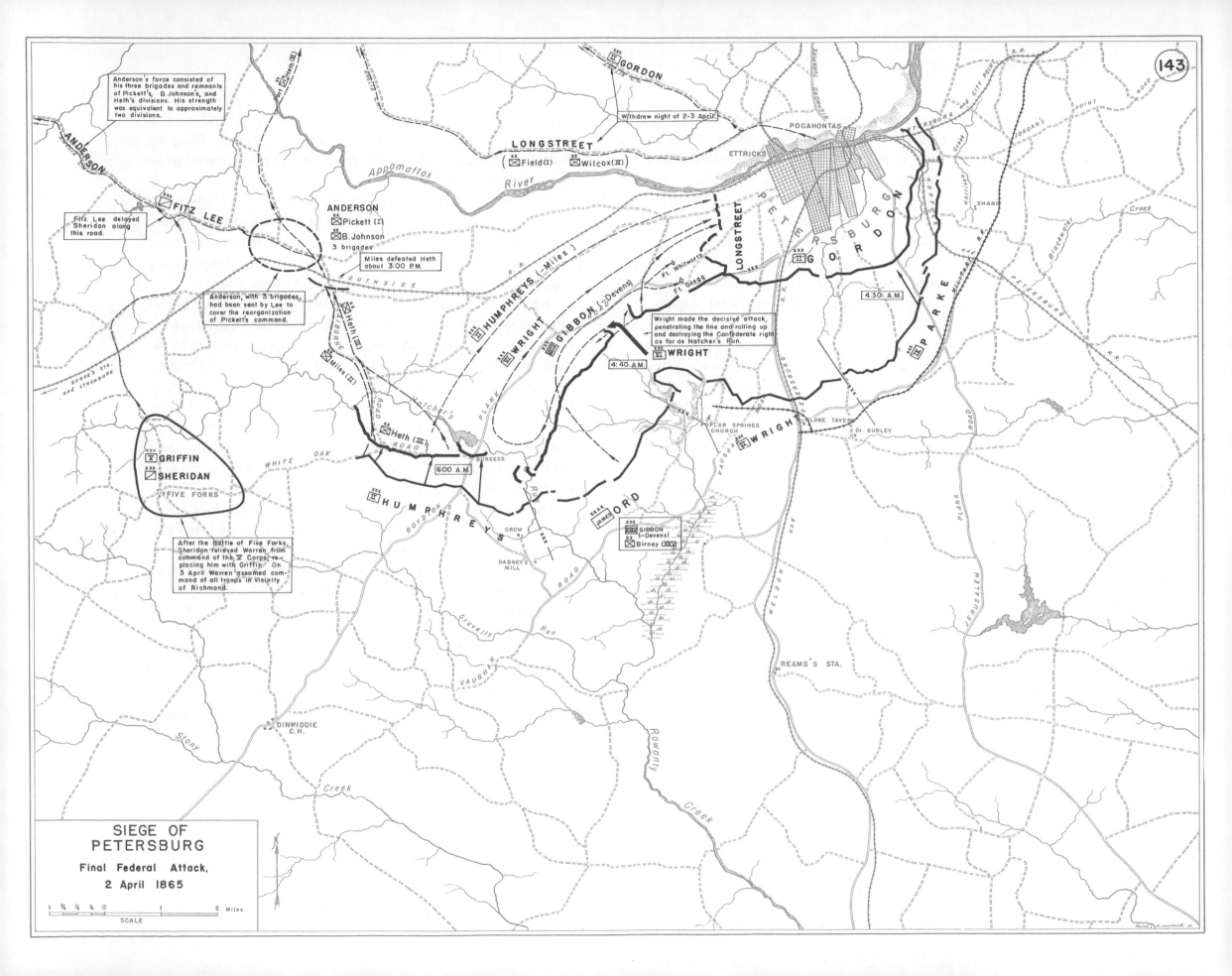

143

Anderson's force consisted of his three brigades and remnants of Pickett's, B. Johnson's, and Heth's divisions. His strength was equivalent to approximately two divisions.

GORDON

Withdrew night of 2-3 April.

POCAHONTAS

ETTRICKS

LONGSTREET

(XX Field(I)   XX Wilcox(III))

ANDERSON

FITZ LEE

Fitz Lee delayed Sheridan along this road.

ANDERSON
XX Pickett(I)
XX B. Johnson
3 brigades

Miles defeated Heth about 3:00 P.M.

Anderson, with 3 brigades, had been sent by Lee to cover the reorganization of Pickett's command.

Appomattox River

SOUTHSIDE

Heth (III)

Miles (II)

HUMPHREYS (-Miles)

WRIGHT

GIBBON (-Devens)

Ft. Whitworth

Ft. Gregg

LONGSTREET

GORDON

4:30 A.M.

PARKE

Wright made the decisive attack, penetrating the line and rolling up and destroying the Confederate right as far as Hatcher's Run.

WRIGHT

4:40 A.M.

Heth (III)

GRIFFIN

SHERIDAN

FIVE FORKS

Hatcher's

BURGESS

6:00 A.M.

POPLAR SPRINGS CHURCH

GLOBE TAVERN

Dr. Gurley

WRIGHT

After the Battle of Five Forks, Sheridan relieved Warren from command of the V Corps, replacing him with Griffin. On 3 April Warren assumed command of all troops in vicinity of Richmond.

HUMPHREYS

ORD

JAMES

GIBBON
(-Devens)
Birney

CROW H.

DABNEY'S MILL

Gravelly Run

VAUGHAN ROAD

REAMS'S STA.

DINWIDDIE C.H.

Stony Creek

Rowanty Creek

SIEGE OF PETERSBURG

Final Federal Attack,
2 April 1865

1 ¾ ½ ¼ 0   1   2 Miles
SCALE

Lee's last hope was to withdraw either southwest to Danville (*off map, bottom left*) or west to Lynchburg—at either of which localities Johnston, now in North Carolina, could possibly join him. This would do little except uselessly prolong the war, and Lee undoubtedly knew it. But Lee's sense of duty kept him from capitulating. His army was but a shadow—approximately 30,000 infantrymen, plus another 20,000 cavalry, artillery, engineer, naval, and miscellaneous troops for a total of no more than 50,000. They were weak from short rations and lack of sleep, and encumbered by some 200 guns and over 1,000 wagons. Horses were underfed and frequently unable to get their loads through the muddy roads.

Amelia Court House (*center*) had been designated as the rallying point. Lee had ordered rations sent there from Richmond before the retreat began. He expected to have his army concentrated and resupplied by late 4 April.

Aware of the two routes which Lee could follow, Grant had immediately taken steps to intercept him, whichever route he chose. Initially, the main effort would be to get across the Richmond & Danville Railroad to block any Confederate move south. By the afternoon of the 4th, Federal cavalry was nipping at Lee's south flank.

Confederate staff work and supply were bad to the last, greatly aiding the Federal pursuit. Lee found no rations waiting at Amelia Court House. Little food was left in the immediate vicinity. Everything now depended upon moving swiftly down the railroad toward Burke's Station before the Federals cut that line and dashed the hope of receiving food by train from Danville. But, again, there was a delay: Ewell and Anderson could not close up until the morning of the 5th.

At 1:00 P.M. that day, Lee marched south from Amelia Court House, but found Union infantry and cavalry across his path. He could not risk an assault; instead, he urged his troops westward toward Farmville, where there was hope of receiving rations from Lynchburg. This meant a killing night march. Discipline broke in some units; exhausted, starving men fell out. Union cavalry harried the Confederate left flank and rear, repeatedly delaying the retreat. Meade had quickly detected Lee's change of route and was following swiftly.

At Sailor's Creek, the Federals caught up. The II Corps overwhelmed Gordon, who was covering the Confederate trains, and captured the larger part of the wagons he tried to protect. Farther south, along the same creek, Wright's VI Corps and the cavalry trapped Ewell's corps and about half of Anderson's.

Early on 7 April, the remaining Confederates reached Farmville, where some were issued rations for the first time since the retreat had begun. Lee continued his withdrawal, crossing to the north bank of the Appomattox River and setting fire to the bridges behind him. The II Corps, however, was able to save those at High Bridge and again struck Lee's rear. Lee formed a line of battle to save his remaining trains, and held Humphreys at bay. But, while he succeeded in this, Ord's infantry and Sheridan's cavalry came up rapidly past Lee's south flank. On the evening of the 8th, the cavalry reached Appomattox Station (*not shown, southwest of Appomattox Court House*), capturing four trains that had been dispatched from Lynchburg with rations, and getting across Lee's line of march.

On the morning of the 9th, Lee sent Gordon and Fitzhugh Lee to break through Sheridan. Initially, the attack forced the Federal cavalry back, only to encounter the infantry masses of Ord's two corps. At the same time, the II Corps closed against the Confederate rear. At 4:00 P.M., 9 April, the formalities of Lee's surrender were completed.

Grant's pursuit still stands as one of the best operations of its type in the history of warfare. Lee was never able to break contact with the Federal forces. Sheridan, Ord, and Griffin served as an encircling force to head off the retreating Confederates, while the rest of the Army of the Potomac maintained constant pressure against their rear guard. Lee could not halt to fight one of these forces without exposing himself to an attack from the other.

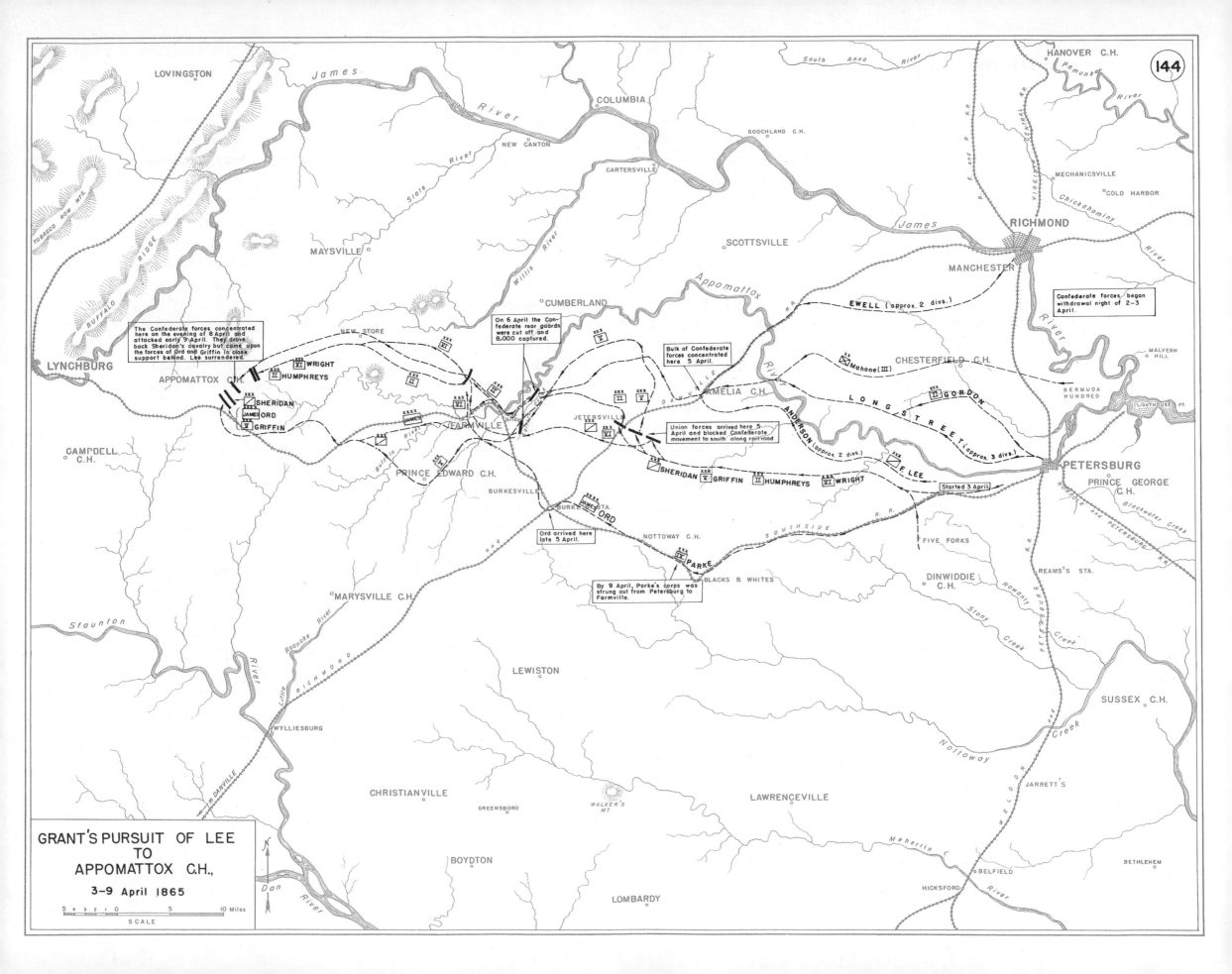

144

The Confederate forces concentrated here on the evening of 8 April and attacked early 9 April. They drove back Sheridan's cavalry but came upon the forces of Ord and Griffin in close support behind. Lee surrendered.

On 6 April the Confederate rear guards were cut off and 8,000 captured.

Bulk of Confederate forces concentrated here 5 April.

Confederate forces began withdrawal night of 2-3 April.

Union forces arrived here 5 April and blocked Confederate movement to south along railroad

Started 3 April

Ord arrived here late 5 April.

By 9 April, Parke's corps was strung out from Petersburg to Farmville.

LOVINGSTON

HANOVER C.H.

COLUMBIA

NEW CANTON

GOOCHLAND C.H.

CARTERSVILLE

RICHMOND

MAYSVILLE

SCOTTSVILLE

MANCHESTER

MECHANICSVILLE

COLD HARBOR

LYNCHBURG

BUFFALO

TOBACCO ROW MTS

CUMBERLAND

EWELL (approx. 2 divs.)

CHESTERFIELD C.H.

MALVERN HILL

APPOMATTOX C.H.

WRIGHT

HUMPHREYS

Mahone (III)

AMELIA C.H.

BERMUDA HUNDRED

LIGHTHOUSE PT.

SHERIDAN

ORD

JAMES

GRIFFIN

LONGSTREET (approx. 3 divs.)

GORDON

FARMVILLE

JETERSVILLE

ANDERSON (approx. 2 divs.)

PETERSBURG

CAMPBELL C.H.

PRINCE EDWARD C.H.

SHERIDAN GRIFFIN HUMPHREYS WRIGHT

F. LEE

PRINCE GEORGE C.H.

BURKESVILLE

JAMES STA. ORD

NOTTOWAY C.H.

SOUTHSIDE R.R.

FIVE FORKS

REAMS'S STA.

DINWIDDIE C.H.

PARKE

BLACKS & WHITES

MARYSVILLE C.H.

LEWISTON

SUSSEX C.H.

WYLLIESBURG

JARRETT'S

CHRISTIANVILLE

GREENSBORO

WALKER'S MT.

LAWRENCEVILLE

BELFIELD

BOYDTON

LOMBARDY

HICKSFORD

BETHLEHEM

GRANT'S PURSUIT OF LEE TO APPOMATTOX C.H.,

3-9 April 1865

5 4 3 2 1 0   5   10 Miles

SCALE

After the Chattanooga campaign (late November, 1863; *see map 116*), Bragg retreated to a position on Rocky Face Ridge *(this map, upper left)*. No major activity occurred in this theater until the following May; by then, Johnston had taken over Bragg's former command. (Davis made Bragg his military advisor, despite his performance at Chattanooga.) Sherman had succeeded Grant as commander of the Military Division of the Mississippi. His forces consisted of the Army of the Tennessee (Sherman's old command, now under McPherson), the Army of the Cumberland (under Thomas), and the Army of the Ohio (Burnside's former command in the Knoxville area, now under Schofield). On paper, Sherman's army was almost twice the size of Johnston's; actually, the Veteran Volunteer Act, allowing furloughs for reenlistment, had depleted its ranks. This situation, coupled with harsh weather and problems of supply build-up, delayed Sherman's advance until early May. Meanwhile, Johnston resisted unrealistic exhortations from Davis, Bragg, and Longstreet to move into Tennessee and Kentucky against Union communications.

Sherman's advance on Atlanta was part of Grant's over-all design for winning the war. He had instructed Sherman "to move against Johnston's army, break it up, and to get into the interior as far as you can, inflicting all the damage you can against their war resources. . . ." As will be seen, Sherman gradually became so obsessed with the final provision of this mission (which, to him, meant the capture of Atlanta) that Johnston's army was not destroyed, but survived to create further trouble.

On 7 May, 1864, Sherman began his advance as shown *(upper left)*. McPherson was to move along the route Lafayette–Villanow–Snake Creek Gap to sever Johnston's rail communications, while Thomas demonstrated on Johnston's front and Schofield moved south against the Confederate right flank. Johnston had left Snake Creek Gap *(center, left)* exposed and had only one brigade *(not shown)* at Resaca. McPherson passed through the gap on the 9th and drove the Confederate brigade at Resaca into its defenses *(action not shown)*. But then he withdrew to the gap (a move sanctioned by his discretionary orders), feeling that he

was not strong enough to cut the Confederate supply line—thus, through overcaution, abandoning an excellent opportunity to bring on the defeat of Johnston's army. On 13 May, Johnston withdrew to Resaca, where he joined Polk's corps, which had arrived from Mississippi on the 11th. Here he took up a precarious position in front of the Oostanaula River *(center, left)*. (It was Johnston's strategy to fall back progressively on the many good defensive positions the terrain provided, hoping to lure Sherman into some rash attack which would give him the chance to deliver a crushing counterblow.)

Sherman attacked halfheartedly on the 14th; the next day, he sent the forces shown to turn the position on its left. Johnston withdrew that night. On the 16th, Sherman took up the pursuit, his three armies taking the routes shown *(bottom left)*. Brig. Gen. Kenner Garrard, reinforced by Brig. Gen. Jefferson C. Davis, moved to attack Rome, an important supply center and ironworks site. On the 18th, Johnston took up a position just north of Cassville. That day he hoped to destroy Schofield's column, which was in advance, before it could be aided by Sherman's other two armies. While Hardee blocked the approach from Kingston and Polk held the valley, Hood, from his position on the hill, was to strike Schofield's flank. But Hood, under the impression that McCook had gotten in his rear, faced north. In the resulting confusion and delay, Sherman's columns closed up, and the opportunity to crush Schofield vanished. Johnston now fell back to a position south of Cassville *(upper center)*, but when Schofield approached on the 19th, and Hood and Polk expressed skepticism as to the Confederate ability to hold, he withdrew to Allatoona Pass.

Sherman rested at Kingston for three days, repairing the railroad and filling his wagons with twenty days' supplies. Then, having no intention of assaulting Johnston's strong position at Allatoona Pass, he cut loose from his railroad (emulating Grant at Vicksburg) and marched toward Dallas *(center)*. Johnston thereupon moved to block him at New Hope Church.

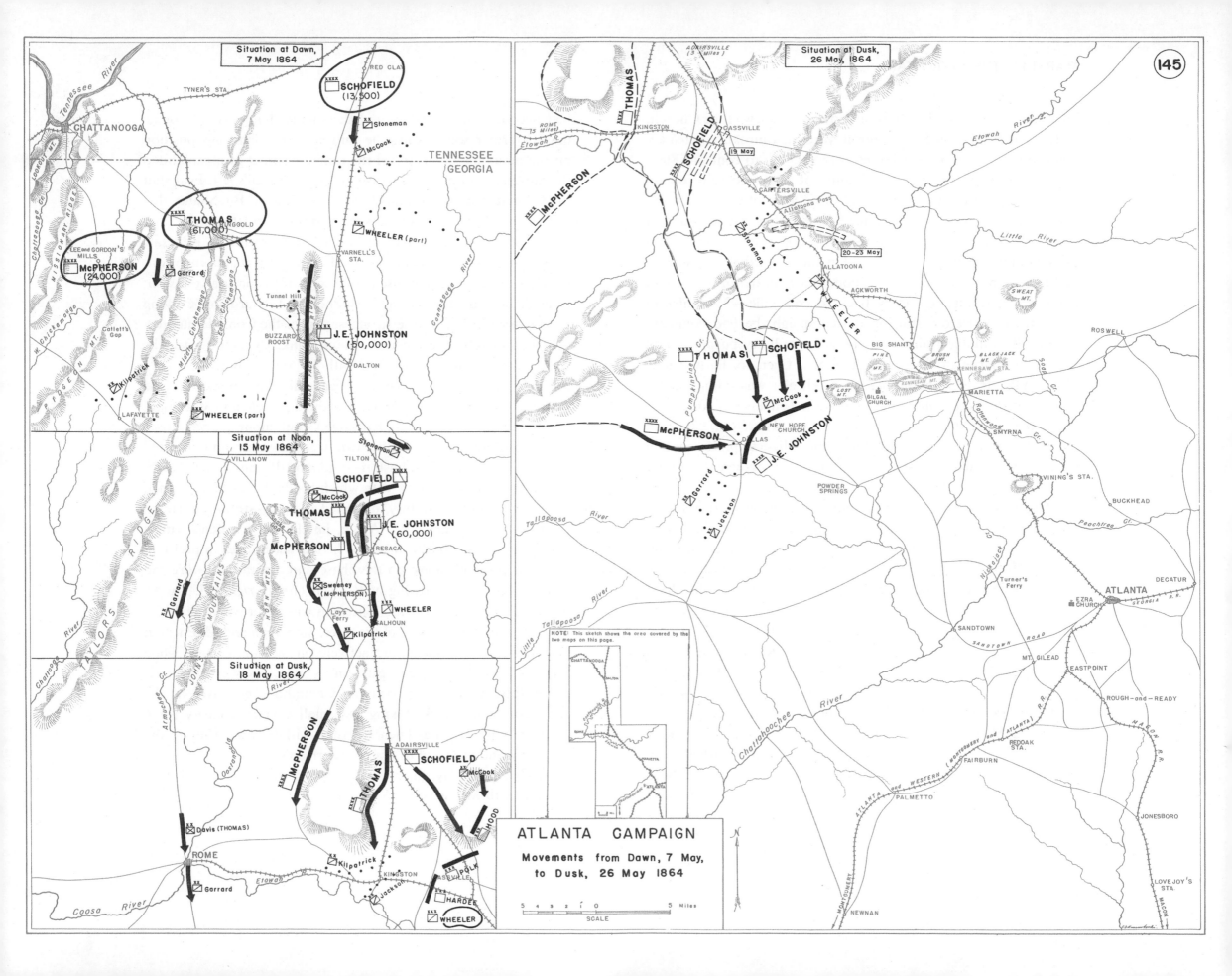

Situation at Dawn,
7 May 1864

Situation at Noon,
15 May 1864

Situation at Dusk,
18 May 1864

Situation at Dusk,
26 May 1864

145

SCHOFIELD
(13,500)

Stoneman

McCook

TENNESSEE
GEORGIA

WHEELER (part)

THOMAS
(61,000)

RINGGOLD

VARNELL'S STA.

LEE and GORDON'S MILLS

McPHERSON
(24,000)

Garrard

Tunnel Hill

BUZZARD ROOST

J. E. JOHNSTON
(50,000)

DALTON

Kilpatrick

Catlett's Gap

LAFAYETTE

WHEELER (part)

Stoneman

VILLANOW

TILTON

SCHOFIELD

McCook

THOMAS

J. E. JOHNSTON
(60,000)

McPHERSON

RESACA

Sweeney
(McPHERSON)

Lay's Ferry

CALHOUN

WHEELER

Kilpatrick

Garrard

McPHERSON

ADAIRSVILLE

SCHOFIELD

McCook

THOMAS

HOOD

Davis (THOMAS)

ROME

Kilpatrick

POLK

KINGSTON

CASSVILLE

Jackson

HARDEE

WHEELER

Garrard

Coosa River

CHATTANOOGA

Tennessee River

Lookout Mt.

Missionary Ridge

W. Chickamauga Cr.

Pigeon Mt.

Middle Chickamauga Cr.

East Chickamauga Cr.

Chattooga River

Chickamauga River

TAYLORS RIDGE

JOHNS MOUNTAINS

HORN MTS.

Armuchee Cr.

Oostanaula River

Conasauga River

Coosawattee River

TYNER'S STA.

RED CLAY

ATLANTA CAMPAIGN

Movements from Dawn, 7 May,
to Dusk, 26 May 1864

5 4 3 2 1 0   5 Miles
SCALE

NOTE: This sketch shows the area covered by the two maps on this page.

CHATTANOOGA
DALTON
ROME
MARIETTA
ATLANTA

ADAIRSVILLE
(3 Miles)

THOMAS

KINGSTON

SCHOFIELD

CASSVILLE

19 May

ROME
(5 Miles)

Etowah R.

Etowah River

Little River

McPHERSON

CARTERSVILLE

Allatoona Pass

Stoneman

20-23 May

ALLATOONA

WHEELER

ACKWORTH

SWEAT MT.

BLACK JACK MT.

ROSWELL

THOMAS

SCHOFIELD

BIG SHANTY

PINE MT.

BRUSH MT.

KENNESAW STA.

McCook

LOST MT.

GILGAL CHURCH

Kennesaw Mt.

MARIETTA

New Hope Church

McPHERSON

DALLAS

J. E. JOHNSTON

Garrard

POWDER SPRINGS

SMYRNA

Jackson

Pumpkinvine Cr.

Tallapoosa River

Tallapoosa River

Little River

Chattahoochee River

Nickajack Cr.

Sandtown Road

VINING'S STA.

BUCKHEAD

Peachtree Cr.

Turner's Ferry

DECATUR

ATLANTA

EZRA CHURCH

Georgia R.R.

SANDTOWN

MT. GILEAD

EASTPOINT

ROUGH-and-READY

REDOAK STA.

FAIRBURN

Montgomery and Atlanta R.R.

Atlanta and West Point R.R.

PALMETTO

MACON R.R.

JONESBORO

LOVEJOY'S STA.

MACON

NEWNAN

Sherman did not attack Johnston's position at New Hope Church; instead, he leapfrogged his troops toward the railroad (*sketch* a). Johnston abandoned his defenses at the church to confront Sherman in the new position. On 1 June, it began to rain, handicapping all operations. On 8 June, Blair's corps of veteran troops, who had been on furlough, joined McPherson. By 11 June, a destroyed bridge about ten miles north had been repaired, and rail communication was established as far forward as Big Shanty, just in rear of McPherson's position. But Sherman now worried about his long line of supply back to Nashville—250 miles to the northwest. Before starting the campaign, he had commandeered all available trains exclusively for military purposes, and had moved large stocks to Chattanooga. Even so, he was now ninety miles from Chattanooga, and Wheeler was raiding in his rear. Also, Forrest—operating in western Tennessee—could well strike the Nashville-Chattanooga rail line. Therefore, Sherman directed sizable forces from along the Mississippi to contain Forrest, while troops from Chattanooga strengthened security forces along the railroad.

The Federals now began building up supplies at Big Shanty and exerting pressure on Johnston's line. Both sides had been employing field fortifications extensively since the initial contact at New Hope Church. Every time a new position was taken up, sturdy fortifications sprang into being within hours—in sharp contrast to their absence at Shiloh two years earlier. The constant Union pressure made itself felt, and Johnston gradually contracted his line, dropping his right back to Kenesaw Mountain and pulling in his left toward Marietta (*sketch* b). During this period, Polk was killed by Federal artillery fire; Loring assumed temporary command of his corps. The rains continued, severely restricting Sherman's ability to move supplies over the muddy roads. He shrank from an assault on the heavily fortified Confederate position, but, by 25 June, the Federal line had been extended far to the south. Schofield's supply haul to the railroad

had become impracticable; and the supply dumps could not be moved farther south along the railroad, for Johnston's position on the mountain commanded the route. Weather also prohibited the movement of a sizable force around Johnston's left. Fear that the Confederates might launch an attack toward Big Shanty dictated maintenance of McPherson's army at top strength.

So Sherman decided to hazard an assault on the Kenesaw Mountain position. The attack, made at 9:00 A.M., 27 June, was poorly planned. Sherman used no deception to confuse Johnston; instead, he sent Thomas and McPherson forward in headlong frontal assaults against the strongest part of the Confederate line. Schofield merely threatened the south flank. By 11:00 A.M., the Union attack had been repulsed with 3,000 casualties.

Now Sherman reverted to a campaign of maneuver, the weather having turned hot and dry again. Schofield and Stoneman, during the fight on the 27th, had edged south along the Sandtown Road. McPherson was withdrawn from the line and directed down the same road. Johnston—undoubtedly discouraged over the monotonous regularity with which his flank was being turned—withdrew and, on 4 July, occupied the very strongly fortified position shown (*sketch* c). Again, he elected to defend with a river at his back, though this time he had six bridges in position. Sherman promptly took up the chase and, on the 4th, directed Garrard to seize a crossing at Roswell (*upper right*). Upon arriving at Johnston's position, Sherman was surprised to find him defending on the west side of the river. Stoneman and McPherson were directed to demonstrate actively on the south flank, while Schofield stealthily moved upstream to find a likely crossing site. On 9 July, Schofield crossed the Chattahoochee River at the mouth of Soap Creek, taking the small cavalry security force completely by surprise. Then Johnston withdrew his army to the east bank and prepared to oppose Sherman's latest turning movement. The next day, Sherman reinforced Garrard's crossing at Roswell with McPherson's XV Corps.

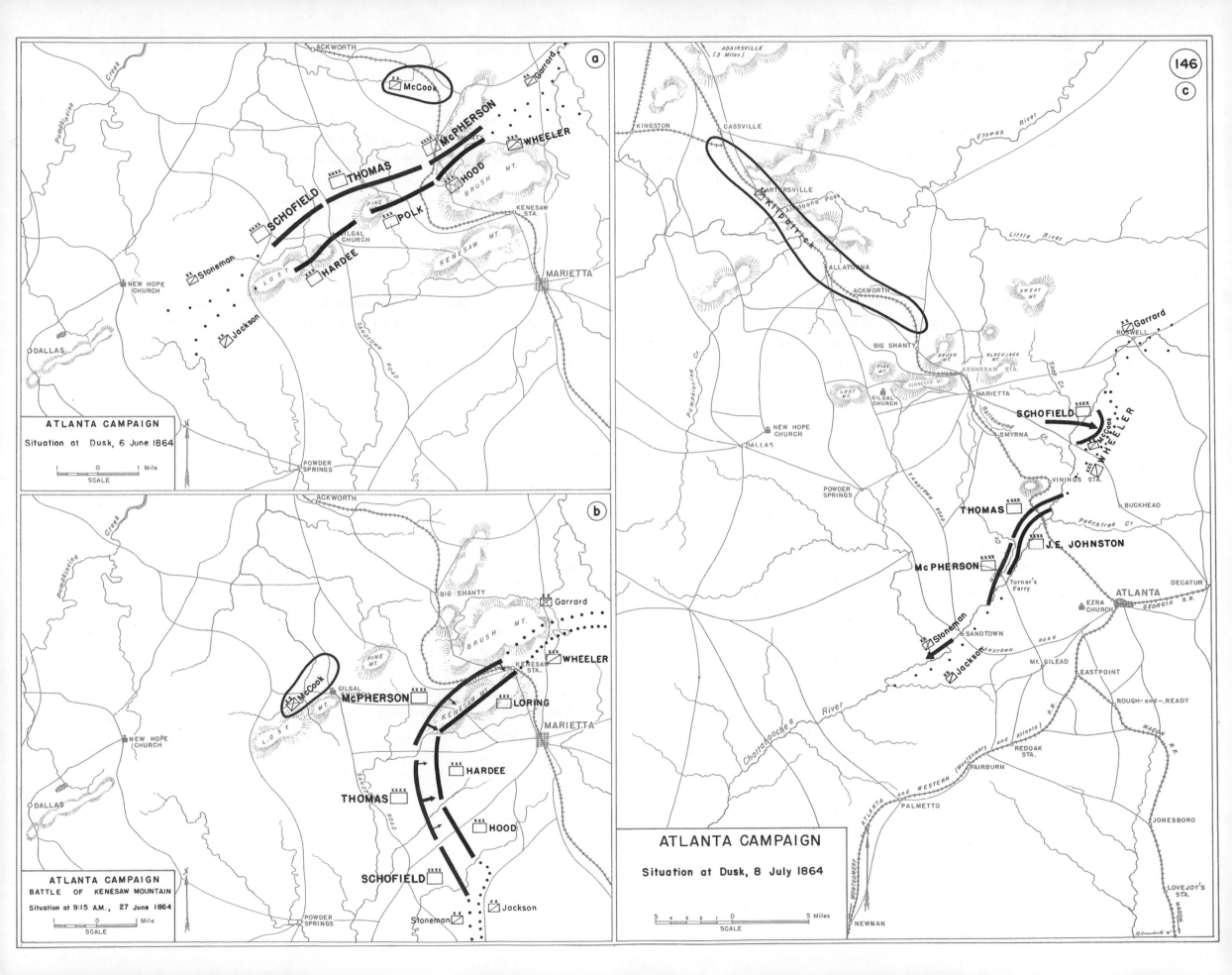

a

ATLANTA CAMPAIGN

Situation at Dusk, 6 June 1864

SCALE

0   1 Mile

b

ATLANTA CAMPAIGN

BATTLE OF KENESAW MOUNTAIN

Situation at 9:15 A.M., 27 June 1864

SCALE

1   0   1 Mile

c

146

ATLANTA CAMPAIGN

Situation at Dusk, 8 July 1864

SCALE

5 4 3 2 1 0   5 Miles

Sherman busied himself from 10 to 17 July moving supplies forward, preparatory to crossing the Chattahoochee in strength. Meanwhile, Davis—who had never been a great admirer of Johnston—had become exasperated by Johnston's Fabian defensive tactics and had sent Bragg to learn if he intended to fight. As a result of the conference, Johnston was replaced by Hood on 17 July. Sherman considered the change to the Union's advantage, for Hood, though admittedly a hard fighter, was reputed to be rash and reckless.

By 18 July, Sherman's armies had crossed the Chattahoochee and had begun to wheel clockwise on Thomas as a pivot; by the 20th, they had reached the positions shown (*sketch* a). That morning, Hood launched an offensive—in truth, his mandate would allow little else. Howard's corps had become overextended during the advance; the attack struck his exposed westernmost division and, in addition, Hooker's corps. Hood attacked in oblique order, progressively from right to left. Thus Hardee had been contained before Lt. Gen. Alexander P. Stewart (who had replaced Loring) came into action. Before Hardee could renew the attack, Hood, worried by McPherson's approach along the railroad, sent Hardee's best division (Cleburne) to reinforce Cheatham, and operations at Peachtree Creek were suspended. Sherman, in response to Grant's warning that the Confederates might transfer troops to Atlanta from Virginia, had dispatched McPherson to break up the railroad leading to Atlanta to prevent such a move.

Hood now withdrew into the defenses of Atlanta (*sketch* b); Sherman followed on the 21st, being under the impression that the city had been evacuated. By noon, he had learned otherwise when Hardee struck McPherson's south flank. As there was no cavalry on that flank to give warning, the attack came as a surprise. Fortunately for Sherman, Maj. Gen. Grenville M. Dodge's corps, which had been pinched out as the line contracted, was moving toward the open flank and arrived just as Hardee struck. Blair and Dodge joined forces and bent back parallel to the railroad. Hardee could make no progress; neither could Wheeler against the Union trains at Decatur. McPherson moved part of

the XV Corps to the scene, and a stalemate resulted. Too late, Hood sent Cheatham forward, but Schofield and Logan handily repulsed his charge. Early in the engagement, McPherson, having directed the movement described above, had ridden into the fighting and been killed—thus perished one of the Union's outstanding soldiers.

Howard (McPherson's replacement) moved toward Ezra Church on 27 July (*sketch* c) in furtherance of Sherman's plan to sever the railroads below Atlanta—Hood's last link to the Confederacy. McCook's and Stoneman's cavalry were to converge on Jonesboro (*bottom right*) to aid the over-all scheme. Learning of Howard's departure, Hood sent S. D. Lee (who had relieved Cheatham) to attack Howard. This he did on the 28th, reinforced by Stewart; but, for the third time within a week, the Confederates failed before hastily erected Federal fortifications. Meanwhile, the Confederate cavalry frustrated the juncture of McCook and Stoneman at Jonesboro; Stoneman went off to release Federal prisoners at Andersonville (*off map, southeast*), and was captured with 700 of his men. Kilpatrick followed with another futile raid on the Confederate railroads. Hood sent Wheeler to break up Sherman's communications, which he could not do, though he caused considerable damage—meanwhile, Hood was left without cavalry to scout Sherman's maneuvers.

Finally, on 26 August, Sherman set all his forces in motion as shown (*sketch* d) and reached the Macon Railroad on the 31st. Hood believed at first that Sherman was withdrawing to the north, and arranged a victory ball in Atlanta; but, by the 28th, he had learned the true situation and hastened Hardee south. Hardee tried to block the advance, but his attack was repulsed. The Union armies now concentrated at Jonesboro; Hood evacuated Atlanta and joined Hardee at Lovejoy's Station.

From Atlanta, Sherman wired Lincoln: "Atlanta is ours and fairly won." More concerned with the city than with Hood's army, he had allowed the latter to escape; but he had gained a victory, sorely needed to aid Lincoln in his election campaign against the Democratic candidate, McClellan. Union casualties totaled 21,656; Confederate, 27,565.

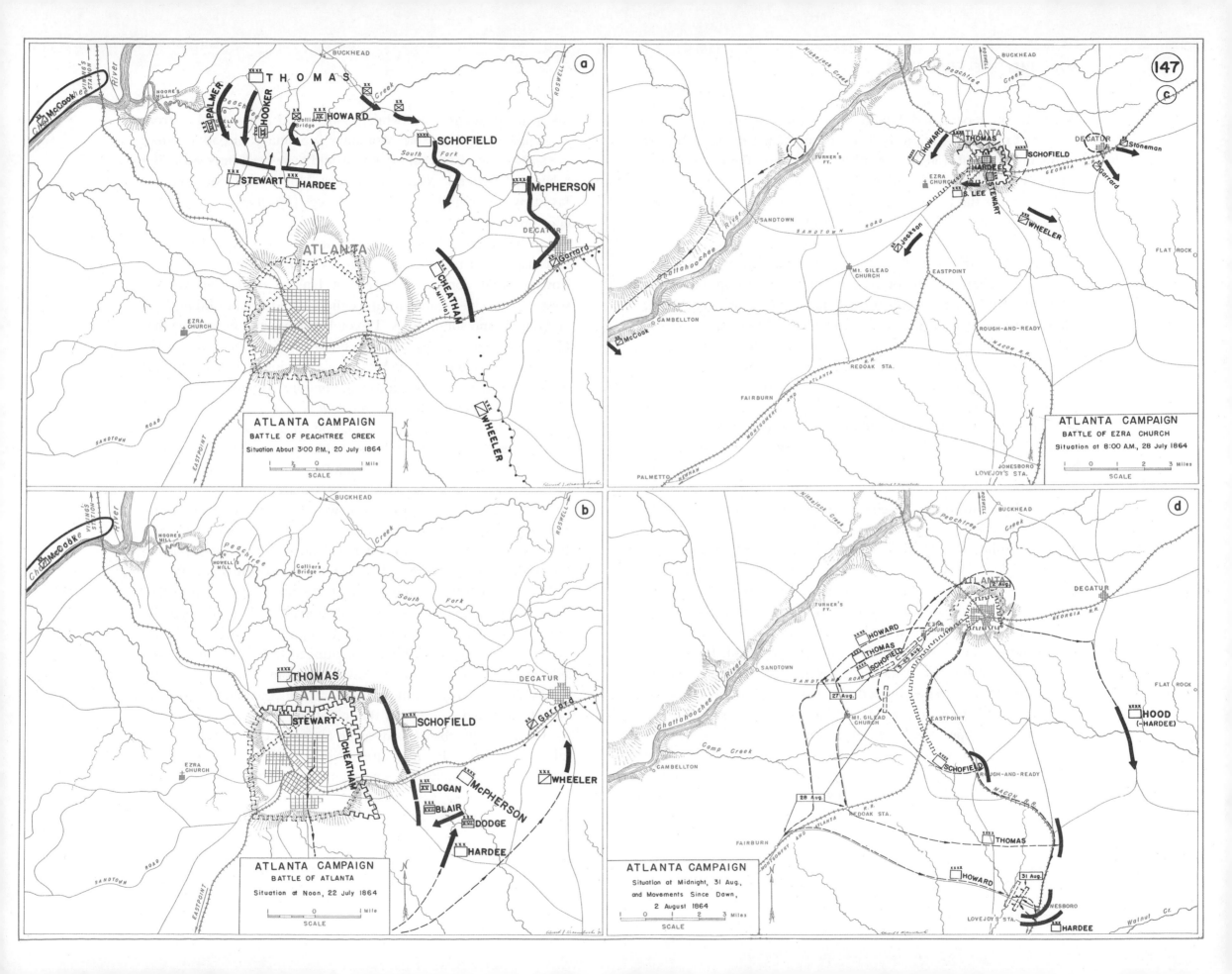

a

THOMAS

PALMER HOOKER HOWARD

SCHOFIELD

STEWART HARDEE

McPHERSON

ATLANTA

CHEATHAM
(+ Militia)

Garrard

WHEELER

ATLANTA CAMPAIGN
BATTLE OF PEACHTREE CREEK
Situation About 3:00 P.M., 20 July 1864
SCALE

b

THOMAS

ATLANTA
STEWART
SCHOFIELD
Garrard

CHEATHAM

EZRA
CHURCH

LOGAN McPHERSON
BLAIR WHEELER
DODGE
HARDEE

ATLANTA CAMPAIGN
BATTLE OF ATLANTA
Situation at Noon, 22 July 1864
SCALE

147

c

HOWARD THOMAS
ATLANTA
HARDEE SCHOFIELD DECATUR Stoneman
Garrard
EZRA
CHURCH
S. LEE STEWART
WHEELER

Jackson

Mt. GILEAD
CHURCH EASTPOINT

McCook

FAIRBURN

REDOAK STA.

ROUGH-AND-READY

JONESBORO
LOVEJOY'S STA.

ATLANTA CAMPAIGN
BATTLE OF EZRA CHURCH
Situation at 8:00 A.M., 28 July 1864
SCALE

d

ATLANTA DECATUR

HOWARD
THOMAS
SCHOFIELD
EZRA
CHURCH
27 Aug.

Mt. GILEAD
CHURCH EASTPOINT
HOOD
(-HARDEE)

SCHOFIELD
ROUGH-AND-READY
28 Aug.

FAIRBURN REDOAK STA.
THOMAS

HOWARD
31 Aug.
JONESBORO
LOVEJOY'S STA.
HARDEE

ATLANTA CAMPAIGN
Situation at Midnight, 31 Aug.,
and Movements Since Dawn,
2 August 1864
SCALE

When Sherman occupied Atlanta on 2 September and left Hood's army at Lovejoy's Station, he had accomplished the second part of his mission but not the first part—to destroy the Confederate army. Herein lay a real source of embarrassment, for by maneuvering against the Union supply line, Hood might force Sherman to evacuate his brilliantly won prize of Atlanta. This was the exact strategy that Hood decided to follow.

Upon his arrival in Atlanta, Sherman displayed a lethargy hitherto not characteristic of his operations. The troops lay about idly; many men whose enlistments had expired left for home; Blair and Logan went north to mend political fences; and Schofield returned to Cincinnati to check on his department. Thus, Sherman surrendered the initiative. Meanwhile, he engaged in an exchange of letters with Hood, occasioned by the Confederate general's taking vehement exception to Sherman's decision to evacuate all civilians from Atlanta. In fairness to Sherman, it should be noted that the month of inactivity was not entirely of his own making. Already, his fertile mind was exploring the possibilities of a march across Georgia, but he had to fit his operations into Grant's over-all scheme—and Grant could not decide how best to employ Sherman's armies.

Meanwhile, on 21 September, Hood moved to Palmetto (*lower right*). Here, on the 27th, he was visited by Jefferson Davis. His army was refitting as much as possible, preparatory to moving into Alabama. Davis' visit had two purposes: to bolster Confederate morale, which had plummeted after the fall of Atlanta; and to devise a campaign strategy with Hood. He accomplished little in the first instance, but was more successful in the second. It was apparently agreed that Hood should move toward Chattanooga (*center, right*), operating against Sherman's communications. If Sherman followed, as was expected, Hood would seek a favorable opportunity to entice him into battle. Their plan was a bit nebulous as to what would be done if Sherman ignored Hood and advanced on Savannah; presumably, Hood was to use

his own judgment. Meanwhile, Hood could draw supplies from Alabama along the Blue Mountain & Selma Railroad (*bottom center*). (Use of this supply line would have been impossible if a scheduled Federal expedition against Mobile had not been delayed by the inability of Canby's forces [*off map, southwest*] to coordinate with Sherman.)

In the interim, Sherman, concerned for the safety of his rear, had dispatched reinforcements to key points. In mid-September, Forrest—that constant scourger of Union commanders in the west—had moved into central Tennessee and begun raiding Federal depots and supply lines. To combat him—and suspecting that Hood, too, was preparing a march northward—Sherman, on the 24th, sent Brig. Gen. John M. Corse's division to Rome and that of Brig. Gen. John Newton to Chattanooga. He alerted all of his detachment commanders (*small blue circles*) to be especially vigilant. On the 29th, urged by Grant to dispose of Forrest, he sent General Thomas back to Nashville to organize all the troops in Tennessee. That same day, another division—that of Brig. Gen. James D. Morgan—was sent to Chattanooga.

The Confederate strategy was working. Sherman was beginning to disperse his strength along his line of communications. But the wily Union commander had no intention of displacing his entire army to the rear. He intended to provide Thomas with sufficient strength—including reinforcements sent from other theaters to Nashville—to cope with Forrest and Hood, while he himself watched Hood and sought an opportunity to deal him a decisive blow. All the while, he continued to urge Grant to consider his plan to strike out for Savannah, pointing out that Hood, almost at his mercy one month earlier, now could maneuver, stay out of his grasp, and retain the initiative.

On 29 September, Hood began his advance across the Chattahoochee River. He had already ordered Wheeler, absent on raiding missions since 15 August, to rejoin the army.

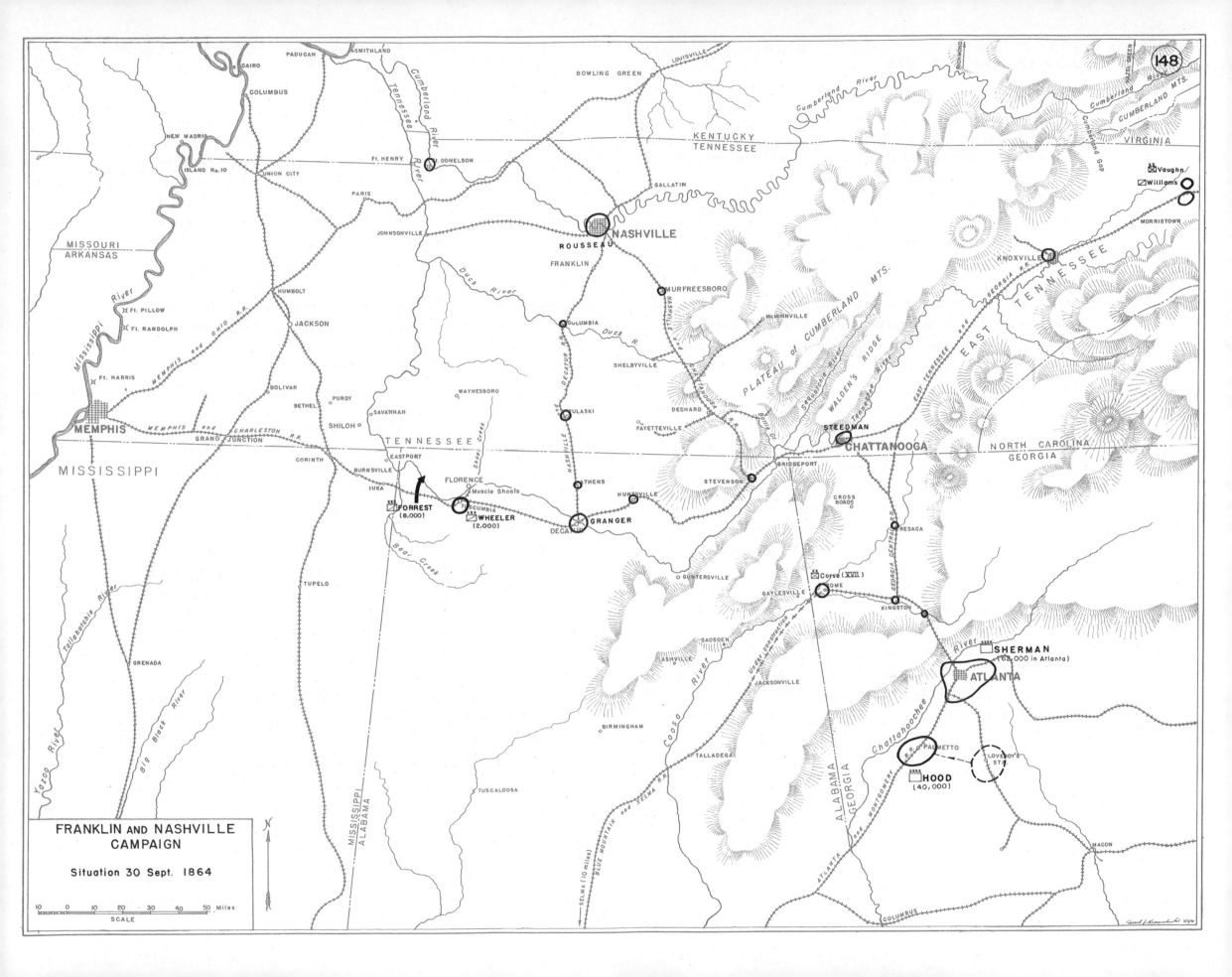

FRANKLIN AND NASHVILLE
CAMPAIGN

Situation 30 Sept. 1864

SCALE

10   0   10   20   30   40   50 Miles

By 1 October, Hood and his 40,000 men had crossed the Chattahoochee and had started north for the railroad. His cavalry (under Jackson) was intercepted by Sherman's (under Kilpatrick and Garrard) in a raid on the railroad near Marietta (*inset sketch*) that day (*action not shown*); but Sherman was still uncertain of Hood's location. Actually, for the next three weeks, Sherman had difficulty keeping abreast of Hood's movements. Hood moved rapidly, screened his marches well, and—by virtue of having the initiative—consistently baffled his adversary. Sherman, served poorly by his cavalry—which he had apparently neglected to train and mold to the desired pattern—trailed after Hood, seeking an opportunity to attack. But, in so doing, he never so dispersed his forces as to leave them exposed to the attack Hood's strategy envisioned.

On 3 October, Sherman, having now learned of Hood's direction of march, left Slocum at Atlanta and moved toward Marietta with a force of about 55,000 men. He reached Marietta on the 4th and learned that large numbers of Confederates were moving along the railroad toward Allatoona (*inset sketch*). Corse, at Rome (*center*), was immediately notified to reinforce the garrison at Allatoona; he sprang to action, ordered a train from Kingston, and had moved 1,000 men to the town by 1:00 A.M., 5 October.

Hood, late on 3 October, had split his forces, sending Stewart to the railroad and the rest of his command to Dallas (*inset sketch*). Stewart laid waste to the railroad between Big Shanty and Ackworth, while French moved on Allatoona. On the morning of the 5th, Stewart rejoined Hood near Dallas, while French attacked Corse. By 8:00 A.M., Corse was surrounded, but refused French's demand for his surrender. At 9:00 A.M., the attack began; Sherman watched anxiously from Kenesaw Mountain. Corse made a gallant defense and stopped the repeated Confederate charges. At 4:00 P.M., the Confederates gave up and

marched away to rejoin Hood, having seen Union reinforcements hurrying forward.

Hood now veered to the west, crossed the Coosa River west of Rome—to which point Corse had been hurriedly returned on 7 October—and headed for Resaca (*upper center*). En route, Wheeler's cavalry (*not shown*), previously raiding in Tennessee, joined him. Sherman arrived at Allatoona on the 9th, but not until the next day did he learn from Corse that Hood was in the vicinity of Rome. On the 12th—the day that Hood demanded the surrender of the brigade at Resaca and left Lee there to enforce the demand—Sherman personally was at Rome, while most of his army was closing on Kingston. There he learned of Hood's true location. He at once ordered reinforcements to move from Kingston to Resaca, which Lee had partially invested. Lee declined to attack the Union position—a decision well within his discretionary orders—because he believed that an assault would be too costly. Meanwhile, Hood sent Stewart as far as Tunnel Hill (*top center*) to burn and damage the railroad as much as possible; en route, Stewart captured a regiment of Negro troops at Dalton. Sherman moved his entire army toward Resaca on the 12th, arriving there with his advance elements on the 13th.

In the past week, the two armies had been coming ever nearer a major battle, but Hood's mobility kept him several jumps ahead of Sherman. The latter, realistically appraising his inability to prevent Hood's raiding of his communications, continued to beseech Grant to allow him to march to Savannah while Thomas contained Hood. As for Hood, he had reached the point where he had to decide whether or not to fight a major battle with Sherman. Having lured Sherman north in consonance with his plan, the stage was set. Continuing to destroy the railroad offered little advantage because, as Hood had discovered to his chagrin, Sherman's efficient repair crews could rebuild it with great speed.

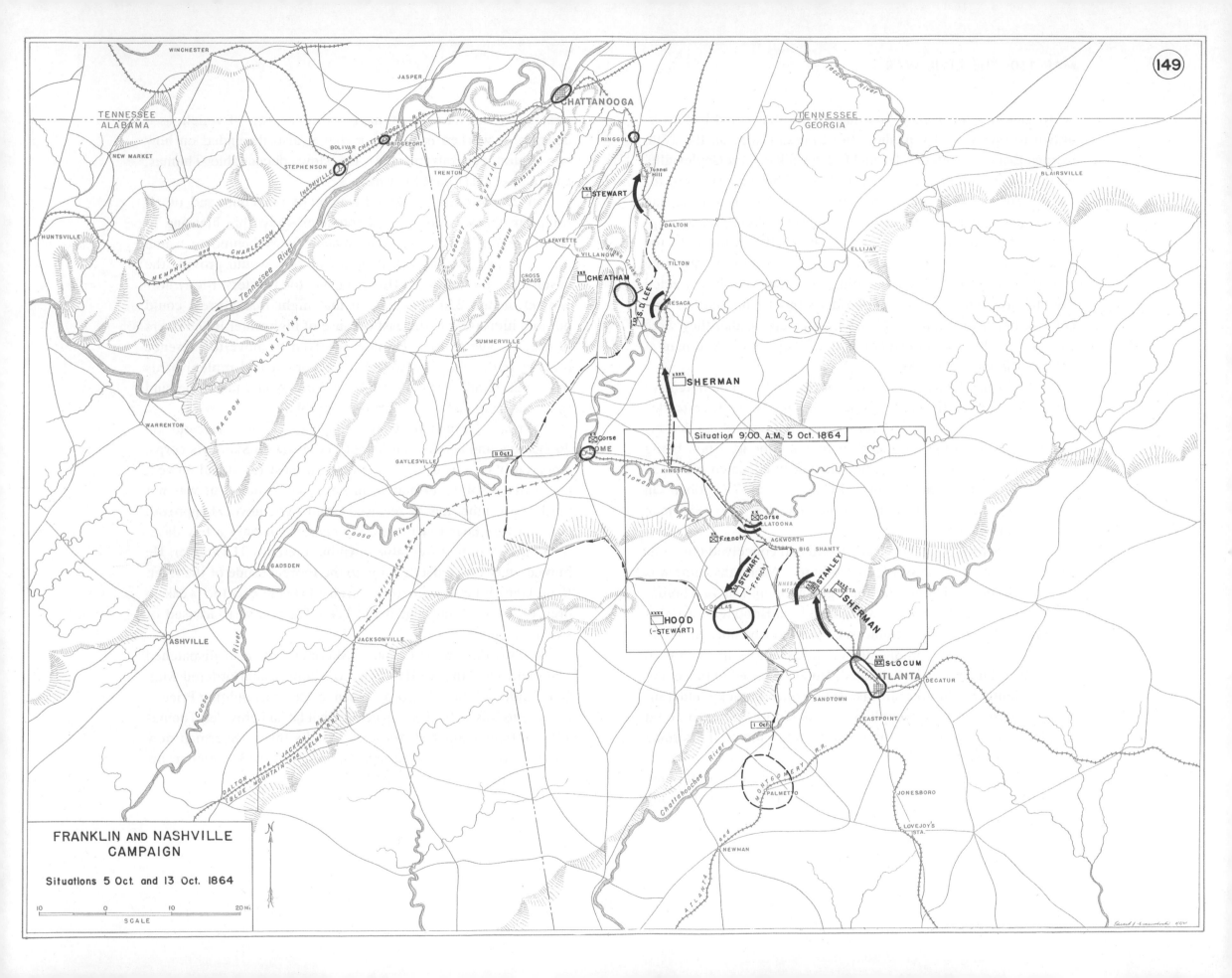

149

FRANKLIN AND NASHVILLE
CAMPAIGN

Situations 5 Oct. and 13 Oct. 1864

Situation 9:00 A.M. 5 Oct. 1864

SCALE
10   0   10   20 Mi.

At Resaca (*center, right*), Sherman found that Hood had withdrawn to the west. He pushed on in pursuit and, on the 16th, learned that the Confederates had fallen back toward Gaylesville. At this time, in a message from Halleck, Sherman received for the first time an intimation that Grant was favorably considering his Savannah march. Though he now began making mental preparations for this momentous move, he applied himself to the task at hand and once more set his forces in motion after the swift-moving Hood. Before doing so, however, he directed Thomas to send back two of the divisions he had earlier dispatched northward; on the 17th, Thomas replied that they were en route, with Schofield in command. They joined Sherman at Gaylesville on 23 October.

But why had Hood—near Cross Roads and in good defensive country—given up the chance to test Sherman's mettle in battle? Fully intending to fight at Cross Roads, Hood had queried his commanders as to the state of their troops' morale. Upon being advised not to risk an attack, he reluctantly canceled his plans and continued to withdraw toward Gadsden on 17 October. On 20 October, he arrived at that point; one day later, Sherman reached Gaylesville.

While resting at Cross Roads, Hood had conceived the strategy that soon led to the Battle of Nashville. Aware that time was on the side of the Union and that, given enough of it, Thomas would unite with Sherman to overwhelm him, Hood reasoned that if he moved swiftly into Tennessee, he might be able to defeat Thomas before that commander could assemble his scattered army. Once Thomas was eliminated, Hood proposed to move into central Kentucky and recruit his army from Kentucky and Tennessee. He hoped to accomplish all this before Sherman could decide whether to follow him or march on Savannah. If Sherman followed, Hood would fight in Kentucky; he felt that, whether successful or defeated, he could thereafter move eastward through the Cumberland Gap to aid Lee. Such was Hood's far-reaching strategy. It was based upon many variables, few of which, as it developed, worked in his favor; but it also depended on how two Union generals reacted—the slow, dependable Thomas, and the fiery, brilliant Sherman.

On 21 October, General Beauregard—in command of all forces in the west since 28 September—gave his blessing to Hood's plan, but directed that Wheeler stay behind to watch Sherman; instead, Forrest, then at Jackson, would provide the cavalry for the advance. Hood set out for Guntersville (*lower center*) on the 22d, but learned that night that Forrest could not join him so far to the east because of high water in the rivers he would have to ford. He now resolved to move to Florence (*center, left*), where he would meet Forrest and replenish his trains before advancing north. But all this would take time, and time was Thomas' most immediate problem.

Sherman learned of Hood's appearance near Decatur on 26 October and at once reinforced Thomas with Stanley's corps. Apparently on this date, seeing how far west Hood had moved, he finally resolved to march on Savannah—though it was not until 2 November that he received Grant's unequivocal approval. Hood tarried near Decatur (*lower center*) for only a few days, then moved on to Tuscumbia, arriving there on 31 October. He immediately crossed a division to the Florence side of the river. Brig. Gen. John T. Croxton's cavalry brigade was too weak to prevent the crossing, but it did keep Thomas well advised of Hood's actions.

Meanwhile, on 30 October, Sherman had also dispatched Schofield with the XXIII Corps to Thomas, and ordered Maj. Gen. Andrew J. Smith's corps—then in Missouri fighting Price—to move to Nashville. Feeling certain that he had provided Thomas with sufficient numbers to parry Hood's thrust, Sherman now prepared for his march through Georgia. By 10 November, his troops were en route back to Atlanta.

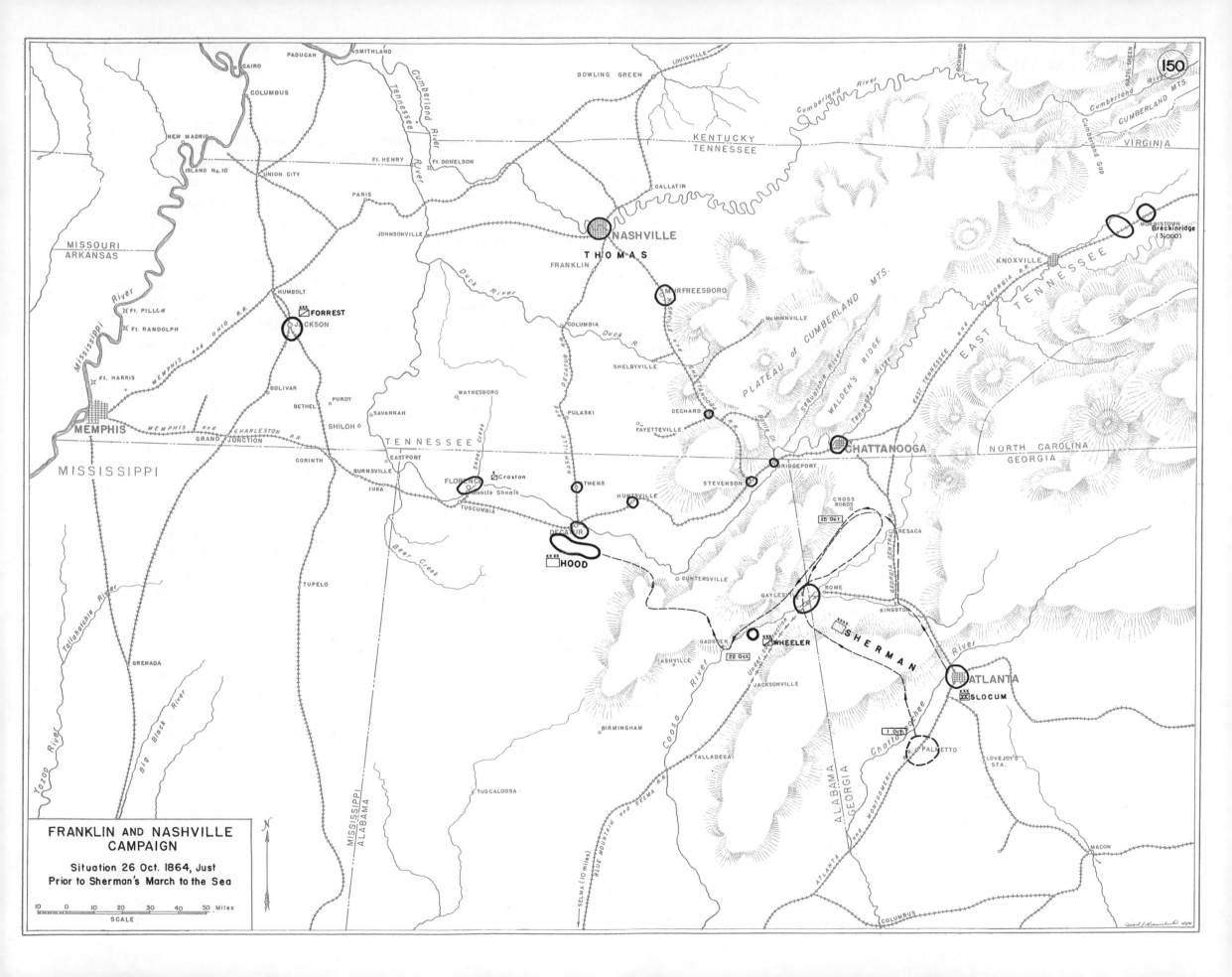

150

FRANKLIN AND NASHVILLE
CAMPAIGN

Situation 26 Oct. 1864, Just
Prior to Sherman's March to the Sea

10   0   10   20   30   40   50 Miles
SCALE

At Tuscumbia (*sketch* a, *lower left*), Hood learned with dismay that his march north would have to be delayed. Forrest had not yet arrived, and destroyed rail lines coupled with bad weather had prevented assembly of the needed supplies. For three weeks, he remained there, slowly replenishing his wagon train; Thomas, almost as slowly, gathered his scattered troops. Hood contemplated advancing despite supply deficiencies, but his troops had been on very short rations, and their morale was dangerously low. Forrest finally arrived on 17 November, and Hood ordered the advance for the following day.

Thomas, meanwhile, though pressed by Sherman to abandon "all minor points and unite... into one army," seems to have failed to appreciate the urgency. Schofield had been sent to Johnsonville (*top left*) as a result of Forrest's raid on that town; and, through good fortune, returned in time to oppose Hood's advance. Brig. Gen. Robert S. Granger was left in the Decatur area (*lower center*) until 22 November, and was then sent to Murfreesboro (*upper right*). He did not participate in the coming battles at Spring Hill, Franklin, or Nashville; neither did Maj. Gen. Lovell Rousseau, who was at Tullahoma.

Hood advanced, as shown, in an attempt to seize the Duck River crossing at Columbia (*upper center*) and thus separate Schofield, at Pulaski, from Thomas. On 22 November, Schofield, alerted to his danger, rushed two divisions north to secure Columbia. The first arrived early on the 24th, just in time to check Forrest, who was about to seize the bridges. That night, Schofield's entire force was at Columbia; Hood was concentrated there by the 26th.

Schofield said that he took his initial position south of the Duck River because Thomas had directed him to hold a bridgehead there until reinforcements could be brought forward and a Federal offensive launched. But, on the 27th, convinced that Hood would turn his position, he withdrew to the north bank (*sketch* b, *lower left*). Indeed, this was Hood's plan. Leaving most of Lee's corps to demonstrate at Columbia, he crossed Stewart and Cheatham at Davis's Ford early on the 29th and

started them north, The night before, Forrest had started on a wider movement and gradually forced Wilson's cavalry back to Hurt's Corner (*center, right*). (The fiery and energetic Wilson had been sent by Grant to bolster Sherman's cavalry, which had been ineffectual up to now.) Schofield, learning of the Confederate movements from Wilson by daylight of the 29th, sent Stanley with Brig. Gen. George D. Wagner's and Kimball's divisions to secure Spring Hill (*upper center*) at 8:00 A.M. Meanwhile, he retained Maj. Gen. Thomas H. Ruger, Cox, and Wood in the now dangerous position at the river. Stanley left Kimball at Rutherford's Creek as ordered, and arrived with Wagner at Spring Hill just in time to repulse Forrest. Forrest had driven Wilson north of Mount Carmel and had ridden on to Spring Hill. Upon his repulse here by Wagner, he withdrew to Thompson's Station, his troops too exhausted and low in ammunition to play any important part in the coming battle.

Meanwhile, Cheatham reached Spring Hill and attacked Wagner in piecemeal fashion at 3:00 P.M. The assault failed through a combination of Confederate tactical errors and excellent Union artillery fire. For some unfathomable reason, Hood had left Stewart farther south in the position shown. Despite Cheatham's pleas for support, Hood did not send Stewart forward until after dark. It is difficult to determine what orders, if any, Hood actually issued at this time. Nevertheless, the following events transpired: Stewart bivouacked near Cheatham, but did nothing; Cheatham made one weak attempt to block the Columbia Pike, but desisted when erroneously informed that no Union troops were moving on the road; all the Confederates believed there would be time to fight on the morrow.

Schofield perceived his opportunity to get back to Franklin and hurried his troops northward all night. By midnight, Ruger had driven Forrest to the east of Thompson's Station, clearing the road there. By 6:00 A.M., 30 November, all Union troops were north of Spring Hill, except the rear-guard brigade. Hood, furious with his subordinates—Cheatham in particular—now took up the pursuit.

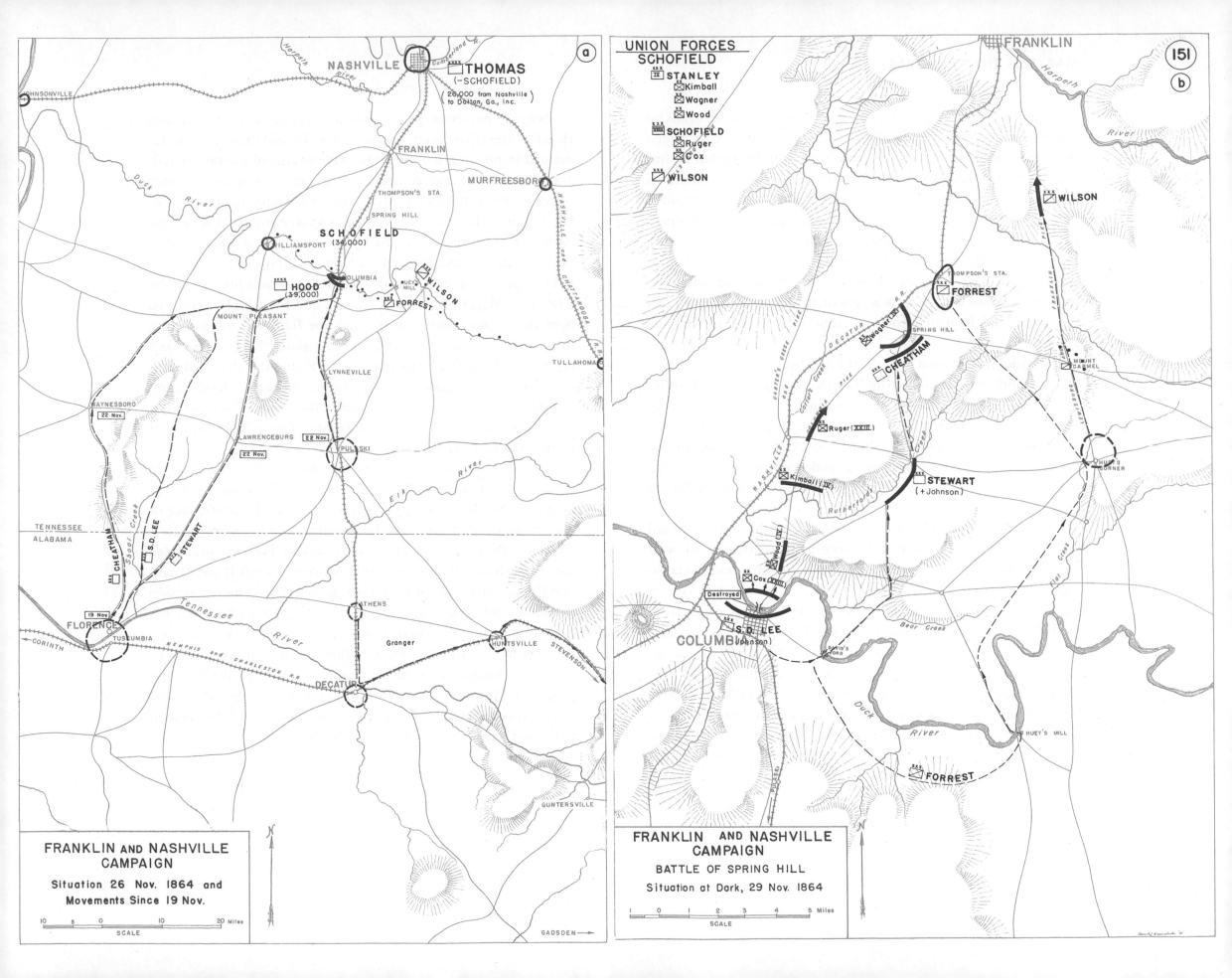

a

NASHVILLE

Cumberland R.

☐ THOMAS
(-SCHOFIELD)

(26,000 from Nashville
to Dalton, Ga., inc.)

JOHNSONVILLE

Harpeth River

FRANKLIN

THOMPSON'S STA.

MURFREESBORO

SPRING HILL

SCHOFIELD
(34,000)

WILLIAMSPORT

Duck River

COLUMBIA

HUEY'S MILL

WILSON

☐ HOOD
(39,000)

☐ FORREST

MOUNT PLEASANT

Nashville and Chattanooga R.R.

LYNNVILLE

TULLAHOMA

WAYNESBORO

22 Nov.

LAWRENCEBURG   22 Nov.

PULASKI

22 Nov.

River

Elk River

TENNESSEE
ALABAMA

CHEATHAM

School Creek

S.D. LEE

STEWART

19 Nov.

FLORENCE

TUSCUMBIA

Tennessee River

ATHENS

Granger

HUNTSVILLE

STEVENSON

CORINTH

MEMPHIS AND CHARLESTON R.R.

DECATUR

GUNTERSVILLE

GADSDEN →

**FRANKLIN AND NASHVILLE
CAMPAIGN**

Situation 26 Nov. 1864 and
Movements Since 19 Nov.

10   5   0   10   20 Miles
SCALE

N

b

151

FRANKLIN

Harpeth River

UNION FORCES
SCHOFIELD

IV STANLEY
⊠ Kimball
⊠ Wagner
⊠ Wood

XXIII SCHOFIELD
⊠ Ruger
⊠ Cox

WILSON

WILSON

THOMPSON'S STA.

FORREST

DECATUR R.R.

Wagner   SPRING HILL

CHEATHAM

MOUNT CARMEL

Carter's Creek Pike

Carter's Creek

Ruger (XXIII)

STEWART
(+ Johnson)

Rutherford's Creek

RALLY'S CORNER

Nashville Pike

Kimball (IV)

Wood (IV)

Cox (XXIII)

Destroyed

S.D. LEE
(Johnson)

COLUMBIA

Davis's Ford

Bear Creek

Flat Creek

Duck River

HUEY'S MILL

FORREST

**FRANKLIN AND NASHVILLE
CAMPAIGN**

BATTLE OF SPRING HILL

Situation at Dark, 29 Nov. 1864

1   0   1   2   3   4   5 Miles
SCALE

N

Schofield's advance guard (Cox's division) reached Franklin (*sketch* a, *top left*) about 6:00 A.M., 30 November. Cox's men were exhausted from days of marching and fighting, but he immediately put them to work throwing up earthworks south of the town. As the other divisions came up, the line was extended; by noon, when it was finished, both flanks rested on the Harpeth River. Two brigades of Wagner's division were placed as a covering force south of Franklin; Colonel Emerson U. Opdycke's brigade, now the rear guard, would become the army reserve upon its arrival. Wood's division was sent on across the river to protect the trains and to watch for any attempt by Hood to turn the position.

Schofield's decision to fight at Franklin, with the river at his back, requires explanation. Withdrawing under pressure at Columbia, he had destroyed his pontons because of lack of vehicles to haul them. The bridges at Franklin needed repair, but since this work would not be completed until noon, Schofield had ordered the defensive line prepared. It was a moderately strong line, which took advantage of the few slight hills in the area, and it afforded good fields of fire.

In the meantime, Hood had been urging his men forward along Columbia Pike since early morning. By 2:00 P.M., Stewart had reached the vicinity of Wagner's position and had begun to deploy for the attack. By 3:00 P.M., Hood's army—less two of Lee's divisions that were still far to the rear, en route from Columbia—was in position as shown. Though Forrest urged a repetition of the Columbia turning movement, Hood was determined to carry the Union lines by a frontal assault. Nettled ever since Atlanta by Hood's sarcastic references to how fortifications had dulled the army's offensive spirit, and particularly by his acrimonious remarks at Spring Hill, the corps and division commanders were incensed. Though logic dictated against a frontal assault, they vowed to demonstrate that their troops could storm fortifications as bravely as any.

Wagner had been placed forward, presumably to ascertain Hood's intentions, after which he was to withdraw. But he remained in position too long. Quickly enveloped by the Confederate attack, his troops turned and fled; the Confederates became intermingled with them. Consequently, the Union main line hesitated to fire. The remnants of Wagner's force streamed across the earthworks, closely followed by the exultant Confederates. A green regiment, recently arrived from Nashville, broke and fled with Wagner, and thus a gap opened in Schofield's line (*sketch* b). Cleburne, Maj. Gen. John C. Brown, and French all converged here and seemed about to roll back the flanks of the gap. But, just then, the courageous Opdycke, assisted by two of Cox's regiments, launched a counterattack which, after thirty minutes of bitter fighting, sealed the gap. Again and again, Hood's commanders hurled their troops against the Union line, but they could not break it. Maj. Gen. Edward Johnson's division was committed just before dark, but without success.

By 9:00 P.M., the fighting had died down; Hood had again failed to defeat his foe. This time, his casualties had been very heavy; he had lost twelve general officers and the confidence of his troops. Confederate casualties totaled 6,252; Union, 2,326.

While the fighting raged around Franklin, Forrest had crossed the Harpeth and attempted to turn Schofield's left flank. Weakened by the diversion of Brig. Gen. James R. Chalmers' division to Hood's left flank, and opposed by the determined Wilson, Forrest was roughly handled and forced back across the river.

That night, at 11:00 P.M., Schofield began to move his troops across the bridges en route to Nashville. Though the crossing progressed for an hour, and the Union army was divided by the river, Hood passively remained in position. On 1 December, Schofield's tired force entered the works at Nashville.

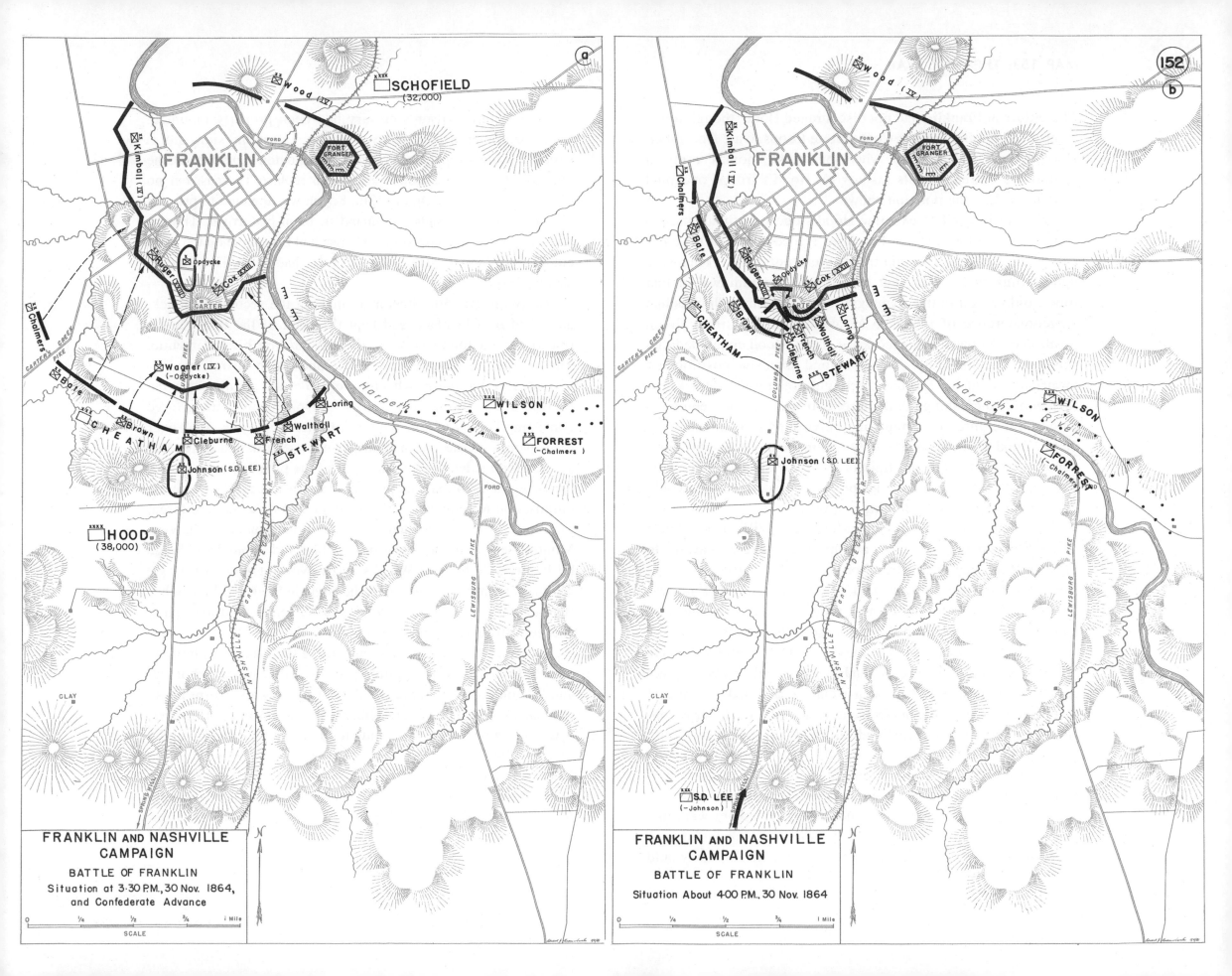

a

Wood (IV)

xxxx
SCHOFIELD
(32,000)

Kimball (IV)

FRANKLIN

FORD

FORT
GRANGER

Ruger (XXIII)

Opdycke

Cox (XXIII)

CARTER

Chalmers

CARTER'S CREEK PIKE

COLUMBIA PIKE

Wagner (IV)
(-Opdycke)

Bate

Loring

Harpeth River

xxx
WILSON

CHEATHAM

Brown

Walthall

Cleburne

French

xxx
STEWART

xxx
FORREST
(-Chalmers)

Johnson (S.D. LEE)

NASHVILLE AND DECATUR R.R.

SPRING HILL PIKE

FORD

LEWISBURG PIKE

xxxx
HOOD
(38,000)

CLAY

**FRANKLIN AND NASHVILLE
CAMPAIGN**

BATTLE OF FRANKLIN

Situation at 3·30 P.M., 30 Nov. 1864,
and Confederate Advance

0   ¼   ½   ¾   1 Mile

SCALE

N

152

b

Wood (IV)

Kimball (IV)

FRANKLIN

FORD

FORT
GRANGER

Chalmers

Bate

Ruger (XXIII)

Opdycke

Cox (XXIII)

Brown

French

Walthall

Loring

Cleburne

CHEATHAM

CARTER'S CREEK PIKE

COLUMBIA PIKE

xxx
STEWART

Harpeth River

xxx
WILSON

Johnson (S.D. LEE)

xxx
FORREST
(-Chalmers)

NASHVILLE AND DECATUR R.R.

LEWISBURG PIKE

CLAY

S.D. LEE
(-Johnson)

**FRANKLIN AND NASHVILLE
CAMPAIGN**

BATTLE OF FRANKLIN

Situation About 4·00 P.M., 30 Nov. 1864

0   ¼   ½   ¾   1 Mile

SCALE

N

The failure at Franklin had not discouraged Hood, though it had an enervating effect on the Confederate troops. On 2 December, Hood arrived at Nashville, where he found Thomas' army in formidable entrenchments (*sketch* a). Hood's troops occupied and entrenched the position shown.

It might be well to examine Hood's decision to advance to Nashville after his defeat at Franklin. The condition of his command and the morale of his troops were not good. Perhaps he underestimated his men, but he felt that a withdrawal at that time would result in the disintegration of his army. Thomas had a preponderance of force, so an assault on the strong Union position could hardly be successful. Thus, Hood concluded that if he could establish his army in a good defensive position and await an assault by Thomas, he might contain that attack and then deliver a crushing counterstroke. In addition, he seemed to entertain the unrealistic hope of receiving reinforcements from Texas. Hood's estimate was overly optimistic, for his highly competent foe was to plan and fight one of the classic battles of the war—a battle in which the once proud Confederate army would be driven from the field fleeing and broken.

On 5 December, Hood sent Maj. Gen. William B. Bate's division of Cheatham's corps and most of Forrest's cavalry to observe Rousseau at Murfreesboro (*off map, right center*). Instead, the Confederates attacked and were repulsed. Bate was recalled to Nashville, but Forrest remained near Murfreesboro and thus was absent from the Battle of Nashville.

Thomas' army consisted of the corps of A.J. Smith (who had arrived from Missouri on 30 November), Schofield, and Wood (successor to Stanley, who had been wounded at Franklin), and of Steedman's 'provisional detachment' (actually a weak corps consisting of service troops divided into two 'divisions,' one commanded by Steedman himself and the other under Brig. Gen. Charles Cruft). Slowly, Thomas made his plans. Now the authorities in Washington intervened. Hood's advance through Tennessee and Grant's current stalemate at Petersburg were disconcerting. Pressure was exerted on Thomas to attack; Grant himself sent orders to start moving. But the stoical Thomas would

not attack until Wilson's cavalry had been properly mounted. By 8 December, he was ready, but then a sleet and snow storm struck, forcing postponement. Again, Washington exploded. On the 9th, Schofield was actually selected to replace Thomas, but no orders were sent out. On the 13th, Logan was directed to proceed to Nashville and assume command if, upon his arrival, Thomas had not yet initiated operations. He reached Louisville on the 15th, but went no farther—Thomas on that day had struck Hood a devastating blow.

Early on the 15th, Steedman, making the secondary attack, advanced on Cheatham and kept the right of the Confederate line occupied for the rest of the day (*sketch* b). Meanwhile, Thomas' main attack—Smith, Wood, and Hatch (dismounted)—had advanced at dawn, wheeling left to a line parallel with the Hillsboro Pike. Maj. Gen. James L. Donaldson, with a force consisting largely of armed quartermaster employees, took over the trenches on the Union right. By noon, Smith and Hatch had seized Hood's detached works west of the pike and had reached the pike itself; Wood was preparing to assault the Confederate outposts on Montgomery Hill (*center*). Hood, seeing the threat to his left, ordered Cheatham to send reinforcements to Stewart. Montgomery Hill was taken in a gallant and impetuous charge by Beatty's division of Wood's corps. Now, at about 1:00 P.M., Thomas ordered Wood to attack the angle in Stewart's line, Schofield to come up on Smith's right, and Wilson to reinforce Hatch and get astride the Granny White Turnpike.

By 1:30 P.M., Stewart's position along Hillsboro Pike became untenable as the overwhelming forces of Smith, Wood, Schofield, and Wilson pounded it. Shortly thereafter, Stewart's corps broke and began to stream toward Granny White Turnpike. However, it was not a complete rout, and Hood, aided by nightfall and a break in the fighting, was able to gather enough men to resume the battle on the next day. Wilson, many of whose troopers were fighting dismounted, had not been able to place a large enough force astride the Granny White Turnpike to hamper the Confederates seriously.

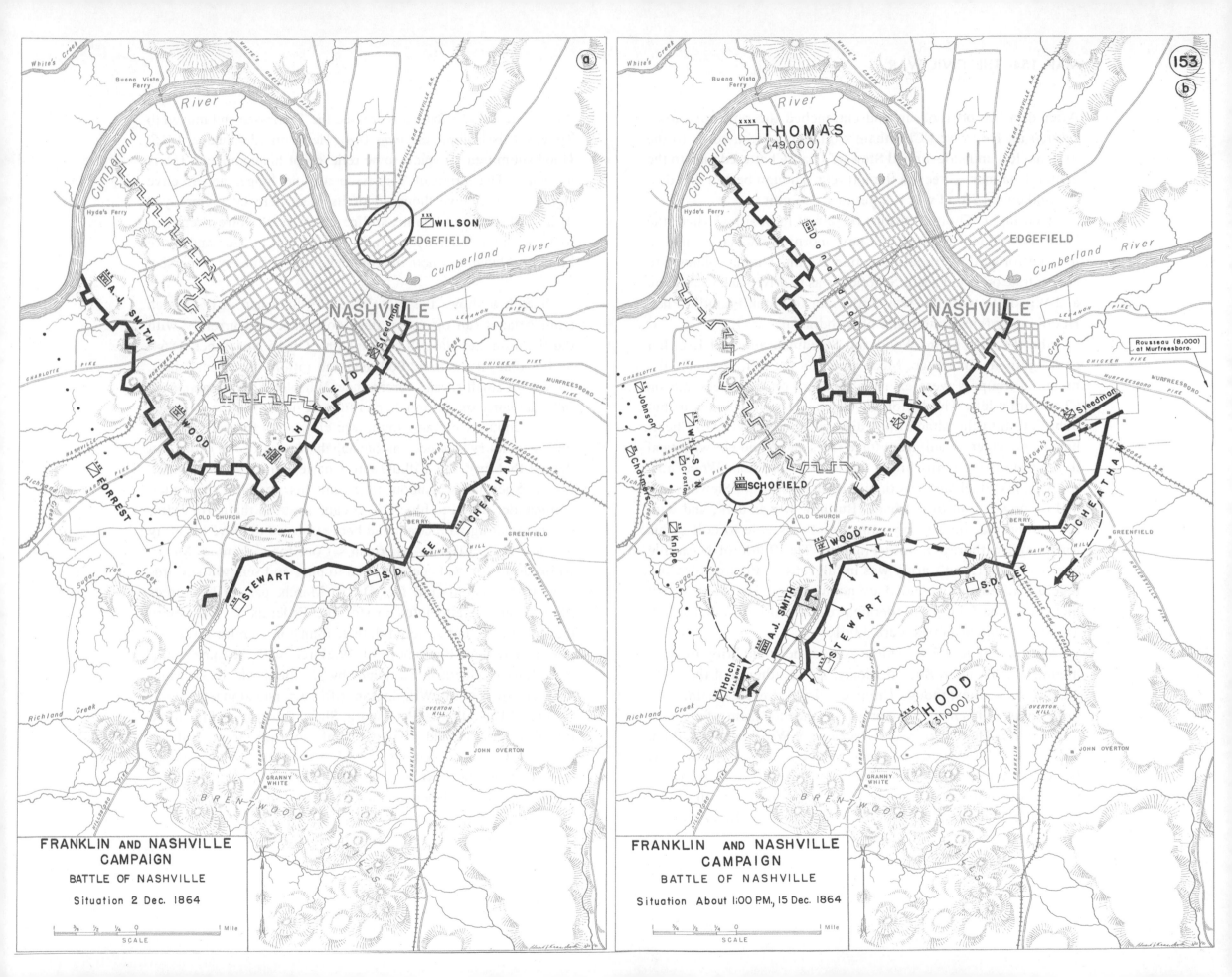

a

WILSON

EDGEFIELD

Cumberland River

NASHVILLE

A. J. SMITH

WOOD

SCHOFIELD

Steedman

FORREST

CHEATHAM

LEE

S. D.

STEWART

153

b

×××× THOMAS (49,000)

River

EDGEFIELD

Cumberland River

Donaldson

NASHVILLE

Rousseau (8,000) at Murfreesboro.

Steedman

Johnson

WILSON

Croxton

Chambers

SCHOFIELD

Knipe

WOOD

CHEATHAM

S. D. LEE

STEWART

A. J. SMITH

Hatch (Wilson)

×××× HOOD (31,000)

JOHN OVERTON

FRANKLIN AND NASHVILLE
CAMPAIGN

BATTLE OF NASHVILLE

Situation 2 Dec. 1864

¾ ½ ¼ 0 _____ 1 Mile
SCALE

FRANKLIN AND NASHVILLE
CAMPAIGN

BATTLE OF NASHVILLE

Situation About 1:00 P.M., 15 Dec. 1864

¾ ½ ¼ 0 _____ 1 Mile
SCALE

After dark, Hood took up and entrenched the position shown (*sketch* a). He moved Cheatham's relatively fresh corps to the extreme left and sideslipped Stewart's badly battered men to the center. Chalmers screened the left rear. Though beaten that day, the undaunted Hood was not yet ready to quit.

That night, Thomas' troops remained in position where the battle had ended. Most of the next morning was consumed in moving forward to Hood's new line. Again, Thomas planned to concentrate on Hood's left. Schofield was to drive back Cheatham, and Wilson to work his way to the rear to block Franklin Pike, Hood's only remaining route of withdrawal.

Shortly after noon, Wood and Steedman attacked Lee, but could gain no advantage. Meanwhile, on the left, Wilson's dismounted troopers were exerting pressure on Chalmers and on Cheatham's left. The Union cavalryman urged Thomas to put Schofield into the attack immediately. About 4:00 P.M., Cheatham came under assault from three sides and could not withstand the pressure; his corps broke and fled to the rear. Wood now renewed his attack and this time was successful, for Stewart, too, had by now begun to fall back. But now it was dark, and with the darkness came a heavy rain. Hood was able to collect his forces and withdraw toward Franklin. The Battle of Nashville was over, and Hood's army was in full retreat. Figures for Confederate killed and wounded are not available. Hood stated that they were small, but Confederate prisoners alone totaled 4,462. Thomas' total casualties were 3,061.

Wilson took up the pursuit as soon as he could bring forward mounts for his men. But this delay, the weather, and the night were Hood's allies; though Union cavalry followed, Chalmers—losing most of his men in the process—checked them a few miles to the south. The next day (17 December), Wilson continued the pursuit, aided by Wood, but Hood was better organized by now. Forrest rejoined him at Columbia on the 18th and managed to hold off Wilson during the next week, as the remnants of the Confederate army retreated to the Tennessee River. On the 25th–27th, the Confederates crossed the Tennessee and moved to Tupelo, Mississippi (*see map* 148). Here, on 13 January, 1865, Hood submitted a request to be relieved of his command. Davis accepted. The Army of Tennessee was no longer an effective fighting force. Five thousand of its men were later employed against Sherman in South Carolina, to no avail. Forrest returned to Mississippi, but Wilson moved against him in 1865 and drove him into Alabama, where his command was ultimately dispersed.

Sketch *b* shows the route taken by Sherman in his march from Atlanta (an operation that took place concurrently with the Franklin and Nashville campaign). On 15 November, 1864, he left that city with 62,000 men and rations for twenty days. Except for small cavalry forces under Wheeler, he was unopposed in his advance on Savannah; en route, he destroyed the railroads and any industry of value to the war effort, and foraged liberally on the country. Hardee, at Savannah (*lower center*), did not defend that city, but withdrew to Charleston on 21 December, just as Sherman was about to assault his position; the Union commander failed to block his escape route to the north. After communicating with Grant and being ordered to move his army to Petersburg, Virginia, Sherman set out for Columbia. Meanwhile, Johnston had been recalled to duty and sent to the Carolinas to oppose his old foe. On 16 March, part of his forces (under Hardee) attempted to stop the Federals at Averysboro (*center, right*), but suffered defeat. Johnston's entire force opposed Sherman at Bentonville on 19 March, with the same result. At Goldsboro, Sherman was joined by Schofield, who had brought his corps by water to Wilmington. After a personal meeting with Grant and Lincoln near Petersburg, Sherman organized his force into three armies and set out to link up with Grant. But, on 13 April, Johnston—having learned of Lee's surrender—sought an armistice; the next day, he surrendered. Except for some minor actions in Alabama and west of the Mississippi, the war was over.

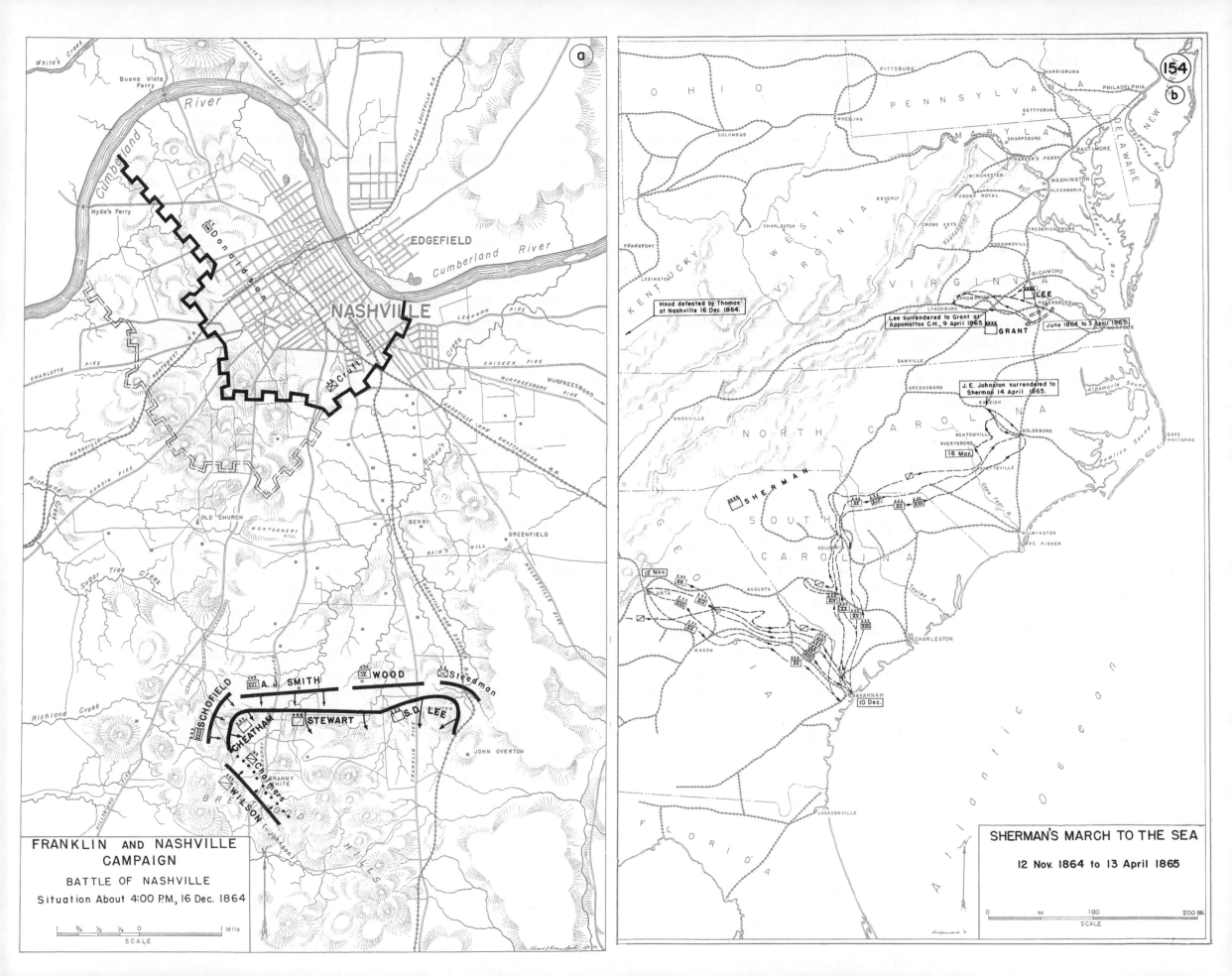

a

White's Creek

Buena Vista Ferry

Cumberland River

Hyde's Ferry

Donaldson

EDGEFIELD

Cumberland River

NASHVILLE

CHARLOTTE PIKE

NORTHWEST R.R.

LEBANON PIKE

CHICKEN PIKE

MURFREESBORO PIKE

OLD CHURCH

MONTGOMERY HILL

BERRY

GREENFIELD

RAIN'S HILL

Richland Creek

Sugar Tree Creek

XVI A. J. SMITH   IV WOOD   Steedman

SCHOFIELD

CHEATHAM   STEWART   S. D. LEE

Chalmers

GRANNY WHITE

WILSON (Johnson)

JOHN OVERTON

BRENTWOOD HILLS

FRANKLIN AND NASHVILLE CAMPAIGN

BATTLE OF NASHVILLE

Situation About 4:00 P.M., 16 Dec. 1864

¾ ½ ¼ 0   1 Mile
SCALE

b

OHIO   PENNSYLVANIA   PITTSBURG   HARRISBURG   PHILADELPHIA

COLUMBUS   WHEELING   GETTYSBURG   NEW JERSEY

MARYLAND   SHARPSBURG   BALTIMORE   DELAWARE

HARPER'S FERRY   WINCHESTER   WASHINGTON

FRANKFORT   WEST VIRGINIA   BEVERLY   FRONT ROYAL   ALEXANDRIA

LEXINGTON   KENTUCKY   VIRGINIA   GORDONSVILLE   RICHMOND

Hood defeated by Thomas at Nashville 16 Dec. 1864.

LYNCHBURG   APPOMATTOX   LEE   PETERSBURG

Lee surrendered to Grant at Appomattox C.H., 9 April 1865.   GRANT   June 1864 to 3 April 1865

DANVILLE

GREENSBORO

J. E. Johnston surrendered to Sherman 14 April 1865.

KNOXVILLE   NORTH CAROLINA   RALEIGH   GOLDSBORO

BENTONVILLE   AVERYSBORO

16 Mar.   FAYETTEVILLE   WILMINGTON

SHERMAN   SOUTH   FT. FISHER

CAROLINA   COLUMBIA

12 Nov.   GEORGIA   AUGUSTA   CHARLESTON

ATLANTA

MACON

SAVANNAH   10 Dec.

FLORIDA   JACKSONVILLE

SHERMAN'S MARCH TO THE SEA

12 Nov. 1864 to 13 April 1865

0   50   100   200 Mi.
SCALE

Two major problems confronted the United States at the beginning of the Spanish-American War: first, to improvise an army; second, to gain control of the seas in order to permit employment of that army against the Spanish possessions in the West Indies.

As in all previous wars, the United States found itself woefully unprepared. There were 28,183 regular troops, of whom part had to be held in the West to guard against renewed Indian troubles. In Cuba, there were about 25,000 insurgents, of little real military value to the Americans. The War Department lacked the organization and the personnel for efficient mobilization; there was no effective staff, no accurate knowledge of the actual strength and disposition of the Spanish forces in Cuba, and no accurate maps of that country. The United States Navy completely outclassed the Spanish Navy, but was inexperienced in fleet operations. The Spanish army in Cuba was superior to the American Army in armament and equipment, but it suffered from a shortage of ammunition and supplies—and still more from the ineptness and pessimism of its high command.

The American plans for war varied day by day in response to public pressure incited by the then-uninhibited press. As many as 250,000 volunteers were demanded and called; the commanding general of the Army, Maj. Gen. Nelson A. Miles, wanted only 80,000 trained men. The fluctuating government plans finally culminated in a proposed expedition of 70,000 men against Havana (*sketch* a, *left center*), for which neither men, ammunition, nor transports were available. Meanwhile, the limited forces at hand were being concentrated at Tampa, Florida.

Then Admiral Pascual Cervera sailed slowly from Spain (*sketch* b) with his squadron—four armored cruisers with three torpedo boats in tow, all poorly equipped. With this news, the American Eastern seaboard went into panic. So politically potent was the civilian fear that the Navy was compelled, against its better judgment, to leave part of the fleet, under Commodore Winfield S. Schley, on the East Coast. Cervera could not get

sufficient coal at Martinique or Curaçao and, as a last resort, put into Santiago Harbor—the only major unblocked Cuban port. Schley eventually located him there, and Admiral William T. Sampson brought up the remainder of the fleet. A gallant attempt to block the narrow harbor mouth by sinking the collier *Merrimac* failed (*sketch* c). Sampson then seized Guantánamo Bay (*sketch* a, *bottom right*) as a forward base, and called for assistance from the Army.

The response was a hasty, confused embarkation of Maj. Gen. William R. Shafter's V Corps at Tampa. After a week's delay, during which the Navy investigated a false report of Spanish warships off the coast of Cuba, Shafter arrived on 20 June off Santiago. Here, Sampson urged a landing on the eastern side of the harbor mouth (*sketch* c) and the storming of the fortifications —up a steep, 230-foot bluff. After consultation with insurgent leaders, Shafter elected to follow his original plan of surrounding Santiago, and decided to seize Daiquirí (*sketch* d, *bottom right*) as an initial base. To confuse the Spaniards, the fleet shelled Siboney and Aguadores, and one division made a feint at landing at Cabañas.

The troops landed unopposed at Daiquirí. By 23 June, Brig. Gen. Henry W. Lawton, commanding the advance guard, occupied Siboney. Lawton's orders had been to take up a defensive position to cover Siboney as a base of operations until logistical means could be assembled for the advance on Santiago. But the ebullient Maj. Gen. Joseph W. Wheeler advanced northwest of Siboney with part of his dismounted division of cavalry and blundered into the Spanish rear guard at Las Guasimas, sustaining a sharp check. Nevertheless, Wheeler—the senior officer ashore—took both his and Lawton's divisions forward to the vicinity of Sevilla, thus compounding the already difficult supply problem. Shafter thereupon ordered Wheeler not to bring on any further engagements, pending the arrival of reinforcements and supplies.

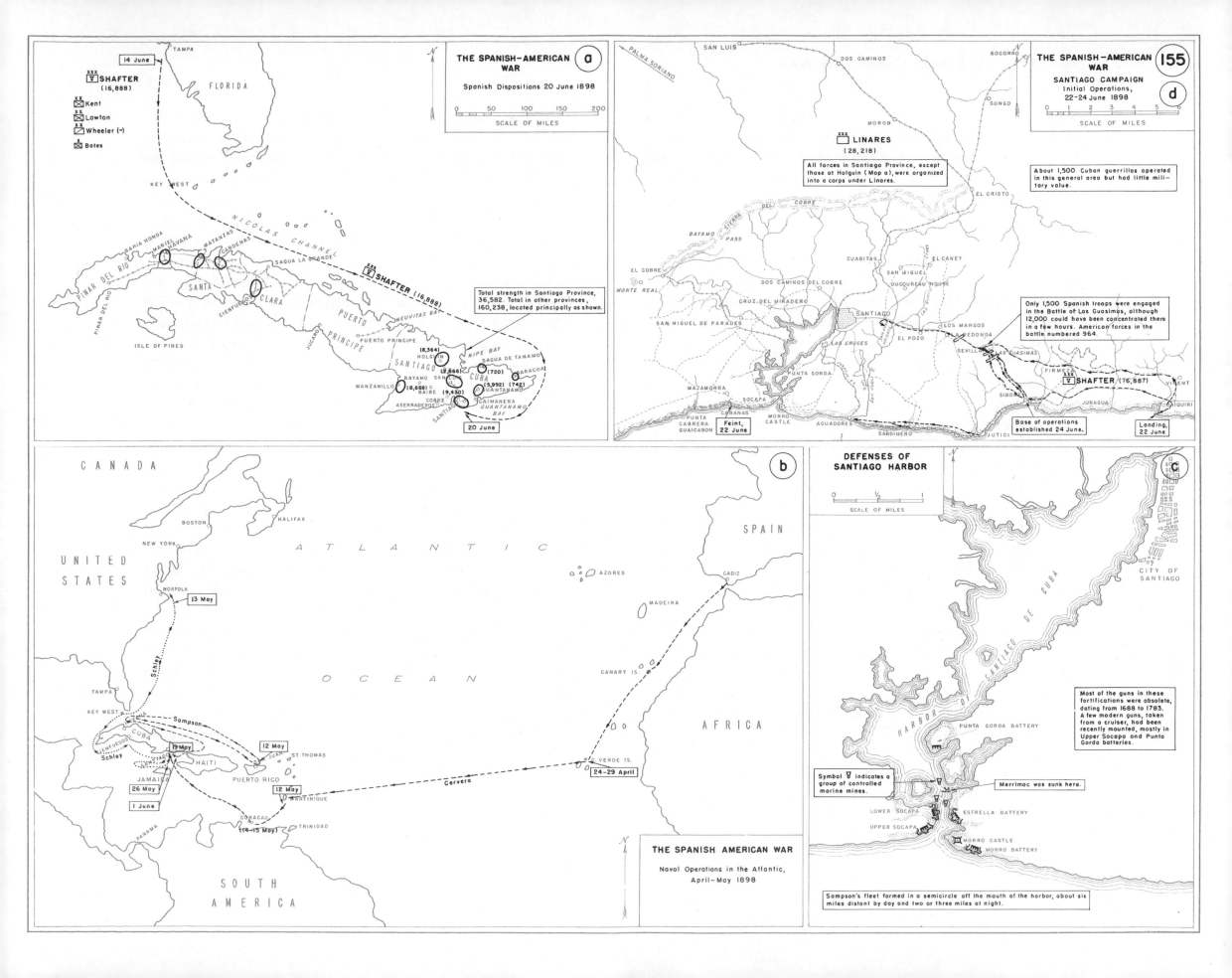

Map (a) — top left

14 June

XXX
V SHAFTER
(16,888)

XX
Kent

XX
Lawton

XX
Wheeler (−)

XX
Bates

TAMPA
FLORIDA
KEY WEST
NICOLAS CHANNEL
BAHIA HONDA
MARIEL
HAVANA
MATANZAS
CARDENAS
SAGUA LA GRANDE
PINAR DEL RIO
SANTA CLARA
CIENFUEGOS
PUERTO PRINCIPE
NEUVITAS BAY
JUCARO
ISLE OF PINES
SANTIAGO
CUBA
NIPE BAY
SAGUA DE TANAMO
BARACOA
HOLGUIN (8,364)
BAYAMO SAN LUIS (2,666)
MANZANILLO
BAIRE (8,668)
GUANTANAMO (9,430)
(5,992) (742)
(720)
CAIMANERA
GUANTANAMO BAY
COBRE
ASERRADEROS
SANTIAGO

XX
SHAFTER (16,888)

Total strength in Santiago Province, 36,582. Total in other provinces, 160,238, located principally as shown.

20 June

Map (d) — top right

THE SPANISH–AMERICAN WAR 155

SANTIAGO CAMPAIGN
Initial Operations,
22–24 June 1898 d

SCALE OF MILES
0 1 2 3 4 5

PALMA SORIANO
SAN LUIS
DOS CAMINOS
SOCORRO
MORON
SONGO
EL CRISTO
SIERRA DEL COBRE
BAYAMO PASS
EL COBRE
MONTE REAL
CUABITAS
SAN MIGUEL
EL CANEY
DOS CAMINOS DEL COBRE
DUCOUREAU HOUSE
CRUZ DEL MIRADERO
SANTIAGO
SAN MIGUEL DE PARADES
LAS CRUCES
EL POZO
PUNTA GORDA
LOS MANGOS
REDONDA
LAS GUASIMAS
SEVILLA
FIRMEZA
MAZAMORRA
SOCAPA
PUNTA CABRERA GUAICABON
CABANAS
MORRO CASTLE
AGUADORES
SARDINERO
SIBONEY
JURAGUA
JUTICI
DAIQUIRI

XXX
LINARES
(28,218)

All forces in Santiago Province, except those at Holguin (Map a), were organized into a corps under Linares.

About 1,500 Cuban guerrillas operated in this general area but had little military value.

Only 1,500 Spanish troops were engaged in the Battle of Las Guasimas, although 12,000 could have been concentrated there in a few hours. American forces in the battle numbered 964.

XXX
V SHAFTER (16,887)

Feint, 22 June

Base of operations established 24 June.

Landing, 22 June

Map (b) — bottom left

CANADA
BOSTON
HALIFAX
NEW YORK
NORFOLK
13 May
UNITED STATES
TAMPA
KEY WEST
CUBA
CIENFUEGOS
Schley
Schley
Sampson
19 May
JAMAICA
26 May
1 June
PANAMA
HAITI
SANTIAGO
JUAN
ST. THOMAS
12 May
PUERTO RICO
12 May
MARTINIQUE
CORACAO
(14–15 May)
TRINIDAD
SOUTH AMERICA
Cervera
C. VERDE IS.
24–29 April
ATLANTIC OCEAN
AZORES
MADEIRA
CANARY IS.
CADIZ
SPAIN
AFRICA

Map (c) — bottom right

HARBOR OF SANTIAGO DE CUBA
CITY OF SANTIAGO
PUNTA GORDA BATTERY
LOWER SOCAPA
UPPER SOCAPA
ESTRELLA BATTERY
MORRO CASTLE
MORRO BATTERY

Most of the guns in these fortifications were obsolete, dating from 1688 to 1783. A few modern guns, taken from a cruiser, had been recently mounted, mostly in Upper Socapa and Punta Gorda batteries.

Symbol ⊻ indicates a group of controlled marine mines.

Merrimac was sunk here.

Sampson's fleet formed in a semicircle off the mouth of the harbor, about six miles distant by day and two or three miles at night.

Shafter experienced great difficulty in trying to establish a forward supply base. His ships had been loaded haphazardly, unloading facilities at Siboney were few and poor, and the road inland was abominable. On 28 June, he received a report that some 8,000 Spanish (*off map, northwest*) were moving east to reinforce Santiago, and decided that he must attack the city before their arrival.

The attack was planned for 1 July. At daybreak, Lawton's division would clear the right flank by capturing El Caney (*top right*)—an action that was expected to require about two hours. Then he would move southwest to envelop the north flank of the Spanish entrenchments on San Juan Heights and Kettle Hill (*center*). Such an advance would also cut off Santiago from Cuabitas (*top center*), the source of its water supply. General Calixto García, the local insurgent leader, was asked to block the Cobre Road (*upper left*) against Spanish reinforcements. Brig. Gens. Jacob F. Kent's and Samuel S. Sumner's divisions were to advance and deploy in front of San Juan Heights, ready to attack when Lawton rejoined them. One regiment (*not shown*) was to attack Aguadores (*off map, bottom left*) to prevent its garrison from moving to Santiago; the Navy was to demonstrate at Santiago Harbor.

The plan was good, but its execution was unexpectedly difficult. Except for some open ground around El Caney and the bare slopes of San Juan Heights, the country to be traversed was heavily wooded, restricting movement to the few poor roads. The Spanish fortifications were strong, centering around small stone forts and blockhouses; some were covered by barbed-wire entanglements. On the night of 30 June, the Americans bivouacked as shown (*dashed blue circles*); the next morning, they advanced along the routes indicated.

Lawton's attack on El Caney found a stubborn little garrison, well dug in and not inclined to surrender. American artillery, firing at long range, was ineffective. Smoke from the old-fashioned, black-powder cartridges of the 2d Massachusetts Regiment made its personnel conspicuous targets for the Spanish, who—armed with modern Mauser rifles—forced the regiment back out of line.

Brig. Gen. John C. Bates's brigade was sent to reinforce Lawton, but still no progress was made until the middle of the afternoon, when the Spaniards began to run out of ammunition and the American artillery moved forward. The key stone fort was stormed shortly after 4:00 P.M.; the heroic Spanish commander, Brig. Gen. Joaquín Vara de Ray, was killed; few of the garrison escaped.

Meanwhile, Kent's and Sumner's divisions had made a slow, confused advance along the road to Santiago. An observation balloon, towed along, provided an excellent aiming point for Spanish artillery. Obsolescent American field pieces on the hill south of El Pozo (*lower center*) tried to support the advance, firing black-powder ammunition; two Krupp quick-firing guns soon forced them to cease fire. The balloonist finally reported a poor trail south of the main road; Kent promptly moved troops onto it to speed up the advance and deployment. Here, his leading regiment—the 71st New York—panicked and refused to advance, but the regulars behind it kept going. (Regular Army regiments are indicated on the map by single numbers.) Eventually, both divisions took up a straggling line along the San Juan River. The situation grew increasingly tense: artillery support had ceased, ammunition was running low, casualties were serious, and communications almost nonexistent; no help could be expected from Lawton. At this critical moment, 1st Lt. John H. Parker brought his detachment of Gatling guns recklessly forward and opened fire on the Spanish entrenchments. Immediately, the defenders began withdrawing. Various subordinate commanders appear to have ordered an assault; it overran both Kettle Hill and San Juan Heights. The Spaniards fell back to the defenses around Fort Cañosa; the exhausted and hungry attackers did not pursue.

Having finally taken El Caney, Lawton started for San Juan Heights. After dark, his advance guard came under fire near the Ducoureau House (*upper center*). Not wanting to risk a night action in unknown country, Lawton took the circuitous route back through El Caney and El Pozo, coming into line about noon on 2 July—less than a mile west of the Ducoureau House (*see map 157*).

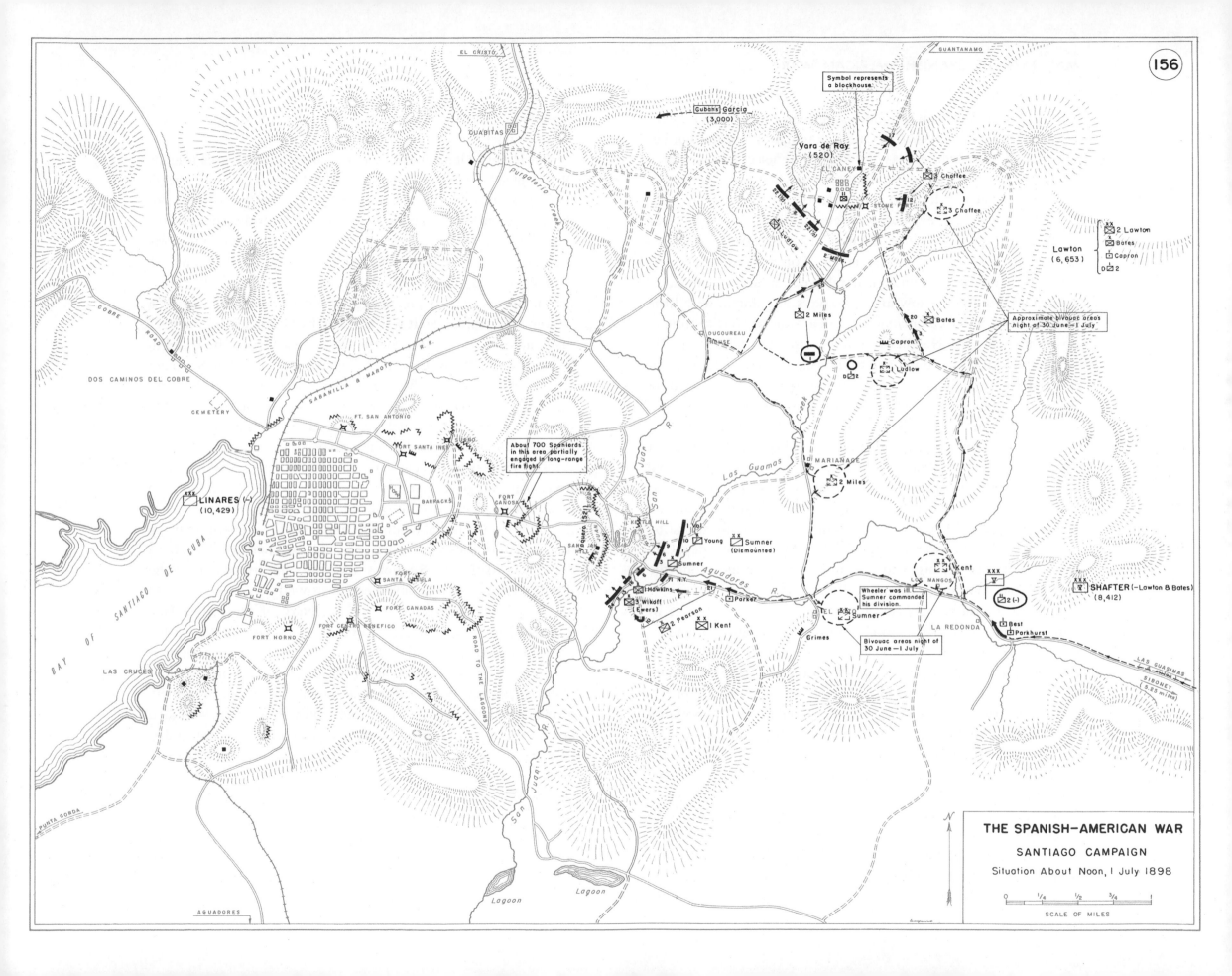

156

Symbol represents
a blockhouse.

Cubans' Garcia
(3,000)

GUABITAS

Vara de Ray
(520)

EL CANEY

3 Chaffee

STONE FORT

3 Chaffee

Lawton
(6,653)

XX 2 Lawton
X Bates
□ Capron
□ ☒ 2

2 Miles

Ludlow

2 Mass.

20 Bates

Capron

3

Approximate bivouac areas
night of 30 June—1 July

DUCOUREAU
HOUSE

□ ☒ 2

1 Ludlow

MARIANAGE

2 Miles

FT. SAN ANTONIO

FORT SANTA INES

CUERO

About 700 Spaniards
in this area partially
engaged in long-range
fire fight.

LINARES (—)
(10,429)

BARRACKS

FORT
CANOSA

KETTLE HILL

1 Vol.

10 Young

Sumner
(Dismounted)

9

SANTA JAG

3 Sumner

Sumner

1 Hawkins

Parker

Kent

XXX
V

XXX
V SHAFTER (—Lawton & Bates)
(8,412)

3 Wikoff
(Ewers)

2 Pearson

1 Kent

Aguadores R.

Wheeler was ill.
Sumner commanded
his division.

LOS MANGOS

☒ 2 (—)

FORT
SANTA URSULA

EL

Sumner

LA REDONDA

Best
Parkhurst

Bivouac areas night of
30 June—1 July

Grimes

FORT CANADAS

FORT CENTRO BENEFICO

FORT HORNO

ROAD TO THE LAGOONS

LAS GUASIMAS

SIBONEY
(8.25 miles)

BAY OF SANTIAGO DE CUBA

LAS CRUCES

PUNTA GORDA

Lagoon

Lagoon

AGUADORES

N

THE SPANISH—AMERICAN WAR

SANTIAGO CAMPAIGN

Situation About Noon, 1 July 1898

0   1/4   1/2   3/4   1

SCALE OF MILES

The capture of San Juan Heights had left the United States forces disorganized and shaken. They held dominating terrain, but between them and Santiago lay the Spanish inner defenses, which were considerably stronger than those they had just taken.

Lawton put his division into position on the extreme right of the American line, eventually extending his front almost to the head of Santiago Bay. García and his Cubans occupied the heights northwest of the city to command the Cobre Road. There was some firing on 2 July, with considerable casualties on both sides. American morale was low after two days of combat, with little sleep or food. Some commanders urged a withdrawal to a stronger position on Sevilla Heights (*off map, east*), but Shafter finally decided to hold his ground and to demand the surrender of Santiago. His initial demand was refused, but negotiations were begun. Shafter also urged the Navy to force the entrance of Santiago Harbor, but Sampson considered that too hazardous.

On 3 July, the entire situation changed abruptly. Acting under positive orders from Madrid and Havana, Cervera made a suicidal attempt to escape. His sortie momentarily surprised the far superior American fleet, which was blockading the harbor; but it had no hope of success, and his ships were destroyed one by one as they fled westward along the coast. On that same day, Col. Federico Escario brought his column into Santiago along the Cobre Road, García making no effort to halt him.

Shafter thereupon pressed his demand for the surrender of Santiago and its garrison. Some reinforcements arrived, and he used them to replace the Cubans on his right flank. He lacked the necessary artillery for an attack on the city; approximately half of his command was more or less sick with malaria, typhoid, and dysentery, and cases of what was thought to be—possibly incorrectly—the dreaded yellow fever were beginning to appear; his supply problem was still critical; and the arrival of the hurricane season might wreck his tenuous line of communications. Nevertheless, aided by a long-range naval bombardment on 10 and 11 July, he secured the surrender not only of Santiago and its garrison but of the entire Spanish IV Corps. This included approximately 12,000 troops at nearby Guantánamo, San Luis, and some minor posts. An agreement was reached on 14 July, and the capitulation was signed the next day; American troops entered Santiago on 17 July.

On 11 July, General Miles arrived off Santiago with a brigade of volunteers, ready to cooperate with the Navy by an assault landing against the Spanish coastal batteries on the west side of the harbor entrance. Finding the negotiations for the Spanish surrender well advanced, he held his troops aboard their transports until the formal surrender, afterward sailing for Puerto Rico.

Early in August, it became necessary to withdraw Shafter's command because of increasing sickness and the danger of a yellow-fever epidemic. It was replaced by "Immune Regiments," made up of men from the Southern states who were believed to be immune to the disease. The Spaniards captured at Santiago were shipped home by the United States, but even after the signing of the peace treaty—the Treaty of Paris, 10 December, 1898—there was considerable delay in evacuating the remaining Spanish forces and restoring law and order.

The success of this campaign can only be regarded as fortuitous. An energetic Spanish commander in the Santiago area could have concentrated his overwhelming forces (*see map 155* a) and opposed the initial landing or exploited the numerous strong defensive positions at Las Guasimas and elsewhere. Had this been done, it is likely that Shafter's V Corps—the better part of the Regular Army—would have been destroyed.

"That splendid little war," as Secretary of State John Hay termed it, proved in the end to be a costly one for the United States. Of the almost 250,000 men mobilized for it through public pressure, it is doubtful that even 20,000 even fired a shot. Nonetheless, nearly 5,500 Americans died in the various theaters of operation and later in the United States. Fewer than 400 died as a result of battle, however; the vast majority were lost to disease and other factors. Financially, the immediate cost of the war was $250 million. Sixty-one years after the fighting had concluded, about 100,000 men—and an almost equal number of dependents—continued to receive pensions. Almost $4 billion dollars in pensions had been paid to that point, at an annual cost of $150 million. The subsequent cost—financial and political—to the United States of administering the territories acquired is incalculable.

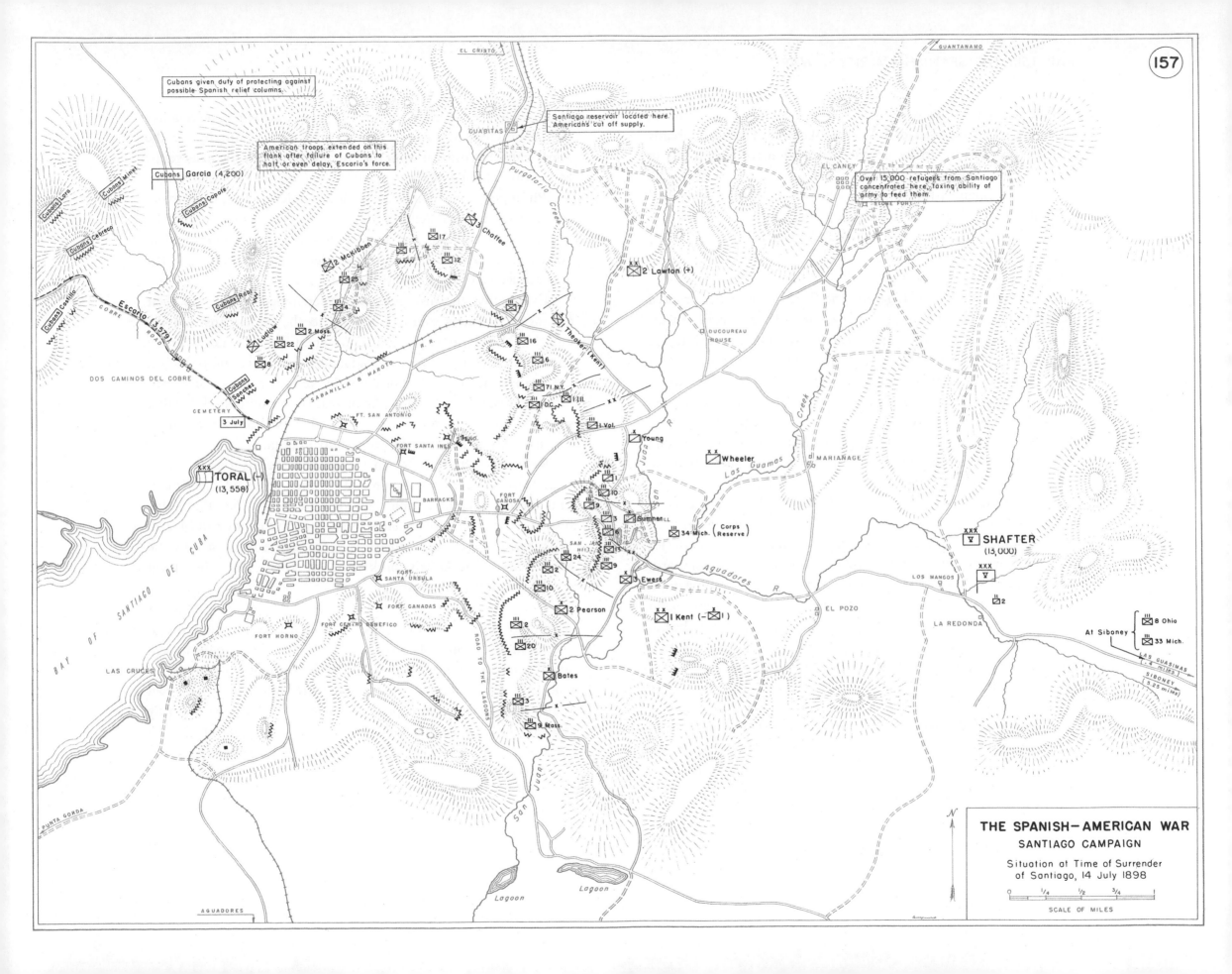

157

Cubans given duty of protecting against possible Spanish relief columns.

Santiago reservoir located here. Americans cut off supply.

American troops extended on this flank after failure of Cubans to halt, or even delay, Escario's force.

Over 15,000 refugees from Santiago concentrated here, taxing ability of army to feed them.

Cubans Garcia (4,200)

Escario (3,579)

DOS CAMINOS DEL COBRE

CEMETERY

3 July

TORAL (-)
(13,558)

BAY OF SANTIAGO DE CUBA

LAS CRUCES

PUNTA GORDA

AGUADORES

FT. SAN ANTONIO

FORT SANTA INES

BARRACKS

FORT CANOSA

FORT SANTA URSULA

FORT CANADAS

FORT CENTRO BENEFICO

FORT HORNO

SAN JUAN HILL

3 Chaffee

2 McKibben

17

12

2 Lawton (+)

Theaker (Kent)

16

6

71 N.Y.

D.C.

I Vol.

Young

Wheeler

Sumner

34 Mich. (Corps Reserve)

Ewers

2 Pearson

I Kent (-I)

Bates

2 Mass.

Ludlow

22

8

SHAFTER
(13,000)

EL POZO

LOS MANGOS

LA REDONDA

At Siboney

8 Ohio

33 Mich.

El Caney

EL CRISTO

GUANTANAMO

GUABITAS

Purgatorio Creek

DUCOUREAU HOUSE

MARIANAGE

Las Guamas Creek

Aguadores R.

San Juan R.

Las Guasimas

Siboney

9 Mass.

Lagoon

Lagoon

N

THE SPANISH-AMERICAN WAR

SANTIAGO CAMPAIGN

Situation at Time of Surrender
of Santiago, 14 July 1898

0   1/4   1/2   3/4   1

SCALE OF MILES

Commodore George Dewey's Asiatic Squadron was at Hong Kong when the Spanish-American War broke out. He had already received instructions to be prepared for offensive operations in the Philippine Islands. Consequently, he had made a thorough study of the Spanish forces in the islands, and was confident of his ability to destroy the Spanish squadron there. He had also established contact—through the American consul at Singapore —with General Emilo Aguinaldo, the leader of an insurgent movement in the Philippines.

Since he was now a belligerent, the British authorities ordered Dewey to leave Hong Kong (*sketch* a, *inset*) by 25 April. Dewey, who had just received (24 April) direct orders to proceed to the Philippines and capture or destroy the Spanish fleet there, left Hong Kong on 25 April, anchoring in nearby Chinese territorial waters until two Filipino leaders joined him on 27 April. Immediately thereafter, he sailed for the Philippine Islands, putting the insurgent leaders ashore on the western coast of Luzon. Finding that the Spanish squadron was not at its base in Subic Bay, he then entered Manila Bay on the night of 30 April–1 May. The tiny Spanish squadron made its fight anchored off its Cavite naval base, and was completely destroyed. Dewey exacted a promise from the Spanish Governor General that the Manila batteries would not fire on him—under threat of an immediate bombardment of the city. Since he lacked sufficient men to occupy Manila, he could only establish a blockade, but gathering insurgents soon surrounded the city on the land side, while the insurrection began to spread through the other islands. Dewey furnished these forces some weapons and, in late May, brought Aguinaldo from Hong Kong to Cavite.

With Dewey's victory (the Battle of Manila Bay), troops under Maj. Gen. Wesley Merritt were dispatched from the United States to reinforce him. The first units to arrive encountered vastly superior insurgent forces. The political situation between the United States and its informal allies became increasingly delicate. The insurgents were between Merritt's forces and Manila (*sketch* b). Aguinaldo had proclaimed a Philippine Republic and hoped for American recognition; he was ready to attack Manila whenever Dewey would cooperate with him. The Spanish Governor General was willing to surrender, eventually, to the Americans, but did not want the city taken over by the insurgents. Meanwhile, the United States, undecided whether it would annex the Philippines or recognize their independence, sought to avoid any appearance of a definite commitment. To further complicate this involved situation, warships of various European powers had appeared in Manila Bay, and the German squadron gave the appearance of trying to provoke hostilities.

Eventually, the insurgents were persuaded to give up their advanced positions south of Manila to the Americans. On the night of 31 July, the Spaniards did a great deal of random firing. On 13 August, the Americans advanced in two columns against the Spanish defenses, supported by Dewey's warships. There was little serious fighting, and the Spaniards soon capitulated. Neither side was aware that the war had ended two days previously, because Dewey had cut the cable into Manila.

Relations between the Americans and the insurgents deteriorated; on 4 February, Aguinaldo's troops attacked the Americans around Manila. Serious fighting on Luzon—the "Philippine Insurrection"—largely ended with Aguinaldo's capture in March, 1901. On some of the southern islands, savage resistance by the Moro tribes was largely broken up by June, 1901, but local revolts continued for years.

The occupation of Puerto Rico (*sketch* c) was a final, minor operation of the Spanish-American War, carried out against occasional local resistance. General Miles had originally planned to land at Punta Fajardo (*right center*) and advance against San Juan (*top center*), the capital. After leaving Cuba, he abruptly changed his objective to Guanica (*lower left*)—apparently both to obtain surprise and to avoid another joint Army-Navy operation (relations having been badly strained during the Santiago operation). Troop convoys from the United States reinforced Miles and landed at the three other points shown. The Puerto Ricans welcomed the Americans, and the peace treaty put an end to this almost bloodless operation.

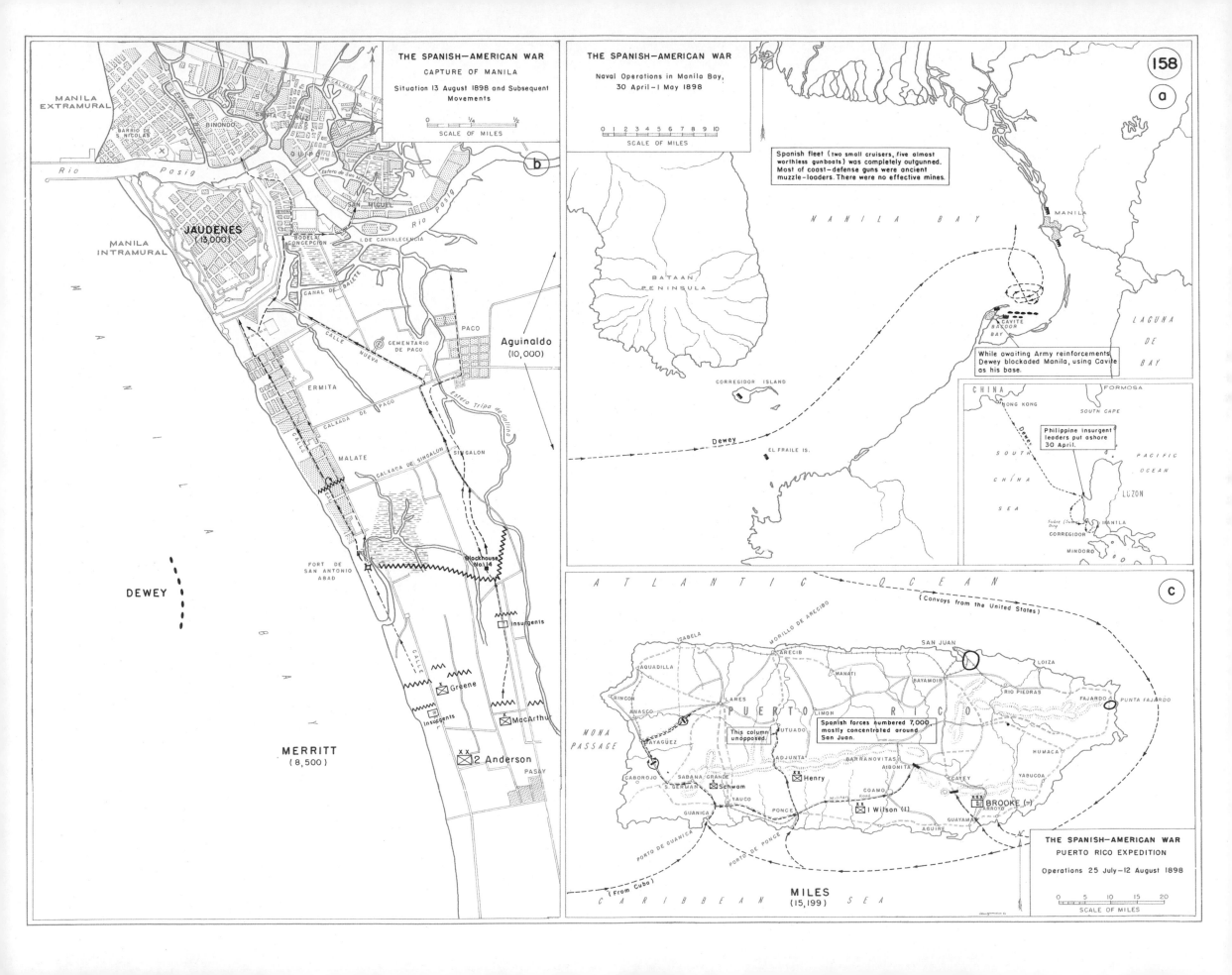

a

b

c

THE SPANISH-AMERICAN WAR
CAPTURE OF MANILA
Situation 13 August 1898 and Subsequent Movements

0   ¼   ½
SCALE OF MILES

THE SPANISH-AMERICAN WAR
Naval Operations in Manila Bay,
30 April-1 May 1898

0 1 2 3 4 5 6 7 8 9 10
SCALE OF MILES

Spanish fleet (two small cruisers, five almost worthless gunboats) was completely outgunned. Most of coast-defense guns were ancient muzzle-loaders. There were no effective mines.

MANILA BAY

MANILA

BATAAN PENINSULA

LAGUNA DE BAY

CAVITE BACOOR BAY

While awaiting Army reinforcements Dewey blockaded Manila, using Cavite as his base.

CORREGIDOR ISLAND

Dewey

EL FRAILE IS.

CHINA   FORMOSA

HONG KONG   SOUTH CAPE

Philippine insurgent leaders put ashore 30 April.

SOUTH CHINA SEA

PACIFIC OCEAN

LUZON

Subic (Subig) Bay   MANILA

CORREGIDOR

MINDORO

MANILA EXTRAMURAL

BINONDO   SANTA CRUZ

BARRIO DE S. NICOLAS

QUIAPO

Rio Pasig

Esterode San Miguel

SAN MIGUEL

JAUDENES (13,000)

MANILA INTRAMURAL

BODELAO CONCEPCION

I. DE CANVALECENCIA

Rio Pasig

CANAL DE BALETE

PACO

CEMENTARIO DE PACO

Aguinaldo (10,000)

CALLE NUEVA

Estero Tripa de Gallina

ERMITA

CALZADA DE PACO

MALATE

SINGALON

CALZADA DE SINGALON

Blockhouse No. 14

FORT DE SAN ANTONIO ABAD

DEWEY

Insurgents

× Greene

Insurgents

× MacArthur

×× 2 Anderson

PASAY

MERRITT (8,500)

THE SPANISH-AMERICAN WAR
PUERTO RICO EXPEDITION
Operations 25 July-12 August 1898

ATLANTIC OCEAN

(Convoys from the United States)

ISABELA   MORILLO DE ARECIBO   SAN JUAN

AQUADILLA   ARECIBO   MANATI   BAYAMOIR   LOIZA

RINCON   LARES   LIMON   RIO PIEDRAS   FAJARDO   PUNTA FAJARDO

ANASCO   PUERTO   RICO

MONA PASSAGE   This column unopposed.   UTUADO   Spanish forces numbered 7,000 mostly concentrated around San Juan.

MAYAGÜEZ   ADJUNTA   BARRANOVITAS   HUMACA

CABOROJO   SABANA GRANDE   × Henry   AIBONITA   CAYEY   YABUCOA

S. GERMAN   × Schwam   COAMO   ××× BROOKE (-)

YAUCO   Military Road   GUAYAMA

GUANICA   PONCE   ×× 1 Wilson (1)   AGUIRE   ARROYO

PORTO DE GUANICA   (From Cuba)

PORTO DE PONCE

CARIBBEAN SEA

MILES (15,199)

0   5   10   15   20
SCALE OF MILES

RECOMMENDED READING LIST

This list does not purport to contain *all* the good books on the military history of the periods covered. The selections should provide the reader with worthwhile references for further study, however.

BASIC WORKS: MILITARY HISTORY and PHILOSOPHY

CLAUSEWITZ, CARL VON. *On War*. 1832. Ed. and trans. by Michael Howard and Peter Paret. Indexed ed., Princeton, New Jersey: Princeton University Press, 1984.

COFFMAN, EDWARD M. *The Old Army: A Portrait of the American Army in Peacetime, 1784–1898*. New York: Oxford University Press, 1986.

CORBETT, JULIAN STAFFORD. *Some Principles of Maritime Strategy*. Reprint, New York: AMS Press, 1976 (originally published by Conway Press Ltd., 1911; 1st Reprint by Naval Institute Press, 1972).

EARLE, EDWARD MEADE, ed. *Makers of Modern Strategy: Military Thought from Machiavelli to Hitler*. Reprint, Princeton, New Jersey: Princeton University Press, 1971, paperback (originally published by Princeton University Press in 1943).

HACKETT, SIR JOHN. *The Profession of Arms*. New York: Macmillan, 1983.

HELLER, CHARLES E., AND WILLIAM A. STOFFT, eds. *America's First Battles: 1776–1965*. Lawrence, Kansas: University Press of Kansas, 1986.

HUNTINGTON, SAMUEL. *The Soldier and the State: The Theory and Politics of Civil-Military Relations*. Reprint, Cambridge, Massachusetts: Belknap Press of Harvard University Press, 1981, paperback (originally published by Random House, 1957).

HUSTON, JAMES. *The Sinews of War: Army Logistics, 1775–1953*. Washington, D.C.: U.S. Government Printing Office, 1966.

JOMINI, ANTOINE HENRI. *The Art of War*. 1838. Trans. by G.H. Mendell and W.P. Craighill. Reprint, Westport, Connecticut: Greenwood Press, 1971.

JONES, ARCHER. *The Art of War in the Modern World*. Urbana, Illinois: University of Illinois Press, 1987.

KOHN, RICHARD H. *Eagle and Sword: The Federalists and the Creation of the Military Establishment in America, 1783–1802*. New York: Free Press, 1975, paperback 1985.

MAHAN, ALFRED THAYER. *The Influence of Sea Power Upon History, 1660–1783*. 1890. Reprint, New York: Hill and Wang, 1957. Paperback, New York: Dover Books, 1987.

MAHON, JOHN K. *History of the Militia and the National Guard*. Macmillan series, *The Wars of the United States*, Gen. ed. Louis Morton. New York: Macmillan, 1983.

MILLETT, ALLAN R. AND PETER MASLOWSKI. *For the Common Defense: A Military History of the United States of America*. New York: Free Press, 1984.

PARET, PETER, ed. *Makers of Modern Strategy: From Machiavelli to the Nuclear Age*. Princeton, New Jersey: Princeton University Press, 1986, paperback.

POTTER, ELMER B., ed. *Sea Power*. 2d ed. Annapolis, Maryland: Naval Institute Press, 1982.

ROPP, THEODORE. *War in the Modern World*. New York: Macmillan, 1985, paperback (previously published by Collier, 1959, revised, 1962, and by Greenwood Press, 1981).

SKELTON, WILLIAM B. *An American Profession of Arms: The Army Officer Corps, 1784–1861*. Lawrence, Kansas: University of Kansas Press, 1992.

STEFFEN, RANDY. *The Horse Soldier, 1776–1943*. 4 vols. Norman, Oklahoma: University of Oklahoma Press, 1977.

SUN TZU. *The Art of War*. 4th century B.C. Trans. with commentary by J. H. Huang. New York: Quill, 1993, paperback.

WEIGLEY, RUSSELL F. *History of the United States Army*. Enlarged edition. Macmillan series, *The Wars of the United States*, Gen. ed. Louis Morton. Bloomington, Indiana: Indiana University Press, 1984, paperback.

———. *The American Way of War: A History of United States Military Strategy and Policy*. Macmillan series, *The Wars of the United States*, Gen. ed. Louis Morton. Bloomington, Indiana: Indiana University Press, 1977, paperback.

THE COLONIAL WARS

FERLING, JOHN. *Struggle for a Continent: The Wars of the Colonial Age*. Arlington Heights, Illinois: Harlan Davidson, Inc., 1993, paperback.

FREEMAN, DOUGLAS S. *George Washington* (Vols. I and II). New York: Charles Scribner's Sons, 1948–49.

HAMILTON, EDWARD P. *The French and Indian Wars: The Story of Battles and Forts in the Wilderness*. Garden City, New York: Doubleday, 1962.

JENNINGS, FRANCES. *Empire of Fortune: Crowns, Colonies and Tribes in the Seven Years War in America*. New York: W.W. Norton and Company, 1988.

KOPPERMAN, PAUL E. *Braddock at the Monongehela*. Pittsburgh: The University of Pittsburgh Press, 1977.

LEACH, DOUGLAS E. *Arms for Empire: A Military History of the British Colonies in North America, 1607–1763*. Macmillan series, *The Wars of the United States*, Gen. ed. Louis Morton. New York: Macmillan, 1973 (currently out of print).

———. *Roots of Conflict: British Armed Forces and Colonial America, 1677–1763*. Chapel Hill, North Carolina: University of North Carolina Press, 1986.

PARGELLIS, STANLEY M., ed. *Military Affairs in North America, 1748–1765*. New York: Appleton-Century Company, 1936.

PARKMAN, FRANCIS. *Count Frontenac and New France Under Louis XIV*. Boston: Little, Brown and Company, 1903.

PECKHAM, HOWARD H. *The Colonial Wars 1689–1762*. Chicago: University of Chicago Press, 1964.

THE AMERICAN REVOLUTION

CHIDSEY, DONALD B. *Valley Forge*. New York: Crown Publishers, 1959.

CUNLIFFE, MARCUS. *George Washington: Man and Monument*. New York: New American Library, 1984 (originally published by Little, Brown, and Company, 1958).

DEARBORN, HENRY. *The Revolutionary War Journals of Henry Dearborn, 1775–1783*. Lloyd A. Brown and Howard H. Peckham, eds. New York: DaCapo Press, 1971.

FREEMAN, DOUGLAS S. *George Washington*. 6 vols. New York: Charles Scribner's Sons, 1948–54.

FREY, SYLVIA R. *The British Soldier in America: A Social History of Military Life in the Revolutionary Period*. Austin, Texas: University of Texas, Press, 1981.

FURNEAUX, RUPERT. *The Battles of Saratoga*. New York: Stein and Day, 1983.

HIGGINBOTHAM, DON. *The War for American Independence: Military Attitudes, Policies, and Practice, 1763–1789*. Macmillan series, *The Wars of the United States*, Gen. ed. Louis Morton. New York: Macmillan, 1971.

MACKESY, PIERS. *The War for America, 1775–1783*. Cambridge, Massachusetts: Harvard University Press, 1964. Reprint, paperback, Lincoln, Nebraska: University of Nebraska Press, 1993.

MAHAN, ALFRED T. *Major Operations of the Navies in the War of American Independence*. Boston: Little, Brown and Company, 1913.

MARTIN, JAMES KIRBY AND MARK E. LENDER. *A Respectable Army: The Military Origins of the Republic, 1763–1789*. Arlington Heights, Illinois: Harlan Davidson, Inc., 1982.

ROYSTER, CHARLES. *A Revolutionary People at War: The Continental Army and American Character, 1775–1783*. Chapel Hill, North Carolina: University of North Carolina Press, 1979.

SHY, JOHN W. *A People Numerous and Armed: Reflections on the Military Struggle for American Independence*. New York: Oxford University Press, 1976. Revised edition, Ann Arbor, Michigan: University of Michigan Press, 1990.

WOOD, W. J. *Battles of the Revolutionary War*. Chapel Hill, North Carolina: Algonquin Books, 1990.

THE WAR OF 1812

COLES, HARRY L. *The War of 1812*. Chicago: University of Chicago Press, 1965.

MAHAN, ALFRED T. *Seapower in its Relation to the War of 1812*. Boston: Little, Brown and Company, 1905.

MAHON, JOHN K. *The War of 1812*. Gainesville, Florida: University of Florida Press, 1972. Paperback, New York: Da Capo, 1991.

STAGG, J.C.A. *Mr. Madison's War: Politics, Diplomacy, and Warfare in the Early American Republic, 1783–1830*. Princeton, New Jersey: Princeton University Press, 1983.

THE MEXICAN WAR

BAUER, KARL JACK. *The Mexican War, 1846–1848*. Macmillan series, *The Wars of the United States*, Gen. ed. Louis Morton. New York: Macmillan, 1974.

BILL, ALFRED H. *Rehearsal for Conflict*. New York: Alfred A. Knopf, 1947.

EISENHOWER, JOHN S.D. *So Far From God: The U.S. War With Mexico, 1846–48*. New York: Random House, 1989. Paperback, New York: Doubleday, 1990.

RECOMMENDED READING LIST

ELLIOTT, CHARLES W. *Winfield Scott*. New York: Macmillan, 1937.

FERRELL ROBERT H., ed. *Monterrey is Ours: The Mexican War Letters of Lt. Dana, 1845–1847*. Lexington, Kentucky: University of Kentucky Press, 1990.

LEWIS LLOYD. *Captain Sam Grant*. Boston: Little, Brown & Company, 1950.

SINGLETARY, OTIS A. *The Mexican War*. Chicago: University of Chicago Press, 1960.

SMITH, GEORGE WINSTON AND CHARLES JUDAH, eds. *Chronicles of the Gringos*. Albuquerque, New Mexico: University of New Mexico Press, 1968.

SMITH, JUSTIN H. *The War with Mexico*. 2 vols. New York: Macmillan, 1919.

THE AMERICAN CIVIL WAR

OFFICIAL HISTORIES

QUARTERMASTER GENERAL OF THE ARMY. *Commanders of Army Corps, Divisions, and Brigades*. Philadelphia: Burk, McFetridge, 1887.

UNITED STATES ARMY. *The War of the Rebellion: Official Records of the Union and Confederate Armies*. 130 vols. Washington: Government Printing Office, 1882–1900.

UNITED STATES NAVY. *War of the Rebellion: Official Records of the Union and Confederate Navies*. 30 vols. Washington: Government Printing Office, 1894–1922.

GENERAL HISTORIES and REFERENCES

ALBAUGH, WILLIAM A. AND EDWARD N. SIMMONS. *Confederate Arms*. Harrisburg, Pennsylvania: Stackpole Books, 1958.

ANDERSON, BERN. *The Naval History of the Civil War*. New York: Alfred A. Knopf, 1962.

BLACK, ROBERT C. *The Railroads of the Confederacy*. Chapel Hill, North Carolina: University of North Carolina Press, 1952.

BRUCE, ROBERT B. *Lincoln and the Tools of War*. Indianapolis and New York: The Bobbs-Merrill Company, 1956.

CATTON, BRUCE. *This Hallowed Ground*. New York: Doubleday & Company, 1956.

CORNISH, DUDLEY TAYLOR. *The Sable Arm: Black Troops in the Union Army, 1861–1865*. Lawrence, Kansas: University Press of Kansas, 1956. Reprint, 1987, paperback.

COULTER, E. MERTON. *The Confederate States of America, 1861–1865*. Vol. 2 of *A History of the South*, Wendell H. Stephenson and E. Merton Coulter, eds. Baton Rouge, Louisiana: Louisiana State University Press, 1950.

EATON, CLEMENT. *A History of the Southern Confederacy*. New York: Macmillan, 1954.

ELIOT, ELLSWORTH. *West Point in the Confederacy*. New York: G.A. Baker & Company, 1941.

FREEMAN, DOUGLAS S. *Lee's Lieutenants: A Study in Command*. 3 vols. New York: Charles Scribner's Sons, 1942–44.

GLATTHAAR, JOSEPH T. *Forged in Battle: The Civil War Alliance of Black Soldiers and White Officers*. New York: The Free Press, 1990.

———. *Partners in Command: The Relationships Between Leaders in the Civil War*. New York: The Free Press, 1994.

GOFF, RICHARD. *Confederate Supply*. Durham, North Carolina: Duke University Press, 1969.

HATTAWAY, HERMAN AND ARCHER JONES. *How the North Won: A Military History of the Civil War*. Urbana, Illinois: University of Illinois Press, 1983, paperback 1991.

JOHNSON, ROBERT U., AND CLARENCE C. BUEL, eds. *Battles and Leaders of the Civil War*. 4 vols. New York: The Century Company, 1884–87.

KEMBLE, C. ROBERT. *The Image of the Army Officer in America: Background for Current Views*. Westport, Connecticut: Greenwood Press, 1973.

LINDERMAN, GERALD F. *Embattled Courage: The Experience of Combat in the American Civil War*. New York: The Free Press, 1987.

LIVERMORE, THOMAS L. *Numbers and Losses in the Civil War*. Bloomington, Indiana: Indiana University Press, 1957.

LUVAAS, JAY. *The Military Legacy of the Civil War*. Chicago, Illinois: The University of Chicago Press, 1959. Reprint, Lawrence, Kansas: University Press of Kansas, 1988, paperback.

MCPHERSON, JAMES. *Battle Cry of Freedom: The Civil War Era*. New York: Ballantine, 1988.

MILLER, FRANCIS T. *The Photographic History of the Civil War*. New York: Review of Reviews Company, 1912.

MORRISON, JAMES L. *The Best School in the World: West Point, the Pre-Civil War Years, 1833–1866*. Kent, Ohio: The Kent State University Press, 1986.

REED, ROWENA. *Combined Operations in the Civil War*. Annapolis, Maryland: Naval Institute Press, 1978.

RHODES, JAMES F. *History of the Civil War, 1861–1865*. New York: Macmillan, 1917.

ROLAND, CHARLES P. *An American Iliad: The Story of the Civil War*. New York: McGraw-Hill, Inc., 1991.

SHANNON, FRED A. *The Organization and Administration of the Union Army, 1861–1865*. 2 vols. Cleveland: The Arthur H. Clark Company, 1928.

TURNER, GEORGE E. *Victory Rode the Rails*. Indianapolis and New York: The Bobbs-Merrill Company, 1953.

WEST, RICHARD S. *Mr. Lincoln's Navy*. New York: Longmans, Green & Company, 1957.

WILLIAMS, KENNETH P. *Lincoln Finds a General*. 5 vols. New York: Macmillan, 1949–56.

WOODWORTH, STEVEN E. *Jefferson Davis and His Generals: The Failure of Confederate Command in the West*. Lawrence, Kansas: University Press of Kansas, 1990.

BATTLES and CAMPAIGNS

CASTEL, ALBERT. *Decision in the West: The Atlanta Campaign of 1864*. Lawrence, Kansas: University Press of Kansas, 1992.

CODDINGTON, EDWIN B. *The Gettysburg Campaign*. New York: Charles Scribner's Sons, 1968.

COX, JACOB D. *The March to the Sea: Franklin and Nashville*. New York: Charles Scribner's Sons, 1894.

COZZENS, PETER. *No Better Place to Die: The Battle of Stones River*. Urbana, Illinois: University of Illinois Press, 1990.

———. *This Terrible Sound: The Battle of Chickamauga*. Urbana, Illinois: University of Illinois Press, 1992.

DAVIS, WILLIAM C. *Battle at Bull Run: A History of the First Major Campaign of the Civil War*. Garden City, New York: Doubleday & Company, 1977.

DOUBLEDAY, ABNER. *Chancellorsville and Gettysburg*. New York: Charles Scribner's Sons, 1892.

DOWDEY, CLIFFORD. *The Seven Days: The Emergence of Lee*. Boston: Little, Brown and Company, 1964. Reprint, New York: The Fairfax Press, 1978.

FURGURSON, ERNEST B. *Chancellorsville 1863: The Souls of the Brave*. New York: Alfred A. Knopf, 1992.

GALLAGHER, GARY W. ed. *The First Day at Gettysburg: Essays on Confederate and Union Leadership*. Kent, Ohio: The Kent State University Press, 1992.

GOSNELL, H. ALLEN. *Guns on the Western Waters: The Story of the River Gunboats in the Civil War*. Baton Rouge, Louisiana: Louisiana State University Press, 1949.

GLATTHAAR, JOSEPH T. *The March to the Sea and Beyond: Sherman's Troops in the Savannah and Carolinas Campaigns*. New York: New York University Press, 1986.

HENNESSY, JOHN J. *Return to Bull Run: The Campaign and Battle of Second Manassas*. New York: Simon and Schuster, 1993.

HORN, STANLEY F. *The Decisive Battle of Nashville*. Baton Rouge, Louisiana: Louisiana State University Press, 1956.

HUGHES, NATHANIEL C. *The Battle of Belmont: Grant Strikes South*. Chapel Hill, North Carolina: University of North Carolina Press, 1991.

JOSEPHY, ALVIN M. *The Civil War in the American West*. New York: Alfred A. Knopf, 1991.

MAHAN, ALFRED T. *The Gulf and Inland Waters*. New York: Charles Scribner's Sons, 1883.

MATTER, WILLIAM D. *If It Takes All Summer: The Battle of the Spotsylvania*. Chapel Hill, North Carolina: The University of North Carolina Press, 1988.

MCDONOUGH, JAMES L. *Shiloh—In Hell Before Night*. Knoxville, Tennessee: University of Tennessee Press, 1977.

MIERS, EARL S. *The Web of Victory*. New York: Alfred A. Knopf, 1951.

MILLIGAN, JOHN D. *Gunboats Down the Mississippi*. Annapolis, Maryland: United States Naval Institute, 1965.

MONAGHAN, JAY. *Civil War on the Western Border, 1854–1865*. Boston: Little, Brown & Company, 1955.

PALFREY, FRANCIS W. *The Antietam and Fredericksburg Campaigns*. New York: Charles Scribner's Sons, 1890.

PFANZ, HARRY W. *Gettysburg: The Second Day*. Chapel Hill, North Carolina: The University of North Carolina Press, 1987.

RHEA, GORDON C. *The Battle of the Wilderness*. Baton Rouge, Louisiana: Louisiana State University Press, 1994.

SEARS, STEPHEN W. *Landscape Turned Red: The Battle of Antietam*. New York: Ticknor & Fields, 1983.

———. *To the Gates of Richmond*. New York: Ticknor and Feilds, 1992. Paperback reprint, 1994.

SHEA, WILLIAM L. AND EARL J. HESS. *Pea Ridge: Civil War Campaign in the West*. Chapel Hill, North Carolina: University of North Carolina Press, 1992.

STACKPOLE, EDWARD J. *The Fredericksburg Campaign: Drama on the Rappahannock*. Harrisburg, Pennsylvania: Stackpole Books, 1957.

RECOMMENDED READING LIST

STEERE, EDWARD. *The Wilderness Campaign: The Meeting of Grant and Lee.* Mechanicsburg, Pennsylvania: Stackpole Books, 1960.

STEWART, GEORGE R. *Pickett's Charge: A Microhistory of the Final Attack at Gettysburg.* Boston: Houghton Mifflin Company, 1959.

TRUDEAU, NOAH A. *The Last Citadel: Petersburg, Virginia, June 1864–April 1865.* Boston: Little, Brown & Company, 1991.

TURNER, MAXINE. *Navy Grey: The Story of the Confederate Navy on the Chattahoochee and Apalachicola Rivers.* Tuscaloosa, Alabama: The University of Alabama Press, 1988.

WISE, STEPHEN A. *Lifeline of the Confederacy: Blockade Running During the Civil War.* Columbia, South Carolina: University of South Carolina Press, 1988.

MEMOIRS and PERSONAL ACCOUNTS

AGASSIZ, GEORGE R., ed. *Meade's Headquarters, 1863–1865: Letters of Colonel Theodore Lymann.* Boston: Atlantic Monthly Press, 1922.

ALEXANDER, EDWARD P. *Military Memoirs of a Confederate.* New York: Charles Scribner's Sons, 1907.

———. *Fighting for the Confederacy: The Personal Recollections of General Edward Porter Alexander.* Gary W. Gallagher, ed. Chapel Hill, North Carolina: University of North Carolina Press, 1989.

BILLINGS, JOHN D. *Hardtack and Coffee: The Unwritten Story of Army Life.* Boston: George M. Smith & Company, 1887.

BUTLER, BENJAMIN F. *Butler's Book.* Boston: A.M. Thayer & Company, 1892.

COMMAGER, HENRY STEELE, ed. *The Blue and the Gray: The Story of the Civil War as Told by Participants.* 2 vols. Reprint, New York: Outlet Book Company, 1982 (originally published by Fairfax, 1950).

DANA, CHARLES A. *Recollections of the Civil War.* New York: D. Appleton & Company, 1899.

DANIEL, LARRY J. *Soldiering in the Army of Tennessee: A Portrait of Life in a Confederate Army.* Chapel Hill, North Carolina: University of North Carolina Press, 1991.

DOUGLAS, HENRY K. *I Rode With Stonewall.* Chapel Hill, North Carolina: University of North Carolina Press, 1940.

EARLY, JUBAL A. *Autobiographical Sketch and Narrative of the War Between the States.* Philadelphia: J.B. Lippincott Company, 1912.

GORDON, JOHN B. *Reminiscences of the Civil War.* New York: Charles Scribner's Sons, 1904.

GRANT, ULYSSES S. *Personal Memoirs of U.S. Grant.* 2 vols. New York: The Century Company, 1895.

HAUPT, HERMAN. *Reminiscences of General Herman Haupt.* Milwaukee, Wisconsin: Wright & Joy Company, 1901.

HUMPHREYS, ANDREW A. *The Virginia Campaign of '64 and '65.* New York: Charles Scribner's Sons, 1937.

JOHNSTON, JOSEPH E. *Narrative of Military Operations.* New York: D. Appleton & Company, 1874.

LONGSTREET, JAMES. *From Manassas to Appomattox.* Philadelphia: J.B. Lippincott Company, 1896.

MCCLELLAN, GEORGE B. *McClellan's Own Story.* New York: C.L. Webster & Company, 1887.

MEADE, GEORGE G. *The Life and Letters of George Gordon Meade.* New York: Charles Scribner's Sons, 1913.

PORTER, HORACE. *Campaigning With Grant.* New York: The Century Company, 1907.

ROSENBLATT, EMIL AND RUTH, eds. *Hard Marching Every Day: The Civil War Letters of Private Wilbur Fisk, 1861–1865.* Lawrence, Kansas: University of Kansas Press, 1992.

SCHOFIELD, JOHN M. *Forty-Six Years in the Army.* New York: The Century Company, 1897.

SCOTT, ROBERT G., ed. *Fallen Leaves: The Civil War Letters of Major Henry Livermore Abbott.* Kent, Ohio: The Kent State University Press, 1991.

SEMMES, RAPHAEL. *Service Afloat or the Remarkable Career of the Confederate Cruisers Sumter and Alabama.* Baltimore, Maryland: Baltimore Publishing Company, 1887.

SHERIDAN, PHILIP H. *Personal Memoirs of P.H. Sheridan.* 2 vols. New York: C.L. Webster & Company, 1888.

SHERMAN, WILLIAM T. *Memoirs of General William T. Sherman.* Reprint, New York: Da Capo, 1984, paperback (originally published in 1875; 1st reprint, Indiana University Press, 1957; 2nd reprint, Greenwood Press, 1972).

SORRELL, C. MOXLEY. *Recollections of a Confederate Staff Officer.* Jackson, Mississippi: McCowatt-Mercer Press, 1958.

WELLS, GIDEON. *Diary of Gideon Wells.* 3 vols. Boston: Houghton-Mifflin Company, 1903.

WILEY, BELL I. *The Life of Johnny Reb.* Indianapolis and New York: The Bobbs-Merrill Company, 1943.

———. *The Life of Billy Yank.* Indianapolis and New York: The Bobbs-Merrill Company, 1952.

WILSON, JAMES H. *Under the Old Flag.* 2 vols. New York: D. Appleton & Company, 1912.

BIOGRAPHIES

BRIDGES, HAL. *Lee's Maverick General: Daniel Harvey Hill.* New York: McGraw-Hill, 1961.

CATTON, BRUCE. *U.S. Grant and the Military Tradition.* Boston: Little, Brown & Company, 1954.

CONNELLY, THOMAS L. *The Marble Man: Robert E. Lee and His Image in American Society.* New York: Alfred A. Knopf, 1977.

DAVIS, WILLIAM C. *Jefferson Davis: The Man and His Hour.* New York: Harper Collins, 1991.

DYER, JOHN P. *The Gallant Hood.* Indianapolis and New York: The Bobbs-Merrill Company, 1950.

———. *"Fightin' Joe Wheeler.* Baton Rouge, Louisiana: Louisiana State University Press, 1941.

ECKERT, RALPH L. *John Brown Gordon: Soldier, Southerner, American.* Baton Rouge, Louisiana: Louisiana State University Press, 1989.

FREEMAN, DOUGLAS SOUTHALL. *R.E. Lee, A Biography.* 4 vols. New York: Charles Scribner's Sons, 1934–1935. Paperback, New York: Macmillan, 1993.

FULLER, J.F.C. *Grant & Lee: A Study in Personality and Generalship.* Bloomington, Indiana: Indiana University Press, 1957.

———. *The Generalship of Ulysses S. Grant.* New York: Dodd, Mead & Company, 1929.

GERSON, NOEL B. *Yankee Admiral: A Biography of David Dixon Porter.* New York: D. McKay Company, 1968.

HALLOCK, JUDITH L. *Braxton Bragg and Confederate Defeat.* Vol. 2. Tuscaloosa, Alabama: The University of Alabama Press, 1991.

HASSLER, WILLIAM W. *A.P. Hill: Lee's Forgotten General.* Richmond, Virginia: Garrett & Massie, 1957.

HENDERSON, G.F.R. *Stonewall Jackson and the American Civil War.* London, England: Longmans, Green & Company, 1936.

HENRY, ROBERT S. *"First with the Most" Forrest.* Indianapolis and New York: The Bobbs-Merrill Company, 1944.

HOLZMAN, ROBERT S. *Stormy Ben Butler.* New York: Macmillan, 1954.

JORDAN, DAVID M. *Winfield Scott Hancock: A Soldier's Life.* Bloomington, Indiana: Indiana University Press, 1988.

LEWIS, CHARLES L. *David Glasgow Farragut: Our First Admiral.* Annapolis, Maryland: The Naval Institute Press, 1943.

MARSZALEK, JOHN F. *Sherman: A Soldier's Passion for Order.* New York: The Free Press, 1993.

MARVEL, WILLIAM. *Burnside.* Chapel Hill, North Carolina: University of North Carolina Press, 1991.

MCCLELLAN, H.B. *The Life and Campaigns of Major-General J.E.B. Stuart.* Boston: Houghton Mifflin Company, 1885.

MCWHINEY, GRADY. *Braxton Bragg and Confederate Defeat.* Vol. 1. New York: Columbia University Press, 1969.

NOLAN, ALAN T. *Lee Considered: General Robert E. Lee and Civil War History.* Chapel Hill, North Carolina: University of North Carolina Press, 1991.

O'CONNOR, RICHARD. *Thomas: Rock of Chickamauga.* New York: Prentice-Hall, 1948.

———. *Sheridan the Inevitable.* Indianapolis and New York: The Bobbs-Merrill Company, 1953.

PARISH, T. MICHAEL. *Richard Taylor: Soldier Prince of Dixie.* Chapel Hill, North Carolina: University of North Carolina Press, 1992.

PEMBERTON, JOHN. *General Pemberton: Defender of Vicksburg.* Chapel Hill, North Carolina: University of North Carolina Press, 1942.

PISTON, WILLIAM G. *Lee's Tarnished Lieutenant: James Longstreet and His Place in Southern History.* Athens, Georgia: University of Georgia Press, 1987.

PRATT, FLETCHER. *Stanton: Lincoln's Secretary of War.* New York: W.W. Norton & Company, 1953.

SANDBURG, CARL. *Abraham Lincoln: The War Years.* 4 vols. New York: Harcourt, Brace & Company, 1939.

SEARS, STEPHEN W. *George B. McClellan: The Young Napoleon.* New York: Ticknor & Fields, 1988.

SWANBERG, W.A. *Sickles the Incredible.* New York: Charles Scribner's Sons, 1956.

THOMAS, EMORY. *Bold Dragoon: The Life of J.E.B. Stuart.* New York: Random House, 1988.

TRULOCK, ALICE R. *In the Hands of Providence: Joshua L. Chamberlain & the American Civil War.* Chapel Hill, North Carolina: University of North Carolina Press, 1992.

RECOMMENDED READING LIST

WALLACE, WILLIARD M. *Soul of the Lion: A Biography of General Joshua L. Chamberlain.* New York: Thomas Nelson & Sons, 1960.

WARNER, EZRA J. *Generals in Grey: Lives of the Confederate Commanders.* Baton Rouge, Louisiana: Louisiana State University Press, 1959.

———. *Generals in Blue: Lives of the Union Commanders.* Baton Rouge, Louisiana: Louisiana State University Press, 1964.

WERT, JEFFREY D. *General James Longstreet: The Confederacy's Most Controversial Soldier: A Biography.* New York: Simon and Schuster, 1993.

WILLIAMS, THOMAS HARRY. *Lincoln and His Generals.* Reprint, Westport, Connecticut: Greenwood Press, 1981 (originally published by Vintage, 1952; paperback edition, Vintage, 1967).

———. *P.G.T. Beauregard: Napoleon in Gray.* Baton Rouge, Louisiana: Louisiana State University Press, 1954.

———. *Hayes of the Twenty-third: The Civil War Volunteer Officer.* New York: Alfred A. Knopf, 1965.

UNIT HISTORIES

CATTON, BRUCE. *Mr. Lincoln's Army.* Garden City, New York: Doubleday, 1949.

———. *Glory Road.* Garden City, New York: Doubleday, 1952.

———. *A Stillness at Appomattox.* Garden City, New York: Doubleday, 1953.

CIST, HENRY M. *The Army of the Cumberland.* New York: Charles Scribner's Sons, 1890.

CONNELLY, THOMAS L. *Army of the Heartland: The Army of Tennessee, 1861–1862.* Baton Rouge, Louisiana: Louisiana State University Press, 1967.

———. *Autumn of Glory: The Army of Tennessee, 1862–1865.* Baton Rouge, Louisiana: Louisiana State University Press, 1971.

HIGGINSON, T.W. *Army Life in a Black Regiment.* Boston: Fields, Osgood & Company, 1870.

HORNE, STANLEY F. *The Army of the Tennessee.* Indianapolis and New York: The Bobbs-Merrill Company, 1941.

JONES, TERRY L. *Lee's Tigers: The Louisiana Infantry in the Army of Northern Virginia.* Baton Rouge, Louisiana: Louisiana State University Press, 1987.

LOSSON, CHRISTOPHER. *Tennessee's Forgotten Warriors: Frank Cheatham and His Confederate Division.* Knoxville, Tennessee: The University of Tennessee Press, 1990.

McMURRAY, RICHARD M. *Two Great Rebel Armies: An Essay in Confederate Military History.* Chapel Hill, North Carolina: The University of North Carolina Press, 1989.

———. ed. *Footprints of a Regiment: A Recollection of the 1st Georgia Regulars, 1861–1865.* Atlanta, Georgia: Longstreet Press, 1992.

NOLAN, ALAN T. *The Iron Brigade: A Military History.* New York: Macmillan, 1961.

SMALL, ABNER R. *The Road to Richmond.* Berkeley, California: University of California Press, 1957.

SWINTON, WILLIAM. *Campaigns of the Army of the Potomac.* New York: Charles Scribner's Sons, 1882.

WATKINS, SAM R. *"Co. Aytch."* Nashville, Tennessee: Cumberland Presbyterian Publishing House, 1882.

WERT, JEFFREY D. *Mosby's Rangers.* New York: Simon and Schuster, 1990.

THE INDIAN WARS

BOURKE, JOHN G. *On the Border with Crook.* 1891. Reprint, Lincoln, Nebraska: University of Nebraska Press, 1971 (1st reprint, Rio Grande Press, 1969).

CONNELL, EVAN S. *Son of the Morning Star: Custer and the Little Bighorn.* New York: Harper and Row, 1984.

HUTTON, PAUL ANDREW. *Phil Sheridan and His Army.* Lincoln, Nebraska: The University of Nebraska Press, 1985.

MAHON, JOHN K. *The History of the Second Seminole War, 1835–1842.* Gainesville, Florida: University Presses of Florida, 1967, paperback, 1992.

PRUCHA, PAUL FRANCIS. *The Sword of the Republic. The United States Army on the Frontier, 1783–1846.* Reprint, Lincoln, Nebraska: University of Nebraska Press, 1986, paperback (originally published by Macmillan, 1969).

SWORD, WILEY. *President Washington's Indian War: The Struggle for the Old Northwest, 1790–1795.* Norman, Oklahoma: University of Oklahoma Press, 1985.

UTLEY, ROBERT M. *Cavalier in Buckskin: George Armstrong Custer and the Western Military Frontier.* Norman, Oklahoma: U. of Oklahoma Press, 1988.

———. *Frontiersmen in Blue: The United States Army and the Indian, 1848–1865.* Reprint, Lincoln, Nebraska: University of Nebraska Press, 1981 (originally published by Macmillan, 1974).

———. *Frontier Regulars: The U.S. Army and the Indian, 1866–1890.* Reprint, Lincoln, Nebraska: University of Nebraska Press, 1984 (originally published by Macmillan, 1973).

THE SPANISH-AMERICAN WAR

ABRAHAMSON, JAMES L. *America Arms for a New Century: The Making of a Great Military Power.* New York: Free Press, 1981.

COSMAS, GRAHAM A. *An Army for Empire: The United States Army in the Spanish-American War.* Columbia, Missouri: University of Missouri Press, 1971.

GATES, JOHN MORGAN. *Schoolbooks and Krags: The United States Army in the Philippines, 1898–1902.* Westport, Connecticut: Greenwood Press, 1973.

JAMIESON, PERRY D. *Crossing the Deadly Ground: U.S. Army Tactics, 1865–1899.* Tuscaloosa, Alabama: University of Alabama Press, 1994.

LINN, BRIAN M. *The U.S. Army and Counterinsurgency in the Philippine War, 1899–1902.* Chapel Hill, North Carolina: University of North Carolina Press, 1989.

MILLER, STUART C. *"Benevolent Assimilation": The American Conquest of the Philippines.* New Haven, Connecticut: Yale University Press, 1982.

REARDON, CAROL. *Soldiers and Scholars: The U.S. Army and the Use of Military History, 1865–1920.* Lawrence, Kansas: University of Kansas Press, 1990.

TRASK, DAVID F. *The War With Spain in 1898.* Macmillan series, *The Wars of the United States,* Gen. ed. Louis Morton. New York: Macmillan, 1981.